Lecture Notes in Artificial Intelligence 12520

Subseries of Lecture Notes in Computer Science

Series Editors

Randy Goebel
University of Alberta, Edmonton, Canada
Yuzuru Tanaka
Hokkaido University, Sapporo, Japan
Wolfgang Wahlster
DFKI and Saarland University, Saarbrücken, Germany

Founding Editor

Jörg Siekmann
DFKI and Saarland University, Saarbrücken, Germany

More information about this subseries at http://www.springer.com/series/1244

Nick Bassiliades · Georgios Chalkiadakis ·
Dave de Jonge (Eds.)

Multi-Agent Systems and Agreement Technologies

17th European Conference, EUMAS 2020
and 7th International Conference, AT 2020
Thessaloniki, Greece, September 14–15, 2020
Revised Selected Papers

 Springer

Editors
Nick Bassiliades 🆔
Aristotle University of Thessaloniki
Thessaloniki, Greece

Georgios Chalkiadakis 🆔
Technical University of Crete
Chania, Greece

Dave de Jonge 🆔
IIIA-CSIC
Bellaterra, Spain

ISSN 0302-9743   ISSN 1611-3349   (electronic)
Lecture Notes in Artificial Intelligence
ISBN 978-3-030-66411-4   ISBN 978-3-030-66412-1   (eBook)
https://doi.org/10.1007/978-3-030-66412-1

LNCS Sublibrary: SL7 – Artificial Intelligence

This Springer imprint is published by the registered company Springer Nature Switzerland AG
The registered company address is: Gewerbestrasse 11, 6330 Cham, Switzerland

Preface

This volume constitutes the revised post-conference proceedings of the 17th European Conference on Multi-Agent Systems (EUMAS 2020) and the 7th International Conference on Agreement Technologies (AT 2020). The conferences were originally planned to be held in Thessaloniki, Greece, in April 2020, but were eventually held online between September 14–15, 2020. The 38 full papers presented in this volume were carefully reviewed and selected from a total of 53 submissions. The papers report on both early and mature research and cover a wide range of topics in the field of multi-agent systems.

EUMAS 2020 followed the tradition of previous editions (Oxford 2003, Barcelona 2004, Brussels 2005, Lisbon 2006, Hammamet 2007, Bath 2008, Agia Napa 2009, Paris 2010, Maastricht 2011, Dublin 2012, Toulouse 2013, Prague 2014, Athens 2015, Valencia 2016, Evry 2017, Bergen 2018) in aiming to provide the prime European forum for presenting and discussing agents research as the annual designated event of the European Association for Multi-Agent Systems (EURAMAS).

AT 2020 was the seventh instalment in a series of events (after Dubrovnik 2012, Beijing 2013, Athens 2015, Valencia 2016, Evry 2017, Bergen 2018) that focus on bringing together researchers and practitioners working on computer systems in which autonomous software agents interact, typically on behalf of humans, in order to come to mutually acceptable agreements. A wide scope of technologies can help provide the support needed for reaching mutually acceptable agreements, such as argumentation and negotiation, trust and reputation, computational social choice, coalition and team formation, coordination and distributed decision-making, and semantic alignment, to name a few.

This year, for the fifth time, the two events were co-located and run as a single, joint event. This joint organization aimed to encourage and continue cross-fertilization among the broader EUMAS and the more specialized AT communities, and to provide a richer and more attractive program to participants. While the technical program was put together by their independent committees, the conferences shared keynote talks and aligned their schedules to minimize overlap and enable participants to make the best possible use of the combined program of the two conferences. Traditionally, both conference series have always followed a spirit of providing a forum for discussion and an annual opportunity for primarily European researchers to meet and exchange ideas. For this reason, they have always encouraged submission of papers that report on both early and mature research.

The peer-review processes carried out by both conferences put great emphasis on ensuring the high quality of accepted contributions. The 90-person EUMAS Program Committee accepted 32 submissions as full papers. The AT review process resulted in the acceptance of six full papers by the 54-person AT program committee.

This volume is structured in sections mirroring the presentation sessions of the joint event (https://eumas2020.csd.auth.gr/). In addition to the papers included in this volume, the program was highlighted by two great keynote talks, the first one by Professor Sarvapali (Gopal) Ramchurn of the Department of Electronics and Computer Science, University of Southampton, UK, on "Emerging Challenge Areas for AI and Multi-Agent Systems: From Sports to Maritime", and the second one by Professor Pavlos Moraitis of the Department of Mathematics and Computer Science, University of Paris, France, on "Computational Argumentation: From Theory to Market". Two papers of EUMAS stood out from the rest and were nominated by the EUMAS Program Chairs as candidates for the best paper award. These two papers were presented in a special session and then a committee composed of all the EUMAS and AT program chairs and one of the keynote speakers, Prof. Pavlos Moraitis, decided that the award should be shared between them.

The editors would like to thank all authors for submitting to EUMAS and AT, all participants, the invited speakers, the members of the Program Committees, and the additional reviewers for putting together a strong joint program. We also thank the local organizers for their hard work organizing the events. Finally, we would like to express our gratitude to the sponsors of the conferences: Aristotle University of Thessaloniki for providing technical and human resources, the MDPI journal *Computers* for sponsoring the EUMAS Best Paper Award, the journal *Autonomous Agents and Multi-Agent Systems* for agreeing to publish extended versions of the EUMAS best and runner-up papers, and the journal SN Computer Science for agreeing to publish a special issue with selected extended EUMAS papers.

November 2020

Nick Bassiliades
Georgios Chalkiadakis
Dave de Jonge

Organization

EUMAS 2020 Program Chairs

Nick Bassiliades   Aristotle University of Thessaloniki, Greece
Georgios Chalkiadakis   Technical University of Crete, Greece

AT 2020 Program Chair

Dave de Jonge   Spanish National Research Council (CSIC), Spain

EUMAS 2020 Program Committee

Stergos Afantenos   IRIT, CNRS/Université Paul Sabatier
Thomas Ågotnes   University of Bergen
Juan Antonio Rodriguez   IIIA-CSIC
  Aguilar
Stéphane Airiau   LAMSADE - Université Paris-Dauphine
Charilaos Akasiadis   NCSR Demokritos
Samir Aknine   Université Claude Bernard Lyon 1
Fred Amblard   IRIT - Université Toulouse 1 Capitole
Merlinda Andoni   Heriot-Watt University
Costin Badica   University of Craiova
Ana L. C. Bazzan   Universidade Federal do Rio Grande do Sul
Antonis Bikakis   University College London
Filippo Bistaffa   IIIA-CSIC
Olivier Boissier   Mines Saint-Étienne
Vicent Botti   Universitat Politècnica de València
Ioana Boureanu   University of Surrey
Nils Bulling   Technische Universität Clausthal and BCG Platinion
Cristiano Castelfranchi   Institute of Cognitive Sciences and Technologies
Alberto Castellini   Verona University
Sofia Ceppi   PROWLER.io
Angelos Chliaoutakis   Technical University of Crete
Massimo Cossentino   National Research Council of Italy
Natalia Criado   King's College London
Aleksander Czechowski   Delft University of Technology
Mathijs De Weerdt   Delft University of Technology
Catalin Dima   LACL, Université Paris-Est Créteil
Dragan Doder   University of Belgrade
Sylvie Doutre   Université Toulouse 1 Capitole - IRIT
Edith Elkind   University of Oxford
Alessandro Farinelli   Verona University

Nicoletta Fornara	Università della Svizzera italiana
Malvin Gattinger	University of Groningen
Benoit Gaudou	UMR 5505 CNRS, IRIT, Université de Toulouse
Nina Gierasimczuk	Technical University of Denmark
Gianluigi Greco	University of Calabria
Davide Grossi	University of Groningen
Andreas Herzig	CNRS, IRIT, Univ. Toulouse
Magdalena Ivanovska	University of Oslo
Antonis Kakas	University of Cyprus
Petros Kefalas	The University of Sheffield
Franziska Klügl	Örebro University
Michał Knapik	ICS PAS
Dušan Knop	TU Berlin
Nadin Kokciyan	The University of Edinburgh
Manolis Koubarakis	National and Kapodistrian University of Athens
Kalliopi Kravari	Aristotle University of Thessaloniki
Michail Lagoudakis	Technical University of Crete
Jérôme Lang	CNRS, LAMSADE, Université Paris-Dauphine
Dominique Longin	IRIT-CNRS
Maite Lopez-Sanchez	University of Barcelona
Emiliano Lorini	IRIT
Marin Lujak	IMT Lille Douai
John-Jules Meyer	Utrecht University
Sanjay Modgil	King's College London
Frederic Moisan	Carnegie Mellon University
Pavlos Moraitis	LIPADE, Paris Descartes University
Stefano Moretti	CNRS UMR7243 – LAMSADE, Université Paris-Dauphine
Svetlana Obraztsova	Hebrew University of Jerusalem
Andrea Omicini	Alma Mater Studiorum-Università di Bologna
Nir Oren	University of Aberdeen
Nardine Osman	Artificial Intelligence Research Institute (IIIA-CSIC)
Sascha Ossowski	University Rey Juan Carlos
Athanasios Aris Panagopoulos	California State University, Fresno
Theodore Patkos	Institute of Computer Science, FORTH
Giuseppe Perelli	University of Gothenburg
Euripides Petrakis	Technical University of Crete
Maria Polukarov	King's College London
Zinovi Rabinovich	Nanyang Technological University
Sarvapali Ramchurn	University of Southampton
Alessandro Ricci	University of Bologna
Emmanouil Rigas	Aristotle University of Thessaloniki
Valentin Robu	Heriot-Watt University
Michael Rovatsos	The University of Edinburgh
Jordi Sabater Mir	IIIA-CSIC

Ilias Sakellariou	University of Macedonia
Sebastian Sardina	RMIT University
Marija Slavkovik	University of Bergen
Nikolaos Spanoudakis	Technical University of Crete
Sebastian Stein	University of Southampton
Nimrod Talmon	Ben-Gurion University of the Negev
Ingo J. Timm	University of Trier
Paolo Torroni	University of Bologna
Paolo Turrini	The University of Warwick
Laurent Vercouter	LITIS lab, INSA de Rouen
Angelina Vidali	University of Athens and IOHK Research
Vasilis Vlachokyriakos	Newcastle University and Open Lab Athens
George Vouros	University of Piraeus
Pinar Yolum	Utrecht University
Neil Yorke-Smith	Delft University of Technology
Leon van der Torre	University of Luxembourg

AT 2020 Program Committee

Estefania Argente	Universitat Politècnica de València
Reyhan Aydogan	Delft University of Technology
Holger Billhardt	Universidad Rey Juan Carlos
Elise Bonzon	LIPADE - Université Paris Descartes
Annemarie Borg	Utrecht University
Henrique Lopes Cardoso	University of Porto
Carlos Chesñevar	UNS (Universidad Nacional del Sur)
Sylvie Doutre	IRIT
Alberto Fernandez	University Rey Juan Carlos
Katsuhide Fujita	Tokyo University of Agriculture and Technology
Adriana Giret	Universitat Politècnica de València
Stella Heras	Universitat Politècnica de València
Mirjana Ivanovic	University of Novi Sad
Vicente Julian	Universitat Politècnica de València
Mario Kusek	University of Zagreb
Emiliano Lorini	IRIT
Yasser Mohammad	Assiut University
Viorel Negru	West University of Timisoara
Eva Onaindia	Universitat Politècnica de València
Marcin Paprzycki	IBS PAN and WSM
Jordi Sabater Mir	IIIA-CSIC
Milos Savic	University of Novi Sad
Francesca Toni	Imperial College London
László Zsolt Varga	ELTE IK
Marin Vukovic	University of Zagreb
Remi Wieten	Utrecht University

EUMAS 2020 External Reviewers

Ioannis Antonopoulos	Heriot-Watt University
Thanasis Baharis	Technical University of Crete
Benoit Barbot	LACL, Université Paris-Est Créteil
Jinke He	TU Delft
Can Kurtan	Utrecht University
Salvatore Lopes	National Research Council of Italy
Ouri Poupko	Weizmann Institute of Science
Dimitrios Troullinos	Technical University of Crete
Onuralp Ulusoy	Utrecht University
Xingyu Zhao	Heriot-Watt University

Local Organizing Committee

Konstantinos Gounis	Aristotle University of Thessaloniki
Kalliopi Kravari	Aristotle University of Thessaloniki
Ioannis Mollas	Aristotle University of Thessaloniki
Emmanouil Rigas	Aristotle University of Thessaloniki
Alexandros Vassiliades	Aristotle University of Thessaloniki

Contents

EUMAS 2020 Session 3: Autonomous Agents

EUMAS 2020 Best Papers Session

EUMAS-AT 2020 Joint Session

**EUMAS 2020 Session 4: Agent-Based Models, Social Choice,
Argumentation, Model-Checking**

EUMAS 2020 Session 1: Intelligent Agents and MAS Applications

Towards a Theory of Intentions
for Human-Robot Collaboration

Rocio Gomez[1], Mohan Sridharan[2(⊠)] (iD), and Heather Riley[1]

[1] Electrical and Computer Engineering, The University of Auckland,
Auckland, New Zealand
m.gomez@auckland.ac.nz, hril230@aucklanduni.ac.nz
[2] School of Computer Science, University of Birmingham, Birmingham, UK
m.sridharan@bham.ac.uk

Abstract. The architecture described in this paper encodes a theory of intentions based on the principles of non-procrastination, persistence, and relevance. The architecture reasons with transition diagrams at two different resolutions, with the fine-resolution description defined as a refinement of, and hence tightly-coupled with, a coarse-resolution description. For any given goal, non-monotonic logical reasoning with the coarse-resolution description computes an activity, i.e., a plan, comprising a sequence of abstract actions to be executed to achieve the goal. Each abstract action is implemented as a sequence of concrete actions by automatically zooming to and reasoning with the part of the fine-resolution transition diagram relevant to the coarse-resolution transition and the goal. Each concrete action is executed using probabilistic models of the uncertainty in sensing and actuation, and the corresponding coarse-resolution observations are added to the coarse-resolution history. Experimental results in the context of simulated and physical robots indicate improvements in reliability and efficiency compared with an architecture that does not include the theory of intentions, and an architecture that does not include zooming for fine-resolution reasoning.

1 Introduction

Consider a robot[1] assisting humans in dynamic domains, e.g., a robot helping a human arrange objects in different configurations on a tabletop, or a robot delivering objects to particular places or people—see Fig. 1. These robots often have to reason with different descriptions of uncertainty and incomplete domain knowledge. This information about the domain often includes commonsense knowledge, especially default knowledge that holds in all but a few exceptional circumstances, e.g., "books are usually in the library but cookbooks may be in the kitchen". The robot also receives a lot more sensor data than it can process, and it is equipped with many algorithms that compute and use a probabilistic quantification of the uncertainty in sensing and actuation, e.g., "I am

---

[1] A journal article based on this work has been accepted for publication in the *Annals of Mathematics and Artificial Intelligence* [11].

© Springer Nature Switzerland AG 2020
N. Bassiliades et al. (Eds.): EUMAS 2020/AT 2020, LNAI 12520, pp. 3–19, 2020.
https://doi.org/10.1007/978-3-030-66412-1_1

90% certain the robotics book is on the table". Furthermore, while it is difficult to provide robots comprehensive domain knowledge or elaborate supervision, reasoning with incomplete or incorrect information can provide incorrect or suboptimal outcomes. This loss in performance is more pronounced in scenarios corresponding to unexpected success or failure, which are common in dynamic domains. For instance, consider a robot trying to move two books from an office to a library. After moving the first book to the library, if the robot observes the second book in the library, or if it observes the second book in the kitchen on the way back to the office, it should stop executing its plan, reason about what may have happened, and compute a new plan if necessary. One way to achieve this behavior is to augment a traditional planning approach with the ability to reason about observations of all domain objects and events during plan execution, but this approach is computationally intractable in complex domains. Instead, the architecture described in this paper seeks to enable a robot pursuing a particular goal to automatically reason about the underlying *intention* and related observations of its domain during planning and execution. It does so by building on an architecture that uses declarative programming to reason about intended actions to achieve a given goal [5], and on an architecture that reasons with tightly-coupled transition diagrams at different levels of abstraction [18]. This work has been described in detail in a recently published journal article [11]. Here, we describe the following key characteristics of the architecture:

- An action language is used to describe the tightly-coupled transition diagrams of the domain at two different resolutions. At the coarse resolution, non-monotonic logical reasoning with commonsense knowledge, including default knowledge, produces a sequence of intentional abstract actions for any given goal.
- Each intended abstract action is implemented as a sequence of concrete actions by automatically zooming to and reasoning with the relevant part of the fine-resolution system description defined as a refinement of the coarse-resolution system description. The outcomes of executing the concrete actions using probabilistic models or uncertainty are added to the coarse-resolution history.

In this paper, the coarse-resolution and fine-resolution action language descriptions are translated to programs in CR-Prolog, an extension of Answer Set Prolog (ASP) [9], for commonsense reasoning. The execution of each concrete action using probabilistic models of uncertainty in sensing and actuation is achieved using existing algorithms. The architecture thus reasons about intentions and beliefs at two resolutions. We demonstrate the capabilities of our architecture in the context of (i) a simulated robot assisting humans in an office domain; (ii) a physical robot (Baxter) manipulating objects on a tabletop; and (iii) a wheeled robot (Turtlebot) moving objects in an office domain. Experimental results indicate that the proposed architecture improves reliability and computational efficiency of planning and execution in dynamic domains in comparison with an architecture that does not support reasoning about intentional actions.

(a) Baxter robot.   (b) Turtlebot.

Fig. 1. (a) Baxter robot manipulating objects on a tabletop; and (b) Turtlebot moving objects to particular locations in a lab.

2 Related Work

There is much work in the modeling and recognition of intentions. Belief-desire-intention (BDI) architectures model the intentions of reasoning agents and guide reasoning by eliminating choices inconsistent with current intentions [6,14]. However, such architectures do not learn from past behavior, adapt to new situations, or include an explicit representation of (or reasoning about) goals. Other work has reasoned with domain knowledge or used models learned from training samples to recognize intentions [13].

An architecture formalizing intentions based on declarative programming was described in [3]. It introduced an action language that can represent intentions based on two principles: (i) *non-procrastination*, i.e., intended actions are executed as soon as possible; and (ii) *persistence*, i.e., unfulfilled intentions persist. This architecture was also used to enable an external observer to recognize the activity of an observed agent, i.e., for determining what has happened and what the agent intends to do [8]. However, this architecture did not support the modeling of agents that desire to achieve specific goals. The *Theory of Intentions* ($\mathcal{TI}$) [4,5] builds on [3] to model the intentions of goal-driven agents. $\mathcal{TI}$ expanded transition diagrams that have physical states and physically executable actions to include mental fluents and mental actions. It associated a sequence of agent actions (called an "activity") with the goal it intended to achieve, and introduced an *intentional agent* that only performs actions that are intended to achieve a desired goal and does so without delay. This theory has been used to create a methodology for understanding of narratives of typical and exceptional restaurant scenarios [20], and goal-driven agents in dynamic domains have been modeled using such activities [15]. A common requirement of such theories and their use is that all the domain knowledge, including the preconditions and effects of actions and potential goals, be known and encoded in the knowledge base, which is difficult to do in robot domains. Also, the set of states (and actions, observations) to be considered can be large in robot domains, which makes efficient reasoning a challenging task. In recent work [20], the authors attempt to

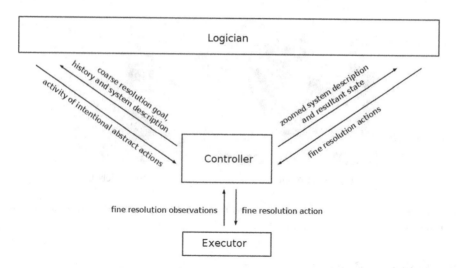

Fig. 2. Architecture combines the complementary strengths of declarative programming and probabilistic reasoning, representing intentions and beliefs as coupled transition diagrams at two resolutions; may be viewed as interactions between a controller, logician, and executor.

address this problem by clustering indistinguishable states [16] but these clusters need to be encoded in advance. Furthermore, these approaches do not consider the uncertainty in sensing and actuation.

Logic-based methods have been used widely in robotics, including those that also support probabilistic reasoning [12,21]. Methods based on first-order logic do not support non-monotonic logical reasoning or the desired expressiveness for capabilities such as default reasoning, e.g., it is not always meaningful to express degrees of belief by attaching probabilities to logic statements. Non-monotonic logics such as ASP address some of these limitations, and they have been used in cognitive robotics applications by an international research community [7]. However, classical ASP formulations do not support the probabilistic models of uncertainty that are used by algorithms for sensing and actuation in robotics. Approaches based on logic programming also do not support one or more of the capabilities such as incremental addition of probabilistic information or variables to reason about open worlds. Towards addressing these limitations, prior work in our group developed a refinement-based architecture that reasoned with tightly-coupled transition diagrams at two resolutions; each abstract action in a coarse-resolution plan computed using ASP was executed as a sequence of concrete actions computed by probabilistic reasoning over the relevant part of the fine-resolution diagram [18]. This paper explores the combination of these ideas with those drawn from $\mathcal{TI}$; specific differences from prior work are described in the relevant sections below.

3   Cognitive Architecture

Figure 2 presents a block diagram of the overall architecture. Similar to prior work [18], this architecture may be viewed as consisting of three components: a controller, a logician, and an executor. In this paper, the controller is responsible for holding the overall beliefs regarding domain state, and for the transfer of control and information between all components. For any given goal, the logician performs non-monotonic logical reasoning with the coarse-resolution representation of commonsense knowledge to generate an activity, i.e., a sequence of intentional abstract actions. Each abstract action is implemented as a sequence of concrete actions by zooming to and reasoning with a fine-resolution representation defined as a refinement of the coarse-resolution representation. The executor uses probabilistic models of the uncertainty in sensing and actuation to execute each concrete action, with the outcomes being communicated to the controller and added to the coarse-resolution history of the logician. These components of the architecture are described below, along with differences from prior work, using variants of the following illustrative domain.

Example Domain 1 *[Robot Assistant (RA) Domain]*. Consider a robot assisting humans in moving particular objects to desired locations in an indoor office domain with:

- Sorts such as *place, thing, robot, object,* and *book,* arranged hierarchically, e.g., *object* and *robot* are subsorts of *thing.*
- Places: $\{office_1, office_2, kitchen, library\}$ with a door between neighboring places—see Fig. 3; only the door between *kitchen* and *library* can be locked.
- Instances of sorts, e.g., $rob_1, book_1, book_2.$
- Static attributes such as *color, size* and parts (e.g., *base* and *handle*) of objects. Other agents that may change the domain are not modeled.

Office 1	Office 2	Kitchen	Library

Fig. 3. Four rooms considered in Example 1, with a human in the *kitchen* and two books in $office_1$. Only the library's door can be locked; all other rooms remain open.

3.1   Action Language and Domain Representation

We first describe the action language encoding of domain dynamics, and its translation to CR-Prolog programs for knowledge representation and reasoning.

Action Language: Action languages are formal models of parts of natural language used for describing transition diagrams of dynamic systems. We use action language $\mathcal{AL}_d$ [10] to describe the transition diagrams at different resolutions. $\mathcal{AL}_d$ has a sorted signature with *statics*, *fluents* and *actions*. Statics are domain attributes whose truth values cannot be changed by actions, whereas fluents are domain attributes whose truth values can be changed by actions. Fluents can be *basic* or *defined*. Basic fluents obey the laws of inertia and can be changed by actions. Defined fluents do not obey the laws of inertia and are not changed directly by actions—their values depend on other fluents. Actions are defined as a set of elementary operations. A domain attribute p or its negation $\neg p$ is a *literal*. $\mathcal{AL}_d$ allows three types of statements: causal law, state constraint, and executability condition.

Coarse-Resolution Knowledge Representation: The coarse-resolution domain representation consists of system description $\mathcal{D}_c$, a collection of statements of $\mathcal{AL}_d$, and history $\mathcal{H}_c$. System description $\mathcal{D}_c$ has a sorted signature Σ_c and axioms that describe the transition diagram τ_c. Σ_c defines the basic sorts, domain attributes and actions. Example 1 introduced some basic sorts and ground instances of the RA domain. Σ_c also includes the sort *step* for temporal reasoning. Domain attributes (i.e., statics and fluents) and actions are described in terms of their arguments' sorts. In the RA domain, statics include relations such as $next\_to(place, place)$, which describes the relative location of places in the domain; and relations representing object attributes such as *color* and *size*, e.g., $obj\_color(object, color)$. Fluents include $loc(thing, place)$, the location of the robot or domain objects; $in\_hand(robot, object)$, which denotes a particular object is in the robot's hand; and $locked(place)$, which implies a particular place is locked. The locations of other agents, if any, are not changed by the robot's actions; these locations are inferred from observations obtained from other sensors. The domain's actions include $move(robot, place)$, $pickup(robot, object)$, $putdown(robot, object)$, and $unlock(robot, place)$; we also consider exogenous actions $exo\_move(object, place)$ and $exo\_lock(place)$, which are used for diagnostic reasoning. Σ_c also includes the relation $holds(fluent, step)$ to imply that a particular fluent holds true at a particular time step. Axioms for the RA domain include causal laws, state constraints and executability conditions such as:

> $move(rob_1, P)$ **causes** $loc(rob_1, P)$
> $loc(O, P)$ **if** $loc(rob_1, P)$, $in\_hand(rob_1, O)$
> **impossible** $pickup(rob_1, O)$ **if** $loc(rob_1, L_1)$, $loc(O, L_2)$, $L_1 \neq L_2$

The history $\mathcal{H}_c$ of the domain contains the usual record of fluents observed to be true or false at a particular time step, i.e., $obs(fluent, boolean, step)$, and the execution of an action at a particular time step, i.e., $occurs(action, step)$. In [18] this notion was expanded to represent defaults describing the values of fluents in the initial state, e.g., "books are usually in the library and if it not there, they are normally in the office". We can also encode exceptions to these defaults, e.g., "cookbooks are in the kitchen". This representation, which does not quantitatively model beliefs in these defaults, supports elegant reasoning with generic defaults and their specific exceptions.

Reasoning: The coarse-resolution domain representation is translated into a program $\Pi(\mathcal{D}_c, \mathcal{H}_c)$ in CR-Prolog[2], a variant of ASP that incorporates consistency restoring (CR) rules [2]. ASP is based on stable model semantics and supports concepts such as *default negation* and *epistemic disjunction*, e.g., unlike "$\neg a$" that states *a is believed to be false*, "*not a*" only implies *a is not believed to be true*. ASP can represent recursive definitions and constructs that are difficult to express in classical logic formalisms, and it supports non-monotonic logical reasoning, i.e., it is able to revise previously held conclusions based on new evidence. An ASP program Π includes the signature and axioms of $\mathcal{D}_c$, inertia axioms, reality checks, and observations, actions, and defaults from $\mathcal{H}_c$. Every default also has a CR rule that allows the robot to assume the default's conclusion is false to restore consistency under exceptional circumstances. Each *answer set* of an ASP program represents the set of beliefs of an agent associated with the program. Algorithms for computing entailment, and for planning and diagnostics, reduce these tasks to computing answer sets of CR-Prolog programs. We compute answer sets of CR-Prolog programs using the system called SPARC [1].

3.2   Adapted Theory of Intention

For any given goal, a robot using ASP-based reasoning will compute a plan and execute it until the goal is achieved or a planned action has an unexpected outcome; in the latter case, the robot will try to explain the outcome (i.e., diagnostics) and compute a new plan if necessary. To motivate the need for a different approach in dynamic domains, consider the following scenarios in which the goal is to move $book_1$ and $book_2$ to the *library*; these scenarios have been adapted from scenarios in [5]:

- **Scenario 1 (planning):** Robot rob_1 is in the kitchen holding $book_1$, and believes $book_2$ is in the kitchen and the library is unlocked. The plan is: $move(rob_1, library)$, $put\_down(rob_1, book_1)$, $move(rob_1, kitchen)$, $pickup(rob_1, book_2)$, followed by $move(rob_1, library)$ and $put\_down(rob_1, book_2)$.
- **Scenario 2 (unexpected success):** Assume that rob_1 in Scenario-1 has moved to the *library* and put $book_1$ down, and observes $book_2$. The robot should explain this observation (e.g., $book_2$ was moved there) and realize the goal has been achieved.
- **Scenario 3 (not expected to achieve goal, diagnose and replan, case 1):** Assume $rob1$ in Scenario-1 starts moving $book_1$ to *library*, but observes $book_2$ is not in the *kitchen*. The robot should realize the plan will fail to achieve the overall goal, explain the unexpected observation, and compute a new plan.
- **Scenario 4 (not expected to achieve goal, diagnose and replan, case 2):** Assume $rob1$ is in the kitchen holding $book1$, and believes $book2$ is in $office_2$ and *library* is unlocked. The plan is to put $book_1$ in the *library*

---

[2] We use the terms "ASP" and "CR-Prolog" interchangeably.

before fetching $book_2$ from $office_2$. Before rob_1 moves to $library$, it observes $book_2$ in the $kitchen$. The robot should realize the plan will fail and compute a new plan.

- **Scenario 5 (failure to achieve the goal, diagnose and replan):** Assume rob_1 in Scenario-1 is putting $book_2$ in the $library$, after having put $book_1$ in the $library$ earlier, and observes that $book_1$ is no longer there. The robot's intention should persist; it should explain the unexpected observation, replan if necessary, and execute actions until the goal is achieved.

One way to support the desired behavior in such scenarios is to reason with all possible observations of domain objects and events (e.g., observations of all objects in the sensor's field of view) during plan execution. However, such an approach would be computationally intractable in complex domains. Instead, we build on the principles of non-procrastination and persistence and the ideas from $\mathcal{TI}$. Our architecture enables the robot to compute actions that are intended for any given goal and current beliefs. As the robot attempts to implement each such action, *it obtains all observations relevant to this action and the intended goal*, and adds these observations to the recorded history. We will henceforth use $\mathcal{ATI}$ to refer to this adapted theory of intention that expands both the system description $\mathcal{D}_c$ and history $\mathcal{H}_c$ in the original program $\Pi(\mathcal{D}_c, \mathcal{H}_c)$. First, the signature Σ_c is expanded to represent an *activity*, a triplet of a *goal*, a *plan* to achieve the goal, and a specific *name*, by introducing relations such as:

$$activity(name), \quad activity\_goal(name, goal), \quad activity\_length(name, length)$$
$$activity\_component(name, number, action)$$

These relations represent each named activity, the goal and length of each activity, and actions that are components of the activity; when ground, these relations are statics.

Next, the existing fluents of Σ are considered to be *physical fluents* and the set of fluents is expanded to include *mental fluents* such as:

$$active\_activity(activity), \quad in\_progress\_goal(goal), next\_action(activity, action),$$
$$in\_progress\_activity(activity), \quad active\_goal(goal), \quad next\_activity\_name(name),$$
$$current\_action\_index(activity, index)$$

where the first four relations are defined fluents, and other relations are basic fluents. These fluents represent the robot's belief about a particular activity, action or goal being active or in progress. None of these fluents' values are changed directly by executing any physical action. The value of $current\_action\_index$ changes if the robot has completed an intended action or if a change in the domain makes it impossible for an activity to succeed. The values of other mental fluents are changed by expanding the set of existing *physical actions* of Σ to include *mental actions* such as $start(name)$, $stop(name)$, $select(goal)$, and $abandon(goal)$, where the first two mental actions are used by the controller to start or stop a particular activity, and the other two are exogenous actions that are used (e.g., by human) to select or abandon a particular goal.

In addition to the signature Σ_c, history $\mathcal{H}_c$ is also expanded to include relations such as $attempt(action, step)$ and $\neg\ hpd(action, step)$, which denote that a particular action was attempted at a particular time step, and that a particular action was not executed successfully at a particular time step. Figuring out when an action was actually executed (or not executed) requires reasoning with observations of whether an action had the intended outcome(s).

We also introduce new axioms in $\mathcal{D}_{c_*}$ e.g., to represent the effects of the physical and mental actions on the physical and mental fluents, e.g., starting (stopping) an activity makes it active (inactive), and executing an action in an activity keeps the activity active. The new axioms also include state constraints, e.g., to describe when a particular activity or goal is active, and executability conditions, e.g., it is not possible for the robot to simultaneously execute two mental actions. In addition, axioms are introduced to generate intentional actions, build a consistent model of the domain history, and to perform diagnostics.

The revised system description $\mathcal{D}'_c$ and history $\mathcal{H}'_c$ are translated automatically to CR-Prolog program $\Pi(\mathcal{D}'_c, \mathcal{H}'_c)$ that is solved for planning or diagnostics. The complete program for the RA domain is available online [17]. Key differences between $\mathcal{ATI}$ and prior work on $\mathcal{TI}$ are:

- $\mathcal{TI}$ becomes computationally expensive, especially as the size of the plan or history increases. It also performs diagnostics and planning jointly, which allows it to consider different explanations during planning but increases computational cost in complex domains. $\mathcal{ATI}$, on the other hand, first builds a consistent model of history by considering different explanations, and *uses this model to guide planning*, significantly reducing computational cost in complex domains.
- $\mathcal{TI}$ assumes complete knowledge of the state of other agents (e.g., humans or other robots) that perform exogenous actions. In many robotics domains, this assumption is rather unrealistic. $\mathcal{ATI}$ instead makes the more realistic assumption that the robot can only infer exogenous actions by reasoning with the observations that it obtains from sensors.
- $\mathcal{ATI}$ does not include the notion of sub-goals and sub-activities (and associated relations) from $\mathcal{TI}$, as they were not necessary. Also, the sub-activities and sub-goals will need to be encoded in advance, and reasoning with these relations will also increase computational complexity in many situations. The inclusion of sub-activities and sub-goals will be explored in future work.

Any architecture with $\mathcal{ATI}$, $\mathcal{TI}$, or a different reasoning component based on logic-programming or classical first-order logic, has two key limitations. First, reasoning does not scale well to the finer resolution required for many tasks to be performed by the robot. For instance, the coarse-resolution representation discussed so far is not sufficient if the robot has to grasp and pickup a particular object from a particular location, and reasoning logically over a sufficiently fine-grained domain representation will be computationally expensive. Second, we have not yet modeled the actual sensor-level observations of the robot or the uncertainty in sensing and actuation. Section 2 further discusses the limitations of other approaches based on logical and/or probabilistic reasoning for robotics domains. Our architecture seeks to address these limitations by combining $\mathcal{ATI}$ with ideas drawn from work on a refinement-based architecture [18].

3.3   Refinement, Zooming and Execution

Consider a coarse-resolution system description $\mathcal{D}_c$ of transition diagram τ_c that includes $\mathcal{ATI}$. For any given goal, reasoning with $\Pi(\mathcal{D}_c, \mathcal{H}_c)$ will provide an activity, i.e., a sequence of abstract intentional actions. In our architecture, the execution of the coarse-resolution transition corresponding to each such abstract action is based on a fine-resolution system description $\mathcal{D}_f$ of transition diagram τ_f, which is a *refinement* of, and is tightly coupled to, $\mathcal{D}_c$. We can imagine refinement as taking a closer look at the domain through a magnifying lens, potentially leading to the discovery of structures that were previously abstracted away by the designer [18]. $\mathcal{D}_f$ is constructed automatically as a step in the design methodology using $\mathcal{D}_c'$ and some domain-specific information provided by the designer.

First, the signature Σ_f of $\mathcal{D}_f$ includes each basic sort of $\mathcal{D}_c$ whose elements have not been *magnified* by the increase in resolution, or both the coarse-resolution copy and its fine-resolution *counterparts* for sorts with magnified elements. For instance, sorts in the RA domain include cells that are components of the original set of places, and any *cup* has a *base* and *handle* as components; any *book*, on the other hand, is not magnified and has no components. We also include domain-dependent statics relating the magnified objects and their counterparts, e.g., *component(cup_base, cup)*. Next, domain attributes of Σ_f include the coarse-resolution version and fine-resolution counterparts (if any) of each domain attribute of Σ_c. For instance, in the RA domain, Σ_f include domain attributes, e.g.: $loc^*(thing^*, place^*)$, $next\_to^*(place^*, place^*)$, $loc(thing, place)$, and $next\_to(place, place)$, where relations with and without the "*" represent the coarse-resolution counterparts and fine-resolution counterparts respectively. The specific relations listed above describe the location of each thing at two different resolutions, and describe two places or cells that are next to each other. Actions of Σ_f include (a) every action in Σ_c with its magnified parameters replaced by fine-resolution counterparts; and (b) knowledge-producing action $test(robot, fluent)$ that checks the value of a fluent in a given state. Finally, Σ_f includes *knowledge fluents* to describe observations of the environment and the axioms governing them, e.g., basic fluents to describe the direct (sensor-based) observation of the values of the fine-resolution fluents, and defined domain-dependent fluents that determine when the value of a particular fluent can be tested. The *test* actions only change the values of knowledge fluents.

The axioms of $\mathcal{D}_f$ include (a) coarse-resolution and fine-resolution counterparts of all state constraints of $\mathcal{D}_c$, and fine-resolution counterparts of all other axioms of $\mathcal{D}_c$, with variables ranging over appropriate sorts from Σ_f; (b) general and domain-specific axioms for observing the domain through sensor inputs; and (c) axioms relating coarse-resolution domain attributes with their fine-resolution counterparts. If certain conditions are met, e.g., each coarse-resolution domain attribute can be defined in terms of the fine-resolution attributes of the corresponding components, there is a path in τ_f for each transition in τ_c—see [18] for formal definitions and proofs.

Reasoning with $\mathcal{D}_f$ does not address the uncertainty in sensing and actuation, and becomes computationally intractable for complex domains. We address this problem by drawing on the principle of *zooming* introduced in [18]. Specifically, for each abstract transition T to be implemented at fine resolution, we automatically determine the system description $\mathcal{D}_f(T)$ relevant to this transition; we do so by determining the relevant object constants and restricting $\mathcal{D}_f$ to these object constants. To implement T, we then use ASP-based reasoning with $\Pi(\mathcal{D}_f(T), \mathcal{H}_f)$ to plan a sequence of *concrete* (i.e., fine-resolution) actions. In what follows, we use "refinement and zooming" to refer to the use of both refinement and zooming as described above. Note that fine-resolution reasoning does not (need to) reason with activities or intentional actions.

The actual execution of the plan of concrete action is based on existing implementations of algorithms for common robotics tasks such as motion planning, object recognition, grasping and localization. These algorithms use probabilistic models of uncertainty in sensing and actuation. The high-probability outcomes of each action's execution are elevated to statements associated with complete certainty in $\mathcal{H}_f$ and used for subsequent reasoning. The outcomes from fine-resolution execution of each abstract transition, along with relevant observations, are added to $\mathcal{H}_c$ for subsequent reasoning using $\mathcal{ATI}$. The CR-Prolog programs for fine-resolution reasoning and the program for the overall control loop of the architecture are available online [17].

Key differences between the current representation and use of fine-resolution information, and the prior work on the refinement-based architecture [18] are:

- Prior work used a partially observable Markov decision process (POMDP) to reason probabilistically over the zoomed fine-resolution system description $\mathcal{D}_f(T)$ for any coarse-resolution transition T; this can be computationally expensive, especially when domain changes prevent reuse of POMDP policies [18]. In this paper, CR-Prolog is used to compute a plan of concrete actions from $\mathcal{D}_f(T)$; each concrete action is executed using algorithms that incorporate probabilistic models of uncertainty, significantly reducing the computational costs of fine-resolution planning and execution. The disadvantage is that the uncertainty associated with each algorithm is not considered explicitly during planning at the fine-resolution.
- Prior work did not (a) reason about intentional actions; (b) maintain any fine-resolution history; or (c) extract and exploit all the information from fine-resolution observations. The architecture described in this paper keeps track of the relevant fine-resolution observations and adds appropriate statements to the coarse-resolution history to use all the relevant information. It also explicitly builds a consistent model of history at the finer resolution.

4   Experimental Setup and Results

This section reports the results of experimentally evaluating the capabilities of our architecture in different scenarios. We evaluated the following hypotheses:

- **H1:** using $\mathcal{ATI}$ improves the computational efficiency in comparison with not using it, especially in scenarios with unexpected success.
- **H2:** using $\mathcal{ATI}$ improves the accuracy in comparison with not using it, especially in scenarios with unexpected goal-relevant observations.
- **H3:** the architecture that combines $\mathcal{ATI}$ with refinement and zooming supports reliable and efficient operation in complex robot domains.

We report results of evaluating these hypotheses experimentally: (a) in a simulated domain based on Example 1; (b) on a Baxter robot manipulating objects on a tabletop; and (c) on a Turtlebot finding and moving objects in an indoor domain. We also provide some execution traces as illustrative examples of the working of the architecture. In each trial, the robot's goal was to find and move one or more objects to particular locations. As a baseline for comparison, we used an ASP-based reasoner that does not include $\mathcal{ATI}$—we refer to this as the "traditional planning" ($\mathcal{TP}$) approach in which only the outcome of the action currently being executed is monitored. Note that this baseline still uses refinement and zoom, and probabilistic models of the uncertainty in sensing and actuation. Also, we do not use $\mathcal{TI}$ as the baseline because it includes components that make it much more computationally expensive than $\mathcal{ATI}$—see Sect. 3.2 for more details. To evaluate the hypotheses, we used one or more of the following performance measures: (i) total planning and execution time; (ii) number of plans computed; (iii) planning time; (iv) execution time; (v) number of actions executed; and (vi) accuracy.

4.1   Experimental Results (Simulation)

We first evaluated hypotheses H1 and H2 extensively in a simulated world that mimics Example 1, with four places and different objects. Please also note the following:

- To fully explore the effects of $\mathcal{ATI}$, the simulation-based trials did not include refinement, i.e., the robot only reasons with the coarse-resolution domain representation. We also temporarily abstracted away uncertainty in perception and actuation.
- We conducted paired trials and compared the results obtained with $\mathcal{TP}$ and $\mathcal{ATI}$ for the same initial conditions and for the same dynamic domain changes (when appropriate), e.g., a book is moved unknown to the robot and the robot obtains an unexpected observation.
- To measure execution time, we assumed a fixed execution time for each concrete action, e.g., 15 units for moving from a room to the neighboring room, 5 units to pick up an object or put it down; and 5 units to open a door. Ground truth is provided by a component that reasons with complete domain knowledge.

Table 1. Experimental results comparing $\mathcal{ATI}$ with $\mathcal{TP}$ in different scenarios. Values of all performance measures (except accuracy) for $\mathcal{TP}$ are expressed as a fraction of the values of the same measures for $\mathcal{ATI}$. $\mathcal{ATI}$ improves accuracy and computational efficiency, especially in dynamic domains.

Scenarios	Average ratios					Accuracy	
	Total time	Number plans	Planning time	Exec. time	Exec. steps	$\mathcal{TP}$	$\mathcal{ATI}$
1	0.81	1.00	0.45	1.00	1.00	100%	100%
2	3.06	2.63	1.08	5.10	3.61	100%	100%
3	0.81	0.92	0.34	1.07	1.12	72%	100%
4	1.00	1.09	0.40	1.32	1.26	73%	100%
5	0.18	0.35	0.09	0.21	0.28	0%	100%
All	1.00	1.08	0.41	1.39	1.30	74%	100%
3 - no failures	1.00	1.11	0.42	1.32	1.39	100%	100%
4 - no failures	1.22	1.31	0.49	1.61	1.53	100%	100%
All - no failures	1.23	1.30	0.5	1.72	1.60	100%	100%

Table 1 summarizes the results of ≈800 paired trials in each scenario described in Sect. 3.2; all claims made below were tested for statistical significance. The initial conditions, e.g., starting location of the robot and objects' locations, and the goal were set randomly in each paired trial; the simulation ensures that the goal is reachable from the chosen initial conditions. Also, in suitable scenarios, a randomly-chosen, valid (unexpected) domain change is introduced in each paired trial. Given the differences between paired trials, it does not make sense to average the measured time or plan length across different trials. In each paired trial, the value of each performance measure (except accuracy) obtained with $\mathcal{TP}$ is thus expressed as a fraction of the value of the same performance measure obtained with $\mathcal{ATI}$; each value reported in Table 1 is the average of these computed ratios. We highlight some key results below.

Scenario-1 represents a standard planning task with no unexpected domain changes. Both $\mathcal{TP}$ and $\mathcal{ATI}$ provide the same accuracy (100%) and compute essentially the same plan, but computing plans comprising intentional actions takes longer. This explains the reported average values of 0.45 and 0.81 for planning time and total time (for $\mathcal{TP}$) in Table 1. In Scenario-2 (unexpected success), both $\mathcal{TP}$ and $\mathcal{ATI}$ achieve 100% accuracy. Here, $\mathcal{ATI}$ stops reasoning and execution once it realizes the desired goal has been achieved unexpectedly. However, $\mathcal{TP}$ does not realize this because it does not consider observations not directly related to the action being executed; it keeps trying to find the objects of interest in different places. This explains why $\mathcal{TP}$ has a higher planning time and execution time, computes more plans, and executes more plan steps.

Scenarios 3–5 correspond to different kinds of unexpected failures. In all trials corresponding to these scenarios, $\mathcal{ATI}$ leads to successful achievement of the goal, but there are many instances in which $\mathcal{TP}$ is unable to recover from the unexpected observations and achieve the goal. For instance, if the goal is to move two books to the library, and one of the books is moved to an unexpected location when it is no longer part of an action in the robot's plan, the robot may not reason about this unexpected occurrence and thus not achieve the goal. This phenomenon is especially pronounced in Scenario-5 that represents an extreme case in which the robot using $\mathcal{TP}$ is never able to achieve the assigned goal because it never realizes that it has failed to achieve the goal. Notice that in the trials corresponding to all three scenarios, $\mathcal{ATI}$ takes more time than $\mathcal{TP}$ to plan and execute the plans for any given goal, but this increase in time is more than justified given the high accuracy and the desired behavior that the robot is able to achieve in these scenarios using $\mathcal{ATI}$.

The row labeled "All" in Table 1 shows the average of the results obtained in the different scenarios. The following three rows summarize results after removing from consideration all trials in which $\mathcal{TP}$ fails to achieve the assigned goal. We then notice that $\mathcal{ATI}$ is at least as fast as $\mathcal{TP}$ and often faster, i.e., takes less time (overall) to plan and execute actions. In summary, $\mathcal{TP}$ results in faster planning but results in lower accuracy and higher execution time than $\mathcal{ATI}$ in dynamic domains, especially in the presence of unexpected successes and failures that are common in dynamic domains. All these results provide evidence in support of hypotheses H1 and H2. For extensive results in more complex domains, including a comparison with an architecture that does not use zooming at the fine-resolution, please see [11].

4.2   Execution Trace

The following execution trace illustrates the differences in the decisions made by a robot using $\mathcal{ATI}$ in comparison with a robot using $\mathcal{TP}$. This trace corresponds to scenarios in which the robot has to respond to the observed effects of an exogenous action.

Execution Example 1 *[Example of Scenario-2]*
Assume that robot rob_1 is in the *kitchen* initially, holding $book_1$ in its hand, and believes that $book_2$ is in $office_2$ and the *library* is unlocked.

– The goal is to have $book_1$ and $book_2$ in the *library*. The computed plan is the same for $\mathcal{ATI}$ and $\mathcal{TP}$, and consists of actions:

$$move(rob_1, library), \; put\_down(rob_1, book_1), move(rob_1, kitchen),$$
$$move(rob_1, office_2), pickup(rob_1, book_2), \; move(rob_1, kitchen)$$
$$move(rob_1, library), \; putdown(rob_1, book_2)$$

– Assume that as the robot is putting $book_1$ down in the *library*, someone has moved $book_2$ to the *library*.
– With $\mathcal{ATI}$, the robot observes $book_2$ in the *library*, reasons and explains the observation as the result of an exogenous action, realizes the goal has been achieved and stops further planning and execution.

– With $\mathcal{TP}$, the robot does not observe or does not use the information encoded in the observation of $book_2$. It will thus waste time executing subsequent steps of the plan until it is unable to find or pickup $book_2$ in the *library*. It will then replan (potentially including prior observation of $book_2$) and eventually achieve the desired goal. It may also compute and pursue plans assuming $book_2$ is in different places, and take more time to achieve the goal.

4.3   Robot Experiments

We also ran experimental trials with the combined architecture, i.e., $\mathcal{ATI}$ with refinement and zoom, on two robot platforms. These trials represented instances of the different scenarios in variants of the domain in Example 1.

First, consider the experiments with the Baxter robot manipulating objects on a tabletop. The goal is to move particular objects between different "zones" (instead of places) or particular cell locations on a tabletop. After refinement, each zone is magnified to obtain grid cells. Also, each object is magnified into parts such as *base* and *handle* after refinement. Objects are characterized by *color* and *size*. The robot cannot move its body but it can use its arm to move objects between cells or zones.

Next, consider the experiments with the Turtlebot robot operating in an indoor domain. The goal is to find and move particular objects between places in an indoor domain. The robot does not have a manipulator arm; it solicits help from a human to pickup the desired object when it has reached the desired source location and found the object, and to put the object down when it has reached the desired target location. Objects are characterized by *color* and *type*. After refinement, each place or zone was magnified to obtain grid cells. Also, each object is magnified into parts such as *base* and *handle* after refinement.

Although the two domains differ significantly, e.g., in the domain attributes, actions and complexity, no change is required in the architecture or the underlying methodology. Other than providing the domain-specific information, no human supervision is necessary; most of the other steps are automated. In ≈50 experimental trials in each domain, the robot using the combined architecture is able to successfully achieve the assigned goal. The performance is similar to that observed in the simulation trials. For instance, if we do not include $\mathcal{ATI}$, the robot has lower accuracy or takes more time to achieve the goal in the presence of unexpected success or failure; in other scenarios, the performance with $\mathcal{ATI}$ and $\mathcal{TP}$ is comparable. Also, if we do not include zooming, the robot takes a significantly longer to plan and execute concrete, i.e., fine-resolution actions. In fact, as the domain becomes more complex, i.e., there are many objects and achieving the desired goal requires plans with multiple steps, there are instances when the planning starts becoming computationally intractable. All these results provide evidence in support of hypothesis H3.

Videos of the trials on the Baxter robot and Turtlebot corresponding to different scenarios can be viewed online [19]. For instance, in one trial involving the Turtlebot, the goal is to have both a cup and a bottle in the *library*, and these objects and the robot are initially in $office_2$. The computed plan has the robot pick up the bottle, move to the *kitchen*, move to the *library*, put the bottle down, move back to the *kitchen* and then to *office₂*, pick up the cup, move to the *library* through the *kitchen*, and put the cup down. When the Turtlebot is moving to the *library* holding the bottle, someone moves the cup to the *library*. With $\mathcal{ATI}$, the robot uses the observation of the cup, once it has put the bottle in the *library*, to infer the goal has been achieved and thus stops planning and execution. With just $\mathcal{TP}$, the robot continued with its initial plan and realized that there was a problem (unexpected position of the cup) only when it went back to *office₂* and did not find the cup.

5   Discussion and Future Work

In this paper we presented a general architecture that reasons with intentions and beliefs using transition diagrams at two different resolutions. Non-monotonic logical reasoning with a coarse-resolution domain representation containing commonsense knowledge is used to provide a plan of abstract intentional actions for any given goal. Each such abstract intentional action is implemented as a sequence of concrete actions by reasoning with the relevant part of a fine-resolution representation that is a refinement of the coarse-resolution representation. Also, the architecture allows the robot to automatically and elegantly consider the observations that are relevant to any given goal and the underlying intention. Experimental results in simulation and on different robot platforms indicate that this architecture improves the accuracy and computational efficiency of decision making in comparison with an architecture that does not reason with intentional actions and/or does not include refinement and zooming.

This architecture opens up directions for future research. First, we will explore and formally establish the relationship between the different transition diagrams in this architecture, along the lines of the analysis provided in [18]. This will enable us to prove correctness and provide other guarantees about the robot's performance. We will also instantiate the architecture in different domains and to further demonstrate the applicability of the architecture. The long-term goal will be enable robots to represent and reason reliably and efficiently with different descriptions of knowledge and uncertainty.

References

1. Balai, E., Gelfond, M., Zhang, Y.: Towards answer set programming with sorts. In: International Conference on Logic Programming and Nonmonotonic Reasoning, Corunna, Spain, 15–19 September 2013 (2013)
2. Balduccini, M., Gelfond, M.: Logic programs with consistency-restoring rules. In: AAAI Spring Symposium on Logical Formalization of Commonsense Reasoning, pp. 9–18 (2003)
3. Baral, C., Gelfond, M.: Reasoning about intended actions. In: Proceedings of the National Conference on Artificial Intelligence, vol. 20, p. 689 (2005)

4. Blount, J., Gelfond, M., Balduccini, M.: Towards a theory of intentional agents. In: Knowledge Representation and Reasoning in Robotics. AAAI Spring Symposium Series, pp. 10–17 (2014)
5. Blount, J., Gelfond, M., Balduccini, M.: A theory of intentions for intelligent agents. In: Calimeri, F., Ianni, G., Truszczynski, M. (eds.) LPNMR 2015. LNCS (LNAI), vol. 9345, pp. 134–142. Springer, Cham (2015). https://doi.org/10.1007/978-3-319-23264-5_12
6. Bratman, M.: Intention, Plans, and Practical Reason. Center for the Study of Language and Information (1987)
7. Erdem, E., Patoglu, V.: Applications of ASP in robotics. Kunstliche Intelligenz **32**(2–3), 143–149 (2018)
8. Gabaldon, A.: Activity recognition with intended actions. In: International Joint Conference on Artificial Intelligence (IJCAI), Pasadena, USA, 11–17 July 2009 (2009)
9. Gelfond, M., Kahl, Y.: Knowledge Representation, Reasoning, and the Design of Intelligent Agents: The Answer-Set Programming Approach. Cambridge University Press, Cambridge (2014). https://books.google.co.nz/books?id=99XSAgAAQBAJ
10. Gelfond, M., Inclezan, D.: Some properties of system descriptions of AL_d. J. Appl. Non-Class. Log. Spec. Issue Equilibr. Logic Answ. Set Program. **23**(1–2), 105–120 (2013)
11. Gomez, R., Sridharan, M., Riley, H.: What do you really want to do? Towards a theory of intentions for human-robot collaboration. Ann. Math. Artif. Intell. (2020). https://doi.org/10.1007/s10472-019-09672-4
12. Hanheide, M., et al.: Robot task planning and explanation in open and uncertain worlds. Artif. Intell. **247**, 119–150 (2017)
13. Kelley, R., Tavakkoli, A., King, C., Nicolescu, M., Nicolescu, M., Bebis, G.: Understanding human intentions via hidden Markov models in autonomous mobile robots. In: International Conference on Human-Robot Interaction (HRI), Amsterdam, Netherlands, 12–15 March 2008 (2008)
14. Rao, A.S., Georgeff, M.P.: BDI agents: from theory to practice. In: 1st International Conference on Multiagent Systems, San Francisco, CA, pp. 312–319 (1995)
15. Saribatur, Z.G., Baral, C., Eiter, T.: Reactive maintenance policies over equalized states in dynamic environments. In: Oliveira, E., Gama, J., Vale, Z., Lopes Cardoso, H. (eds.) EPIA 2017. LNCS (LNAI), vol. 10423, pp. 709–723. Springer, Cham (2017). https://doi.org/10.1007/978-3-319-65340-2_58
16. Saribatur, Z.G., Eiter, T.: Reactive policies with planning for action languages. In: Michael, L., Kakas, A. (eds.) JELIA 2016. LNCS (LNAI), vol. 10021, pp. 463–480. Springer, Cham (2016). https://doi.org/10.1007/978-3-319-48758-8_30
17. Software and results corresponding to the evaluation of our architecture (2019). https://github.com/hril230/theoryofintentions/tree/master/code
18. Sridharan, M., Gelfond, M., Zhang, S., Wyatt, J.: REBA: a refinement-based architecture for knowledge representation and reasoning in robotics. J. Artif. Intell. Res. **65**, 87–180 (2019)
19. Videos demonstrating the use of our architecture on robot platforms (2019). https://drive.google.com/open?id=1m-jVV25vFvi35Ai9N7RYFFOPNaZIUdpZ
20. Zhang, Q., Inclezan, D.: An application of ASP theories of intentions to understanding restaurant scenarios. In: International Workshop on Practical Aspects of Answer Set Programming (2017)
21. Zhang, S., Khandelwal, P., Stone, P.: Dynamically constructed (PO)MDPs for adaptive robot planning. In: AAAI Conference on Artificial Intelligence (AAAI), San Francisco, USA, February 2017 (20)

Decentralised Control of Intelligent Devices: A Healthcare Facility Study

Sacha Lhopital[1], Samir Aknine[2], Vincent Thavonekham[1], Huan Vu[2(✉)] [iD],
and Sarvapali Ramchurn[3] [iD]

[1] VISEO Technologies, Lyon, France
{sacha.lhopital,vincent.thavonekham}@viseo.com
[2] Université de Lyon, CNRS, Université Lyon 1, LIRIS, UMR5205,
69622 Lyon, France
samir.aknine@univ-lyon1.fr, huan.vu@liris.cnrs.fr
[3] University of Southampton, Southampton, UK
sdr1@soton.ac.uk

Abstract. We present a novel approach to the management of notifications from devices in a healthcare setting. We employ a distributed constraint optimisation (DCOP) approach to the delivery of notification for healthcare assistants that aims to preserve the privacy of patients while reducing the intrusiveness of such notifications. Our approach reduces the workload of the assistants and improves patient safety by automating task allocation while ensuring high priority needs are addressed in a timely manner. We propose and evaluate several DCOP models both in simulation and in real-world deployments. Our models are shown to be efficient both in terms of computation and communication costs.

Keywords: IoT · Healthcare · DCOP · DPOP

1 Introduction

The penetration of novel Internet-of-things technology in the healthcare setting is growing rapidly. Many of these devices serve to monitor patients and alert healthcare professionals whenever abnormalities are detected (for instance, a syringe pump is going to ring when it detects an air bubble in its mechanism) or when routine checks are needed (about every four hours).

Nevertheless, operating and monitoring these devices take a considerable amount of time ranging from 5 to 10% a day. As a result, a healthcare provider has to check all those devices on a regular basis. As part of this project, a series of interviews with hospital staff were conducted. The following conclusions were drawn from these interviews. Every time a device encounters a technical problem (e.g. running out of power) or the device is ending its program (e.g. the syringe pump will finish its program in less than ten minutes), the device produces a very loud tone in order to alert the medical staff. Attending to such notifications rapidly becomes intractable with large departments with hundreds of patients.

© Springer Nature Switzerland AG 2020
N. Bassiliades et al. (Eds.): EUMAS 2020/AT 2020, LNAI 12520, pp. 20–36, 2020.
https://doi.org/10.1007/978-3-030-66412-1_2

Thus, when a device rings, the medical staff cannot remember which one it is and what action is expected. Therefore, the staff needs to: (1) go in the room (2) notice the defective equipment (3) act accordingly (for instance: get a medication stored in another room). Limiting these tasks (by only checking rooms requiring an intervention, where it used to be every room of the department every x hours for instance) can improve healthcare professionals' work conditions. With this in mind, several issues were noticed: (1) most of the devices are not integrated into an information system, thus forcing healthcare professionals to individually check them regularly, thereby wasting precious time on monitoring actions; (2) audible notifications from multiple devices at the same time can raise levels of stress and confusion among staff.

Against this background, in this paper we propose a novel approach that looks to minimise the intrusiveness of such devices. Specifically, we develop a solution that: (1) Detects anomalies and manages tasks division by combining data from multiple sources; (2) Constructs and suggests an action plan for healthcare provider. The aim is to provide staff with situational awareness and help them anticipate future interventions. The purpose of our system is to warn the medical staff before devices ring, but without increasing the frequency of their interventions. We formulate the problem as a Distributed Constraint Optimization Problem (DCOP) which has been shown to be effective in itinerary optimization [6,15] and scheduling problems [7]. This decentralized approach has the benefit of distributing the main computations across all available devices. Specifically, this paper advances the state of the art in the following ways.

1. We propose a DCOP approach that limits the amount of data transmitted to a central node.
2. Our DCOP approach allows the seamless integration or removal of IoT devices.
3. We show that a DCOP approach is a natural way of modelling the problem. Our system was simulated using Raspberry Pi's to help represent the problem in a more realistic way. This specific deployment method is very important since it adds development constraints to our system (execution time, machine resources, interactions with the staff).

The remainder of this article is organized as follows. First, the paper introduces the problem statement. After that, we describe the DCOP model we propose to solve this problem. Then, we detail the proposed solution. We pursue with an evaluation of our work. In the conclusion, we summarize the work done and we provide some perspectives.

2   Related Work

MobiCare [1], designed by Chakravorty in 2006, provides a wide-area mobile patient monitoring system to facilitate continuous monitoring of the patients physiological status. Like CodeBlue [9,11] is a popular healthcare project based on BSN framework (Body Sensor Network). In this system, sensors on the patient's body transmit information wirelessly to other devices for further analysis (like laptops and personal computers). While CodeBlue is using a wireless architecture, there have been many efforts in the medical field to design gateways for specific applications. For example, [2,16] suggest the use of gateways instead of wireless or Ethernet to connect networks with different protocols.

Beyond these first solutions, DCOP algorithms have already been tested in practical scenarios such as travel optimization [6,15] or planning [7]. Among the DCOP algorithms, three are particularly well known: ADOPT [12], DPOP [14], OptAPO [10].

[6] compared these main algorithms in situations where the environment changes dynamically. Their study shows that these algorithms offer good performance but also highlight some limitations. DPOP is the fastest algorithm at runtime, but it is extremely greedy about the size of the messages exchanged. ADOPT gives variable results depending on the constraints. Indeed, if the system is not subject to many conflicting constraints, the algorithm will be efficient. On the other hand, if many constraints conflict, ADOPT does not provide efficient results. OptAPO was proven to be incomplete and therefore, a complete variant has been proposed [5]. Both variants are based on a mediator agent, so the resolution is not fully distributed. [7] proposed another algorithm to solve dynamic problems called DCDCOP (*Dynamic Complex DCOP*) based on a case study of time use optimization in a medical context. This algorithm - mainly based on the addition of a *Degree of Unsatisfaction* measure - dynamically guides agents through the resolution process. This method is more appropriate where agents try to optimize several variables at the same time.

The mechanism we propose is based on the DPOP algorithm [13]. We propose an improved version of the algorithm proposed by [13]. We have designed new heuristics for the *Depth First Search* (DFS) tree generation to improve the execution speed. This is the first model for device management using DCOPs.

3   Problem Statement

We consider a hospital facility made up of several departments. Each department includes a set of rooms. Within a room, several devices are deployed to monitor the status of each patient. Each room has a neighborhood formed by a set of rooms. The objective of the system is to determine the times when healthcare providers pass through each of these rooms and prioritize them in order to perform the operations required for each patient (e.g. recharging a syringe pump, etc.). The intervention time consists of a number of minutes before the situation becomes critical. Thus, we prioritize the rooms depending on which one is the most urgent. The emergency "level" is calculated dynamically and depends on several parameters. A room deadline is the time when a device of this room will ring. We define, a configuration O_t as the set of times for all the rooms in the department for a time step t. Each configuration O_t must satisfy the following rules: (1) a room must have only one intervention time at a time t_i; (2) the current configuration must be accessible by all rooms so that they share the same information; (3) all the rooms should not call the healthcare providers at the same time, except the rooms in the same neighbourhood. In order to build this configuration, we model the problem as follows. Let $A = \{a_1, \ldots, a_n\}$ be the set of agents (which manage the rooms) with n the total number of rooms. Each room i is modeled by an agent a_i. For a room i, each agent a_i will compute a value v_i which represents the time (in minutes) before the next intervention. Let $D = \{d_1, \ldots, d_n\}$ be all the possible values for v_i. If $d_i = +\infty$, then no intervention is required in the room i. Let t be the current time step. A configuration $O_t = \{v_1, \ldots, v_n\}$ is optimal if, and only if, it respects all the constraints of each room in the department. The system's inputs are the agents A and the previous configuration O_{t-1}. Thus, the O_t configuration is optimal if F, the interventions cost function, is minimal according to the next intervention dates v_i. Our goal is to seek a minimization:

$$\arg \min_{O_t} F(O_t) = \sum_{i=1}^{n} C_i \qquad (1)$$

For a specific v_i, C_i returns a global cost $\in \mathbb{R} \cup \{\infty\}$. This global cost, to satisfy F, is defined regarding all the following structural constraints.

- **c1. Device number constraint:** If there are no devices in the room, the agent will not ask for intervention: Let $M_i = \{m_1, \ldots, m_l\}$ be the set of all the devices of the room i.

$$\forall a_i \in A, |M_i| = 0 \Rightarrow v_i = +\infty \qquad (2)$$

- **c2.a Simple device rescheduling constraint:** Healthcare professionals have to check the room just before a device ends its program. We define the function $isInCriticState(m_i)$ which returns $true$ if the device m_i is in a critical state.

$$\forall a_i \in A, \forall m_l \in M_i,$$
$$isInCriticState(m_l) \Rightarrow v_i < 10 \qquad (3)$$

- **c2.b Critical device rescheduling constraint:** Healthcare professionals have to reschedule machines when they come to a critical state. Therefore, we define the function $programState(m_i)$ to return the remaining time (minutes) before m_i ends its program. If the remaining time is not computable (i.e. the device does not require an intervention), the function returns $+\infty$. As a consequence, if a device in the room i ends its program in less than $30\,\text{min}$ than v_i has to be less than this value.

$$\forall a_i \in A, \exists m_l \in M_i,$$
$$\neg\, isInCriticState(m_l) \wedge programState(m_l) \leq 30 \qquad (4)$$
$$\Rightarrow v_i \leq programState(m_l)$$

- **c3. Neighbourhood constraint:** If two rooms are in the same location, they can synchronize their decisions to avoid multiple interventions in a short time. In other words: two neighbours should not ask for interventions with less than $t_{synchro}$ minutes interval (except if they both call at the same time). We define the function $neighbours(a_i, a_j)$ as a function returning $true$ when the agents a_i and a_j are neighbours.

$$\forall a_i, a_j \in A^2, neighbours(a_i, a_j) \Rightarrow \tag{5}$$
$$(|v_i - v_j| > t_{synchro} \vee |v_i - v_j| = 0)$$

- **c4.a Patient's condition constraint:** If a patient uses multiple devices (more than five), we consider that he needs more attention than others. His state should be checked at least every three hours instead of four otherwise. Let τ_i be the elapsed time since a medical staff came into the room i.

$$\forall a_i \in A, (|M_i| > 5 \wedge \tau_i \geq 180) \Rightarrow v_i < 30 \tag{6}$$

- **c4.b Time between two visits constraint:** The elapsed time between two interventions in a room cannot exceed four hours. This constraint is derived from the interviews we made. If more than 3 h and 30 min have passed since the last visit, the system should plan another visit within 30 min.

$$\forall a_i \in A, (|M_i| \geq 1 \wedge \tau_i \geq 210) \Rightarrow v_i < 30 \tag{7}$$

- **c5. Quietness constraint:** Each agent a_i verifies if there is no device in the room i that needs intervention. If it is the case, healthcare staff can ignore the room:

$$\forall a_i \in A, \forall m_l \in M_i,$$
$$(\neg isInCriticState(m_l) \wedge$$
$$programState(m_l) > 30 \wedge \tau_i < 180) \tag{8}$$
$$\Rightarrow v_i \geq 240$$

Example 1. *Consider the following scenario with 6 rooms (a_1, a_2, a_3, a_4, a_5 and a_6) in a medical department. None of the rooms has devices to monitor except the room a_3 which is monitoring 3 devices programmed to end respectively in 40 min, 60 min, and the last is in a critical state. The neighbourhood is the following: a_1 is surrounded by a_3 and a_2; a_4 is surrounded by a_3 and a_5; And a_5 is also neighbour with a_6. Therefore, a_1, a_3, a_4, a_5 have two neighbours, while a_2 and a_6 have only one neighbour (cf. Fig. 1).*

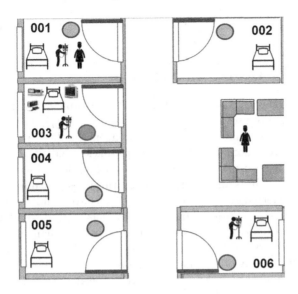

Fig. 1. Illustration scenario with the 6 rooms in the medical department. None of the rooms have devices to monitor except agent a_3 which is monitoring 3 devices programmed to end respectively in 40 min, 60 min, and the last (in red) is in a critical state. All adjacent rooms are neighbours. Therefore, a_1, a_3, a_4, a_5 have two neighbours, while a_2 and a_6 have only one neighbour. (Color figure online)

Also, assuming that:

- $M_3 = \{m_{31}, m_{32}, m_{33}\}$
  with $isInCriticState(m_{32}) = True$ *(the device is in a critical state),* $programState(m_{31}) = 60$ *and* $programState(m_{33}) = 40$.
- $M_4 = M_5 = M_1 = M_2 = M_6 = \{\emptyset\}$.
- $\tau_3 = 60$.
- *We also set* $t_{synchro} = 30$.

The structural constraints can be described as:

c1: v_4, v_5, v_1, v_2 *and* v_6 *will take the value* $+\infty$.
c2: *The device* m_{32} *needs intervention. Thus,* $v_3 < 10$. *The device* m_{31} *ends its program in 60 min and the device* m_{33} *in 40 min. Hence:* $v_3 \leq 60$; $v_3 \leq 40$.
c3: *Given the neighbourhood in the scenario, we deduce that* $|v_3 - v_4| > t_{synchro}$ *and* $|v_3 - v_1| > t_{synchro}$.
c4: *The last intervention is very recent (because* $\tau_3 < 180$ *and* $|M_3| < 5$*), so this constraint will not be applied.*
c5: *This constraint does not apply here.*

Next, we formalize the problem as a distributed constraint optimization problem.

Centralized solutions to scheduling have a lack of scalability and adaptability to dynamic events such as the arrival of an emergency. In such a dynamic

context, using a decentralized approach allows to be proactive to any change of
the devices.

4   DCOPs for Device Management

We formalise the Device Management DCOP as a tuple $\{A, V, D, C\}$, where:
$A = \{a_1, a_2, \ldots, a_n\}$ is a set of n agents; $V = \{v_1, v_2, \ldots, v_n\}$ are variables owned
by the agents, where variable v_i is owned by agent a_i; $D = \{d_1, d_2, \ldots, d_n\}$ is
a set of finite-discrete domains. A variable v_i takes values in $d_{v_i} = v_1, \ldots, v_k$;
$C = \{c_1, \ldots, c_m\}$ is a set of constraints, where each c_i defines a cost $\in \mathbb{N} \cup \{\infty\}$.
A solution to the DCOP is an assignment to all variables that minimizes $\sum_{i=1}^{n} c_i$.

DCOP is a preferred solution to deal with stochastic and dynamic environments with data gathered from different agents. It is applied to numerous different applications in multi-agent systems such as disaster management, meeting
scheduling, sensor network [3].

There are several ways to formalize our problem as a DCOP, depending on
what agents, variables and constraints are representing. Here we present three
approaches to formalize the medical optimization problem as a DCOP: a fully
decentralized room-based approach (**Room Approach**), a semi-decentralized
area-based approach (**Area Approach**) and finally a semi-decentralized multi-
variable approach (**Multi-variable Area-based Approach**). We intend to
show the effect of different levels of decentralization on the quality of time computing. We evaluate and show the performance of each approach which may be
suitable for different medical device conditions.

4.1   Room-Based Approach

The **Room Approach** consists of modelling all the rooms as agents. The number of agents corresponds to the number of rooms to monitor. Each agent has
a variable that corresponds to the desired intervention time, depending on the
devices conditions in the room. The domain of the variables varies from 0, which
is the most critical call, to ∞ which means that no call is planned. We then map
the structural constraints described in the Eqs. (2) to (8) as follows:

Device number constraint

$$c_1(v_i) = \begin{cases} \infty, & \text{if } |M_i| = 0 \text{ and } v_i \neq +\infty \\ 0, & \text{otherwise} \end{cases} \tag{9}$$

Device rescheduling constraint

$$c_2(v_i) = \begin{cases} \infty, & \text{if } \exists m_l \in M_i, \\ & isInCriticState(m_l) \text{ and } v_i \geq 10 \\ 1, & \text{if } \exists m_l \in M_i, (\neg isInCriticState(m_l) \\ & \text{and } programState(m_l) \leq 30) \\ & \text{and } v_i > programState(m_l) \\ 0, & \text{otherwise} \end{cases} \tag{10}$$

Neighbourhood constraint

$$c_3(v_i, v_j) = \begin{cases} 1, & \text{if } neighbours(a_i, a_j) \\ & \text{and } |v_i - v_j| \leq t_{synchro} \\ & \text{and } |v_i - v_j| \neq 0 \\ 0, & \text{otherwise} \end{cases} \qquad (11)$$

Patient's condition and time between two visits constraint

$$c_4(v_i) = \begin{cases} \infty, & \text{if } ((|M_i| > 5 \text{ and } \tau_i \geq 180) \\ & \text{or } (|M_i| \geq 1 \text{ and } \tau_i \geq 210)) \text{ and } v_i \geq 30 \\ 0, & \text{otherwise} \end{cases} \qquad (12)$$

Quietness constraint

$$c_5(v_i) = \begin{cases} 1, & \text{if } \forall m_l \in M_i, \ v_i < 240 \\ & \text{and } \neg isInCriticState(m_l) \\ & \text{and } programState(m_l) > 30 \text{ and } \tau_i < 180 \\ 0, & \text{otherwise} \end{cases} \qquad (13)$$

The objective of our DCOP is to minimize $\sum_{i=1}^{n} c_i$. This optimization represents the goal of the system (i.e. minimizing the number of rooms making calls without violating any structural constraint).

4.2   Area-Based Approach

Instead of considering each room as an agent, we can consider a hospital area as an agent which monitors multiple rooms. We consider that the department is divided into several areas. As an area agent, it holds a unique variable v that contains the most critical intervention time among all monitored rooms. By gathering information from several rooms in this way, the system solves the problem using the same constraints as in the previous approach. However, these constraints are applied to all the rooms instead of a single room. On the other hand, the neighbourhood constraint no longer concerns the rooms, but rather the areas. Therefore, the global cost C_i is also computed by area as follows:

$$C_i = \begin{cases} \infty, & \text{if } \exists r_k \in R_i, \ \exists m_l \in M_k \\ & isInCriticState(m_l) \\ \sum_{k=1}^{p} \sum_{q=2}^{m} c_q(v_i), & \text{otherwise} \end{cases} \qquad (14)$$

In this approach, the device number constraint is no more used. We define a similar constraint to take all rooms R_i into account and no longer a single one.

This approach also requires us to consider the impact on privacy and, more specifically, the transit of data. For security and data protection reasons, the centralization of data is very sensitive.

4.3 Multi-variable Area-Based Approach

To go further in the area-based modelling, a slightly more specific approach was also considered where each area defines an intervention time for each room. In this last approach, we still consider that each one of the rooms in the area has the knowledge on all the other rooms. Thus, we still have a single area agent, but this agent will calculate a time set $V_{a_i} = \{v_{r_1}, v_{r_2}, \ldots, v_{r_k}\}$ where k is the number of rooms of the area i. This approach also requires us to consider the impact on privacy, like the area-based approach.

Now that we have formalized the problem as a DCOP, we discuss the quality of the solution and the usefulness of the method.

5   A DPOP Solution for the Device Management Problem

To solve the DCOP presented above, we use the DPOP algorithm (*Dynamic Parameter Optimization Problem*) [14], based on the exchange of messages between agents. We chose to use DPOP as it is one of the fastest DCOP algorithms [6], working by *tree aggregation* [4]. In more details, DPOP operates on a matrix handling algorithm. To communicate agents use a tree graph (DFS): an undirected graph, which contains a variable node v_i for each agent, and an edge connecting a variable node v_i with another variable node v_j if and only if v_i is a neighbour of v_j. Each agent in DPOP takes the role of the variable node which represents its own variable. Figure 2 shows the tree graph of the room-based approach for the scenario presented in the Example 1. The main process of DPOP consists in computing and exchanging messages between variable nodes through the tree graph constructed. At each iteration k of the process, all agents execute 3 phases. In the first phase, a proper tree graph is generated to serve as a communication structure for the next steps. To do so, agents exchange messages through their neighbourhood in order to generate the tree graph. When this graph is complete, the second phase starts: starting from the leaves of the tree, each agent a_i computes its own cost matrix $Util_i$ (depending on its v_i value and on its children v values) and propagates it upward through the tree edges. Those matrices summarize the influence of the sending agent and its neighbours on the next steps. The third phase is started by the root when phase 2 is over. Each agent computes its optimal value for v based on the $Util$ matrix and the $Value$ message it received from its parent. Then it sends this value as a $Value$ message to its own children.

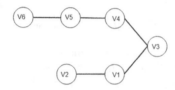

Fig. 2. Room-based approach tree graph for the scenario presented in Example 1. There are 6 agents (v_1 to v_6), each is connected to its neighbours.

Example 2. *Consider the tree graph presented in Fig. 2. Let $D = \{0, 30, 241\}$.
The message that the variable v_2 sends to its parent v_1 for the iteration k is the
following: $Util_2 = \begin{bmatrix} a \\ b \\ c \end{bmatrix}$, where each matrix value is the result of a cost $(\sum_{l=1}^{5} c_l)$.
The abscissa axis represents the lowest possible value for v_2, while the ordinate
represents all possible values for v_1 in D. When v_1 is set up with the best value
for this iteration (let us say b), v_1 sends this value back to v_2.*

During the propagation of messages, an agent is able to calculate locally its
next intervention time that minimizes the sum of the costs over all neighbours
functions. Classic DPOP does not always guarantee convergence at the end of an
iteration. In our context, we overcome this issue with the use of the **Quietness
constraint**.

Event Detection and Management. Dynamic events should be taken into account
during the resolution. For instance, we need to detect when a medical staff is
in a room (or when she is near). Every event will dynamically impact some
constraints. Thus, the system will detect healthcare staff interventions and can
update the different constraints parameters, for instance, the time since the last
intervention (τ), the states of the devices, the number of interventions $(|M|,
isInCriticState(m), programState(m))$.

Event detection is essential when a device enters in a critical state. The
healthcare provider needs to be called right away because the situation corresponds to an emergency.

Priority Management. After each iteration, all agents set their next intervention
time v depending on their knowledge about their devices. However, if an agent
i asks for a quicker intervention than its neighbours, i will not necessarily be
satisfied if it is not the most critical in the system.

In order to deal with this issue, we define the concept of priority for the
DCOP solver. The classic DPOP algorithm generates a DFS tree for the problem
to solve. But for the same problem, several DFS trees may be generated. Yet,
depending on the generated tree, the algorithm finds a local solution (possibly
the best solution, but not necessarily).

Yet, in our case study, finding a local solution is not enough. We therefore
search for the best solution because healthcare providers need to check on the
most urgent patients first. To do so, we define some specific rules for the DPOP
that allow agents to declare themselves as more important. More precisely, those
rules impact the tree graph construction in the first phase of DPOP by putting
the most important agents at the top of the DSF tree. This allows them to choose
their intervention time first. Three specific priority rules are defined:

- **Critical Priority** is triggered when a device enters a critical state. The
  concerned agent will ask other agents to start a new DCOP computation
  handling its condition. This priority is the most important. When this rule

applies, it overcomes all the others. When triggered, all agents will start a
new computation of the DCOP algorithm.

– **Time Priority** is triggered when a device needs intervention since the last
iteration, but no healthcare provider has been able to intervene. At each iteration, the agent will increase its priority until a healthcare provider answers
the call.
– **Intervention Consequence Priority** is triggered after a healthcare assistant provides an intervention. When triggered, the priority of the concerned
agent is reduced to the lowest value.

6   Empirical Evaluation

We have evaluated the performance of our method using the DPOP algorithm.
The algorithm was implemented in Python 3.6 and deployed on Raspberry Pi
devices, using Broadcom BCM2837 64-bit processor with four ARM Cortex-A53
hearts - 1,2 GHz. The use of Raspberry pi allows us to physically distribute our
agents - as it will be the case in a real situation. DPOP was also implemented
using Frodo [8]. In order to communicate, the Mqtt protocol was used with a
Mqtt Server running on a local gateway. All compared values are averages on
up to 10 to 50 consecutive simulations (the exact number depends on the used
method with the Frodo simulator or with the deployed system and their multiple
parameters). All algorithms are evaluated according to their execution time. We
ran our experiments with all our different approaches: room-based approach,
area-based approach and the multi-variable area-based approach.

6.1   Benchmarking

The Fig. 3a represents the execution time of each approach: **Room Approach**
in solid line; **Area Approach** in big dots; and **Multi-variable Area-based
Approach** with dashed lines. Multiple curves are shown for different numbers of
agents in the system. Whatever the situation, these curves show that the fastest
approach is the **Area Approach** (execution time between 1,29 and 2,68 s by
agent). The **Room Approach** also gives good results (between 3,75 and 5,6 s).
This evaluation shows that the **Area Approach** can offer faster results but it
will be at the detriment of the precision of the results. The Fig. 3b summarizes
these results. Figures 5a and 6a present the results with 6 agents. Among them, 3
agents run on Raspberry Pi devices and 3 agents run on Windows 10 computers.
Figures 5b and 6b show a similar situation but with 10 agents (3 agents on
Raspberry Pi devices and others on Windows 10 computers). Also, dotted lines
represent a specific simulation performed with simulated Raspberry Pi devices
(QEMU). The use of this simulator drastically increased the execution time
because this simulator uses more computer resources. Therefore, we will focus
on the analysis of the results represented in solid lines. The total execution time
of our deployed system is higher than the execution time we observed with the
DPOP simulation (cf. Fig. 4). For 6 agents (cf. Fig. 5a), we provide a solution in

---

Algorithm 1. Scheduling Agent pseudo-code

Require: root = NULL
  for all agents **do**
    if root == NULL **then**
      send starting signal
    else
      send starting signal with root as a parameter
    end if
  end for
  while results size < number of agents **do**
    wait
  end while
  for all results **do**
    if result == 0 **then**
      root = agent
      Start over
    end if
    if result < 30 **and** agent.priority > 0 **then**
      agent.priority = agent.priority + 1
    end if
    if result > 30 **and** agent.priority > 0 **then**
      agent.priority = 0
    end if
  end for

Algorithm 2. DPOP Agent pseudo-code when receiving a message to start

---

  if root != NULL **then**
    run DPOP algorithm with root as the DFS Tree root
  else
    run DPOP classic algorithm
  end if
  return result

---

less than 1 s using the simulator and in less than 5 s with our deployed system. This can be explained by the fact that our system provides an optimal solution, whereas FRODO provides a local optimum. This is the case because the "priority constraint" cannot be taken into account by Frodo without completely rewriting the DPOP algorithm. Secondly, regardless of the number of agents, the execution time is quite similar. Against the **Room Approach**, the **Area Approach** runs the algorithm much faster. For instance, 10 rooms divided into 4 areas give results in 1,64 s, and 10 rooms divided into 6 areas give results in 2,15 s. This semi-decentralized approach allows the system to produce more relevant results for great numbers of rooms (more than 30). Furthermore, the algorithm gives 4,64 s for 50 rooms divided into 4 areas and 9,29 s for 6 areas. This is consistent since the system only has 4 to 6 agents instead of 50 agents for the **Room Approach**.

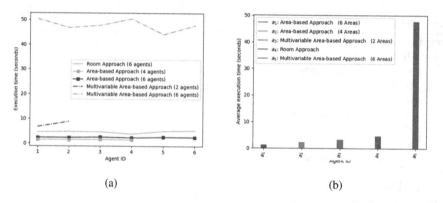

Fig. 3. Evaluations of our algorithm. (a) Execution time of the system deployed on Raspberry Pi devices depending on the approach for a medical department of 6 rooms. (b) Average execution time of the system deployed on Raspberry Pi devices depending on the approach for a medical department of 6 rooms.

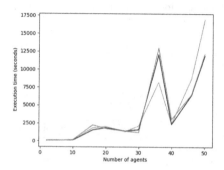

Fig. 4. Execution time depending on the number of agents using FRODO.

Table 1 gives the execution times for the **Multi-variable Area-based Approach**. If the method takes more time to execute, we observed some considerable differences between two agents, execution times for the same iteration. For instance, in the Table 1, agent 6 takes 1571 s to execute and agent 4 takes 129 s while others take less than 65 s. Those major differences can be explained by the new data structure that the agents use. Indeed, instead of using matrices of $|D|$ dimensions, the agents are computing matrices of $|D|^{NbRoomsArea(a_i)}$ dimensions where $NbRoomsArea(a_i)$ is the number of rooms managed by the agent a_i. Therefore, depending on their positions in the tree graph in the DPOP algorithm, some agents will have to deal with much more data because each parent in the tree will receive as much matrix $|D|^{NbRoomsArea(a_i)}$ as it has children. The resulting matrix will then have the following dimension: $|D|^{NbRoomsArea(a_i)} \times NbChildren(a_i)$ where $NbChildren(a_i)$ is the number of children for the agent a_i in the DFS tree.

Table 1. Execution time for 12 Rooms and 6 Areas (with a **Multi-variable Area-based Approach**).

Area	1	2	3	4	5	6
Time (s)	66.95	66.67	66.91	129.3	60.99	1571.99

6.2   Message Size

Our algorithm (and DPOP in general) requires a linear number of messages. This is explained by the DFS construction which requires $2 \times l$ messages, where l is the number of edges in the tree graph. For n agents, $Util$ DPOP phase requires $n - 1$ messages (from the bottom to the top of the tree). The $Value$ propagation requires $n - 1$ messages (from the top to the bottom of the tree). The maximum message size and memory requirements grow exponentially with the number of agents. More precisely, DFS and $Value$ messages are size and memory linear. But the complexity lies in the size of the $Util$ messages, which is space and time exponential. Figures 6a and b give the size of the exchanged messages between the agents (respectively for 6 agents in the system, and for 10 agents). Those curves show the average size of the received messages for each agent depending on different tested situations. Our system exchanges very tiny messages compared to a Frodo simulation. For example with 10 agents (plain curves), the agent number 3 is the one receiving huge messages (average of 3800 bytes). But with Frodo, average messages size is in the order of 102 Kbytes. These results are explained by the fact that we use the Mqtt communication protocol, which allows to define a specific message structure. Also, regarding the Figs. 6a and b, we observe important variations from one agent to another. Those results are explained by the algorithm processing method. Indeed, depending on the DFS tree generated during the first phase, the agents at the top of this tree will receive bigger messages because their children will send them bigger matrices during the $Util$ propagation phase. The $Util$ matrix is a multidimensional matrix, with one dimension for each variable of the problem to solve. Therefore, every time an agent received a $Util$ matrix from one of its children, the current agent increases the dimensions of the matrix (because the agent adds its own variable to solve to the matrix). In the DPOP algorithm as described by A. Petcu, each dimension of the matrix corresponds to the possible value of an agent. Each agent who receives a matrix from one of these children (in the DFS tree) actually receives a cost matrix based on the value the child will take. The more the matrix goes up in the DFS tree, the more children are to be taken into account, so the more dimensions there are. For instance, in the Fig. 6b, agents 1 to 3 received bigger messages than other agents because they are at the top of the tree and they have to compute more data. The same effect is observed for the agent 2 in the Fig. 6b.

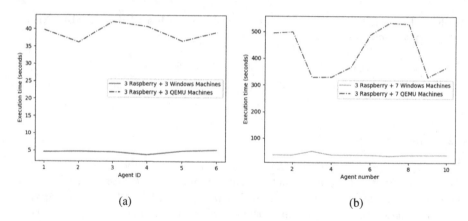

(a)   (b)

Fig. 5. Execution time comparison between our system and QEMU simulations. (a) Comparison for 6 agents. The figure shows the quality of the solutions and that our system performed better on Raspberry Pi devices. (b) Comparison for 10 agents.

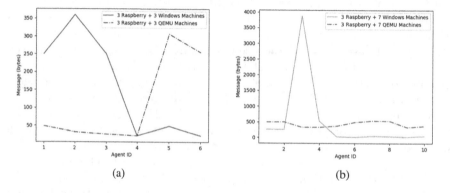

(a)   (b)

Fig. 6. Evaluation of the messages size. (a) Average received messages size comparison between our system deployed on Raspberry Pi devices and our system deployed with QEMU simulator (for 6 agents). (b) Average received messages size comparison between our system deployed on Raspberry Pi devices and our system deployed with QEMU simulator (for 10 agents).

7   Conclusion

In this paper, we have proposed an intelligent system to ease the daily work of the medical staff in helping patients. Our work offers a new method to supervise and monitor the various devices running in the rooms of the medical department and leaves the medical staff to focus on their patients. We provided a DCOP formalization of the problem and showed how we use the DPOP algorithm to solve it. Our method produces an efficient solution in terms of alerting healthcare professionals in intervention times. We showed the robustness of this solution to dynamic events. We also provided different formulations of the model with different degrees of privacy preservation when it comes to the messages passed around. While our work has shown the potential of the DCOPs to solve the medical device management problem, in the future, we aim to extend our method to consider a more sophisticated system with cameras to detect healthcare providers movements in the medical department. More precisely, we want to deploy our system on Arduino instead of the Raspberry to follow up on this work. We also aim to test our system with real devices like syringe pumps and multi-parameter monitor as they are the most common ones in most medical services.

References

1. Chakravorty, R.: A programmable service architecture for mobile medical care. In: Proceedings of the 4th IEEE Annual Conference on Pervasive Computing and Communications Workshops (PERSOMW), Pisa, Italy, March 2006, pp. 531–536. IEEE Computer Society (2006)
2. Emara, K., Abdeen, M., Hashem, M.: A gateway-based framework for transparent interconnection between WSN and IP network. In: Proceedings of the EUROCON, pp. 1775–1780 (2009)
3. Fioretto, F., Pontelli, E., Yeoh, W.: Distributed constraint optimization problems and applications: a survey. J. Artif. Intell. Res. **61**, 623–698 (2018)
4. Freuder, E.C.: A sufficient condition for backtrack-bounded search. J. ACM (JACM) **32**, 755–761 (1985). JACM Homepage archive
5. Grinshpoun, T., Meisels, A.: Completeness and performance of the APO algorithm. J. Artif. Intell. Res. **33**, 223–258 (2008)
6. Junges, R., Bazzan, A.L.C.: Evaluating the performance of DCOP algorithms in a real world, dynamic problem. In: Padgham, L., Parkes, D.C., Müller, J.P., Parsons, S. (eds.) Proceedings of the of 7th International Conference on Autonomous Agents and Multiagent Systems, AAMAS 2008, Estoril, Portugal, May 2008, pp. 599–606 (2008)
7. Khanna, S., Sattar, A., Hansen, D., Stantic, B.: An efficient algorithm for solving dynamic complex DCOP problems. In: Proceedings of the 2009 IEEE/WIC/ACM International Conference on Intelligent Agent Technology, IAT 2009, October 2009 (2009)
8. Léauté, T., Ottens, B., Szymanek, R.: FRODO 2.0: an open-source framework for distributed constraint optimization. In: Proceedings of the IJCAI'09 Distributed Constraint Reasoning Workshop, DCR 2009, Pasadena, California, USA, pp. 160–164 (2009)
9. Lorincz, K., et al.: Sensor networks for emergency response: challenges and opportunities. IEEE Pervasive Comput. **3**, 16–23 (2004)
10. Mailler, R., Lesser, V.: Solving distributed constraint optimization problems using cooperative mediation. In: Proceedings of the International Joint Conference on Autonomous Agents and Multiagent Systems, New York, USA, pp. 438–445. IEEE Computer Society (2004)
11. Malan, D., Fulford-Jones, T., Welsh, M., Moulton, S.: CodeBlue: an ad hoc sensor network infrastructure for emergency medical care. In: Proceedings of the MobiSys Workshop on Applications of Mobile Embedded Systems (WAMES), Boston, MA, USA, June 2004, pp. 1–8 (2004)
12. Modi, P.J., Shen, W., Tambe, M., Yokoo, M.: Adopt: asynchronous distributed constraint optimization with quality guarantees. Artif. Intell. **161**, 149–180 (2005)

13. Petcu, A.: DPOP, a dynamic programming optimization protocol for DCOP. In: A Class of Algorithms for Distributed Constraint Optimization, pp. 52–57. IOS Press BV, Amsterdam (2009)
14. Petcu, A., Faltings, B.: A scalable method for multiagent constraint optimization. In: Proceedings of the 19th International Joint Conference on Artificial Intelligence, Edinburgh, Scotland, pp. 266–271. Professional Book Center (2005)
15. Vu, H., Aknine, S., Ramchurn, S.D.: A decentralised approach to intersection traffic management. In: International Joint Conference on Artificial Intelligence (IJCAI), Stockholm, Sweden (2018)
16. Zhu, Q., Wang, R., Chen, Q., Liu, Y., Qin, W.: IOT gateway: bridging wireless sensor networks into internet of things. In: 2010 IEEE/IFIP International Conference on Embedded and Ubiquitous Computing, December 2010, pp. 347–352 (2010)

Decentralised Multi-intersection Congestion Control for Connected Autonomous Vehicles

Huan Vu[1]([✉])(iD), Samir Aknine[1], Sarvapali Ramchurn[2](iD),
and Alessandro Farinelli[3](iD)

[1] Université de Lyon, CNRS, Université Lyon 1, LIRIS, UMR5205,
69622 Lyon, France
`huan.vu@liris.cnrs.fr, samir.aknine@univ-lyon1.fr`
[2] University of Southampton, Southampton, UK
`sdr1@soton.ac.uk`
[3] Department of Computer Science, University of Verona, Verona, Italy
`alessandro.farinelli@univr.it`

Abstract. This paper presents a decentralised mechanism for traffic control of connected autonomous vehicles in settings where multiple road intersections have to be managed and optimised. We propose a solution based on the distributed constraint optimisation approach (DCOP). We build upon state of the art algorithm for single-intersection management in order to manage congestion both across and within intersections. Furthermore, to solve the DCOP, we propose an improved node ordering policy for the Max-sum_AD_VP algorithm. Empirical evaluation of our model and algorithm demonstrate that our approach outperforms existing benchmarks by up to 32% in terms of average delay for both single and multiple intersection setup.

Keywords: Congestion control · Connected vehicles · Distributed constraints optimisation

1 Introduction

Autonomous cars are predicted to number several millions by 2025. Crucially, these cars will be able to communicate and coordinate with vehicles in range, opening up opportunities to mitigate congestion and the risk of accidents. This ability to communicate and coordinate underpins the notion of Connected Autonomous Vehicles (CAVs).

Specifically, previous works from the AI community as well as the transportation community have considered different strategies to use CAVs to mitigate traffic congestion. Some notable ones are [2,4,16,18,19]. They either use First Come First Served (FCFS) [4], alternating [16], Distributed Constraint Optimisation Problem (DCOP) [18] to optimise traffic at an intersection. However, the lack of communication and coordination between intersections can result,

© Springer Nature Switzerland AG 2020
N. Bassiliades et al. (Eds.): EUMAS 2020/AT 2020, LNAI 12520, pp. 37–51, 2020.
https://doi.org/10.1007/978-3-030-66412-1_3

as we show in this paper, in highly congested situations across neighbouring intersections, and thus, reduce the overall performance. [4] is further extended in [17], a market-based approach where drivers constantly submit bids to get the permission to cross the intersection. This mechanism can be applied to the road network, however, it turns the network into a competitive set up with no guarantees on performance as the bids are not optimised in any way. Recent work [1] proposes a solution to deal with multi-intersection traffic management. However, at a single intersection, this model relies on the one proposed earlier [7], in which, the computation is centralised in an intersection controller, which results in having a single point of failure.

Against this background, we propose a congestion management model based on a DCOP representation, both at the intersection and the network level. In more detail, this paper advances the state of the art in the following ways. First, we propose a more efficient way to model space inside an intersection than previous models. Second, we propose a novel mechanism that makes it possible for intersections to distribute vehicles and reduce congestion across the network, while avoiding computationally expensive global optimisation. Third, we propose an improvement to the Max-sum_AD_VP algorithm [20], one of the best incomplete DCOP algorithms, to account for the particular structure of our problem. Finally, we empirically evaluate the performance of each proposition and show the potential of using such approach for traffic management.

The remainder of the paper is organised as follows: Section 2 discusses existing intersection models while Sect. 3 extends one of these models using a precise approach. Section 4 presents a novel solution to the multi-intersection problem. Section 5 formalises our problem as a DCOP and presents a variant of the Max-sum_AD_VP algorithm, along with an improvement to the algorithm by ordering nodes using priority levels. Section 6 evaluates our model on a single and multiple intersection setup, and Sect. 7 concludes the paper.

2   Background on Intersection Model and Rules for Vehicles

To be able to understand our multi-intersection approach, we need to first understand the existing single intersection microscopic transportation model. Most of these models aim to propose a regulation method for an individual intersection. To deal with the lack of coordination between intersections, we will propose in latter sections, a novel method that enables the use of the information in the global traffic conditions to improve the overall performance.

CAVs, each guided by an agent, will replace the current flow-centric control based on optimising the traffic light system [11]. In future CAV-based road networks, an intersection will no longer be regulated by traffic lights, but by using intelligent agents that manage the right-of-way of each individual vehicle so that we can optimise the use of resources (e.g. space and time, infrastructure, fuel).

When opting for intelligent intersection management, one crucial step is to model the intersection area and define rules for vehicles crossing this area. In most works proposed earlier in multi-agent systems, cellular-based presentations are often the authors' choice [4,17,18]. However, using cellular-based model might lead to a higher use of space than necessary (e.g. in the model proposed by [4], the area that a vehicle reserved is always higher than its exact length and width), or a lack of precision (e.g. in the model proposed by [18], each vehicle is counted as one cell, regardless of their length).

In every existing intersection model, rules for vehicles are the same. They aim to give each vehicle a reservation [4,17], which is a set of cells for each time step or an admission time [18], which is the time that the vehicle can enter the intersection. The rules for reservations or admission times to be accepted is that vehicles can cross the intersection without stopping and without any conflict between them. Conflicts are often detected if vehicles try to use the same cell at the same time.

In reality, depending on the infrastructure installed at the intersection level, vehicles might be able to know their exact position. They also have information about their velocity and their length. Thus, instead of using a cellular model and checking for conflict between vehicles using their reserved cells, they might be able to apply the exact formula computed based on this information. Before heading to our main contribution, namely the multi-intersection problem, we will first define how to check for conflicts between vehicles by proposing this exact formula.

3   A Space-Efficient Intersection Model

We notice that when using the cellular model, vehicles are often not precisely represented. Therefore, a vehicle can occupy multiple cells at a time based on its position. This may lead to an inefficient way of using space and thus, can reduce the performance of the model. In this section, we will present a precise way to model trajectories of vehicles to avoid conflict, while being more space-efficient.

Definition 1. *Let t be the current time step and V_t the set of all vehicles approaching the intersection. Each vehicle $v_i \in V_t$ is modelled with: its relative distance to the intersection d_i, its velocity s_i and its length ℓ_i.*

Definition 2. *An intersection is modelled with several incoming lanes, several outgoing lanes, and a central zone called conflict zone. The path of a vehicle across the intersection is called a trajectory. The shared area between two trajectories is called a conflict spot (cf. Fig. 1).*

3.1   Structural Constraints

We model each intersection using a DCOP model described in [18], as it is a recent model that can outperform existing approaches at the intersection level. This model aims to find, for each time step t, a configuration Φ_t, which consists of one admission time for each vehicle. Vehicles are able to cross the intersection

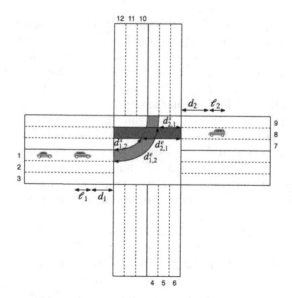

Fig. 1. Intersection with 12 incoming lanes, 12 outgoing lanes and a conflict zone. *Incoming lanes* are numbered from 1 to 12. The conflict zone is crossed by various trajectories. There are 3 vehicles v_1 (light blue), v_2 (green) and v_3 (orange). The trajectories τ_1 of v_1 and τ_3 of v_3 are the same and are coloured in light blue, and τ_2 of v_2 in green. The conflict spot between the two trajectories is coloured in red (Color figure online).

at a constant speed at their admission time. The conflict free property is guaranteed. As mentioned earlier, we extend the existing model by using the exact information about vehicle location, velocity and length. Thus, the rules in that model can be rewritten as follows:

Let L be the set of incoming lanes and $l_k \in L$ be lane k. For each $v_i \in V_t$, let $l_{v_i} \in L$ be the lane in which the vehicle v_i is present and τ_i be v_i's trajectory inside the conflict zone. Let $d_{i,j}^s$ the distance between the beginning of τ_i and the starting point of the *conflict spot* between τ_i and τ_j and $d_{i,j}^e$ the distance between τ_i and the end of this *conflict spot*. Let $varphi_i$ be the time v_i starts crossing the intersection.

c1. Distance constraint. A vehicle has to cross the distance separating it from the conflict zone before entering it:

$$\forall v_i \in V, \varphi_i > t + \frac{d_i}{s_i} \tag{1}$$

c2. Anteriority constraint. A vehicle v_i cannot enter the conflict zone before the vehicle v_j preceding it on its lane completely enters the *conflict zone*. In our model, we consider the area close to an intersection. Therefore, no overtaking is possible. Thus a vehicle v_i cannot enter the conflict zone before the vehicle v_j preceding it on its lane completely enters the *conflict zone*. We have:

$$\forall v_i, v_j \in V_t^2, l_{v_i} = l_{v_j}, d_i > d_j \Rightarrow \varphi_i > \varphi_j + \frac{\ell_j}{s_j} \tag{2}$$

c3. Conflict constraint. Two vehicles must not be present at the same time in their conflict spot. Given all the information, if the trajectories of v_i and v_j have a *conflict spot*, v_i has to leave it before v_j arrives or vice-versa[1]. Note that the time it takes for v_i to completely leave the *conflict spot* is the time it travels the distance $d_{i,j}^e + \ell_i$. We have:

$$\forall v_i, v_j \in V_t^2,$$
$$(\varphi_i + \tfrac{d_{i,j}^s}{s_i}) > (\varphi_j + \tfrac{d_{j,i}^e + \ell_j}{s_j})$$
$$\vee (\varphi_j + \tfrac{d_{j,i}^s}{s_j}) > (\varphi_i + \tfrac{d_{i,j}^e + \ell_i}{s_i}) \tag{3}$$

3.2 Objective of Each Intersection and Discussion

The average delay of vehicles has been the common benchmark at the intersection level [4,17,18]. Let w_i be the waiting time of v_i, this minimisation can be described as finding the minimum value for $\sum_{v_i \in V_t} w_i$. However, from a network point-of-view, simply evacuating vehicles in front of the intersection as quickly as possible can create high density traffic in the *outgoing lanes*. Indeed, several studies [9,10,14] have shown that traffic flow speed in a lane is not linear in the lane's density, but rather follows complex rules. Hence, in a road network, continuing to send vehicles to a lane that has a high density may result in a significant slowdown. In the market-based regulation system [17], authors have introduced a dynamic pricing policy to improve the performance of the network. Building upon that policy, we will next introduce a priority setting technique that can be used to regulate traffic in a multi-intersection settings.

4 Priority Levels for Multi-intersection Settings

To date, intersection management algorithms have mainly been shown to optimise traffic flow for individual intersections. However, they do not acknowledge the fact that it is not always possible to evacuate vehicles through the outgoing lanes as they might be the neighbouring intersections' incoming lane and thus might have a long queue. This leads to the fact that optimising traffic at an intersection might lead to further conflict at another intersection. In this section, we present a novel dynamic individual priority level, that can be used to distribute vehicles among intersections, or even guide vehicles to a better trajectory.

Similar to a dynamic pricing problem [3,6] where resources might have different costs each time, a vehicle's delay should be continuously evaluated using

---

[1] This solution aims to work for settings with a large number of CAVs. In transitional periods where non-autonomous vehicles are presented, this constraint can be extended by adding a time lapse between the two vehicles to keep a safe distance.

several criteria. Formally, we define for each vehicle v_i a strictly positive real value priority level ρ_i. This priority level is updated using traffic information such as the vehicle's past trajectories, the current traffic density at its destination and the nature of the vehicle. A priority is defined by its type (e.g., emergency vehicles, buses, road maintenance vehicle) whilst a dynamic factor is added using the other information (e.g., trajectory, destination, delay). Next we propose two ways to update vehicles' priority level, namely the *Priority by history* and the *Priority by destination*.

4.1   Calculating Priority Levels

The priority of a vehicle represents the contribution of its delay in the solution (i.e. a vehicle with higher priority contributes more to the quality of the solution). Therefore, dynamically updating this priority can guide the mechanism to different solutions as time progresses. In this paper, we propose two ways to calculate and update a vehicle's priority based on its information and on the global traffic condition.

Priority by History: *Priority by history* is computed based on the total delay of a vehicle from the beginning of its trajectory. Assuming that every ordinary vehicle that enters the road network has the same priority level and each intersection will try to minimise average delays, the method would favour the more crowded lanes. This makes vehicles that travel in a less crowded trajectory wait for an extremely long time in dense traffic. To be able to balance a vehicle's waiting time and the global objective of the intersection, we dynamically change vehicles' *priority by history*. In this paper, we consider the distribution of *priority by history*, ranging from 0 for vehicles that recently entered the system to 10 for vehicles that are suffering lots of delay (cf. Fig. 2a). In certain cases, this priority can also help evacuating vehicles from a congested area as they tend to have higher delays and thus, higher priority than others.

Priority by Destination: *Priority by destination* is computed based on the density of the next destination of a vehicle to avoid sending vehicles to a congested area. In a simple intersection model, it is often assumed that the *outgoing lanes* are always free and capable of taking vehicles. However, this assumption breaks down in real-world settings as the conditions at the neighbouring intersections will determine how fast cars can move along. For example, if an intersection cannot shift vehicles from one of its *incoming lanes*, a neighbouring intersection cannot and should not shift more vehicles to this lane. Such situation can also create a deadlock if the first CAV in the lane has to stop because its destination doesn't have enough free space. Hence, redistributing priority so that an intersection can avoid sending vehicles to a more congested intersection can also be useful. Furthermore, giving a priority bonus to a certain direction also encourages vehicles to take a less congested route when they have multiple options

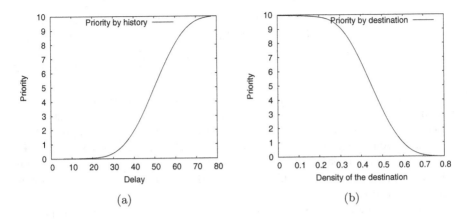

Fig. 2. Priority distribution (a) *Priority by history* (b) *Priority by destination*

to complete their journey. The bonus *priority by destination* is also distributed from 0 to 10, according to the expected density of their destination communicated by the neighbouring intersection (cf. Fig. 2b). Furthermore, intersections can exchange information with their neighbours in case of blocked lanes due to unpredictable events so that traffic flows can be eased.

Optimising Weighted Delay. Since each vehicle has its priority level, we will build, for each time step t, a configuration Φ_t for all vehicles in V_t in front of the intersection that minimises their total weighted delay whilst being able to satisfy all the structural constraints described above. The input is the set of vehicles V_t presented in front of an the intersection at the current time step and the configuration at the last time step Φ_{t-1}. Let w_i be the waiting time of vehicle v_i (i.e. the difference between the admission time of v_i in fluid condition and its actual admission time) and Φ be the set of all possible configurations, our goal can be expressed as follows:

$$f : (t, V_t, \Phi_{t-1}) \mapsto \arg\min_{\Phi_t \in \Phi} \sum_{v_i \in V_t} w_i * \rho_i \tag{4}$$

We next discuss the formalisation of the model using a DCOP and show how existing DCOP solution algorithms can be optimised to consider the parameters of our problem.

5   DCOPs for Intersection Management

Distributed constraint optimisation is a general way to formulate multi-agent coordination problems. A Distributed Constraint Optimisation Problem (or DCOP) is a tuple $\{\mathcal{A}, \mathcal{X}, \mathcal{D}, \mathcal{C}\}$, where: $\mathcal{A} = \{a_1, \ldots, a_n\}$ is a set of n agents;

$\mathcal{X} = \{x_1, \ldots, x_n\}^2$ are variables owned by the agents, where variable x_i is owned by agent a_i; $\mathcal{D} = \{\mathcal{D}_{x_1}, \ldots, \mathcal{D}_{x_n}\}$ is a set of finite-discrete domains. A variable x_i takes values in $\mathcal{D}_{x_i} = v_1, \ldots, v_k$; $\mathcal{C} = \{c_1, \ldots, c_m\}$ is a set of constraints, where each c_i defines a cost $\in \mathbb{R} \cup \{\infty\}$. A solution to the DCOP is an assignment to all variables that minimise $\sum_i c_i$.

There are several ways in which we can formalise our problem as a DCOP, depending on what we choose to represent with agents, variables and constraints. The choices have an impact in both computational load and communication overhead of agents. Here we evaluate our model using two formalisations, namely the vehicle-based approach where each vehicle is considered as an agent and the lane-based approach where the sub-problem of the lane is solved before the global optimisation problem.

To give some more details, in the vehicle-based approach, each vehicle participates in the DCOP formulation as an agent. They each have one variable representing their admission time. The vehicles then perform a fully decentralised process in order to find a global solution that does not cause any conflict, and that optimises the overall delay.

On the other hand, in the lane-based approach, each lane is represented by an agent. This solution sacrifices some decentralisation in exchange for less computational time. Vehicles in the same lane are affected with the anteriority constraint, and may often cross the intersection using the same trajectory. Thus, the lane agent can solve the sub-problem of only exchanging solutions that do not violate the anteriority constraint. The lane agent uses a pseudo variable which is the Cartesian product of the admission time of all the vehicles in the lane.

The lane-based approach has been shown to outperform the vehicle-based approach in standard Max-sum setting [18]. However, when switching to a recent variant of the algorithm, the Max-sum_AD_VP [20], the success rate becomes higher and thus we reevaluate their performances and notice that each approach is preferred in different traffic densities.

As can be seen, most of our constraints are hard constraints. Since the state of the intersection constantly changes and the number of vehicles at rush hours can be quite high, it is important to produce solutions rapidly, trading off optimality for robustness to changes in traffic condition. Hence, instead of optimal DCOP algorithms, we opt for heuristic, anytime algorithms that have been shown to produce solutions of relatively high quality. In what follows, we first propose our adaptations of the Max-sum algorithm [5] to improve performance on the traffic management problem.

5.1 Optimisation

To exploit the two models presented above, we use message-passing approaches. We chose a variant of the Max-sum algorithm [5] as it has been shown to be one of the fastest and most efficient algorithms in many multi-agent domains

---

[2] The number of variables can be different. In this paper, we assume only one variable per agent.

[12,13,15]. The Max-sum algorithm uses two kinds of messages. At each iteration i of the process, a message is sent from each variable node x to a factor node c, including for each value $d \in \mathcal{D}_x$, the sum of the costs for this value she received from all factor node neighbours apart from c in iteration $i-1$. Formally, for each value $d \in \mathcal{D}_x$ the message $R^i_{x \to c}(d)$ includes: $\sum_{c' \in C_x \backslash c} cost(f'.d) - \alpha$, where C_x is the set of factor neighbours of variable x and $cost(c'.d)$ is the cost for value d included in the message received from c' in iteration $i-1$. α represents a scalar to prevent the message to increase endlessly in cyclic factor graphs. The message sent from a factor node c to a variable node x contains for each possible value $d \in \mathcal{D}_x$ the minimum cost that can be achieved from any combination of other variables involved in c. Formally, for each value $d \in \mathcal{D}_x$, the message $Q^i_{f \to x}(d)$ includes $min_{PA_{-x}} cost(\langle x, d \rangle, PA_{-x})$ where PA_{-x} is a possible combination of assignments to all variables involved in c except x. The cost of an assignment $a = (\langle x, d \rangle, PA_{-x})$ is $c(a) + \sum_{x' \in X_f \backslash x} cost(x'.d')$. $c(a)$ is the original cost in the constraint c for the assignment a and $cost(x', d')$ is the cost which was received from variable node x' during iteration $i-1$, for the value d' which is assigned to x' in a. These messages are exchanged between graph nodes until the convergence criteria is reached[3].

5.2   The Max-Sum_AD_VP Algorithm and the Importance of Node Ordering

Max-sum_AD_VP is a recent variant of Max-sum and is empirically proven to converge faster and to a better solution than the standard version [20]. It operates on a directed factor graph. The transformation between these two graphs is produced by giving each agent a unique index to create an order. At each phase, messages are only computed and sent in one direction (e.g. upstream direction in odd phases and downstream direction in even phases). From the third phase, Max-sum_AD_VP adds value propagation, a technique where each variable node selects a currently optimal assignment and sends it alongside the standard message. Factor nodes then, based on the value chosen, compute messages by minimising only over assignments that are consistent with the value chosen.

To transform the original factor graph into an acyclic directed graph, Max-sum_AD_VP has no preference and often uses the variable indices. Since the solution quality of Max-sum_AD_VP is highly related to the initial assignments, we aim to find a good way to organise nodes to improve its performance. In our system, vehicles come with different priorities and we can see that the optimal solution is more likely to favour vehicles with high priority. Thus, we conjecture that by arranging the nodes in the priority order so that the algorithm can converge faster to a better solution. This is due to the fact that during the value propagation phases, the nodes with higher priority propagate their values first. In Sect. 6.2 we will evaluate the performance of ordering nodes in different traffic conditions.

---

[3] In our experiments the algorithm stops when convergence is achieved or when the timeout is reached.

In the lane-based approach, instead of the priority of the vehicles, lane agents use the sum of the priorities over the vehicles presented in the lane.

6   Empirical Evaluation

In this section, we evaluate the performance of our mechanism and the efficiency of the improvements that we proposed for the Max-sum_AD_VP algorithm. The experiments were performed using an Intel Core i5 clocked at 2.9 GHz with 32 GB RAM, under Ubuntu 16.04. The Max-sum_AD_VP algorithm is implemented in Java as per [20]. We compare values from at least 50 simulations, with 95% confidence interval as error bars. The insertion rate of vehicles to the intersection ranges from 0.1 (off-peak) to 0.5 (rush hour) [8].

6.1   Evaluating Space Efficiency at Individual Intersections

In this first benchmark, we aim to compare the performance of our model and the standard cellular model used in [18]. The intersection evaluated is the one from Fig. 1. Each incoming lane has a width of 3 m. We decided to use such intersections as they are one of the most complicated scenarios in urban settings. Vehicles are generated without any priority and both models are evaluated using the lane-based approach with the same standard Max-sum algorithm. A time step is set at 2 s and is also the timeout of the DCOP algorithms. If the algorithm fails to provide a solution before timing out, the intersection will automatically apply the FCFS solution as it is very simple to compute and advance to the next time step. Based on the results in Fig. 3a, we observe an improvement in dense traffic only from using space more efficiently, without changing the algorithm.

6.2   Evaluating the Efficiency of the Max-Sum_AD_VP Algorithm at Individual Intersections

Next, we evaluate in detail our mechanism at a single intersection. Here we evaluate all combinations of the approaches: Vehicle-based approach with node ordering (VB-NO), Lane-based approach with node ordering (LB-NO), standard vehicle-based approach (VB) and standard lane-based approach (LB). Vehicles are generated with a random priority ranging from 1 to 10. We measure the quality of the solution (i.e. the total weighted delay of vehicles) during off-peak and rush hours. For reference we also put the results from the model proposed by [18] on the same weighted delay problem (i.e. using a cellular, standard Max-sum resolution). The intersection and timeout conditions stay the same as the first experiment.

Figure 3b shows the average success rate of each approach (i.e. the percentage of iterations where the algorithm converges to a better solution than the one provided by FCFS). We can see that in dense traffic, VB fails to respond to the 2-s timeout and thus, has the worst success rate of about 24% whilst LB converges about 80% of the time with node ordering and 70% of the time

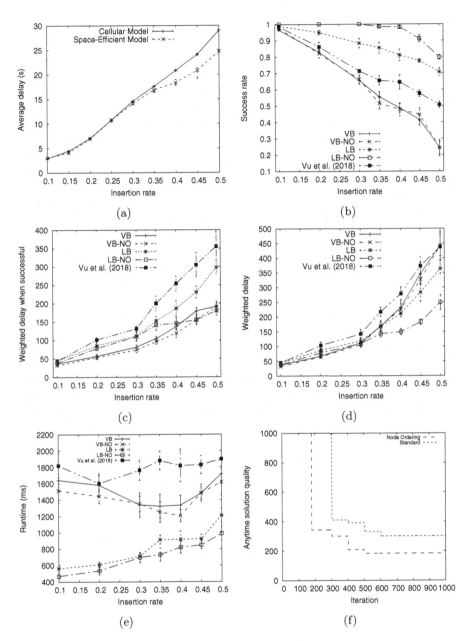

Fig. 3. Empirical evaluations on the single intersection setting. Figure (a) shows the performance of our space efficient model. Figure (b) shows success rate of each approach on a weighted delay problem. Figure (c) shows the average solution quality when successful. Figure (d) shows the average weighted delay. Figure (e) shows the average runtime of each algorithm when successful. Figure (f) shows the anytime cost of Ordered and Standard versions of Max-sum_AD_VP running on the lane-based approach.

without. Figure 3c shows the average solution quality when successful. We note that VB tends to converge to a better solution in off-peak conditions. In VB, the solution is less likely to favour vehicles with high priority since it depends more on the number of vehicles in the lane. Therefore, using node ordering with this approach does not always result in a better outcome, and at times pushes Max-sum_AD_VP to greedily pick a worse solution. For LB, since lanes with more vehicles/higher priority are more likely to have shorter delays, using node ordering causes Max-sum_AD_VP to converge faster with higher success rate, especially in dense traffic. Figure 3d shows the overall quality of the solution, i.e. the average weighted delay of all vehicles. VB is the solution that gives the best performance in off-peak conditions. In dense traffic, since it often has to take the FCFS solution when it fails to converge, its overall cost is higher than the cost of LB. LB-NO provides a fairly good result in dense traffic and is the best one in rush hour. It outperforms the existing approach by up to 32%. Hence, switching between approaches for different traffic conditions could lead to a better solution for single intersection traffic management. Figure 3f shows the anytime quality of the solution to compare the performance between the ordered and the standard versions of the lane-based approach Max-sum_AD_VP. We can clearly observe a better convergence when ordering nodes using priority levels.

6.3   Multi-intersection Efficiency

To be able to measure the effect of dynamic vehicle priorities, we evaluate our mechanism in two different scenarios using a 2×2 intersection model. In the scenario A, we consider the East-West direction through I_1 and I_2 in the rush

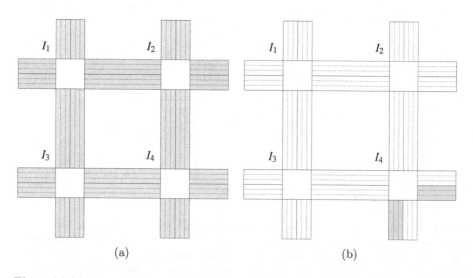

(a)   (b)

Fig. 4. Multi-intersection scenario (a) The east-west direction through I_1 and I_2 (in red) is more crowded than the other directions. (b) The east and south *outgoing lanes* of I_4 (in red) have a limited capacity (Color figure online).

hour conditions whilst the other directions in normal conditions (cf. Fig. 4a). This is a common scenario during rush hours in urban traffic.

In the scenario B, we consider the east and south *outgoing lanes* of I_4 can only evacuate 1 vehicle every 3 time steps and get crowded (cf. Fig. 4b).

Table 1 shows results achieved using each individual priority, a combined version using the sum of the priorities, and the standard version.

Table 1. Average delay of vehicles in different scenarios.

	Priority by history only	Priority by destination only	Combined priority	No priority
Scenario A	24.74 ± 3.13	27.88 ± 3.86	**21.25 ± 2.25**	32.19 ± 6.29
Scenario B	21.98 ± 3.01	**12.85 ± 2.66**	13.12 ± 3.84	21.16 ± 4.42

In the scenario A, both priorities contribute to the improvement of the overall solution. Indeed, when we take a closer look at the intersections I_3 and I_4, their north lanes often have to evacuate more vehicles. The *priority by history* speeds up this evacuation since the vehicles in these lanes have suffered from higher delays. On the other hand, the *priority by destination* prevents I_3 and I_4 to send vehicles to the north, since the northern *outgoing lanes* might not be able to evacuate a large number of vehicles.

In the scenario B, we noticed that the *priority by destination* contributes much more to the congestion avoidance. In fact, without the *priority by destination*, vehicles continue to be sent to the intersection I_4, creating a congested situation. This congestion further leads to the impossibility of sending vehicles from I_2 and I_3 to the east and south directions respectively, thus blocked vehicles from entering I_2 and I_3. The average delay grows rapidly due to deadlocks. The *priority by history* makes the performance slightly worse (but not significant) while sending unnecessary vehicles to I_4. In this simulation, we consider that vehicles have a fixed trajectory before entering the network but to extend the model, vehicles might choose to go from I_2 to I_3 or vice-versa through I_1 instead of I_4 to reduce their delays and optimise the use of traffic network.

6.4 Discussion on the Lane-Based Approach

As shown in the empirical results, the lane-based approach can sometimes be outperformed by the vehicle-based approach, especially in the lower density settings. However, there is also another aspect we should take a closer look at, namely the communication range of the vehicles. Communication between vehicles can be achieved via the infrastructures installed at the intersection level. However, there are always areas where intersections may not have any computation capability (e.g., in rural areas or non-urban settings). This can be important in mass evacuations following fires or floods [13].

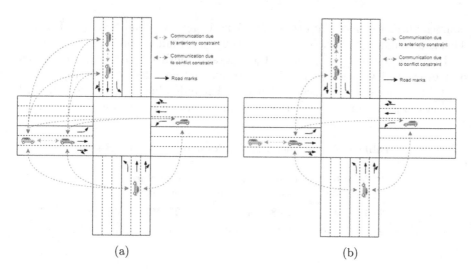

(a)   (b)

Fig. 5. Communication range required for (a) the vehicle-based approach. (b) the lane-based approach.

In Figs. 5a and b we can see that the lane-based approach also helps reducing communication range, because only the vehicle representing the lane is required to communicate with vehicles representing conflicting lanes. Therefore, in the lane-based approach, the lane agent should be the first vehicle in the lane due to the reduction of communication range.

7   Conclusions

In this paper, we proposed a novel approach for managing CAVs to reduce traffic congestion. Our results show that we outperform benchmark solutions by up to 32% at a single intersection. Our dynamic priority assignment technique is proven to be efficient in multi-intersection settings. Since the combined version might not be the best in some cases, future work will look at a detailed evaluation of combination between several priority distribution functions to adapt to traffic conditions. Other performance metrics such as fuel consumption and comfortability of passengers (due to acceleration, deceleration and stop-and-go) can also be used for evaluation.

References

1. Ashtiani, F., Fayazi, S.A., Vahidi, A.: Multi-intersection traffic management for autonomous vehicles via distributed mixed integer linear programming. In: 2018 Annual American Control Conference (ACC), pp. 6341–6346 (2018)
2. Azimi, R., Bhatia, G., Rajkumar, R., Mudalige, P.: Ballroom intersection protocol: synchronous autonomous driving at intersections. In: IEEE International Conference on Embedded and Real-Time Computing Systems and Applications (2015)

3. Do Chung, B., Yao, T., Friesz, T.L., Liu, H.: Dynamic congestion pricing with demand uncertainty: a robust optimization approach. Transp. Res. Part B Methodol. **46**, 1504–1518 (2012)
4. Dresner, K., Stone, P.: A multiagent approach to autonomous intersection management. JAIR **31**(1), 591–656 (2008)
5. Farinelli, A., Rogers, A., Petcu, A., Jennings, N.R.: Decentralised coordination of low-power embedded devices using the max-sum algorithm. In: AAMAS 2008, pp. 639–646 (2008)
6. Faruqui, A., Sergici, S.: Household response to dynamic pricing of electricity: a survey of 15 experiments. J. Regul. Econ. **38**, 193–225 (2010). https://doi.org/10. 1007/s11149-010-9127-y
7. Fayazi, S.A., Vahidi, A., Luckow, A.: Optimal scheduling of autonomous vehicle arrivals at intelligent intersections via MILP. In: 2017 American Control Conference (ACC), pp. 4920–4925 (2017)
8. Junges, R., Bazzan, A.L.C.: Evaluating the performance of DCOP algorithms in a real world, dynamic problem. In: AAMAS 2008, pp. 599–606 (2008)
9. Lighthill, M.J., Whitham, G.B.: On kinematic waves. I. Flood movement in long rivers. Proc. Roy. Soc. Lond. A **229**, 281–316 (1995)
10. Lighthill, M.J., Whitham, G.B.: On kinematic waves. II. A theory of traffic flow on long crowded roads. Proc. Roy. Soc. Lond. Ser. A **229**, 317–345 (1955)
11. Litman, T.: Autonomous vehicle implementation predictions. Victoria Transport Policy Institute (2013)
12. Macarthur, K., Stranders, R., Ramchurn, S., Jennings, N.R.: A distributed anytime algorithm for dynamic task allocation in multi-agent systems. In: AAAI 2011, pp. 701–706 (August 2011)
13. Ramchurn, S., Farinelli, A., Macarthur, K., Jennings, N.R.: Decentralized coordination in RoboCup rescue. Comput. J. **53**, 1447–1461 (2010)
14. van Rijn, J.: Road capacities. Indevelopment (2014)
15. Stranders, R., Farinelli, A., Rogers, A., Jennings, N.R.: Decentralised coordination of mobile sensors using the max-sum algorithm. In: IJCAI 2009, pp. 299–304 (2009)
16. Tlig, M., Buffet, O., Simonin, O.: Decentralized traffic management: a synchronization-based intersection control. In: ICALT 2014 (2014)
17. Vasirani, M., Ossowski, S.: A market-inspired approach for intersection management in urban road traffic networks. JAIR **43**, 621–659 (2012)
18. Vu, H., Aknine, S., Ramchurn, S.D.: A decentralised approach to intersection traffic management. In: IJCAI 2018, pp. 527–533 (2018)
19. Xu, B., et al.: Distributed conflict-free cooperation for multiple connected vehicles at unsignalized intersections. Transp. Res. Part C Emerg. Technol. **93**, 322–334 (2018)
20. Zivan, R., Parash, T., Cohen, L., Peled, H., Okamoto, S.: Balancing exploration and exploitation in incomplete min/max-sum inference for distributed constraint optimization. JAAMAS **31**(5), 1165–1207 (2017)

Congestion Management for Mobility-on-Demand Schemes that Use Electric Vehicles

Emmanouil S. Rigas[1]($\boxtimes$) and Konstantinos S. Tsompanidis[2]

[1] Department of Informatics, Aristotle University of Thessaloniki,
54124 Thessaloniki, Greece
erigas@csd.auth.gr
[2] Department of Computing, The University of Northampton,
Northampton NN1 5PH, UK
ktsompanidis@hotmail.com

Abstract. To date the majority of commuters drive their privately owned vehicle that uses an internal combustion engine. This transportation model suffers from low vehicle utilization and causes environmental pollution. This paper studies the use of Electric Vehicles (EVs) operating in a Mobility-on-Demand (MoD) scheme and tackles the related management challenges. We assume a number of customers acting as cooperative agents requesting a set of alternative trips and EVs distributed across a number of pick-up and drop-off stations. In this setting, we propose congestion management algorithms which take as input the trip requests and calculate the EV-to-customer assignment aiming to maximize trip execution by keeping the system balanced in terms of matching demand and supply. We propose a Mixed-Integer-Programming (MIP) optimal offline solution which assumes full knowledge of customer demand and an equivalent online greedy algorithm that can operate in real time. The online algorithm uses three alternative heuristic functions in deciding whether to execute a customer request: (a) The sum of squares of all EVs in all stations, (b) the percentage of trips' destination location fullness and (c) a random choice of trip execution. Through a detailed evaluation, we observe that (a) provides an increase of up to 4.8% compared to (b) and up to 11.5% compared to (c) in terms of average trip execution, while all of them achieve close to the optimal performance. At the same time, the optimal scales up to settings consisting of tenths of EVs and a few hundreds of customer requests.

Keywords: Electric vehicles · Mobility-on-demand · Scheduling · Heuristic search · Cooperative

1 Introduction

We live in a world where the majority of the population is living in, or around, large cities. Given that this trend tends to increase, the current personal transportation model is not sustainable as this is based to a large extend on privately

N. Bassiliades et al. (Eds.): EUMAS 2020/AT 2020, LNAI 12520, pp. 52–66, 2020.
https://doi.org/10.1007/978-3-030-66412-1_4

owned internal combustion engine vehicles [1]. These vehicles cause high air and sound pollution and usually have low utilization rates [21]. Electric Vehicles (EVs) can be an efficient alternative to those using internal combustion engines in terms of running costs [8], quality of driving, and environmental impact. At the same time, their main disadvantages are their short ranges and long charging times. To address such issues, cities aim to build many charging stations. Charging facilities though, are only worth building if there are enough EVs to use them. However, drivers will not buy EVs if charging stations are not first available, leading to a catch-22 situation.

Mobility-on-Demand (MoD) schemes [14] are considered as a way to increase vehicle utilization. MoD involves vehicles that are used by either individuals, or small groups of commuters, and provides them with an alternative from using their privately owned vehicles. Such systems have the potential to reduce traffic congestion in urban areas, as well as the need for large numbers of parking spots and increase the vehicle utilization rates as few vehicles will cover the transportation needs of many commuters.

Given these benefits of EVs and MoD schemes, in this paper we study a setting where EVs are used within MoD schemes, and propose solutions for the related optimization challenges. By addressing these challenges, the advantages of the two transportation modes can be combined [3,14]. Moreover, the use of EVs in MoD schemes offers an opportunity to better market EVs to potential car owners as they get to try the technology before buying it. In this way, EV-equipped MoD schemes would help popularize EVs, while at the same time having a positive impact in urban traffic conditions as well as the environment.

Against this background, we model the MoD scheme for EVs and develop novel algorithms to solve the problem of scheduling trips for MoD consumers in order to maximize the number of trip requests serviced while coping with the limited range of EVs. We step upon the work presented in [17] and study the problem of assigning EVs to customers in a MoD scheme and we solve it offline and optimally using Mixed Integer Programming (MIP) techniques, as well as online using heuristic search. In doing so, we advance the state of the art as follows:

1. We extend the optimal scheduling algorithm "Off-Opt-Charge" presented in [17] which considers single travel requests by customers, by covering the option for customers to express their demand for more than one tasks, where as a task we consider a trip between a pair of locations starting a particular point in time.
2. We develop an online greedy scheduling algorithm for the problem of selecting the tasks to execute and the assignment of EVs to customers and we propose three alternative heuristic functions.

The rest of the paper is structured as follows: Section 2 presents related work, Sect. 3 formally defines the problem, Sect. 4 presents the optimal offline solution of the problem and Sect. 5 the equivalent online one. Section 6 provides a detailed evaluation of the algorithms and finally, Sect. 7 concludes and presents ideas for future work.

2   Related Work

In this context, Pavone et al. propose mathematical programming-based rebalancing mechanisms to decide on the relocation of vehicles to restore imbalances across a MoD network, either using robotic autonomous driving vehicles [16], or human drivers [15], while Smith et al. [19] use mathematical programming to optimally route such rebalancing drivers. Moreover, Carpenter et al. [4] develop solutions for the optimal sizing of shared vehicle pools. These works assume normal cars, while EVs present new challenges for MoD schemes as EVs have a limited range that requires them to charge regularly. Moreover, if such MoD schemes are to become popular, it is important to ensure that charging capacity is managed and scheduled to allow for the maximum number of consumer requests to be serviced across a large geographical area. In addition, in order for MoD schemes to be economically sustainable, and given the higher cost of buying EVs compared to conventional vehicles, it is important to have them working at maximum capacity and servicing the maximum number of customers around the clock.

In such a setting, Drwal et al. [10] consider on-demand car rental systems for public transportation. To balance the demand across the stations and to maximise the operator's revenue, they adjust the prices between origin and destination stations depending on their current occupancy, probabilistic information about the customers' valuations and estimated relocation costs. Using real data from an existing on-demand mobility system in a French city, they show that their mechanisms achieve an up to 64% increase in revenue for the operator and at the same time up to 36% fewer relocations. In addition, Rigas et al. [17] use mathematical programming techniques and heuristic algorithms to schedule EVs in a MoD scheme taking into consideration the limited range of EVs and the need to charge their batteries. The goal of the system is to maximize serviced customers. Cepolina and Farina [5] study the use of single-sitter compact-sized EVs in a MoD scheme operating in a pedestrian zone. The vehicles are shared throughout the day by different users and one way trips are assumed. However, here the authors also assume open ended reservation to exist (i.e., the drop-off time is not fixed), thus adding one more dimension to the problem. Given this, they propose a methodology that uses a random search algorithm to optimize the fleet size and distribution to maximize the number of serviced customers. Moreover, Turan et al. [22] study the financial implications of smart charging in MoD schemes and they conclude that investing in larger battery capacities and operating more vehicles for rebalancing reduces the charging costs, but increases the fleet operational costs. Finally, Gkourtzounis et al. [12] propose a software package that allows for efficient management of a MoD scheme from the side of a company, and easy trip requests for customers.

From an algorithmic point of view, similarities can be found with problems such as the capacitated vehicle routing problem [6] which is a special case of the Vehicle Routing Problem [7], where each vehicle has a limited carrying capacity, the project scheduling problem [20], and the machine scheduling problem [13].

Overall, the need for battery charging as well as the strict order of task execution differentiate our problem compared to the majority of the works presented so far, and make it harder to find the optimal solution. Also the efficient online algorithms make it more applicable in real-world deployments. In the next section, the problem is formally defined.

3 Problem Definition

In a MoD scheme which uses EVs, customers may choose to drive between pairs of predefined locations. They can choose at least one starting point and at least one end point. Since the MoD company's aim is to serve as many requests as possible, the system selects to execute the task which keeps the system in balance (i.e., trying to match demand across supply). A task is defined as a trip from a pick-up to drop-off location starting a particular point in time. Thus, based on the number of start and end points the customer has defined, all possible combinations are calculated and the equivalent tasks are created. We consider a network of pick-up and drop-off stations where the EVs can park and charge their batteries. The stations are considered as nodes aiming to be kept neither empty nor overloaded. The system needs to be in balance since the overloading of one station may cause major disruption to the network. A summary of all notations can be found in Table 1.

We consider a fully connected directed graph $G(L, E)$ where $l \in L \subseteq \mathbb{N}$ is the set of locations where the stations exist and $e \in E \subseteq \mathbb{N}$ are the edges connecting all locations combinations. Each station has a maximum capacity $c_l^{max} \in \mathbb{N}$ declaring the number of EVs that can reside at it simultaneously. We assume a set of discrete time points $t \in T \subseteq \mathbb{N}$ where the time is global for the system and the same for all agents. We have a set of tasks $r \in R \subseteq \mathbb{N}$ where a task is a trip initiating a particular point in time. Thus, each task has a starting location l_r^{start}, an end location l_r^{end}, as well as a starting time t_r^{start}, a duration τ_r and an equivalent energy demand $e_r \in \mathbb{N}$.

We denote the set of EVs $a \in A \subseteq \mathbb{N}$. Each EV has a current location $l_{a,t} \in L$, a current battery level $e_{a,t} \in \mathbb{N}$, a maximum battery level $e_a^{max} \in \mathbb{N}$, an energy consumption rate $con_a \in \mathbb{N}$ where $con_a =$ (energy unit/time point), a maximum travel time $\tau_a = e_a^{max}/con_a$ and a charging rate $ch_a \in \mathbb{N}$. Note that an EV changes location only when being driven by a customer and no relocation of vehicles exists.

Finally, we have a set of customers $i \in I \subseteq \mathbb{N}$ where a customer needs to travel between one or more pairs of locations $dem_i \subseteq R$. Customers act as fully cooperative agents when communicating their demand to the MoD company. After the demand is communicated to the company, an EV-to-customer assignment algorithm is applied. In doing so, a set of assumptions are made:

1. The MoD company is a monopoly. At this point competition between companies is not taken into consideration. This would introduce different approaches

in decision making strategy and should include more variables into the problem domain (energy and labor cost, building rents, taxes, etc.), which are not the case in this paper.

2. The MoD company uses the same EV model. For simplification reasons it is considered that all EVs are of the same make and model.
3. All stations have one charger for each parking spot. This means that if there is a parking spot available, there is also a charger available. There is no waiting queue for charging.
4. EVs' full battery capacity is sufficient to make a journey from one station to any other without extra charge needed. No stops are required, and no charging time needs to be spent in between two locations. Travelling to locations beyond the maximum range of an EV needs a different formulation and induce challenges which will be solved in future work.

Table 1. Notations used in problem definition and algorithms.

Notation	Explanation
l	Location of a station
e	Edge connecting two stations
c_l^{max}	Maximum capacity of a station
t	Time point
r	A task
l_r^{start}	Start location of a task
l_r^{end}	End location of a task
t_r^{start}	Start time of a task
τ_r	Duration of a task
e_r	Energy demand of a task
a	An EV
$l_{a,t}$	Current location of EV
$e_{a,t}$	Energy level of EV
e_a^{max}	Max battery capacity of EV
ch_a	Charging rate of EV
con_a	Consumption rate of EV
τ_a	Max travel time of EV
i	A customer
dem_i	Travel demand of customer
λ_r	Task r accomplished (Boolean)
$\epsilon_{a,r,t}$	True if EV a is working on task r at time t (Boolean)
$prk_{a,t,l}$	True if EV a is parked at location l at time t (Boolean)
$bch_{a,t}$	Charging rate of EV a at time t

4   Optimal Offline Scheduling

In this section, we assume that customer requests are collected in advance and we propose an optimal offline algorithm for the assignment of EVs to customers. This formulation aims to maximize the number of tasks that are completed (i.e., customer service) (Eq. 1). To achieve this, we present a solution based on Mixed Integer Programming (MIP), where we use battery charging to cope with the EVs' limited range. MIP techniques have been particularly useful to solve such large combinatorial problems (e.g., combinatorial auctions [2,18], travelling salesman problem [9]). We will refer to this algorithm as *Optimal*. As a solver we have selected the IBM ILOG CPLEX 12.10. In this formulation, we define four decision variables: 1) $\lambda_r \in \{0, 1\}$ denoting whether a task r is accomplished or not, 2) $\epsilon_{a,r,t} \in \{0, 1\}$ denoting whether EV a is executing task r at time t or not, 3) $prk_{a,t,l} \in \{0, 1\}$ denoting whether EV a is parked at time point t at location l or not and 4) $bch_{a,t} \in [0, ch_a]$ which denotes whether an EV a is charging at time point t and at which charging rate (i.e., the charging rate can be any between 0 and the maximum charging rate - ch_a).

Objective Function:

$$max \sum_{r \in R} (\lambda_r) \tag{1}$$

Subject to:

– *Completion constraints:*

$$\sum_{a \in A} \sum_{t_r^{start} \leq t < t_r^{end}} \epsilon_{a,r,t} = \tau_r \times \lambda_r, \forall r \tag{2}$$

$$\sum_{a \in A} \sum_{t_r^{start} > t, t \geq t_r^{end}} \epsilon_{a,r,t} = 0, \forall r \tag{3}$$

$$\epsilon_{a,r,t+1} = \epsilon_{a,r,t} \forall a, \forall r, \forall t : t_r^{start} \leq t < t_r^{end} - 1 \tag{4}$$

$$bch_{a,t} \leq \sum_{l \in L} prk_{a,t,l} \times ch_a, \forall a, \forall t \tag{5}$$

$$0 \leq e_{a,t=0} + \sum_{t'=0}^{t} bch_{a,t'} - \sum_{r \in R} \sum_{t''=t_r^{start}}^{t} \epsilon_{r,a,t''} \times con_a \leq 100, \forall a, \forall t \tag{6}$$

$$\sum_{r \in dem_i} \lambda_r \leq 1, \forall i \tag{7}$$

The *completion* constraints ensure the proper execution of tasks. Thus, for each executed task, the time traveled must be equal to the duration of the trip

concerned (Eq. 2), and no traveling must take place when a task is not executed
(Eq. 3). Moreover, each task is executed by exactly one EV at a time (Eq. 4) and
Eq. 9). Equation 5 ensures that each EV a can charge only while being parked.
When an EV is parked, it can charge with a charging rate up to its maximum
one. However, when it is driving and $prk_{a,t,l} = 0$ it cannot charge. Regarding
the time points the EV will charge, the solver will choose any time points, as
long as the available range will not compromise the task execution ability. At
the same time, Eq. 6 ensures that the battery level of an EV a never goes above
100%, or below 0%. Thus, no EV a will execute a task r for which it does not
have enough range, nor will it charge more than its battery capacity. Note that
we assume all EVs to have the same fixed average consumption. Finally, for each
customer at most one of her alternative tasks dem_i must be executed (Eq. 7).

– *Temporal, spatial, and routing constraints:*

$$\sum_{l \in L} prk_{a,t,l} = 1 - \sum_{r \in R} \epsilon_{a,r,t}, \forall a, \forall t \tag{8}$$

$$2 \times \sum_{r \in R} \epsilon_{a,i,t_r^{start}} = \sum_{l \in L} \sum_{t \in T-1} |prk_{a,t+1,l} - prk_{a,t,l}|, \forall a \tag{9}$$

$$prk_{a,t_r^{start}-1,l_r^{start}} \geq \epsilon_{a,r,t_r^{start}}, \forall r, \forall a \tag{10}$$

$$prk_{a,t_r^{end},l_r^{end}} \geq \epsilon_{a,r,t_r^{end}}, \forall r, \forall a \tag{11}$$

$$\sum_{a \in A} (prk_{a,t,l}) \leq c_l^{max}, \forall l, \forall t \tag{12}$$

$$prk_{a,t=0,l} = l_a^{start}, \forall a, \forall l \tag{13}$$

$$\epsilon_{a,r,t=0} = 0, \forall a, \forall r \tag{14}$$

The *temporal, spatial and routing* constraints ensure the proper placement of
the EVs over time. Equation 8 ensures that for each time point at which an EV
is executing a task, this EV cannot be parked at any location and also assures
(together with Eq. 4) that any time point, each EV executes at most one task.
Moreover, Eq. 9 ensures that no EVs change location without executing a task
(the sum of all changes of EVs' locations as denoted in prk decision variable,
must be double the total number of tasks that are executed). Note that, this
constraint is linearized at run time by CPLEX. This is usually done by adding
two extra decision variables and two extra constraints.

Now, whenever a task is to be executed, the EV that will execute this task
must be at the task's starting location one time point before the task begins
(Eq. 10), and similarly, whenever a task has been executed, the EV that has
executed this task must be at the task's end location the time point the task

ends (Eq. 11). Moreover, at every time point, the maximum capacity of each location must not be violated (Eq. 12). Finally, at time point $t = 0$, all EVs must be at their initial locations (Eq. 13), which also means that no tasks are executed at $t = 0$ (Eq. 14).

– *Cut constraints:*

$$\sum_{a \in A} prk_{a,t,l} = \sum_{a \in A} prk_{a,t-1,k} + \sum_{R^{start}(t,l)} \lambda_r - \sum_{R^{end}(t,l)} \lambda_r, \forall t, \forall l \qquad (15)$$

Equation 15 ensures that for every location, the total number of EVs at charging stations changes only when EVs depart or arrive to execute a task, or after executing tasks. Although this constraint is covered by Eq. 9, when added to the formulation, it significantly speeds up the execution time. In fact, it is known that the introduction of additional *cut constraints* into a MIP problem may cut off infeasible solutions at an early stage of the branch and bound searching process and thus reduce the time to solve the problem [11]. Given that MoD schemes should also work in a dynamic setting, in the next section we present an online greedy scheduling algorithm that uses alternatively three heuristic functions to solve the task execution problem.

5   Greedy Online Scheduling

In the previous section, we presented an optimal offline solution for the EV to customer assignment problem in a MoD setting. However, this algorithm assumes full knowledge of supply and demand in advance. In this section, in order to have a more complete set of tools to tackle the pre-defined problem we propose a greedy online algorithm that calculates an EV to task assignment in real time as requests arrive to the system. This algorithm applies a one-step look ahead heuristic search mechanism and achieves near optimal performance and scales to thousands of EVs and tasks.

Given that EVs change locations only when being driven by customers, the tasks that an EV will be able to execute in the future are directly related to the ones it has already executed in the past (i.e., the end location of one task will be the start location for the next one). In large settings, normally not all tasks can be executed. Thus the selection of the ones to execute is of great importance, since each decision can affect future task execution.

The proposed scheduling algorithm uses three heuristic functions in deciding on whether to execute a task or not. The first is the sum of squares of parked EVs at each station (see Eq. 16). The larger this number, the more imbalance for the system. In this case, we select to execute the task that will lead the EV to the location that minimizes this sum and causes the least imbalance to the system. For example if we consider two stations each having three parking spots, and three EVs. If all three EVs are parked in one station (when a task/request will be accomplished), the outcome would be: $3^2 + 0^2 = 9$. However, if two EVs were parked at one station and one at the other, the outcome would be: $2^2 + 1^2 = 5$. We refer to this heuristic as *Square*.

The second heuristic is the destination station capacity percentage (see Eq. 17). In this case, we divide the sum of the parked EVs at location l by its total capacity and we select to execute the task that will lead an EV to the location with the highest current capacity (i.e., the lower number of existing EVs). This calculation is used to discover each location's capacity percentage separately and aims to move EVs to locations where the supply is low. We refer to this heuristic as *Destination*.

Finally, the third heuristic is a simple random choice of the task to execute. We refer to this heuristic as *Random*.

$$sq_t = \sum_{l \in L} (\sum_{a \in A} \epsilon_{a,t,l})^2, t \in T \qquad (16)$$

$$dcp_{l,t} = (\sum_{a \in A} \epsilon_{a,t,l})/c_l^{max} \qquad (17)$$

In what follows, we provide a step-by-step description of the greedy scheduling algorithm (see Algorithm 1). Based on the online execution of the algorithm, if at time point t a new customer i arrives and expresses her demand, then the set dem_i of all possible tasks is created (line 2). Then, we update the energy level for all EVs. EVs are assumed to charge their battery every time point they are parked unless the battery is fully charged (lines 3–8). Note that in contrast to the optimal algorithm, here the EVs charge with the maximum rate. For each task in dem_i, we check whether the end location of it has enough capacity to receive one vehicle. If this is true, then we search the set of EVs to find the ones that are parked at the starting location of the task and have enough energy to execute the task. If at least one such EV exists, then this task is added to the set dem_i^* that contains the list of feasible tasks (lines 9–23). The next step is to calculate for each of the feasible tasks, the $score_r$ using one of the three heuristic functions (lines 24–27). These scores are later sorted on ascending order and the task with the lower score is selected to be executed (lines 27–28). Once the task has been selected, the EV is assigned to it and its location is updated accordingly (lines 29–39). In the next section we present a detailed evaluation of our algorithms.

6   Evaluation

In this section, we present a detailed evaluation of our algorithms using a number of different settings. In doing so, we use real locations of pick-up and drop-off points owned by ZipCar[1] in Washington DC, USA which are available as open data.[2] The distance and duration of all trips were calculated using Google maps. The evaluation of our algorithms takes place in two main parts:

---

[1]   https://www.zipcar.com/washington-dc.
[2]   http://opendata.dc.gov/datasets/.

Algorithm 1. EV-to-Customer assignment algorithm.

Require: $A, T, L, dem_i, \forall a, l, r : e_{a,t}, \epsilon_{a,t,l}, w_{a,t,r}, l_r^{start}, l_r^{end}, e_r, \tau_r$

1: {If a new customer i arrives at time point t then:}
2: Create dem_i which consists of the combination of all start and end points defined by the customer.
3: **for all** $(a \in A)$ **do**
4:     **for all** $(t' \in T : t' < t)$ **do**
5: {Update the energy level of each EV}
6:         $e_{a,t} = e_{a,t} + (\sum_{l \in L} \epsilon_{a,t',l}) \times cha - (\sum_{r \in R} w_{a,t',r}) \times con_a$
7:     **end for**
8: **end for**
9: **for all** $(r \in dem_i)$ **do**
10: {If the end location of the task has enough capacity for an incoming vehicle:}
11:     **if** $(c_{l_r^{end}, t + \tau_r} < C_{l_r^{end}, t + \tau_r})$ **then**
12:         $FoundEV \leftarrow False$
13:         $a = 0$
14:         **while** $(Found = False$ AND $a < |A|)$ **do**
15: {Search the set of EVs until an EV with current location equal to the initial location of the task that has enough energy to execute the task is found.}
16:             **if** $(\epsilon_{a,t,l_r^{start}} = 1$ AND $e_{a,t} > e_r)$ **then**
17:                 $Found \leftarrow True$
18:             **end if**
19:             $a = a + 1$
20:         **end while**{Update the set of feasible tasks.}
21:         $(dem_i^* \leftarrow dem_i^* + r)$
22:     **end if**
23: **end for**
24: **for all** $(r \in dem_i^*)$ **do**
25:     Calculate $score$ for each task using one of the three heuristic functions.
26: **end for**
27: Sort $score$ in ascending order.
28: Select to execute task r that minimizes the heuristic function.
29: **for all** $(t' \in T : t' \geq \tau_r)$ **do**
30: {Set the new location of the EV after the execution of the task.}
31:     $\epsilon_{a,t',l_r^{end}} = 1$
32: **end for**
33: **for all** $t' \in T : t' > t$ **do**
34:     $\epsilon_{a,t',l_r^{start}} = 0$
35: **end for**
36: **for all** $(t' \in T : t' \geq t$ AND $t' < t + \tau_r)$ **do**
37: {Set the EV to be working on the task for the equivalent time points. }
38:     $w_{a,t',r} = 1$
39: **end for**

- EXP1: The performance of the online and offline algorithms in terms of the average number of serviced customers (i.e., executed tasks).
- EXP2: The execution time and the scalability of the algorithms.

To perform the experiments we used the following setting: 1) One time point is equal to 15 min and totally 58 time points exist which is equivalent to the execution of the MoD service from 7:00 to 18:00. 2) 8 locations exist and tasks can be formulated based on one of 56 possible trips (i.e., the trips are the combinations of the locations that form the MoD scheme. However, locations too close to each other were ignored) and trips as well as starting times were randomly selected. Each location has a maximum capacity $c_l^{max} = 10$. 3) Each customer i has a demand dem_i of up to three alternative tasks. 4) The energy consumption rate for each EV a is selected to be $con_a = 10$ and the charging rate $cha_a = 25$. This means that for each time point that an EV is working the battery level is reduced by 10 units of energy, and for each time point an EV is charging the battery level is increased by up to 25 units of energy (fast battery charging): The average range of an EV is currently at around 150 km. We assume an average speed of 40 km/hour which means that an EV can drive for 3.75 h. In our evaluation setting, one time point is equal to 15 min, and 3.75 h equal to 15 time points. Thus, $con_a = 10\%$ of battery for each time point. A fast charger can fully charge an EV at around one hour. Thus, $cha_a = 25\%$ of the battery for each time point. Both con_a and cha_a are configuration parameters and can be selected by the user. All experiments were executed on a Windows PC using an Intel i7-4790K CPU and 16 GB of RAM running at 2400 MHz.

6.1   EXP1: Customer Service

Here we investigate the performance trade-off incurred by the online algorithms in terms of average customer service against the optimal offline one. Initially, we study a setting with 15 EVs and up to 70 customers. Note that each customer expresses her demand for up to 3 alternative tasks, with an average number of 2, so the average number of tasks is approximately double the number of customers. As we observe in Fig. 1, all online algorithms are close to the optimal with the best being the Squared having a 94.2% efficiency in the worst case, then is the Destination with a 93.3% efficiency in the worst case and last is the Random with a 86.9% efficiency in the worst case.

Aiming to see how the number of EVs affects the performance of the online algorithms, we set up an experiment with 100 customers and up to 35 EVs. As we can observe in Fig. 2 the overall image is similar to the previous case with the Squared being the best, the Destination second and the Random third. However, it is interesting to notice that when the number of EVs is low (5 EVs) or large (35 EVs) the performance deficit of the Destination and Random is smaller compared to the case where 20 EVs exist. This can be explained by the fact that when the number of EVs is low the heuristics, as they are connected to the number of EVs, cannot make a big difference, while when the number of EVs is high the problem becomes easier to solve.   Finally, in order to evaluate the performance of the online algorithms in larger settings, we set up an experiment with 100

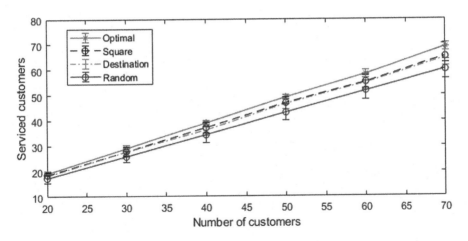

Fig. 1. Average number of serviced customers

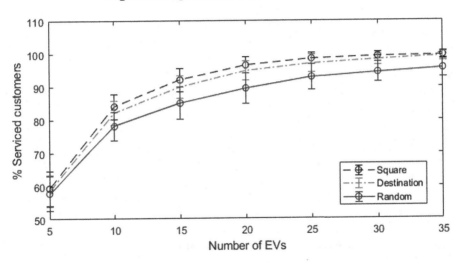

Fig. 2. Average number of serviced customers- Varying number of EVs

EVs, 100 time points and up o 1200 customers. As we can observe in Fig. 3, up to around 500 customers all three algorithms have a similar performance, but later the Squared and Destination have a better performance and for 1200 customer the Destination has a 95.4% efficiency compared to the Squared and the Random a 89.7% efficiency compared to the Squared.

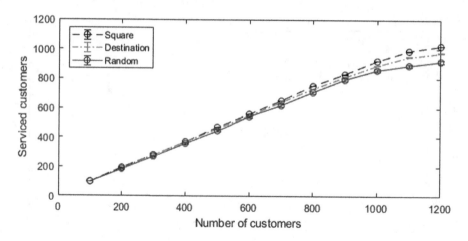

Fig. 3. Average number of serviced customers- Online algorithms

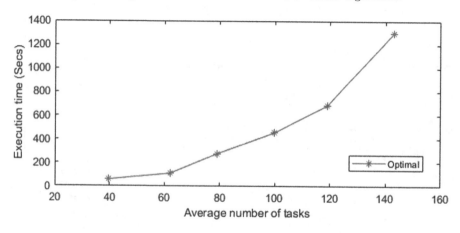

Fig. 4. Execution time of the Optimal algorithm

6.2   EXP2: Execution Time and Scalability

Execution time and scalability are typical metrics for scheduling algorithms. In a setting with 15 EVs and up to around 140 tasks (i.e., 70 customers), we see in Fig. 4 that the execution time of the Optimal algorithm increases polynomially. Using MATLAB's Curve Fitting Toolbox we see that the Optimal's execution time is second degree polynomial with $R^2 = 97.11$. At the same time, the online algorithms have a very low execution time, as they all run in well under 0.05 s even in large settings.

7   Conclusions and Future Work

In this paper, we studied the problem of scheduling a set of shared EVs in a MoD scheme. We proposed an offline algorithm which collects the customers' demand in advance and calculates an optimal EV to customer assignment which maximizes the number of serviced customers. This algorithm scales up to medium sized problems. We also proposed three variations of an online algorithm which operates in a customer-by-customer basis and has shown to achieve near optimal performance while it can scale up to settings with thousands of EVs and locations.

Currently, we assume that the customer-agents are cooperative when communicating their demand to the system. As future work we aim to extend this by including non-cooperative agents and to apply mechanism design techniques in order to ensure truthful reporting. Moreover, we aim to improve the charging procedure of the EVs by trying to maximize the use of limited and intermittent energy from renewable sources. Finally, we want to enhance our algorithms in handling possible uncertainties in arrival and departure times, while aiming to maximize customer satisfaction and their profit.

Acknowledgment. This research is co-financed by Greece and the European Union (European Social Fund - ESF) through the Operational Programme "Human Resources Development, Education and Lifelong Learning" in the context of the project "Reinforcement of Postdoctoral Researchers - 2nd Cycle" (MIS-5033021), implemented by the State Scholarships Foundation (IKY).

References

1. U.S. Energy Information Administration: Annual energy outlook 2020. Technical report (2020)
2. Andersson, A., Tenhunen, M., Ygge, F.: Integer programming for combinatorial auction winner determination. In: 2000 Proceedings of the 4th International Conference on MultiAgent Systems, pp. 39–46 (2000). https://doi.org/10.1109/ICMAS.2000.858429
3. Burns, L.D.: Sustainable mobility: a vision of our transport future. Nature **497**(7448), 181–182 (2013)
4. Carpenter, T., Keshav, S., Wong, J.: Sizing finite-population vehicle pools. IEEE Trans. Intell. Transp. Syst. **15**(3), 1134–1144 (2014). https://doi.org/10.1109/TITS.2013.2293918
5. Cepolina, E.M., Farina, A.: A new shared vehicle system for urban areas. Transp. Res. Part C Emerg. Technol. **21**(1), 230–243 (2012). https://doi.org/10.1016/j.trc.2011.10.005
6. Chandran, B., Raghavan, S.: Modeling and solving the capacitated vehicle routing problem on trees. In: Golden, B., Raghavan, S., Wasil, E. (eds.) The Vehicle Routing Problem: Latest Advances and New Challenges. Operations Research/Computer Science Interfaces, vol. 43, pp. 239–261. Springer, Boston (2008). https://doi.org/10.1007/978-0-387-77778-8_11
7. Dantzig, G.B., Ramser, J.H.: The truck dispatching problem. Manage. Sci. **6**(1), 80–91 (1959)

8. Densing, M., Turton, H., Bäuml, G.: Conditions for the successful deployment of electric vehicles-a global energy system perspective. Energy **47**(1), 137–149 (2012)
9. Dorigo, M., Gambardella, L.M.: Ant colony system: a cooperative learning approach to the traveling salesman problem. IEEE Trans. Evol. Comput. **1**(1), 53–66 (1997). https://doi.org/10.1109/4235.585892
10. Drwal, M., Gerding, E., Stein, S., Hayakawa, K., Kitaoka, H.: Adaptive pricing mechanisms for on-demand mobility. In: Proceedings of the 16th Conference on Autonomous Agents and MultiAgent Systems, pp. 1017–1025. International Foundation for Autonomous Agents and Multiagent Systems (2017)
11. Floudas, C.A., Lin, X.: Mixed integer linear programming in process scheduling: modeling, algorithms, and applications. Ann. Oper. Res. **139**(1), 131–162 (2005)
12. Gkourtzounis, I., Rigas, E.S., Bassiliades, N.: Towards online electric vehicle scheduling for mobility-on-demand schemes. In: Slavkovik, M. (ed.) EUMAS 2018. LNCS (LNAI), vol. 11450, pp. 94–108. Springer, Cham (2019). https://doi.org/10.1007/978-3-030-14174-5_7
13. Lomnicki, Z.A.: A "branch-and-bound" algorithm for the exact solution of the three-machine scheduling problem. J. Oper. Res. Soc. **16**(1), 89–100 (1965). https://doi.org/10.1057/jors.1965.7
14. Mitchel, W.J., Borroni-Bird, C.E., Burns, L.D.: Reinventing the Automobile: Personal Urban Mobility for the 21st Century. MIT Press, Cambridge (2010)
15. Pavone, M., Smith, S.L., Emilio, F., Rus, D.: Robotic load balancing for mobility-on-demand systems. Robot. Sci. Syst. **31**, 839–854 (2011)
16. Pavone, M., Smith, S.L., Frazzoli, E., Rus, D.: Robotic load balancing for mobility-on-demand systems. Int. J. Robot. Res. **31**(7), 839–854 (2012). https://doi.org/10.1177/0278364912444766
17. Rigas, E.S., Ramchurn, S.D., Bassiliades, N.: Algorithms for electric vehicle scheduling in large-scale mobility-on-demand schemes. Artif. Intell. **262**, 248–278 (2018). https://doi.org/10.1016/j.artint.2018.06.006
18. Sandholm, T., Suri, S., Gilpin, A., Levine, D.: Winner determination in combinatorial auction generalizations. In: Proceedings of the 1st International Joint Conference on Autonomous Agents and Multiagent Systems: Part 1, AAMAS 2002, pp. 69–76. ACM, New York (2002). https://doi.org/10.1145/544741.544760
19. Smith, S., Pavone, M., Schwager, M., Frazzoli, E., Rus, D.: Rebalancing the rebalancers: optimally routing vehicles and drivers in mobility-on-demand systems. In: 2013 American Control Conference (ACC), pp. 2362–2367 (2013). https://doi.org/10.1109/ACC.2013.6580187
20. Talbot, F.B., Patterson, J.H.: An efficient integer programming algorithm with network cuts for solving resource-constrained scheduling problems. Manage. Sci. **24**(11), 1163–1174 (1978)
21. Tomic, J., Kempton, W.: Using fleets of electric-drive vehicles for grid support. J. Power Sources **168**(2), 459–468 (2007). https://doi.org/10.1016/j.jpowsour.2007.03.010
22. Turan, B., Tucker, N., Alizadeh, M.: Smart charging benefits in autonomous mobility on demand systems. In: 2019 IEEE Intelligent Transportation Systems Conference (ITSC), pp. 461–466 (2019)

Disaster Response Simulation as a Testbed for Multi-Agent Systems

Tabajara Krausburg[1,2]([✉]) [ID], Vinicius Chrisosthemos[1] [ID], Rafael H. Bordini[1] [ID], and Jürgen Dix[2] [ID]

[1] School of Technology, Pontifical Catholic University of Rio Grande do Sul,
Porto Alegre, Brazil
{tabajara.rodrigues,vinicius.teixeira99}@edu.pucrs.br,
rafael.bordini@pucrs.br
[2] Department of Informatics, Clausthal University of Technology,
Clausthal-Zellerfeld, Germany
dix@tu-clausthal.de

Abstract. We introduce a novel two-dimensional simulator for disaster response on maps of real cities. Our simulator deals with logistics and coordination problems and allows to plug-in almost any approach developed for simulated environments. In addition, it (1) offers functionalities for further developing and benchmarking, and (2) provides metrics that help the analysis of the performance of a team of agents during the disaster. Our simulator is based on software made available by the multi-agent programming contest, which over the years has provided challenging problems to be solved by intelligent agents. We evaluate the performance of our simulator in terms of processing time and memory usage, message exchange, and response time. We apply this analysis to two different approaches for dealing with the mining dam disaster that occurred in Brazil in 2019. Our results show that our simulator is robust and can work with a reasonable number of agents.

Keywords: Disaster response · MAS · Testbed

1 Introduction

Disaster Response has long been used as a scenario for multi-agent systems, but it remains a relevant problem to be addressed by real-world applications. Each year, many countries suffer from devastating natural disasters [2,13,14]. Such disaster events often overwhelm local authorities in dealing with the many tasks that must be accomplished in order to recover quickly. With that in mind, we have developed a new disaster response simulator where agents control simulated entities that represent autonomous vehicles, human professional rescuers, and volunteers. The simulation happens on a realistic map, where affected areas and victims are placed.

In the beginning of 2019, a dam for mining tailings collapsed, inundating with mud all over a sparse area; in fact, 12 million cubic meters of mining tailings were

© Springer Nature Switzerland AG 2020
N. Bassiliades et al. (Eds.): EUMAS 2020/AT 2020, LNAI 12520, pp. 67–81, 2020.
https://doi.org/10.1007/978-3-030-66412-1_5

spread out over more than 46 kilometres [2]. Buildings, cars, animals, and people were swamped by mud. Then, a massive operation was carried out to respond to that disaster event. Three months after the disaster, confirmed fatal victims toll was 225 with 68 missing people [2]. In our simulator, which was mostly being used for flooding scenarios, a new type of scenario based on mud events is introduced in order to analyse and experiment with Multi-Agent System (MAS) approaches that could support *tactical response* of such disasters.

We aim to provide a realistic simulation environment for benchmarking intelligent software agents in disaster response context. Although this topic has already been addressed in the Agent-Based Modelling (ABM) community [8,9], in most approaches decision-making is limited to reactive reasoning (e.g., rule-based system) [11], and in others, AI techniques are constrained to a few situations in a given scenario [15]. However, simulation tools should not constrain, in any way, decision-making capabilities of agents in coping with the posed problem. In contrast with this, authors in [1] decoupled agents from the environment to evaluate different MAS frameworks in a challenging scenario. By doing so, they let agents act freely to fully exploit their reasoning capabilities. With that in mind, we apply the concepts introduced in [1] to simulations in disaster response episodes in which developers are free to choose the degree of agent's reasoning and AI techniques that fit them best. Therefore techniques are not evaluated in isolation, but as part of a complex system.

This paper is organised as follows. Section 2 describes relevant related work in disaster environments and explains why we need a new simulator for this particular domain. In Sect. 3, the reasoning engine and all features of our simulator are described using several examples illustrating the core ideas. Section 4 contains some experiments performed in order to evaluate our simulator. Finally, Sect. 5 concludes with future directions.

2   Related Work

Disaster response simulation has been addressed in the multi-agent systems literature for a long time. We review some of the main work and discuss the differences with respect to our simulator.

Different disaster response scenarios have been proposed in the literature, most of them use an ABM approach. Mancheva et al. [9] model a *bushfire* episode in which Belief Desire Intention (BDI) agents simulate human behaviour and interactions. Hilljegerdes and Augustijn [6] explore a *hurricane* season to simulate a evacuee procedure during two consecutive hurricane events. In both work, a general platform for simulating ABM is used, GAMA[1] and NetLogo[2] respectively. By contrast, Klein et al. [8] implement a resilience scenario considering a cross-border disaster event using Repast[3] framework, which is based on Java. This scenario demands coordination between parties that have differences in the

---

[1] http://gama-platform.org.

[2] https://ccl.northwestern.edu/netlogo/.

[3] https://repast.github.io/.

way they are organised and even in their cultural collective behaviour. The main focus of those approaches is to simulate some predefined behaviour, for this purpose, they take advantage of a ABM tool to implement and solve their designed problem.

Another approach is to provide a problem and ask for solutions from the MAS community: RoboCup-Rescue [15] is one of the most successful simulators which intends to simulate disaster response episodes. It offers two major competitions for participants. The first one focuses on *virtual robots* working together to assess the situation of a devastated area. The second one is a agent-based simulation of an earthquake in which agents try to minimise the impact of the disaster. Teams implement their algorithms in ADF modules [7]. This enables modularity in team's code and organisers are then able to run the code and swap modules of same purpose around to collect performance results. RoboCup-Rescue, in the agent-based simulation, focuses on certain aspects of the scenario (e.g., task allocation, team formation, and route planning), in which teams develop techniques for those isolated problems.

An even more general approach is to simply provide the problem and leave it entirely open to the MAS community to choose strategies and techniques of how to solve it. In the Multi-Agent Programming Contest (MAPC) [1], the aim is to identify key problems, collect suitable benchmarks, and gather test cases for MAS community, in particular to MAS programming languages. Agents are decoupled from the environment server and interact with it by sending actions and receiving perceptions. Doing so, agents chose strategies and AI techniques that fit them best. The environment is designed to enforce coordinated actions and to be highly dynamic; which means it changes as new events are announced and as teams of agents act upon the shared environment.

Our simulator is inspired by MAPC; in particular by the contests of 2016, 2017, and 2018, with the *"Agents in the City"* scenario [1]. In that scenario agents of two different teams control various autonomous vehicles to solve logistic problems simulated on the map of a real city. We leave it to the developers of agents to choose and apply what are the possibly best approaches to address the overall disaster response problem. Doing so, we work to shift MAS community's attention to relevant problems of real-world in which developers can fully exploit the entire potential that MAS solutions can offer.

3   A Simulator for Disaster Response Episodes

In a disaster episode, usually, a sparse area is affected [10] and the experts, robots, and volunteers accomplish certain tasks in order to minimise the suffering and loss caused by the disaster event. We simulate some tasks related to a collapse of a dam for mining tailings occurred in Brumadinho in 2019.

In our setting, tasks for rescuing victims, collecting mud samples, and taking photographs[4]: These are announced by the Centre for Disaster Management (CDM). Some victims may have their location already revealed and others are hidden in the middle of the mud. Information about the area is collected and then analysed in order to decide whether there might be or not victims at that location. The CDM also tags specific locations in which the mud must be sampled. As new information is received during the disaster response operation, new tasks are announced and require further investigation.

In disaster response episodes volunteers support disaster response in many ways (e.g., as a workforce) [3]. For this reason, recent work concentrates on integrating those persons into the operation [12]. To represent that need, we define the idea of *social assets* that represents volunteers in disaster response context. We distinguish between agents that connect before the simulation starts (i.e., regular agents) and agents that connect after the simulation has begun (i.e., social assets) to help some other agent. For instance, if an agent has to finish a task but it does not have the skill to do so, it can try to find some social assets that are able to perform that particular task. The reader can find the code and additional information about this simulator in our repository[5].

3.1 Problem Set-Up

The disaster response simulator generates an environment model (where agents will be situated) based on the parameters established in a configuration file. It is organised into five sections:

- **Map:** contains all the information regarding the simulator itself and the map in which the simulation will take place (Open Street Map (OSM)).
- **Regular Agents:** sets how many agents should be instantiated at the beginning of the simulation as well as their skills and resources.
- **Social Assets:** similar to regular agents in which one can define the amount of social assets and their skills and resources.
- **Actions:** specifies the actions available to the agents stating which skills and resources are needed in order to perform them in the environment.
- **Events:** sets the chance to occur, size, and number of occurrences of mud events. Such events are noticed by the CDM that announces tasks (i.e., photos, samples, and rescuing victims) to be accomplished by the agents. A photo task has a chance of an agent finding out victims at that location.

Agents have physical and virtual storage in addition to their move capability. Three types of movement are supported in our simulated environment: by air, ground, or water. The skill of an agent indicates which movement the simulation

---

[4] Photo in our context is an abstraction that represents a further investigation that must be carried out in order to find out whether a victim is or is not hidden under the mud. Usually, experts may use some device that provides data that must be analysed to draw a conclusion.

[5] https://github.com/smart-pucrs/MASiRe.

engine should perform for that agent (e.g., skill `airMovement`). Air movement enables agents to reach any coordinate in the map (i.e., latitude and longitude). The underlying map is compounded by a set of nodes that could form a route from one place to another. These nodes are affected by the disaster events, for instance, in a mud episode, spawned nodes are tagged and pose speed constraints on the agents' locomotion to represent the effects of mud on the ground surface. Note that agents' skills and resources should match (i.e., a string match) the skills and resources required by an action in order to be performed.

Agents interact with the simulator through actions. Actions are designed to meet the model of the mud episode in which the CDM announces tasks that must be accomplished by the agents. The actions available for the agents are:

pass does nothing in the environment;

move moves an agent towards a specific coordinate;

charge recharges, at the CDM, the agent's energy used by other actions (e.g., move action);

rescue achieves task `rescue victim` and puts a volume in the agent's physical storage;

collect achieves task `collect sample` and puts a volume in the agent's physical storage;

take-photo achieves task `take photo` and puts a volume in the agent's virtual storage;

analyse-photo analyses a photo, at the CDM, to figure out whether there is or not a victim at that location;

search-social-asset searches for a social asset in a given perimeter;

request-social-asset asks for opening a connection for a social asset;

provide-retrieve-physical synchronised actions between agents to exchange physical volume;

provide-retrieve-virtual synchronised actions between agents to exchange virtual volume;

carry-becarried synchronised actions that put one agent into the physical storage of another;

deliver delivers an item from the agent's storage in the agent's current position (it could be an physical item, virtual item, or even an agent).

Agents that are being carried by other agent cannot perform any action but **pass**. This feature us useful when an agent is out of battery or cannot move at the current terrain.

Agents play in discrete steps, in which at each step an action is expected from each connected agent. A step represents a notion of time unit in the simulation (i.e., seconds, minutes, etc.) and it also has a timeout for waiting for actions from the agents. We call a match a run of **n** steps (set in the configuration file) for a team of agents in the simulated disaster environment. Events, and consequently tasks, may have a duration span (in steps) that poses time constraints to the agents. This is also the case for the people stuck in the mud, once the duration is set to 0 in the environment model the victim is considered dead.

3.2 Architecture of the Disaster Response Simulator

The architecture of our simulator is divided into three components:

- **Simulation Engine:** responsible for creating the environment, events, agents, processing the actions received from agents, and computing metrics at the end of the simulation;
- **Application Program Interface (API)** interfaces the communication between agents and the simulation engine, as well as refreshes the graphical interface with new data;
- **Monitor:** receives data from the API and shows it in the browser.

Figure 1 gives an overview of the components and libraries used in our simulator.

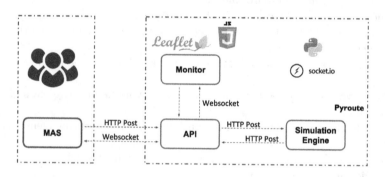

Fig. 1. Architecture of the simulator.

Although for agents a graphical interface is not needed during the simulation, for humans carrying out the experimentation, it is a very useful tool to see what is going on. Experts can visually analyse the behaviour adopted by a team of agents and it is also useful in order to find flaws in strategies.

3.3 Communication with Multi-Agent Platforms

The communication between the simulator and a MAS is established by a well-defined protocol similar to the one in MAPC [1]. The protocol consists of four types of messages:

Initial Percepts: Sent to an agent as soon as it connects to the API. It contains all percepts related to the map and the agent's role in the simulation. These percepts do not change during a match.

Percepts: Sent to the agent at each new simulation step. It contains all the percepts for the current state of the environment and of the agents (an agent does not receive percepts of other agents).

End: Sent to the agent at the end of a match. It contains a report of the performance of the team of agents during the match (this is further discussed in Sect. 3.5).

Bye: Received by all agents when all matches have finished. It contains the report of the performance of the agents in all matches; similar to the end message but for when the whole simulation is finished.

All the messages of the protocol are in JSON object format and can be easily parsed by a MAS to Prolog-like syntax. Note that any Multi-Agent System platform is able to connect and interact with our simulator as long as it implements the communication protocol described above. All the messages are generated by the simulation engine which is detailed in the next section.

3.4 Simulation Cycle

So far we have illustrated the configuration of the simulator and how to exchange messages. We are now introducing how the simulator itself works.

The simulation engine first checks the configuration file and generates all events that will take place in the simulated environment as well as all the social assets options. Note that a social asset is available for a period (e.g., it can be called from step 120 to 150). Once this phase is finished, the API begins accepting connections from agents. When a request is made, the API generates a *token* that will be used during the whole simulation to represent that agent, and sends to the agent the `initial percepts`. When all agents get connected (or the timeout is reached), the simulator enters the cycle until the end of the match. The cycle consists of:

1. sending `percepts` for the current step (Simulation Engine $\mapsto$ API $\mapsto$ MAS);
2. updating the graphical interface (API to Monitor);
3. waiting for the connected agents' actions (API);
4. sending actions to the simulator (API to Simulation Engine);
5. Simulation Engine processes actions;
6. goes back to the first step.

If no action is received from an agent in time (i.e., before the timeout for that simulation step be reached), the API assigns a `pass` action to it. If all steps are processed the simulation engine sends an `end` message and disconnects all social assets. If there are no more matches to simulate (i.e., other maps), it sends the `bye` message and disconnects all agents.

A special treatment is needed when a *social asset* is requested by a regular agent. This action is processed by the simulation engine that asks to the API to wait for a new connection. If a timeout is reached, a *failure* is returned to the requester agent. This social asset is always linked to a regular agent and can be disposed of at any time by its creator. After being connected, a social asset is considered a regular agent: It receives perceptions and performs actions in the environment.

At the beginning of a simulation a mud event is always generated (i.e., at the first step), after that, other events may occur dynamically over the simulation. A mud event only disappears when there are no more tasks to be completed in the affected area. Our simulation focuses only on the response phase of a disaster [10].

3.5   Simulation Metrics

A final but important part of the simulation are the results generated about the performance of the team(s) of agents. We collect during the simulation some metrics that help developers of the MAS and experts to analyse the advantages and drawbacks of the adopted strategies.

At the end of each match, we record the performance of team of agents in accomplishing all the tasks announced by the CDM. The simulator provides metrics for:

Victims: This metric states the total number of victims in the simulation, including both the victims already known in the mud events as well as victims hidden under the mud. We also count the number of victims delivered to the CDM, alive or dead. Finally, we count all the generated victims (i.e., in the mud events and in the photo events) that were not rescued by the agents.

Photos: This metric refers to the total number of photo tasks that were generated. It represents locations of the affected area that should have been evaluated by the agents in order to look for new victims. Every time an agent takes a photo or analyses a photo, we record that information. Photo tasks that were not completed are also counted.

Samples: For this metric we show the quantity of mud-sample tasks requested by the disaster response command. Although this kind of task has not the same priority as rescuing a victim in disaster operations, it represents secondary tasks that agents should also take into account during their activities. We also keep track of how many these tasks were completed by the agents.

The simulator also allows the user to record matches for future replay. This enables further analysis of what happened during the simulation and is a very powerful feature during the development of MAS teams.

4   Evaluating the Simulator

After introducing how our simulator works, we present some results regarding its performance. We start describing the simulator performance over a range of parameter in the configuration file. Then we illustrate how to compare different approaches using the metrics provided by the simulator's report.

4.1   Simulator Performance

We experiment with some configuration parameters in order to monitor memory usage, processing time, message exchange and response time. As the experiments were directed to the assessment of the simulator engine, we decided not to consider the influence of graphic monitoring. In addition, the connection with a MAS platform will not be considered in these experiments, that is, we instantiate "fake agents"[6] that connect to the simulator to experiment with its performance only.

---

[6] Fake agents are agents that do not perform any reasoning; they just send a predefined action at each step.

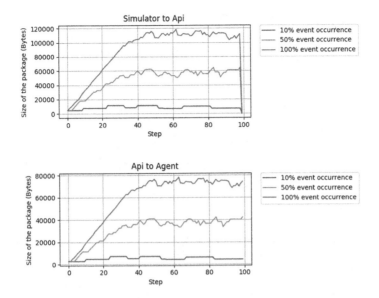

Fig. 2. Package size of the messages exchanged between the sim-engine, API, and MAS.

All experiments were executed in a MacPro 5 server with 32 Gigabyte of RAM and two hexa core Intel Xeon of 2.4 GHz processor.

To clearly explain the experiments, we define a basic setting of the parameters used during all the simulations (in the following we only state the parameters that have different values in this setting). In the basic configuration, the number of steps is set to 100, the chance of a event to occur to 10%, the number of agents to one, and the number of mapped nodes to 49634 (i.e., subset of nodes from the map that are loaded into the simulation). The mud events have a duration of 30 to 50 steps.

We start describing the experiments with package size and response time for sent actions. All the messages exchanged between the simulation engine and the API, and also between the API and the MAS, are evaluated. We set the simulation to 100 steps and only one agent is instantiated. We experiment with the chance of a mud event to occur in the simulation. We remind the reader that mud events lead the CDM to announce tasks for rescuing victims, taking photos, and collecting samples. The results are depicted in Fig. 2.

At the end of each step, percepts and activated events are sent to the API; this is depicted in the first chart of Fig. 2. As the simulation progresses, we can notice a growth in the size of the packages as new events are being announced. However, the growth gets stable around step 40. This is due to the configured duration of an event, at that point, as new events are announced, others disappear. We can see that the size of packages depends on the number of events occurring in the disaster scenario as well as on the number of agents. If we instantiate more agents, the size of the packages exchanged between the simulation engine and API will increase only in the part that represents the agents' current states.

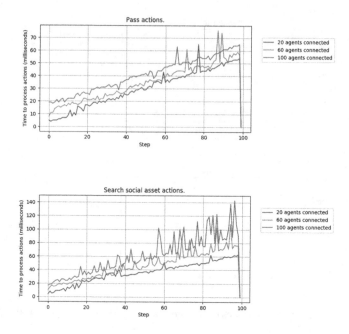

Fig. 3. Response time of the simulation engine considering two different actions; `pass` is the least expensive action and `searchSocialAssets` is the most expensive one.

However, from the API to MAS we have to multiply the package size by the number of agents, as agents need to receive their own state and the state of the environment (see the second chart in Fig. 2). Disaster scenarios in which new events are announced frequently are unlikely, for instance, in a simulation of 100 steps, 100 events being announced. By observing the simulation with 10% event occurrence, a more realistic value, we have acceptable packet sizes for the communication between the components of the overall simulation.

Next, we experiment with the actions sent by the agents in order to evaluate the simulation engine's response time. Agents send the same action at each step. We analyse a simulation instance in which all agents send a `pass` action. The `pass` action is the least expensive action in terms of computation for the simulator; it changes nothing in the environment. We also analyse the response time when the agents send the `searchSocialAsset` action. This action is the most expensive one, because the engine must go through all the elements of the set of social assets, evaluating their distance to the requesting agent in order to send back only the assets that are within the specified perimeter. For this experiment, we set the incidence of events to 100% in which they stay activated throughout the simulation. Each mud event will contain only one task of each type and one new social asset will be made available at each step. We vary the number of agents between 20, 60, and 100. The results are depicted in Fig. 3.

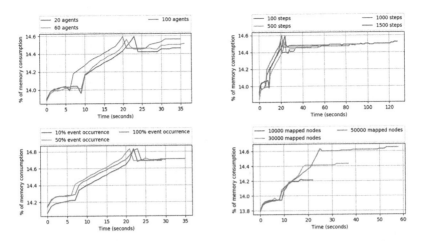

Fig. 4. Memory usage: varying # of agents, steps, event occurrence, and mapped nodes.

The first chart in Fig. 3 depicts the time taken to process the **pass** action. In order to advance a step, the simulator performs the agents' actions in the environment, updates the current status of the other entities (i.e., victims' life-time), generates the new state, and sends the information back to the agents. For both actions the simulation response time grows linearly, as expected; this is due to the number of events generated at each step (i.e., one new event being announced). However, when comparing the response time for both actions, we can see that the search action is slightly slower than the pass action.

The next two experiments are for memory usage and processing time. We instantiate simulations varying the number of connected agents (20, 60, and 100 agents), the number of steps that a match takes (100, 500, 1000, and 1500 steps), the complexity of the simulated problem which means the incidence of events throughout the simulation (10%, 50%, 100% chance that a new mud event occurs in a step), and the number of nodes mapped in the OSM file (10000, 30000, and 50000 nodes). We analyse from the moment the simulator is instantiated, going through the generation of events, loading the map, and getting agents connected until the initial percepts are sent to the agents (i.e., before the first simulation step). We depict the results for memory usage in Fig. 4.

When the simulator is started, all events that will occur in the simulation are generated and stored in memory; the event only gets activated at the step indicated by the event generation procedure. In this sense, the number of steps could indeed have an impact on the performance of the simulation initialisation. However, as we can see in Fig. 4, as we change the parameters of the simulation, the memory usage increases linearly. Moreover, we can see that the size of the map (i.e., mapped nodes) has not a significant impact on memory usage. The memory used by the simulator increases a little as we change the configuration settings, therefore we can conclude that simulating more complex scenarios seems to be feasible.

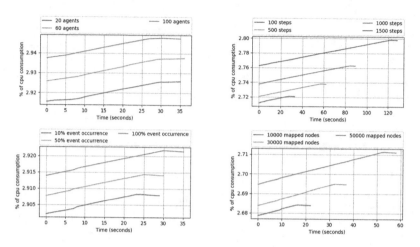

Fig. 5. Processing time: varying # of agents, steps, event occurrence, mapped nodes.

In addition to memory usage, we analyse the processing time required to generate the shared environment. We used the same parameters as in the memory experiment to run those simulation instances. The results are depicted in Fig. 5. We can see a similar behaviour for the number of agents, steps, and event occurrences. The processing time requirement grows linearly with increasing the parameters. For the size of the map, we still notice a small increase when compared with the memory usage experiment.

4.2   Comparison Between Different MAS Approaches

Having shown that our simulator is robust, we now aim to demonstrate how MAS researchers can use our simulator metrics to analyse the performance of a team of agents[7]. We evaluate two approaches in the same disaster scenario: (i) a MAS with only very simple reasoning; and (ii) a MAS using a coalition formation approach to partition the set of agents. Both approaches are developed using the JaCaMo platform [4] in which the communication protocol (Sect. 3.3) is implemented in a CArtAgO artefact.

In this scenario, we consider a mud disaster environment in which 30 experts receive tasks from the CDM and must establish a coordination between themselves to perform all announced tasks. We assume experts are able to teleoperate robots. The configuration file is set as the following:

- 500 steps in a match;
- two types of regular agents: *drone* for aerial locomotion (7 agents), and Unmanned Ground Vehicles (UGV) for ground locomotion (23 agents);
- ground vehicles suffer speed reduction of 50% in a zone affected by mud;

---

[7] Although we compare the two approaches to show how to use our metrics, our main goal does not lie to state which approach is better.

- new mud events occur at each step with chance of 2% containing: four to eight mud sample tasks; four to ten photo tasks; and one to three victims.
- each photo has a chance of 80% to reveal one to three victims in that area;
- victims stay alive in the simulation for 50 to 100 steps.

Any change in the disaster scenario can be easily set in our configuration file. For instance, it is completely feasible to declare other types of agents and skills according to the range of experts and unmanned (or manned) vehicles that are available in the operation. However, to better illustrate the use of simulator's metrics, we prefer to keep the experiment simple.

Both approaches have some characteristics in common related to the agents' reasoning. Drones are capable of taking photos, analysing them, and collecting mud samples. They always prefer collecting photos and analysing them rather than collecting mud samples. UGV are capable of rescuing victims and collecting mud samples; both must be delivered at the CDM. They always prefer rescuing victims rather than collecting mud samples. Note that the agents are not aware of the current health situation of the victim, they try to save the first victim they find in the disaster zone. After completing a task, an agent always returns to the CDM to report on what was done, to recharge, and to choose a new task. Agents use a simple coordination mechanism in order to pick a task. An agent queries if there is no other agent performing that task, then it broadcasts to the other agents that it is now attempting to achieve that particular task.

In the simple MAS team, agents always consider all the active mud events in order to pick a task. They only attempt to execute the first task returned when querying its belief base for known events (preserving the preferences of each role over the tasks).

In the MAS team that uses coalition formation, we use the C-Link algorithm introduced by Farinelli et al. [5][8]. It is a heuristic algorithm for coalition formation based on hierarchical clustering. We aim to partition the agents for the set of active mud events. An agent post as contribution to act upon a mud event the number of tasks it could accomplish in that event, plus the distance to get there (long distances have smaller contributions). The *characteristic function* evaluates the contribution of each agent divided by the number of agents of that same type in the coalition. For instance, in a mud event in which two mud samples must be collected, a drone agent would have contribution value of two for that event (we ignore the distance values in this example). However, if a coalition contains two drone agents, each will contribute only one to the total value, so the coalition value will still be two. After the *coalition structure* is formed, coalition members only act upon the mud event related to the coalition they belong. We generate a new coalition structure every time a new mud event occurs in the scenario, and agents may be reallocated to work on different areas.

---

[8] As our main goal is not to evaluate the technique itself but to demonstrate how to compare different approaches, we omit implementation details.

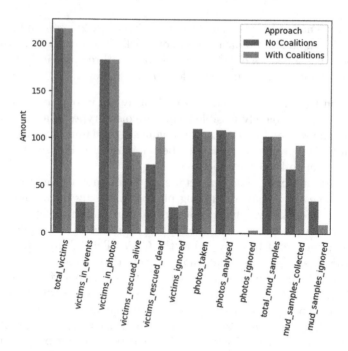

Fig. 6. Metrics for the mud disaster response considering two MAS approaches.

We execute both teams in the same scenario (i.e., same events at the same steps) and collect their performance results which are depicted in Fig. 6. For this setting, the simple reasoning MAS team rescued more victims alive, but it did not accomplish many mud sample tasks. Drones and UGV always try to achieve their most preferred tasks (i.e., taking photos and rescuing victims respectively), and ignore the rest. In contrast, the coalition formation MAS team accomplished more of the tasks announced by CDM, however, the priority system for rescuing victims was applied only locally in the mud regions which led to a higher number of rescued bodies. This shows how to use the simulator's metrics as a guide for decision-making.

5   Conclusions and Future Work

In this paper, we have introduced a new disaster response simulator to be used by the scientific community during the design and benchmark of different MAS approaches for coordinating autonomous agents. It differs from previous approaches in the literature about simulating disaster response environments by *not constraining* the MAS approach to a few reasoning mechanisms or AI techniques: Any methods can be plugged-in and evaluated in a long-term simulation. The present simulator was first designed to cope with floods, but with the occurrence of a collapse of a dam for mining tailings in Brumadinho in 2019, we adapted it to suit better some characteristics of this disaster.

For future work, we aim to expand the range of disasters that our simulator is capable of simulating. We also intend to improve the tasks and actions provided by our simulator, in particular providing other predefined actions that require agents to cooperate and coordinate themselves. Moreover, we want to bring also the recovery phase [10, described therein] into the simulations, in order to investigate how we can improve disaster preparation and response. We aim to work along with experts and professionals that act on various types of disasters, taking into account the usability of our simulator.

References

1. Ahlbrecht, T., Dix, J., Fiekas, N.: Multi-agent programming contest 2017. Ann. Math. Artif. Intell. **84**, 1–16 (2018). https://doi.org/10.1007/s10472-018-9594-x
2. Armada, C.A.S.: The environmental disasters of mariana and brumadinho and the brazilian social environmental law state (2019). https://doi.org/10.2139/ssrn.3442624
3. Betke, H.J.: A volunteer coordination system approach for crisis committees. In: Proceedings of 15th ISCRAM, pp. 786–795 (2018)
4. Boissier, O., Bordini, R.H., Hübner, J.F., Ricci, A., Santi, A.: Multi-agent oriented programming with JaCaMo. Sci. Comput. Program **78**, 747–761 (2013). https://doi.org/10.1016/j.scico.2011.10.004
5. Farinelli, A., Bicego, M., Bistaffa, F., Ramchurn, S.D.: A hierarchical clustering approach to large-scale near-optimal coalition formation with quality guarantees. Eng. Appl. Artif. Intell. **59**, 170–185 (2016). https://doi.org/10.1016/j.engappai.2016.12.018
6. Hilljegerdes, M., Augustijn, P.: Evaluating the effects of consecutive hurricane hits on evacuation patterns in dominica. In: Proceedings of 16th ISCRAM, pp. 462–472 (2019)
7. Iwata, K., Jaishy, S., Ito, N., Takami, S., Takayanagi, K.: Agent-development framework based on modular structure to research disaster-relief activities. Int. J. Softw. Innov. **6**, 1–15 (2018). https://doi.org/10.4018/IJSI.2018100101
8. Klein, M., et al.: A multi-agent system for studying cross-border disaster resilience. In: Proceedings of 15th ISCRAM, pp. 135–144 (2018)
9. Mancheva, L., Adam, C., Dugdale, J.: Multi-agent geospatial simulation of human interactions and behaviour in bushfires. In: Proceedings of 16th ISCRAM (2019)
10. Murphy, R.R.: Disaster Robotics. The MIT Press, Cambridge (2014)
11. Ramchandani, P., Paich, M., Rao, A.: Incorporating learning into decision making in agent based models. In: Oliveira, E., Gama, J., Vale, Z., Lopes Cardoso, H. (eds.) EPIA 2017. LNCS (LNAI), vol. 10423, pp. 789–800. Springer, Cham (2017). https://doi.org/10.1007/978-3-319-65340-2_64
12. Ramsell, E., Granberg, T.A., Pilemalm, S.: Identifying functions for smartphone based applications in volunteer emergency response. In: Proceedings of 16th ISCRAM (2019)
13. UNESCAP: Asia-pacific disaster report 2019 (August 2019). https://www.unescap.org/publications/asia-pacific-disaster-report-2019
14. UNISDR: Global assessment report on disaster risk reduction 2019. technical report, United Nations (2019)
15. Visser, A., Ito, N., Kleiner, A.: Robocup rescue simulation innovation strategy. In: RoboCup 2014: Robot World Cup XVIII, pp. 661–672 (2015). https://doi.org/10.1007/978-3-319-18615-3_54

EUMAS 2020 Session 2: Mechanisms, Incentives, Norms, Privacy

Rewarding Miners: Bankruptcy Situations and Pooling Strategies

Marianna Belotti[1,2]([✉]), Stefano Moretti[3]([✉]), and Paolo Zappalà[4,5]([✉])

[1] CEDRIC, CNAM, 75003 Paris, France
[2] Caisse des Dépôts, 75013 Paris, France
marianna.belotti@caissedesdepots.fr
[3] LAMSADE, CNRS, Université Paris-Dauphine, Université PSL,
75016 Paris, France
stefano.moretti@dauphine.fr
[4] LIP6, CNRS, Sorbonne Université, 75005 Paris, France
paolo.zappala@lip6.fr
[5] Politecnico di Milano, 20133 Milan, Italy

Abstract. In Proof-of-Work (PoW) based blockchains (e.g., Bitcoin), mining is the procedure through which miners can gain money on regular basis by finding solutions to mathematical crypto puzzles (*i.e.,* full solutions) which validate blockchain transactions. In order to reduce the uncertainty of the remuneration over time, miners cooperate and form pools. Each pool receives rewards which have to be split among pool's participants. The objective of this paper is to find an allocation method, for a mining pool, aimed at redistributing the rewards among cooperating miners and, at the same time, preventing some malicious behaviours of the miners.

Recently, Schrijvers et al. (2017) have proposed a rewarding mechanism that is *incentive compatible*, ensuring that miners have an advantage to immediately report full solutions to the pool. However, such a mechanism encourages a harmful inter-pool behaviour (*i.e.,* pool hopping) when the reward results insufficient to remunerate pool miners, determining a loss in terms of pool's computational power.

By reinterpreting the allocation rules as outcomes of *bankruptcy situations*, we define a new rewarding system based on the well-studied *Constrained Equal Losses* (CEL) rule that maintains the incentive compatible property while making pool hopping less advantageous.

Keywords: Blockchain · Mining · Mining pool · Reward · Bankruptcy situation

1 Introduction

In the blockchain systems transactions are collected in blocks, validated and published on the distributed ledger. Nakamoto [5] proposed a Proof-of-Work system based on Back's Hashcash algorithm [1] that validates blocks and chains them

© Springer Nature Switzerland AG 2020
N. Bassiliades et al. (Eds.): EUMAS 2020/AT 2020, LNAI 12520, pp. 85–99, 2020.
https://doi.org/10.1007/978-3-030-66412-1_6

one to another. The Proof-of-Work system requires finding an input of a predefined one-way function (*e.g.*, hash function) generating an output that meets the difficulty target. More precisely, the goal for the block validators (*miners*) is to find a numerical value (*nonce*) that added to an input data string and "hashed" gives an output which is lower than the predefined threshold. A miner who finds a *full solution* (*i.e.*, a nonce meeting the difficulty target) broadcasts it across the network.

Miners compete to be the first to find a full solution in order to publish the block and gain a reward consisting in new minted crypto-currencies. Mining is a competitive crypto puzzle (a *mining race*) that participants try to solve as fast as possible. The difficulty D of the crypto puzzle limits the rate at which new transaction blocks are generated by the blockchain (*e.g.*, it takes approximately 10 min to find a full solution in the Bitcoin network). This difficulty value is adjusted periodically in order to meet the established validation rate. At the time of writing, in order to validate a block in the Bitcoin blockchain, miners needs to generate (on average) a number $D = 15,47T$ of hashes.

Mining is a procedure through which miners can gain a substantial amount of money. Nowadays, due to the high difficulty values, solo miners (*i.e.*, miners who work alone with a personal device) find a full solution with a time variance range of billions of years. Small miners survive in this new industry by joining mining pools. A mining pool is a cooperative approach in which multiple miners share their efforts (*i.e.*, their computational power) in order to validate blocks and gain rewards. Once a full solution is found, pool's reward is split among the miners. In this way small miners, instead of waiting for years to be rewarded, gain a fraction of the reward on a regular basis.

Miners' reward is based on their contribution in finding a full solution. In order to give proof of their work, miners submit to the pool partial solutions, *i.e.*, nonces that do not meet the original threshold, but a higher one. The solutions of this easier crypto puzzle are considered "near to valid" solutions and called *shares*. For those blockchains that adopt a SHA-256 function, every *hash value* (*i.e.*, output of the hash function) is a full solution with probability $\frac{1}{2^{32}D}$, and each hash has a probability of $\frac{1}{2^{32}}$ to be a share. Hence, a share is a full solution with probability $p := \frac{1}{D}$.

Miners are rewarded according to the number of shares that they provide. Whenever a share is also a full-solution a block is validated and the pool gains a reward that is split among pool participants according to the number of shares that they have reported.

Mining pools are managed by a pool manager that establishes the way in which miners should be rewarded. Each pool adopts its own rewarding system. There exist several rewarding approaches that can be more or less attractive to miners (see for instance [6]).

1.1 Mining Pool Attacks

An attack to a mining pool refers to any miner's behavior which differs from the default practice (the honest one) and that jeopardizes the collective welfare of the pool. Rosenfeld provided in [6] an overview of the possible malicious behaviours regarding pools whose profitability depends on their own rewarding mechanism. Miners may attack their pool at the time of reporting their Proof-of-Work. More precisely they can (*i*) delay in reporting a share (*i.e., block withholding*) and/or (*ii*) report a share elsewhere (*i.e., pool-hopping*).

The former is a practice consisting in delaying in reporting shares and full solutions to a mining pool. This practice implies delaying a block validation and the consequent possession of the reward, that in some cases may be profitable for attackers. Pool-hopping consists in an attack where miners "hop" from a pool to another one according to pools' attractiveness.

1.2   Related Works on Rewarding Mechanisms

The problem for a pool manager is to establish how to redistribute the rewards among pool participants in order to prevent malicious behaviours (as the ones listed above). In other words, the pool manager must choose an "appropriate" rewarding mechanism preventing (possibly, all) different types of attacks. Concerning the block withholding practice, *Schrivers et al.* [7] make use of non-cooperative game theory to propose a rewarding mechanism (denoted as *incentive compatible*) that prevents this attack. This specific rewarding system is robust against malicious actions operated inside a pool, however it does not behave as well in an inter-pool environment since it cannot prevent pool-hopping. In this case, Rosenfeld [6] shows that malicious miners can gain at the expenses of the honest ones, who receive a lower reward than the expected one. In [4] the authors use cooperative games to prove that pool-hopping is not preventable, thus mining pools are not stable coalitions.

Our contribution. Starting from the model in [7], the goal of this work is to propose an alternative incentive compatible rewarding mechanism discouraging the pool-hopping practice. By reinterpreting the reward function in [7] as an outcome of a bankruptcy situation, we construct, analyze and test a new rewarding mechanism adoptable by pools to remunerate contributing miners.

The paper is structured as follows. Section 2 presents the basic model for mining pool and some definitions about bankruptcy situations. In Sect. 3, we introduce a reward function from the literature, we compare it with a new one (based on a modified version of the CEL rule for bankruptcy situation) and we show that the two are equivalent with respect to incentives in reporting shares or full solutions. Then, in Sect. 4, we compare these two methods from a multi-pool perspective by showing (also with the aid of simulations) that the CEL-based reward function performs better than the one from the literature in discouraging miners to hop from a pool to another. Section 5 concludes the paper.

2   Preliminaries

2.1   The Model

Let $N = \{1, \ldots, n\}$ be a finite set of miners. Time is split into *rounds*, *i.e.*, the period it takes any of the miner in the pool to find a full solution. During a round miners participate in the mining race and report their shares (and the full solution) to the pool manager. Once the full solution is submitted, the pool manager broadcasts the information to the network and receives the block reward B. Then, the pool manager redistributes the block reward B among the miners according to a pre-defined reward function. The round is then concluded and a new one starts. For the sake of simplicity we set $B = 1$.

The situation is represented by the vector $\mathbf{s} = (s_1, s_2, \ldots, s_n) \in \mathbb{N}^N$, defined as *history transcript*, that contains the number of shares s_i reported by each miner $i \in N$ in a round. Letting $S = \sum_{i \in N} s_i$ be the total number of reported shares, the reward function $R : \mathbb{N}^N \to [0, 1]^n$, according to [7], is a function assigning to each history transcript $\mathbf{s}$ an allocation of the reward $(R_1(\mathbf{s}), \ldots, R_n(\mathbf{s}))$, where R_i denotes the fraction of reward gained by the single miner $i \in N$ and $\sum_{i \in N} R_i = B = 1$.

Following the approach in [7], under the assumption of rationality, miners want to maximize their individual revenues over time. Let K be the numbers of rounds that have been completed at time t and let $\mathbf{s}_j$ be the transcript history for any round $j \in K$. Given a reward function R, a miner $i \in N$ will adopt a strategy (*i.e.*, the number of reported shares at each round j) aimed at maximizing her total reward given by

$$\lim_{t \to +\infty} \sum_{j \in K} R_i(\mathbf{s}_j),$$

where a strategy affects both the number of completed rounds and the number of reported shares. In [7], a reward function R is said to be *incentive compatible* if each miner's best response strategy is to immediately report to the pool a share and a full solution. Assuming that (i) one single pool represents the total mining power (normalized to 1) of the network and that (ii) each miner $i \in N$ has a fraction α_i of the hashing power, then the probability for a miner i to find a full solution is α_i. Under this assumption, Schrijvers et al. [7] show that a miner $i \in N$ has an incentive to immediately report her shares if and only if the reward function R is monotonically increasing (*i.e.*, $R_i(\mathbf{s} + \mathbf{e}^i) > R_i(\mathbf{s})$ for all history transcripts $\mathbf{s}$, where $\mathbf{e}^i = (e_1^i, \ldots, e_n^i) \in \{0, 1\}^N$ is a vector such that $e_j^i = 0$ for each $j \in N \setminus \{i\}$ and $e_i^i = 1$.). Moreover, they show that a miner $i \in N$, finding a full solution at time t, has an incentive to immediately report it if and only if the following condition holds:

$$\sum_{j=1}^{n} \alpha_j \cdot \left(R_i(\mathbf{s}^t + \mathbf{e}^j) - R_i(\mathbf{s}^t) \right) \leq \frac{\mathbb{E}_{\mathbf{s}}[R_i(\mathbf{s})]}{D} \tag{1}$$

for all vectors of mining powers $(\alpha_i)_{i=1}^n$ and all history transcripts $\mathbf{s}^t$, where $\mathbb{E}_{\mathbf{s}}[R_i(\mathbf{s})]$ is the expected reward for miner i over all possible history transcripts.

Condition (1) results from the comparison of the withholding strategy – *i.e.*, $\sum_{s:S=1} \mathbb{P}(\text{find } s) \cdot \left(R_i(s^t + s)\right)$ – with the honest one – *i.e.*, $R_i(s^t) + \frac{\mathbb{E}_s[R_i(s)]}{\mathbb{E}_s[S]}$ – knowing the fact that the total number of submitted shares in a round, $S = \sum_{i \in N} s_i$, follows a geometrical distribution of parameter $p = \frac{1}{D}$ (*i.e.*, the probability for a share to be a full solution), where D is the difficulty of the crypto puzzle. Therefore, the value of the parameter D corresponds to the average number of submitted shares in a round.

2.2   Bankruptcy Situations

We now provide some game-theoretical basic definitions. A *bankruptcy situation* arises whenever there are some agents claiming a certain amount of a divisible estate, and the sum of the claims is larger than the estate. Formally, a *bankruptcy situation* on the set N consists of a pair $(\mathbf{c}, E) \in \mathbb{R}^N \times \mathbb{R}$ with $c_i \geq 0 \; \forall i \in N$ and $0 < E < \sum_{i \in N} c_i = C$. The vector $\mathbf{c}$ represents agents' demands (each agent $i \in N$ claims a quantity c_i) and E is the estate that has to be divided among them (and it is not sufficient to satisfy the total demand C).

We denote by $\mathbb{B}^N$ the class of all bankruptcy situations $(\mathbf{c}, E) \in \mathbb{R}^N \times \mathbb{R}$ with $0 < E < \sum_{i \in N} c_i$ A *solution* (also called *allocation rule* or *allocation method*) for bankruptcy situations on N is a map $f : \mathbb{B}^N \to \mathbb{R}^N$ assigning to each bankruptcy situation in $\mathbb{B}^N$ an *allocation vector* in $\mathbb{R}^N$, which specifies the amount $f_i(\mathbf{c}, E) \in \mathbb{R}$ of the estate E that each agent $i \in N$ receives in situation $(\mathbf{c}, E)$.

A well-known allocation rule in the literature is the *Constrained Equal Losses* (CEL) rule, which is defined in the following definition (see, for instance, [3,8] for more details on bankruptcy situations and the CEL rule).

Definition 1 (Constrained equal losses rule (CEL)). *For each bankruptcy situation* $(\mathbf{c}, E) \in \mathbb{B}^N$, *the constrained equal losses rule is defined as* $CEL_i(\mathbf{c}, E) = \max(c_i - \lambda, 0)$ *where the parameter* λ *is such that* $\sum_{i \in N} \max(c_i - \lambda, 0) = E$.

3   Incentive Compatible Reward Functions

Schrijvers et al. [7] introduce a reward mechanism that fulfills the property of incentive compatibility using the identity of the full solution discoverer w. Given a vector $\mathbf{e}^w = (e_1^w, \dots, e_n^w) \in \{0,1\}^N$ such that $e_i^w = 0$ for each $i \in N \setminus \{w\}$ and $e_w^w = 1$, the incentive compatible reward function R is the following:

$$R_i(\mathbf{s}; w) = \begin{cases} \frac{s_i}{D} + e_i^w \left(1 - \frac{S}{D}\right), & \text{if } S < D \\ \frac{s_i}{S}, & \text{if } S \geq D \end{cases} \quad \forall i \in N, \qquad (2)$$

where s_i is the number of shares reported by miner i, S is the total number of reported shares in a round and D is the crypto puzzle difficulty. This function rewards miner i proportionally to the submitted shares in the case $S \geq D$. On the other hand, in the case $S < D$, each miner receives a fixed reward-per-share equal to $\frac{1}{D}$ and the discoverer w of the full solution receives, in addition, all the remaining amount $1 - \frac{S}{D}$. So, in both cases, $\sum_{i \in N} R_i(\mathbf{s}; w) = B = 1$. Roughly speaking, the reward function R is the combination of two distinct allocation methods. In a *short round*, i.e., when the total amount of reported shares is smaller than the difficulty D of the original problem, the reward function allocates a fixed amount-per-share to all agents equal to $\frac{1}{D}$, but the agent w who finds a solution is rewarded with an extra prize. Instead, in a *long round*, i.e., when the total amount of reported shares exceeds the difficulty of the problem, the reward function allocates the reward proportionally to the individual shares.

Remunerating miners in a per-share fashion, for long rounds, would lead pool going bankrupt since the reward B results insufficient to pay out all the reported shares. For long rounds, the rewarding mechanism proposed in [7] is nothing more than a solution to a bankruptcy situation. Therefore, it is possible to create new reward functions by simply substituting in long rounds (*i.e.*, in bankruptcy situations) different bankruptcy solutions.

Let us now create a new rewarding mechanism based on the CEL rule defined in Sect. 2.2 and let us compare the properties of the two allocation methods in long rounds. In order to preserve incentive compatibility we define a CEL-based reward function.

Definition 2. *Given the identity of the full solution discoverer w, for all $i \in N$ the CEL-based reward function $\widehat{R}$ is defined as follows:*

$$\widehat{R}_i(\mathbf{s}; w) = \begin{cases} \frac{s_i}{D} + e_i^w\left(1 - \frac{S}{D}\right), & \text{if } S < D \\ \frac{e_i^w}{D} + \max\left(\frac{s_i}{D} - \lambda, 0\right), \ \lambda : \sum_i \max\left(\frac{s_i}{D} - \lambda, 0\right) = 1 - \frac{1}{D}, & \text{if } S \geq D \end{cases},$$

where $\mathbf{e}^w = (e_1^w, \ldots, e_n^w) \in \{0,1\}^N$ is a vector such that $e_w^w = 1$ and $e_i^w = 0 \ \forall i \in N \setminus \{w\}$, s_i is the number of shares reported by miner i, $S = \sum_{i \in N} s_i$ is the total number of reported shares in a round and D is the crypto puzzle difficulty.

We assign to agent w, who finds the solution during a long round, an extra prize of $\frac{1}{D}$ to add to the allocation established by the classical CEL rule for the bankruptcy situation $(\mathbf{c}, E) = \left(\frac{1}{D} \cdot \mathbf{s}, 1 - \frac{e_i^w}{D}\right)$, with the estate reduced by $\frac{1}{D}$. More precisely, in long rounds $\widehat{R}_i(\mathbf{s}; w) = \frac{e_i^w}{D} + CEL_i\left(\frac{1}{D} \cdot \mathbf{s}, 1 - \frac{e_i^w}{D}\right)$. In other words, it means that 1 is added to the count of the shares s_i reported by the full solution discoverer w. If the value $\frac{s_i}{D} - \lambda$ is negative, by default, the agent w is receiving $\frac{1}{D}$. This incentive is sufficient to make the reward function incentive compatible.

Before proving this statement, let us compare the allocations provided by the classical CEL rule and $\widehat{R}$ through an example with $n = 3$, $D = 10$ and $E = 1$.

Example 1. Given the following bankruptcy situation: $\mathbf{s} = (2, 7, 8)$, miner 1 finds the full solution ($w = 1$) and $(\mathbf{c}, E) = ((0.2, 0.7, 0.8), 1)$. By Definition 1, it is easy to check that $\lambda = 0.25$, hence:

$$CEL(\mathbf{c}, E) = (0, 0.45, 0.55).$$

Now, consider the new CEL-based rule $\widehat{R}$, a prize of $\frac{1}{D} = 0.1$ is allocated to miner 1, and a new bankruptcy situation $(\mathbf{c}, E')$ arises where the estate is reduced by 0.1; $(\mathbf{c}, E') = ((0.2, 0.7, 0.8), 0.9)$. By Definition 2, now $\lambda = 0.3$ and we have that:

$$\widehat{R}((2, 7, 8); 1) = (0.1, 0, 0) + CEL((0.2, 0.7, 0.8), 0.9) =$$
$$= (0.1, 0, 0) + (0, 0.4, 0.5) = (0.1, 0.4, 0.5).$$

In order to prove that the CEL-based rule is incentive compatible we need to present some preliminary results. More precisely, to express Condition (1) for this new reward function we need to focus on the parameter λ of the definition. This parameter depends on miners' demands and it changes value from round to round. It is important to analyze how the parameter varies if an additional share is found. Let us denote by:

(i) λ_1 the value of the parameter λ when miner i finds the full solution and immediately reports it to the pool and,
(ii) λ_2 the value of the parameter after delaying in reporting the full solution by one additional share. By convention, if miner i finds the additional share the parameter is denoted as λ_2^1, while if any other miner finds it we have λ_2^2.

By analyzing the different values of the parameter λ it is possible to derive the following result:

Proposition 1. *Let us consider* $CEL_i(\mathbf{c}, E) = \max(c_i - \lambda_1, 0)$ *and* $CEL_i(\mathbf{c} + \mathbf{e}_j, E) = \max(c_i' - \lambda_2, 0)$. *For each* $(\mathbf{c}, E) \in \mathbb{B}^N, i, j \in N$ *we have that* $\lambda_1 \leq \lambda_2$.

Proof. Let us report the efficiency condition for the two allocations:

$$\max(c_j - \lambda_1, 0) + \sum_{i \in N \setminus \{j\}} \max(c_i - \lambda_1, 0)$$
$$= \max(c_j + 1 - \lambda_2, 0) + \sum_{i \in N \setminus \{j\}} \max(c_i - \lambda_2, 0).$$

If $c_j \leq \lambda_1$, efficiency condition implies that $\sum_{i \in N \setminus \{j\}} \max(c_i - \lambda_1, 0) \geq \sum_{i \in N \setminus \{j\}} \max(c_i - \lambda_2, 0)$. Hence, $\lambda_1 \leq \lambda_2$. For $c_j > \lambda_1$ let us assume, by contradiction, that $\lambda_1 > \lambda_2$. The assumption implies that $\sum_{i \in N \setminus \{j\}} \max(c_i - \lambda_1, 0) \leq \sum_{i \in N \setminus \{j\}} \max(c_i - \lambda_2, 0)$. However, $\max(c_j - \lambda_1, 0) = c_j - \lambda_1 < c_j - \lambda_2 < c_j + 1 - \lambda_2 = \max(c_j + 1 - \lambda_2, 0)$ and this leads to contradiction.

Corollary 1. *Given the situation of Proposition 1 we have that:* $\lambda_2 - \frac{1}{D} \leq \lambda_1 \leq \lambda_2$.

Now, we are ready to prove the incentive compatibility of the new reward function based on the CEL rule.

Proposition 2. *The CEL-based reward function* $\widehat{R}$ *of Definition 2 satisfies the property of incentive compatibility.*

Proof. Let us write down Condition (1) for $\widehat{R}$:

$$\alpha_i \left(\frac{1}{D} + \max\left(\frac{s_i + 1}{D} - \lambda_2^1, 0 \right) - \frac{1}{D} - \max\left(\frac{s_i}{D} - \lambda_1, 0 \right) \right)$$

$$+ (1 - \alpha_i) \left(\max\left(\frac{s_i}{D} - \lambda_2^2, 0 \right) - \frac{1}{D} - \max\left(\frac{s_i}{D} - \lambda_1, 0 \right) \right) \leq \frac{\mathbb{E}_s[\widehat{R}_i(\mathbf{s}; w)]}{D}.$$

Since the average reward $\mathbb{E}_s[\widehat{R}_i(\mathbf{s}; w)]$ is positive, the right hand side is positive. Therefore, the condition is fulfilled if the left hand side is not positive.

Due to Proposition 1 and Corollary 1 we have that: $\frac{s_i}{D} - \lambda_2^2 \leq \frac{s_i}{D} - \lambda_1 \leq \frac{s_i+1}{D} - \lambda_2^1$.

If all the terms in the form $\max(\cdot, 0)$ are positive, then the condition is fulfilled:

$$\alpha_i \left(\frac{1}{D} - \lambda_2^1 + \lambda_1 \right) + (1 - \alpha_i) \left(-\lambda_2^2 - \frac{1}{D} + \lambda_1 \right) \leq$$

$$\leq \max(\alpha_i, 1 - \alpha_i)(-\lambda_2^1 - \lambda_2^2 + 2\lambda_1) \leq 0.$$

If $\frac{s_i}{D} - \lambda_2^2 \leq 0 \leq \frac{s_i}{D} - \lambda_1$ we get:

$$\alpha_i \left(\frac{1}{D} - \lambda_2^1 + \lambda_1 \right) + (1 - \alpha_i) \left(-\frac{s_i}{D} - \frac{1}{D} + \lambda_1 \right) \leq$$

$$\leq \max(\alpha_i, 1 - \alpha_i)(-\lambda_2^1 - \frac{s_i}{D} + 2\lambda_1) \leq 0.$$

If $\frac{s_i}{D} - \lambda_1 \leq 0 \leq \frac{s_i+1}{D} - \lambda_2^1$ we get:

$$\alpha_i \left(\frac{s_i + 1}{D} - \lambda_2^1 \right) + (1 - \alpha_i) \left(-\frac{1}{D} \right) \leq \max(\alpha_i, 1 - \alpha_i) \left(\frac{s_i}{D} - \lambda_2^1 \right) \leq$$

$$\leq \max(\alpha_i, 1 - \alpha_i) \left(\frac{s_i}{D} - \lambda_1 \right) \leq 0.$$

In the end, if all the terms in the form $\max(\cdot, 0)$ are equal to 0, then the condition is fulfilled, since the left hand side is negative.

4 A Multi-pool Analysis

Pool-hopping consists of a practice in which miners leave a pool to join another one that is considered more attractive in terms of remuneration. More precisely, during a round a miner performing pool hopping (*i.e.*, a *hopper*) stops submitting shares to the pool she was working with at the beginning of the round and starts submitting shares to a different one. A hopper leaves, during a mining race, a pool entering (or already in) a long round for a pool that is currently in a short round. The hopping miner receives an increasing reward from the brand new pool (in short round) and a decreasing reward from the pool left (facing a bankruptcy situation where the resource B is insufficient to remunerate the working miners).

In a multi-pool framework, the total mining power of the network is represented by different mining pools each with its own computational power. Differently from Sect. 2.1, each miner $i \in N$ is characterized by α_i that now represents a fraction of the pool hashing rate. Indeed, in the single-pool framework, we denote with α_i the fraction of the total hashing power.

Hopping affects the actual rewards of a pool. If a miner performs pool hopping the pool loses computational power and so on average the full solution is found later, i.e., the rounds become longer.

In our multi-pool analysis, we assume that pool hopping is performed at the very beginning of a long round and that miners hop between two pools adopting the same rewarding mechanism. Every mean denoted as $\mathbb{E}[\cdot]$ is considered conditioned to the fact that the miner is in a long round: $\mathbb{E}_s[\cdot|S > D]$. From now on, we mark with an asterisk (*) every variable defining the reward of miners once pool hopping is performed.

4.1 Hopping Analysis on Schrijver's Rewarding Function

When miner i is remunerated with reward function R her incentive to perform pool hopping can be measured as the difference between (i) the average reward when hopping $\mathbb{E}[R_i^*]$ and (ii) the average reward $\mathbb{E}[R_i]$ when working for the pool:

$$\delta_{hop} := \mathbb{E}[R_i^*] - \mathbb{E}[R_i].$$

Proposition 3. *The reward function R proposed by Schrijvers et al. always gives miners a positive incentive $\delta_{hop} > 0$ to perform pool hopping.*

Proof. As shown in [7], the average reward of an honest miner $i \in N$, i.e., not hopping, is:

$$\mathbb{E}[R_i] = \alpha_i.$$

A hopper (hopping at time t) receives an increasing reward from the new pool in a short round and a decreasing one from the pool left. The sum of the two represents the total reward. On average at the end of a short round ($S = D$) a miner has found $\alpha_i \cdot D$ shares. The round finishes after $D + t$ shares are found, with $t \in [0, +\infty)$, hence the reward for the miner who performs pool hopping is the following:

$$\mathbb{E}[R_i^*] = \sum_{t=0}^{\infty} \left(\frac{\alpha_i t}{D} + \frac{\alpha_i D}{D+t} \right) p'(1 - p')^t > \frac{\alpha_i}{1 - \alpha_i} > \alpha_i,$$

where $p' = \frac{1-\alpha_i}{D}$ is the probability that a share found by an honest miner is a full solution, t is the time taken by an honest miner (working for the old pool) to find a new share and R_i^* is the reward obtained by a miner who hops from a pool rewarding with R to another pool using the same reward function. Hence, the incentive to perform pool hopping is always positive:

$$\delta_{\text{hop}} = \mathbb{E}[R_i^*] - \mathbb{E}[R_i] > \alpha_i - \alpha_i = 0.$$

A second result deriving from Proposition 3 is the fact that, on average, the hopping miners gain more than their hashing ratio α_i. This has been empirically verified on the Bitcoin network in [2]. The average reward for a hopper, between pools adopting R, can be analytically computed according to the following result.

Proposition 4. *The average reward of miner $i \in N$ hopping between two different pools remunerating miners according to the reward function R is the following:*

$$\mathbb{E}[R_i^*] = \frac{\alpha_i}{1 - \alpha_i} + \alpha_i^*,$$

where $\alpha_i^* = \alpha_i(1 - \alpha_i)e^{1-\alpha_i}(-Ei(\alpha_i - 1))$ with $Ei(x) = \int_{-\infty}^{x} \frac{e^t}{t}$ denoting the exponential integral.

Proof. On average, a miner with computational power α_i who performs pool hopping receives:

$$\mathbb{E}[R_i^*] = \sum_{t=0}^{\infty} \frac{\alpha_i t}{D} p'(1 - p')^t + \sum_{t=0}^{\infty} \frac{\alpha_i D}{D + t} p'(1 - p')^t.$$

The first term represents the reward received by the new pool in short round that can be easily computed as follows:

$$\frac{\alpha_i}{D} \sum_{t=0}^{\infty} t \cdot p'(1 - p')^t = \frac{\alpha_i}{D} \cdot \frac{D}{1 - \alpha_i} = \frac{\alpha_i}{1 - \alpha_i}.$$

The second term (denoted as α_i^*) corresponds to the reward assigned by the pool left by the hopping miner. In order to compute this term we need to consider an approximation for $D \to \infty$:

$$\alpha_i^* = \sum_{t=0}^{\infty} \frac{\alpha_i D}{D + t} \frac{1 - \alpha_i}{D} \left(1 - \frac{1 - \alpha_i}{D}\right)^t \approx \alpha_i(1 - \alpha_i)e^{1-\alpha_i} \sum_{t=D}^{\infty} \frac{1}{t} e^{-\frac{1-\alpha_i}{D}t}.$$

The computations can be solved by defining:

$$f(x) := \lim_{D \to \infty} f_D(x) = \lim_{D \to \infty} \sum_{t=D}^{\infty} \frac{1}{t} e^{-\frac{tx}{D}}.$$

Using Lebesgue's theorem and given the constraint $\lim_{x \to \infty} f(x) = 0$ we get:

$$f(x) = -Ei(-x).$$

Hence:

$$\alpha_i^* \approx \alpha_i(1 - \alpha_i)e^{1-\alpha_i} f(1 - \alpha_i) = \alpha_i(1 - \alpha_i)e^{1-\alpha_i}(-Ei(\alpha_i - 1)).$$

Thanks to the result provided by Proposition 4 we note that the shares submitted in the pool left by the hopping miner (α_i^*) represent an important part of her average reward. More precisely, for values of $\alpha_i < 0.39$, α_i^* is more than the 50% of the average reward a miner would have got by not leaving the pool (*i.e.*, her computational power α_i). For instance, if a miner has $\alpha_i = 0.2$ as computational power, she will get $\alpha_i^* \approx 0.11$.

4.2   Hopping Analysis on CEL-Based Rewarding Function

Following similar arguments, we can analyze the incentive to perform pool hopping when adopting the CEL-based rule $\widehat{R}$. We can, then, compare the results obtained for the reward function R with the ones provided by $\widehat{R}$. We denote as β_i the average reward of function $\widehat{R}$ (corresponding to α_i for function R) that can be computed as follows since the probability for a miner i to find a full solution and to receive the extra prize $\frac{1}{D}$ is α_i:

$$\beta_i = \mathbb{E}[\widehat{R}_i] = \frac{\alpha_i}{D} + \mathbb{E}\left[\max\left(\frac{s_i}{D} - \lambda, 0\right)\right] \quad \lambda : \sum_i \max\left(\frac{s_i}{D} - \lambda, 0\right) = 1 - \frac{1}{D}.$$

Like in Sect. 4.1, let us define the incentive to perform pool hopping $\widehat{\delta}_{hop} := \mathbb{E}[\widehat{R}_i^*] - \mathbb{E}[\widehat{R}_i]$ and let us compute the average reward received by a hopper:

$$\mathbb{E}[\widehat{R}_i^*] = \sum_{t=0}^{\infty} \left(\frac{\alpha_i t}{D} + \max\left(\frac{\alpha_i D}{D} - \lambda, 0\right)\right) p'(1 - p')^t = \frac{\alpha_i}{1 - \alpha_i} + \mathbb{E}\left[\max(\alpha_i - \lambda, 0)\right],$$

where $p' = \frac{1 - \alpha_i}{D}$, t is the time taken by an honest miner to find a new share and $\widehat{R}_i^*$ is the reward obtained by a hopping miner. Analogously to α_i^* for function R, we denote by β_i^* the reward given by the pool the hopper left:

$$\beta_i^* = \mathbb{E}\left[\max(\alpha_i - \lambda, 0)\right].$$

Hence we have that:

$$\widehat{\delta}_{hop} = \mathbb{E}[\widehat{R}_i^*] - \mathbb{E}[\widehat{R}_i] = \frac{\alpha_i}{1 - \alpha_i} + \beta_i^* - \beta_i.$$

4.3   Comparison of the Two Rewarding Functions in a Multi-pool Framework

We have, now, the metrics to compare the performance of the reward functions R and $\widehat{R}$ in hopping situations. Both rewarding systems present an incentive to hop in long rounds, however the miner rewarded with the CEL-based reward function are less incentivized. It is possible to compare the incentives $\delta_{hop}, \widehat{\delta}_{hop}$ given by the two functions $R, \widehat{R}$ through the variables introduced in Sect. 4.2 since:

$$\widehat{\delta}_{hop} \leq \delta_{hop} \Leftrightarrow \beta_i - \beta_i^* \geq \alpha_i - \alpha_i^*.$$

In order to show that the hopping incentive for the CEL-based reward function is lower with respect to the incentive given by R it is sufficient to prove that $\beta_i - \beta_i^* \geq \alpha_i - \alpha_i^*$.

Proposition 5. *Let N be the ordered set of miners: $\alpha_1 \leq \alpha_2 \leq \cdots \leq \alpha_n$, let us define $\alpha_{>i} := \sum_{j>i} \alpha_j$, as the global computational powers of the miners that are more powerful than α_i. Then, $\beta_i - \beta_i^* \geq \alpha_i - \alpha_i^*$ if $(1 - \alpha_i)(\alpha_{>i} - \alpha_i)e^{-\alpha_i + (\alpha_{>i} - \alpha_i)^{-1}}(-Ei(\alpha_i - 1)) \geq 1$ where $Ei(\cdot)$ is the exponential integral function.*

Proof. Given the definitions of β_i and β_i^*:

$$\beta_i = \frac{\alpha_i}{D} + \sum_{t=0}^{\infty} \max\left(\alpha_i + \frac{\alpha_i t}{D} - \lambda, 0\right) p(1-p)^t \quad \text{and}$$

$$\beta_i^* = \sum_{t=0}^{\infty} \max\left(\alpha_i - \lambda, 0\right) p'(1-p')^t,$$

let us recall that $p = \frac{1}{D}$ is the probability for a share to be a full solution and that $p' = \frac{1-\alpha_i}{D}$ represents the probability for a share reported by an honest miner to be a full solution.

For $t \to \infty$ (*i.e.*, for very long rounds) the function $\max(\cdot, 0)$ either tends to 0 or to 1 since in long rounds eventually the most powerful miner is receiving all the reward ($\max(\cdot, 0) \to 1$) and the other miners are receiving none of it ($\max(\cdot, 0) \to 0$). The limit value 0 is reached for $t = \gamma_i \cdot D$, where $\gamma_i \in \mathbb{R} \cup \{+\infty\}$ is defined as follows; $\gamma_i := \mathrm{argmin}_\gamma \{\frac{\alpha_i t}{D} - \lambda < 0, \forall t \geq \gamma D\}$. Roughly speaking, $\gamma_i \cdot D$ represents the number of shares after which miner i is not rewarded.

Hence, it is possible to rewrite β_i and β_i^* in this form:

$$\beta_i = \frac{\alpha_i}{D} + \sum_{t=0}^{\gamma_i D} \left(\alpha_i + \frac{\alpha_i t}{D} - \lambda\right) p(1-p)^t \quad \text{and} \quad \beta_i^* = \sum_{t=0}^{\gamma_i D} (\alpha_i - \lambda) p'(1-p')^t.$$

The value of γ_i might change if the miner is performing pool hopping, but for the sake of simplicity we approximate by considering the same γ_i in both cases. Assuming that $\sum_t \lambda \cdot p(1-p)^t \approx \sum_t \lambda \cdot p'(1-p')^t$ we can approximate the difference between β_i and β_i^* as follows:

$$\beta_i - \beta_i^* \approx \frac{\alpha_i}{D} + \sum_{t=0}^{\gamma_i D} \frac{\alpha_i t}{D} p(1-p)^t.$$

Due to the value of the difficulty D, we can consider the limit for $D \to \infty$, then:

$$\beta_i - \beta_i^* \approx \frac{\alpha_i}{D} + \sum_{k=0}^{\gamma_i D} \frac{\alpha_i k}{D} \frac{1}{D} e^{-k/D} = \frac{\alpha_i}{D} + \alpha_i \frac{1}{D^2} \sum_{k=0}^{\gamma_i D} k e^{-k/D} \to \alpha_i(1 - e^{-\gamma_i}(1+\gamma_i)).$$

Let us now compute explicitly γ_i. If $i = N$ (*i.e.*, $\alpha_i = \mathrm{argmax}_j\{\alpha_j\}$) then $\gamma_i = \infty$. Otherwise at time $t = \gamma_i \cdot D$ the miners who receive a positive reward are all the $j \in N : \alpha_j > \alpha_i$, *i.e.*, all the ones having larger computational power than i. According to the CEL rule definition we get the following balance equation:

$$\sum_{j>i} \left(\alpha_j \left(1 + \frac{t}{D}\right) - \lambda\right) = 1 - \frac{1}{D} \approx 1.$$

Since the time $t = \gamma_i \cdot D$ is the moment when the value $\max(\alpha_i(1 + \frac{t}{D}) - \lambda, 0)$ turns from positive to null, we can say that $\alpha_i(1 + \frac{t}{D}) - \lambda \approx 0$. Therefore we have that:

$$\sum_{j>i}\left(\alpha_j\left(1+\frac{t}{D}\right)-\alpha_i\left(1+\frac{t}{D}\right)\right)=1.$$

Replacing the value of t with $\gamma_i \cdot D$ we get $(\alpha_{>i}-(N-i)\alpha_i)(1+\gamma_i)=1$, then:

$$\gamma_i=((\alpha_{>i}-(N-i)\alpha_i)^{-1}-1).$$

Now we can find a lower bound for γ_i (since $N-i\geq 1$) and so for $\beta_i-\beta_i^*$:

$$\gamma_i\geq\bar\gamma_i:=((\alpha_{>i}-\alpha_i)^{-1}-1)\implies\beta_i-\beta_i^*\geq\alpha_i(1-e^{-\bar\gamma_i}(1+\bar\gamma_i)).$$

The sufficient condition for $\beta_i-\beta_i^*\geq\alpha_i-\alpha_i^*$ is:

$$\alpha_i(1-e^{-\bar\gamma_i}(1+\bar\gamma_i))\geq\alpha_i-\alpha_i^*.$$

We get the statement of the proposition by replacing $\bar\gamma_i$ and α_i^* with their explicit formulas.

Thanks to Proposition 5, given miner i's hashing ratio (*i.e.*, α_i) and the power of the miners who are stronger than i (*i.e.*, $\alpha_{>i}$), we can check whether $\widehat R$ is giving a lower hopping incentive than the one given by R (*i.e.*, check whether $\widehat\delta_{\text{hop}}\leq\delta_{\text{hop}}$) by simply applying the sufficient condition introduced above that we denote as $f(\alpha_i,\alpha_{>i})$:

$$f(\alpha_i,\alpha_{>i}):=(1-\alpha_i)(\alpha_{>i}-\alpha_i)e^{-\alpha_i+(\alpha_{>i}-\alpha_i)^{-1}}(-Ei(\alpha_i-1))\geq 1.$$

Let us analyze the hopping performance of R and $\widehat R$ in the following example.

Example 2. Given 5 miners ordered according to their hash rates: $\alpha_1=0.10$, $\alpha_2=0.15$, $\alpha_3=0.20$, $\alpha_4=0.25$, $\alpha_5=0.30$, using the condition provided by Proposition 5 we get:

- $f(\alpha_1,\alpha_{>1})=f(0.10,0.90)=0.59<1$, miner 1 has a greater incentive to perform pool hopping if rewarded with $\widehat R$ rather than with R;
- $f(\alpha_2,\alpha_{>2})=f(0.15,0.75)=0.66<1$, miner 2 has a greater incentive to perform pool hopping if rewarded with $\widehat R$ rather than with R;
- $f(\alpha_3,\alpha_{>3})=f(0.20,0.55)=1.24>1$, miner 3 has a greater incentive to hop if rewarded with R rather than with $\widehat R$;
- $f(\alpha_4,\alpha_{>4})=f(0.25,0.30)>10^6>1$, miner 4 has a greater incentive to hop if rewarded with R rather than with $\widehat R$;
- $f(\alpha_5,\alpha_{>5})=f(0.30,0)\to\infty>1$, miner 5 has a really low incentive to perform pool hopping if rewarded with $\widehat R$.

We can see that miners representing the 75% of the pool's computational power have a lower incentive to perform pool hopping when the CEL-based rewarding mechanism is adopted.

By analyzing function $f(\cdot, \alpha_{>i}) - i.e.$, fixing $\alpha_{>i}$ – we can identify the cases in which $\hat{\delta}_{\text{hop}} \leq \delta_{\text{hop}}$ (where $\widehat{R}$ performs better than R). For instance, $f(\cdot, \alpha_{>i}) > 1$ for every $\alpha_{>i} < 0.4$, means that with $\widehat{R}$ not only the miners representing the most powerful 40% of the pool have a lower incentive to perform pool hopping, but also the miner i who just follows in the ranking.

To compare the two reward functions, it is necessary to estimate the percentage of miners who have a lower incentive to perform pool hopping. In Example 2 this percentage is $p(\alpha = \{0.1, 0.15, 0.2, 0.25, 0.3\}) = 75\%$. Formally we would like to estimate:

$$p(\alpha) := \sum_i \alpha_i \cdot \mathbf{1}_{\{\beta_i - \beta_i^* \geq \alpha_i - \alpha_i^*\}}.$$

We know that $p(\alpha) > 40\%$ thanks to the analysis of function f. In order to get a better idea of the range of the value of function p we perform a simulation.

Simulation. Due to the unpredictability of α, we assume that it comes from a random distribution. More precisely, given $X_i \sim U[0, 1]$, α_i is defined as follows: $\alpha_i := \frac{X_i}{\sum_j X_j}$.

We run a simulation with 100 different samples of α for n miners, with $n \in \{3, 10, 20, 30, 50\}$, and estimate the CDF of $p_n(\alpha)$ for every n. We compute explicitly β_i and β_i^*, without using the approximation above introduced.

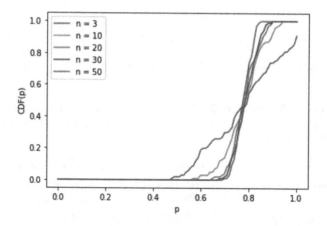

Fig. 1. CDF of every $p_n(\alpha)$, with $n \in \{3, 10, 20, 30, 50\}$.

The functions $p_n(\alpha)$ have *almost always* values over 0.5 (*i.e.*, in just two cases out of 100 with $n = 3$, $p_3(\alpha)$ achieves value between 0.47 and 0.5) (Fig. 1).

This means that in most of the cases the majority of the miners have a lower incentive to perform pool-hopping with $\widehat{R}$ rather than R.

5   Conclusion

The paper analyzes the robustness of two different rewarding mechanisms in both intra-pool and inter-pool environments. Schrijvers et al. introduce in [7] a reward function R that is incentive compatible. However, this rule gives miners an incentive to leave pools in long rounds to join pools in short rounds that adopt the same rewarding system (*i.e.,* pool-hopping).

By reinterpreting R, in long rounds, as an allocation rule for a bankruptcy situation, we create a new rewarding function $\widehat{R}$ inspired to the well-known Constrained Equal Loss (CEL) rule.

We show that this CEL-based rule is incentive compatible as R but it provides to most of the miners a lower incentive to perform pool hopping in long rounds. In conclusion, if a pool wants to tackle this issue, the proposed rewarding function $\widehat{R}$ is the one to be recommended.

References

1. Back, A.: Hashcash - a denial of service counter-measure (2002)
2. Belotti, M., Kirati, S., Secci, S.: Bitcoin pool-hopping detection. In: 2018 IEEE 4th International Forum on Research and Technology for Society and Industry (RTSI), pp. 1–6. IEEE (2018)
3. Herrero, C., Villar, A.: The three musketeers: four classical solutions to bankruptcy problems. Math. Soc. Sci. **42**(3), 307–328 (2001)
4. Lewenberg, Y., et al.: Bitcoin mining pools: a cooperative game theoretic analysis. In: Proceedings of the 2015 International Conference on Autonomous Agents and Multiagent Systems, pp. 919–927. Citeseer (2015)
5. Nakamoto, S.: Bitcoin: A peer-to-peer electronic cash system (2008)
6. Rosenfeld, M.: Analysis of bitcoin pooled mining reward systems. arXiv preprint arXiv:1112.4980 (2011)
7. Schrijvers, O., Bonneau, J., Boneh, D., Roughgarden, T.: Incentive compatibility of bitcoin mining pool reward functions. In: Grossklags, J., Preneel, B. (eds.) FC 2016. LNCS, vol. 9603, pp. 477–498. Springer, Heidelberg (2017). https://doi.org/10.1007/978-3-662-54970-4_28
8. Thomson, W.: Axiomatic and game-theoretic analysis of bankruptcy and taxation problems: an update. Math. Soc. Sci. **74**, 41–59 (2015)

A Game-Theoretical Analysis of Charging Strategies for Competing Double Auction Marketplaces

Bing Shi[1,2,3(✉)] and Xiao Li[1]

[1] Wuhan University of Technology, Wuhan 430070, China
{bingshi,xiaoli}@whut.edu.cn
[2] Shenzhen Research Institute of Wuhan University of Technology,
Shenzhen 518000, China
[3] State Key Laboratory for Novel Software Technology at Nanjing University,
Nanjing 210023, China

Abstract. The double auction marketplaces usually charge fees to traders to make profits, but little work has been done on analyzing how marketplaces charge appropriate fees to make profits in multiple marketplaces competing environment. In this paper, we investigate this problem by using game theory. Specifically, we consider four typical types of fees, and use Fictitious Play algorithm to analyze the Nash equilibrium market selection and bidding strategy of traders in competing environment when different types of fees are charged. Building on this, we draw insights about how the marketplaces charge strategies in equilibrium when sellers and buyers have made the choice of the marketplace and bid in Nash equilibrium. Furthermore, we investigate which type of fees is more competitive in terms of maximizing profits while keeping traders staying in the marketplaces. Our experimental results provide useful insights on setting charging strategies for competing double auction marketplaces.

Keywords: Double auction · Market fee · Game theory · Bidding strategy · Nash equilibrium · Fictitious play

1 Introduction

Double auction [14] is a particular two-sided market mechanism with multiple buyers (one side) and multiple sellers (the other side). In such a mechanism, traders can submit offers at any time in a specified trading round and they will be matched by the marketplace at a specified time. The advantages of this mechanism are that traders can enter the marketplace at any time and they can trade multiple homogeneous or heterogeneous items simultaneously [7]. Due to its high allocative efficiency between buyers and sellers of goods [23], this market mechanism has been widely adopted by realistic exchanges, such as commodities exchanges. The high efficiency has also led many online marketplaces to use this format, including stock exchanges, business-to-business commerce, bandwidth

© Springer Nature Switzerland AG 2020
N. Bassiliades et al. (Eds.): EUMAS 2020/AT 2020, LNAI 12520, pp. 100–115, 2020.
https://doi.org/10.1007/978-3-030-66412-1_7

allocation [12], spectrum allocation [25], and smart grid energy exchange [1]. In the real world, such double auction marketplace is often run by commercial enterprise that seeks to maximize profit by charging fees to traders such as eBay makes profit by charging sellers [20]. Nevertheless, in today's global economy, each marketplace needs to compete with other homogeneous marketplaces. For example, stock exchanges compete with each other worldwide [18]. Therefore, it's crucial to set optimal charging strategy for double auction marketplaces. In this paper, we will analyze how the double auction marketplaces charge fees to maximize profits in a competing environment.

In the real world, the marketplaces can charge different types of fees to make profits. For example, with respect to the time of charging fees, the marketplaces can charge fees before sellers and buyers make any transactions (i.e. *ex-ante* fees) or charge fees after they have made transactions (i.e. *ex-post* fees). The double auction markets' charging strategies play an important role on affecting traders' profits. Thus it will affect the traders' market choices and bidding strategies, which in turn affect the competition result of double auction markets. Hence, we need to analyze how to determine the charging strategies for competing double auction marketplaces. Furthermore, some traders may leave the marketplaces if they can't trade when market fees are charged.

Specifically, in this paper, we assume that marketplaces adopt a so-called clearing-house double auction mechanism, where matching of sellers and buyers occurs once all sellers and buyers have submitted their offers, and the transaction price is set in the middle of the matched sellers and buyers. We also assume that traders are heterogeneous with continuous privately known types (the type is traders' preferences on the goods). According to the time of charging fees and fee values, in this paper, we will analyze four typical types of fees that marketplaces usually charge, such as registration fee, transaction fee, profit fee and transaction price percentage fee [4,24]. In such a context, intuitively, we know that the behavior of traders and marketplaces are affected by each other. Therefore, game theory [8], which mathematically studies such strategies interactions between self-interested agents, is appropriate to be used to analyze this system (where an individual's success in making choices depends on the choices of others). Specially, we consider the competing environment where there exist two marketplaces competing with each other and then analyze the marketplaces' charging strategies in this environment in detail.

The structure of the rest of the paper is as follows. In Sect. 2 introduced the related work about this field. In Sect. 3, we describe the basic settings, and derive the expected utilities of traders and marketplace in this setting. In Sect. 4, we describe the algorithm used in this paper. In Sect. 5, we analyze how different types of fees can affect the sellers and buyers' market selection and bidding strategies. In Sect. 6, we analyze how the marketplace charges fees in Nash equilibrium. Finally, we conclude in Sect. 7.

2   Related Works

Since the charging strategies of the marketplaces are affected by traders' bidding strategies, first we introduce the related work about traders' bidding strategies in the double auction marketplace, then we introduce the related works about marketplaces charging strategies.

Firstly, many heuristic bidding strategies have been proposed for traders bidding in double auction, such as [9,10,13]. Besides, there are also research works related to traders' bidding strategies based on game theory. Phelps et al. [16] use evolutionary game theory to investigate the Nash equilibrium given a restricted strategy space. However, these restricted strategies do not necessarily constitute a Nash equilibrium when considering the entire space of possible strategies. Jackson et al. [11] show the existence of a non-trivial mixed-strategy equilibrium for double auctions in a variety of settings given a finite set of offers, and Reny et al. [19] show that when there are sufficiently many buyers and sellers with a finite set of discrete offers, there exists a monotonic pure equilibrium bidding strategy for traders. Chowdhury et al. [6] proposed a dynamic Monte Carlo Tree Search (MCTS) bidding strategy that preforms a more comprehensive search of the policy space using an anytime algorithm. But when the bidding space is large, this algorithm may not longer been suitable. However, these researches are not suitable for traders to bid across multiple marketplaces because they do not consider the choice of marketplaces.

Next, In the context of multiple double auctions, Cai et al. [3] experimentally analyze how standard economic measures are affected by the presence of multiple marketplaces when traders select marketplaces and submit offers in a heuristic way, and then Miller et al. [15] experimentally analyse traders' market selection strategies in the competing marketplaces trading environment. Shi et al. [22] analyse the Nash equilibrium market selection strategy in the context of multiple competing double auction marketplaces using evolutionary game theory(EGT), but they emphasise traders adpot a fixed bid factor for the bidding strategy rather than Nash equilibrium bidding strategy. All the above works do not consider interaction between the markets' charging strategies and the traders' trading strategies, and only a small number of traders are considered.

There also exist works on analyzing how the competing marketplaces charge fees to make profits. Caillaud et al. [5] analyze the competition between two marketplaces. They assume that traders are homogeneous and the market selection only depends on the number of traders of the other side, the result show that when traders can only enter one marketplace at a time, by adopting the "divide-and-conquer" strategy, in equilibrium, one marketplace will attract all traders, but it has to give up all profit. however, the number of traders of the own side also affects traders' bidding strategies, but they don't consider this factor. Shi et al. [22] investigate how the competing double auction marketplaces make profits by charging fees, the results show that when competing marketplaces charging different type of fees, the competing marketplaces are more likely to co-exist in equilibrium. But when the marketplaces charge the same type of fees, competing marketplaces can't co-exist any more.

However, the above works only consider a small number of traders, and they don't consider how competing marketplaces set fees to make profits while keep traders. Our work investigates the problem from another perspective. We investigate how competing marketplaces charge appropriate fees to make profits while keep traders in Nash equilibrium, by the way, due to the number of traders have an impact on the traders' bidding strategies, which in turn affect the markets' competitive results. Thus, we will also consider the situation of a large number of traders with continuous privately known types, and analyze traders' bidding strategies in Nash equilibrium.

3 Framework

In this section, we first introduce the basic setting for analysing our problems. Then in order to undertake the theoretical analysis, we derive the equations to calculate the expected utilities of the traders in this setting, which the FP algorithm needs to approximate the Nash equilibrium bidding strategy. Furthermore, we also derive the equations to calculate the expected profit and the expected number of traders when the marketplaces charge fees.

3.1 Basic Setting

We assume that there is a set of buyers, $\mathcal{B} = \{1, 2, ...B\}$, and a set of sellers, $\mathcal{S} = \{1, 2, ...S\}$. Each buyer and each seller can only trade a single unit of the goods in one marketplace. All goods are identical. Each buyer and seller has a type[1], which is denoted as θ^b and θ^s respectively. We assume that the types of all buyers are i.i.d drawn from the cumulative distribution function F^b, with support $[0, 1]$, and the types of all sellers are i.i.d drawn from the cumulative distribution function F^s, with support $[0, 1]$. The distributions F^b and F^s are assumed to be common knowledge and differentiable. The probability density functions are f^b and f^s respectively. In our setting, the type of each specific trader is not known to the other traders, i.e. private information.

According to the time of charging fees and the fee value, we consider four typical fees: registration fee r, which is charged to traders when they enter the marketplace (ex-ante and flat fee); transaction fee t, which is charged to buyers and sellers when they make transactions (ex-post and flat fee); profit fee q, which is charged on profits made by buyers and sellers (ex-post and percentage fee); and transaction price percentage fee o, which is charged on the transaction price of buyers and sellers (ex-post and percentage fee). Note that the ex-ante and percentage fee usually does not exist. Moreover, we further make an assumption that traders will incur a small cost ι when they enter the marketplace (such as time cost for trading online). We do this so that they slightly prefer choosing no marketplace than choosing a marketplace but making no transactions (even

---

[1] The type of a buyer is its *limit price*, the highest price it is willing to buy the item for, and the type of a seller is its *cost price*, the lowest price it is willing to sell the item for.

if $r = 0$). This small cost will help us to distinguish buyers' behaviour between bidding the lowest allowed offer and not choosing the marketplace, and sellers' behaviour between bidding the highest allowed offer and not choosing the marketplace.

Furthermore, we assume that the marketplace adopts a clearing-house mechanism, which means that the marketplace matches sellers with buyers when all sellers and buyers have submitted their offers. We also assume that the marketplace matches buyers with sellers according to the **equilibrium matching** policy, which means that the marketplace matches the buyer with v-th highest offer with the seller with v-th lowest offer if the seller's offer is not greater than the buyer's offer. By adopting the clearing-house mechanism and the equilibrium matching policy, the marketplace can match sellers and buyers in a highly efficient way. Moreover, we assume that the transaction price of a successful transaction in the marketplace is determined by a parameter $k \in [0, 1]$ (i.e. a *discriminatory k-pricing* policy), which sets the transaction price of a matched buyers and sellers at the point determined by k in the interval between their offers.

We now describe the offers that sellers and buyers take in this setting. In this paper, we call the offers of the buyers *bids* and the offers of the sellers *asks*. Specifically, we make the assumption that there is a finite number of bids and asks and that these are discrete. The ranges of possible bids and asks constitute the *bid space* and *ask space* respectively. For convenience, we further assume that buyers and sellers have the same offer space, which is given by $\Delta = \{0, \frac{1}{D}, \frac{2}{D}, ..., \frac{D-1}{D}, 1\} \cup \{\ominus\}$, i.e. the bid(ask) space comprises $D + 1$ allowable bids(asks) from 0 to 1 with step size $1/D$ (D is a natural number), and $\ominus$ means not submitting an offer in the marketplace (i.e. not choosing the market). Note that the expected utility of a seller or buyer is directly dependent on its beliefs about other sellers or buyers' offer choices. Therefore, instead of looking at their strategies, in what follows, the expected utility is expressed directly in terms of sellers and buyers' offer distributions. Specifically, we use ω_i^b to denote the probability of bid d_i^b being chosen by a buyer, and use ω_i^s to denote the probability of ask d_i^s being chosen by a seller. Furthermore, we use $\Omega^b = \left(\omega_1^b, \omega_2^b, ..., \omega_{|\Delta|}^b\right)$, $\sum_{i=1}^{|\Delta|} \omega_i^b = 1$, to represent the probability distribution of buyers' bids, and $\Omega^s = (\omega_1^s, \omega_2^s, ..., \omega_{|\Delta|}^s)$ for the sellers' ask distribution.

3.2 Trader's Expected Utility

Before analysing the strategies of the traders, we first need to derive the equations to calculate their expected utilities. Which are defined as the expected profits that traders can make in the marketplaces. In what follows, we derive the expected utility of a buyer, but the seller's is calculated analogously. A buyer's expected utility depends on its type, its own bid, and its beliefs about offer choices of other sellers and buyers. In the following, we calculate the expected utility of a buyer with type θ^b bidding d^b given other buyers' bid distribution Ω^b and sellers' ask distribution Ω^s, and the market fees.

Since the marketplace adopts the equilibrium matching policy, we need to know the position of the buyer's bid in the marketplace, which determines its matching with sellers. When knowing other buyers' bid choices, we can know the buyer's position. Specifically, we use a $|\Delta|$-tuple $\bar{x} = \langle x_1, ... x_{|\Delta|} \rangle \in \mathcal{X}$ to represent the number of buyers choosing different bids, where x_i is the number of buyers choosing bid d_i^b, $\mathcal{X}$ is the set of all such possible tuples and we have $\sum_{i=1}^{|\Delta|} x_i = B - 1$ (note that we need to exclude the buyer for which we are calculating the expected utility). The probability of exactly x_i buyers choosing bid d_i^b is $\left(\omega_i^b \right)^{x_i}$, and then the probability of the tuple $\bar{x}$, which denotes the number of buyers choosing different bids, is:

$$\rho^b(\bar{x}) = \binom{B-1}{x_1, ..., x_{|\Delta|}} \times \prod_{i=1}^{|\Delta|} \left(\omega_i^b \right)^{x_i} \tag{1}$$

Now for a particular $\bar{x}$, we determine the buyer's position as follows. Firstly, we obtain the number of other buyers whose bids are greater than the buyer's bid d^b, which is given by:

$$X^>(\bar{x}, d^b) = \sum_{d_i^b \in \Delta : d_i^b > d^b} x_i \tag{2}$$

Similarly, we use $X^=(\bar{x}, d^b)$ to represent the number of buyers whose bids are equal to the buyer's bid (excluding the buyer itself):

$$X^=(\bar{x}, d^b) = \sum_{d_i^b \in \Delta : d_i^b = d^b} x_i \tag{3}$$

Due to having discrete bids and given $X^>(\bar{x}, d^b)$ buyers bidding higher than the buyer's bid d^b and $X^=(\bar{x}, d^b)$ buyers bidding equal to d^b, the buyer's position $v_{\bar{x}}$ given $\bar{x}$ could be anywhere from $X^>(\bar{x}, d^b) + 1$ to $X^>(\bar{x}, d^b) + X^=(\bar{x}, d^b) + 1$, which constitutes the buyer's position range. We use $\mathcal{V}_{\bar{x}} = \{ X^>(\bar{x}, d^b) + 1, ..., X^>(\bar{x}, d^b) + X^=(\bar{x}, d^b) + 1 \}$ to denote the position range. Since $X^=(\bar{x}, d^b) + 1$ buyers have the same bid, as we said previously, a tie-breaking rule is needed to determine the buyer's position. Here we adopt a standard rule where each of these possible positions occurs with equal probability, i.e. $1/(X^=(\bar{x}, d^b) + 1)$.

The buyer's expected utility also depends on sellers' ask choices. Specifically, we use a $|\Delta|$-tuple $\bar{y} = \langle y_1, ... y_{|\Delta|} \rangle \in \mathcal{Y}$ to represent the number of sellers choosing different asks, where y_i is the number of sellers choosing ask d_i^s, and $\mathcal{Y}$ is the set of all such possible tuples and we have $\sum_{i=1}^{|\Delta|} y_i = S$. The probability of the tuple $\bar{y}$, which indicates the number of sellers choosing different asks, is:

$$\rho^s(\bar{y}) = \binom{S}{y_1, ..., y_{|\Delta|}} \times \prod_{i=1}^{|\Delta|} \left(\omega_i^s \right)^{y_i} \tag{4}$$

Now given the buyer's positions $v_{\bar{x}}$ and the number of sellers choosing different asks $\bar{y}$, next we calculate the buyer's expected utility. Given the tuple $\bar{y}$, we can sort the asks of the sellers descendingly. The ask which is $v_{\bar{x}}$-th highest will be matched with the buyer's bid. We denote this ask as d^s. Now the buyer's expected utility can be calculated:

$$U\left(v_{\bar{x}}, \bar{y}, \theta^b, d^b, \Omega^B, \Omega^S, r, t, q, o\right) = \begin{cases} 0 & \text{if } d^b = \ominus \\ \theta^b - TP - \mathcal{P} & \text{if } d^b \geq d^S \\ -r - \iota & \text{if } d^b < d^s \end{cases} \quad (5)$$

where $\mathcal{P} = r + t + (d^b - TP) \times q + TP \times o + \iota$ is the seller and buyer's payment in the transaction and $TP = d^s \times k + d^b \times (1 - k)$ is the transaction price.

Finally, by considering all possible numbers of sellers choosing different asks, all possible positions and all possible numbers of buyers choosing different bids, the buyer's expected utility is given by:

$$\tilde{U}\left(\theta^b, d^b, \Omega^b, \Omega^s, r, t, q, o\right) = \sum_{\bar{x} \in \mathcal{X}} \rho^b(\bar{x}) \times \sum_{v_{\bar{x}} \in \mathcal{V}_{\bar{x}}} \frac{1}{X = (\bar{x}, d^b) + 1}$$

$$\times \sum_{\bar{y} \in \mathcal{Y}} \rho^s(\bar{y}) \times U\left(v_{\bar{x}}, \bar{y}, \theta^b, d^b, \Omega^B, \Omega^S\right) \quad (6)$$

$$r, t, q, o)$$

3.3   The Marketplace's Expected Utility

After deriving equations to calculate the expected utilities of sellers and buyers, we now calculate the expected utility of the marketplace (i.e. its profit) when it charges fees. Specifically, in the following, we derive equations to calculate the marketplace's expected utility given the offer distributions of buyers and sellers, Ω^b and Ω^s. Intuitively, we can see that the expected utility depends on the number of sellers and buyers choosing each allowed offer. Similarly, we use a $|\Delta|$-tuple $\bar{x} = \langle x_1, ..., x_{|\Delta|} \rangle \in \mathcal{X}'$, $\sum_{i=1}^{|\Delta|} x_i = B$, to denote the number of buyers choosing different bids, where x_i is the exact number of buyers choosing bid d_i^b, and $\mathcal{X}'$ is the set of all such possible tuples. We use $\bar{y} = \langle y_1, ..., y_{|\Delta|} \rangle \in \mathcal{Y}$, $\sum_{i=1}^{|\Delta|} y_i = S$, to denote the number of sellers choosing different asks. Given the number of buyers and sellers choosing different offers, $\bar{x}$ and $\bar{y}$, we will know what exact bids and asks are placed in the marketplace. Then the marketplace's expected utility is calculated as follows. Since the marketplace uses equilibrium matching to match sellers and buyers, we first sort the bids descendingly and asks ascendingly in the marketplace, and then match high bids with low asks. Specifically, we assume that there are T transactions in total in the marketplace, and in transaction t, we use d_t^b and d_t^s to represent the matched bid and ask. Then the transaction price of this transaction is $TP_t = d_t^s \times k + d_t^b \times (1 - k)$. The marketplace's utility is:

$$U(r,t,q,o,\bar{x},\bar{y}) = \sum_{d_i^b \in \Delta : d_i^b \neq \ominus} x_i \times r + \sum_{d_i^s \in \Delta : d_i^s \neq \ominus} y_i \times r$$

$$+ \sum_{t=1}^{T} \left(2t + \left(d_t^b - \mathrm{TP}_t\right) \times q + \left(\mathrm{TP}_t - d_t^s\right)\right) \tag{7}$$

$$\times q + \mathrm{TP}_t \times o \times 2)$$

In this equation, the former two parts are profits from charging registration fees to buyers and sellers respectively, and the last part is the profit from charging transaction fees, profit fees and transaction price percentage fees.

Now we have obtained the marketplace's expected utility given the number of buyers and sellers choosing different offers, which are denoted by $\bar{x}$ and $\bar{y}$ respectively. Furthermore, the probability of $\bar{x}$ appearing is:

$$\varrho^b(\bar{x}) = \binom{B}{x_1, \dots, x_{|\Delta|}} \times \prod_{i=1}^{|\Delta|} \left(\omega_i^b\right)^{x_i} \tag{8}$$

and the probability of $\bar{y}$ appearing is:

$$\varrho^s(\bar{y}) = \binom{S}{y_1, \dots, y_{|\Delta|}} \times \prod_{i=1}^{|\Delta|} \left(\omega_i^s\right)^{y_i} \tag{9}$$

At this moment, we can compute the marketplace's expected utility given offer distributions Ω^b and Ω^s:

$$\tilde{U}(r,t,q,o,\Omega^b,\Omega^s) = \sum_{\bar{x} \in \mathcal{X}'} \varrho^b(\bar{x}) \times \sum_{\bar{y} \in \mathcal{Y}} \varrho^s(\bar{y}) \times U(r,t,q,o,\bar{x},\bar{y}) \tag{10}$$

4   Solving the Nash Equilibrium Charging Strategy

In this section, we describe how to solve the Nash equilibrium charging strategy of the marketplace when competing with other marketplaces. As we mentioned before, we analyze the Nash equilibrium of charging strategies given all sellers and buyers adopting Nash equilibrium marketplace selection and bidding strategies in different types of fees. Therefore, we first need to obtain the Nash equilibrium strategies of sellers and buyers. Given sellers and buyers having privately known types, we can only approximate the Nash equilibrium strategies when the marketplaces charge different types of fees. In Sect. 4.1 we introduce how to use Fictitious Play algorithm (FP) to do this. After knowing sellers and buyers' Nash equilibrium strategies, i.e. offer distribution Ω^b and Ω^s in Nash equilibrium, we can compute the expected utility of the competing marketplace using Eq. 10 when marketplaces charge different fees. Then the expected utilities of competing marketplaces in different fees consists of a payoff matrix, and we can use Gambit[2] to find Nash equilibrium charging strategies in this matrix, and the payoff matrix is shown in three-dimensional graph.

---

[2] http://gambit-project.org.

4.1   The Fictitious Play Algorithm

In game theory, fictitious play (FP) is a learning rule first introduced by George W. Brown [2]. In it, each player presumes that the opponents are playing stationary (possibly mixed) strategies. Each player selects an action according to a probability distribution that represents that player's strategy, then each player could, via repeated play, learn this distribution by keeping a running average of opponent actions [21]. Based on there own distribution, each player thus best responds to the empirical frequency of play of their opponent. However, The standard FP algorithm is not suitable for analyzing Bayesian games where the player's type is not known to other players. To ameliorate this, we adopt a generalized FP algorithm [17] to derive the strategies of the Bayesian game with continuous types and incomplete information, and it is often used to approximate the Bayes-Nash equilibrium (i.e. deriving the ϵ-Bayes-Nash equilibrium) by running the FP algorithm for a limited number of rounds.

We first describe how to compute the best response actions against current FP beliefs. Previously, we used Ω^b and Ω^s to denote the probability distributions of buyers' and sellers' offers respectively. In the FP algorithm, we use them to represent FP beliefs about the buyers and sellers' offers respectively. Then, given their beliefs, we compute the buyers' and the sellers' best response functions. In the following, we describe how to compute the buyers' best response function σ^{b*}, where $\sigma^{b*}(\theta^b, \Omega^b, \Omega^s, r, t, q, o) = argmax_{d^b \in \Delta} \tilde{U}(\theta^b, d^b, \Omega^b, \Omega^s, r, t, q, o)$ is the best response action of the buyer with type θ^b against FP beliefs Ω^b and Ω^s. The optimal utility that a buyer with type θ^b can achieve is $\tilde{U}^*(\theta^b, \Omega^b, \Omega^s, r, t, q, o) = max_{d^b \in \Delta} \tilde{U}(\theta^b, d^b, \Omega^b, \Omega^s, r, t, q, o)$. From the equations to calculate the buyer's expected utility in Sect. 3.2, we find the buyer's expected utility $\tilde{U}(\theta^b, d^b, \Omega^b, \Omega^s)$ is linear in its type θ^b for a given bid. Given this, and given a finite number of bids, the best response function is the upper envelope of a finite set of linear functions, and thus is piecewise linear. Each line segment corresponds to a type interval, where the best response action of each type in this interval is the same. We can create the set of distinct intervals I^b, which constitute the continuous type space of buyers, i.e. $\bigcup_{\Psi^b \in I^b} \Psi^b = [0, 1]$, which satisfy the following conditions:

- For any interval Ψ^b, if $\theta_1^b, \theta_2^b \in \Psi^b$, then $\sigma^{b*}(\theta_1^b, \Omega^b, \Omega^s) = \sigma^{b*}(\theta_2^b, \Omega^b, \Omega^s)$, i.e. types in the same interval have the same best response action.
- For any distinct $\Psi_1^b, \Psi_2^b \in I^b$, if $\theta_1^b \in \Psi_1^b$, $\theta_2^b \in \Psi_2^b$, then $\sigma^{b*}(\theta_1^b, \Omega^b, \Omega^s) \neq \sigma^{b*}(\theta_2^b, \Omega^b, \Omega^s)$

Based on the above computation, we can calculate the best response action distribution of buyers, which is done as follows. We know that given the buyers' type distribution function F^b and probability density function f^b, the probability that the buyer has the type in the interval Ψ^b is $\int_{\Psi^b} f(x)dx$, denoted by $F^b(\Psi^b)$. When the best response action corresponding to the interval Ψ_i^b is d_i^{b*}, the probability that the bid d_i^{b*} is used by buyers is $\omega_i^b = F^b(\Psi_i^b)$. By calculating the probability of each bid being used, we obtain the current best response action distribution of buyers, denoted by Ω_{br}^b, which is against current FP beliefs. We can then update the FP beliefs of buyers' bids, which is given by:

$$\Omega_{\tau+1}^b = \frac{\tau}{\tau+1} \times \Omega_\tau^b + \frac{1}{\tau+1} \times \Omega_{br}^b \tag{11}$$

where $\Omega_{\tau+1}^b$ is the updated FP beliefs of the buyers' bids for the next iteration round $\tau + 1$, Ω_τ^b is the FP beliefs on the current iteration round τ, and Ω_{br}^b is the probability distribution of best response actions against FP beliefs Ω_τ^b. This equation actually gives the FP beliefs on the current round as the average of FP beliefs of all previous rounds. The computation of the sellers' best response function and belief updates is analogous.

Since we approximate the Nash equilibrium, if the difference between the expected utility of a buyer (seller) in current best response action distributions and its expected utility of adopting best response action against current best response action distributions is not greater than ϵ, the FP algorithm stops the iteration process, and the current best response actions with corresponding type intervals constitute an ϵ-Bayes-Nash equilibrium. Specifically, we set $\epsilon = 0.00001$.

5   Nash Equilibrium Strategies of Sellers and Buyers

In this section, we will use the FP algorithm to analyse traders' Nash equilibrium bidding strategies when the marketplaces charge different types of fees. The reason why we first analyze the traders' bidding strategies is that traders' Nash equilibrium bidding strategies can directly affect marketplace's utility according to Sect. 3.3. Therefore, in order to investigate how each fee type combination can affect bidding strategies, in the following analysis, we assume that the marketplace only charges one type of fees at a time. For illustrative purposes, we show our results in a specific setting with 50 buyers and 50 sellers, and 11 allowable bids(asks) unless mentioned otherwise[3]. Furthermore, we assume that the small cost for traders entering a marketplace is $\iota = 0.0001$. For the transaction price, we assume $k = 0.5$, i.e. the transaction price is set in the middle of the matched bid and ask, which means the marketplace has no bias in favor of buyers or sellers. Finally, we assume that both buyers and sellers' types are independently drawn from a uniform distribution.

We now consider sellers and buyers' equilibrium strategies when there are two competing marketplaces[4]. We first consider the case where the marketplaces charge no fees to seller and buyers. By using FP, we find that, sellers and buyers eventually converge to one marketplace in equilibrium. The result is shown in Fig. 1(a). The gray line represents buyers' bids in equilibrium and the black line represents sellers' asks in equilibrium. From this figure, We find that buyers shade

---

[3] We also tried other settings. However, we still obtained the similar results.

[4] Note that our algorithms allow more than two competing marketplaces and more sellers and buyers. However, in this paper, we focus on the typical setting with two marketplaces.

their bids by decreasing their bids, and sellers shade their asks by increasing their asks, in order to keep profits. We also find that when buyers' (sellers') types are lower (higher) than a certain point they will not enter the marketplace because of the small cost ι.

Now we consider the case where marketplace 1 charges a profit fee and marketplace 2 charges a registration fee. For example, marketplace 1 charges a very high profit fee of 90%, and marketplace 2 charges a registration fee of 0.1. If initial beliefs are uniform (i.e. all actions are chosen with the same possibility), we find that all traders eventually converge to marketplace 1 and the equilibrium bidding strategies are shown in Fig. 1(b). there exists a bigger range of types of sellers and buyers not choosing the marketplace, sellers and buyers only ask or bid for 0.5. The reason of they converging to marketplace 1, is as follows. When a high profit fee is charged, the traders shade their offers more to keep profits, they will both bid (ask) 0.5 offers, and won't pay for profit fee. However, shading has no effect in the case of registration fees. Therefore, sellers and buyers will prefer the marketplace charging profit fees compared to registration fees. Furthermore, we also run simulations with many other fee combinations, and always find that all sellers and buyers converge to one marketplace.

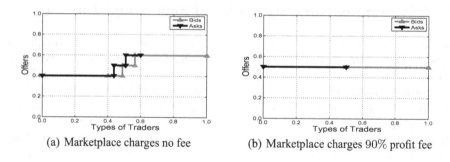

(a) Marketplace charges no fee   (b) Marketplace charges 90% profit fee

Fig. 1. Equilibrium strategies with 50 sellers and 50 buyers.

6   Equilibrium Analysis of Marketplace's Charging Strategies

In Sect. 5, we have analyzed sellers and buyers' strategies when competing marketplaces charge different types of fees. Based on this, we now start to analyze the Nash equilibrium charging strategies of marketplaces.

In more detail, in the following analysis, we discretize fees from 0 to 1 with step size 0.01. Then we obtain different fee combinations. For each fee combination, we repeat the experiments by trying different initial FP beliefs. For each set of initial FP beliefs, we run the FP algorithm and obtain the sellers and buyers' Nash equilibrium offer distributions Ω^b and Ω^s (i.e. converged FP beliefs). By using Eq. 10, we compute the marketplace' expected utilities for the given fee combination when starting from a particular FP beliefs. When repeating the experiments from different initial FP beliefs, we obtain the average utilities (i.e. profits) of marketplaces for this given fee combination. We repeat this process for different possible fee combinations, and consists of a profit matrix, from which we can use Gambit to compute the Nash equilibrium charging strategies. In the following, we analyze how to set fees in equilibrium in ten different cases. The marketplaces' profits in different fee combinations when sellers and buyers have used Nash equilibrium strategies are shown in Fig. 2.

Registration Fee and Registration Fee: Firstly, we analyze the case of both marketplaces charging registration fees. The results are shown in Fig. 2(a). We can see that their profits are symmetric, and both marketplaces charging 0.15 registration fees constitutes a Nash equilibrium charging strategy.

Transaction Fee and Transaction Fee: In the second case, we consider that both charges transaction fees. The results are shown in Fig. 2(b). Both marketplaces charging 0.05 transaction fee constitutes a Nash equilibrium charging strategy. Note that comparing this result to Fig. 2(a), both marketplaces charge a lower value of transaction fee.

Profit Fee and Profit Fee: In the third case marketplaces charge profit fees. The results are shown in Fig. 2(c). We find that both marketplaces charging a 11% profit fee constitutes a Nash equilibrium charging strategy.

Transaction Price Percentage Fee and Transaction Price Percentage Fee: In this case marketplaces charge transaction price percentage fees. The results are shown in Fig. 2(d). Both marketplaces charging a 5% transaction price percentage fee constitutes a Nash equilibrium charging strategy.

In the above four cases, both marketplaces charge the same types of fees. We can find that two marketplaces' payoff are symmetrical. In the following, we analyze the cases of marketplaces charging different types of fees.

Registration Fee and Transaction Fee: In the fifth case, marketplace 1 charges a registration fee and 2 charges a transaction fee. The results are shown in Fig. 2(d). We find that marketplace 1 charges 0.1 registration fee, marketplace 2 charges 0.15 transaction fee, constitutes a Nash equilibrium charging strategy.

Registration Fee and Profit Fee: In the sixth case, marketplace 1 charges a registration fee and marketplace 2 charges a profit fee. The results are shown in Fig. 2(f), we can see that the payoff of marketplace 2 is higher than marketplace 1. This is because compared with registration fee, sellers and buyers prefer to enter the marketplace which charges a profit fee since they can hide their true profit by shading their offers, and thus reduce the absolute payment of profit fees. Marketplace 1 charging 0.23 registration fee and Marketplace 2 charging 31% profit fee constitutes a Nash equilibrium charging strategy.

Registration Fee and Transaction Price Percentage Fee: In this case, marketplace 1 charges a registration fee and marketplace 2 charges a transaction price percentage fee. The results are shown in Fig. 2(g). Marketplace 1 charging

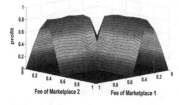

(a) Both marketplaces charge registration fees.

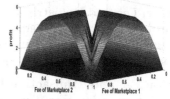

(b) Both marketplaces charge transaction fees.

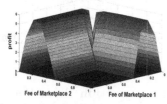

(c) Both marketplaces charge profit fees.

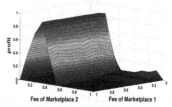

(d) Both marketplaces charge transaction price percentage fees.

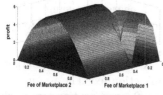

(e) marketplace 1 charges a registration fee and marketplace 2 charges a transaction fee.

(f) marketplace 1 charges a registration fee and marketplace 2 charges a profit fee.

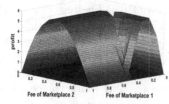

(g) marketplace 1 charges a registration fee and marketplace 2 charges a transaction price percentage fee.

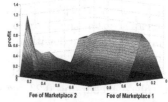

(h) marketplace 1 charges a transaction fee and marketplace 2 charges a profit fee.

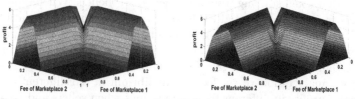

(i) marketplace 1 charges a transaction fee and marketplace 2 charges a transaction price percentage fee.

(j) marketplace 1 charges a profit fee and marketplace 2 charges a transaction price percentage fee.

Fig. 2. Marketplaces' profits when sellers and buyers have adopted Nash equilibrium strategies in different fee combinations.

0.05 registration fee and marketplace 2 charging 15% transaction price percentage fee constitutes a Nash equilibrium strategy, and marketplace 2 charging a transaction price percentage fees is more attractive to sellers and buyers.

Transaction Fee and Profit Fee: In this case, marketplace 1 charges a transaction fee and marketplace 2 charges a profit fee. The results are shown in Fig. 2(h). Marketplace 1 charging 0.05 transaction fee and marketplace 2 charging 28% profit fee constitutes a Nash equilibrium charging strategy. Sellers and buyers prefer the marketplace charging a profit fee.

Transaction Fee and Transaction Price Percentage Fee: In the ninth case, the results are shown in Fig. 2(i). When marketplace 1 charges 0.05 transaction fee and marketplace 2 charges 8% transaction price percentage fee, it constitutes a Nash equilibrium charging strategy. We find that when marketplace 1 charges 0.5 or above, no sellers and buyers will enter marketplace 1.

Profit Fee and Transaction Price Percentage Fee: Finally, we consider that marketplace 1 charges a profit fee and marketplace 2 charges a transaction price percentage fee, and the results are shown in Fig. 2(j). We find that the profit of marketplace 2 increases quickly and then decreases rapidly. This is because when marketplace's fee increases, sellers and buyers will leave quickly to enter marketplace 1. Marketplace 1 charging 18% profit fee and marketplace 2 charging 5% transaction price percentage fee constitutes a Nash equilibrium charging strategies.

Furthermore, what we can see from Fig. 2(g) is that if the marketplace charges a registration fee, traders need to pay regardless of whether or not the transaction is successful, which will cause the traders to be reluctant to enter this marketplace. Therefore, in a competitive market environment, the marketplace charges registration fee will not be competitive. Then, comparing Fig. 2(c), (f), (h) and (j) where profit fees are charged, with other figures where no profit fees are charged, we find marketplaces make less profits when profit fee is charged. This is because in this situation, sellers and buyers can hide their actual profits by shading their offers, and thus make less payments to marketplaces. Furthermore, when one marketplace charges a profit fee, its opponent, who charges another type of fees, has to charge a lower fee in order to attract sellers and buyers. This result further indicates that charging profit fee is better to keep sellers and buyers, but is worse of making profit. Moreover, in Fig. 2(g) and (i), we find that the transaction price percentage fee is better than the registration fee and transaction fee to attract sellers and buyers, and makes profits at a good level.

7   Conclusion

In this paper, we use game theory to analyze how double auction marketplaces charge fees in Nash equilibrium when competing with other homogeneous marketplaces. We first use FP algorithm to derive the Nash equilibrium marketplace selection and bidding strategies of seller and buyers in competitive double auction marketplaces. We find that in our setting, all sellers and buyers will converge to one marketplace in Nash equilibrium, i.e. another marketplace cannot survive, moreover, traders shade their offers in equilibrium and the degree to which they do this depend on the amount and types of fees that are charged by marketplaces. Based on the sellers and buyers' Nash equilibrium behavior, we further analyze the Nash equilibrium charging strategies of marketplaces when charging different types of fees. We find that different fees can affect marketplaces' profits significantly. In a competitive environment, the marketplace that charges a registration fee will not be competitive, and traders will not choose to enter this marketplace. The profit fee and transaction price percentage fee are more competitive to attract sellers and buyers than another two types of fees. This result provides a theoretical basis for how competing double auction marketplaces charge fees to maximize their profits in real economic world.

Acknowledgement. This paper was funded by the Humanity and Social Science Youth Research Foundation of Ministry of Education (Grant No. 19YJC790111), the Philosophy and Social Science Post-Foundation of Ministry of Education (Grant No. 18JHQ060), Shenzhen Basic Research Foundation (General Program, Grant No. JCYJ20190809175613332) and the Innovation Foundation for Industry, Education and Research in Universities of Science and Technology Development Center of Ministry of Education (Grant No. 2018A02030).

References

1. An, D., Yang, Q., Yu, W., Yang, X., Fu, X., Zhao, W.: Soda: strategy-proof online double auction scheme for multimicrogrids bidding. IEEE Trans. Syst. Man Cybern. Syst. **48**(7), 1177–1190 (2017)
2. Brown, G.W.: Iterative solution of games by fictitious play. Act. Anal. Prod. Alloc. **13**(1), 374–376 (1951)
3. Cai, K., Niu, J., Parsons, S.: On the economic effects of competition between double auction markets. In: Ketter, W., La Poutré, H., Sadeh, N., Shehory, O., Walsh, W. (eds.) AMEC/TADA -2008. LNBIP, vol. 44, pp. 88–102. Springer, Heidelberg (2010). https://doi.org/10.1007/978-3-642-15237-5_7
4. Cai, K., Niu, J., Parsons, S.: On the effects of competition between agent-based double auction markets. Electron. Comm. Res. Appl. **13**(4), 229–242 (2014)
5. Caillaud, B., Jullien, B.: Chicken & egg: competition among intermediation service providers. RAND J. Econ. **34**, 309–328 (2003)
6. Chowdhury, M.M.P., Kiekintveld, C., Son, T.C., Yeoh, W.: Bidding strategy for periodic double auctions using Monte Carlo tree search. In: Proceedings of the 17th International Conference on Autonomous Agents and Multi-agent Systems, pp. 1897–1899. International Foundation for Autonomous Agents and Multi-agent Systems (2018)
7. Friedman, D., Rust, J.: The Double Auction Market: Institutions. Santa Fe Institute Studies in the Science of Complexity, vol. XIV. Theories And Evidence. Perseus Publishing, New York (1993)
8. Fudenberg, D., Tirole, J.: Game Theory. The MIT Press, Cambridge (1991)

9. Gjerstad, S., Dickhaut, J.: Price formation in double auctions. Games Econ. Behav. **22**, 1–29 (1998)
10. Gode, D.K., Sunder, S.: Allocative efficiency of markets with zero-intelligence traders: Market as a partial substitute for individual rationality. J. Polit. Econ. **101**(1), 119–137 (1993)
11. Jackson, M.O., Swinkels, J.M.: Existence of equilibrium in single and double private value auctions 1. Econometrica **73**(1), 93–139 (2005)
12. Kelly, F.P., Maulloo, A.K., Tan, D.K.: Rate control for communication networks: shadow prices, proportional fairness and stability. J. Oper. Res. Soc. **49**(3), 237–252 (1998)
13. Ma, H., Leung, H.F.: An adaptive attitude bidding strategy for agents in continuous double auctions. Electron. Comm. Res. Appl. **6**(4), 383–398 (2007)
14. Milgrom, P.: Auctions and bidding: a primer. J. Econ. Perspect. **3**(3), 3–22 (1989)
15. Miller, T., Niu, J.: An assessment of strategies for choosing between competitive marketplaces. Electron. Comm. Res. Appl. **11**(1), 14–23 (2012)
16. Phelps, S., McBurney, P., Parsons, S.: Evolutionary mechanism design: a review. Auton. Agents Multi-Agent Syst. **21**(2), 237–264 (2010)
17. Rabinovich, Z., Gerding, E.H., Polukarov, M., Jennings, N.R.: Generalised fictitious play for a continuum of anonymous players. In: Proceedings of the 21st Joint Conference on Artificial Intelligence, pp. 245–250 (2009)
18. Ramos, S.B.: Competition between stock exchanges: a survey. In: FAME Research Paper (77) (2003)
19. Reny, P.J., Perry, M.: Toward a strategic foundation for rational expectations equilibrium. Econometrica **74**(5), 1231–1269 (2006)
20. Rogers, A., David, E., Jennings, N.R., Schiff, J.: The effects of proxy bidding and minimum Bid increments within eBay auctions. ACM Trans. Web (TWEB) **1**(2), 9 (2007)
21. Shamma, J.S., Arslan, G.: Dynamic fictitious play, dynamic gradient play, and distributed convergence to Nash equilibria. IEEE Trans. Autom. Control **50**(3), 312–327 (2005)
22. Shi, B., Gerding, E.H., Vytelingum, P., Jennings, N.R.: An equilibrium analysis of market selection strategies and fee strategies in competing double auction marketplaces. Autonom. Agents Multi-Agent Syst. **26**(2), 245–287 (2013)
23. Smith, V.L.: An experimental study of competitive market behavior. J. Polit. Econ. **70**, 111–137 (1962)
24. Tatur, T.: On the trade off between deficit and inefficiency and the double auction with a fixed transaction fee. Econometrica **73**(2), 517–570 (2005)
25. Wang, S., Xu, P., Xu, X., Tang, S., Li, X., Liu, X.: Toda: Truthful online double auction for spectrum allocation in wireless networks. In: 2010 IEEE Symposium on New Frontiers in Dynamic Spectrum (DySPAN), pp. 1–10. IEEE (2010)

Agents for Preserving Privacy: Learning and Decision Making Collaboratively

Onuralp Ulusoy$^{(\boxtimes)}$ and Pınar Yolum

Utrecht University, Utrecht, The Netherlands
{o.ulusoy,p.yolum}@uu.nl

Abstract. Privacy is a right of individuals to keep personal information to themselves. Often online systems enable their users to select what information they would like to share with others and what information to keep private. When an information pertains only to a single individual, it is possible to preserve privacy by providing the right access options to the user. However, when an information pertains to multiple individuals, such as a picture of a group of friends or a collaboratively edited document, deciding how to share this information and with whom is challenging as individuals might have conflicting privacy constraints. Resolving this problem requires an automated mechanism that takes into account the relevant individuals' concerns to decide on the privacy configuration of information. Accordingly, this paper proposes an auction-based privacy mechanism to manage the privacy of users when information related to multiple individuals are at stake. We propose to have a software agent that acts on behalf of each user to enter privacy auctions, learn the subjective privacy valuations of the individuals over time, and to bid to respect their privacy. We show the workings of our proposed approach over multiagent simulations.

Keywords: Multiagent systems · Online social networks · Privacy

1 Introduction

Collaborative systems enable users to interact online while sharing content that pertains to more than one user. Consider an online social network (OSN), where a user can share pictures that include other users, who are many times able to tag themselves or others, comment on it, and even reshare it with others. Or, an IoT system, in which one security camera would like to share footage of a setting to guarantee security for the people, while one individual would prefer to keep the location of herself secret. In both of these cases, the content being in question relates to multiple entities, who have different privacy concerns or expectations from each other. Even though the content is meant to be shared by a single entity, the content is related to more than the uploader and hence is actually *co-owned* by others [11,21].

When co-owners have different privacy constraints, they should be given the means to make a decision as to either share or not to share the content. However,

N. Bassiliades et al. (Eds.): EUMAS 2020/AT 2020, LNAI 12520, pp. 116–131, 2020.
https://doi.org/10.1007/978-3-030-66412-1_8

current systems enable only the uploader to set privacy settings while publishing contents, but does not allow co-owners to state their constraints. As a result, individuals are left to resolve conflicts via offline methods [14].

Ideally, systems should provide privacy management mechanisms to regulate how content will be shared. Recently, multiagent agreement techniques, such as negotiation [12,21] and argumentation [13] have been used. These approaches have been successful but require heavy computations; that is, they can only be used when the entities can reason on its privacy policies and communicate with others intensively. Moreover, the agents in these systems follow predefined rules but do not learn better ways to preserve their users' privacy over time. An alternative to this is to use auctions [20] where each user bids based on how much she wants to see a content public or private. The decisions are then made based on the winning bids [4,6].

Accordingly, this paper first explains an *agent-based* approach PANO for collaborative privacy management. When a content is about to be shared, agents of co-owners interact over a mechanism to reach a decision. Similar to Squicciarini *et al.* [20], PANO uses Clarke-Tax mechanism, but adapts it to protect users against abuses, and at the same time encourages users to share content online. PANO incorporates a group-wise budget system that ensures that advantages gained by interactions with certain individuals can only be used against the same individuals. Thus, the agents support users in biding automatically for their behalf. Next, we propose an agent architecture called PRIVACY AUCTIONING LEARNING AGENT (PANOLA) that uses user's privacy policy as an initial point to bid but then learns to adjust its bidding strategy over time. Learning has been used in context of privacy before, mostly to enable agents to classify whether a user would consider a content private or not [7,18]. However, the learning problem addressed here is different. First, since the content to be shared is co-owned, other agents' actions influence the outcome of a privacy decision. Second, what needs to be learned is not whether a content is private or not, but what the agent would bid to share or not to share the content, given what it has observed and shared before.

Our main contributions in this paper are as follows:

- We provide a fair privacy respecting auctioning method based on Clarke-Tax mechanism, where software agents represent users' privacy requirements and appropriately bid on behalf of the users.
- We develop a privacy-aware bidding strategy for the agents based on reinforcement learning. This gives them the ability to fine-tune their auction bids according to previous experiences and adjust their privacy respecting strategies over time.
- We evaluate the proposed approach over multiagent simulations and show that it achieves superior privacy protection than non-learning cases.

The rest of this paper is organized as follows: Sect. 2 explains PANO in detail, with a focus on how automatic bidding is done for protecting privacy. Section 3 proposes an agent architecture that learns bidding strategies over time. Section 4 describes our multiagent simulation environment and evaluates the effectiveness of learning. Finally, Sect. 5 discusses our work in relation to existing methods in the literature.

2   Agent-Based Auctioning for Privacy: PANO

To enable decisions on co-owned content, we propose co-owners to be represented with software agents. Agents keep track of the privacy preferences of entities and act on behalf of them to reach a decision. We propose PANO, an agent-based privacy decision system, where agents employ auctioning mechanisms to reach decisions on privacy conflicts [24]. PANO uses an extended version of Clarke-Tax Mechanism as an underlying mechanism.

2.1   Background: Clarke-Tax Mechanism

Clarke-Tax mechanism [4] provides an auction mechanism, where participants bid for different, possible actions in the environment. The action that receives the highest total bids from the participants wins and is executed. Different from an English auction, participants who aid in the winning action to be chosen, i.e., that bid towards it, are taxed according to the value they put on it. This is achieved by subtracting the bid values of every single user from the overall values. If the subtraction of a single user's bid changes the overall decision, it shows that the user's bid on this action had a *decisive* value. Thus, the user is taxed with the difference of the actual action's score and the score of action to be taken if that user were not present in the auction [4]. In the context of collaborative privacy, Clarke-Tax mechanism is used to decide on how a content is going to be shared. Squicciarini *et al.* [20] consider three types of sharing actions: *no share*, *limited share*, and *public share*. We follow the same scheme here. When an image is about to be shared, all the relevant participants bid on these three possible actions.

2.2   PANO Auctions

The Clarke-Tax auctions are beneficial for decision making for multiple participants with different opinions, as they support truthfulness [20]. If Clarke-Tax auctions are applied in commerce, then each participant would have their own budget (e.g., money) to bid with. However, since we are emulating the auction idea, the participants are given budgets at the beginning of each auction, which they can use to bid in the current auction or save to bid later. As usual, a participant cannot bid more than her current budget.

When Clarke-Tax auctions are applied in privacy as opposed to commerce, there are two points that need attention: First, users can enter into arbitrary auctions in arbitrary groups to increase their budgets. If budgets earned with one group of users is used to set the privacy in a second group by overbidding, then the system is abused. Second, it is not clear to assign a bid value for privacy.

In commerce, the valuation for an item can be identified more easily, however, for privacy, the difference between values is not easily interpreted. Without clear boundaries to specify the range for bids, agents are left with an uncertainty to express their preferences accurately. We address these two points by offering only group-wise budgets and ensuring boundaries for bid ranges [24].

Group-wise Spending: To prevent abuse of using budgets for trivial auctions with different users, earned budgets can only be used in new contents with the same co-owners. With this, we improve robustness of the system, where malicious users cannot collaborate for increasing their budget and forcing the other users about their own choices. For example, without group-wise Spending, two agents might share arbitrary content over a social network without spending budget for privacy actions, thus increasing their total budget. When they co-own a content with others, they will have extra budget from these previous efforts, and can bid high amounts to force sharing a content over on OSN, while in fact it is a sensitive content for another user that can't outbid the malicious users. With group-wise spending, each agent would have a separate budget for each co-owner group, hence cannot use previously earned budget against a co-owner group if the earned previously budget was with another co-owner group.

Boundaries: Boundaries enable all the agents to bid inside a predefined range. This is beneficial for preventing users that are richer in the budget from dominating the decisions. This also helps agents that participate in the auctions to have better evaluation functions, because they can have a better opinion about the other participants' bids. When the agents know what would be the maximum bid from the others, they can set their bidding strategy accordingly. For example, without the boundaries in place, when an agent considers a content for a privacy action, she would try to bid as much as possible since she would considers others doing the same for the opposite action. But with boundaries, the agent would have a clearer idea about how much to bid, since she will know the amount to outbid in the worse case scenario, where all the agents bid the amount of the maximum boundary for the opposite action.

Definition 1 *PANO:* PANO *auction is defined as a 6-tuple:*
$AUC = \{c, AC, A, m, M, BD\}$, *which consists of the auction's related content c, a set of privacy actions (AC), the set of agents (A) that participate in the auction, minimum possible bid (m), maximum possible bid (M) and the set of placed bids (BD), where each bid $b_{t,a}$ ($b_{t,a} \in BD$) is related to one single action t (t $\in$ AC) and one single agent a (a $\in$ A).*

Given a PANO auction defined as in Definition 1, a system can compute the outcome for the agents, and update their budgets accordingly. At the end of each auction, each participant is given an amount that is equal to the half of the maximum possible bid. This prohibits the agent to bid for the maximum possible bid for each auction. That is, the agent would need to save its acquired budget for the next auction to be able to bid higher than average possible bid. Our reason to employ this half of the maximum boundary is that if an agent acquires more budget than she should use, she would be able to bid the maximum allowed amount for every auction. In this case, it would not make sense for an agent to deliberate the bid amount, since a higher bid would increase her chances to force the action she wants, regardless of the significance of the action. On the extreme opposite case, if the agents would earn very little amount for every auction, they would not be able to bid for many decisions when they consider the content sensitive. In this situation, many privacy violations might occur, and agents would be forced to save their budget for many cases to be able to have a decision in one. Our decision to give half the amount of the maximum possible bid aims to find a balance between these two extreme cases, where agents should deliberate about placing their bids to be able to enforce their decisions only when necessary, but they would still be able to enforce their decisions in the sensitive cases, if they bid reasonably.

2.3 Privacy Policy

Each agent should have an evaluation mechanism on the importance of a content, and how much it is willing to bid for its preferred actions. Since the action set can differ significantly in terms of size, the evaluation mechanism of the agents should rely on some generic, but still comprehensive representation of the represented individuals' privacy preferences. Thus, we propose a 5-tuple privacy policy structure to represent the privacy related choices of the individuals.

Definition 2 *PANO Policy: A* PANO *policy P is a 5-tuple P = {a,n,p,q,i}, where a is the agent that the policy belongs to, n is the audience of the policy who are the users affected by the outcome, p is the contextual properties for the content that the policy will be applied, q is the privacy related action and i is the importance of the policy, which is a rational value between 0 and 1.*

An example policy of an agent that represents Alice, who wants to share its blood pressure information received from an IoT device with her doctor and nurse can be defined as:

$P = \{Alice, \{doctor[Alice], nurse[Alice]\}, info[BloodPressure], share, 0.9\}.$

3   Learning to Bid

Existing work in PANO assumes that the agents are homogeneous and bid in a predefined manner. However, this is rarely the case in real life. First, different users have different privacy understandings that can affect their bidding strategies. Second, users do not know their valuations accurately. Third, some users' privacy expectations can change over time, requiring them to bid differently for the same content at two different time points.

In general, users (and thus agents) are not experts of privacy domains. Even though users claim that they care about privacy and can express their privacy concerns, they tend to act differently and their actions can possibly contradict with their privacy requirements [1]. Hence, presenting privacy related actions in a way that users can understand and fit their privacy requirements with ease becomes essential. For a privacy auctioning mechanism, agents would find it difficult to place an exact bid on a privacy action, but presenting a range from which they can provide their bids, rather than a single value could be easier. Depending on the context, the extent of the range can vary and providing bids on one end of the range versus the other can significantly change the outcome of the bid. For this reason, it is best if an agent can learn over time a range from which it can generate its bids.

In order to facilitate this, we use reinforcement learning [22]. With reinforcement learning, agents can learn how to improve their privacy actions over time by making use of the only few possible visible outcomes in the system and with simple computations. In our adoption of reinforcement learning to PANO; over time, agents' desired actions are rewarded or their bad choices are penalized. According to these, agents explore their set of actions, in order to adapt and act in the best possible way for the current state of the environment. The convergence to learn the best possible action depends on the exploration/exploitation balance of the agents. An adventurous agent can explore from a wider range of actions while risking being penalized, while a conservative agent can avoid taking risk and adapt slowly, but might get stuck in local minima since the best possible action has a bigger probability of never being explored.

In light of the aspects mentioned above that can affect the privacy decisions, we introduce our learning agent, called *Privacy Auctioning Learning Agent (PANOLA)*. PANOLA employs reinforcement learning to learn the bidding ranges, build strategies using defined coefficients and adapt its bidding according to the outcome of previous decisions. In addition, we ensure that PANOLA can act coherently with agents' privacy policies even when previous decisions are not available.

3.1 Bidding Ranges

With the given minimum and maximum boundaries for PANO, we introduce bidding ranges, where the agents can pick from the possible ranges within the boundaries and bid integers between the picked ranges. All the possible bidding ranges within boundaries are stored by the agents themselves; each of them accompanied by a rational *utility* value, in the range of [0–1] that denotes how suitable a range is for bidding for a privacy action; 0 meaning the least suitable and 1 the most suitable. Since the agents cannot have any previous experience when first introduced to a domain, the initial utilities are computed according to the distance of the ranges' mean values to the agents' initial bid evaluations extracted from their privacy policies.

Example 1 Figure 1 depicts two bidding range examples ($r_1 = [4, 12]$ and $r_2 = [14, 18]$) for action t between minimum and maximum boundaries (m and M respectively), assigned as 0 and 20. The set of ranges contains more than these two, since we include all possible integer ranges between m and M. $b_{t,a}$ shows the initial bidding evaluation for action t, which is given as 6 and means that the agent would initially bid 6 for t for the incoming content.

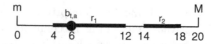

Fig. 1. A depiction of two ranges between minimum (m) and maximum (M) bidding boundaries and the initial bidding evaluation of agent a for action t

In time, utility values of bidding ranges change according to success or failure of the picked bids. Agents do not share the utility values with the environment or other agents. Each agent updates its utilities independently according to the outcome of the auctions. Reinforcement learning is used to make agents learn to pick the most suitable range for a given content type, using information that results from PANO auctions, such as the amount they paid from their budget according to their bids, the deducted tax amount if any tax was paid and the action chosen by the auction, which can be considered as the most important factor for the learning process. We employ all these factors in our computations for learning the suitability of the ranges. The agents pick the range with the highest utility for a given content and bid an integer value inside this range according to their bidding strategy for their preferred action.

3.2   Effective Auctions

An important aspect in facilitating reinforcement learning is to balance exploration of new bid ranges with exploitation of already found ones. The exploration/exploitation balance is not binary in most of the real life domains, since the uncertainty and non-determinism is usually present. Therefore, we make use of continuous utility ranges with several coefficients that represent properties of the auction outcomes to compute the balance.

Like most of the approaches in reinforcement learning [3,5,23], the unsuccessful range pickings are penalized with a decrease in the utility value, while the successful ones have an increase in the utility. In our approach, the utilities are based on the *effectiveness* of the previous auctions. Intuitively, an auction has been effective for an agent if a preferred action has been decided, while the agent did not bid too high and was not taxed too much. We formalize this intuition below using three coefficient values. Table 1 summarizes the important parameters for the proposed approach.

– Bid Coefficient (BC) captures the preference of winning an auction with lower bids. Having a higher BC means that spending less is more important while winning. This is essential when an agent has a limited budget, since winning with a lower bid would enable the agent to have spare budget for the future auctions. In contrast, a rich agent would prefer a lower BC value since bidding more than it should would still leave budget for the future auctions, without the need to search of another winning bid with a lower value.

Table 1. Coefficients and values for utility calculations

Name Abbreviation	Short description	Equation/Function	Range
Bid Coef. BC	Used for distinguishing between winning with lower and higher bids	$BC \rightarrow 0$: decrease effect of BC $BC \rightarrow 0.5$: increase effect of BC	$[0\text{--}0.5$
Tax Coef. TC	Changes the importance of taxes in utility calculation	$TC \rightarrow 0$: decrease effect of TC $TC \rightarrow 0.5$: increase effect of TC	$[0\text{--}0.5]$
Action Coef. AC	Assigned by the agents according to their action choice preferences	$AC \rightarrow BC + TC$: decrease effect of AC $AC \rightarrow 1$: increase effect of AC	$[(BC + TC) - 1]$
Distance D	Used in the initial utility value calculations	$D = (M - |Mean(rng) - b_{t,a}|)/M$	$[0\text{--}1]$
Effectiveness E	Calculates agent's effectiveness in an auction	$E = AC - (BC * b_{t,a}/M + TC * Tax/M)$	$[0\text{--}1]$

- Tax Coefficient TC has a similar purpose to BC, but it focuses on the amount of taxed budget on winning bids instead of the bids themselves. Similar to BC, a higher TC increases the importance of taxes in utility computation.
- AC enables each agent to decide the importance order of the privacy actions. Agents assign coefficient values between $BC + TC$ and 1 to each action according to their action ordering preferences, the highest coefficient value being the AC of the most important action.

These three aforementioned coefficients are used in computing the final effectiveness. For the Effectiveness (E) value, a higher amount means that the agent's preferred action has been chosen with lower bidding and lower taxing. The ratio of $b_{t,a}$ to the maximum possible bid M gives the magnitude of the bid. The higher this value, the less effective the auction will be. This magnitude is adjusted with BC to account for the fact that different agents would care about this differently. The ratio of Tax to maximum possible bid M gives the magnitude of the budget loss for the agent. Again, the higher this amount, the less effective the auction would be. Adjusting it with TC enables the agent to account for different contexts, e.g., when the agent has high budget and would not be affected by being taxed. The effectiveness of the auction is then the difference between the value gained by the decided action AC and the cost of bidding and taxing as shown in Table 1. The sum of Tax Coefficient TC and the Bid Coefficient BC should be lower than the Action Coefficient AC, so that when an auction is successful,

E will have a positive value and can increase the utility of the picked range for the auction.

The effectiveness of an auction will determine the likelihood of a bidding range to be picked again. However, at the beginning, the agent does not have any effectiveness values, as it has not participated in any previous auctions. Yet, they still need a mechanism to assign bids. Distance (D) formula is used for this purpose of initial utility value calculations. This formula favors bidding ranges that are closer to the agent's initial privacy policy. That is, the distance formula assigns higher utility values to the ranges that have a close mean value to the agents' initial bid evaluations, and lower values to the distant ranges. According to D (in Table 1), if the mean of all the integer values within a range is equal to the initial bid evaluation of the agent, D will be equal to 1, which will be a top pick for the first auction for a related content. The normalization according to the maximum auction boundary ensures that the furthest difference between the range mean and initial bid evaluation would be the difference between the maximum boundary and the minimum boundary (zero for our simulation), since the furthest distance could be the initial bid evaluation to be at one end of the boundary and the mean of the range on the other end. In such case, $|Mean(range) - b_{t,a}|$ part of the D calculation will always be equal to the maximum boundary M, thus the D value will be computed as 0. In addition to enabling first time utilities with D, we also ensure that initial bids are as close as possible to the agents' intended privacy requirements. A utility value closer to 1 would mean that the agent is indeed willing to bid around the mean of the picked range, and the privacy action outcome of the first auction would be similar with when the agent does not employ a learning strategy and bids a value according to its own privacy policies.

Example 2 Referring back to the examples of two ranges in Fig. 1, the mean of r_1 and r_2 are 8 and 16 respectively. If we assume that there are no previous auctions for agent a, the initial bid $b_{t,a}$ is given as 6, which is the amount a is willing to bid for action t, if the learning process with ranges are not available. According to the equation of D, r_1 has the initial utility of 0.9 and r_2 has 0.5. As the mean of r_1 is closer to $b_{t,a}$, it has a higher D value than r_2 and can be considered a better candidate for a bidding range of t for an incoming auction.

3.3   Utility Update

After the initialization with the Distance value, utility computation depends on the Effectiveness value and the total number of auctions entered. Utility for a range called r_x is simply computed with the formula below:

$$Utility\{r_x\} = \frac{\sum_{i=1}^{n} E_i + D_{r_x}}{n+1} \tag{1}$$

According to Formula 1, utility value of r_x after n auctions is the sum of all previous E values and the initial D value divided by the number of entered auctions plus one, considering D.

Example 3 According to the example in Fig. 1, the initial utilities of the ranges according to D value would be $[0-1] : 0.725, [0-2] : 0.75, ..., [4-12] : 0.9, ..., [14-18] : 0.5, ..., [18-20] : 0.35, [19-20] : 0.325$.

If we ignore the ranges that are not shown in the examples above, r_1 ($[4-12]$) is the one to be picked for the next bid, since it has the highest utility. Assume that the agent picked r_1, won the auction with a bid within the range, and got an E value of 0.8 out of it. The utility of r_1 will become $(0.9 + 0.8)/2$, equaling to 0.85. Since this value is still higher than other ranges above, it will have the highest probability to be picked for the next auction.

4   Evaluation of Learning for Preserving Privacy

The above setup shows us how reinforcement learning can be used by the agents to generate bids. Some important questions that follow are: does this approach enable agents to learn accurately, do the agents that learn bidding ranges perform better in PANO auctions, do other personal values affect preserving privacy and if so, how.

In order to answer these questions, we design and implement a multiagent simulation environment, where PANO and PANOLA agents with different privacy policies enter PANO auctions. The environment consists of a set of agents, and different types of contents, where the agents have predetermined evaluations to rely on. According to these content evaluations, agents have an initial opinion about which privacy actions to support in an auction, and how much they are willing to bid for it. The environment also keeps track of the budget balances of the agents, and their success rate (i.e., the percentage of won auctions in all entered auctions) for further performance evaluations. The content types and the number of actions may vary in the environment, and the required information is fully observable to the agents so they can evaluate on how to bid for a given content type and the set of privacy actions. As in the original Clarke-Tax algorithm, the agents cannot see the bids of the other agents before or after an auction, but they are informed of the winning action as well as the amount of tax to pay, in case they are taxed.

4.1   Simulation System

We have developed a simulation system to evaluate the performance of PANOLA agents in different setups. The environment supports both PANO agents, which do not employ any learning for bidding and PANOLA agents, which learn how to bid over time. The simulation includes multiple action choices and all the agents have predetermined evaluations about how important they consider different action types and how much their initial bid should be accordingly. After the agents are loaded into environment, the simulation cycles for all the contents, and agents enter PANO auctions to collaboratively decide which action to take for the given auctions.

To understand whether an agent is successful, we use a success metric, which calculates the percentage of auctions for which an agent's preferred privacy action is chosen. Recall that the auctions are set up in a such a way that the privacy expectations of the agents conflict. As a result, if an agent's most preferred action is the result of the auction, then this agent has won and the remaining agents have lost. That said, it is possible to have two privacy actions that end with the same highest bid. In those cases, we disregard the auction from calculations of success. Thus, the total wins of all the agents equals the total count of the auctions. This simple metric enables us to see which agents have been the most successful in selecting privacy actions as measured by the percentage of total auctions.

4.2   PANOLA vs. PANO Agents

In our multiagent simulations, there are PANOLA agents that learn how to bid over time and the remaining agents are opposing PANO agents that have different action choices than PANOLA agents. These opposing PANO agents have a static strategy, meaning that they always bid the same pre-evaluated amount for the same type of content.

We perform ten simulation runs of 100 contents for each to evaluate preservation of total budget, amount spent for each content and success for entered auctions (e.g. successful if the first action choice of the agent is the outcome of an auction and unsuccessful if not). The experiments where we include both PANO agents and PANOLA are executed with a single PANOLA against a PANO agent setup, since we aim to measure PANOLA's success with different characteristics against PANO agent opponents that do not learn how to bid over time. The experiments for comparing PANOLA agents with different values against each other are conducted with one-against-one auctions, since our purpose for this comparison is to measure a learning characteristic against another one.

In our first experiment, we evaluate the success of PANOLA against PANO agents in terms of privacy decisions. For all 100 content, our scenario sets the privacy actions of PANOLA and PANO agents always in conflict, thus in each auction the agents oppose each other to ensure their own privacy action becoming the final privacy decision. One of the goals of PANO auctions is to enable every agent to participate for making privacy decisions in the long run, by taxing the winners of the auctions to give a higher chance for the losing agents for the future auctions. Referring back to Sect. 2.2, since we allow agents to earn limited budget (i.e., half of the maximum possible bid) after each auction, even when the agent learns the right bidding range, they might not be able to bid due to lack of budget. Hence, we evaluate whether PANOLA agents learn the right bidding range, we perform auctions with and without budget restrictions. Figure 2 shows the privacy success percentages of PANOLA against PANO agent in both conditions.

As expected, PANOLA learns to outbid the PANO agent after a few auctions, and wins every auction afterwards for the unlimited budget condition.

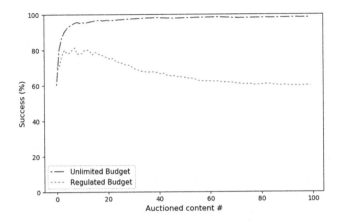

Fig. 2. Privacy success of PANOLA against PANO agents in unlimited and regulated budget scenarios.

This shows that PANOLA indeed learns the correct range to bid from and if PANOLA owns enough budget, it will always choose the correct amount to bid for its privacy actions. When the budget regulation is in place, it is expected for both agents to decide on some privacy actions in the long run, as this is a desired outcome in our mechanism. For the evaluation with the regulated budget, PANOLA still performs better in the long run than PANO agent (~60% privacy success after 100 auctions); but this time PANO agent is able to give the decisive privacy action for some auctions. The main reason for this is that even though PANOLA learns how to outbid the opponent, it will run out of budget after winning some auctions, and in that case the opponent can win the auction. However, we can also conclude that learning how to bid is beneficial for agents, since adapting the bids for their desired privacy actions enables them to obtain significantly more desired collaborative privacy decisions in their favor than the agents that do not adapt over time.

4.3   Exploration Within Bid Ranges

While learning which range a bid will be given from is the first step, deciding on the actual bid is an important second step. Intuitively, the agent can pick a bid from the range based on a given distribution. Currently, we implement two types of agents, namely *adventurous* and *conservative*. *Adventurous* agents bid randomly within the picked bidding range, while *conservative* agents bid according to normal distribution in Gaussian.

We compare the performance of the adventurous and conservative PANOLA agents against each other. We investigate the success rate and total owned budget of the agents over 100 auctions. Figure 3 shows the success rates and total owned budget over 100 auctions for both agents.

According to Figure 3, it can be seen that conservative bidding achieves slightly more successful results after the agent learns the environment through

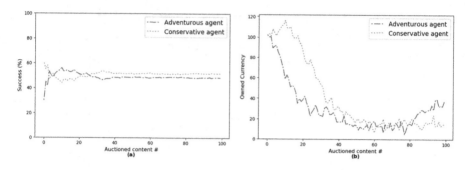

Fig. 3. Success (a) and Owned Budget (b) of adventurous and conservative PANOLA against each other

some auctions. It is also more successful at the first few auctions, while spending more reasonably than the adventurous bidding with random distribution. Around the tenth auction, adventurous agent's success passes conservative, since the adventurous agent tries to increase its bids to beat conservative, while conservative does not increase its bids since it already wins auctions. But after the next few auctions, conservative agent also adjusts its bids accordingly, and stays steadily around 4% more successful than the adventurous agent. The main reason for this difference relies on the Clarke-Tax mechanism; when a conservative agent outbids the adventurous, the tax amount payed tends to be a small amount, since the conservative agent sticks closer to its winning range and not reaching the maximum boundaries. In the opposite position, an adventurous agent can win by trying bids closer to the maximum boundary, but get taxed with a bigger amount which decreases its budget significantly for the next auction. According to this evaluation, it can be said that when two learning agents have the same importance evaluation for an incoming content, using a conservative approach leads to more successful bids in the long run.

With these results, we can conclude that employing conservative strategy in biddings is more beneficial than the adventurous strategy in most cases. However, the learning curve of an adventurous agent while losing is steeper than the conservative one. Thus, when the agent loses most of the bids, trying an adventurous strategy while trying to pick from higher ranges could be useful to find out the winning privacy bids over opponents.

5   Discussion

Privacy in ubiquitous systems started to receive attention around early2000 s, with the Internet becoming accessible to most of the people in the world and enabling easy sharing and access of private information over the web. Langheinrich [15] is one of the first works that investigate the open issues for privacy-respecting approaches for ubiquitous computing. Spiekermann and Cranor [17] and Gürses *et al.* [10] study the grounds of engineering privacy, explaining how information related domains can be designed to employ privacy-preserving methods. Paci *et al.* [16] provide an extensive survey for literature about access control over community centric collaborative systems; laying down the key issues and giving a roadmap for future challenges. Bahri *et al.* [2] show the challenges of preserving privacy over decentralized OSNs, and provides a review of previous work done for overcoming these challenges. These studies all show that privacy is an important aspect of collaborative information systems and address the need for effective mechanisms.

Even though the systems the main goal is intended to satisfy the general good for the collaborative privacy decisions, the agents that represent entities naturally have the goal to force their privacy requirements to the others.

Collaborative privacy management is investigated in the literature for different domains. Fong [9] introduce Relationship Based Access Control (ReBAC) mechanism, and provides a model to make it applicable to OSNs, where users can define their privacy constraints related to the relations that are available in OSNs, such as friends or colleagues. Multi-party Access Control Model by Hu *et al.* [11] is another work which focuses on determining a single final policy according to privacy requirements of the users. PANO offers [24] a fair mechanism to decide on which action to take, which uses Clarke-Tax auctions at its core with some economic modifications such as group-wise spending, bidding boundaries and income-expenditure balance levels. For the competitiveness of the agents, we introduce a learning mechanism that is based on reinforcement learning, where agents can adapt according to the visible information resulting from the outcome of previous auctions. We also use an evaluation distance coefficient to overcome the cold start problem for the agents that have no prior information about auctions or their opponents.

The use of machine learning for privacy is gaining momentum and the research area is still open for further improvement. Fogues *et al.* [8] provide an agent-based approach which requires user input when required to learn incrementally about user policies, and recommends privacy policies for sharing content for multiuser scenarios. Vanetti *et al.* [25] propose a machine learning approach for filtering unwanted textual contents in OSNs. Squicciarini *et al.* [19] infer privacy policies of OSN users for photographic contents. Zhong *et al.* [26] employ contextual image properties in a different way: they extract and learn from the image features in a way to detect possible privacy conflicts to take further action.

Our work on this paper opens up interesting research directions. The first direction is to use the findings of this paper to build an agent that can change its behavior as needed as well as build models of other agents' in the auctions to make better decisions. The second direction is to capture the dynamics between agents, especially that of trust. When agents trust each other more, they could reflect that differently when bidding, leading to better overall decisions. The third direction is understanding and derivation of social norms into PANO, which could be beneficial to create learning agents according to their normative behavior.

References

1. Acquisti, A., Brandimarte, L., Loewenstein, G.: Privacy and human behavior in the age of information. Science **347**(6221), 509–514 (2015)
2. Bahri, L., Carminati, B., Ferrari, E.: Decentralized privacy preserving services for online social networks. Online Soc. Netw. Media **6**, 18–25 (2018)
3. Barto, A.G., Mahadevan, S.: Recent advances in hierarchical reinforcement learning. Discr. Event Dyn. Syst. **13**(4), 341–379 (2003)
4. Clarke, E.: Multipart pricing of public goods. Pub. Choice **11**(1), 17–33 (1971)
5. Diuk, C., Cohen, A., Littman, M.L.: An object-oriented representation for efficient reinforcement learning. In: Proceedings of the 25th International Conference on Machine Learning, pp. 240–247. ICML 2008, ACM, New York, NY, USA (2008)
6. Ephrati, E., Rosenschein, J.S.: The clarke tax as a consensus mechanism among automated agents. In: Proceedings of the Ninth National Conference on Artificial Intelligence, Vol. 1, pp. 173–178. AAAI 1991, AAAI Press (1991)
7. Fang, L., LeFevre, K.: Privacy wizards for social networking sites. In: Proceedings of the 19th International Conference on World Wide Web, pp. 351–360. WWW 2010, ACM, New York, NY, USA (2010)
8. Fogues, R.L., Murukannaiah, P.K., Such, J.M., Singh, M.P.: SoSharP: recommending sharing policies in multiuser privacy scenarios. IEEE Internet Comput. **21**(6), 28–36 (2017)
9. Fong, P.W.: Relationship-based access control: protection model and policy language. In: Proceedings of the First ACM Conference on Data and Application Security and Privacy, pp. 191–202. CODASPY 2011, ACM (2011)
10. Gürses, S., Troncoso, C., Diaz, C.: Engineering privacy by design. Comput. Priv. Data Prot. **14**(3), 25 (2011)
11. Hu, H., Ahn, G.J., Jorgensen, J.: Multiparty access control for online social networks: model and mechanisms. IEEE Trans. Knowl. Data Eng. **25**(7), 1614–1627 (2013)
12. Kekulluoglu, D., Kökciyan, N., Yolum, P.: Preserving privacy as social responsibility in online social networks. ACM Trans. Internet Technol. **18**(4), 42:1–42:22 (2018)
13. Kökciyan, N., Yaglikci, N., Yolum, P.: An argumentation approach for resolving privacy disputes in online social networks. ACM Trans. Internet Technol. **17**(3), 27:1–27:22 (2017)
14. Lampinen, A., Lehtinen, V., Lehmuskallio, A., Tamminen, S.: We're in it together: interpersonal management of disclosure in social network services. In: Proceedings of the SIGCHI Conference on Human Factors in Computing Systems, pp. 3217–3226. CHI 2011, ACM, New York, NY, USA (2011)
15. Langheinrich, M.: Privacy by design — principles of privacy-aware ubiquitous systems. In: Abowd, G.D., Brumitt, B., Shafer, S. (eds.) UbiComp 2001. LNCS, vol. 2201, pp. 273–291. Springer, Heidelberg (2001). https://doi.org/10.1007/3-540-45427-6_23
16. Paci, F., Squicciarini, A., Zannone, N.: Survey on access control for community-centered collaborative systems. ACM Comput. Surv. **51**(1), 6:1–6:38 (2018)
17. Spiekermann, S., Cranor, L.F.: Engineering privacy. IEEE Trans. Softw. Eng. **35**(1), 67–82 (2009)
18. Squicciarini, A., Caragea, C., Balakavi, R.: Toward automated online photo privacy. ACM Trans. Web **11**(1), 2:1–2:29 (2017)

19. Squicciarini, A.C., Lin, D., Sundareswaran, S., Wede, J.: Privacy policy inference of user-uploaded images on content sharing sites. IEEE Trans. Knowl. Data Eng. **27**(1), 193–206 (2015)
20. Squicciarini, A.C., Shehab, M., Paci, F.: Collective privacy management in social networks. In: Proceedings of the 18th International Conference on World Wide Web, pp. 521–530. WWW 2009, ACM, New York, NY, USA (2009)
21. Such, J.M., Rovatsos, M.: Privacy policy negotiation in social media. ACM Trans. Auton. Adapt. Syst. **11**(1), 41–429 (2016)
22. Sutton, R.S., Barto, A.G.: Reinforcement Learning: An Introduction. MIT Press, Cambridge (2018)
23. Tan, M.: Multi-agent reinforcement learning: Independent vs. cooperative agents. In: Proceedings of the Tenth International Conference on Machine Learning, pp. 330–337. Morgan Kaufmann (1993)
24. Ulusoy, O., Yolum, P.: Collaborative privacy management with auctioning mechanisms. In: Ito, T., Zhang, M., Aydoğan, R. (eds.) ACAN 2018. SCI, vol. 905, pp. 45–62. Springer, Singapore (2021). https://doi.org/10.1007/978-981-15-5869-6_4
25. Vanetti, M., Binaghi, E., Ferrari, E., Carminati, B., Carullo, M.: A system to filter unwanted messages from OSN user walls. IEEE Trans. Knowl. Data Eng. **25**(2), 285–297 (2013)
26. Zhong, H., Squicciarini, A., Miller, D.: Toward automated multiparty privacy conflict detection. In: Proceedings of the 27th ACM International Conference on Information and Knowledge Management, pp. 1811–1814. CIKM 2018, ACM, New York, NY, USA (2018)

Open Social Systems

Nardine Osman[1], Carles Sierra[1], Ronald Chenu-Abente[2], Qiang Shen[3],
and Fausto Giunchiglia[2(✉)]

[1] Artificial Intelligence Research Institute (IIIA-CSIC), Barcelona, Spain
{nardine,sierra}@iiia.csic.es
[2] Dipartimento di Ingegneria e Scienza dell'Informazione, Univerità di Trento,
Trento, Italy
{chenu,fausto}@disi.unitn.it
[3] College of Computer Science and Technology, Jilin University, Changchun, China
shenqiang19@mails.jlu.edu.cn

Abstract. While normative systems have excelled at addressing issues
such as coordination and cooperation, they have left a number of open
challenges. The first is how to reconcile individual goals with community
goals, without breaching the individual's privacy. The evolution of norms
driven by individuals' behaviour or argumentation have helped take the
individual into consideration. But what about individual norms that one
is not willing to share with others? Then there are the ethical considerations that may arise from our interactions, such as, how do we deal
with stereotypes, biases, or racism, or how to avoid the abuse of community resources. This paper is concerned with accounting for individual
needs while respecting privacy and adhering to the community's ethical code. We propose a decentralised architecture for normative systems
that, along with the community norms, introduces individual's requirements to help mediate the interaction between members.

Keywords: Normative systems · Privacy by design

1 Introduction

Normative systems have attracted a lot of attention in the multi agent systems
community as one approach to maintain the autonomy of agents while ensuring
community goals and aspirations are fulfilled. Norms essentially specify the rules
of interaction: what one can (or cannot) do, when, under what conditions, etc.
Normative systems copy how human societies function, and they can be compared to social norms that govern society's behaviour or organisational norms
that mediate interactions in organisations [8].

While normative systems have excelled at addressing issues such as coordination and cooperation [1], they have left a number of open challenges. The first
is how to reconcile individual goals with community goals, without breaching
the individual's privacy. A number of approaches have been studied to take the
individual into consideration, such as norm synthesis techniques that would help

© Springer Nature Switzerland AG 2020
N. Bassiliades et al. (Eds.): EUMAS 2020/AT 2020, LNAI 12520, pp. 132–142, 2020.
https://doi.org/10.1007/978-3-030-66412-1_9

norms evolve based on individuals' behaviour [6], or norm evolution that would allow the individuals to reason about norms through argumentation [7]. But what about individual norms that one is not willing to share with their fellow community member? For example, imagine a community norm that states that a donation cannot be below 5€ and an individual norm that states that a donation cannot exceed 50€. Another open challenge are the ethical considerations that may arise from our interactions, such as, how do we deal with stereotypes, biases, or racism, or how to avoid the abuse of community resources, to name a few.

In other words, the question this paper addresses is how can we make sure that an individual will have their needs taken into consideration while we ensure their privacy is respected and the community's ethical code is not violated. To address these issues, this paper proposes a decentralised architecture for normative systems that, along with the community norms, introduces individual's requirements to help mediate the interaction between members. Section 2 presents our proposal in brief, Sect. 3 introduces the notation used in this paper, Sect. 4 introduces the decentralised architecture addressing the challenges discussed above, while Sect. 5 provides a motivating example, before concluding with Sect. 6.

2   Proposal

To address the issues presented above, we first say that in addition to community norms, there are also individual norms that describe the individual's rules of interaction with others.

Norms, as illustrated earlier, specify what actions are acceptable for that specific individual, who can the individual interaction with, and under what circumstances. While normative systems have focused a lot on the action, 'what' can one do, we highlight in this paper the other crucial aspect of interactions: 'who' can one interact with. The 'who' aspect has been implicit until now, usually hidden under the 'what' action specification. In an increasingly hyperconnected world, we choose to make the 'who' more explicit in our proposal. To achieve this, we require users to have profiles describing them, such as describing their gender, their age, their relationships, etc. With such profiles, rules on who to interact with can then be specified. For example, one individual norm can then say 'only seek the support of female friends during my breakup period', while another can say 'never ask my ex-husband for help'. As such, and in addition to community norms and individual norms, the individual profile becomes another crucial element for mediating our interactions.

Both the individual's norms and profile may be divided into a private and shared part. In what follows, we present the norms and the profiles in more detail.

2.1 Norms

As per the above we distinguish between community norms and individual norms.

- **Community norms.** These norms are the community's agreed upon norms. Any action (represented by a message exchange) in the peer-to-peer network must be coherent with them. We consider an action acceptable by the community when it doesn't violate any of the community's norms.

  We note community norms can be categorised into a number of groups (Fig. 1). For example, institutional norms can describe the rules of behaviour in the given community (following the concept of electronic institutions [2]). Governance norms can describe the rules of who has the right to change existing norms and how. Ethical norms can describe what is considered ethical and what actions are deemed unethical, and hence, unacceptable in the community. Incentivising norms can help provide incentives for community members to behave in a certain way, such as encouraging benevolent behaviour, say to help maintaining the community and fulfilling its objectives. One can even imagine re-using, adapting, or building on top of existing norms. For example, a new social network may re-use the institutional norms of an existing social network and adapt them to their community's particular needs.

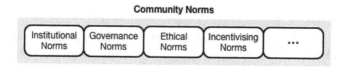

Fig. 1. Community norms

- **Individual norms.** These norms represent particular aspects of the relationship of the human with her machine and with the community. For instance, a prohibition to pop-up a message during a siesta unless coming from a relative. Or one can filter messages coming from people that they do not deem trustworthy. As most individual norms are private, some 'unethical' behaviour may be codified at this level and remain unnoticed, such as a private norm requiring to never show messages coming from old men.

  In general, individual norms may implement certain behaviour that may not be fully aligned with the community values and norms. In cases of conflict between community norms and individual private ones, community norms prevail concerning actions within the community. For example, if community norms prohibit discriminating against women, then an action like excluding females from a given activity will be prohibited. However, individual private norms prevail when concerning actions local to one's machine. For instance, while community norms may prohibit discriminating against women, one's private norms can enforce requests coming from women to be suppressed (ignored).

We note that individual norms can further be divided into two parts: private norms and shared norms.

- **Private norms** are norms that are private and are never shared with other machines (e.g. 'never show messages coming from old men'). Their impact is restricted as other machines do not have access to these norms.
- **Shared norms** are norms that travel with messages so that other people's machines can take them into consideration (e.g. when specifying 'do not ask the help of people outside Barcelona', the receiving machine can check the location of its human, even if this data is private as this data never leaves the machine and is not shared with others).

2.2   Profiles

Generally speaking we assume we have two types of profiles that we can intuitively describe as follows.

- **Private profile.** This is the set of features that are private to (and hence, accessible only by) the human's own machine. For instance, if gender("A",female) is part of Alice's private profile this means that Alice's machine has permission to use Alice's gender in the reasoning.
- **Shared profile.** This is a set of features that can be shared with (or made accessible to) others, both the humans and their machines. There are several approaches, both centralised and decentralised, that one can choose from for making information public. However, in this proposal, we suggest sharing the public profile by communicating it to other machines on an as-needed basis.

Of course, humans decide what part of their profile is public and what part is kept private.

The notion of private profile is quite intuitive. We want to keep private what we do not want the others to know. This issue of privacy has always been around but it has become of paramount importance with the pervasive use of the Web and the Social Media. In the past we were protected for free by our space and time limitations: it would take some time to from place A to place B and this time would increase with distance. The phone lifted some time barriers, but the propagation of information would still be limited by the fact that we were able to choose who to interact with and, in any case, the communication would only happen in pairs. Television lifted other barriers, allowing for zero time one-to-many communication, but still information was very much verified and under control and in many cases regulated by law. The Social Media have lifted the last barrier: now everybody can talk with everybody and say whatever they prefer with basically no limitations (the first limitations being established by the most recent legislation, for instance, GDPR in Europe).

The social media have made it possible to replicate and hugely expand what has always been the case in the real world. Now anybody can share information with anybody, virtually the entire world population, in zero time and no space constraints. This motivates the focus on privacy and hence the need for a private profile.

But this is only part of the story. First of all, *the notion of privacy is not an absolute notion.* There is information that I may be willing to share with my family but not with my friends and even less with my enemies. For example people are usually very happy to share information about the location of their children in a certain moment of time, for instance the fact that they go to a school with a certain address and that lectures will end at 1pm, with a person with a car that maybe has a child who goes to the same school. But they would never be willing to share this information with a person they do not fully trust. In social relations, the notion of *privacy is fully contextual* in the sense that it depends on the current situation and also in the objectives that one wants to achieve.

The contextuality, and therefore non-absoluteness, of privacy brings up the key observation which underlies the need for both a public and a private profile. To provide another example which integrates the one about the child who needs to be picked up from school, suppose I have a certain disease, e.g., diabetes. This is sensitive information, namely information with many more constraints for its circulation. In general, most people would not talk about their disease, but, for instance, a person with diabetes, if too low in her level of sugar in the blood, would be very happy to let others know about this. And not only of the need for sugar but also of the fact that the reason is diabetes, as this would increase the urgency of the intervention. In social relations there is always *a tension between privacy and transparency.* In almost any interaction with other people we trade-off some privacy (about us, about our family, friends, ..., anybody) as a key enabler for obtaining information, support, information from others.

The notion of public profile captures exactly this need of transparency, meaning by this the sharing information as key to enabling social interactions. Clearly, the public profile is *contextual*, where the person we interact with is a crucial component of the relevant context, and mostly *dynamic*. There is in fact very little information, if any, that we are willing to always share with others; maybe our name, but also in this case it is easy to think of exceptions. Furthermore the public profile, like the private profile, will change in time because of multiple reasons, e.g., change of one's job or of the place where one lives. The contextuality and dynamicity of the public profile will require its continuous update and revision. This consists of a process which will be enforced by the local peer, as driven by its user, and which will consist of performing a set of abstraction operations [4] on the private profile.

3 Notation

We first present, in this Section, the notation used in the remainder of this paper. We say let CN describe the set of community norms, PrR and ShR describe the sets of private and shared norms, respectively, and PrP and ShP describe the private and share profiles, respectively. We view a profile as a set of features. To specify which agent does a set of norms or profile describe, we use the sub index of that agent. For example, PrR_A describe's A's private norms whereas ShP_B describes B's shared profile.

We say a profile is a set of features, and we specify features as propositions. For example, we say $gender(``A",female)$ to state that A's gender is female and $loc(``A",barcelona)$ to state that A's location is in Barcelona. As for norms, we specify these as "if then" statements that talk about actions (similar to the rule-based norms of [3]), and we use the deontic operators O and F to describe obligations and prohibitions, accordingly. For example, $F(display(``A",M))$ states that it is forbidden to display the message M to A.

4   Architecture and Associated Operational Model

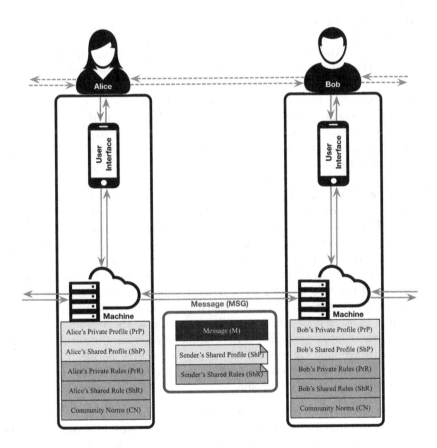

Fig. 2. Basic (distributed) architecture

In Fig. 2, the schema of the peer-to-peer architecture for our proposed normative system is presented. Each user has a machine, that may run all or some of its computations on a remote server (depending on the complexity of the norms and their computational requirements). Each user interacts with its machine through a user interface.

As illustrated in Sect. 2, each user specifies their profile and individual norms. The profile is divided into private (PrP) and shared (ShP) parts, and the norms into private (PrR) and Shared (ShR) parts.

The norm engine at each machine will have both a reactive and proactive behaviour.

- **Reactive Behaviour.** This allows the norm engine to react to messages received (usually representing the actions being performed), and there are two types of messages that a machine can receive:

  - *A message from the user interface.* When a user performs an action, it is translated into a message that is sent to the machine through the user interface. The message includes the shared norms and a copy of the sender's shared profile. Upon the receipt of such a message, the norm engine needs to first verify that the message does not violate any of the norms, this includes the community norms and the sender's individual norms (both private and shared). A conflict resolution mechanism should address any conflicting norms that may arise. If the action violates any of those norms, an error message is sent back to the user. However, if the action obeys the norms, then the norm engine needs to decide what to do next, usually translated into sending messages to other peers. This decision follows from the community and individual norms (both private and shared), and takes the user's profile (both public and shared) into account as needed.
  - *A message from another machine.* As in the previous case, the norm engine needs to first verify that the message does not violate any of the community norms. This re-checking upon receipt ensures that the sender's norm engine has not been manipulated to cheat. If the message violates any of the community norms, then it may either be discarded, or if the community norms require sanctioning, then the appropriate sanctions should be executed.

    However, if the action obeys the community norms, then the norm engine needs to decide what to do next, which is usually translated into sending messages to other peers and/or sending messages to the user interface. This decision takes into consideration the community norms, the norms attached to the message, and the individual private and shared norms. This ensures that the machine abides with its human's private norms without leaking any of their private norms and profile.

- **Proactive Behaviour.** This allows the norm engine to proactively perform actions as required by the norms. For example, incentivising norms might remind a user to complete their profile, if this has been neglected for some time, or remind the user of how much their contribution to their community is valued, if they haven't been active lately. To be proactive, a machine will require access to the community norms and individual private norms, as well as its human's private and public profile.

5 Motivating Example

In this example we will specify the interaction between three people with the uHelp use case in mind. uHelp [5] is an app that allows one to find help with everyday tasks, such as picking up one's child from school, or finding a friend to play squash with. uHelp works by crawling one's social network looking for trusted volunteers. In this example, imagine having four people involved: Alice (A), Bob (B), Carol (C), and Dave (D). Say Bob, Carol and Dave are on Alice's contact list, and Bob is on Carol's contact list. The community norms (CN), or the uHelp norms, specify how a help request is propagated in the social network. They state that every time a machine receives a help request, it needs to decide whether it displays it to its user (Lines 32–35, Fig. 3), and whether it needs to forward it and to whom (Lines 24–31, Fig. 3). We note that the person making the request will decide the maximum number of hops accepted when looking for volunteers (Hops) and the minimum trustworthiness required (Trust). As these are specified for a given task, they are sent along with the help request message (Line 38, Fig. 3).

As for individual norms, imagine Carol has a private norm that says ignore help requests from females (i.e. do not display such requests, as show in Lines 13–17, Fig. 3). Alice, on the other hand, has a private norm and a shared one. The private one specifies that only those who are close by (in Barcelona) get to see her help requests (Lines 10–12, Fig. 3). The shared one specifies that none of her requests may be displayed to Bob (Lines 19–22, Fig. 3). As Bob is her ex-husband, she prefers that Bob does not see her requests, though she is happy for his machine to still receive her requests as she is interested in using his social network. Hence, she only prohibits the display of the message to Bob.

Now concerning people's profiles, some information such as gender, location, or trust in others may be kept private (Lines 1–4, Fig. 3), or made public (Lines 6–8, Fig. 3). For example, Alice's private profile specifies her trust in her contacts: in this case, 'low' for Bob and 'high' for Carol and Dave. Similarly, Carol's private profile specifies her trust in her contact Bob as 'high' and her current location as being in London. Bob, Dave and Alice are happy to make share their gender and location with others through their shared profiles.

Now given these profiles and norms, imagine that Alice is running late at work and she needs someone to pick up her child from school (message M). She accepts friends of friends (Hops=2, for connection level 2), but is looking for trustworthy volunteers only (Trust="high"), as illustrated in Line 38, Fig. 3. For these norms to be enforced by other machines, Alice shares these norms along with her other shared norms and profiles by attaching them to the help request (M), resulting in the message, MSG.

As soon as the help request is sent by Alice, the norm interpreter at her machine will check whether the message applies with the community norms (CN), in which case it does. The interpreter then needs to decide what are the actions that this message entails, taking into consideration Alice's profile (private and shared), her norms (private and shared), and the community norms. According to the community norm on Lines 24–31, the interpreter decides to forward the help request to Carol and Dave, as they satisfy the requested hops and trustworthiness constraints (the trustworthiness of Bob, on the other hand, is low).

Upon receiving the message, Dave's machine now needs to check whether the message applies with the community norms, which it does. It then needs to decide what are the resulting actions of receiving this message, taking into consideration Dave's profile and norms (both private and shared), the norms attached to the message (that is, Alice's shared norms), and the community norms. According to the community norm on Lines 32–35, the request is then displayed to Dave, despite the fact that Alice forbids it in its private norm. This is because Alice's private norm is private and cannot be taken into consideration by other people's machines.

Upon receiving this message, again, Carol's machine needs to check whether the message applies with the community norms, which it does. After that, it needs to decide what are the resulting actions of receiving this message, taking

```
1    PrP_A = { trust("A","B",low) ;
2              trust("A","C",high) ;
3              trust("A","D",high) }
4    PrP_C = { trust("C","B",high) ; loc("C",london) }
5
6    ShP_A = { gender("A",female) ; loc("A",barcelona)}
7    ShP_B = { gender("B",male) ; loc("B",barcelona) }
8    ShP_D = { gender("D",male) ; loc("D", rome) }
9
10   PrR_A = { IF ¬loc(X,barcelona) ∧ requester(M)="A" THEN
11              F(display(X,M))
12            END IF }
13   PrR_C = { IF rcv_help_rqst(Sndr,"C",Trust,Hops,MSG) ∧
14              gender(Sndr)=female ∧
15              MSG=M+ShR_M+ShR_Sndr+ShP_Sndr THEN
16                F(display("C",M))
17            END IF}
18
19   ShR_A = { IF rcv_help_rqst(Sndr,"B",Trust,Hops,MSG) ∧
20              MSG=M+ShR_M+ShR_Sndr+ShP_Sndr THEN
21              F(display("B",M))
22            END IF }
23
24   CN = {IF rcv_help_rqst(Sndr,Rcvr,Trust,Hops,MSG) THEN
25          FOR ALL X∈Rcvr.Contacts
26            IF trust(Rcvr,X,Y) ∧
27            Y≥Trust ∧ Hops>0 THEN
28              O(snd_help_rqst(Rcvr,X,Trust,Hops-1,MSG))
29            END IF
30          END FOR
31        END IF ;
32        IF rcv_help_rqst(Sndr,Rcvr,Trust,Hops,MSG) ∧
33          type(Sndr)=machine ∧ MSG=M+ShR_M+ShR_Sndr+ShP_Sndr THEN
34            O(display(Rcvr,M))
35        END IF }
36
37   M = "Can you pick up my son from school at 5pm?"
38   ShR_M = { O(snd_help_rqst("A",machine("A"),"high",2,MSG_M)) }
```

Fig. 3. uHelp example: profiles and norms

into consideration Carol's profile (private and shared), her norms (private and shared), the norms attached to the message (that is, Alice's shared norms), and the community norms. In this case, and according to Carol's private norm on Lines 13–17, the help request is not displayed on Carol's mobile as it comes from a female. However, the help request is forwarded to Bob, according to the community norm at Lines 24–31. Note that while Alice's trust in Bob was low, her trust in Carol is high, and Carol's trust in Bob is also high, allowing the message to be forwarded to Bob through Carol.

Upon receiving the message, Bob's machine again checks its adherence to community norms. Then, as above, it needs to decide what are the resulting actions of receiving this message, taking into consideration Bob's profile (private and shared), his norms (private and shared), the norms attached to the message (that is, Alice's shared norms), and the community norms. In this case, and according to Alice's shared norm on Lines 19–22, the help request is not displayed on Bob's mobile as Alice forbids it.

This example illustrates how our proposed system ensures the interaction between people adheres to both community norms and individual ones without jeopardizing people's privacy. It also illustrates the impact of private and shared information. For instance, private norms are better suited to control local behaviour, whereas shared norms are better suited for controlling the behaviour of other machines.

6   Conclusion

This paper has proposed a decentralised architecture for normative systems that introduces individual norms, while ensuring the privacy of people. One aspect that has been overlooked in this paper and left for future work is the conflict resolution mechanism. Having people specify their own norms will probably result in conflicting rules, and a mechanism will be needed to address such conflicts.

Our current next steps will be to implement the proposed system by extending the existing uHelp platform to introduce the different types of norms (adding private and shared ones) and different types of profiles (splitting them into private and shared). Furthermore, we plan to integrate uHelp with an extended version of iLog [9] that automatically learns people's profiles from their online activity.

As illustrated in our discussion of community norms, these norms can be used to specify the rules of interaction in a community, but also to introduce more specialised rules, such as rules specifying what is considered ethical and unethical, or rules specifying how to motivate people to act in a certain way. Future work will be experimenting with these specialised different, focusing on ethics and incentives.

Acknowledgements. This research has received funding from the European Union's Horizon 2020 FET Proactive project "WeNet – The Internet of us" (grant agreement

No 823783), as well as from the Spanish Ministry of Economy, Industry and Competitiveness' Retos 2017 project "CIMBVAL" (project No TIN2017-89758-R), and the RecerCaixa 2017 project "AppPhil".

References

1. Andrighetto, G., Governatori, G., Noriega, P., van der Torre, L.W.N. (eds.): Normative Multi-Agent Systems, Vol. 4. Dagstuhl Publishing (2013)
2. d'Inverno, M., Luck, M., Noriega, P., Rodriguez-Aguilar, J., Sierra, C.: Communicating open systems. Artif. Intell. **186**, 38–94 (2012)
3. García-Camino, A., Rodríguez-Aguilar, J.A., Sierra, C., Vasconcelos, W.W.: Constraint rule-based programming of norms for electronic institutions. Autonom. Agents Multi-Agent Syst. **18**(1), 186–217 (2009)
4. Giunchiglia, F., Walsh, T.: A theory of abstraction. Artif. Intell. **57**(2–3), 323–389 (1992)
5. Koster, A., et al.: U-help: supporting helpful communities with information technology. In: Proceedings of the 2013 International Conference on Autonomous Agents and Multi-agent Systems, pp. 1109–1110. AAMAS 2013, International Foundation for Autonomous Agents and Multi-agent Systems, Richland, SC (2013)
6. Morales, J., López-Sánchez, M., Esteva, M.: Using experience to generate new regulations. In: Proceedings of IJCAI 2011, pp. 307–312 (2011)
7. Oren, N., Luck, M., Miles, S., Norman, T.: An Argumentation Inspired Heuristic for Resolving Normative Conflict. Unknown Publisher (2008)
8. Shoham, Y., Tennenholtz, M.: On social laws for artificial agent societies: off-line design. Artif. Intell. **73**, 231–252 (1995). https://doi.org/10.1016/0004-3702(94)00007-N
9. Zeni, M., ad Zaihrayeu, I., Giunchiglia, F.: Multi-device activity logging. In: ACM International Joint Conference on Pervasive and Ubiquituous Computing, pp. 299–302. ACM (2014)

A Faithful Mechanism for Privacy-Sensitive Distributed Constraint Satisfaction Problems

Farzaneh Farhadi$^{(\boxtimes)}$ and Nicholas R. Jennings

Department of Computing, Imperial College London, London, UK
{f.farhadi,n.jennings}@imperial.ac.uk

Abstract. We consider a constraint satisfaction problem (CSP) in which constraints are distributed among multiple privacy-sensitive agents. Agents are self-interested (they may reveal misleading information/constraints if that increases their benefits) and privacy-sensitive (they prefer to reveal as little information as possible). For this setting, we design a multi-round negotiation-based incentive mechanism that guarantees truthful behavior of the agents, while protecting them against unreasonable leakage of information. This mechanism possesses several desirable properties, including Bayesian incentive compatibility and individual rationality. Specifically, we prove that our mechanism is faithful, meaning that no agent can benefit by deviating from his required actions in the mechanism. Therefore, the mechanism can be implemented by selfish agents themselves, with no need for a trusted party to gather the information and make the decisions centrally.

Keywords: Constraint satisfaction problems · Incentive mechanism design · Privacy

1 Introduction

Distributed constraint satisfaction problems (DisCSP) in which decision variables and constraints are distributed among multiple agents are common in many multi-agent systems. They are popular because they are a good representation of many real world applications including resource allocation [1], scheduling [16], electronic commerce [22] and logistics [18].

To solve distributed CSPs, agents need to exchange messages until a solution is found or until one agent finds out that there is no solution to the problem. In many cases, there is also a natural desire for the agents to minimize the amount of information revealed during the problem solving process. This is particularly true in cases where the agents are self-interested. Such privacy-sensitive encounters [10] involve the design of mechanisms that strike a balance between the amount of

This work was supported and funded by Samsung Electronics R&D Institute UK (SRUK).

N. Bassiliades et al. (Eds.): EUMAS 2020/AT 2020, LNAI 12520, pp. 143–158, 2020.
https://doi.org/10.1007/978-3-030-66412-1_10

information revealed and the desire to reach an acceptable solution. For example exchanging no information minimizes the amount of information revealed but is unlikely to lead to a solution, whereas all agents revealing all their constraints maximizes the chance of finding a socially-optimal solution but at the cost of all privacy.

When the agents are self-interested, the mechanism needs to be robust to the possibility of receiving misleading information from the agents. However, such agents will only provide truthful information if they are motivated by relevant incentives to do so. In an incentive mechanism, the agents give each other rewards (or penalties) based on the information they share with each other. These rewards must be designed so as to align the agents' individual objectives and eventually to motivate them to not reveal fake information.

The literature on incentive mechanism design mostly focuses on centralized mechanisms where a trusted entity performs as a manager and processes the mechanism procedures centrally [3,25]. However, in many cases, a trusted entity does not always exist. To tackle this drawback, we design a faithful incentive mechanism that can be run by selfish agents. A mechanism is faithful if an agent cannot benefit by deviating from any of his required actions, including information-revelation, computation and message passing [17].

In more detail, our faithful incentive mechanism strikes a balance between privacy and social efficiency. This mechanism is based on the *score-voting* idea which is used in the literature for designing centralized incentive mechanisms [12]. Specially, we design a multi-round negotiation-based mechanism in which at each round, the agents first rate a set of candidate solutions and then decide if any of them is acceptable. To make this voting mechanism Bayesian truthful, we present a reward function that is based on the agents' beliefs about the likely effectiveness of their votes on the final outcome. We guarantee faithfulness of the mechanism by setting non-manipulable rules and show that the minimum number of solutions being discussed at each round is a control parameter that balances the tradeoff between privacy leakage and social efficiency. We illustrate this mechanism via the domain of distributed meeting scheduling, which is a canonical example of a DisCSP with self-interested and privacy-sensitive agents.

This work presents the first faithful mechanism for a DisCSP with selfish and privacy-sensitive agents. Moreover, our mechanism has the flexibility to adjust the relative importance of privacy leakage and social efficiency. DisCSPs show quite different behaviors based on the relative importance of privacy and efficiency. Therefore, designing a unified mechanism than can plausibly handle a diverse range of DisCSPs is a key advance.

2   Related Literature

DisCSP was first introduced in [26]. Most existing mechanisms in this area require that all decision variables and constraints are known by the corresponding agents in advance; i.e. they are offline mechanisms. Two strands of works are prevalent in the category of offline mechanisms: complete mechanisms [7,13] and incomplete mechanisms [23,28]. The former are guaranteed to find the social-welfare maximizing solution, but require exponential time in the worst case. The latter find suboptimal solutions but run quickly enough to be applied to real-world applications. However, offline mechanisms do not fit dynamic applications such as meeting scheduling, where new decision variables and constraints are introduced over time. Thus, to solve practical dynamic DisCSPs, we need to design online mechanisms that make decisions based on partial available information.

Distributed online mechanisms often use negotiation between agents to find a solution [9,21]. During such encounters, agents usually need to adjust their negotiating strategy based on their information about others' preferences to change the outcome to their favorite one. Some cooperative negotiation mechanisms assume that agents' preferences are public information [19]. In a competitive environment (non-cooperate negotiation), however, self interested agents keep their preferences private to avoid being exploited by their opponents [11,20]. Without the knowledge of opponents' preferences, agents may have difficulty in adjusting their negotiation strategies properly. This difficulty has been addressed in the literature of incentive mechanism design [25].

There is a long tradition of using centralized incentive mechanisms within distributed systems [14]. However, there are very few known methods for distributed problem solving in the presence of self-interested agents. The first steps in providing a distributed incentive mechanism were the works presented in [5,6]. However, the rules of these mechanisms are not robust to manipulation, and hence are not suitable for distributed implementation. Starting from [15], researchers have attempted to design faithful mechanisms that incentivize agents to follow all the rules [17]. These mechanisms do not consider privacy leakage and so are not directly applicable for our purposes.

There are a number of papers that are starting to address privacy issues in DisCSP [2,10,27]. These papers describe techniques, such as encryption [27], obfuscation [2], and codenames [2], that can be used with DisCSP algorithms such as DPOP, ADOPT, and NCBB, to provide privacy guarantees. However, these works do not take agents' selfish behavior into account.

3 Multi-agent Meeting Scheduling

We view meeting scheduling as a distributed and dynamic CSP where the decisions are about when to hold each meeting and the constraints are the attendees' calendar availabilities. The problem is distributed as the agents are only aware of their own calendars and is dynamic as the needs for different meetings arise over time. In this setting, the agents need to decide about the time of different meetings one-by-one, and without knowing what will happen next. Attendees of the meetings are self interested and privacy-sensitive; they wish to maximize their own utility and reveal as little information about their availabilities and preferences as possible. Therefore, we need to design an incentive mechanism that guarantees truthful behavior of the agents, while protecting them against unreasonable leakage of information.

Formally, we model each meeting m by a tuple $m = (A, I, l)$ where A is the set of mandatory attendees, $I \in A$ is the initiator who is responsible for setting the meeting time, and l is the meeting's required length in terms of time slots. We denote the set of all available time slots in a meeting scheduling problem by $S = \{s^1, \ldots, s^T\}$, where s^j represents the j-th available time slot.

Attendees of the meetings, including the initiator, are selfish. They have some preferences over the outcomes and attend to their desires without any regard to the preferences of others. Agent i's preferences are captured by a utility function $U_i(.)$, which is a function of five variables:

1. Meeting start time ($s \in S$): We denote agent i's valuation for having a meeting at time t by the valuation function $V_i(t) \in \{-\infty\} \cup [V_{min}, V_{max}]$. The valuation is $-\infty$ when the meeting scheduling fails or when the meeting is set at a time the agent cannot attend. Agent i's valuation for a meeting with length l which starts at time s is the minimum value he assigns to attending a meeting at times $s, s+1, \ldots, s+l-1$.
2. The messages sent in the mechanism (M_i): The agents are privacy-sensitive and prefer not to share their calendar's information with others. We denote by $L(M_i)$ the amount of agent i's privacy which is leaked by sending messages M_i. This privacy leakage adversely affects the agent's utility. We will discuss thoroughly how to design the leakage function in Sect. 4.
3. Number of rounds of mechanism (n): Each agent's utility is a decreasing function of the number of rounds. This is because, the longer the mechanism takes, more communication resources agents need to use in the process.
4. Reward received at the mechanism (R_i): In an incentive mechanism, the agents may give some rewards to others to incentivize them to behave as they want. These rewards can come in the form of points, badges and leveling that can help the agents advance in the future [24]. In this paper, we consider rewards to be convenience points that can be used by the agents to influence the future meeting scheduling processes.
5. Convenience points spent at the mechanism (C_i): This is the number of convenience points that agent i used to influence the outcome of the meeting scheduling process. In general, more points are required to express higher interests in a specific time for a meeting.

Based on the discussion above, we model agent i's utility function in a quasi-linear way as follows:

$$U_i(s, l, M_i, n, R_i) = \delta_i^{n-1} \min_{s \leq t \leq s+l-1} V_i(t) - \theta_i L(M_i) - C_i + R_i, \tag{1}$$

where $\delta_i \in (0, 1)$ is agent i's discount factor by which agent i's future profits is multiplied to find its present value, and $\theta_i \in (0, 1)$ is agent i's sensitivity to his privacy. Agent i's discount factor displays his patience in the mechanism, while his privacy sensitivity represents his attitude toward revealing his private information to others.

Agents' valuation functions and hence their calendar availabilities are assumed to be their own private information. Therefore, selfish agents have to be motivated by a suitably designed incentive mechanism to reveal their calendar availabilities truthfully. This mechanism needs to limit the leakage of agents' privacy, as agents do not participate in a mechanism if it is overly detrimental to their privacy. In the next section, we introduce a privacy leakage function $L(.)$. Then, in Sect. 5, we detail our incentive mechanism that induces honest behavior by all selfish and privacy-sensitive agents.

4   Privacy Leakage

In a meeting scheduling process, the agents care about the privacy of their information. They want to protect the privacy of their respective availability schedules, as well as the lists of meetings they are involved in. Moreover, the initiator who is responsible for scheduling a meeting may not want to share the details, such as the number or identities of the participants, with them before the meeting starts[1].

To satisfy these requirements, we restrict our attention to the following class of mechanisms.

Definition 1. Define by $\Gamma^{1\rightarrow 1}$ the class of incentive mechanisms that satisfy the following two properties:

1. Message passing occurs only between the initiator and the responders, and not between responders themselves. The initiator does not pass the information he receives from a responder to the others.
2. The initiator never asks the reason why an agent is free or busy at a time slot. He also never describes the meeting's details for the responders.

We call this class non-curious one-to-one (NC 1-1) mechanisms.

Restricting attention to this class of mechanisms guarantees that the details of the current meeting, as well as the other appointments or meetings the agents might have, are not leaked. However, in order to find a feasible time for the meeting, revealing some information about the free/busy (F/B) status of the agents is inevitable. In the following, we propose a function that measures the leakage of the agents' F/B information in an NC 1-1 mechanism.

In an NC 1-1 mechanism, no F/B information of a responder is leaked to the other responders. Therefore, the only possible leakage is from the initiator to the responders, and vice versa. Before revealing any information, the initiator and the responders have a prior belief about the F/B information of each other. This belief is based on the previous knowledge they may have about each other. When no such information is available, the belief assigns probability 0.5 to both free and busy status of the others for each time slot.

When a meeting scheduling mechanism runs, the initiator and the responders learn some new information about each other's calendars. This new information

---

[1] This leak of information may enable responders to collude with each other to alter the outcome in their favor.

constitutes a posterior belief about the F/B information of the other agent. The agents' posterior beliefs about each agent i is constructed based on the messages he has sent to them. Therefore, agent i is able to track the evolution of the beliefs.

We define the privacy of a responder i at each instant of time as the distance between the initiator's belief about his F/B status and his true F/B information. The privacy leakage of agent i is the difference between his privacy at the start and end of the mechanism.

To formalize this idea, we denote the true probability distribution of agent i's availability at time slot s^j by $t_i^j : \{F, B\} \to \{0, 1\}$, where t_i^j assigns a probability 0 or 1 to the free (F) and busy (B) status of agent i at time s^j. We have $t_i^j(F) = 1$ and $t_i^j(B) = 0$, if agent i is free at s^j, and $t_i^j(F) = 0$ and $t_i^j(B) = 1$, if he is busy at that time.

At each instant of time, the initiator assigns a probability distribution to the F/B status of agent i for time slot s^j. We denote this probability distribution at the beginning and end of the mechanism by $b_{I,i}^j : \{F, B\} \to [0, 1]$ and $e_{I,i}^j : \{F, B\} \to [0, 1]$, where $b_{I,i}^j(F)$ and $b_{I,i}^j(B)$ ($e_{I,i}^j(F)$ and $e_{I,i}^j(B)$) are the prior (posterior) beliefs the initiator has on the free and busy state of agent i, respectively, at time slot s^j.

Now, to define agent i's privacy before and after running the mechanism, we compare the prior and posterior beliefs with the true distribution. We do this comparison based on the total variation distance metric [8]. For two probability distributions p and q on a random variable $x \in X$, the total variation distance is defined as

$$\delta(p, q) = \frac{1}{2}\|p - q\|_1 = \frac{1}{2} \sum_{x \in X} |p(x) - q(x)|, \tag{2}$$

where $\|.\|_1$ represents the L_1 norm. Using this distance, we measure the privacy of responder i at the beginning and end of a mechanism as

$$Pr_i^b = \sum_{j=1}^{T} \delta(t_i^j, b_{I,i}^j) = \sum_{j=1}^{T} \left| t_i^j(F) - b_{I,i}^j(F) \right|, \tag{3}$$

and

$$Pr_i^e = \sum_{j=1}^{T} \delta(t_i^j, e_{I,i}^j) = \sum_{j=1}^{T} \left| t_i^j(F) - e_{I,i}^j(F) \right|, \tag{4}$$

respectively. The privacy leakage of responder i is the difference between his privacy at the start and end of the mechanism. That is,

$$L_i = Pr_i^b - Pr_i^e. \tag{5}$$

In a similar way, we define the initiator's privacy at the start and end of a mechanism, as:

$$Pr_I^b = \frac{1}{|A| - 1} \sum_{i \in A, i \neq I} \sum_{j=1}^{T} \delta(t_I^j, b_{i,I}^j) = \frac{1}{|A| - 1} \sum_{i \in A, i \neq I} \sum_{j=1}^{T} \left| t_I^j(F) - b_{i,I}^j(F) \right|, \tag{6}$$

and

$$Pr_I^e = \frac{1}{|A| - 1} \sum_{i \in A, i \neq I} \sum_{j=1}^{T} \delta(t_I^j, e_{i,I}^j) = \frac{1}{|A| - 1} \sum_{i \in A, i \neq I} \sum_{j=1}^{T} \left| t_I^j(F) - e_{i,I}^j(F) \right|. \quad (7)$$

The only fundamental difference between (6)–(7) and (3)–(4) is that irrespective of the responders who only communicate with the initiator, the initiator communicates with all of the responders. Therefore, his messages could affect all responders' beliefs. We define the initiator's privacy as the average of the privacy he gets in his communications with the responders. The privacy leakage of the initiator is defined as

$$L_I = Pr_I^b - Pr_I^e. \quad (8)$$

The privacy leakage function proposed above has two main features.

1. This privacy metric takes the possible correlation among an agent's availabilities at different time slots into account. In some cases, an agent has some side information about the pattern of an agent's calendar. This side information could be the length or repeat frequency of his meetings, or the length of breaks he normally has between them. In these cases, the F/B information of one time slot may reveal parts of the F/B information of other time slots. This indirect leakage of information reflects in functions (4) and (7) through the posterior beliefs $e_{I,i}^j$ and $e_{i,I}^j$. This capability is missing in most of the available privacy metrics, such as entropy and information content.
2. The privacy value of each time slot is finite and normalized to one. One of the drawbacks of the logarithmic-based privacy metrics, such as Information content and KL divergence, is that they do not provide any upper bound for the privacy leakage; by using these metrics, the privacy leakage could go to infinity even if the information of just one time slot is leaked.

Measuring privacy leakage with the function proposed above, in the next section we present our negotiation-based mechanism that guarantees truthfulness.

5   A Negotiation-Based Incentive Mechanism

The initiator has some candidate start times for a meeting that needs to be scheduled. The responders have different valuations and availabilities for these time intervals, but this information is not available to the initiator. To extract this information with low privacy leakage, at each round, the initiator offers at least L_{min} start times to the responders and asks them to rate the offers on a scale of 0 to $D - 1$, where 0 means "busy/unavailable", 1 means "Available but completely dissatisfied" and $D - 1$ means "Available and completely satisfied".

Increasing the lower bound L_{min} increases the chance of finding a socially acceptable solution in a shorter length of time, but at the cost of a higher privacy leakage. Therefore, L_{min} is a control parameter that can be used to balance the tradeoff between speed and social efficiency on one side, and privacy leakage on the other.

The agents who rate time slot s at $d \in \{1, 2, \ldots, D-2\}$ attend the meeting at s only if the initiator compensates them for the hardship they endure by giving them some convenience points. Two examples of hardship could be attending a meeting after work hours and rescheduling an existing meeting so as to open room for this one. The agents use these convenience points to rate future time slots. The number of points awarded by the initiator to a responder is a decreasing function of his reported satisfaction d for that time slot, but it is also a function of the satisfaction levels he reported for the other offered time slots. Thus, if a responder announces to be generally more satisfied with the offered time slots, he will get more points if one of his undesirable time slots is selected. This rule is used so as to prevent the responders from falsely reporting low satisfaction levels in order to get more points.

In more detail, the mechanism is a multi-round negotiation, where at each round the initiator offers at most L_{max} meeting start times to the responders. If the number of offers made at round n, denoted by L_n, is greater than or equal to a lower threshold L_{min}, the initiator is permitted to go to the next round and offer some new start times, if he couldn't find a suitable time for the meeting at the current round n. However, if $L_n < L_{min}$, the negotiation ends at the end of round n, independent of whether or not the meeting scheduling was successful. This rule is designed to encourage the initiator to make at least L_{min} offers at each round, if he is able to do so.

We denote the time slots offered by the initiator at round n for starting the meeting by $\{s_n^1, \ldots, s_n^{L_n}\}$. Receiving this offer, each responder should rate each of the offered times $s_n^1, \ldots, s_n^{L_n}$ on a scale of 0 to $D-1$. We denote responder i's ratings at round n by $\mathbf{r}_{i,n} = (r_{i,n}^1, \ldots, r_{i,n}^{L_n})$, where $r_{i,n}^j \in \{0, 1, \ldots, D-1\}$ indicates how satisfied responder i is with starting the meeting at the j-th time slot offered to him at round n.

At each round n of the mechanism, each agent i has $b_{i,n}$ convenience points that can be used to rate the offered time slots. Giving rates 0 and 1 does not require spending points, however to give a rate $d \geq 2$ to an offer, the agent needs to assign $d-1$ points to that offer. We define $N_{i,n}^d$, $d = 0, 1, \ldots, D-1$, as the number of time slots to which responder i gives rate d at round n. Using this notation, the number of points agent i spends at round n to give rating $\mathbf{r}_{i,n}$ can be derived as

$$C_{i,n} = \sum_{d=2}^{D-1} (d-1) N_{i,n}^d. \tag{9}$$

At each round n of negotiation, we must have $C_{i,n} \leq b_{i,n}$.

Let us define $A_{i,n}$ as the number of time slots responder i announces availability at round n. We can derive this parameter as $A_{i,n} = \sum_{d=1}^{D-1} N_{i,n}^d$. We define the total flexibility responder i shows at round n of negotiation as follows:

$$F_{i,n} = \sum_{d=1}^{D-1} (A_{i,n} + 1)^{d-1} N_{i,n}^d. \tag{10}$$

This function gives the decimal value of number $(N_{i,n}^{D-1}, \ldots, N_{i,n}^1)$ in base $A_{i,n} +$ 1. Therefore, a greater value of $F_{i,n}$ means responder i is more satisfied with the time slots offered at round n. Function F is invertible; meaning that for each i, n, given $A_{i,n} + 1$, the vector $(N_{i,n}^{D-1}, \ldots, N_{i,n}^1)$ can be reconstructed from the flexibility $F_{i,n}$. We use this property and represent hereafter, the cost $C_{i,n}$ of agent i's rating at round n by $C(A_{i,n}, F_{i,n})$.

After receiving the responders' ratings, the initiator checks to see if any of $\{s_n^1, \ldots, s_n^{L_n}\}$ is a good time for the meeting. If he finds none of these time slots appealing, he can go to the next round and make some new offers, provided that $L_n \geq L_{min}$. But if he does so, the mechanism doesn't let him go back to time slots $\{s_n^1, \ldots, s_n^{L_n}\}$ in the future. This rule is designed to encourage the initiator to decide about the meeting time as soon as possible. If the initiator neglects a time, in which all attendees are available, and goes to the next round, there is a risk that no other feasible time slots can be found in the future, and hence the meeting scheduling fails. To avoid this risk, the initiator prefers to set up the meeting time as soon as he can.

The presence of all responders at the meeting is necessary. Therefore, the initiator does not schedule the meeting at a time at which at least one responder gave a zero rating. If the initiator chooses time slot s_n^j, $j = 1, \ldots, L_n$, as the meeting start time, he should award some convenience points to the following two groups of responders:

1. Responders who announce they are not completely satisfied with time slot s_n^j. These responders who rate time slot s_n^j at $d \in \{1, 2, \ldots, D-2\}$, must receive a compensation for the hardship they will endure if they attend the meeting at interval $[s_n^j, s_n^j + l - 1]$;
2. Responders who announce complete satisfaction with all offered time slots at round n at which they are available. Although these responders are completely satisfied with the possible choices and will unconditionally attend the meeting if any of them is selected, the initiator gives them a reward to appreciate their high flexibility.

The number of points that must be awarded to a responder i if time slot s_n^j is selected as the meeting start time is denoted by $t(r_{i,n}^j, A_{i,n}, F_{i,n}, L_n)$. This function is decreasing in $r_{i,n}^j \in \{1, 2, \ldots, D-2\}$ and increasing in $F_{i,n}$, when the other parameters are fixed.

To incentivize agents to rate the offered time slots truthfully, we design reward function $t(.)$ such that it satisfies the following conditions:

(a)

$$\sum_{d=1}^{D-1} P(d, A, F)\, t(d, A, F, L) - C(A, F) = P(1, A, A)\, t(1, A, A, L),$$

$$\forall L \le L_{max}, \forall A \le L, \forall F \text{ st. } F \pmod{A+1} > 0,$$

(11)

where $P(d, A, F)$ is the probability a responder with flexibility F who announced availability at A time slots at round n, assigns to the fact that one of the time slots he rates at d will be selected by the initiator.

(b) $t(D-1, A, F, L) = 0$, if $F \ne A(A+1)^{D-2}$.

(c) $t(d, A, F, L)$ is a decreasing function of d for $d \in \{1, \dots, D-2\}$.

(d) $t(.)$ is invariant to shifting of the ratings. That is, $\mathbf{r}'_{i,n} = (\mathbf{r}_{i,n} + c)\, \text{sign}(\mathbf{r}_{i,n})$, where $c \in \{1, \dots, D-2\}$, implies that $t(d', A', F', L) = t(d, A, F, L)^2$.

The intuitions behind the above conditions are as follows. Condition (a) guarantees that provided the agent gives rate 1 to at least one offer, the expected number of points he gets minus the points he used depends only on the number of time slots he reports to be available, and not on the specific ratings he gives to the offers. This expectation is computed based on the agent's belief about the likely effectiveness of his ratings on the final outcome. Condition (b) ensures that a responder who is announced to be completely satisfied with the chosen meeting time receives no reward, unless he rated all the offers at $D-1$. Condition (c) means that the agents who are less satisfied with the selected time slot receive higher rewards. Condition (d) determines the reward for ratings with F $(\text{mod } A + 1) = 0$ and guarantees that the reward function is only sensitive to the relative ratings the agent give to the offers and not on the absolute values. Based on the definition provided in condition (d), we call ratings r and $\mathbf{r}'$ shifted versions of each other, if 1) they mark the same time slots as unavailable, and 2) they differ only by a constant factor in the available time slots.

Theorem 1. For any fixed belief profile $\{P(d, A, F)\}_{d,A,F}$ which is invariant to shifting of the ratings, the system of equations defined in (11) has a solution that satisfies (b)-(d). We say a belief profile is invariant to shifting if $\mathbf{r}'_{i,n} = (\mathbf{r}_{i,n} + c)\, \text{sign}(\mathbf{r}_{i,n})$, where $c \in \{1, \dots, D-2\}$, implies that $P(d', A', F') = P(d, A, F)$.

We present the proofs of all the theorems and lemmas in [4].

The probabilities $\{P(d, A, F)\}_{d,A,F}$ depend on 1) the responders' belief about the number of other people who should attend the meeting, and 2) the initiator's strategy for selecting the meeting start time. At each round n, when the initiator receives the responders' reports $\mathbf{r}_{i,n}$, $i = 1, \dots, N$, he evaluates all offers $\{s_n^1, \dots, s_n^{L_n}\}$ and decides which, if any, of them are suitable to be selected as the meeting start time. Since the initiator is selfish, he does this evaluation based on his own utility. According to (1), the initiator's utility for any start time s_n^j is the difference between the discounted value interval $[s_n^j, s_n^j + l - 1]$ has for him

---

[2] It is clear that by this transformation, we have $A' = A$.

Algorithm 1: Reward Design

---

1 **Initialize** reward function $t(.)$ such that it satisfies condition (c)-(d);
2 $err \leftarrow \infty$;
3 **while** $err > th$ **do**
4 $\quad$ Calculate probabilities $\{P(d, A, F)\}_{d,A,F}$ based on $t(.)$;
5 $\quad$ $t_{new} \leftarrow$ Solution of the set of Eq. (11) that satisfies condition (b)–(d);
6 $\quad$ $err \leftarrow Norm(t - t_{new})$;
7 $\quad$ $t \leftarrow t_{new}$;
8 **end**

---

and the sum of his privacy leakage and the points he should spend to incentivize responders to attend the meeting at that time. This utility would be $-\infty$, if at least one responder cannot attend the meeting at that time. That is,

$$U_I(s_n^j) = \begin{cases} \delta_I^{n-1} \min_{s_n^j \leq t \leq s_n^j + l - 1} V_I(t) - \theta_I L(M_I) - \\ \sum_{i \in A} t(r_{i,n}^j, A_{i,n}, F_{i,n}, L_n), & \text{If } r_{i,n}^j > 0 \text{ for all } i, \\ -\infty, & \text{Otherwise.} \end{cases}$$

(12)

It is clear from (12) that the initiator's strategy for selecting the meeting's time and hence the probabilities $\{P(d, A, F)\}_{d,A,F}$ depend on the reward function $t(.)$. Therefore, for each $L \leq L_{max}$, to derive a reward function that satisfies the set of constraints (11) we have to run Algorithm 1. This algorithm works by first considering an arbitrary reward function $t(.)$ that satisfies conditions (c)–(d). These conditions are weak and easily satisfied. Then it calculates probabilities $\{P(d, A, F)\}_{d,A,F}$ that matches with the selected reward function and updates function $t(.)$ based on equation (11) and conditions (b)-(d). This procedure repeats until convergence is reached. Theorem 1 ensures that the algorithm will never stick in Line 5 because of not finding a solution to the set of equations (11).

We represent the Negotiation-based Meeting Scheduling (NMS) mechanism designed in this section by $\Gamma = (L_{min}, L_{max}, D, t(.))$. The corresponding pseudo-code of this mechanism is shown by Algorithm 2. Briefly, the NMS mechanism starts with designing a reward function $t(.)$ that satisfies conditions (a)-(d) and announcing it to the agents. Then, when the need for a meeting arises, the meeting's initiator starts a negotiation process by offering some of his desirable time slots. The number of offers at each round is one of the initiator's decision variables. Receiving the offers, the responders use their convenience points to express their preferences over them. Then, the initiator evaluates each offer based on the utility it provides to him, considering the cost $\sum_{i \in A} t(r_{i,n}^j, A_{i,n}, F_{i,n}, L_n)$ he should pay to incentivize the responders to participate in the meeting (12). If the initiator finds any of the offers acceptable, he will set up the meeting at that time and terminates the negotiation. Otherwise, he will go to the next round if $L_n \geq L_{min}$.

Algorithm 2: NMS mechanism $\Gamma = (L_{min}, L_{max}, D, t(.))$

---

1 The system announces reward function $t(.)$ to all agents.;
2 **for** *each meeting $m = 1, 2, \ldots$* **do**
3 │   System chooses parameters L_{min} and L_{max} based on the relative importance of privacy and efficiency.;
4 │ $n \leftarrow 1$;
5 │   Meeting start time $s_m \leftarrow 0$;
6 │   **while** $s_m = 0$ **do**
7 │   │   Initiator offers $L_n \leq L_{max}$ time slots to the responders.;
8 │   │   Each responder i rates the offered time slots on a scale of 0 to $D - 1$ as $\mathbf{r}_{i,n} = (r_{i,n}^1, \ldots, r_{i,n}^{L_n})$.;
9 │   │   **if** *Initiator finds any of the offered time slots appealing* **then**
10 │   │   │   A suitable time slot s_n^j is selected as the meeting start time.;
11 │   │   │ $s_m \leftarrow s_n^j$;
12 │   │   │   Initiator awards $t(r_{i,n}^j, A_{i,n}, F_{i,n}, L_n)$ points to each responder i;
13 │   │   **else**
14 │   │   │   **if** $L_n \geq L_{min}$ **then**
15 │   │   │   │ $n \leftarrow n + 1$.;
16 │   │   │   **else**
17 │   │   │   │   Meeting scheduling fails.;
18 │   │   │   │ $s_m \leftarrow \infty$.;
19 │   │   │   **end**
20 │   │   **end**
21 │   **end**
22 **end**

---

6 Properties of the Mechanism

In this section, we show that the NMS mechanism $\Gamma = (L_{min}, L_{max}, D, t(.))$ is faithful. To this end, we need to prove that both the responders and the initiator have no incentive to deviate from their required actions. We prove the faithfulness of the responders and the initiator in Sects. 6.1 and 6.2, respectively.

6.1 Responders' Faithfulness

The responders must have an incentive to 1) participate in the mechanism and 2) rate the offers truthfully. The first property is called individual rationality and the second is incentive compatibility. In the following, we investigate and prove these two properties for the privacy-sensitive responders (the proofs are given in [4]).

Property 1 (Individual Rationality): Individual rationality, also referred to as voluntary participation, is a desirable feature of a mechanism as it guarantees that the agents voluntarily participate in the mechanism. This property is important as agents are not forced to participate in a mechanism but can decide whether or not to participate.

Theorem 2. The NMS mechanism is individually rational for privacy-sensitive responders. That is, each responder prefers the outcome of the mechanism to the utility he gets when he does not participate.

Property 2 (Incentive Compatibility): The NMS mechanism is Bayesian incentive compatible from the responders' view point if each privacy-sensitive responder can achieve his maximum expected utility by adopting a truthful strategy. We focus on Bayesian incentive compatibility, as the agents have incomplete information and hence try to maximize their expected utility. To prove this property we first need to define what exactly a truthful strategy is.

Definition 2. We say that responder i is truthful in the mechanism $\Gamma = (L_{min}, L_{max}, D, t(.))$, if his report $\mathbf{r}_{i,n}$ at each round n satisfies the following conditions:

(I) For each $j = 1, \ldots, L_n$, $r_{i,n}^j = 0$ if and only if the responder is busy at time s_n^j.
(II) The ratings are non-decreasing in the value of the time slots, i.e. $V_i(s_n^j) > V_i(s_n^k)$ implies that $r_{i,n}^j \geq r_{i,n}^k$.
(III) The ratings are as discriminant as possible. That is, time slots with different values get different ratings, as long as both the number of satisfaction levels D and the budget $b_{i,n}$ allow.

Definition 2 provides a formal description of a responder's truthful behavior. In the following, we show that the mechanism Γ is powerful enough to incentivize privacy-sensitive responders to adopt a truthful strategy.

Lemma 1. The privacy-sensitive responders do not have any incentive to lie about their availability, i.e.giving rate 0 to a time-slot is efficient for a responder if and only if he is busy at that time slot.

Lemma 1 proves that condition (I) of Definition 2 is satisfied. In the next lemma, we prove that condition (II) is also satisfied.

Lemma 2. It is never optimal for a responder to give a higher rating to a time slot he likes less.

To prove satisfaction of condition (III), we need the following lemma. This lemma states an important property of the proposed mechanism that is key to proving incentive compatibility.

Lemma 3. It is optimal for each responder i to give rate 1 to at least one offer. In this case, the expected number of points he gets at each round of the mechanism minus the number of points he spends is independent of how he rates his available time slots.

As a result of Lemma 3, when a responder wants to decide on the ratings for his available time slots, he does not need to consider the points; he only needs to consider the effect of his ratings on the selected time slot. This property helps us to prove the next lemma.

Lemma 4. The ratings are as discriminant as possible. That is, as long as the number D of satisfaction levels and the responder's budget al.low, it is optimal for him to give unequal ratings to time slots with unequal values.

Based on Lemmas 1–4, we can state the following main theorem.

Theorem 3. For any L_{min}, L_{max}, and D, the mechanism $\Gamma = (L_{min}, L_{max}, D, t(.))$ where reward function $t(.)$ is derived by Algorithm 1 is Bayesian incentive-compatible from the view point of privacy-sensitive responders.

6.2 Initiator's Faithfulness

In the NMS mechanism, the initiator is supposed to 1) participate in the mechanism voluntarily, 2) make at least L_{min} offers at each round, if he is able to do so, 3) choose a feasible start time, and 4) award convenience points to the responders according to reward function $t(.)$. In the following, we discuss briefly why the initiator has no incentive to deviate from any of the above-mentioned actions.

Voluntarily participation of the initiator can be proved following similar steps to Theorem 2. The initiator offers at least L_{min} time slots at each round to preserve the chance of continuing the negotiation. Since otherwise, he may end up failing the scheduling, while a feasible time slot exists. In this case, the utility of the initiator is $-\infty$ and hence, he does his best to avoid it.

Setting the meeting at a time when some agents are busy is equivalent to failing the meeting scheduling, which values $-\infty$ to the initiator. Therefore, the initiator never chooses a time slot to which at least one agent give 0 rating. The attendance of responders at the meeting is conditioned by receiving the corresponding rewards. Therefore, if the initiator does not award the promised points to the responders, they do not participate in the meeting. This fact prevents the initiator from deviating from giving responders the promised rewards.

7   Conclusions

Using a score-voting approach, we described an incentive mechanism for DisCSPs with selfish and privacy-sensitive agents. Our mechanism is online and can be implemented in dynamic situations where the decision variables and constraints are evolving over time. Moreover, we showed that the mechanism is faithful and can be run by selfish agents, with no need to a central trusted entity. Devising a control parameter, we made the mechanism adjustable to different scenarios in which agents assign different weights to privacy and efficiency. We presented the mechanism via the domain of meeting scheduling, however, this mechanism can be easily applied to a wide range of multi-agent systems.

References

1. Brooks, R.R.: Distributed sensor networks: a multiagent perspective. Int. J. Distrib. Sens. Netw. **4** (2008)
2. Faltings, B., Leaute, T., Petcu, A.: Privacy guarantees through distributed constraint satisfaction. In: Web Intelligence and Intelligent Agent Technology (2008)
3. Farhadi, F., Golestani, S.J., Teneketzis, D.: A surrogate optimization-based mechanism for resource allocation and routing in networks with strategic agents. IEEE Trans. Autom. Control **64**, 464–479 (2019)
4. Farhadi, F., Jennings, N.R.: A faithful mechanism for privacy-sensitive distributed constraint satisfaction problems. Technical report. https://github.com/ffarhadi20/Paper/blob/master/Main.pdf
5. Feigenbaum, J., Papadimitriou, C., Sami, R., Shenker, S.: A BGP-based mechanism for lowest-cost routing. Distrib. Comput. **18** (2002)
6. Feigenbaum, J., Shenker, S.: Distributed algorithmic mechanism design: recent results and future directions. In: DIAL (2002)
7. Gershman, A., Meisels, A., Zivan, R.: Asynchronous forward bounding for distributed cops. J. Artif. Intell. Res. **34**, 61–88 (2009)
8. Gibbs, A.L., Su, F.E.: On choosing and bounding probability metrics. Int. Stat. Rev. **70** (2002)
9. Jennings, N., Jackson, A.: Agent-based meeting scheduling: a design and implementation. Electron. Lett. **31**, 350–352 (1995)
10. Leaute, T., Faltings, B.: Privacy-preserving multi-agent constraint satisfaction. In: International Conference on Computational Science and Engineering, vol. 3 (2009)
11. Leu, S.S., Son, P.V.H., Nhung, P.T.H.: Hybrid Bayesian fuzzy-game model for improving the negotiation effectiveness of construction material procurement. J. Comput. Civ. Eng. **29** (2015)
12. Majumdar, D., Sen, A.: Ordinally Bayesian incentive compatible voting rules. Econometrica **72**, 523–540 (2004)
13. Modi, P.J., Shen, W.M., Tambe, M., Yokoo, M.: Adopt: asynchronous distributed constraint optimization with quality guarantees. Artif. Intell. **161**, 149–180 (2005)
14. Parkes, D.C., Kalagnanam, J.R., Eso, M.: Achieving budget-balance with vickrey-based payment schemes in exchanges. In: 17th IJCAI (2001)
15. Parkes, D.C., Shneidman, J.: Distributed implementations of vickrey-clarke-groves mechanisms. In: AAMAS (2004)
16. Pascal, C., Panescu, D.: On applying discsp for scheduling in holonic systems. In: 20th International Conference on System Theory, Control and Computing (2016)
17. Petcu, A., Faltings, B., Parkes, D.C.: M-DPOP: faithful distributed implementation of efficient social choice problems. J. Artif. Intell. Res. **32** (2008)
18. Pultowicz, P.: Multi-agent negotiation and optimization in decentralized logistics. Ph.D. thesis, University of Vienna (2017)
19. Rosenchein, J.S., Zlotkin, G.: Rules of Encounter. MIT Press, Cambridge (1994)
20. Rubinstein, A.: Perfect equilibrium in a bargaining model. Econometrica **50**, 97–109 (1982)
21. Sen, S., Durfee, E.H.: A formal study of distributed meeting scheduling. Group Decis. Negot. **7**, 265–289 (1998)
22. Singh, D.K., Mazumdar, B.D.: Agent mediated negotiation in e-commerce: a review. Int. J. Mod. Trends Eng. Res. **9**, 285–301 (2017)
23. Teacy, W.T.L., Farinelli, A., Grabham, N.J., Padhy, P., Rogers, A., Jennings, N.R.: Max-sum decentralised coordination for sensor systems. In: 7th International Joint Conference on Autonomous Agents and Multiagent Systems (2008)

24. Thom-Santelli, J., Millen, D., DiMicco, J.: Removing gamification from an enterprise SNS (2012)
25. Yokoo, M.: Protocol/mechanism design for cooperation/competition. In: 3rd International Joint Conference on Autonomous Agents and Multiagent Systems (2004)
26. Yokoo, M., Ishida, T., Durfee, E.H., Kuwabara, K.: Distributed constraint satisfaction for formalizing distributed problem solving. In: International Conference on Distributed Computing Systems (1992)
27. Yokoo, M., Suzuki, K., Hirayama, K.: Secure distributed constraint satisfaction: reaching agreement without revealing private information. Artif. Intell. **161**, 229–245 (2005)
28. Zivan, R., Okamoto, S., Peled, H.: Explorative anytime local search for distributed constraint optimization. Artif. Intell. **212**, 1–26 (2014)

Incentivising Exploration and Recommendations for Contextual Bandits with Payments

Priyank Agrawal[1]([✉])(iD) and Theja Tulabandhula[2](iD)

[1] University of Illinois at Urbana-Champaign, Urbana, USA
priyank4@illinois.edu
[2] University of Illinois at Chicago, Chicago, USA
tt@theja.org

Abstract. We propose a contextual bandit based model to capture the learning and social welfare goals of a web platform in the presence of myopic users. By using payments to incentivize these agents to explore different items/recommendations, we show how the platform can learn the inherent attributes of items and achieve a sublinear regret while maximizing cumulative social welfare. We also calculate theoretical bounds on the cumulative costs of incentivization to the platform. Unlike previous works in this domain, we consider contexts to be completely adversarial, and the behavior of the adversary is unknown to the platform. Our approach can improve various engagement metrics of users on e-commerce stores, recommendation engines and matching platforms.

Keywords: Multi agent learning · Contextual bandit · Incentivizing exploration

1 Introduction

In several practical applications such as recommendation systems (mobile health apps, Netflix, Amazon product recommendations) and matching platforms (Uber, Taskrabbit, Upwork, Airbnb), the platform/firm has to learn various system parameters to optimize resource allocation while only *partially* being able to control learning rates. This is because, the users who transact on such platforms can take autonomous actions that maximize their own utility based on potentially inaccurate information, sometimes to the detriment of the learning goals.

It is well known that users are influenced by the ratings and reviews of previous users provided by the platform while making their purchase decisions on e-commerce platforms. For such settings, it is standard to associate the different products on the platform with parameters (or attributes). Similarly, the users who arrive on the platform can be identified by their preference which we subsequently refer as *contexts*. The true attributes are unknown to both the platform

© Springer Nature Switzerland AG 2020
N. Bassiliades et al. (Eds.): EUMAS 2020/AT 2020, LNAI 12520, pp. 159–170, 2020.
https://doi.org/10.1007/978-3-030-66412-1_11

and the users, however, estimates of these attributes can be learnt as the users purchase products on the platform based on their preferences and reveal their utility via ratings and reviews. Generally, e-commerce platforms are assumed to have complete knowledge of the user contexts, e.g., by users logging into the platform before making a purchase. The most common behavior model of the users is myopic, i.e., they make greedy decisions based on the attributes of different items revealed by the platform. A myopic user's decision based on these attributes can be sub-optimal if attributes have not been learned well enough from previous transactions. Because of the positive feedback loop, the platform's estimates of these attributes may be very different from their true values, leading to loss of social welfare. While users are myopic, the platform tends to be long-term focused, and has to incentivise its users through discounts, promotions and other controls to learn these attributes accurately and increase the overall social welfare.

Similarly in the area of mobile health apps (e.g., for chronic care management, fitness & general health, medication management) incentivization in learning can help the app serve users better, but might get impeded by users being immediate reward focused. Here, the platform typically sends recommendations for users to partake in activities with the goal of improved health outcomes [5]. The quality of recommendations can be high if the platform knows the utility model of the users and their preferences for different activities. To learn these preferences, the platform could devise incentives to nudge the user to prefer a different activity than their currently preferred choice, where the latter is based on current low quality recommendations. If it can restrict the amount of nudging while still being able to learn enough to give good activity recommendations (based on what it has learned so far), then all users will be better off.

In the above two applications and many others, the platform's goal is to maximize social welfare of the myopic users by learning the system parameters just enough to make the best recommendations (or equivalently, ensuring that the users take the best actions for their contexts) over time, when compared to the clairvoyant benchmark of making recommendations when the system parameters are known. The paper focuses on modeling a *principal-agent* variation of online learning in the *contextual bandit* setting that allows the platform (principal) to use payments as auxiliary controls. Typically, the platform needs to give payments (which are costly) since in most practical settings the choices of the users based on current data may not be exploratory enough. Our objective then is to design such payments schemes that allow learning and improving social welfare, while simultaneously not costing too much to the platform.

Contextual bandits, a popular framework to learn and maximize revenue in online advertising and recommendation domains [2,13,17], are problems where users are modeled as contexts (feature vectors) and the learner picks an action tailored to the context for which it is rewarded (bandit feedback). The methods developed here learn the parameters of the reward generation model while simultaneously exploiting current information on the quality of the arms (popular algorithms include EXP4, ϵ-greedy, RegCB etc.). While limited in their expressivity compared to Markov Decision Processes (MDPs) (there are no states), they tend to capture learning problems where the reward for an action (such as purchasing an item or walking for 10 min or standing up) has an immediate outcome (such as a positive utility or a better mood) fairly accurately. While MDPs are also a suitable approach, they are typically harder to learn and analyse theoretically.

Only a few works have considered the principal-agent variations which involves incentivization in learning through payments or otherwise in the recent past. In [3] show that a constant amount of payments is enough if the users are heterogeneous, however, in their setting the platform is aware of the arriving contexts and the distribution from which contexts are drawn. The role of user heterogeneity is further explored in [1,11] as *covariate diversity*. In the former work, the authors consider contexts to be stochastic and prove that myopic arm selection is enough for certain distributions of contexts when the number of arms is two, while in the later, the authors use controlled and known perturbations to the contexts and show that greedy (myopic) selection of arms gives sub-linear regret. In [10], the authors propose a randomized algorithm without an explicit user heterogeneity criteria. However, their technique requires use of ridge estimator to estimate arm attributes leading to unbiased estimates.

A related but orthogonal approach is pursued in [4,9,15,16], where the authors consider principal-agent settings but only allow the use of information asymmetry under incentive compatibility constraints to explore, unlike payments in our setting. A similar setting was also investigated in [8] where they explore various unbiased disclosure policies that the platform can use to explore. In [7] the authors also consider a principal-agent setting, and assuming that the principal knows the distribution from which the contexts arrive as well as that each arm is preferred by at least some contexts, provide regret and payment bounds for an incentivization algorithm (building on their earlier results in [6]). In a vanilla multi-armed bandit setting, the authors in [18] have studied how payments can help explore and achieve sublinear regret.

Main Contributions: First, we propose a contextual bandit based principal-agent model where payments can be used as auxiliary controls to induce exploration and learning. Second, we develop qualitative and quantitative characterization of payments as means of ensuring exploratory behaviour by agents. We develop a novel algorithm and show that the expected aggregate payments it makes in such regimes is sub-linear in the time horizon T. Finally, we compare regret performance and payments requirements of our approach and other competitors on both synthetic and real datasets. We find that the greedy approach with no payments (i.e., the platform does not explore at all) work well with real data, however, there are synthetic data instances where its regret performance is consistently surpassed by algorithms such as ours. Our proposed algorithm works with the most general agent behavior (adversarial contexts), moreover, the payments scheme does not require the principal to have the knowledge of the current context (see Sect. 2).

2 Problem Statement

Users (or agents) arrive sequentially over a period T on a platform V and make choices. The context vector corresponding to an agent arriving at time step $t \in [T]$ is represented as $\theta_t \in \mathbb{R}^d$ (w.l.o.g. assume $\|\theta_t\|_2 \leq 1$). Each choice is represented as an arm $i \in \mathcal{N}$ (with $|\mathcal{N}| = N$), which is associated with a fixed d-dimensional attribute vector μ_i (w.l.o.g. assume $\|\mu_i\|_2 \leq 1$). We can think of each coordinate of μ_i as an attribute of arm i that may influence the user to choose it over the others. True arms attributes are unknown to both platform and the agents a priori, and the platform shows its estimate of these attributes to arriving agents.

User Choice and Reward Model: The user choice behavior is myopic in nature: she is presented with the empirical estimates of $\{\mu_i\}_{i \in \mathcal{N}}$: $\{\hat{\mu}_i\}_{i \in \mathcal{N}}$, corresponding to the arms available on the platform (e.g., via metadata, tags or auxiliary textual information) and then she makes a singleton choice. In this notation, $\hat{\mu}_i^t$ denotes the latest estimate for the arm i available at the time t. She may have a random utility for each arm i, whose mean is $\theta_t.\mu_i$ (an inner product), where θ_t is her context vector. Given these utilities, she picks an arm with the highest perceived utility. In the special case where there is no randomness in the utilities, then her decision is simply $\arg\max_{j \in \mathcal{N}} \theta_t.\hat{\mu}_j$. For simplicity, we will work under this restriction for the rest of the paper. Let the chosen arm be denoted as i_t at round t. The reward accrued by the user is $\theta_t.\mu_{i_t}$.

Feedback Model: Although the platform keeps track of all interaction history, it can only observe the context after the agent has arrived on the platform. The platform computes and displays the empirical estimates $\{\hat{\mu}_i\}_{i \in \mathcal{N}}$ based on the measurements it is able to make. The measurements include the context of the user that arrived and the random utility that she obtained: $y_t = \theta_t.\mu_{i_t} + \eta_t$, where η_t is a zero mean i.i.d. sub-Gaussian noise random variable. The platform estimates $\{\hat{\mu}_i\}_{i \in \mathcal{N}}$ by using the observed contexts and the reward signals for each arm at each time step, most often by solving a regression problem. Some useful notations are as follows: Θ is the $T \times d$-dimensional *design matrix* whose rows are the contexts θ_t. Also $\forall i \in \mathcal{N}$, $S_{i,t} := \{s < t | i_s = i\}$. Further, $\Theta(S_{i,t})$ represents the design matrix corresponding to the contexts arriving at the time steps denoted by $S_{i,t}$, and $Y(S_{i,t})$ denotes the collection of rewards corresponding to these contexts at time steps $S_{i,t}$.

Learning Objective: The platform incurs an instantaneous regret r_t if the arm picked by the user is not the best arm for that user. That is, $r_t = \max_j \theta_t.\mu_j - \theta_t.\mu_{i_t}$. The goal of the platform is to reduce the expected cumulative regret $R_T = \mathbb{E}[\sum_{t=1}^T r_t]$ over the horizon T. Intuitively, if the platform had the knowledge and could display the true attributes of the arms, then the users would pick the items that are best suited to them, and the cumulative regret would be zero. But since the platform does not know the attributes of the arms a priori and the users are acting myopically, it has to incentivise some of these users to explore (based on the history of contexts and rewards generated thus far). The platform does so by displaying a payment/discount vector $\mathbf{p}^t$ in addition to the estimated arm attributes. The corresponding user's decision is $\arg\max_{j\in\mathcal{N}}(\theta_t.\hat{\mu}_j + p_j^t)$. The goal of the platform is to design incentivization schemes that minimize the cumulative regret, while keeping the total payments made as small as possible. We assume all ties to be broken arbitrarily. Hence at each round t, an agent with context θ_t (unknown to the platform when it is deciding payments) arrives on the platform. The platform presents the agent with arm estimates $\{\hat{\mu}_i\}_{i\in\mathcal{N}}$ and a payment vector $\mathbf{p}^t$. The agent makes a singleton choice, thereby accruing some reward. The platform observes the context and a noisy measurement of this reward, and updates its estimates.

3   Algorithms and Guarantees

In this section, we propose a new algorithm (CBwHETEROGENIETY, see Algorithm 1) that uses randomized payments to incentivize agents, enabling the platform to incur sub-linear regret. Essentially we identify a way to adapt and extend the non principal-agent setting of [11] to our platform-user interaction model. One way to reduce the cost that the platform incurs towards incentivization is to work with a special class of contexts (those having *covariate diversity*, see Definition 1), which would provide *exploration* of the arms naturally, leading to learning and low-regret. More specifically, in the contextual bandit setting of [11], the authors assume that a known perturbation (i.i.d. noise) is added to the contexts before they are picked up by the platform. They show that because of this perturbation the power of adversary (in choosing the contexts) is reduced and a myopic selection of arms enjoys sublinear regret (Theorem 1).

In our setting, the choice of context at a given round is purely adversarial and we make no assumption on the contexts. Our key idea is to *use payments to mimic perturbations*. We show that with the proposed payment scheme, *covariate diversity* can be infused into our model, even if the arriving contexts are adversarial. Finally, we bound the expected cumulative payments in our scheme and show that it is sub-linear in T.

Our algorithm CBwHETEROGENIETY is described in Algorithm 1. The key idea is to first generate perturbations that can satisfy the covariate diversity condition, and then transform these perturbations to a payment vector, which is then presented to the user. The user then myopically picks the best action, given these payments (one for each arm), ensuring fair compensation if this choice was different from their original choice. The platform updates the estimates of the selected arm's attribute vector by performing a regression while taking the payment information into account. As we show below, this approach enjoys sublinear (in horizon T) upper bounds on regret and the payment budget.

Lemma 1. *In* CBwHETEROGENIETY *(Algorithm 1), there exists a suitable payment for each arm such that* $\arg\max_i(\hat{\mu}_i^t.\theta_t + p_i^t) = \arg\max_i \hat{\mu}_i^t.(\theta_t^\circ)$ *for all $t > m$ (m is the number of initial forced exploration rounds). And θ_t° satisfies*

Input: Arms: $\mathcal{N}$, time horizon: T, and initial exploration parameter: m.
InitialExploration()
for $t = m + 1$ *to* T **do**
    Agent with context θ_t arrive at the Platform.
    $\{p_i^t\}_{i \in \mathcal{N}} = $ CalcPayment().
    Agent choose arm $\pi_t = \arg\max_i(\hat{\mu}_i^t.\theta_t + p_i^t)$.
    UpdateEstimate()
end
Procedure CalcPayment()
    $p_i^t = \zeta_t.\hat{\mu}_i^t$, where $\zeta_t \sim \mathcal{N}(0, \sigma^2 I_d)$ for all arms.
Procedure UpdateEstimate()
    Updating History:
        $\Theta(S_{\pi_t, t+1}) = [\Theta(S_{\pi_t, t})|(\theta_t + \zeta_t)]$ with ζ_t obtained above, and
        $Y(S_{\pi_t, t+1}) = [Y(S_{\pi_t, t})|(\hat{\mu}_{\pi_t}.\theta_t + p_{\pi_t}^t)]$.
    Updating Parameter:
        $\hat{\mu}_{\pi_t}^{t+1} = (\Theta(S_{\pi_t, t})^T \Theta(S_{\pi_t, t}))^{-1} \Theta(S_{\pi_t, t})^T Y(S_{\pi_t, t})$.

Algorithm 1: CBwHETEROGENIETY

covariate diversity (Definition 1). Additionally, expected payments made by the platform are sub-linear in horizon T, specifically the average cumulative payments are $\mathcal{O}\left(N\sqrt{2T\log(NT)}\right)$.

Proof. First, we make some observations. The platform can offer *negative* payments implying users would incur some penalty if they select certain actions. Hence, the platform can influence the choice of the myopic user by providing a collection of payments and penalties (one for each arm). Enforcing payments as: $p_i^t = \zeta_t.\hat{\mu}_i^t$ where $\zeta_t \sim \mathcal{N}(0, \sigma^2 I_d)$, ensures that the perceived context, $\theta_t + \zeta_t$ at any given round t satisfies the *covariate diversity condition*. Hence, in the proposed payments scheme, the platform pays a random payments vector $\mathbf{p}^t$ where each arm may receive a non-zero value, depending on the estimates $\hat{\mu}^t$.

The cumulative payments for an arm i can be expressed as:

$$Payment(T, i) = \sum_{t=1}^{T} \zeta_t.\hat{\mu}_{i_t}^t, \tag{1}$$

Notice that, $\zeta_t.\hat{\mu}_i^t$ is a sum of sub-Gaussian random variables as $\zeta_t.\hat{\mu}_i^t = \sum_{l=1}^{d} \zeta_t^{(l)}.\hat{\mu}_i^{(l),t}$. Hence $\zeta_t.\hat{\mu}_i^t$ is a sub-Gaussian random variable with the variance-proxy parameter, $||\hat{\mu}_i^t||$. Since we assume that $||\mu_i|| \leq 1$, estimate (in our algorithm) $||\hat{\mu}_i^t|| \leq 1$ as well. Thus we can use sub-Gaussian tail bounds to upper bound the absolute value of the payments in Eq. (1). Consider the following standard tail bound for sub-Gaussian random variable:

Lemma 2. *Let $Y_1, Y_2..Y_t$ be an s-sub-Gaussian martingale, i.e, each Y_j is distributed as mean-0 and s-sub-Gaussian conditioned on $Y_1,..Y_{j-1}$. Then:*

$$\mathbb{P}\left[\sum_{j=1}^{t} Y_j < \sqrt{2ts\log(1/\delta)}\right] > 1 - \delta$$

Thus we bound the sum $\sum_{t=1}^{T} \zeta_t.\hat{\mu}_{i_t}^t$ with probability at least $1 - \delta$ with the quantity:

$$\sum_{t=1}^{T} \zeta_t.\hat{\mu}_{i_t}^t < \sqrt{2T\log(1/\delta)}. \tag{2}$$

In Eq. (2), we apply a union bound to obtain a bound for all arms $i \in \mathcal{N}$ simultaneously with probability $1 - \delta'$, as shown below:

$$\sum_{t=1}^{T} \zeta_t.\hat{\mu}_{i_t}^t < \sqrt{2T\log(N/\delta')}$$

Hence, the cumulative payments across all arms is upper bounded by:

$$\sum_{i=1}^{N} Payments(T, i) < N\sqrt{2T\log(N/\delta')},$$

with probability at least $1 - \delta'$. To realize the final bound we use $\delta' = 1/T$.

We now provide a proof of the regret claim. First, we re-write the definition of *covariate diversity* from [11] as below.

Definition 1. *For any distribution $\mathcal{D}$ with $\zeta \sim \mathcal{D}$ and $\zeta \in \mathbb{R}^d$ and $\theta_t^\circ := \theta_t + \zeta$, for any arbitrary $\theta_t \in \mathbb{R}^d$ such that: (a) if ζ is a "centrally bounded", i.e. $w.\zeta \leq r$, $\forall w : ||w|| \leq 1$ with high probability, and (b) if the minimum eigenvalue of the expected outer product $\mathbb{E}[\theta_t^\circ.(\theta_t^\circ)^T]$ is lower bounded, i.e:*

$$\lambda_{\min}\left[\mathbb{E}\left[\theta_t^\circ.(\theta_t^\circ)^T\right]\right] \geq \lambda_\circ,$$

then, the perturbed context, θ_t° has covariate diversity.

Remark 1. In the Algorithm 1, an agent makes a choice after receiving the payment vector from the platform and hence to the platform, the perceived context θ_t° has Gaussian ("centrally bounded" distribution) perturbation baked-in providing co-variate diversity to the context. Such a condition on the context implies that there is non-trivial variance in all dimensions and intuitively such an arrangement allows convergence of the least square estimator of arm attributes.

Since (a) the payments scheme proposed in the proof of Lemma 1 establishes *covariate diversity*, and (b) in the Algorithm 1, we update history with perturbed contexts, it is intuitive to see that the regret upper bound of Theorem 4.1 of [11] (derived in the non principal-agent setting) also applies here.

Theorem 1. *With an appropriate initial exploration (parameterized by m),* CBwHETEROGENIETY *has the following regret upper bound with probability at least* $1 - \delta''$:

$$R(T) \leq \tilde{O}\left(\sqrt{TN} \log{(TN)}^{3/2}\right),$$

where the notation $\tilde{O}(.)$ *hides dependence on instance specific parameters and* δ''.

Remark 2. Note that for the regret guarantee to hold, Algorithm 1 must have an initial exploration phase, during which the agents are made to play arms uniformly at random or in a round-robin fashion. Intuitively, this warm-start is required to build up robustness of estimates against adversarial contexts.

3.1 Other Payments Scheme and Lower Bound

In the previous section, we established a payments scheme with bounded cumulative cost to the platform that also allowed for sub-linear regret without any additional assumption on the instance or the adversarial choice of the contexts. It is natural to ask the following question: does there exist a payments scheme which is even more frugal for the platform (i.e., costs less) and still ensures sublinear regret? Could there be a principal-agent setting where initial exploration is not needed? The first question has been partially addressed before. In [3], the authors show that only a constant (in T) total amount of payment is required for a sub-linear regret bound. However, in their model the platform knows the distribution of the contexts as well as views the context of the arriving agent before deciding on the payments, this is in addition to the heterogeneity assumption on the contexts, which is equivalent to the *covariate diversity* described above. In [10], the authors presents a randomized algorithm which does not need any initial exploration phase as the exploration is baked-into the randomization. Their scheme, however requires that the agents and the platform maintain the estimate of the arm attributes using a ridge estimator.

In the previous section and in the above works, cumulative payment scales up with instance parameters. We claim that, this is essential if we ought to perform better than a vanilla explore-then-commit strategy[1], as shown in the following lemma.

Lemma 3. *Consider* $\mathcal{A}$ *to be the set of all explore-then-commit algorithms (without incentivization) for the contextual bandit that does not make any addition assumptions on the instance or the contexts. With a restricted upper cap* B *on the cumulative payments budget, no algorithm can do better than the best algorithm in the set* $\mathcal{A}$ *even with an initial exploration.*

---

[1] In a typical explore-then-commit learning strategy, there is an initial pure exploration phase by the end of which the learner commits to a single best action till the end of the horizon T [12].

Proof. Firstly, we make an observation that the best algorithm (denoted by *Alg*) in the set $\mathcal{A}$: it has the best regret guarantee of all algorithms that do not explicitly incentivize by payments and have an initial exploration phase. Consider an instance with two arms and let t be the first round after the initial exploration phase. Let $\hat{\mu}_1$ and $\hat{\mu}_2$ be the corresponding estimates of the arm attributes, visible to the arriving agents on the platform. As the agent arrival is purely adversarial, $\exists$ context θ', such that $(\hat{\mu}_1 - \hat{\mu}_2) \cdot \theta' > B$. Further, if the adversary opts for this context for all the following rounds till T, then incentivizing through payments is fruitless. This is because, the fixed budget B is too less to induce any change to the myopic behavior of the agents. Hence, in fixed budget regimes, *Alg* has the best regret guarantee.

4   Simulations

In this section we compare the learning performance (regret) and payment requirements for our proposed strategy Algorithm 1 and other standard baselines for both synthetic and real datasets. For ease of referencing we name the algorithms as: (1) CBwHETEROGENIETY (Algorithm 1); (2) CBwPAYMENTS (an algorithm in which the platform provides as much payment as required so that the myopic agents choose arms as if they are deploying LinUCB [14]); (3) CBCHAINEDUNRESTRICTED (an algorithm based on the chaining method of [10]); (4) CBCHAINEDRESTRICTED (an instance of the algorithm CBCHAINE-DUNRESTRICTEDwith a fixed upper cap on the total cumulative payments) and (5) NOPAYMENTS (the platform is passive and agents make myopic choice without any influence).

In our first experiment, the contexts are drawn from a multivariate Gaussian distribution with a non-zero mean. We set the number of arms to be $|\mathcal{N}| = 8$, the context dimension as $d = 4$, and the time horizon as $T = 800$, while averaging over 10 Monte Carlo runs (refer to Fig. 1). The NOPAYMENTS strategy, i.e., where the platform has no control on exploration, perform very well and has a sub-linear regret. However, in our simulation studies its performance was consistently surpassed by other algorithms, especially CBwPAYMENTS with Lin-UCB as the underlying strategy. One interesting result (which is also observed in the next experiment) is that CBwHETEROGENIETY has good performance in terms of payments required to ensure sub-linear regret. This reinforces our theoretical guarantees for the same (see Lemma 1, where upper bounds on the expected total payments were stated). On the other hand, LinUCB (implemented within CBwPAYMENTS) incurred large incentivization costs in these synthetic principal-agent instances.

Next, we use the same experimental setup as before, but use a publicly available data set to mimic arm attribute learning: the EEG data set from the OpenML platform. This data set contains 14-dimensional feature vectors with two possible class labels ($|\mathcal{N}| = 2$). We use this classification instance to generate contexts and assign rewards. We standardize the feature vectors as a pre-processing step. Taking the time horizon as $T = 2500$, we randomize the

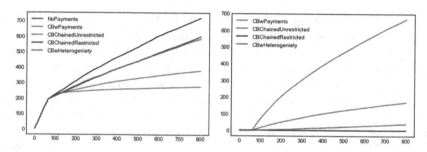

Fig. 1. Left plot shows cumulative regret, right shows the total payments made by various algorithms. In both plots, x-axis is the time horizon and y-axis represents either cumulative regret or cumulative payments made.

arrival of contexts and report results averaged over 10 Monte Carlo runs (refer Fig. 2). Interestingly, the NoPayments strategy performs very well, followed by the payment based schemes (note that our algorithm is quite competitive in this setting and has regret and payment guarantees while NoPayments does not without addtional assumptions).

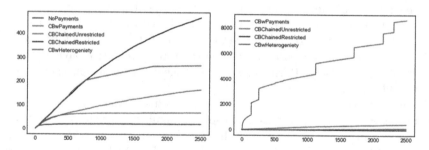

Fig. 2. Left plot shows the cumulative regret, right shows the total payments made by various algorithms. In both, x-axis is the time horizon and y-axis represents either cumulative regret or cumulative total payments.

5 Conclusion

In this paper, we studied the principal-agent variants of online learning under the contextual bandit framework, where a platform sends recommendations and users act on those that are most valuable to them, and the platform can use payments to incentivize exploration and fasten learning.

This paper is among only a handful of recent works which have tackled the problem of incentivization/recommendation in principal-agent settings, hence several fruitful avenues for extending this initial foray remain.

- In Algorithm 1, platform uses payments to infuse heterogeneity in the arriving contexts. It is easy to ensure sub-linear regret with $\Omega(T)$ payments. Similarly, if the allowed regret is upto $O(T)$, the platform does not need to pay at all. It would an interesting problem to calculate lower bounds on payments required for a reasonable regret guarantee.

- It seems to be the case that notions such as covariate diversity may be necessary for unbiased estimation of arm attributes. Hence, a study which ties together the efficacy of various algorithms (including ours) to covariate diversity in the contexts could be an interesting contribution in the incentivized exploration literature.
- Although assuming myopic behavior of the agents is an intuitive modeling choice, it may not cover all the practical possibilities. Hence, extending algorithm design and analysis to situations where the agents are non-myopic, for instance, they are anticipating payments, are partially observed, or are governed by a rich discrete choice model. All these would also be of significant interest.
- More complex user behaviors can modeled if the platform can inform the estimate of each arm's attributes along with their variance. This can better inform the users, especially the ones that are risk-averse.

References

1. Bastani, H., Bayati, M., Khosravi, K.: Mostly exploration-free algorithms for contextual bandits. arXiv preprint arXiv:1704.09011 (2017)
2. Bietti, A., Agarwal, A., Langford, J.: A contextual bandit bake-off. arXiv preprint arXiv:1802.04064 (2018)
3. Chen, B., Frazier, P., Kempe, D.: Incentivizing exploration by heterogeneous users. In: Conference On Learning Theory, pp. 798–818 (2018)
4. Cohen, L., Mansour, Y.: Optimal algorithm for Bayesian incentive-compatible. arXiv preprint arXiv:1810.10304 (2018)
5. Dantzig, S., Geleijnse, G., Halteren, A.T.: Toward a persuasive mobile application to reduce sedentary behavior. Pers. Ubiquit. Comput. **17**(6), 1237–1246 (2013)
6. Frazier, P., Kempe, D., Kleinberg, J., Kleinberg, R.: Incentivizing exploration. In: Proceedings of the Fifteenth ACM Conference on Economics and Computation, pp. 5–22. ACM (2014)
7. Han, L., Kempe, D., Qiang, R.: Incentivizing exploration with heterogeneous value of money. In: Markakis, E., Schäfer, G. (eds.) WINE 2015. LNCS, vol. 9470, pp. 370–383. Springer, Heidelberg (2015). https://doi.org/10.1007/978-3-662-48995-6_27
8. Immorlica, N., Mao, J., Slivkins, A., Wu, Z.S.: Incentivizing exploration with unbiased histories. arXiv preprint arXiv:1811.06026 (2018)
9. Immorlica, N., Mao, J., Slivkins, A., Wu, Z.S.: Bayesian exploration with heterogeneous agents. In: The World Wide Web Conference, pp. 751–761. ACM (2019)
10. Kannan, S., et al.: Fairness incentives for myopic agents. In: Proceedings of the 2017 ACM Conference on Economics and Computation, pp. 369–386. ACM (2017)
11. Kannan, S., Morgenstern, J.H., Roth, A., Waggoner, B., Wu, Z.S.: A smoothed analysis of the greedy algorithm for the linear contextual bandit problem. Adv. Neural Inf. Process. Syst. **31**, 2227–2236 (2018)
12. Langford, J., Zhang, T.: The epoch-greedy algorithm for contextual multi-armed bandits. In: Proceedings of the 20th International Conference on Neural Information Processing Systems, pp. 817–824. Citeseer (2007)

13. Lattimore, T., Szepesvári, C.: Bandit Algorithms. Cambridge University Press, Cambridge (2020)
14. Li, L., Chu, W., Langford, J., Schapire, R.E.: A contextual-bandit approach to personalized news article recommendation. In: Proceedings of the 19th International Conference on World Wide Web, pp. 661–670. ACM (2010)
15. Mansour, Y., Slivkins, A., Syrgkanis, V.: Bayesian incentive-compatible bandit exploration. In: Proceedings of the Sixteenth ACM Conference on Economics and Computation, pp. 565–582. ACM (2015)
16. Mansour, Y., Slivkins, A., Syrgkanis, V., Wu, Z.S.: Bayesian exploration: incentivizing exploration in Bayesian games. arXiv preprint arXiv:1602.07570 (2016)
17. Riquelme, C., Tucker, G., Snoek, J.: Deep Bayesian bandits showdown: an empirical comparison of Bayesian deep networks for thompson sampling. In: International Conference on Learning Representations, ICLR (2018)
18. Wang, S., Huang, L.: Multi-armed bandits with compensation. In: Advances in Neural Information Processing Systems, pp. 5114–5122 (2018)

Emotional Agents Make a (Bank) Run

Konstantinos Grevenitis[1] (ID), Ilias Sakellariou[1]([envelope]) (ID), and Petros Kefalas[2] (ID)

[1] Department of Applied Informatics, University of Macedonia, Thessaloniki, Greece
{mai16028,iliass}@uom.edu.gr
[2] Department of Computer Science, The International Faculty of the University
of Sheffield City College, Thessaloniki, Greece
kefalas@citycollege.sheffield.eu
http://www.uom.gr/, http://citycollege.sheffield.eu

Abstract. Agent-based Computational Economics (ACE) is an area
that has gained significant attention, since it offers the possibility to
model economic phenomena in a more fine-grained manner than other
approaches. One such phenomenon is "bank panic" in which the term
"panic" implies the existence of emotional bias towards to the sudden
withdrawal of deposits from financial institutions (simultaneous bank
runs). However, research towards complex emotional agents in ACE has
not been extensively conducted. The paper employs a formal state-based
model enhanced with explicit emotional states, mood and personality
characteristics in order to describe the agents behavior. A NetLogo simulation of a multi-agent system in a limited economic environment is
attempted in order to study the effects of emotions, emotion contagion
and the role of various players in the genesis of a bank panic crisis. The
aim is to investigate further whether such agent models that are already
used in other areas, such as evacuation simulation, could also provide a
better insight on the evolution of such economic phenomena.

Keywords: Agent based simulation · Emotional agents · Agent-based
computational economics · Bank runs

1 Introduction

Agent based Computational Economics (ACE) is a thriving area of research,
offering the potential to model economic phenomena. Existing conventional
methods are based on mathematical models, which describe a set of definitions and assumptions that lead to proofs of theorems. A number of economists
consider such models too restrictive to address real problems and thus moved
towards other computational alternatives [13]. ACE modelling has been applied
to the same problems, for instance how an economic system reaches an equilibrium. ACE conveys a methodological novelty since the models consist of relatively simple agents that collectively exhibit rich behaviour with the overall
outcome naturally emerging as a result of their interactions. Thus, agent-based

© Springer Nature Switzerland AG 2020
N. Bassiliades et al. (Eds.): EUMAS 2020/AT 2020, LNAI 12520, pp. 171–187, 2020.
https://doi.org/10.1007/978-3-030-66412-1_12

modeling enables the development of macroeconomic models using a bottom up approach [28].

ACE can be applied to a broad spectrum of micro or macro economic systems, where agents can be represented as interactive goal-directed entities, i.e. BDI agents. However, in many economics applications, BDI agents need to be infused with emotions that may affect their reasoning and decision-making. Emotions affect an agent's goals, hence affecting their actions [18], that is common in the real world. In addition, incorporating human aspects such as personality and emotion leads to more believable simulations [17].

The paper aims to investigate further whether emotional agent models, used in other areas such as evacuation simulation, could provide a better insight on the evolution of economic phenomena. Our motivation was to demonstrate the potential of ACE in an emotionally intensive economic phenomenon, namely a bank panic. Thus, the main contribution of the paper is an agent model and the corresponding simulation based on a formal method that supports emotions including emotion contagion.

The rest of the paper is structured as follows. Section 2 presents an overview of the related work in ACE, bank runs and emotional agents; Sect. 3 provides a brief description of the emotions X-Machine model, which was used as the basis to specify the behaviour of agents in the simulation environment. Section 4 describes the agent model used, including the emotional inputs and how they affect agent behaviour, with Sect. 5 presenting the preliminary experimental results. Finally, Sect. 6 concludes the paper.

2   Background and Related Work

2.1   Emotions

Emotions are meant to be short, short term states of mind the individual passively experiences instigated by events or objects [7]. Mood, on the other hand, is used to describe a long standing emotional state. In psychological studies, the emotions that influence the deliberation and practical reasoning of an agent are considered as heuristics for preventing excessive deliberation [4]. Emotions affect an agent's goals, hence affecting their actions. Emotional effects on goals can manifest via reordering existing goals, or by introducing completely new goals. The goals' success or failure can affect emotional states.

In addition to emotions and moods, personality is an important aspect which affects perception and how quickly the emotional state changes. The final factor that is of great importance to communication intensive socioeconomic environments is contagion, i.e. how an agent's emotional state affect another agent's emotional state. All these integrated, make an individual's behaviour completely different from pure rational behaviour in the absence of emotions.

Agents can be potentially enhanced by infusing emotions in their functionality leading to Emotional-BDI agents, i.e. agents whose behaviour is guided not only by beliefs, desires and intentions, but also by the influence of emotions (such as fear, anxiety etc.) in reasoning and decision-making. The existing formal systems for rational agents [20] do not allow a straightforward representation of emotions. However, they have properties which can be inherited in order to properly model Emotional-BDI agents [18].

2.2 Emotional Agents in Socioeconomic Scenarios

Several models for emotions in agent systems have been reported. ESCAPES is a multi-agent simulation tool, that reproduces phenomena on evacuation scenarios, such as an escape scenario at the International Terminal of Los Angeles International Airport [29].

Elsewhere, a Group Decision Support System was developed focused on the negotiation process improvement through argumentation, by using the affecting characteristics of the involved parties [25]. The system uses both personality and emotional inputs in order to select the best arguments to reach a decision. The results revealed that aggressive agents achieve more preferred solutions than negotiator agents.

In [1], another agent based model of the financial domain was introduced; leveraged investors (banks) that used a Value-at-Risk constraint. This constraint was established on historical market data (e.g. asset prices) to predict the portfolio risk. The model took under consideration pro-cyclical leverage (low risk results in high leverage). It was shown that it resulted in endogenous irregular oscillations. This means that when the stock prices were increased the market collapsed. When the leverage was regulated to correct the risk (using a counter-cyclical leverage policy) prices reached a plateau which stabilized the system.

2.3 Bank Runs

A bank run is defined as the situation "where depositors withdraw their deposits from banks because of fear of the safety of their deposits" [12]. The term "bank panic" is often associated with the existence of emotional bias towards a sudden simultaneous withdrawal of deposits from different financial institutions (simultaneous bank runs). Bank runs often appeared in the course of time, such as the Great Depression in the US. The 2007 global financial crisis, has also been characterized by bank runs internationally (e.g., Countrywide Bank, IndyMac Bank, Northern Rock Bank, etc.). To avoid bank runs, several actions have been taken, such as increasing deposit insurance in bank of the US and UK [12].

There have been several approaches in simulating bank run scenarios with ACE. The frequency of occurrence in bank runs has been studied in [27], where panic is spread among agents that focus on the neighborhood influence. The assumption is that different equilibria are likely to be established in different neighbourhoods. The model included synchronization effects which generate bank runs and is based on three important interacting factors which influence the patient agents' strategies (withdraw or wait), the proportion of patient agents (those that wait), the activation threshold and the interaction neighborhood of agents [6]. A similar approach with regards to focusing on neighborhood influence is taken in [26], which showed that the number of bank run incidents decreases with the size of the banks, i.e. number of clients. The work reported in [8] focuses on rumors spreading. The model described is predicated on dynamic rumor-based bank runs with endogenous information acquisition by incorporating bank liquidity uncertainties into a asynchronous awareness framework. The liquidity event triggers a rumor spread and therefore the bank can be exposed to a bank withdrawal. In such a case, depositors can withdraw or deposit at any time for a tiny low transaction cost, or wait so as to totally withdraw, then redeposit if the bank survives. The risk of collapse of a financial system has been studied in [19], which is calculated through an agent based model that suits the microeconomic framework for this economic analysis. In the model, there are heterogeneous agents that interact through two key channels: direct and informational contagion. Results showed that when bank runs are associated with contagion, then an increase in interconnectedness worsens the outcomes. In [11], the probability of bank runs is reported. Even when the economy is thriving, they proposed that agents' behaviour is influenced by non-favorable news and that can cause a bank run. Agents are modelled as rational or irrational with a wide range of learning models. Irrational thinking increases the chances of the system to collapse. An agent-based model for banking analysis is developed in [3]. The model includes agents types (savers, loans, and banks) which inhabit a world divided into different regions. Results showed that banks which are more vulnerable to credit shocks are also more likely to be under capitalized and eventually have to rely on the European Union's Emergency Liquidity Assistance.

Finally, agents behaviour in simulations can be predicted more accurately if artificial neural networks are utilised [11]. Taking into consideration the multi factorial facets of bank runs, the results demonstrate that if the agents are aware of the whole picture of market then bank run incidents only occur when the economy is at an extremely poor state. There exist a plethora of studies related to economic analysis of bank runs but they fall outside the context of this paper [2,5,12,16].

The novelty of the current work is attributed to three factors: (a) our model is not based on a standard definition of a neighbourhood, e.g. lattice, but it adopts a more dynamic notion of neighborhood, one that depends on the spatial characteristics of the simulation platform, (b) our agents do not attempt to liquidify all their assets from the bank but instead their intention is to have enough cash to make them feel secure, i.e. we consider retail depositors agents relying on the assumption that deposit insurance is guaranteed by the government supervision of banks and (c) agents follow relatively complex behaviours and can be easily extended.

3 Modelling Agents Using X-Machines and Emotions

3.1 A Formal Model of Agents

X-Machines [9] are finite state machines that offer an elegant way to compact states Q by allowing processing of a globally available memory structure M. In addition, transitions F between states are each labeled by a function φ (where $\varphi \in \Phi$) that is triggered by inputs Σ and not just input values as in simple automata, i.e. $F : Q \times \Phi \to 2^Q$. Functions φ also take into account the memory values, i.e. $\varphi : \Sigma \times M \to \Gamma \times M$, they generate an output and change the memory values. These characteristics give X-Machines some important advantages for formal agent modeling: (a) models have less states Q, (b) states, beliefs, goals etc. are nicely represented as Q and M,(c) behaviors map well to transition functions φ and (d) the formal model facilitate transformation to executable code but also is supported by a well established theory for complete testing. The formal definition of X-Machines can be found at [9].

In Fig. 1 we show a partial X-Machine model of a rational (emotionless) agent. In this model, three states are depicted ("at the bank", "at store" and "at home"), four functions-behaviors ("withdraw some cash", "withdraw all cash", "go to store" and "go home") and a partial memory structure containing information that will trigger any behavior. For instance, in this particular case, "withdraw some cash" is triggered, which will allow the agent to get the appropriate amount of cash in order to go to the store.

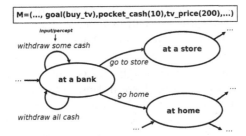

Fig. 1. A partial X-Machine model of a rational agent

3.2 A Formal Model of Emotions

In order to facilitate a simulation of emotional agents, we adopt the formal model of emotions that was presented in [15], extended with a contagion mechanism [23], albeit with minor modifications. In the following, we briefly outline the approach reported in the previously mentioned work for completeness.

The representation of emotions follows the dimensional approach [21,22], i.e. emotions are represented in a two dimensional space [15]. Thus, emotion is a tuple (v_e, a_e), where $v_e \in [-1,1]$ is the *valence* measure, that is how "pleasurable" it is to experience an emotional state and $a_e \in [-1,1]$ the *arousal* measure, representing the likelihood to take some action in the specific state. The tuple defines the *emotional state E* of the agent and will be referred to as the *emotional state vector* of the agent.

Emotional states are subject to change due to *percepts, emotion contagion* (i.e. external stimuli) and *mood*. Thus, there are three stages in computing the overall emotional change in each execution cycle. They all share a similar mechanism for computing the resulting emotional state. The main characteristics of the mechanism is that the emotional state vector shifts closer to the input vector associated with either external stimuli or mood, and the rate of change is regulated by *personality traits* of the agent. The latter allows to represent population diversity in the simulation, i.e. model the fact that some agents might be more receptive to percepts than others.

The emotional effect of a *percept* is represented by a vector (v_{prc}, a_{prc}), i.e. each agent percept is associated with an input emotion vector. Given an emotional state (v_e, a_e) the resulting vector (v'_e, a'_e) is given in Eq. 1.

$$(v'_e, a'_e) = \left(v_e + \frac{f_p^2 \cdot \Delta v}{1 + e^{-f_p \cdot (|\Delta v| - 1)}} \ , \ a_e + \frac{f_p^2 \cdot \Delta a}{1 + e^{-f_p \cdot (|\Delta a| - 1)}} \right) \tag{1}$$

where $\Delta v = v_{prc} - v_e$ and $\Delta a = a_{prc} - a_e$. The personality factor $f_p \in (0, 1]$ determines how quickly the emotion vector converges to an emotional percept.

The contagion model described in [23] is inspired by the ASCRIBE model [10], although simpler, and adapted to the vector representation of emotions. *Emotional contagion* is treated as a form of perception: agents perceive the emotions of other agents in their proximity. Thus, emotion contagion involves computing an overall emotion vector (v_{cnt}, a_{cnt}) based on the emotions of neighboring agents. In order to define the neighbourhood of each agent, it is assumed that agents inhabit a two dimensional world. However, extending the definitions to a three dimensional world is straightforward.

In order to model the spatial characteristics of such a perception, each agent has an *influence-crowd* (IC_i) that consists of all other agents within a radius d_{inf}, i.e. $IC_i = \{Agent_j : d(Pos_i, Pos_j) \le d_{inf}\}$.

Contagion strength w_{ij} (Eq. 2) determines the strength by which an agent j $(j \in IC_i)$, influences agent i and depends on the *expressiveness* of agent j, $expr_j$, a measure of how much the agent manifests its emotions, and the *channel*, that models that closer agents have a larger effect to the emotions of the agent i.

$$w_{ij} = expr_j \cdot \underbrace{\left(1 - \frac{d(Pos_i, Pos_j)}{d_{inf}} \right)}_{channel_{ij}} \tag{2}$$

The overall contagion strength w_i of agent i by all agents in its influence is:

$$w_i = \sum_{j \in IC_i} w_{ij} \tag{3}$$

To form the emotional percept due to contagion (v_{cnt}, a_{cnt}), each emotion contagion vector coordinate is defined as the sum of the corresponding emotion vector coordinates of agents in the influence crowd multiplied by the normalised contagion strength (w_{ij}/w_i):

$$(v_{cnt}, a_{cnt}) = \left(\sum_{j \in IC_i} (w_{ij}/w_i) \cdot v_j \ , \ \sum_{j \in IC_i} (w_{ij}/w_i) \cdot a_j \right) \tag{4}$$

The vector (v_{cnt}, a_{cnt}) is treated in a similar manner as other percepts (Eq. 1), however, the change now depends on the on the openness (opn_i) of the agent i, i.e. how perceptive the agent is to other agents' emotions, and is given in Eq. 5.

$$(v_e'', a_e'') = \left(v_e' + \frac{opn_i^2 \cdot \Delta v_{cnt}}{1 + e^{-opn_i \cdot (|\Delta v_{cnt}| - 1)}} \ , \ a_e' + \frac{opn_i^2 \cdot \Delta a_{cnt}}{1 + e^{-opn_i \cdot (|\Delta a_{cnt}| - 1)}} \right) \tag{5}$$

where $\Delta v_{cnt} = v_{cnt} - v_e'$ and $\Delta a_{cnt} = a_{cnt} - a_e'$, where (v_e', a_e') is the emotion vector computed after the change due to perception (Eq. 1).

Finally, the emotional state of agent is affected by its mood. Mood describes the long term emotional state of the agent, i.e that state in which the agent will eventually settle given that no external stimuli are present. Thus, mood provides the mechanism to model that the effects of a single emotion percept are reduced over time. Change due to mood is given by Eq. 6, where mood is the vector (v_m, v_a), $\Delta v_{me} = v_m - v_e''$ and $\Delta a_{me} = a_m - a_e''$, (v_e'', a_e'') the emotion vector computed in Eq. 5 and d is a discount factor that depends on the simulation model. The vector (v_e^f, a_e^f) is the new emotional state of the agent.

$$(v_e^f, a_e^f) = \left(v_e'' + \frac{d \cdot f_p^3 \cdot \Delta v_{me}}{1 + e^{-f_p \cdot (|\Delta v_{me}| - 1)}} \ , \ a_e'' + \frac{d \cdot f_p^3 \cdot \Delta a_{me}}{1 + e^{-f_p \cdot (|\Delta a_{me}| - 1)}} \right) \tag{6}$$

3.3   A Formal Model of Emotional Agents

The emotional model described above is embedded in an X-Machine model resulting in Emotional X-Machines $^e\mathcal{X}$. The additional component in this model is an emotional structure formalisation E that consists of emotional states ^eQ, moods $\mathcal{M}$, personality traits P and a contagion type mechanism C. In addition, there exist emotions revision functions $^e\varphi$ that given an emotional state, a mood, a contagion model, a personality trait and a memory tuple, it returns a new emotional state. Finally, inputs go through a revision function ρ_σ which given an input transforms it into an emotional percept taking into account the current emotional state, the mood and the personality. The formal definition of Emotional X-Machines can be found at [14]. It should be noted that transitions functions of the original state machine (behaviors) take into account the emotional structure E.

The enhanced model (Emotional X-Machines) allows the description of the behavior of emotional agents which are developed on top of rational agents (simple X-Machines), offering a natural decoupling of the two types. For instance, consider again the partial model of Fig. 1 now extended with the emotional structure as depicted in Fig. 2. Under certain emotional state (e.g. panic due to rumors of financial crisis), the behavior which should be triggered is now "withdraw all cash" and not "withdraw some cash" as it was in the original case.

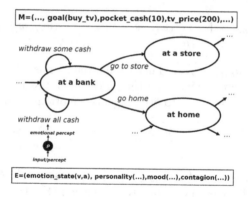

Fig. 2. A partial Emotional X-Machine model of an emotional agent

Emotional X-Machines have been used in a number of simulations involving evacuation scenarios [24]. In this work we focus on economic phenomena, as described in Sect. 4.

4 Modelling Bank Runs

Emotion X-Machines allow for a much richer bank depositor model, than those that have been explored in the literature. The model presented takes advantage of spatial characteristics of agent simulation platforms, since agents are expected to move in a two dimensional space, i.e. the world they inhabit and interact with. This presents the significant advantage of having agents interacting with a variable neighborhood, i.e. the underlying agent interaction links vary with respect to where the agent is located. More specifically, being at different locations during a single 24 h simulation day, an agent interacts with "co-workers" sharing the same workplace, with a *different* set of agents in its home neighborhood, or with *other* agents located in a shopping area. Although the first two sets are invariant during the simulation, since they are fixed at initialisation, the third set al.lows the agent to form ephemeral links with agents that happen to visit the store at the same time. By interaction in this case, we refer to emotion contagion, i.e. the emotional change due the other agents included in an agent's influence crowd IC_i, which is computed dynamically in each time point.

4.1 Environment Setup

Agent movement also allows the opportunity to model the affect of *influencers* in the simulated world, for instance media that spread rumors regarding the imminent bank failure.

By allowing influencers to "move", they interact for short periods with different sets of agents, thus providing a varying perceptual input to the latter. This, we believe, leads to a better modelling of the impact that influencers have to the general population. For instance, in order to be affected by public media an agent could follow some of their broadcasts; since this is not expected to happen continuously during the course of a day, a model should be able to accommodate such an interaction. Additionally, not all agents follow the same media, thus one could model the impact of a highly influential news channels by increasing its number of influencers.

The current model has a very fine grain representation of time, with 15 min corresponding to a single simulation step. Under this assumption, agents stay at their working place for 8 h a day and commute to work for 45 mins (please see Sect. 4.2). Such a fine grain simulation, facilitates experimentation with the evolution of phenomena that occur rather rapidly.

The model simulates a limited part of the economic environment: we consider only retail banks, a market (shops), workplaces, houses, influencers and individual depositors. In this model we are only interested in cash flow and we do not model transactions that occur with electronic forms of money (i.e. credit cards). This restriction of the model was due to the fact that we are concerned about bank panic, i.e. a significant amount of banks failing, a problem that can manifest when depositors withdraw cash for safe keeping at their home. The model has entities that represent:

- *Banks*: Each bank has an initial amount of retail depositor savings (see below) and maintains a 10% fractional reserve in cash. Each retail depositor maintains an account in one of the available banks. Each bank maintains a number of ATMs that "spread" its presence in the environment. It can serve a limited number of customers in each step, thus *queues* can be formed outside banks (a phenomenon common in bank runs).
- *Shops* stand for the marketplace. Shops provide goods to individuals (for the obvious exchange of cash) and at the end of each day deposit their profits to the banks, thus contributing to maintaining adequate cash levels of banks.
- *Influencers*: are agents that move randomly in the experiment world, and "spread rumors" regarding bank solvency. They act as perceptual input to bank depositors, i.e. the latter perceive their presence and form the corresponding emotional percept (see Sect. 4.2).

4.2   Agent Parameters Setup

The main actors are the *Retail Depositors* and we are going to refer to the latter as the *agents* hereafter. The latter have a number of parameters, stored as *memory values* in the corresponding X-Machine:

- *savings* in one of the banks, that is initially set to three times the agent's *salary*,
- the current amount of cash in their *Wallet* (W_i),
- a desired level of cash the agent "feels" safe to have, i.e. its *Cash-Level* (Cl_i),
- a ratio of *Wallet/Cash-Level* ($r_i^{w/cl}$) that determines when the agent needs to withdraw money from the bank.

Obviously the ratio $r_i^{w/cl}$ determines the amount of cash that exist off the system, i.e. cash held outside banks. We define the 10% of their salary as the *Original Cash Level* (OC_i) and initially $Cl_i = W_i = OC_i$.

Agents follow a daily cycle, that consists of an 8-hour working day, after which they return home. When their goods level is low, they visit the market, and when the level of cash in their wallet drops below the threshold $r_i^{w/cl} \cdot Cl_i$ ($W_i < r_i^{w/cl} \cdot Cl_i$), they visit the bank to withdraw money. Agents do not move between locations instantly, but commute so that each transportation requires are least three time steps (45 mins): this allows agent to perceive the status of the environment, as for instance whether a queue is formed in front of a bank, etc. The behavioural model outlined above, was encoded as an emotions X-Machine, with states and transitions depicted in Fig. 3.

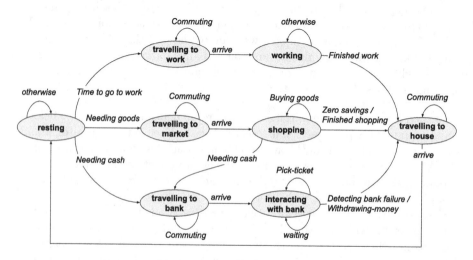

Fig. 3. The Agent state transition X-Machine Model

Following the description of Sect. 3, a subset of the agent percepts is mapped to emotions, i.e. they produce a change to the emotional state of the agent. In the current model, three percepts belong to this subset:

- Perception of an influencer in the agent's proximity, which is mapped to the emotional percept $E_{ifl} = (-0.5, 0.7)$. In the model ifluencers spread negative rumors regarding the solvency of banks and thus cause a negative affect on the agent's valence (value -0.5) and at the same time urge agents to withdraw money from the failing banks (arousal value 0.7).
- Perception of any queues in a bank, mapped to $E_{bankQ} = (-0.5, 0.8)$. Such a perception confirms the negative valence of the emotion attributed to the influencer and further alerts the agent to take some action w.r.t. money withdraw (arousal 0.8).

- Finally, perception of agent's bank failure is mapped to the emotion $E_{bankF} = (-1, 1)$, i.e. the minimum valence and the maximum arousal value, i.e. what could be described as panic.

The above emotional percepts lead to changes to the emotional state of the agent, which affect in the current model, memory values of the X-machine. In particular, the two dimensions of the emotion state vector affect the *Cash-Level* Cl_i) and a ratio *Wallet/Cash-Level* ($r_i^{w/cl}$) of the agent.

Equation 7 shows how the cash level changes with respect to the arousal of the agent. Since arousal measures the incentive of the agent to take action, i.e. withdraw money from the bank, an increase in the arousal coordinate of the emotion vector leads to an increased cash level. As shown in Eq. 7, we define the latter to be at most 5 times the original OC_i, i.e. at most 50% of their monthly salary.

$$Cl_i(a_e) = \begin{cases} OC_i & : a_e \leq 0 \\ (1 + 5 \cdot a_e) \cdot OC_i & : a_e > 0 \end{cases} \tag{7}$$

Valence controls the Wallet/Cash-Level ratio of agents. The rationale behind this choice is that in unpleasant economic situations, agents feel safer if they have more cash in their disposal. Thus, Eq. 8 provides the ratio change with respect to value (obviously lower valence leads to a higher ratio).

$$r_i^{w/cl} = -0.25 \cdot v_e + 0.75 \tag{8}$$

As a final note, the model includes a consumption rate that decreases the level of goods in all agents in every simulation step. The section that follows (Sect. 5) presents the results of our experiments.

5   Experimental Results

We implemented the model[1] using NetLogo [30]. According to our experience, NetLogo can successfully deal with such simulations, even at large scale. We divided the experiments into two phases: (a) experiments in order to calibrate the model, and (b) experiments to show the effect that influencers have on the population. The calibration phase is required to setup appropriate parameters in a state where an equilibrium is achieved, far from any potential bank failures. These parameters are then used in the second phase.

The number of agents is set to 250, the number of banks to 5, with 10 ATMs and 15 workplaces in total. The salary is set to 600 monetary units for all agents. The original cash level for each agent was set to 10% of the salary. As mentioned, each agent has three times its salary as savings in one of the banks minus its cash level.

The personality characteristics of the agents are as follows. The personality factor f_p (Eq. 1), ranges between 0.5 and 0.75, while expressiveness $expr_i$ (Eq. 2)

---

[1] The code can by found at https://github.com/isakellariou/NetLogoBankRun.

and openness opn_i (Eq. 5) have a minimum value of 0.2 with the maximum being 0.4. Agents receive randomly a value within the range mentioned above for each parameter.

5.1   Calibration

In the first set of experiments related to calibration, we expect that the system is in equilibrium, i.e. no bank run event occurs. We set the maximum time period for the experiment to 25 days. The number of influencers is set to 0, meaning that no "bad news" on bank solvency is spread within the simulation world. We test the environment for two cases. The first concerns experiments with no contagion, and as shown in Fig. 4, the system is in equilibrium, i.e. bank reserves are well over the amount of cash desired by the agents. The fluctuations observed are attributed to the fact that agents withdraw money from the bank to cover the needs in market goods by paying in cash, which at the end of each simulation day are deposited by the shops back to the bank. Almost identical results occur for the case of agents interacting under the contagion model described in Sect. 3. Values reported in Fig. 4 are the average values over a set of 10 experiments.

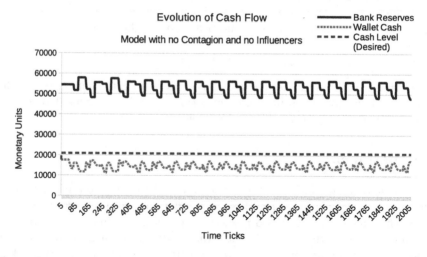

Fig. 4. Experimental results during calibration (No Contagion and No Influencers).

5.2   The Effect of Influencers

Having a set of initial conditions that form an equilibrium, the next set of experiments involves increasing the number of influencers in the simulation world. We consider this number to reflect how strong rumors regarding bank failure are, thus we vary the number of influencers from 5 to 15. Table 1 summarizes the results over a set of 12 runs for each combination of influencers and contagion model, with the column "Failure Rate", reporting the number of experiments over those 12 runs where all banks failed, i.e. the manifestation of the "bank panic". For each set of runs, the column "Simulation Step" reports the time point when the last bank failed with the associated standard deviation. Results, as expected, confirm the belief that stronger bank failure rumors increase likelihood that banks will fail.

Table 1. Bank Failures w.r.t. the number of influencers

	No contagion mechanism			With emotion contagion		
Influencers	Failure Rate	Sim. Step	StdDev	Failure Rate	Sim. Step	StdDev
5	25%	1388.33	414.31	0%	-	-
6	33.3%	1370.25	679.02	16.7%	1271.00	170
7	75%	1088.22	314.50	33.3%	1136.50	158.86
8	91.7%	816.64	171.33	50%	762.83	406.25
9	100%	581.33	58.38	66.7%	848.50	376.51
10	100%	423.50	174.53	83.3%	782.50	491.01
11	100%	393.75	37.01	100%	421.83	37.71
12	100%	293.67	63.88	100%	434.08	98.05
13	100%	309.25	117.43	100 %	343.33	147.51
14	100%	221.92	39.37	100%	301.67	51.53
15	100%	243.83	44.64	100%	269.67	160.23

It is interesting to note that in simulations using the contagion model, the number of total failures (all banks fail) is less compared to no contagion mechanism simulations, and at a much slower rate. Although this appears counter intuitive, it can be explained by the fact that, interaction with neighboring agents reduces the effect to the population, at least in the early stages of spreading rumors, i.e. the effects of influencers are reduced due to interaction among individuals. Recall that according to the emotions model (Sect. 3), emotions induced by influencers and contagion are both treated as percepts, however with a different factor (personality factor vs. openness).

Figure 5 presents the behaviour of agents under emotion contagion, when the number of influencers is 15. Again values reported are averaged over all experimental runs. Note that the desired level of cash increases rather rapidly and thus this leads eventually to banks failing. The steep rise of the desired cash level at the final steps of the simulation is attributed to the fact that once agents learn that their bank has failed, they simply panic, spreading this emotion to other members of the population.

Similar results can be observed in Fig. 6, although the time it takes for the banks to fail is much larger.

It is also interesting to see the time relation between successive banks failures in the world, since not all banks fail at the same time. Figure 7 shows, the average

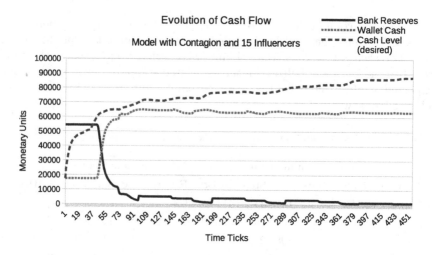

Fig. 5. Experimental results with the emotion contagion model and 15 influencers.

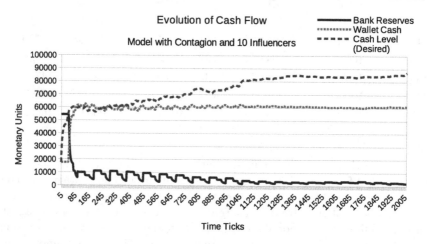

Fig. 6. Experimental results with the emotion contagion model and 10 influencers.

time point of each bank failure in the corresponding set of experiments, i.e. the time point when the first bank fails, the second, etc. As it can be easily observed, experiments with no contagion (labeled as *No-Cont*) fail earlier compared to those with contagion (labeled *Contagion*) for both cases of 10 and 15 influencers, due to the same reasons reported earlier in the section. Another interesting point to note is that when one bank fails, then others follow in a rather short time period, again due to the fact that agents not being able to withdraw money are pushed to a panic state, and this has an effect through the contagion mechanism to all other agents.

Although the present experimental evaluation of the bank run phenomenon is preliminary, it is noticed that a relation exists between strong rumors of bank

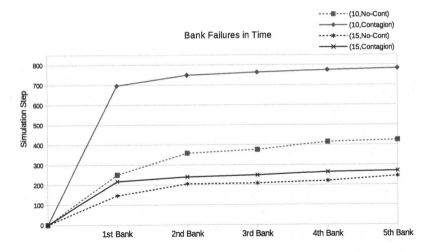

Fig. 7. Bank failures vs. simulation time.

failures incidents and actual bank panic. However, to reach a safe conclusion, a more thorough experimental evaluation is required, one that might take into account more parameters of the system, as for example no-retail depositors and interbank links. However, given the expressive power of X-Machines, modelling more agents, other influencers, global broadcasting models, is not expected to present significant difficulties.

6   Conclusions

Incorporating human aspects such as personality and emotion can be an important research direction for ACE, since it allows modelling of emotionally intensive economic phenomena and can lead to more engaging and believable simulations. The present work attempts, for the first time to the best of our knowledge, to use a formal emotional agent model towards a simulation of bank panic, a phenomenon that is often associated with the emotional state of involved stakeholders. In that direction, the paper presents an emotions X-Machine model, together with an implementation in a well known simulation platform. The experimental results confirm that a relation exists between public opinion influencers (e.g. public media) and the manifestation of such phenomena.

There are a number of research directions towards which this work can be extended. These include a more in-depth analysis of the current experimental model and adding different types of stakeholders in the domain, such as government officials. Finally, it is interesting to build a more complete model of the banking system and include a wider range of economic activities, such as inter-bank links and strategic investors. In all cases, we believe the introduction of formal emotional agent modelling could provide ACE with a set of tools that can increase its potential.

References

1. Aymanns, C., Farmer, J.D.: The dynamics of the leverage cycle. J. Econ. Dyn. Control **50**, 155–179 (2015). https://doi.org/10.1016/j.jedc.2014.09.015

2. Brown, M., Trautmann, S.T., Vlahu, R.: Understanding bank-run contagion. Technical report, European Central Bank (2014). https://www.ecb.europa.eu/pub/pdf/scpwps/ecbwp1711.pdf

3. Chan-Lau, J.A.: ABBA: an agent-based model of the banking system. IMF Working Papers 17/136, International Monetary Fund (2017). https://ideas.repec.org/p/imf/imfwpa/17-136.html

4. Damasio, A.R.: Descartes Error: Emotion, Reason, and the Human Brain. G.P. Putnam, New York (1994)

5. Davis, D.D., Reilly, R.J.: On freezing depositor funds at financially distressed banks: an experimental analysis. J. Money Credit Bank. **48**(5), 989–1017 (2016). https://doi.org/10.1111/jmcb.12324

6. Deng, J., Yu, T., Li, H.: Bank runs in a local interaction model. Phys. Procedia **3**(5), 1687–1697 (2010). https://doi.org/10.1016/j.phpro.2010.07.007

7. Fridja, N.: The psychologists' point of view. In: Lewis, M., Haviland-Jones, J., Feldman-Barrett, L. (eds.) Handbook of Emotions, 3rd edn., pp. 68–87. The Guildford Press, New York (2008). https://hdl.handle.net/11245/1.295660

8. He, Z., Manela, A.: Information acquisition in rumor' based bank runs. J. Financ. **71**(3), 1113–1158 (2016). https://doi.org/10.1111/jofi.12202

9. Holcombe, M., Ipate, F.: The theory of x-machines. In: Correct Systems: Building a Business Process Solution, pp. 135–168. Springer, London (1998). https://doi.org/10.1007/978-1-4471-3435-0_6

10. Hoogendoorn, M., Treur, J., Wal, C., Wissen, A.: Modelling the interplay of emotions, beliefs and intentions within collective decision making based on insights from social neuroscience. In: Neural Information Processing: Theory and Algorithms, LNCS, vol. 6443, pp. 196–206. Springer, Berlin Heidelberg (2010). https://doi.org/10.1007/978-3-642-17537-4_25

11. Huang, W., Huang, Q.: Connectionist agent-based learning in bank-run decision making. Chaos Interdisc. J. Nonlinear Sci. **28**(5), 055910 (2018). https://doi.org/10.1063/1.5022222

12. Iyer, R., Puri, M.: Understanding bank runs: the importance of depositor-bank relationships and networks. Am. Econ. Rev. **102**(4), 1414–1445 (2012). https://doi.org/10.1257/aer.102.4.1414

13. Judd, K.L.: Chapter 17 Computationally intensive analyses in economics. In: Handbook of Computational Economics, pp. 881–893. Elsevier (2006). https://doi.org/10.1016/s1574-0021(05)02017-4

14. Kefalas, P., Sakellariou, I., Basakos, D., Stamatopoulou, I.: A formal approach to model emotional agents behaviour in disaster management situations. In: Likas, A., Blekas, K., Kalles, D. (eds.) SETN 2014. LNCS (LNAI), vol. 8445, pp. 237–250. Springer, Cham (2014). https://doi.org/10.1007/978-3-319-07064-3_19

15. Kefalas, P., Sakellariou, I., Savvidou, S., Stamatopoulou, I., Ntika, M.: The role of mood on emotional agents behaviour. In: Nguyen, N.-T., Manolopoulos, Y., Iliadis, L., Trawiński, B. (eds.) ICCCI 2016. LNCS (LNAI), vol. 9875, pp. 53–63. Springer, Cham (2016). https://doi.org/10.1007/978-3-319-45243-2_5

16. Kiss, H.J., Rodriguez-Lara, I., Rosa-García, A.: Do social networks prevent or promote bank runs? J. Econ. Behav. Organ. **101**, 87–99 (2014). https://doi.org/10.1016/j.jebo.2014.01.019

17. Padgham, L., Taylor, G.: A system for modelling agents having emotion and personality. In: Cavedon, L., Rao, A., Wobcke, W. (eds.) IAS 1996. LNCS, vol. 1209, pp. 59–71. Springer, Heidelberg (1997). https://doi.org/10.1007/3-540-62686-7_28

18. Pereira, D., Oliveira, E., Moreira, N.: Formal modelling of emotions in BDI agents. In: Sadri, F., Satoh, K. (eds.) CLIMA 2007. LNCS (LNAI), vol. 5056, pp. 62–81. Springer, Heidelberg (2008). https://doi.org/10.1007/978-3-540-88833-8_4

19. Provenzano, D.: Contagion and bank runs in a multi-agent financial system. In: Teglio, A., Alfarano, S., Camacho-Cuena, E., Ginés-Vilar, M. (eds.) Managing Market Complexity: The Approach of Artificial Economics, pp. 27–38. LNE, Springer, Berlin, Heidelberg (2013). https://doi.org/10.1007/978-3-642-31301-1_3

20. Rao, A.S., Georgeff, M.P.: Modeling rational agents within a BDI-architecture. In: Principles of Knowledge Representation and Reasoning. Proceedings of the second International Conference. pp. 473–484. Morgan Kaufmann, San Mateo (1991). https://doi.org/10.5555/3087158.3087205

21. Russell, J.A.: A circumplex model of affect. J. Pers. Soc. Psychol. **39**(6), 1161–1178 (1980). https://doi.org/10.1037/h0077714

22. Russell, J.A.: Core affect and the psychological construction of emotion. Psychol. Rev. **110**(1), 145–172 (2003). https://doi.org/10.1037/0033-295X.110.1.145

23. Sakellariou, I., Kefalas, P., Savvidou, S., Stamatopoulou, I., Ntika, M.: The role of emotions, mood, personality and contagion in multi-agent system decision making. In: Iliadis, L., Maglogiannis, I. (eds.) AIAI 2016. IAICT, vol. 475, pp. 359–370. Springer, Cham (2016). https://doi.org/10.1007/978-3-319-44944-9_31

24. Sakellariou, I., Kefalas, P., Stamatopoulou, I.: Evacuation simulation through formal emotional agent based modelling. In: Duval, B., van den Herik, H.J., Loiseau, S., Filipe, J. (eds.) ICAART 2014 - Proceedings of the 6th International Conference on Agents and Artificial Intelligence, vol. 2, ESEO, Angers, Loire Valley, France, 6–8 March, 2014, pp. 193–200. SciTePress (2014). https://doi.org/10.5220/0004824601930200

25. Santos, R., Marreiros, G., Ramos, C., Neves, J., Bulas-Cruz, J.: Personality, emotion, and mood in agent-based group decision making. IEEE Intell. Syst. **26**(6), 58–66 (2011). https://doi.org/10.1109/mis.2011.92

26. dos Santos, T., Nakane, M.: Dynamic bank runs: an agent-based approach. Working Papers Series 465, Central Bank of Brazil, Research Department (2017). https://EconPapers.repec.org/RePEc:bcb:wpaper:465

27. Shi, S., Temzelides, T.: A model of bureaucracy and corruption. Int. Econ. Rev. **45**(3), 873–908 (2004). https://doi.org/10.1111/j.0020-6598.2004.00290.x

28. Tesfatsion, L.: Chapter 16 agent-based computational economics: a constructive approach to economic theory. In: Tesfatsion, L., Judd, K. (eds.) Handbook of Computational Economics, vol. 2, pp. 831–880. Elsevier (2006). https://doi.org/10.1016/s1574-0021(05)02016-2

29. Tsai, J., et al.: Escapes - evacuation simulation with children, authorities, parents, emotions, and social comparison. In: AAMAS 2011: The Tenth International Conference on Autonomous Agents and Multiagent System, vol. 2, pp. 457–464. ACM Digital Library, New York, New York, United States (2011). https://dl.acm.org/doi/abs/10.5555/2031678.2031682

30. Wilensky, U.: NetLogo (1999). http://ccl.northwestern.edu/netlogo/. Center for Connected Learning and Computer-Based Modeling, Northwestern University, Evanston, IL

EUMAS 2020 Session 3: Autonomous Agents

An Interface for Programming Verifiable Autonomous Agents in ROS

Rafael C. Cardoso$^{(\boxtimes)}$ (ID), Angelo Ferrando(ID), Louise A. Dennis(ID),
and Michael Fisher(ID)

Department of Computer Science, The University of Manchester, Manchester, UK
{rafael.cardoso,angelo.ferrando,louise.dennis,
michael.fisher}@manchester.ac.uk

Abstract. Autonomy has been one of the most desirable features for robotic applications in recent years. This is evidenced by a recent surge of research in autonomous driving cars, strong government funding for research in robotics for extreme environments, and overall progress in service robots. Autonomous decision-making is often at the core of these systems, thus, it is important to be able to verify and validate properties that relate to the correct behaviour that is expected of the system. Our main contribution in this paper, is an interface for integrating BDI-based agents into robotic systems developed using ROS. We use the GWENDOLEN language to program our BDI agents and to make use of the AJPF model checker in order to verify properties related to the decision-making in the agent programs. Our case studies include 3D simulations using a simple autonomous patrolling behaviour of a TurtleBot, and multiple TurtleBots servicing a house that can cooperate with each other in case of failure.

Keywords: Autonomous agents · High-level decision-making · Robotic applications · ROS · Model checking

1 Introduction

Belief-Desire-Intention (BDI) [13] agents has been the standard paradigm for agent programming languages over the years. These mental attitudes represent, respectively, the information, motivational, and deliberative states of the agent. Incoming perceptions from the environment can trigger the update of the *belief* base (what the agent believes to be true about its environment and other agents). This update generates more goal options and updates the *desire* base (the desired states that the agent hopes to achieve) accordingly. Finally, given the updated belief and desire base, the *intention* base (a sequence of actions that an agent

---

Work supported by UK Research and Innovation, and EPSRC Hubs for "Robotics and AI in Hazardous Environments": EP/R026092 (FAIR-SPACE), EP/R026173 (ORCA), and EP/R026084 (RAIN).

© Springer Nature Switzerland AG 2020
N. Bassiliades et al. (Eds.): EUMAS 2020/AT 2020, LNAI 12520, pp. 191–205, 2020.
https://doi.org/10.1007/978-3-030-66412-1_13

wants to carry out in order to achieve a desired state) is updated and one intention is chosen to be executed.

There are many agent programming languages that are based on BDI, such as GWENDOLEN [6], Jason [1], 2APL [4], GOAL [9], and more recently ASTRA [2]. Such languages would be ideal for controlling high-level decision-making in autonomous robots. However, despite the various choices in agent languages, there is still a lack of robotic applications that make use of them. Past attempts usually try to mimic or implement their own BDI representation inside of their robotic application, such as in [8]. These attempts are often domain-specific or depend on specific versions of software to work. Moreover, they usually lack any means of verifying the high-level decision-making component of the system.

In this paper, we introduce an interface for the GWENDOLEN agent programming language to communicate with the Robot Operating System (ROS) [11]. This interface allows agent programs to send commands to a robot's actuators and receive feedback from the robot and its sensors. We use GWENDOLEN due to its association with the Agent Java PathFinder (AJPF) [7] model checker. AJPF is an extension of JPF [15], a model-checker that works directly on Java program code instead of on a mathematical model of the program's execution. This extension allows for formal verification of agent programs by providing a property specification language based in Linear-time Temporal Logic that supports the description of terms usually found in BDI agents.

We validate our interface through its practical use in two case studies using the Gazebo 3D simulator, chosen for its association with ROS and its realistic physics plugins. In our first scenario, an agent autonomously controls a TurtleBot3 to keep patrolling four waypoints in a map indefinitely. Our second scenario expands to three agents, each controlling its own TurtleBot3, in a home environment where the agents can cooperate to deliver items throughout the house. Although we focus on GWENDOLEN in this paper, our interface can be used with any AgentSpeak(L) [12] based-language that is implemented in Java.

The remainder of this paper is organised as follows. The next section contains basic concepts about ROS that are used throughout the paper. In Sect. 3, we describe how our interface can be used to allow autonomous agents programs that are capable of performing high-level decision-making in robots that use ROS. Section 4 has two case studies that show our interface in use: a single-agent patrolling a simple environment, and three agents cooperating in a home environment. In Sect. 5, related approaches that combine autonomous agents with robots and/or provide any means of verifying decision-making in robots are presented. We conclude the paper in Sect. 6.

2   Background

ROS [11] is an open-source set of software libraries and tools to develop robotic applications. We chose it because of its modularity, its large community of users, and its compatibility with a variety of robots. ROS applications follow a node-based structure. Each robot inside ROS can be defined as a set of nodes, and each node handles a specific aspect. For example, we can have nodes fetching data from sensors, sending commands to actuators, or even focused on evaluations and computations to support the other nodes in the system.

ROS nodes are inherently distributed and the entire information sharing is obtained through message passing. This simplifies the internal logic of each single node, and allows a natural distribution of the workload on multiple machines (common in cyber-physical systems). When a node enters the system, in order to communicate with the other nodes, it has to register with ROS Master. The ROS Master is a special node which keeps track of the nodes registered in the system, and enables the communication among them, as shown in Fig. 1.

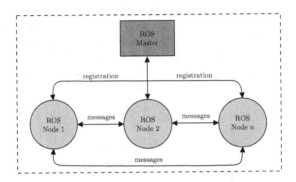

Fig. 1. ROS general structure.

When a node registers to the ROS Master, it has to specify the *topics* for which it is a publisher or a subscriber. A topic in ROS can be seen as a communication channel used by the nodes to exchange information. Each node can be a *publisher*: able to send messages on the channel; or a *subscriber*: able to receive messages from the channel. In Fig. 2 an example with one publisher and two subscribers is shown. For each topic, the ROS Master keeps track of the nodes that are publishing on it. When a new subscriber node registers to the ROS Master, the ROS Master enables peer-to-peer communication between the subscriber node and all the nodes publishing on the requested topic. The ROS Master is involved only at this initial stage. After it, all the consecutive communications are performed directly among the involved nodes. This communication is one-way from (one or more) publishers to (one or more) subscribers.

Communication using topics is flexible, but also many-to-many. It is appropriate when the nodes have to continuously update the system, such as in the case of sensors. When a node wants to make a request to another node (one-to-one), and it expects a response (the result) from it, then using *services* is more appropriate. A node can offer one or multiple services, and each service is specified through its name, and a pair of messages representing its input and output. When a node needs a service, it has to send a message (the message request) to the service (identified by its name) and wait for the response.

Fig. 2. ROS example communication through topics.

Services are synchronous, which can be a problem when the task assigned to the service requires a long time to be completed, or when the requesting node needs to cancel the request. In these cases, the *action library* can be used (Fig. 3), allowing the creation of servers that can accept long-running requests (called goals), and clients that can cancel the execution at any time and receive feedback (intermediate results) dynamically until the goal is completed and the final result is available.

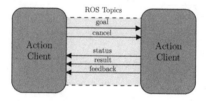

Fig. 3. Action library.

3   Integrating Autonomous Agents with ROS

In this section we describe an interface[1] that can be used to integrate autonomous agents with ROS using the *rosbridge* library. While we use the GWENDOLEN language in our examples and case studies, we note that any agent programming language that uses Java would be able to benefit from our interface. For instance, we have also tested using the Jason [1] language.[2] However, in this paper we focus on the GWENDOLEN language, particularly due to its association with the AJPF model checker, which enables us to verify properties of the agent's program.

---

[1] GWENDOLEN interface source code is available at: https://github.com/autonomy-and-verification-uol/gwendolen-rosbridge.

[2] Jason interface source code is available at: https://github.com/rafaelcaue/jason-rosbridge.

3.1   Connecting to *Rosbridge*

Rosbridge is a library for ROS that allows external programs to communicate with ROS [3]. This is easily achieved through message passing using the JSON format. A message sent from a ROS node to an external program passes through the *rosbridge* node, which translates the message to JSON and then publishes the message to the appropriate topic that the external program is listening to. Conversely, a message sent (in JSON format) from an external program to a ROS node is received by the *rosbridge* node, translated from JSON to ROS messages, and then published to the appropriate topic.

The *rosbridge* library does not alter ROS in any way, it simply provides a ROS API for non-ROS programs. Thus, it is programming language and transport agnostic, making it easy to integrate any external program with ROS, as long as messages are sent in the JSON format. Another advantage of *rosbridge* is that it does not alter ROS core functions in any way, therefore it requires minimal to no changes between new ROS versions. This, in turn, makes external programs agnostic of ROS versions, as long as the ROS message structure remains unchanged from the original version.

Our interface is implemented as a GWENDOLEN environment. It connects to *rosbridge* using the WebSocket protocol, as shown in Listing 1. First the bridge object is instantiated, and then, once the environment starts it attempts to connect to *rosbridge* using the *rosbridge* server URI (localhost in this example) with the default port 9090 (this can be changed in the ROS launch file of *rosbridge*). The second parameter is a flag that determines if the call should be blocked until the connection is established.

```
1    public class RosEnv extends DefaultEnvironment {
2       RosBridge bridge = new RosBridge();
3       public RosEnv() {
4          bridge.connect("ws://localhost:9090", true);
5       }
6    }
```

Listing 1: Sample environment code in GWENDOLEN for connecting to *rosbridge*.

The translation of a message from Java to JSON is done automatically, however the message still has to be defined in Java with the appropriate data types that relate to the data types specified in the ROS message. New message types only have to be defined once, and if added to the interface JAR can then be used subsequently by any program.

3.2   Subscribing

Agents can subscribe to ROS topics through the environment. The subscription is completely transparent to the agent. Perceptions are generated by the environment as messages are published in the subscribed topic. Subscribers can be defined in the constructor method for the environment, or can be declared later on. An example of a subscriber definition in the environment is shown in Listing 2. We make use of the **bridge** object to subscribe to the topic called

"/ros_to_java", where we need to set the ROS message type (with the full type "std_msgs/String"), however the other fields are optional and work the same way as when declaring subscribers in ROS.

```
1    bridge.subscribe(SubscriptionRequestMsg.generate("/ros_to_java")
2       .setType("std_msgs/String")
3       .setThrottleRate(1)
4       .setQueueLength(1),
5       new RosListenDelegate() {
6          public void receive(JsonNode data, String stringRep) {
7          MessageUnpacker<PrimitiveMsg<String>> unpacker =
8             new MessageUnpacker<PrimitiveMsg<String>>(PrimitiveMsg.class);
9          PrimitiveMsg<String> msg = unpacker.unpackRosMessage(data);
10         System.out.println(msg.data);
11         }
12      }
13   );
```

Listing 2: Creating a subscriber in the interface.

Each subscriber has a `receive` method that unpacks the message (this time using the message type as defined in the interface, $PrimitiveMsg<String>$). In this example we simply print the data contents of the message. The case studies shown in the next section cover how to translate the contents of a message into perceptions to be sent to the agent.

It is important to note that messages coming from ROS to the agent usually originate from sensors, which depending on the frequency that is being published could overload the belief base of an agent. This is a known problem in using autonomous agents in robots, and the solution is to either change the frequency to an acceptable value or to apply a filter. The filter can be applied directly to the ROS code of the sensor, to the `receive` method in our interface, or to the belief base revision of the agent. We conjecture that the first would be the most efficient computationally, the second can be easier to change and adapt, and the third is the most difficult since it requires changes to the source code of the language being used.

3.3   Publishing

An agent can publish a message to a ROS topic through actions in its environment. Most agent programming languages delegate the action description to the environment. As such, the code for the environment usually contains a section for describing these actions. In the GWENDOLEN language this occurs inside the `executeAction` method, which is activated when an agent prompts a new action. For example (Listing 3), if we want to add an action called `hello_ros` to the environment, we simply have to match the name of the action received (`actionname`) to the name of the action (a string) we want to deal with.

```
1    public Unifier executeAction(String agName, Action act) throws AILexception {
2        String actionname = act.getFunctor();
3        if (actionname.equals("hello_ros")) {
4            hello_ros();
5        }
6        return super.executeAction(agName, act);
7    }
```

Listing 3: Execute action environment in GWENDOLEN.

We specify the `hello_ros` action that was called in Listing 3 as a method, described in Listing 4. In this method, since we want to send a message to a ROS topic we have to create a new publisher. The first parameter is the topic that the message will be published to (*"/java_to_ros"*), the second parameter is the ROS type of the message (*"std_msgs/String"*), and the third is the `bridge` object. In this example, once the agent calls the `hello_ros` action a string message is published on the *"/java_to_ros"* topic each 500 ms, up to a total of 100 messages. Note that to publish a message it is necessary to associate it with the correct type as defined in the interface, $PrimitiveMsg{<}String{>}$ in this case.

```
1    public void hello_ros() {
2        Publisher pub = new Publisher("/java_to_ros", "std_msgs/String", bridge);
3        for(int i = 0; i < 100; i++) {
4            pub.publish(new PrimitiveMsg<String>("hello from gwendolen " + i));
5            try {
6                Thread.sleep(500);
7            } catch (InterruptedException e) {
8                e.printStackTrace();
9            }
10       }
11   }
```

Listing 4: Creating a publisher in the interface.

4 Case Studies

To validate our interface we have applied it to two different scenarios[3] and have verified certain properties about the behaviour of the agents. In the first scenario, the autonomous agent decides the order to visit waypoints in order to patrol an area. The second scenario has three agents, each controlling its own TurtleBot3 to service several rooms in a home environment.

All of our case studies were simulated using ROS and the Gazebo 3D simulator. Our simulations were performed in both Kinetic and Melodic versions of ROS. We have used the 2019 release of MCAPL (Model-checking Agent Programming Languages) [5], which includes the GWENDOLEN agent language and the AJFP program model checker.

---

[3] Source code of both scenarios are available at: https://github.com/autonomy-and-verification-uol/gwendolen-ros-turtlebot3.

4.1   TurtleBot Autonomous Patrolling

We use a TurtleBot3 to patrol around four different locations in an environment, illustrated in Fig. 4. The robot can start at any point inside the map, however it must patrol the designated waypoints in order (A → B → C → D → A → ...). The robot starts with a complete map of the area, and uses the *move_base* library to move to specific coordinates in the map while avoiding obstacles.

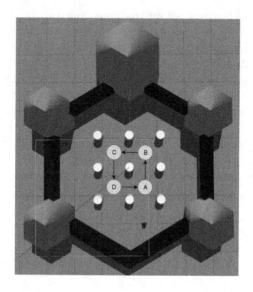

Fig. 4. TurtleBot autonomous patrolling simulated in Gazebo.

Move base is an action library, and as such it has a server that executes actions and a client that requests actions. While our agents cannot serve directly as clients due to the communication barrier between ROS and external programs, the agents can publish a message through the interface and rosbridge, which is received by a ROS node for the move base client. This client can then process the message and create a new request for the move base server.

Agent Implementation. A plan in GWENDOLEN is started by an *event*, for example, a plan for completing a goal *patrol(a)* is activated when the goal (!) *patrol(a)* is added (+); this is known as a goal addition event. The plan will be selected and added to the agent's intention base if the formulae present in the *guard* (i.e. the context or precondition of the plan, goes after a colon and between curly brackets) are true. After a plan is selected, a sequence of actions in the plan body (denoted by ←) is executed.

The complete source code of the agent program is shown in Listing 5. The agent begins with 8 initial beliefs (lines 5–12): four for each waypoint (a, b, c, d) and another four for each coordinate that corresponds to one of the waypoints.

For simplicity the agent already starts with this knowledge, although in a more complex scenario it could learn it during execution from the low-level control of the robot (sensors and/or movement libraries) or from other agents. The initial goal of the agent is to start patrolling waypoint A. This triggers the plan in lines 18–19, which tests in the plan guard if the agent has the belief with the corresponding coordinates. If this is the case, then a belief going(a) is added to the belief base, and the agent executes the move action. This action is sent to the move base library, where a path from the robot's initial position to the destination is computed and altered as the robot moves.

Subsequent plans (lines 20–24) deal with the result of the move base library. The result is returned upon the end of the action with code 3 if it was successful, or with code 2 in case of failure (i.e. the action stopped and the robot has not arrived in its destination). The first four plans respond to a successful action, which means that the robot arrived in its destination and is ready to patrol the next waypoint in the list. Each plan removes the going belief and calls the patrol plan as appropriate.

```
1   GWENDOLEN
2   :name: turtlebot3
3
4   :Initial Beliefs:
5   waypoint(a)
6   waypoint(b)
7   waypoint(c)
8   waypoint(d)
9   waypoint_coordinate(a,1.25,0.0,0.0)
10  waypoint_coordinate(b,2.5,0.0,0.0)
11  waypoint_coordinate(c,2.5,1.0,0.0)
12  waypoint_coordinate(d,1.25,1.0,0.0)
13
14  :Initial Goals:
15  patrol(a) [perform]
16
17  :Plans:
18  +!patrol(Waypoint) [perform] : { B waypoint_coordinate(Waypoint,X,Y,Z) }
19  <- +going(Waypoint), move(X,Y,Z);
20  +movebase_result(Seq,3) : { B going(a) } <- -going(a), +!patrol(b) [perform];
21  +movebase_result(Seq,3) : { B going(b) } <- -going(b), +!patrol(c) [perform];
22  +movebase_result(Seq,3) : { B going(c) } <- -going(c), +!patrol(d) [perform];
23  +movebase_result(Seq,3) : { B going(d) } <- -going(d), +!patrol(a) [perform];
24  +movebase_result(Seq,2) : { B going(W) } <- print("Movement to ",W," failed.");
```

Listing 5: GWENDOLEN agent program for the TurtleBot autonomous patrolling.

The plan on line 24 can be used to deal with failure. In this case, for brevity we simply print a message on the screen. However, the agent could retrieve its target waypoint using the belief going and retry the action, or it could try to move to the next waypoint in the list, and so on. In the real world things often fail or don't work as expected, so it is important for the agent to be able to react and reason about these events at a high-level.

The subscriber for the move base action result is shown in Listing 6. Note that this subscriber uses a message type from the move base library called "*move_base_msgs/MoveBaseActionResult*". In lines 9–12 we create the new perception that is to be sent to the agent. We create the literal *movebase_result* and add the two terms (parameters) that come with the ROS message: seq, an increasing sequence identification; and status, an int value that indicates success or failure. Then, the literal is added as a perception and sent to the agent.

```
1    bridge.subscribe(SubscriptionRequestMsg.generate("/move_base/result")
2      .setType("move_base_msgs/MoveBaseActionResult"),
3    new RosListenDelegate() {
4      public void receive(JsonNode data, String stringRep) {
5        MessageUnpacker<MoveBaseActionResult> unpacker =
6          new MessageUnpacker<MoveBaseActionResult>(MoveBaseActionResult.class);
7        MoveBaseActionResult msg = unpacker.unpackRosMessage(data);
8        clearPercepts();
9        Literal movebase_result = new Literal("movebase_result");
10       movebase_result.addTerm(new NumberTermImpl(msg.header.seq));
11       movebase_result.addTerm(new NumberTermImpl(msg.status.status));
12       addPercept(movebase_result);
13       }
14    }
15  );
```

Listing 6: Move base result subscriber for the TurtleBot autonomous patrolling.

The execution of the move action is processed in the environment, as described in Listing 7. It takes the coordinates, as sent by the agent, and creates a publisher to the topic "/gwendolen_to_move_base" using the Vector3 message type. A move base client is listening to that topic, and upon receiving a message it creates a goal with the coordinates given in the message and sends it to the move base server.

```
1    public void move(double lx, double ly, double lz) {
2      Publisher move_base =
3        new Publisher("/gwendolen_to_move_base", "geometry_msgs/Vector3", bridge);
4      move_base.publish(new Vector3(lx,ly,lz));
5    }
```

Listing 7: Move action for the TurtleBot autonomous patrolling.

Verification. Some of the properties that we verified of the implementation of our agent, consider the following:

$$\Box(A_{\texttt{turtlebot3}}\ patrol(a) \rightarrow \Diamond \neg B_{\texttt{turtlebot3}}\ going(a))$$
$$\Box(A_{\texttt{turtlebot3}}\ patrol(b) \rightarrow \Diamond \neg B_{\texttt{turtlebot3}}\ going(b))$$
$$\Box(A_{\texttt{turtlebot3}}\ patrol(c) \rightarrow \Diamond \neg B_{\texttt{turtlebot3}}\ going(c))$$
$$\Box(A_{\texttt{turtlebot3}}\ patrol(d) \rightarrow \Diamond \neg B_{\texttt{turtlebot3}}\ going(d))$$

These properties state that it is always the case ($\Box$) that if the *turtlebot3* agent executes the action *patrol* (to either A, B, C, or D), then eventually ($\Diamond$) the *turtlebot3* agent will no longer believe that it is on its way to that particular waypoint. That is, it has either arrived or failed.

4.2   The Three TurtleBots: Home Service Robots

In this section, we present a case study involving multiple robots inside a house (Fig. 5). Differently to the example presented in Sect. 4.1, in this scenario the robots have to collaborate to solve specific tasks. The reasoning process followed by each robot is defined by a GWENDOLEN agent. More specifically, each robot has the job to bring supplies and tools around the house. The robots collaborate in two situations; when a robot needs an item from another robot, and, when a robot fails to deliver an item because of some technical difficulties.

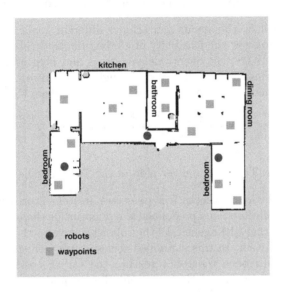

Fig. 5. Map of the house where the three TurtleBots are used.

In order to use multiple robots, each one controlled by a GWENDOLEN agent, we modify a few things in our interface. Until now, there was only one agent publishing messages, and only one robot receiving them; in fact, it was not necessary to keep track of which agent was sending a certain message, and which robot was reacting on the latter. When multiple agents are involved, each one of them needs to distinguish its topics according to its associated robot. This can be achieved straightforwardly by keeping track of the name of the robot in ROS, and adding it as namespace when publishing the messages. In this way, each robot knows where to subscribe to receive the agent's commands and each agents knows where to publish.

For example, consider three robots called ag1, ag2 and ag3, respectively; and a topic corresponding to the action that each agent can ask its corresponding robot to do, act. Thus, ag1 publishes on ag1/act, ag2 on ag2/act and finally, ag3 on ag3/act.

Agent Implementation. Each agent has a set of beliefs (Listing 8) denoting the items to be delivered and where they have to be delivered. For example, the following three beliefs in the agent's mind tell that, the agent has a coke to be delivered to the table in the kitchen, and the table in the kitchen is at some specific coordinates.

```
1    item(coke)
2    delivery(coke, kitchen, table)
3    waypoint_coordinate(kitchen,table,1.25,2.0,1.5)
```

Listing 8: Example of beliefs in the TurtleBot house scenario.

Using these beliefs, the agents can achieve different goals. In this scenario, where our aim is to show the feasibility of guiding multiple robots using a MAS defined in GWENDOLEN, the agents deliver items and help each other in case of technical problems. This is obtained through the `deliver` plan (Listing 9), where the agent checks for item to deliver, and deliver them (base case).

```
1    +!deliver [perform] : { B name(Name), B delivery(Item, Room, Waypoint),
2        B item(Item), B waypoint_coordinate(Room, Waypoint, X, Y, Z) }
3    <- move(Name, X, Y, Z), -delivery(Item, Room, Waypoint), +!deliver [perform];
```

Listing 9: The basic deliver plan in the TurtleBot house scenario.

In this plan, the agent checks if it possesses an item `Item` which has to be delivered to a specific `Room` in a predefined waypoint inside the room (`Waypoint`). If this is the case, then the agent asks the robot to move to the target position, and to deliver the item. In this simplified scenario, the delivery is assumed as being instantaneous; once the robot reaches the target position, the item is instantaneously delivered, and the agent only has to update its beliefs accordingly (by removing the belief about delivering the item).

We defined two other course of actions which may happen when a delivery has to be done. The first case is when the item required is not available, thus the agent has to ask to the other agents to deliver the item, if they have it. This can be achieved with a different `deliver` plan, as shown in Listing 10.

```
1    +!deliver [perform] : { B delivery(Item, Room, Waypoint), ~ B item(Item) }
2    <- -delivery(Item, Room, Waypoint),
3        .send(ag1, :tell, delivery(Item, Room, Waypoint)),
4        ...
5        .send(agn, :tell, delivery(Item, Room, Waypoint));
```

Listing 10: The second deliver plan in the TurtleBot house scenario.

The trigger for this case is different from before. This plan is triggered when a delivery is expected by the agent for an `Item`, but the agent does not have the item (~ stands for negation). Thus, the agent has to ask the other agents to help deliver this item. The messages will simply create beliefs in the receiver agents' belief base. If one of them has the item, then it will execute the base deliver plan (note that we allow multiple agents to deliver the same item).

The last case is when an agent fails and is no longer able to continue with its deliveries. In this case, the agent asks for help to the other agents. The agent which accepts to help it, will move to the position of the broken agent, and fetch all the items from the latter. In this way, even though a robot fails, its items can still be delivered. This can be obtained with a combination of multiple plans, and due to space constraints we only report the plans that send the help requests.

```
1   +!deliver [perform] : { B name(Name), B failure(Room, Waypoint) }
2   <- +!ask_for_help(Name, Room, Waypoint);
3   +!ask_for_help(Name, Room, Waypoint) : { ~ B accept_request_for_help, B agent_to_ask(Ag)}
4   <- .send(Ag, :tell, help_request(Name, Room, Waypoint)),
5        wait(5000),
6        -agent_to_ask(Ag),
7        +!ask_for_help(Name, Room, Waypoint);
8   +!ask_for_help(Name, Room, Waypoint) : { B accept_request_for_help }
9   <- -accept_request_for_help;
```

Listing 11: The third deliver plan in the TurtleBot house scenario.

In Listing 11, the agent that failed asks for help to all the other agents one at a time; after each request, it waits a fixed amount of time (5000 ms), before sending the request to another agent. This is necessary to simplify the communication protocol involved, and to avoid that multiple agents decide to help the agent that failed.

Verification. One of the advantages in defining the agents in GWENDOLEN is that we can also do model checking of their behaviours. For instance, a property we check is:

$$\Box(\mathcal{B}_{tb3\_0} \, delivery(coke, kitchen, table)) \rightarrow \Diamond(\neg\mathcal{B}_{tb3\_0} \, delivery(coke, kitchen, table))$$

Where we check for a specific agent (tb3_0 in this case) if a delivery assigned to it is eventually considered completed. In this case, the delivery of the coke to the kitchen's table. The delivery can be achieved by the agent, or by any helper agent in case of failure.

5   Related Work

In [17], the authors discuss the necessary requirements to integrate agent programming languages with robotic frameworks. These requirements are exemplified using a demo application of a NAO robot in a home-care scenario. The robot is controlled using the 2APL agent language that interacts with ROS through an interface environment. However, the paper limits itself to describing existing solutions that can be used and past work in the literature. The interface itself is never described, and no source code is provided within the paper.

Two similar approaches have been developed to allow the Jason [1] agent programming language to interface with ROS. The first approach [16] makes use of the *rosjava* library. This library re-implements the essential core features of ROS in Java, which is not officially supported in ROS. The authors use this library to then connect the agents through the CArtAgO [14] environment, which Jason agents can then access using CArtAgO artifacts. The second approach [10] changes the default agent architecture to interface with ROS code in C++. Compared to our interface, both approaches have the disadvantage of requiring changes to core ROS functionalities, something that usually changes between new releases of ROS. Whilst our approach remains version agnostic (as long as the ROS message structure remains the same) and can be used by a variety of agent programming languages (as long as they support Java).

6   Conclusion

In this paper we presented an interface that allows the integration of autonomous agents (particularly those programmed in agent languages that support Java) with robots that use ROS. Agents can use the interface to publish messages (e.g. commands to actuators) to a ROS topic or to subscribe to a topic in order to receive messages (e.g. perceptions from sensors). To evaluate our approach we used the interface to develop autonomous agents in GWENDOLEN that are capable of high-level decision-making in the TurtleBot3 robot. In the first case study, the agent controls the patrolling behaviour of the robot. We increase the number of agents and robots in the second case study, using three agents (one for each of the three TurtleBot3 robots) to service multiple rooms in a house. For both scenarios we have used the AJPF model checker to verify some properties of the agents program.

Although verifying the code that is responsible for the robot's decision-making is an important step towards providing assurances about its behaviour, in some scenarios (e.g. safety critical) it may also be necessary to verify other nodes that are part of the system, such as the vision mechanism or the path planner. Other future work include comparing the agent's program with traditional decision-making code in Python/C++ (ROS supported languages), and performing field tests in real world applications.

References

1. Bordini, R.H., Wooldridge, M., Hübner, J.F.: Programming Multi-agent Systems in AgentSpeak using Jason. John Wiley & Sons, Chichester (2007)
2. Collier, R.W., Russell, S., Lillis, D.: Exploring AOP from an OOP perspective. In: Proceedings of the 5th International Workshop on Programming Based on Actors, Agents, and Decentralized Control. In: AGERE! 2015, pp. 25–36. Association for Computing Machinery, New York (2015). https://doi.org/10.1145/2824815.2824818
3. Crick, C., Jay, G., Osentoski, S., Pitzer, B., Jenkins, O.C.: Rosbridge: ROS for non-ROS users. In: Christensen, H.I., Khatib, O. (eds.) Robotics Research. STAR, vol. 100, pp. 493–504. Springer, Cham (2017). https://doi.org/10.1007/978-3-319-29363-9_28

4. Dastani, M.: 2APL: a practical agent programming language. Auton. Agent. Multi-Agent Syst. **16**(3), 214–248 (2008). https://doi.org/10.1007/s10458-008-9036-y
5. Dennis, L.: The MCAPL framework including the agent infrastructure layer and agent Java pathfinder. J. Open Source Softw. **3**(24), 617 (2018). https://doi.org/10.21105/joss.00617
6. Dennis, L.A., Farwer, B.: Gwendolen: A BDI language for verifiable agents. In: Logic and the Simulation of Interaction and Reasoning. AISB, Aberdeen (2008)
7. Dennis, L.A., Fisher, M., Webster, M.P., Bordini, R.H.: Model checking agent programming languages. Autom. Softw. Eng. **19**(1), 5–63 (2012)
8. Gottifredi, S., Tucat, M., Corbatta, D., García, A., Simari, G.R.: A BDI architecture for high level robot deliberation. Inteligencia Artif. **14**(46), 74–83 (2010)
9. Hindriks, K.V., de Boer, F.S., van der Hoek, W., Meyer, J.-J.C.: Agent programming with declarative goals. In: Castelfranchi, C., Lespérance, Y. (eds.) ATAL 2000. LNCS (LNAI), vol. 1986, pp. 228–243. Springer, Heidelberg (2001). https://doi.org/10.1007/3-540-44631-1_16
10. Morais, M.G., Meneguzzi, F.R., Bordini, R.H., Amory, A.M.: Distributed fault diagnosis for multiple mobile robots using an agent programming language. In: 2015 International Conference on Advanced Robotics (ICAR), pp. 395–400, July 2015 https://doi.org/10.1109/ICAR.2015.7251486
11. Quigley, M., et al.: ROS: an open-source robot operating system. In: Workshop on Open Source Software at the International Conference on Robotics and Automation. IEEE, Japan (2009)
12. Rao, A.S.: AgentSpeak(L): BDI agents speak out in a logical computable language. In: Van de Velde, W., Perram, J.W. (eds.) MAAMAW 1996. LNCS, vol. 1038, pp. 42–55. Springer, Heidelberg (1996). https://doi.org/10.1007/BFb0031845
13. Rao, A.S., Georgeff, M.P.: BDI agents: from theory to practice. In: Proceedings of the First International Conference on Multi-agent Systems, pp. 312–319 (1995)
14. Ricci, A., Piunti, M., Viroli, M., Omicini, A.: Environment programming in CArtAgO. In: El Fallah Seghrouchni, A., Dix, J., Dastani, M., Bordini, R.H. (eds.) Multi-Agent Programming, pp. 259–288. Springer, Boston, MA (2009). https://doi.org/10.1007/978-0-387-89299-3_8
15. Visser, W., Havelund, K., Brat, G., Park, S.J., Lerda, F.: Model checking programs. Autom. Softw. Eng. **10**(2), 3–11 (2002)
16. Wesz, R.: Integrating robot control into the Agentspeak(L) programming language. Master's thesis, Pontificia Universidade Catolica do Rio Grande do Sul (2015). http://tede2.pucrs.br/tede2/handle/tede/6941
17. Ziafati, P., Dastani, M., Meyer, J.-J., van der Torre, L.: Agent programming languages requirements for programming autonomous robots. In: Dastani, M., Hübner, J.F., Logan, B. (eds.) ProMAS 2012. LNCS (LNAI), vol. 7837, pp. 35–53. Springer, Heidelberg (2013). https://doi.org/10.1007/978-3-642-38700-5_3

Integrated Commonsense Reasoning and Deep Learning for Transparent Decision Making in Robotics

Tiago Mota[1] , Mohan Sridharan[2(✉)] , and Aleš Leonardis[2]

[1] Electrical and Computer Engineering, The University of Auckland,
Auckland, New Zealand
tmot987@aucklanduni.ac.nz
[2] School of Computer Science, University of Birmingham, Birmingham, UK
{m.sridharan,a.leonardis}@bham.ac.uk

Abstract. A robot's ability to provide explanatory descriptions of its decisions and beliefs promotes effective collaboration with humans. Providing such transparency in decision making is particularly challenging in integrated robot systems that include knowledge-based reasoning methods and data-driven learning algorithms. Towards addressing this challenge, our architecture couples the complementary strengths of non-monotonic logical reasoning with incomplete commonsense domain knowledge, deep learning, and inductive learning. During reasoning and learning, the architecture enables a robot to provide on-demand *explanations* of its decisions, beliefs, and the outcomes of hypothetical actions, in the form of relational descriptions of relevant domain objects, attributes, and actions. The architecture's capabilities are illustrated and evaluated in the context of scene understanding tasks and planning tasks performed using simulated images and images from a physical robot manipulating tabletop objects. Experimental results indicate the ability to reliably acquire and merge new information about the domain in the form of constraints, and to provide accurate explanations in the presence of noisy sensing and actuation.

Keywords: Explainable reasoning and learning · Non-monotonic logical reasoning · Deep learning · Scene understanding · Robotics

1 Introduction

Imagine a robot arranging objects in desired configurations on a table, and estimating the occlusion of objects and stability of object configurations. Figure 1a illustrates a scene in this setting. An object is considered to be occluded if the view of any minimal fraction of its frontal face is hidden by another object, and any given configuration (i.e., a vertical stack of objects) is unstable if any object in the configuration is unstable. To perform these tasks, the robot extracts information from on-board camera images, reasons with this information and incomplete domain knowledge, and executes actions to achieve desired outcomes. The

© Springer Nature Switzerland AG 2020
N. Bassiliades et al. (Eds.): EUMAS 2020/AT 2020, LNAI 12520, pp. 206–225, 2020.
https://doi.org/10.1007/978-3-030-66412-1_14

(a) Test scenario.   (b) Image from robot's camera.

Fig. 1. (a) Motivating scenario of a Baxter robot arranging objects in desired configurations on a tabletop; (b) Image from the camera on the robot's left gripper.

robot also incrementally learns previously unknown constraints, and responds to questions about its plans, actions, associated decisions, and beliefs. For instance, assume that the target configuration in Fig. 1b is to have the pig on the orange block, and that the plan is to move the blue block on to the table before placing the pig on the orange block. When asked to justify a step of the plan, e.g., "why do you want to pick up the blue block first?", the robot answers "I have to put the pig on the orange block. The blue block is on the orange block"; when asked, after executing the plan, to explain why an action was not executed, e.g., "why didn't you pick up the pig first?", the robot responds "Because the blue block is on the orange block".

Realizing the motivating scenario described above poses challenges in knowledge representation, reasoning, learning, and control. This paper focuses on enabling a robot to provide an on-demand *explanation* of its decisions and beliefs in the form of a description comprising relations between relevant objects, actions, and attributes of the domain. Such "explainability" will help establish accountability in the robot's decision making and help the human designer improve the algorithms, but it remains an open problem. It is particularly challenging with integrated robot systems that include knowledge-based reasoning methods (e.g., for planning and diagnostics) and data-driven (e.g., deep learning) algorithms that are the state of the art for many pattern recognition problems. Research in cognitive systems and architectures indicates that relational representations and reasoning with commonsense knowledge help promote transparency in decision making [13,15,29]. Inspired by this insight, our architecture tightly couples the complementary strengths of knowledge-based and data-driven methods, while providing transparent decision making. It builds on and significantly expands our prior work that combined non-monotonic logical reasoning and deep learning for scene understanding in simulated images [21]. This paper contributes the ability to:

– Automatically extract relevant information and construct explanations as relational descriptions provided in response to questions about the robot's decisions and beliefs, including under hypothetical situations.

– Incrementally merge newly acquired information with existing knowledge, exploiting the interplay between representational choices, reasoning methods, and learning algorithms to generate accurate explanations.

These capabilities are evaluated in the context of planning tasks and scene understanding tasks in simulated scenes and on a physical robot manipulating table-top objects. Specifically, the robot (i) computes and executes plans to arrange objects in desired configurations; and (ii) estimates occlusion of scene objects and stability of object configurations. Experimental results indicate the ability to (i) incrementally reduce uncertainty about the scene by learning previously unknown state constraints; and (ii) construct explanations reliably and efficiently by automatically identifying and reasoning with the relevant knowledge despite noisy sensing and actuation.

The remainder of the paper is organized as follows. We first discuss related work in Sect. 2, followed by a description of the architecture in Sect. 3. Experimental results are discussed in Sect. 4, and the conclusions are presented in Sect. 5.

2   Related Work

Early work on explanation generation drew on research in cognition, psychology, and linguistics to characterize explanations in terms of generality, objectivity, connectivity, relevance, and information content [7]. Subsequent studies involving human subjects have also indicated that the important attributes of good explanations include coherence, simplicity, generality, soundness, and completeness [24]. In parallel, fundamental computational methods were developed for explaining unexpected outcomes by reasoning logically about potential causes [10].

With the use of AI and machine learning methods in different domains, there is much interest in understanding the decisions of these methods[1]. This understanding can be used to improve the underlying algorithms, and to make automated decision-making more acceptable or trustworthy to humans [17]. Recent work in *explainable AI* and *explainable planning* can be broadly categorized into two groups [19]. Methods in one group modify or map learned models or reasoning systems to make their decisions more interpretable, e.g., by tracing decisions back to input data [11] or explaining the predictions of any classifier by learning equivalent interpretable models [25], or biasing a planning system towards making decisions easier for humans to understand [33]. Methods in the other group provide descriptions that make a reasoning system's decisions more transparent, e.g., explaining planning decisions [3], or causal and temporal relations [27]. Much of this research is agnostic to how an explanation is structured or assumes comprehensive domain knowledge. Given the use of deep networks and related algorithms in different applications, methods are being developed to understand

---

[1] For a recent debate on whether interpretability is needed in machine learning, please see: https://www.youtube.com/watch?v=93Xv8vJ2acI.

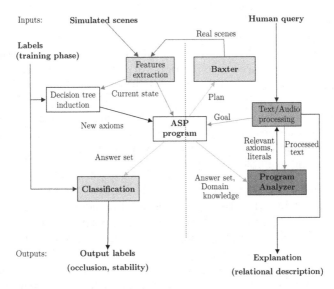

Fig. 2. Architecture combines strengths of non-monotonic logical reasoning with incomplete commonsense domain knowledge, deep learning, and inductive learning. New components to the right of the dashed line support desired explainability.

the operation of these networks, e.g., by computing the features most relevant to a deep network's outputs [2]. As documented in a recent survey, these methods compute gradients and decompositions in a network's layers to obtain heatmaps of the relevant features [26]. There has also been work on reasoning with learned symbolic structure, or with a learned graph encoding scene structure, in conjunction with deep networks to answer questions about images of scenes [23,32]. However, these approaches do not (i) fully integrate reasoning and learning to inform and guide each other; or (ii) use the rich commonsense knowledge, which is available in almost every domain, for reliable and efficient reasoning, learning, and the generation of descriptions of the decisions and beliefs of the system under consideration.

Our focus is on integrated robot systems that use a combination of knowledge-based and data-driven algorithms to represent, reason with, and learn from incomplete domain knowledge and noisy observations. We enable such robots to generate relational descriptions of decisions, beliefs, and hypothetical or counterfactual situations; humans often consider such hypothetical options to infer causal relations [4]. Recent surveys state that these capabilities are not supported by existing systems [1,19]. Our architecture addresses this limitation by extending work in our group on explainable agency [14], a theory of explanations [31], and on combining non-monotonic logical reasoning and deep learning for classification of simulated images [21].

3   Architecture

Figure 2 shows the overall architecture. Components to the left of the dashed vertical line were introduced in our prior work that combined non-monotonic logical reasoning and deep learning for classification in simulated images [21]; we summarize these components for completeness. Components to the right of the dashed line are introduced here to expand reasoning capabilities and answer questions about decisions, beliefs, and hypothetical situations. We describe these new components and revisions to existing components in more detail. We do so using the following example domain.

Example Domain 1. *[Robot Assistant (RA) Domain]*
A Baxter (see Fig. 1a): (i) estimates occlusion of scene objects and stability of object structures, and arranges objects in desired configurations; and (ii) provides relational descriptions of decisions, beliefs, and hypothetical situations as responses to questions and commands. There is uncertainty in the robot's perception and actuation, and the robot uses probabilistic algorithms to visually recognize and move objects. The robot has incomplete (and potentially imprecise) domain knowledge, which includes object attributes such as *size* (small, medium, large), *surface* (flat, irregular) and *shape* (cube, apple, duck); spatial relations between objects (above, below, front, behind, right, left, in); some domain attributes; and some axioms governing domain dynamics such as:

- Placing an object on top of an object with an irregular surface results in an unstable object configuration.
- For any given object, removing all objects blocking the view of any minimal fraction of its frontal face causes this object to be not occluded.

This knowledge may need to be revised over time, e.g., some actions, axioms, and the values of some attributes may not be known, or the robot may find that placing certain objects on an object with an irregular surface results in a stable configuration.

3.1   Knowledge Representation, Reasoning, and Learning

We first describe the knowledge representation, reasoning, and learning components.

Feature Extraction: In our architecture, the sensor inputs are RGB images of simulated scenes, or noisy top and front views of any given scene from the robot's cameras; our previous work considered RGB-D images (i.e., point clouds) of simple simulated scenes [21]. From each image, a probabilistic algorithm is used to extract objects and their attributes. Also, the spatial relations between objects are computed using our prior work that incrementally learns the *grounding*, i.e., the meaning in the physical world, for position-based and distance-based prepositional words such as "above", "in", and "far", in the form of 2D and 1D histograms [20].

Non-monotonic Logical Reasoning: To represent and reason with domain knowledge, we use CR-Prolog, an extension to Answer Set Prolog (ASP) that introduces *consistency restoring* (CR) rules; we use the terms "CR-Prolog" and "ASP" interchangeably in this paper. ASP is a declarative language that represents recursive definitions, defaults, causal relations, and constructs that are difficult to express in classical logic formalisms. ASP is based on the stable model semantics, and encodes *default negation* and *epistemic disjunction*, e.g., unlike "¬a", which implies that "*a is believed to be false*", "not a" only implies "*a is not believed to be true*" [9]. Each literal can hence be true, false, or unknown, and the *robot only believes statements that it is forced to believe*. ASP supports non-monotonic logical reasoning, i.e., adding a statement can reduce the set of inferences, which helps recover from errors due to reasoning with incomplete knowledge. Knowledge-based reasoning paradigms such as ASP are often criticized for requiring considerable prior knowledge, and for being unwieldy in large, complex domains. However, modern ASP solvers are used by an international community to reason efficiently with a large knowledge base or with incomplete knowledge [5].

A domain's description in ASP comprises a *system description* $\mathcal{D}$ and a *history* $\mathcal{H}$. $\mathcal{D}$ comprises a *sorted signature* Σ and axioms encoding the domain's dynamics. Our prior work explored spatial relations for classification tasks; Σ included *basic sorts*, e.g., *object*, *robot*, *size*, *relation*, and *surface*; *statics*, i.e., domain attributes that do not change over time, e.g., *obj_size(object, size)* and *obj_surface(obj, surface)*; and *fluents*, i.e., attributes whose values can be changed, e.g., *obj_relation(above, A, B)* implies object A is *above* object B. *The robot in this paper also plans and executes physical actions that cause changes in the domain.* Such a dynamic domain is modeled in our architecture by first describing the expanded Σ and transition diagram in action language $\mathcal{AL}_d$ [8]; this description is then translated to ASP statements. For the RA domain, Σ now includes the sort *step* for temporal reasoning, additional fluents such as *in_hand(robot, object)*, actions such as *pickup(robot, object)* and *putdown(robot, object, location)*, and the relation *holds(fluent, step)* implying that a particular fluent holds true at a particular timestep. Axioms of the RA domain include ASP statements such as:

$$holds(in\_hand(robot, object), I + 1) \leftarrow occurs(pickup(robot, object), I) \quad \text{(1a)}$$
$$holds(obj\_relation(above, A, B), I) \leftarrow holds(obj\_relation(below, B, A), I) \quad \text{(1b)}$$
$$\neg occurs(pickup(robot, object), I) \leftarrow holds(in\_hand(robot, object), I) \quad \text{(1c)}$$

which encode a causal law, a state constraint, and an executability condition respectively, e.g., Statement 1(a) implies that executing the "pickup" action causes the target object to be in the robot's grasp in the next time step; *our prior work only included state constraints* [21]. The axioms also encode some commonsense knowledge in the form of default statements that hold unless there is evidence to the contrary, e.g., "larger objects placed on smaller objects are unstable" is encoded in ASP as:

$$\neg holds(stable(A), I) \leftarrow holds(obj\_relation(above, A, B), I), \qquad (2)$$
$$size(A, large), \ size(B, small), \ not \ holds(stable(A), I)$$

where "not" denotes default negation. In addition to axioms, information extracted from the input images (e.g., spatial relations, object attributes) with sufficiently high probability is converted to ASP statements at that time step. Also, the domain's history $\mathcal{H}$ comprises records of fluents observed to be true or false at a particular time step, i.e., $obs(fluent, boolean, step)$, and of the execution of an action at a particular time step, i.e., $hpd(action, step)$. In [29] this notion was expanded to represent defaults describing the values of fluents in the initial state, e.g., "it is initially believed that a book is in the library", and exceptions, e.g., "a cookbook is in the kitchen".

To reason with the domain knowledge, our architecture constructs the CR-Prolog program $\Pi(\mathcal{D}, \mathcal{H})$, which includes Σ and axioms of $\mathcal{D}$, inertia axioms, reality checks, closed world assumptions for actions, and observations, actions, and defaults from $\mathcal{H}$. Every default also has a CR rule to let the robot assume the default's conclusion is false to restore consistency under exceptional circumstances. For instance, the statement in the ASP program: $\neg loc(X, library) \xleftarrow{+} book(X)$ is a CR rule that is triggered under exceptional circumstances to assume a book is not in the library as a potential explanation of an unexpected observation. The program for our RA domain is available online [22]. Once Π is constructed, planning, diagnostics, and inference can be reduced to computing *answer sets* of Π [9]. Any answer set represents the beliefs of the robot associated with Π; it is a description of a possible world and the set of literals of domain fluents and statics at any particular time step represents the *state* at that time step. Note that incorrect inferences can be drawn due to incomplete knowledge, noisy sensor input, or the use of a low threshold for elevating probabilistic information to statements in the ASP program. Non-monotonic logical reasoning enables the robot to recover from such errors, and not be very sensitive to the choice of the probability threshold. Also, although we do not describe it here, it is possible to model non-determinism (e.g., in action outcomes) in our architecture. In addition, work by others in our group has combined such logical reasoning at a coarse resolution with probabilistic reasoning over the relevant part of a finer resolution representation of the domain [29]. For ease of understanding and to focus on the interplay between non-monotonic logical reasoning and learning, we limit ourselves to logical reasoning at one resolution in this paper.

Classification: Similar to the approach in our prior work, for any given image, the robot tries to estimate the occlusion of objects and the stability of object configurations using ASP-based reasoning. If an answer is not found, or an incorrect answer is found (on labeled training examples), the robot automatically extracts relevant regions of interest (ROIs) from the corresponding image. Parameters of existing Convolutional Neural Network (CNN) architectures (e.g., Lenet [16], AlexNet [12]) are tuned to map information from each such ROI to the corresponding classification labels. An innovation of our prior work was to reason with knowledge of the task (e.g., estimating occlusion) to identify and ground only the relevant axioms and relations in the image under consideration to determine the ROIs [21]. In this paper, we reason about relevance over a sequence of steps to provide explanations, as described in Subsect. 3.2.

Decision Tree Induction: Images used to train the CNNs are considered to contain information about missing or incorrect constraints related to occlusion and stability. Image features and spatial relations extracted from ROIs in each such image, along with the known labels for occlusion and stability (during training), are used to incrementally learn a decision tree summarizing the corresponding state transitions. The learning process repeatedly splits a node based on an unused attribute likely to provide the highest reduction in entropy. Next, branches of the tree that satisfy minimal thresholds on purity at the leaf ($\geq$95% samples in one class) and on the level of support from labeled examples ($\geq$5%) are used to construct candidate axioms. Candidates are validated and those without a minimal level of support ($\geq$5%) on unseen examples are removed. These thresholds are set to identify a small number of highly likely axioms, and small changes to thresholds do not affect performance. Also, the thresholds can be revised to achieve other outcomes, e.g., they can be lowered significantly to identify default constraints.

Unlike our prior work, we introduce new strategies to process noisy images of more complex scenes. First, we use an ensemble learning approach, retaining only axioms that are identified over a number of cycles of learning and validation. Second, different versions of the same axiom are merged to remove over-specifications, e.g.:

$$\neg stable(A) \leftarrow obj\_relation(above, A, B),\ obj\_surface(B, irregular) \qquad (3a)$$
$$\neg stable(A) \leftarrow obj\_relation(above, A, B),\ obj\_surface(B, irregular), \qquad (3b)$$
$$obj\_size(B, large)$$

where Statement 3(b) can be removed because the size of the object at the bottom of a stack does not provide any additional information about instability given that it has an irregular surface. If the robot later observes that a large object, even with an irregular surface, can support a small object, the axiom will be revised suitably. Specifically, axioms with the same head and some overlap in the body are grouped. Each combination of one axiom from each group is encoded in an ASP program along with axioms that are not in any group. This program is used to classify ten labeled scenes, only retaining axioms in the program that provides the highest accuracy on these scenes. Third, to filter axioms that cease to be useful, the robot associates each axiom with a *strength* that decays exponentially over time if it is not reinforced, i.e., not used or learned again. Any axiom whose strength falls below a threshold is removed. Other work in our group has explored the learning of actions, causal laws, and executability conditions in simulated domains [30]. Here, we only consider the learning of constraints and explore the effect of the learned axioms on the ability to provide explanations.

3.2 Relational Descriptions as Explanations

Our architecture's new components exploit the interplay between representation, reasoning, and learning to provide the desired relational descriptions of decisions, beliefs, and the outcomes of hypothetical events.

Interaction Interface and Control Loop: Human interaction with our architecture is through speech or text. Existing algorithms, software, and a controlled (domain-specific) vocabulary are used to parse human verbal input and to provide a verbal response when appropriate. Specifically, verbal input from a human is transcribed into text drawn from the controlled vocabulary. This (or the input) text is labeled using a part-of-speech (POS) tagger, and normalized with the lemma list [28] and related synonyms and antonyms from WordNet [18]. The processed text helps identify the type of request, which may correspond to a desired goal or a question about decisions, beliefs, or the outcomes of hypothetical events. In the former case, the goal is sent to the ASP program for planning. The robot executes the plan, replanning when unexpected action outcomes cannot be explained, until the goal is achieved. In the latter case, the "Program Analyzer" considers the domain knowledge (including inferred beliefs that are computed as needed) and processed human input to automatically identify relevant axioms and literals. These literals are inserted into generic response templates based on the controlled vocabulary, resulting in human-understandable (textual) descriptions that are converted to synthetic speech if needed.

Program Analyzer: Algorithm 1 describes our approach for automatically identifying and reasoning with the relevant information to construct the desired relational descriptions in the context of four types of *explanatory* questions or requests. The first three question types were introduced as those to be considered by any explainable planning system [6]; we also consider a question about specific beliefs.

1. **Plan description** When asked to describe a particular plan, the robot parses the related answer set(s) to extract a sequence of actions of the form *occurs(action1, step1), ..., occurs(actionN, stepN)* (line 3 in Algorithm 1). These actions are used to construct the response.

2. **Action justification: Why action X at step I?** To justify the execution of any particular action at a particular time step:
   (a) For each action that occurred after time step I, the robot examines relevant executability condition(s) and identifies literal(s) that would prevent the action's execution at step I (lines 5–7). For the goal of placing the *orange_block* on the table in Fig. 1b, assume that the action executed are *occurs(pickup(robot, blue_block), 0), occurs(putdown(robot,*

Algorithm 1. (Program Analyzer) Construct answer to input question

---

Input : Literal of input question; $\Pi(\mathcal{D}, \mathcal{H})$; answer templates.
Output: Answer and answer Literals.

```
// Compute answer set
```
1 AS = AnswerSet(Π)
2 **if** *question = plan description* **then**
```
    // Retrieve all actions from answer set
```
3   answer_literals = Retrieve(AS, actions)
4 **else if** *question = "why action X at step I?"* **then**
```
    // Extract actions after step I
```
5   next_actions = Retrieve(AS, actions for step $> I$)
```
    // Extract axioms influencing these actions
```
6   relevant_axioms = Retrieve(Π, head $= \neg$ next_actions)
```
    // Extract relevant literals from Answer Set
```
7   relevant_literals = Retrieve(AS, Body(relevant_axioms) $\in I \wedge \notin I + 1$)
```
    // Output literals
```
8   answer_literals = pair(relevant_literals, next_actions)
9 **else if** *question = "why not action X at step I?"* **then**
```
    // Extract axioms relevant to action
```
10   relevant_axioms = Retrieve(Π, head $= \neg$ occurs(X))
```
    // Extract relevant literals from Answer Set
```
11   answer_literals = Retrieve(AS, Body(relevant_axioms) $\in I \wedge \notin I + 1$)
12 **else if** *question = "why belief Y at step I?"* **then**
```
    // Extract axioms influencing this belief
```
13   relevant_axioms = Retrieve(Π, head $= Y$)
```
    // Extract body of axioms
```
14   answer_literals = Recursive_Examine(AS, Body(relevant_axioms))
15 Construct_Answer(answer_literals, answer_templates)

---

blue_block), 1), and *occurs(pickup(robot, orange_block), 2)*. If the focus is on the first *pickup* action, an executability condition related to the second *pickup* action:

$$\neg occurs(pickup(robot, A), I) \ \leftarrow \ holds(obj\_relation(below, A, B), I)$$

is ground in the scene to obtain *obj_relation(below, orange_block, blue_block)* as a literal of interest.

(b) If any identified literal is in the answer set at the time step of interest (0 in the current example), and is absent (or its negation is present) in the next step, it is taken to be a reason for executing the action under consideration (line 7).

(c) The condition modified by the execution of the action of interest is paired with the subsequent action to construct the answer to the question (line 8). For instance, the question "Why did you pick up the blue block at time step 0?", receives the answer "I had to pick up the orange block, and the orange block was located below the blue block".

A similar approach is used to justify the selection of any particular action in any particular plan that has been computed but not yet executed.

3. **Hypothetical actions: Why not action X at step I?**   For   questions about actions not selected for execution:
   (a) The robot identifies executability conditions that have the hypothetical action in the head, i.e., conditions that prevent the action from being selected during planning (line 10 in Algorithm 1).
   (b) For each identified executability condition, the robot examines whether literals in the body are satisfied in the corresponding answer set (line 11). If so, these literals are used to construct the answer.

Suppose action *putdown(robot, blue_block, table)* occurred at step 1 in Fig. 1b. For the question "Why did you not put the blue cube on the tennis ball at time step 1?", the following related executability condition is identified:

$$\neg occurs(putdown(robot,\ A,\ B), I) \leftarrow has\_surface(B,\ irregular)$$

which implies that an object cannot be placed on another object with an irregular surface. The answer set indicates that the tennis ball has an irregular surface. The robot provides the answer "Because the tennis ball has an irregular surface".

4. **Belief query: Why belief Y at step I?** To explain any particular belief, the robot searches for support axioms in which the belief is the head and the corresponding body is satisfied in the current state. The search is repeated recursively for literals in the body until no more axioms are found (lines 13–14). These relevant literals are used to construct the answer. For instance, to explain the belief that object ob_1 is unstable in step I, the robot finds the support axiom:

$$\neg holds(stable(ob_1), I) \leftarrow holds(small\_base(ob_1), I)$$

Assume that the current beliefs include that ob_1 has a small base. Searching for why ob_1 is believed to have a small base identifies the axiom:

$$holds(small\_base(ob_1), I) \leftarrow holds(relation(below,\ ob_2,\ ob_1),\ I),$$
$$has\_size(ob_2,\ small),\ has\_size(ob_1,\ big)$$

Asking "why do you believe object ob_1 is unstable at step I?" would provide the answer "Because object ob_2 is below object ob_1, ob_2 is small, and ob_1 is big".

Robot Platform: Our prior work explored scene understanding tasks with simulated images, but this paper considers a robot that also plans and executes actions to achieve the desired goals. As stated earlier, we use a Baxter robot that manipulates objects on a tabletop. The Baxter uses probabilistic algorithms to process inputs from its cameras, e.g., to extract information about the presence of objects, their attributes, and the spatial relations between objects, from images such as Fig. 1b. The Baxter also uses built-in probabilistic motion planning algorithms to execute primitive manipulation actions, e.g., to grasp and pick up objects. Observations obtained with a high probability are elevated to literals associated with complete certainty in the ASP program. Recall that our architecture's non-monotonic logical reasoning capability enables the robot to identify and recover from errors caused by adding incorrect information to the ASP program.

4   Experimental Setup and Results

Subsection 4.1 describes the setup for evaluating the ability to construct relational descriptions of decisions, beliefs, and hypothetical events. Subsection 4.2 then describes some execution traces and Subsect. 4.3 discusses quantitative results.

4.1   Experimental Setup

Experiments were designed to evaluate the following hypotheses:

H1 : reasoning with incrementally learned and merged state constraints improves the quality of plans generated; and

H2 : exploiting the links between reasoning and learning improves the accuracy of the descriptions provided to explain the decisions and beliefs.

These hypotheses and the underlying capabilities of our architecture were evaluated considered four kinds of explanatory requests and questions: (i) describing the plan; (ii) justifying the execution of an action at a given time step; (iii) justifying not choosing a hypothetical action; and (iv) justifying particular beliefs. As stated in Algorithm 1 in Subsect. 3.2, the same methodology can also be adapted to address other requests nd questions. The quality of a plan was measured in terms of the ability to compute minimal plans, i.e., plans with the least number of actions to achieve the desired goals. The quality of an explanation was measured in terms of precision and recall of the literals in the answer provided by our architecture in comparison with the expected response. The expected ("ground truth") response was provided in a semi-supervised manner based on manual input and automatic selection of relevant literals.

Experimental trials considered images from the robot's camera and simulated images. Real world images contained 5–7 objects of different colors, textures, shapes, and sizes in the RA domain of Example 1. The objects included cubes, a pig, a capsicum, a tennis ball, an apple, an orange, and a pot. These objects were either stacked on each other or spread on the table—see Fig. 1b. A total of 40 configurations were created, each with five different goals for planning and four different questions for each plan, resulting in a total of 200 plans and 800

| (a) Execution Example 1. | (b) Execution Example 3. | (c) Additional example. |

Fig. 3. (a) Relation between blue cube and red cube is important for the explanation in Execution Example 1; (b) The rubber duck is the focus of attention in Execution Example 3; and (c) Example of another trial (not described in this paper) in which a tennis ball plays an important role in the explanation constructed by our architecture. (Color figure online)

questions. Since evaluating applicability to a wide range of objects and scenes is difficult on robots, we also used a real-time physics engine (Bullet) to create 40 simulated images, each with 7–9 objects (3–5 stacked and the remaining on a flat surface). Objects included cylinders, spheres, cubes, a duck, and five household objects from the Yale-CMU-Berkeley dataset (apple, pitcher, mustard bottle, mug, and box of crackers). We once again considered five different goals for planning and four different questions for each plan, resulting in the same number of plans (200) and questions (800) as with the real world data.

To explore the interplay between reasoning and learning, we focused on the effect of learned knowledge on planning and constructing explanations. Specifically, we ran experiments with and without some learned constraints in the knowledge base. Learned constraints were revised over time in our architecture, as described in Subsect. 3.1, whereas the learned constraints were not used by the baselines for planning and explanation generation. During planning, we measured the number of optimal, sub-optimal, and incorrect plans, and the planning time. An *optimal* plan is a minimal plan that achieves the goal; a *sub-optimal* plan requires more than the minimum number of steps and/or has to assume an unnecessary exception to default knowledge; and an *incorrect* plan leads to undesirable outcomes and fails to achieve the desired goal. We discuss the quantitative results of these experimental trials after describing some execution traces of our architecture's operation.

4.2 Execution Trace

The following execution traces illustrate our architecture's ability to construct relational descriptions explaining the decisions, beliefs, and the outcomes of hypothetical actions.

Execution Example 1. *[Plans, actions, and beliefs]*
Consider a robot that starts with objects as shown in Fig. 1b. The robot is assigned the goal of achieving a state in which the red block is on top of

the orange block, i.e., *holds(relation(on, red_block, orange_block), I)*. The robot answers the following questions *after executing* a plan and successfully achieving the assigned goal:

- **Human:** "Please describe the plan."
  Baxter: "I picked up the blue block. I put the blue block on the table. I picked up the orange block. I put the orange block on the table. I picked up the red block. I put the red block on the orange block."
- The human may ask the robot to justify a particular action in the executed plan.
  Human: "Why did you pick up the blue block at step 0?"
  Baxter: "Because I had to pick up the red block, and it was below the blue block."
  The constructed answer is also used to automatically highlight the relevant image regions that influenced this answer, as shown in Fig. 3.
- The human now may ask about particular actions that were not considered.
  Human: "Why did you not put down the orange block on the blue block?"
  Baxter: "Because the blue block is small." In the absence of a reference to a particular time step, the robot answers the question based on the single instance (in the executed plan) of putting the orange block on another block or surface. In addition, the answer is based on learned default knowledge, i.e., that objects with a small base are typically unstable.
- The human may also ask about particular beliefs.
  Human: "Why did you believe that the red block was below the blue block in the initial state?"
  Baxter: "Because I observed the red block below the blue block in step zero."

Execution Example 2. *[Reasoning and explanation]*
Continuing with the previous example, the subsequent interactions are as follows:

- **Human:** "Put the tennis ball on the blue cube."
  The goal *holds(relation(on, ball, blue_block), I)* is encoded in the ASP program for planning. The default rule about configurations with small bases being unstable prevents the robot from placing objects on the blue block. At the same time, the robot has to compute plans to achieve the assigned goal. This causes an inconsistency that is resolved by invoking a CR rule and planning to place the ball on the top of the blue block. The following interaction takes place after plan execution:
- **Human:** "Please describe the plan you executed."
  Robot: "I picked up the ball. I put the ball on the blue block."
- The human may now explore the belief of the agent that requires it to consider exceptions to the default knowledge:
  Human: "Why do you believe the ball is on the blue block?"
  Robot: "Because I observed the ball on the blue block in step one."

Combining reasoning with constructing explanations thus allows the robot to adapt to unforeseen exceptions.

Execution Example 3. *[Learning and explanation]*

In some situations, the robot may be unable to respond to the human request or question because it is not possible to achieve the desired object configuration or belief. Even in such cases, our architecture enables the robot to answer explanatory questions. For instance, consider the simulated scene in Fig. 3b, with the following interaction:

- **Human:** "Please put the pitcher on the duck."
  This action is not executed because of a constraint learned during a previous trial that any object configuration that has an object on another object with an irregular surface will be unstable.
- If asked, the robot can justify its decision of not executing the action.
  Human: "Why did you not put the pitcher on the duck?".
  Robot: "Because the duck has an irregular surface."
  The image region relevant to the construction of the robot's answer to the question posed by the human is automatically highlighted in the corresponding image, as indicated in Fig. 3b above.

This example illustrates how integrating reasoning and learning helps justify the decision to not execute a requested action that will have an unfavorable outcome.

Overall, these and other such examples demonstrate how our architecture uses a relational representation, automatically reasons with just the relevant knowledge, incrementally revises axioms, and identifies image regions, attributes, and actions contributing to particular decisions and beliefs. Since the same set of samples are used to learn axioms and train the deep networks, our approach also provides a partial understanding of the behavior of learned deep networks.

4.3   Experimental Results

In this section, we discuss quantitative results of evaluating the desired hypotheses. The first set of experiments was designed as follows to evaluate hypothesis **H1**:

1. Forty initial object configurations were arranged (similar to that in Fig. 1a). The Baxter automatically extracted information (e.g., attributes, spatial relations) from images corresponding to top and frontal views (using the cameras on the left and right grippers), and encoded it in the ASP program as the initial state.
2. For each initial state, five goals were randomly chosen and encoded in the ASP program. The robot reasoned with the existing knowledge to create plans for these 200 combinations (40 initial states, five goals).
3. The plans were evaluated in terms of the number of optimal, sub-optimal and incorrect plans, and planning time.
4. Experiments were repeated with and without the learned axioms.
5. Steps 1–4 (above) were also repeated with the simulated images.

Since the number of plans and planning time vary depending on the initial conditions and the goal, we conducted paired trials with and without the learned constraints included in the ASP program used for reasoning. The initial conditions and goal were identical in each paired trial, and differed between different paired trials. Then, we expressed the number of plans and the planning time with the learned constraints as a fraction of the corresponding values obtained by reasoning without the learned constraints. The average of these fractions over all the trials is reported in Table 1. In addition, we computed the number of optimal, sub-optimal, and incorrect plans in each trial as a fraction of the total number of plans in the trial; we did this separately with and without using the learned axioms for reasoning, and the average over all trials is summarized in Table 2. These results indicate that using the learned axioms for reasoning significantly reduced the search space, resulting in a much smaller number of plans and a substantial reduction in the planning time. In addition, when the robot used the learned axioms for reasoning, it resulted in a much smaller number of sub-optimal plans and eliminated all incorrect plans. Also, each such sub-optimal plan was created only when the corresponding goal could not be achieved without creating an exception to a default, e.g., stacking an object on a small base. Without the learned axioms, a larger fraction of the plans are sub-optimal or incorrect. These results support hypothesis **H1**.

The second set of experiments was designed as follows to evaluate hypothesis **H2**:

Table 1. Number of plans and planning time with the learned axioms expressed as a fraction of the values without the learned axioms. Reasoning with the learned axioms improves performance.

Measures	Ratio (with/without)	
	Real scenes	Simulated scenes
Number of plans	0.36	0.33
Planning time	0.66	0.89

Table 2. Number of optimal, sub-optimal, and incorrect plans expressed as a fraction of the total number of plans. Reasoning with the learned axioms improves performance.

Plans	Real scenes		Simulated scenes	
	Without	With	Without	With
Optimal	0.31	0.82	0.15	0.49
Sub-optimal	0.12	0.18	0.31	0.51
Incorrect	0.57	0	0.54	0

1. For each of the 200 combinations (40 configurations, five goals) from the first set of experiments with real-world data, we considered knowledge bases with and without the learned axioms and had the robot compute plans to achieve the goals.
2. The robot had to describe the plan and justify the choice of a particular action (chosen randomly) in the plan. Then, one parameter of the chosen action was changed randomly to pose a question about why this new action could not be applied. Finally, a belief related to the previous two questions had to be justified.
3. The literals present in the answers were compared against the expected literals in the ideal response, with the average precision and recall scores reported in Table 3.
4. We also performed these experiments separately for simulated images, with the average results summarized in Table 4.

Tables 3 and 4 show that when the learned axioms were used for reasoning, the precision and recall of relevant literals (for constructing the explanation) were higher than when the learned axioms were not included. The improvement in performance is particularly pronounced when the robot has to answer questions about actions that it has not actually executed. The precision and

Table 3. (Real scenes) Precision and recall of retrieving relevant literals for constructing answers to questions with and without using the learned axioms for reasoning. Using the learned axioms significantly improves the ability to provide accurate explanations.

Query type	Precision		Recall	
	Without	With	Without	With
Plan description	91.77%	100%	91.77%	100%
Why X?	91.75%	94.75%	91.98%	94.75%
Why not X?	93.57%	95.16%	87.91%	98.88%
Belief	93.04%	99.35%	93.63%	100%

Table 4. (Simulated scenes) Precision and recall of retrieving relevant literals for constructing answers to questions with and without reasoning with learned axioms. Using the learned axioms significantly improves the ability to provide accurate explanations.

Query type	Precision		Recall	
	Without	With	Without	With
Plan description	90.04%	100%	90.04%	100%
Why X?	93.0%	93.0%	93.0%	93.0%
Why not X?	93.22%	100%	89.43%	98.04%
Belief	97.22%	99.19%	97.9%	100%

recall rates were reasonable even when the learned axioms were not included; this is because not all the learned axioms are needed to accurately answer each explanatory question. When the learned axioms were used for reasoning, errors were very rare and corresponded to some additional literals being included in the answer (i.e., over-specified explanations). In addition, when we specifically removed axioms related to the goal under consideration, precision and recall values were much lower. Furthermore, there was noise in both sensing and actuation, especially in the robot experiments. For instance, recognition of spatial relations, learning of constraints, and manipulation have approximate error rates of 15%, 5–10%, and 15% respectively. Experimental results thus indicate that coupling reasoning and learning to inform and guide each other enables the robot to provide accurate relational descriptions in response to questions about decisions, beliefs, and the outcomes of hypothetical actions. This supports hypothesis **H2**. Additional examples of images, questions, and answers, are in our open source repository [22].

5   Conclusions

This paper described a cognitive systems-inspired approach that enables an integrated robot system to explain its decisions, beliefs, and the outcomes of hypothetical actions. These explanations are constructed on-demand in the form of descriptions of relations between relevant objects, actions, and attributes of the domain. We have implemented this approach in an architecture that combines the complementary strengths of non-monotonic logical reasoning with incomplete commonsense domain knowledge, deep learning, and inductive learning. In the context of some scene understanding and planning tasks performed in simulation and a physical robot, we have demonstrated that our architecture exploits the interplay between knowledge-based reasoning and data-driven learning. It automatically identifies and reasons with the relevant information to efficiently construct the desired explanations, with both the planning and explanation generation performance improving significantly when previously unknown state constraints are learned incrementally and used for subsequent reasoning.

Our architecture opens up multiple avenues for further research. First, we will integrate the ability to learn other kinds of axioms and the corresponding knowledge represented as an ASP program. We will do so by building on the approach developed in our group by combining non-monotonic logical reasoning, active learning, and relational reinforcement learning [30]. Second, we will explore more complex domains, tasks, and explanations, reasoning with relevant knowledge at different tightly-coupled resolutions for scalability [29]. We are specifically interested in exploring scenarios in which there is ambiguity in the questions (e.g., it is unclear which of two occurrences of the *pickup* action the human is referring to), or the explanation is needed at a different level of abstraction, specificity, or verbosity. We will do so by building on a related theory of explanations [31]. Third, we will use our architecture to better understand the behavior of deep networks. The key advantage of using our architecture is that it uses reasoning to guide learning. Unlike "end to end" data-driven learning methods based on deep networks, our architecture uses reasoning to trigger learning only when existing knowledge is insufficient to perform the desired task(s). The long-term objective is to develop an architecture that exploits the complementary strengths of knowledge-based reasoning and data-driven learning for the reliable and efficient operation of robots in complex, dynamic domains.

Acknowledgments. This work was supported in part by the Asian Office of Aerospace Research and Development award FA2386-16-1-4071 and the U.S. Office of Naval Research Science of Autonomy Award N00014-17-1-2434. Reported opinions are those of the authors.

References

1. Anjomshoae, S., Najjar, A., Calvaresi, D., Framling, K.: Explainable agents and robots: results from a systematic literature review. In: International Conference on Autonomous Agents and Multiagent Systems, Montreal, Canada (2019)
2. Assaf, R., Schumann, A.: Explainable deep neural networks for multivariate time series predictions. In: International Joint Conference on Artificial Intelligence, Macao, China, pp. 6488–6490 (2019)
3. Borgo, R., Cashmore, M., Magazzeni, D.: Towards providing explanations for AI planner decisions. In: IJCAI Workshop on Explainable Artificial Intelligence, pp. 11–17 (2018)
4. David, H., Tom, B.: An Enquiry Concerning Human Understanding: A Critical Edition. Oxford University Press, New York (2000)
5. Erdem, E., Patoglu, V.: Applications of ASP in robotics. Künstliche Intelligenz **32**, 143–149 (2018). https://doi.org/10.1007/s13218-018-0544-x
6. Fox, M., Long, D., Magazzeni, D.: Explainable Planning. In: IJCAI Workshop on Explainable AI (2017)
7. Friedman, M.: Explanation and scientific understanding. Philosophy **71**(1), 5–19 (1974)
8. Gelfond, M., Inclezan, D.: Applications of ASP in robotics. J. Appl. Non-Class. Logics **23**(1–2), 105–120 (2013). Special Issue on Equilibrium Logic and Answer Set ProgrammingSpecial Issue on Equilibrium Logic and Answer Set ProgrammingSpecial Issue on Equilibrium Logic and Answer Set ProgrammingSpecial Issue on Equilibrium Logic and Answer Set ProgrammingSpecial Issue on Equilibrium Logic and Answer Set Programming
9. Gelfond, M., Kahl, Y.: Knowledge Representation, Reasoning and the Design of Intelligent Agents. Cambridge University Press, New York (2014)
10. de Kleer, J., Williams, B.C.: Diagnosing multiple faults. Artif. Intell. **32**, 97–130 (1987)
11. Koh, P.W., Liang, P.: Understanding black-box predictions via influence functions. In: International Conference on Machine Learning, pp. 1885–1894 (2017)
12. Krizhevsky, A., Sutskever, I., Hinton, G.E.: ImageNet classification with deep convolutional neural networks. In: Neural Information Processing Systems, pp. 1097–1105 (2012)
13. Laird, J.E.: The Soar Cognitive Architecture. The MIT Press, Cambridge (2012)

14. Langley, P., Meadows, B., Sridharan, M., Choi, D.: Explainable agency for intelligent autonomous systems. In: Innovative Applications of Artificial Intelligence (2017)
15. Langley, P.: Progress and challenges in research on cognitive architectures. In: AAAI Conference on Artificial Intelligence, San Francisco, USA, 4–9 February 2017
16. LeCun, Y., Bottou, L., Bengio, Y., Haffner, P.: Gradient-based learning applied to document recognition. Proc. IEEE **86**(11), 2278–2324 (1998)
17. Lewandowsky, S., Mundy, M., Tan, G.: The dynamics of trust: comparing humans to automation. J. Exp. Psychol. Appl. **6**(2), 104 (2000)
18. Miller, G.A.: WordNet: a lexical database for English. Commun. ACM **38**(11), 39–41 (1995)
19. Miller, T.: Explanations in artificial intelligence: insights from the social sciences. Artif. Intell. **267**, 1–38 (2019)
20. Mota, T., Sridharan, M.: Incrementally grounding expressions for spatial relations between objects. In: International Joint Conference on Artificial Intelligence, pp. 1928–1934 (2018)
21. Mota, T., Sridharan, M.: Commonsense reasoning and knowledge acquisition to guide deep learning on robots. In: Robotics Science and Systems (2019)
22. Mota, T., Sridharan, M.: Scene understanding, reasoning, and explanation generation (2020). https://github.com/tmot987/Scenes-Understanding
23. Norcliffe-Brown, W., Vafeais, E., Parisot, S.: Learning conditioned graph structures for interpretable visual question answering. In: Neural Information Processing Systems, Montreal, Canada, 3–8 December 2018
24. Read, S.J., Marcus-Newhall, A.: Explanatory coherence in social explanations: a parallel distributed processing account. Pers. Soc. Psychol. **65**(3), 429 (1993)
25. Ribeiro, M., Singh, S., Guestrin, C.: Why should I trust You? Explaining the predictions of any classifier. In: International Conference on Knowledge Discovery and Data Mining, pp. 1135–1144 (2016)
26. Samek, W., Wiegand, T., Müller, K.R.: Explainable artificial intelligence: understanding, visualizing and interpreting deep learning models. ITU J. ICT Discoveries Impact Artif. Intell. Commun. Netw. Serv. **1**, 1–10 (2017)
27. Seegebarth, B., Müller, F., Schattenberg, B., Biundo, S.: Making hybrid plans more clear to human users: a formal approach for generating sound explanations. In: International Conference on Automated Planning and Scheduling (2012)
28. Someya, Y.: Lemma list for English language (1998)
29. Sridharan, M., Gelfond, M., Zhang, S., Wyatt, J.: REBA: a refinement-based architecture for knowledge representation and reasoning in robotics. J. Artif. Intell. Res. **65**, 87–180 (2019)
30. Sridharan, M., Meadows, B.: Knowledge representation and interactive learning of domain knowledge for human-robot collaboration. Adv. Cogn. Syst. **7**, 69–88 (2018)
31. Sridharan, M., Meadows, B.: Towards a theory of explanations for human-robot collaboration. Kunstliche Intelligenz **33**(4), 331–342 (2019)
32. Yi, K., Wu, J., Gan, C., Torralba, A., Kohli, P., Tenenbaum, J.B.: Neural-symbolic VQA: disentangling reasoning from vision and language understanding. In: Neural Information Processing Systems, Montreal, Canada, 3–8 December 2018
33. Zhang, Y., Sreedharan, S., Kulkarni, A., Chakraborti, T., Zhuo, H.H., Kambhampati, S.: Plan explicability and predictability for robot task planning. In: International Conference on Robotics and Automation, pp. 1313–1320 (2017)

Combining Lévy Walks and Flocking for Cooperative Surveillance Using Aerial Swarms

Hugo Sardinha[✉], Mauro Dragone, and Patricia A. Vargas

Edinburgh Centre for Robotics, Heriot-Watt University, Scotland, UK
{hs20,m.dragone,p.a.vargas}@hw.ac.uk.com

Abstract. Continuous area coverage missions are a fundamental part of many swarm robotics applications. One of such missions is cooperative surveillance, where the main aim is to deploy a swarm for covering predefined areas of interest simultaneously by k robots, leading to better overall sensing accuracy. However, without prior knowledge of the location of these areas, robots need to continuously explore the domain, so that up-to-date data is gathered while maintaining the benefits of simultaneous observations. In this paper, we propose a model for a swarm of unmanned aerial vehicles to successfully achieve cooperative surveillance. Our model combines the concept of Lévy Walk for exploration and Reynolds' flocking rules for coordination. Simulation results clearly show that our model outperforms a simple collision avoidance mechanism, commonly found in Lévy-based multi-robot systems. Further preliminary experiments with real robots corroborate the idea.

Keywords: Lévy Walk · Swarm intelligence · Reynolds' flocking · Surveillance area coverage · Swarm robotics

1 Introduction

The benefits of swarm intelligence techniques have been widely exploited in cooperative missions [1–7]. A particular advantage of these techniques is the focus on generating decentralized controllers, allowing for greater scalability in real-world applications. Such applications often require the swarm to deal with the lack of prior knowledge of the domain, as well as demanding reliable up-to-date information [8]. This is particularly true in surveillance and monitoring tasks in a variety of domains, such as: inspection and surveillance [9,10], search & rescue [8,11], and agriculture [12–14]. Both surveillance and monitoring tasks focus on developing control laws which enable groups of robots to transverse and observe a given domain, but with a slightly different focus. The goal of surveillance is to maximize some measure of coverage or information gathering, while monitoring focuses on ensuring that certain areas of the domain (usually predefined) are visited with a certain frequency. To tackle these tasks, aerial swarms have been widely employed as the preferred vehicle [15], due to their intrinsic ability to

© Springer Nature Switzerland AG 2020
N. Bassiliades et al. (Eds.): EUMAS 2020/AT 2020, LNAI 12520, pp. 226–242, 2020.
https://doi.org/10.1007/978-3-030-66412-1_15

gather data over a wide field of the ground plane, for example, through a down facing camera. However, as their distance to the ground increases, the resolution of observations decreases [16]. Furthermore, the accuracy of these observations is also affected by the noisy characteristics inherent to any sensor leading to inaccuracies [17]. These factors have led researchers to propose that several simultaneous observations of the same point would yield a more accurate measurement [17,18]. This proposition is extremely useful when considering unmanned aerial vehicles (UAVs), since their overlapping sensing regions (or fields of view) on the ground plane, are the means by which these desired multiple simultaneous observations can be gathered. Figure 1 depicts an example where three quadcopters share points in their respective fields of view. This ability to maintain an overlap of sensing regions, naturally requires robots to be able to coordinate, while on the other hand, the very nature of the surveillance task, requires robots to continuously explore the domain [19].

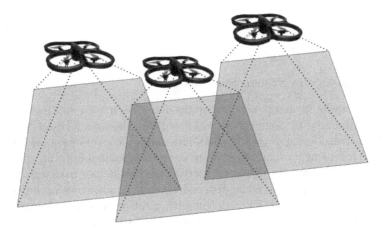

Fig. 1. Fields of view for 3 aerial vehicles, where the darker shades represent the areas sensed simultaneously by more than one UAV.

Examples of such exploratory behaviours are widely found in natural societies, such as in honeybees [20], sharks [21] and primates [22]. In fact, foraging individuals in these societies have been noted to explore an environment by coupling periods of localized random walks with periods of ballistic relocation across the domain [23]. This exploratory behaviour is known as *Lévy Walk* (LW) [24] and has been successfully used as an exploratory behavior for single-agent systems [25], as well as in swarm-based systems [26]. In contrast to previous works, we focus on studying the ability of robots within swarm, not only to coordinate in order to maintain the aforementioned overlapping sensing regions, but to do so while preforming LWs, leveraging exploration. We propose that this can be accomplished by merging a biologically-inspired coordination strategy and a LW controller, in a decentralized manner. Such coordination strategies have long drawn inspiration also from natural agents' inherent ability to coordinate using only simple and local control rules [27]. The most popular of such frameworks was introduced by Reynolds in [28], where the rules to generate *flocking* behaviours were proposed. In our work, we bringing together the *flocking* rules proposed by Reynolds, and the LW motion model, effectively creating a system that seamlessly integrates both coordination and exploration.

1.1 Contribution

The main contribution of this paper is the development of a decentralized model, integrating the coordination mechanism based on Reynolds' rules, with and an exploratory behaviour based on *Lévy Walk*. We test our model in a simulated environment on a cooperative surveillance task. The aim is to explore a given domain, while maintaining an overlap between the regions sensed by robots of the swarm. We also demonstrate our controller with proof-of-concept experiments with two drones.

2 Swarm Systems

2.1 Surveillance in Swarm Systems

Surveillance tasks in multi robot systems have been long addressed by the research community [9]. Some of the initial works in this area focused on optimizing policies, considering trajectory planning, energy consumption and dynamic constraints for a single robot, which were later extrapolated into the multi-robot scenario [29]. Other works developed model-based strategies to determine feasible trajectories in real time while also considering detailed sensing models [30], or considering the task routing problem with a set of predefined locations that need to be visited [31]. More recently authors also applied the *flocking* strategy proposed by Reynolds to address coordination [32], using a pheromone map to guide the swarm to explore new regions. While control actions were computed in a decentralized manner, the pheromone map is treated as a central shared resource, of which every robot is assumed to have knowledge at any point in time. We should highlight that, even if these works focus on the surveillance task by employing an aerial swarm, neither of them address the extra constraint of having overlapping sensing regions.

Another approach to surveillance using aerial swarms was proposed by Saska in [9]. In this work a Particle Swarm Optimization (PSO) based method was used to derive individual robot trajectories before deployment, with prior knowledge of areas of interest to be visited, therefore centralising the method on the planning level. However, authors demonstrate that, after deployment, on-board sensing can be used in a distributed fashion to adjust trajectories using relative-localization methods between UAVs, in cases where external localization is non-existent or lacks the desired precision. Even though this work mentions the benefits that multiple simultaneous observations can bring, the metrics presented focus mainly on the output of their proposed PSO in regards to the areas visited and accuracy of individual pose estimation.

Interestingly, the topic of overlapping sensing regions has been given more attention in the field of Wireless Sensing Networks (WSNs) [33,34]. However, works in this field usually assume that a predefined set of areas exist such that each point needs to be observed by k sensors simultaneously, a task known as k-coverage [35]. Approaches to k-coverage using robots mainly focus on: optimizing the number of robots to be deployed for the desired coverage constraints [36]; optimizing energy efficiency [19], or optimizing network connectivity [37], which tend to require prior knowledge of the set of areas of interest. Nevertheless, k-coverage is a topic relevant to this work and as such we will use this concept as a metric to show that our proposed model enables the swarm to achieve simultaneous observations while exploring the domain.

2.2 Lévy Walks in Swarm Systems

Sutantyo *et al.* introduced the *Lévy Walk* (LW) into swarm applications [38], using the notion of artificial potential fields, as a means of collision avoidance between robots preforming LWs, for a target search task. Later, that work was extended to consider an adaptation of the Lévy parameter (μ) based on the density of targets found [26]. Another work that deals with underwater multi-robot search using LW is presented in [39]. However, contrary to what we will assume, authors consider the scenario where regions of the environment are divided and each robot explores its own assigned region. Suarez and Murphy in their survey [40] also suggest that robots should divide the environment into individual search areas. Nevertheless, they also point out that regions of interest might not clear at the start, and might even change over time, making it difficult to subdivide an environment prior to the mission. However, all the aforementioned works focus on a slightly different problem, since they consider targets in the domain and study their impact on each robot's behaviour. Our approach focuses on a more fundamental aspect of the swarm's behaviour, namely, how can robots both coordinate and explore, while maintaining overlapping sensing regions.

To highlight the benefits of LW in surveillance or coverage tasks, authors in [41] have compared analytical results, considering strategies based on LW and other random walk-based methods to show the clear advantage of the former, in terms of overall robots' displacement. More recent papers on Lévy Walks for swarm systems have also focused primarily on math-based models [42], which tend to abstract real constraints such as robots' dynamics, communication and sensing capabilities, as well as ability to maintain overlapping observations.

In summary, our proposed model differs from the any of the above, in two key aspects: i) absence of predefined search regions for each robot and ii) fully decentralized control of UAVs.

3   Proposed Model

In our model, robots use a behaviour-based controller divided into two components: *Flocking:Interaction*, dealing with the coordination behaviour, and *Lévy Walk*, introducing the exploratory behaviour, each outputting a velocity vector.

3.1   Flocking:Interaction

This component, based on [28], consists of three rules: separation; cohesion; and alignment, defined below.

Separation: Consider the ith robot, with a neighbourhood $\mathbf{N_s}$ of all the j robots below a distance δ_s whose positions $\mathbf{p_j}$ have their centroid at $\mathbf{P_s}$ defined as:

$$\mathbf{P_s} = \left(\sum_{j \in N_s} \mathbf{p_j} \Big/ N_s \right) - \mathbf{p_i} \tag{1}$$

Based on the relative orientation of $\mathbf{P_s}$ to the position of the ith robot (ρ_s^θ) we compute the *separation* contribution, in form of an angular velocity, as:

$$\mathbf{w_s} = \beta \begin{bmatrix} 0 & 0 & w_s^z \end{bmatrix}^T = \beta \begin{bmatrix} 0 & 0 & (\rho_s^\theta + \pi) - \theta_i \end{bmatrix}^T \tag{2}$$

Where θ_i is the orientation of the ith robot. Note that we add π to the computation so that we consider a vector *away* from the geometric center $\mathbf{P_s}$.

Cohesion: Consider the ith robot, with a neighbourhood $\mathbf{N_c}$ of all the j robots below a distance δ_c whose positions $\mathbf{p_j}$ have their centroid at $\mathbf{P_c}$ defined as:

$$\mathbf{P_c} = \left(\sum_{j \in N_c} \mathbf{p_j} \Big/ N_c \right) - \mathbf{p_i} \tag{3}$$

Based on the relative orientation of $\mathbf{P_c}$ to the position of the ith robot (ρ_c^θ) we compute the *cohesion* contribution, in form of an angular velocity, as:

$$\mathbf{w_c} = \gamma \begin{bmatrix} 0 & 0 & w_c^z \end{bmatrix}^T = \gamma \begin{bmatrix} 0 & 0 & \rho_c^\theta - \theta_i \end{bmatrix}^T \tag{4}$$

where θ_i is the orientation of the ith robot. Note that we *do not* add π to the computation so that we consider a vector *towards* the geometric center $\mathbf{P_c}$.

Alignment: Consider i^{th} robot, and the average heading Θ of the j robots in a neighbourhood $\mathbf{N_a}$ within distance $\delta_a > \delta_s$.

$$\Theta = \sum_{j \in \mathbf{N_a}} \theta_j \Big/ \mathbf{N_a} \tag{5}$$

where θ_j is the orientation of robot j in $(r\ p\ y)$ coordinates. The *alignment* contribution, in the form of angular velocity $\mathbf{w_a}$, is computed as:

$$\mathbf{w_a} = \alpha \left[0\ 0\ \omega_a^z\right]^T = \alpha \left[0\ 0\ (\mathbf{\Theta} - \theta_i)\right]^T \tag{6}$$

The contribution from the *interaction* block, for the ith robot in the swarm, is given by Eq. (8), where α, β and γ are weights between 0 and 1:

$$\Phi_i = \begin{bmatrix} \mathbf{v} \\ \mathbf{w_s} + \mathbf{w_a} + \mathbf{w_c} \end{bmatrix} \tag{7}$$

$$= [v_x\ 0\ 0\ 0\ 0\ \beta\omega_s^z + \gamma\omega_c^z + \alpha\omega_a^z]^T \tag{8}$$

3.2 Lévy Walk

To introduce a *Lévy*-based velocity command into the algorithm, we first generate the appropriate variables, i.e., target orientation ψ and walk length L. For that we use the *Lévy Generator* proposed by [43] to randomly draw a Lévy distributed variable r:

$$r = \frac{\sin\left((\mu - 1) * \widetilde{U_1}\right)}{\cos(\widetilde{U_1})^{\frac{1}{1-\mu}}} \left(\frac{\cos\left((2 - \mu) * \widetilde{U_1}\right)}{\widetilde{U_2}}\right)^{\frac{2-\mu}{\mu - 1}} \tag{9}$$

where $\widetilde{U_1} = U_1\pi/2$, $\widetilde{U_2} = (U_2 + 1)/2$, and a random orientation being given by $\psi = U_3\pi$ with $U_1\ U_2\ U_3$ being uniformly distributed random variables between 0 and 1 and μ the Lévy parameter that influences the length of the jump. Figure 2 illustrates this influence.

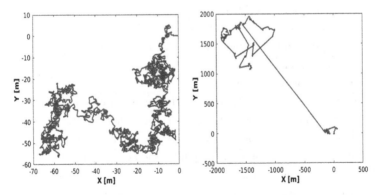

Fig. 2. Trajectories of one robot with different μ values. On the left $\mu = 3$ and on the right $mu = 2$, showing how higher values o μ lead to smaller walks and hence more frequent change of orientation.

Having selected r, we draw an uniformly distributed value of ψ and compute:

$$x = r \cdot \cos(\psi) \tag{10}$$
$$y = r \cdot \sin(\psi) \tag{11}$$
$$L = \sqrt{x^2 + y^2} \tag{12}$$

As robots transverse space, the distance each one travels d is calculated and updated. When this distance reaches L, a new L is generated as well as a new ψ. As this happens and a robot finishes its walk, it starts updating its orientation making its neighbours react to this change and continue their trajectory in a different direction. Similarly to before this change is forced upon a robot through a velocity command:

$$\mathbf{w_l} = \eta \begin{bmatrix} 0 & 0 & \omega_l^z \end{bmatrix}^T = \begin{bmatrix} 0 & 0 & \eta(\psi - \theta) \end{bmatrix}^T \tag{13}$$

where η is a scaling factor and θ is the yaw angle of a robot in the swarm. This angular velocity command overrides both *alignment* and *separation* rules in order to achieve the desired orientation. In this case linear velocity command

Table 1. Notation

$\mathbf{P_s}$	Centroid of the neighbours' positions considered for the Separation rule
$\mathbf{P_c}$	Centroid of the neighbours' positions considered for the Cohesion rule
Θ	Average heading of neighbours considered for the Alignment rule
δ_s	Threshold below which neighbours are considered for the Separation rule
δ_c	Threshold below which neighbours are considered for the Cohesion rule
δ_a	Threshold below which neighbours are considered for the Alignment rule
$\mathbf{N_s}$	Set of neighbours considered for the Separation rule
$\mathbf{N_c}$	Set of neighbours considered for the Cohesion rule
$\mathbf{N_a}$	Set of neighbours considered for the Alignment rule
μ	Lévy parameter
L	Length of generated walk
$\mathbf{w_s}$	Angular velocity component output by the Separation rule
$\mathbf{w_c}$	Angular velocity component output by the Cohesion rule
$\mathbf{w_a}$	Angular velocity component output by the Alignment rule
$\mathbf{w_l}$	Angular velocity component output by the Lévy generator
$\mathbf{\Phi_i}$	Velocity command for agent i based on the Interaction rules
$\mathbf{\Lambda_i}$	Velocity command for agent i based on the Lévy process
$\mathbf{p_i}$	Position of agent i
v_x, v_y	Linear components of the agent's velocity in local frame
θ_i	Orientation of agent i
β, γ, α	Weights for Separation, Cohesion and Alignment rules respectively

Table 2. Values of fixed parameters used in the interaction component.

δ_s [m]	δ_c [m]	δ_a [m]	β	γ	α
1.5	2.5	2.5	5	0.2	1

assumes the type of $\mathbf{v_l} = \begin{bmatrix} v_x, v_y, 0 \end{bmatrix}$ with orientation $(\rho_s^\theta + \pi)$ and therefore the Lévy based contribution to a robot's velocity is given by Eq. (14). Tables 1 and 2 summarize, respectively, the notation used in our proposed model and the fixed parameters used in the interaction component of our model.

$$\mathbf{\Lambda_i} = \begin{bmatrix} \mathbf{v_l} \ \mathbf{w_l} \end{bmatrix}^T = \begin{bmatrix} v_x \ v_y \ 0 \ 0 \ 0 \ \omega_l \end{bmatrix}^T \tag{14}$$

Having set the components of our proposed model, we present below the algorithm for a seamless integration of *Lévy Walks* and coordination rules which runs in a decentralized manner, for each separate UAV. Algorithm 1 shows the conditional relationships between commands $(C(t))$ sent to each agent. While time t is smaller than the total time of the experiment T, each agent computes the interaction rules according to their respective neighbourhoods and check if their walk is completed. The action of each agent is then conditional on its own walk being completed or not.

Algorithm 1. Lévy Swarm Algorithm (LSA)

Initialize distance $d = 0$.
Assign L
Initialize control action $\mathbf{C}(t_0) = \begin{bmatrix} 0 \ 0 \ 0 \ 0 \ 0 \ 0 \end{bmatrix}$
while $t \leq T$ **do**
    Compute Interaction rules
    if $d \geq L$ **then**   ▷ Completed Walk
        Compute new ψ and L
        $d = 0$
        $\mathbf{C}(t) = \mathbf{\Lambda}$ ▷ Lévy Command
    else
        $\mathbf{C}(t) = \mathbf{\Phi}$ ▷ Interaction Command
    end if
    Get pose
    Update distance d
end while

---

4   Experiments and Results

In this section, we illustrate the effectiveness of the proposed model in a number of simulated experiments. We also present a preliminary real robot experiment that was designed to test the main components of our model using 2 Parrot drones. A video demonstrating the results accompanies this paper[1].

---

[1] https://youtu.be/KvEs7wQ0Ti4.

4.1 Simulation Experiments

Simulations were conducted on 20 m by 20 m grid sub-divided into tiles of 0.5 m, for evaluation, and run in `GAZEBO-ROS` framework. The size of the swarm was set to 15 Parrot `ar-drones`, to sufficiently large for the interaction rules to have an effect, but not excessively so, to avoid covering the domain without the need for a strategy. A ROS-based framework was chosen due to its wide adoption in both academia and industry, and the recognition it receives as being the *de-facto* operating system for the development of applications in robotics.

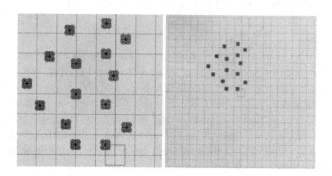

Fig. 3. Initial position of 15 UAVs in an empty arena, for the simulation experiments

Each robot, i.e. Parrot `ar-drone`, has a down-facing camera capable of sensing an area of 2.5 m by 2.5 m. Each robot is assumed to have an accurate estimation of its pose (through GPS in simulation, and through the VICON mocap system in the real experiments) which is communicated directly to its neighbourhood. Such neighbourhood is limited by the robot's communication range considered to be the same as δ_a. Figure 3 shows the initial positions of the UAVs in the simulated area. These simulations considered a varying Lévy parameter (μ) with values $\mu \in]1, 3[$. Each parameter (μ) was run 60 times, for a period of 1,800 s. Simulations were run with $\mu = [1.6, 2.0, 2.4, 2.8]$ to show differences in the behaviour of the swarm, at low, medium and high values of μ. In this work we quantify how many tiles of the grid-domain the swarm is able to maintain under a certain k coverage level over time, defined as $K(t)$. Our metric is defined by, firstly, considering the subset of tiles sensed by UAV i at time t, i.e. $A_i(t)$, and define a set $\Omega(t)$ that contains all these subsets as:

$$\Omega(t) = \{A_i(t)\} \quad \forall i \leq N \tag{15}$$

where N is the number of UAVs. Through set Ω we can enumerate all the combinations of k A subsets and create set S^k, of size $\binom{N}{k}$, where each member is one of said combinations. Therefore, $K(t)$ is the total size of intersections between the A subsets within the elements of S^k, and defined as:

$$K(t) = \sum_{\forall j} |\cap \{S_j^k\}_{j \subset J}| \tag{16}$$

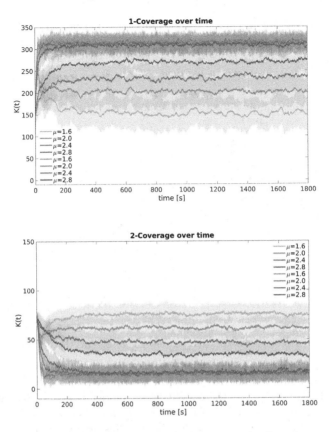

Fig. 4. Number of cells under k-coverage over time for $k \in [1, 2]$, with our model (blue) and the baseline (red) (Color figure online).

where J is the index set of S. Results of our simulations are depicted in Fig. 4 and show our proposed model (blue) and a simpler one with only the avoidance rule (red), hereafter addressed as the baseline, for $k \in [1, 2]$. Our results for $k = 1$, show that it is the baseline case which performs the best. Since robots only interact to avoid each other, this creates a diffusive behaviour, that naturally increases the number of cells sensed only by one UAV. However, in the context of our problem we are mainly interested in the scenario where $k = 2$.

Figures 4.1 and 4.2 both show how much merging the *flocking* rules with the LW component impacts the results. In qualitative terms the results are completely the opposite, showing how this merging of techniques leads to a significant outperforming behaviour when $k = 2$.

It is also interesting to highlight that as the value of μ increases, the performance of the system tends to the baseline case, showing that as μ approaches its maximum value, the local exploratory component of the system dominates the coordination mechanism. However, by observing Fig. 4 alone one cannot assess about the effectiveness of exploration, since there is no indication if the cells sensed at a given point in time are the same, or not, than the cells sensed at a later stage. To assess this, we introduce a random variable $\mathscr{X}_k$, that represents *the total number of different cells sensed by k* **UAVs** and whose probability distribution, $P(\mathscr{X}_k)$, is shown in Fig. 5.

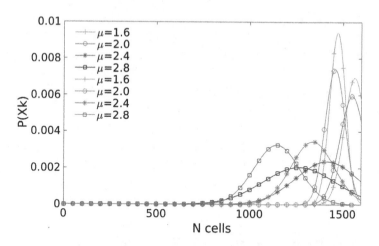

Fig. 5. Simulated $P(\mathscr{X}_k)$ for $k=2$, with our model (blue) and the baseline (red) (Color figure online).

This result also highlights the benefit of our model, which invariably leads to a higher mean of different cells sensed, leading to a higher probability of sensing all the cells of the domain with $k = 2$ robots . This advantage is evident in the results obtained with our model, always outperforming its baseline counterpart for each value of μ.

4.2   Preliminary Real Experiments

In order to further investigate the role of k in the simulation, some preliminary experiments were conducted with two real Parrot **ar-drones** in a 3×3 m arena. To consider a similar ratio between the size of the arena domain and the size of each tile of the grid, tiles are considered to be 0.05×0.05 m. Figure 6 shows this domain as well as the initial positions of the two UAVs.

Similarly to the simulated experiments, we first plot the total number of cells sensed by k UAVs over time t. Figures 7.1 and 7.2 show these results.

The first noticeable difference between simulated and real results is the apparent lack of effect of μ in both cases. In fact, since Lévy processes tend to occur over long distances, the preliminary scenario used is too small for such investigation. Nevertheless one can still draw a parallel with simulated results where values for k are concerned. On one hand, for $k = 1$, the baseline always yields a higher value, as expected since $k = 1$ favours a diffusion behaviour, rather than a coordinated one. On the other hand, for $k = 2$, the results are again reversed, being our model able to outperform the baseline.

Fig. 6. Initial positions of 2 ar-drones

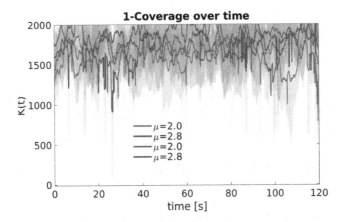

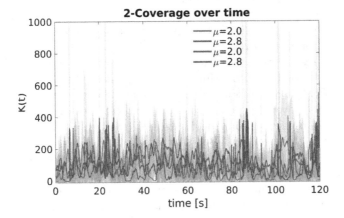

Fig. 7. Experimental number of cells under k-coverage for $k = [1, 2]$ with our model (blue) and the baseline (red) (Color figure online).

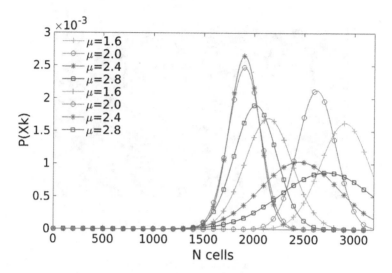

Fig. 8. Experimental $P(\mathscr{X}_k)$ for $k=2$, for our model (blue) and the baseline (red) (Color figure online).

The same is true for the probability distributions of $\mathscr{X}$, depicted in Fig. 8, where our model continues to show a higher average number of cells being sensed by k UAVs simultaneously.

5 Conclusions and Future Work

This paper presented a swarm model that combines coordination and exploration strategies using UAVs for collaborative surveillance. Our model is fully decentralized, with minimal direct communication between robots [44] and does not require global knowledge or partitioning of the domain. This model is, to the best of our knowledge, the first to merge the Reynolds *flocking* rules and the *Lévy Walk* exploration strategy.

Simulation results were assessed based on two metrics. The first, $K(t)$, represents the total number of tiles, in a grid domain, sensed by k UAVs at time t. The second, $P(\mathscr{X}_k)$, represents the distribution of the *number of different cells sensed by k UAVs* over the course of the experiment. Both metrics have shown the advantage of the proposed model for k-coverage when $= 2$. Merging the *flocking* rules with the LW strategy, always increased the performance of the system, when compared to the baseline case where only collision avoidance exists. Our results show that, choosing lower values of μ is preferential when our model is adopted. On the other hand, in the baseline case, the performance of the system, in respect to $K(t)$, seems to be independent of μ. Since the only interaction between agents is collision avoidance, we infer that this aspect, rather than the LW, is the predominant behaviour, pointing towards the need for future work on the study of interference among agents in a swarm.

The effect of μ, in both our model and the baseline, is evident in the second metric, $P(\mathscr{X}_k)$. The results show that higher values of μ tend to lead to a lower mean of (N) different cells being discovered, reflecting the expected behaviour of the LW for values of μ in this range. Noticeably, when comparing the distributions $P(\mathscr{X}_k)$ between our model and the baseline, the mean value of $P(\mathscr{X}_k)$ is always higher in our model, than the respective baseline result. This shows that, for the same mission time, the baseline approach restricts the swarm from sensing a higher number of different cells simultaneously with k UAVs. These results corroborate the hypothesis that merging both behaviours ensures that a larger portion of the domain is covered, maintaining the desired overlapping sensing regions. Despite the positive results favouring our model, the difference between probability distributions is less evident in simulation than in real experiments.

Future work will focus on studying the behaviour of our coordination algorithm with more realistic sensing and communication models as well as performing a sensitivity analysis regarding the swarm size and flocking parameters. We aim to assess the performance of our approach applied to a larger swarms of flying drones, in terms of k-coverage but also in terms of its ability to deal with robots' failures and other unexpected events.

We also would like to conduct experiments on variations of the *Lévy Walk* concept. For instance, by including inertial motion, making the change of orientation not uniformly random but biased towards the current heading. This way we could maximize the crossing of the entire domain. Another example, would be to explore other *Lévy Walk* parameters using machine learning techniques, more specifically, artificial homeostatic systems [45–47], evolutionary approaches [48,49] or a combination of both [50,51].

Acknowledgments. The authors would like to thank Siobhan Duncan, Gissell Estrada, Jakub Stocek and Heiko Gimperlein for the insightful discussions on the model.

References

1. Şahin, E.: Swarm robotics: from sources of inspiration to domains of application. In: Şahin, E., Spears, W.M. (eds.) SR 2004. LNCS, vol. 3342, pp. 10–20. Springer, Heidelberg (2005). https://doi.org/10.1007/978-3-540-30552-1_2
2. Vargas, P.A., Benhalen, A.M., Pessin, G., Osório, F.S.: Applying particle swarm optimization to a garbage and recycling collection problem. In: 2012 12th UK Workshop on Computational Intelligence (UKCI), pp. 1–8. IEEE (2012)
3. Pessin, G., et al.: Swarm intelligence and the quest to solve a garbage and recycling collection problem. Soft. Comput. **17**(12), 2311–2325 (2013)
4. Couceiro, M.S., Rocha, R.P., Ferreira, N.M.F., Vargas, P.A.: Darwinian robotic swarms for exploration with minimal communication. In: 2013 IEEE Congress on Evolutionary Computation, pp. 127–134 (2013)
5. Griffiths Sànchez, N.D., Vargas, P.A., Couceiro, M.S.: A darwinian swarm robotics strategy applied to underwater exploration. In: 2018 IEEE Congress on Evolutionary Computation (CEC), pp. 1–6 (2018)

6. Oliveira, G.M.B., et al.: A cellular automata-based path-planning for a cooperative and decentralized team of robots. In: 2019 IEEE Congress on Evolutionary Computation (CEC), pp. 739–746 (2019)
7. Artaxo, P.G., Bourgois, A., Sardinha, H., Vieira, H., de Paiva, E.C., Fioravanti, A.R., Vargas, P.A.: Autonomous cooperative flight control for airship swarms (2020). https://arxiv.org/abs/2004.07665
8. Couceiro, M.S., Vargas, P.A., Rocha, R.P., Ferreira, N.M.F.: Benchmark of swarm robotics distributed techniques in a search task. Robot. Auton. Syst. $62(2)$, 200–213 (2014)
9. Saska, M., et al.: Autonomous deployment of swarms of micro-aerial vehicles in cooperative surveillance. In: 2014 International Conference on Unmanned Aircraft Systems (ICUAS), pp. 584–595. IEEE (2014)
10. Artaxo, P.G., et al.: Control of multiple airships for autonomous surveillance and target tracking. In: XIII Brazilian International Symposium in Intelligent Automation, pp. 771–778 (2017)
11. Din, A., Jabeen, M., Zia, K., Khalid, A., Saini, D.K.: Behavior-based swarm robotic search and rescue using fuzzy controller. Comput. Electr. Eng. 70, 53–65 (2018)
12. Costa, F.G., Ueyama, J., Braun, T., Pessin, G., Osório, F.S., Vargas, P.A.: The use of unmanned aerial vehicles and wireless sensor network in agricultural applications. In: 2012 IEEE International Geoscience and Remote Sensing Symposium, pp. 5045–5048 (2012)
13. Faiçal, B.S., et al.: The use of unmanned aerial vehicles and wireless sensor networks for spraying pesticides. J. Syst. Architect. $60(4)$, 393–404 (2014)
14. Albani, D., Ijsselmuiden, J., Haken, R., Trianni, V.: Monitoring and mapping with robot swarms for agricultural applications. In: 2017 14th IEEE International Conference on Advanced Video and Signal Based Surveillance (AVSS), pp. 1–6. IEEE (2017)
15. Chung, S.J., Paranjape, A.A., Dames, P., Shen, S., Kumar, V.: A survey on aerial swarm robotics. IEEE Trans. Robot. $34(4)$, 837–855 (2018)
16. Albani, D., Manoni, T., Nardi, D., Trianni, V.: Dynamic UAV swarm deployment for non-uniform coverage. In: Proceedings of the 17th International Conference on Autonomous Agents and MultiAgent Systems, pp. 523–531. International Foundation for Autonomous Agents and Multiagent Systems (2018)
17. Petrlík, M., Vonásek, V., Saska, M.: Coverage optimization in the cooperative surveillance task using multiple micro aerial vehicles. In: 2019 IEEE International Conference on Systems, Man and Cybernetics (SMC), pp. 4373–4380. IEEE (2019)
18. Jiguo, Y., Wan, S., Cheng, X., Dongxiao, Y.: Coverage contribution area based k-coverage for wireless sensor networks. IEEE Trans. Veh. Technol. $66(9)$, 8510–8523 (2017)
19. Elhoseny, M., Tharwat, A., Yuan, X., Hassanien, A.E.: Optimizing k-coverage of mobile WSNs. Exp. Syst. Appl. 92, 142–153 (2018)
20. Reynolds, A.M., Smith, A.D., Menzel, R., Greggers, U., Reynolds, D.R., Riley, J.R.: Displaced honey bees perform optimal scale-free search flights. Ecology $88(8)$, 1955–1961 (2007)
21. Sims, D.W., et al.: Scaling laws of marine predator search behaviour. Nature $451(7182)$, 1098 (2008)
22. Sun, Q., Fei, H., Yeqing, W., Huang, X.: Primate-inspired adaptive routing in intermittently connected mobile communication systems. Wirel. Netw. $20(7)$, 1939–1954 (2014)
23. Bénichou, O., Loverdo, C., Moreau, M., Voituriez, R.: Intermittent search strategies. Rev. Mod. Phys. $83(1)$, 81 (2011)

24. Zaburdaev, V., Denisov, S., Klafter, J.: Lévy walks. Rev. Mod. Phys. **87**(2), 483 (2015)
25. Pasternak, Z., Bartumeus, F., Grasso, F.W.: Lévy-taxis: a novel search strategy for finding odor plumes in turbulent flow-dominated environments. J. Phys. A: Math. Theor. **42**(43), 434010 (2009)
26. Sutantyo, D., Levi, P., Möslinger, C., Read, M.: Collective-adaptive Lévy flight for underwater multi-robot exploration. In: 2013 Mechatronics and Automation (ICMA), pp. 456–462. IEEE (2013)
27. Floreano, D., Mattiussi, C.: Bio-inspired Artificial Intelligence: Theories, Methods, and Technologies. MIT Press, Cambridge (2008)
28. Reynolds, C.W.: Flocks, herds and schools: a distributed behavioral model. ACM SIGGRAPH Comput. Graph. **21**, 25–34 (1987)
29. Nigam, N., Bieniawski, S., Kroo, I., Vian, J.: Control of multiple UAVs for persistent surveillance: algorithm and flight test results. IEEE Trans. Control Syst. Technol. **20**(5), 1236–1251 (2011)
30. Keller, J., Thakur, D., Likhachev, M., Gallier, J., Kumar, V.: Coordinated path planning for fixed-wing UAS conducting persistent surveillance missions. IEEE Trans. Autom. Sci. Eng. **14**(1), 17–24 (2016)
31. Michael, N., Stump, E., Mohta, K.: Persistent surveillance with a team of MAVs. In: 2011 IEEE/RSJ International Conference on Intelligent Robots and Systems, pp. 2708–2714. IEEE (2011)
32. Li, W.: Persistent surveillance for a swarm of micro aerial vehicles by flocking algorithm. Proc. Inst. Mech. Eng. Part G J. Aerosp. Eng. **229**(1), 185–194 (2015)
33. Costa, F.G., Ueyama, J., Braun, T., Pessin, G., Osório, F.S., Vargas, P.A.: The use of unmanned aerial vehicles and wireless sensor network in agricultural applications. In: 2012 IEEE International Geoscience and Remote Sensing Symposium, pp. 5045–5048. IEEE (2012)
34. Faiçal, B.S., et al.: The use of unmanned aerial vehicles and wireless sensor networks for spraying pesticides. J. Syst. Arch. **60**(4), 393–404 (2014)
35. Elhoseny, M., Tharwat, A., Farouk, A., Hassanien, A.E.: K-coverage model based on genetic algorithm to extend WSN lifetime. IEEE Sens. Lett. **1**(4), 1–4 (2017)
36. Kumar, S., Lai, T.H., Balogh, J.: On k-coverage in a mostly sleeping sensor network. In: Proceedings of the 10th Annual International Conference on Mobile Computing and Networking, pp. 144–158. ACM (2004)
37. Khoufi, I., Minet, P., Laouiti, A., Mahfoudh, S.: Survey of deployment algorithms in wireless sensor networks: coverage and connectivity issues and challenges. Int. J. Auton. Adapt. Commun. Syst. **10**(4), 341–390 (2017)
38. Sutantyo, D.K., Kernbach, S., Levi, P., Nepomnyashchikh, V.A.: Multi-robot searching algorithm using lévy flight and artificial potential field. In: 2010 IEEE International Workshop on Safety Security and Rescue Robotics (SSRR), pp. 1–6. IEEE (2010)
39. Keeter, M., et al.: Cooperative search with autonomous vehicles in a 3D aquatic testbed. In: 2012 American Control Conference (ACC), pp. 3154–3160. IEEE (2012)
40. Suarez, J., Murphy, R.: A survey of animal foraging for directed, persistent search by rescue robotics. In: IEEE International Symposium on Safety, Security, and Rescue Robotics (SSRR), pp. 314–320. IEEE (2011)
41. Bartumeus, F., da Luz, M.G.E., Viswanathan, G.M., Catalan, J.: Animal search strategies: a quantitative random-walk analysis. Ecology **86**(11), 3078–3087 (2005)

42. Deshpande, A., Kumar, M., Ramakrishnan, S.: Robot swarm for efficient area coverage inspired by ant foraging: the case of adaptive switching between Brownian motion and Lévy flight. In: ASME 2017 Dynamic Systems and Control Conference (2017)
43. Harris, T.H., et al.: Generalized Lévy walks and the role of chemokines in migration of effector CD8+ T cells. Nature **486**(7404), 545 (2012)
44. Das, B., Couceiro, M.S., Vargas, P.A.: MRoCS: a new multi-robot communication system based on passive action recognition. Robot. Auton. Syst. **82**, 46–60 (2016)
45. Vargas, P., Moioli, R., de Castro, L.N., Timmis, J., Neal, M., Von Zuben, F.J.: Artificial homeostatic system: a novel approach. In: Capcarrère, M.S., Freitas, A.A., Bentley, P.J., Johnson, C.G., Timmis, J. (eds.) ECAL 2005. LNCS (LNAI), vol. 3630, pp. 754–764. Springer, Heidelberg (2005). https://doi.org/10.1007/11553090_76
46. Moioli, R.C., Vargas, P.A., Husbands, P.: A multiple hormone approach to the homeostatic control of conflicting behaviours in an autonomous mobile robot. In: 2009 IEEE Congress on Evolutionary Computation, pp. 47–54 (2009)
47. Vargas, P.A., Moioli, R.C., Von Zuben, F., Husbands, P.: Homeostasis and evolution together dealing with novelties and managing disruptions. Int. J. Intell. Comput. Cybern. **2**(3), 435–454 (2009)
48. Trianni, V., Tuci, E., Ampatzis, C., Dorigo, M.: Evolutionary swarm robotics: a theoretical and methodological itinerary from individual neuro-controllers to collective behaviours. In: The Horizons of Evolutionary Robotics, pp. 153–178 (2014)
49. Vargas, P.A., Di Paolo, E.A., Harvey, I., Husbands, P.: The Horizons of Evolutionary Robotics. MIT Press, Cambridge (2014)
50. Moioli, R.C., Vargas, P.A., Von Zuben, F.J., Husbands, P.: Towards the evolution of an artificial homeostatic system. In: 2008 IEEE Congress on Evolutionary Computation (IEEE World Congress on Computational Intelligence), pp. 4023–4030 (2008)
51. Moioli, R.C., Vargas, P.A., Von Zuben, F.J., Husbands, P.: Evolving an artificial homeostatic system. In: Zaverucha, G., da Costa, A.L. (eds.) SBIA 2008. LNCS (LNAI), vol. 5249, pp. 278–288. Springer, Heidelberg (2008). https://doi.org/10.1007/978-3-540-88190-2_33

Single-Agent Policies for the Multi-Agent Persistent Surveillance Problem via Artificial Heterogeneity

Thomas Kent[1]($\boxtimes$) , Arthur Richards[1] , and Angus Johnson[2]

[1] University of Bristol, Bristol, UK
{thomas.kent,arthur.richards}@bristol.ac.uk
[2] Thales UK, Reading, UK
angus.johnson@uk.thalesgroup.com

Abstract. Modelling and planning as well as Machine Learning techniques such as Reinforcement Learning are often difficult in multi-agent problems. With increasing numbers of agents the decision space grows rapidly and is made increasingly complex through interacting agents. This paper is motivated by the question of if it is possible to train single-agent policies in isolation and without the need for explicit cooperation or coordination still *successfully* deploy them to multi-agent scenarios. In particular we look at the multi-agent Persistent Surveillance Problem (MAPSP), which is the problem of using a number of agents to continually visit and re-visit areas of a map to maximise a metric of surveillance.

We outline five distinct single-agent policies to solve the MAPSP: Reinforcement Learning (*DDPG*); Neuro-Evolution (*NEAT*); a Gradient Descent (*GD*) heuristic; a random heuristic; and a pre-defined 'ploughing pattern' (*Trail*). We will compare the performance and scalability of these single-agent policies to the Multi-Agent PSP. Importantly, in doing so we will demonstrate an emergent property which we call the *Homogeneous-Policy Convergence Cycle* (HPCC), whereby agents following homogeneous policies can get stuck together, continuously repeating the same action as other agents, significantly impacting performance. This paper will show that just a small amount of noise, at the state or action level, is sufficient to solve the problem, essentially creating artificially-heterogeneous policies for the agents.

Keywords: Multi-agent systems · Reinforcement learning · Surveillance · Coverage · Emergent behaviour

1 Introduction and Background

Real-world problems such as reconnaissance and surveillance [13,14], search and rescue [9] and, drone crop-monitoring [11] rely on efficient and continuous ways of visiting areas of the world. For problems covering large areas or when higher-frequency monitoring is desirable it can be useful to deploy multiple agents,

© Springer Nature Switzerland AG 2020
N. Bassiliades et al. (Eds.): EUMAS 2020/AT 2020, LNAI 12520, pp. 243–260, 2020.
https://doi.org/10.1007/978-3-030-66412-1_16

or even swarms [1], in an environment. Modelling and planning for multi-agent problems can often be difficult due to a rapidly growing decision space, made increasing complex through the interacting agents [17]. Additionally, this can result in a need for coordination and communication that may not be possible in many situations. Many Unmanned Aerial Vehicle (UAV) platforms and off-the-shelf solutions are designed in isolation and typically offer only single-agent behaviours. Unless agents have been designed for multi-agent settings or can be coordinated via some centralised control, then policy homogeneity might be unavoidable. However, as we will demonstrate in this paper this can lead to undesirable emergent properties.

The aim this paper is to explore the concept of using single-agent policies, designed and/or trained in isolation, that can be *successfully* deployed in a multi-agent scenario. In particular we focus on the multi-agent Persistent Surveillance Problem (MAPSP), as a simplified use-case pertinent to multi-agent systems research. The MAPSP is the problem of using a number of agents to continually visit and re-visit areas of a map in order to maximise a metric. We outline, in Sect. 3, a range of different action policies, for agents to decide the best action to take given an agent-centric local observation. Policies include (1) *Random*; (2) *Gradient Descent*; (3) *DDPG*; (4) *NEAT* and (5) Trail-Following. In particular, in Sect. 3.2, we will demonstrate that by deploying *homogeneous* single-agent policies in a multi-agent setting can lead to a highly undesirable emergent property that we call the 'Homogeneous Policy Convergence Cycle' (HPCC). Each of the policies will be evaluated for varying numbers of agents and the HPCC problem will be demonstrated. Finally approaches to counteract the HPCC will be discussed where we will show that by essentially making the agents less homogeneous, via the addition of noise, is sufficient to fix the problem.

2   Persistent Surveillance Problem

The Persistent Surveillance Problem (PSP) belongs to a class of problems known as *coverage problems* [4,5]. The aim of Persistent Surveillance is to continually visit and re-visit all areas of a map in order to maximise a surveillance score that sufficiently quantifies performance. To measure this a 2-Dimensional world is divided into regions using a hexagonal-grid structure of N 'hexes', with each of these hexes having an associated surveillance score (as depicted in Fig. 1). The total surveillance score, i.e. the PSP objective, is the sum of all the scores across all the hexes. In this paper we have designed a score-function that quantifies a notion of 'level of surveillance' and its subsequent exponential decay by a relationship dictated by the hex-score function:

$$\mathcal{V}(h^i_{t+1}) = \begin{cases} \mathcal{V}(h^i_t) + C, & \text{if } h^i_t \text{ occupied.} \\ \mathcal{V}(h^i_t)\lambda, & \text{otherwise.} \end{cases} \tag{1}$$

This function defines that when an agent is in a hex, h^i, it increases that hex's score, $\mathcal{V}(h^i)$ by a positive linear constant, C, each time-step it occupies the hex.

Then for any hex unoccupied the score $\mathcal{V}(h^i)$, decays exponentially by a factor $\lambda = (1/2)^{(dt/T_h)}$, which is a constant parametrised by its 'half-life' value T_h such that $\lambda \leq 1$. The score of each hex is also bounded, restricting $\mathcal{V}(h^i_t) \in [0, v_{max}]$.

We define the set $H_t = \{h^i_t \text{ for } i = 1..N\}$ to be the set of all N hexes at time t. Thus the total *surveillance score*, at time t, is sum of all the scores of H_t, that is

$$\mathcal{V}(H_t) = \sum_{\forall h^i_t \in H} \mathcal{V}(h^i_t). \tag{2}$$

The aim of the PSP is to keep the score $\mathcal{V}(H)$ as high as possible at all times, with the max surveillance score defined as

$$\mathcal{V}^*(H) = \max_{\forall t \in T}(\mathcal{V}(H_t)). \tag{3}$$

2.1   PSP Simulation Environment

The Persistent Surveillance Problem has been implemented as an environment in-line with the OpenAI Gym [3] and follows the traditional State, Action, Reward sequence [15]. The Multi-Agent Simulator (MAS) environment keeps track of agent locations and their underlying states. The MAS can be queried for a state (observation) of any agent and in turn the agent can carry out an action in the environment and the MAS simulates the outcome, and returns a reward. In the case when there are multiple agents, all observations and actions happen simultaneously. In addition we assume that agents are unable to communicate with each other and do not attempt to plan for other agents. The environment is defined over the bounded 2-Dimensional world W. All agents are restricted to stay within W, with their motions being 'clipped' at the simulator level ensuring they can only move within the bounds.

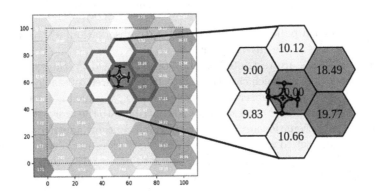

Fig. 1. Agent-centric observation, higher-values green, lower are red, $s^k_t = [20.00, 9.83, 10.66, 19.77, 18.49, 10.12, 9.00]$ (Color figure online)

The specific environmental parameter choices for the results in this paper are as follows. The world, $W = [0, 100] \times [0, 100]$ and is made up a grid of $N = 56$

hexagons each with a height of 15 m (flat edge-to-edge). The simulation updates at a discrete time-step dt, updating all $h^i \in H$, using Eq. (1) with a half-life decay $T_h = 120$, a linear increase $C = 5$ and a maximum value of $v_{\max} = 20$. To help with agent training and performance we also use a technique called frame-skip, (popularised from Deep Learning techniques designed to play Atari games [10]) which limits the rate of decision making to once every $3dt$. Thus an agent receives an observation every third time-step, acts on it and this action is held for $3dt$. Furthermore we define each agent velocity as $5m/dt$, and so every action results in the agent moving $3 \times 5 = 15$ m across the world.

2.2   Local Observations

The PSP simulation environment keeps track of the current global state of the world via the scores of each hex, using the current values, the agent locations and Eq. (1). Agents deployed in the environment will be given access to these states via *observations*, as depicted in Fig. 1, which will be agent-centric, i.e. dependent on the current agent location. The policies outlined in this paper are given only these *local observations* of the state, with which to make their action decision (with the exception of *Trail* which requires a degree of global-localisation to stay on course).

We define the set of hexes directly adjacent to h^i as

$$\text{hexAdj}(h^i) = \{\forall h^j \in H | h^j \text{ adjacent } h^i\}, \tag{4}$$

which is shown in Fig. 1 with h^i in the centre. Then, given an agent k, currently located in hex h^i, the agent's observation $s^k(h^i)$ (we choose to shorten the notation to simply s^k when it is appropriately clear), is defined as

$$s^k(h^i) = \{\mathcal{V}(h) \text{ for } h \in \{h^i \cup \text{hexAdj}(h^i)\}. \tag{5}$$

It is the role of each policy to use this local-state observation, s^k, to decide the best action to take in the environment.

While our agents are restricted to the bounded world W they may observe hexes outside of this, in which case those hexes are declared 'obstacle hexes'. Any obstacle hex, h^{obs}, has its observation value set to v_{obst} which is a value greater than $v_{\max}$ but with $\mathcal{V}(h^{\text{obst}}) = 0$ so as not to contribute to the score. Additionally, in the multi-agent scenarios any observation which contains another agent is also declared h^{obst} and set to v_{obst}. Note that a hex h^{obst} does not physically restrict an agent from moving into it, instead its aim is to deter agents moving there by being a high value while not contributing to the score and in turn not affecting the reward.

2.3   Action Policy

An agent k's decision making is contained entirely within its policy function π^k. The role of the policy to take an observation, s^k, and provide an action,

$a^k \leftarrow \pi(s^k)$, from the set of all possible actions $\mathcal{A}$. In this paper the action, $a^k \in [-1, 1] \times [-1, 1]$, is the two-dimensional trigonometric-encoding of direction in which to travel, that is, the agent heading, θ, encoded by the two values $a^k = [\sin(\theta), \cos(\theta)]$ (with $\theta = 0$ corresponding to East).

Some of the policies outlined in Sect. 3.1 use a discrete action policy, whereby an action is chosen from a set, $a^k \in \mathcal{A}_d$, of 6 possible hexagonal directions, equivalent to the angular encoding $\theta \in \left[\frac{7\pi}{6}, \frac{9\pi}{6}, \frac{11\pi}{6}, \frac{\pi}{6}, \frac{3\pi}{6}, \frac{5\pi}{6}\right]$. These angles correspond to the angular direction from the centre point of the centre hex h^i to the centre of each of $h \in \text{hexAdj}(h^i)$.

2.4 Reward Function

For policies which require 'training' (i.e. *DDPG* and *NEAT*) we must also define a reward function. At each time, t, an agent k chooses an action, a^k via its policy, π^k, the agent carries out that action in the environment and in return is given a reward, r^k. The Machine Learning (ML) agents, *DDPG* and *NEAT*, of Sect. 3.1 require this reward to learn, and the reward function itself is a hugely important factor within ML in shaping *how* and *what* an agent learns [8]. As the agents only have access to local observations the reward is restricted to be a function of these only. For an agent k, at time t in hex h_t^k, we define the reward to be how much the state $s_t^k(h_t^i)$ is improved as a result of taking the action, that is:

$$r_{t+1} = \mathcal{V}(s_{t+1}^k(h^i)) - \mathcal{V}(s_t^k(h^i)) \tag{6}$$

Thus the agent gets positive reward if it leaves the $s^k(h^i)$ better than when it arrived. This reward is provided to the agent by the environment as it keeps track of past hex scores. The mathematical incentive of this reward is to ensure that the linear addition of C from Eq. (1) is better than the loss via the decay of λ of each of the other hexes. By having the bound of $v_{\max}$ it means that agents do not simply try to move between two hexes, instead they should be moving towards hexes of lower values where there is sufficient 'room' to add value.

2.5 Analytical Assessment

Given a world W, the score function of Eq. (1) and a hexagonal-grid structure of the environment we are able to analyse theoretical bounds on PSP problem. For each action-step (i.e. 3 time-steps) the most value an agent can add to a hex is $3 \times C = 15$, and hexes have a maximum value $v_{\max} = 20$, this means that ideally we want to be moving towards hexes that are ideally less than $v_{\max} - 3c = 5$.

If we visit each of the $N = 56$ hexes in some sequence, $H_{\text{seq}} = \{h^0, \ldots, h^n\}$, and spend $3dt$ at each, then each hex will have a score $a_0 = 15$ at the time it is visited and then that value will subsequently decay. The currently occupied hex h_t^n will have the highest value $\mathcal{V}(h_t^n) = a_0$, then the hex visited previously, at the current time-step, h_t^{n-1}, had the same value but has since decayed by λ and thus $\mathcal{V}(h_t^{n-1}) = a_0\lambda$ and for $n - 2$, $\mathcal{V}(h_t^{n-2}) = a_0\lambda^2$. This continues in this fashion until the hex visited n time-steps ago, which has a value $\mathcal{V}(h_t^0) = a_0\lambda^n$.

The sum of these scores, and thus the current surveillance score, is in fact a geometric series:

$$a_0\lambda^0 + a_0\lambda^1 + a_0\lambda^2 + \cdots + a_0\lambda^n = \sum_{k=0}^{n-1} a_0\lambda^k = a_0\left(\frac{1-\lambda^n}{1-\lambda}\right) \tag{7}$$

Therefore, visiting each hex once, for $\lambda = (\frac{1}{2}^{\frac{3}{120}})$ the surveillance score reaches $\mathcal{V}(H_{\text{seq}}) = 542$. The value of the hex visited n time-steps ago H_{seq}, $\mathcal{V}(h_0) = a_0\lambda^n = 15 \times 0.379 = 5.684$. Therefore if we continue to visit the hexes in the order of H_{seq}, that is we now visit h_0 again, and its value becomes $5.684 + 3 \times C = 20.684$, which is above v_{max} and so is capped at 20. Repeating the same logic as before $a_0 \leftarrow 20$ and using Eq. (7) the surveillance score becomes $\mathcal{V}(H_{\text{seq}}) = 723$.

In order to achieve these kinds of scores it is necessary to find an admissible sequence H_{seq} that can be visited in that order. This requires a kind of trail, that visits each hex only once and returns to the starting hex, in graph-theory this is known as a Eulerian cycle. Therefore it is clear that in order to maximise the surveillance score it is necessary to find a policy that best approximates this kind of cycle. With this in mind, in Sect. 3.1 a trail-agent will be outlined, which is able to follow a pre-defined cycle, and used as a benchmark to compare the other agents to (Fig. 2).

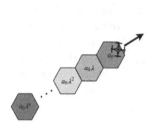

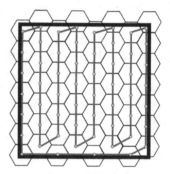

Fig. 2. Ideal hex trail resulting in geometric series

Fig. 3. Pre-defined trail for agent to follow

3 Single-Agent Policies for the PSP

We now outline five single-agent policies designed to solve the Single Agent Persistent Surveillance Problem. The objective of each of these policies will be to achieve the best $\mathcal{V}^*(H)$ during an episode, by deciding, at each step which direction to move around the environment.

3.1   Five Policies for PSP

The first two policies act as *benchmarks* to essentially bound what good and bad performance looks like. The first, *Random*, acts independently of observations and moves randomly and should result in poor performance. While the second, *Trail*, uses the idea of Sect. 2.5, and follows a pre-defined trail, requiring global information and should result in the best performance.

The remaining three, local policies, act on the local agent-centric observations of the world described in Sect. 2.2. A simple heuristic policy called *gradient descent* acts on the *model* that moving towards lower values is best. Finally, we use two different 'off-the-shelf' ML algorithms, *DDPG* and *NEAT*, and apply them to our implementation of the Persistent Surveillance Problem.

All of the methods outlined in this paper have been implemented in Python 3.5 and all the simulations are run on a Dell Precision 3520 laptop running Ubuntu 16.04, with a 2.7 Ghz core i7 CPU and 16 GB of RAM.

Random Policy. The role of the random agent is to act as a minimum benchmark and is essentially a *blind-policy*. The agent is given an observation, s^k, but is not used in its action selection. The agent simple picks, at random, a discrete direction from one of the six possible, $a^k \in \mathcal{A}_d$. Due to the randomness of this policy, it is non-deterministic.

Trail Policy Benchmark. As discussed in Sect. 2.5 an ideal path to take is one travelling through a sequence of hexes in a Eulerian Cycle. Boustrophedon patterns, also known as ploughing patterns, are some of the best known examples of this approach and have long be used in agriculture [7] and in search and rescue missions [12].

For the purposes of providing a benchmark, a pre-defined trail-based policy is implemented as shown in Fig. 3. However, we must note that a direct comparison is not entirely fair as this policy requires a degree of global-state localisation that is not afforded to the local-state policies. An agent running the trail-policy must first work out where it is on the trail in order to determine where to move next. Thus the policy here is to take the trail-point closest to the agent and then select the action in the direction of the next trail-point. An agent will continue around this cycle trying to essentially approximate the geometric sum of Eq. (7).

Gradient Descent Policy. A Gradient Descent (*GD*) approach is used as a simple yet effective heuristic. This acts as a very simplified *model-based* policy, where the model is 'move towards nearby hexes of lowest value'. That is, choose the hex, $h^{\min} = \mathrm{argmin}(s_t^k)$, with the lowest observation value and move towards it. Thus the discrete action $a^k \in \mathcal{A}_d$ is the one corresponding to $h^{\min}$.

Using the example observation of Fig. 1, $s_t^k = [20.00, 9.83, 10.66, 19.77, 18.49, 10.12, 9.00]$, the GD policy would move towards the hex corresponding to minimum value $h^{\min} = 9.00$, i.e. the last value of s_t^k, North-West ($3\pi/6$). In the event of there being more than one minimum value, then one of them chosen at random (this adds a level of uncertainty to this policy).

DDPG Policy. A *Tensorflow* implementation of the Deep Deterministic Policy Gradient algorithm [8] is used, which is a model-free, online, off-policy Reinforcement Learning method. It combines the use of an actor-critic architecture along with target-network updates, replay buffers and stochastic exploration. *DDPG* is designed to be used within environments with continuous actions spaces which is why it was chosen for this problem. *DDPG* is a policy gradient method and as such uses a functional approximation, in this case a Deep Neural Network, to the Q-function. RL is used to train these DNNs through standard *SARSA* structured examples [15] to allow us to compute the optimal action, a, to take for a given state s, that is the action which maximises our Q-function, $\max_a \mathcal{Q}^*(s, a)$.

This implementation uses the standard hyper-parameters of the original paper [8]. With an input layer, two hidden layers one of 400 and one of 300 units, and one output layer. A learning rate of 10^{-4} for the actor networks and 10^{-3} for the critic networks. A discount factor γ of 0.99 is used, a target-network update rate of $\eta = 0.01$. The Ornstein-Uhlenbeck process was used for training-noise [18], with noise parameters of $\theta = 0.05$ and $\sigma = 0.05$. The input to the Neural Network is the state observation of the 7 hex values normalised between 0 and 1. Our *DDPG* has two outputs, activated via hyperbolic-tangent functions, giving output values $o_1, o_2 \in [-1, 1]$ which correspond to the action a^k of Sect. 2.3, $\sin(\theta)$ and $\cos(\theta)$ respectively. The reasoning behind using two output values was to overcome a neuron-saturation [6] issue observed by the authors, a single angle can be easily recovered via the $\theta = \arctan2(\sin(\theta), \cos(\theta))$ function.

The *DDPG* network was trained for 2000 episodes using the reward function of Eq. (6) taking approximately 60 min, at which point training had sufficiently converged.

NEAT Policy. Neuro-Evolution of Augmenting Topologies (*NEAT*) [16] is a method for evolving Neural Networks (NN) via an Evolutionary Algorithm (EA). Here a NN is subjected to an EA process in order to evolve both the structure, the weights and the activation functions of the NN with the key idea of starting by building from small NNs and evolving to add increasing complexity.

The evolutionary approach differs to the standard *SARSA* of RL by way of the Reward. Where, as is the case of *DDPG*, the reward received in RL is at each step, EAs instead use an episodic measure of success known as fitness. Therefore, any network evolved by *NEAT* is evaluated against this fitness value and a selection operator determines whether it is kept for the next generation. The fitness function used in the paper is the cumulative value over the episode of the reward function of Eq. (6).

The NNs take the 7 values of s^k as input, are a single-layer deep, and have 6 output nodes with each corresponding to an action direction $a^k \in \mathcal{A}_d$. A soft-max activation function is used to select the highest-valued output neuron, the corresponding discrete action is then returned. *NEAT* is initialised with a population of fully connected single layer NNs with randomised weights and activations. The process of *NEAT* is for each generation to evolve the population of candidate NNs, test them within the PS environment, evaluate their fitness using the cumulative reward function of Eq. (6) and select the best candidates to be retained for the next generation. *NEAT* continues this standard evolutionary process until a termination condition is met, in this case 2000 generations. The resulting NN is then the *NEAT* policy, taking in the observation s^k, running it through the NN, and taking the resulting action.

3.2 Multi-Agent Deployment of Single-Agent Policies

To deploy multiple agents within the MAS described in Sect. 2.1, we take a given policy and deploy copies of it on each agent within the environment. The MAS provides agents with observations and the agents decide action to take, these observations and actions happen *simultaneously*. The agents are unable to communicate, coordinate or plan for each other except for other agents appearing as obstacles. Outside of getting v_{obst} in an observation there is no enforcement of collision avoidance, instead agents motivation for avoiding one another is intrinsic to the reward function itself.

4 Results and Discussion

The aim of this paper is to assess how well policies, designed in isolation, are able to be deployed on multiple agents in the same environment. Firstly, we will see how well the single-agent policies perform in the single-agent environment. Then for each policy we test how well it performs when being deployed on a given number of agents. In Sect. 4.2 we will discuss how all agents having homogeneous policies leads to highly undesirable emergent behaviour, importantly in Sect. 4.3 we will demonstrate how we are able to overcome this emergent behaviour through noise.

4.1 Homogeneous-Policy Performance

The five single-agent policies outlined above are now tested in a single agent environment to assess performance. Each *trial* will be run 100 times (100 episodes), with an agent with a chosen policy deployed in the environment outlined in Sect. 2, of 100 m 100 m area made up of 56 hexes H. Each episode starts with the agent in a random location in W and then proceeding to run for 200 action-steps (which is 600 dt as each action is held for 3 dt).

For the real world problems needing to continuously surveil an area, there are a number of metrics, based on our surveillance score, which could measure performance. These can be continuous measures such as the average score, the maximum score achieved, time-to-reach a certain value or could be pass-fail such as never dropping below a certain minimum-value. The results presented here will be based on $\mathcal{V}^*(H_t)$ averaged over all runs. Traits of a *good* policy are high average values, which rise quickly and remain stable and ideally have lower variance across runs.

The single-agent deployment results, as shown in Fig. 4a, show that the benchmark policy performs the best with almost no variance, with the 'peaks' of the trail policy, visible at step 56 and 112, depicting when the agent completes each lap of the trail. As expected the random policy performs the worst with the highest levels of variance. The remaining three policies (*GD, DDPG, NEAT*) all perform somewhat similarly, with *DDPG* initially performing well but later being outperformed by *GD*. All agents experience the diminishing rate of reward towards the later parts of the episode due to most of the hexes having high scores, at which point the policies simply maintain them.

However, the results of Figs. 4 and 5 show that when multiple-agents are used, we quickly observe that the three policies *GD, DDPG* and *NEAT* all exhibit the same dramatic drop-off in performance. This is due to an effect we will discuss next in Sect. 4.2 which we call Homogeneous-Policy Convergence Cycle (HPCC). This effect appears to worsen with increasing numbers of agents, exhibiting this performance-drop more quickly. What is equally alarming is that this effect is so bad that for 10 agents it appears that an entirely random policy can outperform them on average.

Notably even the analytical best policy, that is The Trail Policy, also fails to easily transfer to the multi-agent scenario albeit for a different reason to the others. Here it is due to the fact the agents are placed in the world at random and are therefore not necessarily evenly spaced across the trail. This means that you could end up with agents grouped behind one another, and as discussed in Sect. 2.5 agents ideally want to be going to the least visited hexes next, and not to one just visited by another agent. This could be fixed in a number of ways but would require some additional coordination or planning, such as being forced to slow down to space out, or this could utilise the observations more and moving to parts of the trail where the next hex in the trail has a lower score, however these are left for future work.

4.2   Homogeneous-Policy Convergence Cycle

Figures 4 and 5 show a large reduction in performance by simply deploying a homogeneous policy to multiple-agents within the same environment. The cause of this is due to an emergent property that we call *Homogeneous-Policy Convergence Cycle* (HPCC). This property is cyclical in nature and can occur when two or more agents occupy the same hex and essentially get 'stuck' together. The process is depicted in Fig. 6a and happens, at some time t, as follows

(1) Agents move to the same hex h_t;
(2) Agents get an identical local state observation s_t;
(3) Identical, deterministic policies π, return identical action choices a_t
(4) Agents in the same hex, h_t, perform identical actions, and move to the same hex, h_{t+1}, as the other agents - thus returning to step 1)

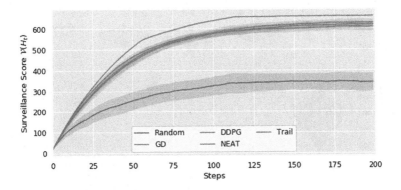

(a) 1 Agent Mean Score $\mu \pm \sigma$

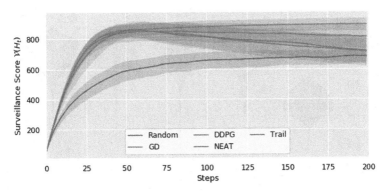

(b) 3 Agents Mean Score $\mu \pm \sigma$

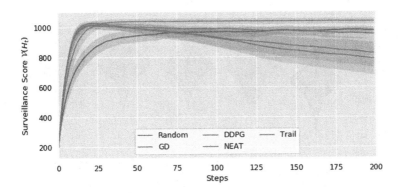

(c) 10 Agents Mean Score $\mu \pm \sigma$

Fig. 4. Multi-agent PSP performance over 200 action steps

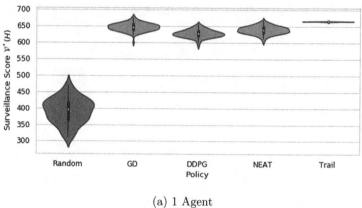

(a) 1 Agent

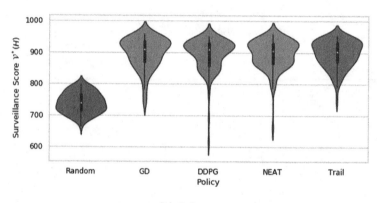

(b) 3 Agents

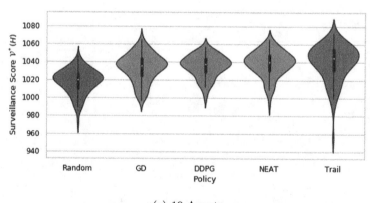

(c) 10 Agents

Fig. 5. v_{max} value distribution for PSP performance for differing number of Agents

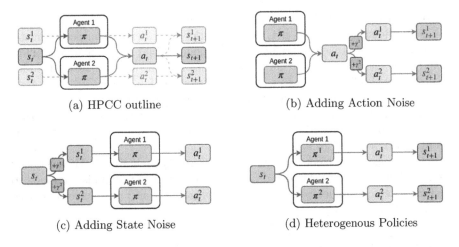

(a) HPCC outline

(b) Adding Action Noise

(c) Adding State Noise

(d) Heterogenous Policies

Fig. 6. Homogeneous Policy Convergence Cycle and potential fixes

The HPCC problem is essentially a product of homogeneity and determinism, something that appears in game-theory, the El Farol Bar problem [2] for example. The solid-line path of Fig. 6a represents this convergence cycle, if we break away from any of the 4-steps above and transition onto one of the dotted paths we can break this cycle, this can be achieved by doing one of the following:

(1) Co-operate to avoid moving into the same hex $\rightarrow h_t^1 \neq h_t^2$
(2) Have differing states $\rightarrow s_t^1 \neq s_t^2$ and therefore $a_t^1 \neq a_t^2$
(3) Have differing action choices $\rightarrow a_t^1 \neq a_t^2$ and therefore $s_{t+1}^1 \neq s_{t+1}^2$
(4) Have differing policies so identical states may result in differing actions

To achieve 1) we would require the addition of coordination which is not the aim of this paper. We could also achieve 4) as we have outlined 5 different PS single-agent policies which are heterogeneous from one another. So for scenarios with 5 agents or fewer we could feasibly deploy a team of agents each with a heterogeneous-policy as depicted in Fig. 6d, however for an increasing number of agents designing new, distinct, policies is more difficult and is unrealistic for large numbers of agents. Instead we focus on 2) and 3) and look at a straightforward method for overcoming the HPCC problem via the addition of noise.

4.3 Artificial Heterogeneity

We will now demonstrate two similar ways, as depicted in Figs. 6b and 6c, to break HPCC through artificial-heterogeneity. By simply adding noise to either an agent's action or to an agent's state observation, we are able to essentially turn homogeneous policies into heterogeneous ones.

Action Noise. The optimal action chosen by our policy $a_t \leftarrow \pi^*(s_t)$ will be the same for an identical state as it is deterministic. To achieve a non-deterministic action, it suffices to take the action a_t of the policy π and add a small amount of noise, γ^i, for each agent i, and for each dimension of the action space. This idea is to increase the likelihood of producing different action choices $a_t^1 \neq a_t^2$, as in Fig. 6b. The noise value is drawn from a uniform distribution $\gamma \sim \mathcal{U}(-0.1, 0.1)$ for each action dimension and added to the output of the policy. Note that the addition of noise results in an action which at an individual policy level is suboptimal $a_t + \gamma \notin \pi^*(a|s_t)$.

Action-noise is sufficient in breaking HPCC, as shown in Fig. 7, the previously exhibited long-term performance drop-off is entirely removed. This allows us to effectively deploy single-agent heterogeneous policies on multiple agents with only a minor adjustment.

State Noise. Instead of directly altering a homogeneous policy's action choice we can instead perturb our state observations, s_t, by again adding small amounts of noise. This is depicted in Fig. 6c, where for each agent i, we add the noise γ^i (the same size as s) to the identical state s_t, so that $s_t^i = s_t + \gamma^i$. The aim is to increase the chances that $s_t^i \neq s_t$. Again, noise γ^i, is taken from a uniform distribution $\gamma \sim \mathcal{U}(-1.0, 1.0)$ for each agent i, with dimensions to match the state observation (this distribution is proportionally similar to the action noise distribution). The aim is that we are able to ensure that even if agents occupy the same hex, the observations they receive differ slightly and thus for a sufficient level of state noise will result in distinct action choices $a_t^1 \neq a_t^2$.

The results of Fig. 8 clearly show just how effective even a small amount of noise added to either the action or state is, fixing HPCC. It appears that for higher agent counts, state noise results in higher max surveillance scores along with lower variance. As expected adding noise to the Trail policy has little effect, as it does not suffer from HPCC and it does not act on the state information.

The choice of where the noise is added has some subtle differences. By adding noise to the state observation you are relying on $s + \gamma^1$ and $s + \gamma^2$ *at some point* being sufficiently different to result in the policy π outputting two different actions, and the agents then moving out of the same hex. Whereas with action noise, assuming $\gamma^1 \neq \gamma^2$, you are *forcing* $a + \gamma^1 \neq a + \gamma^2$, so agents are therefore *always* taking different actions. This is likely the cause of the difference in variance of the two approaches. Additionally, due to the discrete action selection of *GD* and *NEAT*, perturbation in the action space, as we add a continuous amount of noise, allows a little more continuity in the agents movements. With state noise only, discrete actions remain discrete, but if the same state plus noise for two agents can now produce two different actions choice, those two actions will differ by at least the discrete resolution instead of just the smaller action noise.

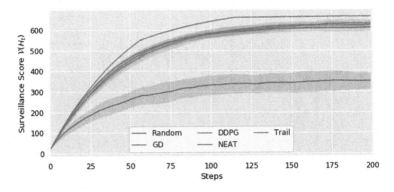

(a) 1 Agent Mean Score $\mu \pm \sigma$

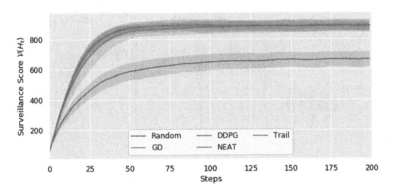

(b) 3 Agents Mean Score $\mu \pm \sigma$

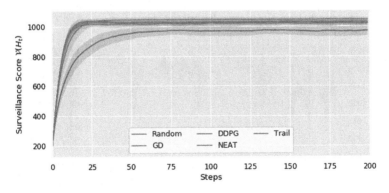

(c) 10 Agents Mean Score $\mu \pm \sigma$

Fig. 7. Multi-Agent PSP performance over 200 action steps with action-noise

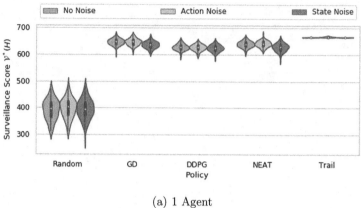

(a) 1 Agent

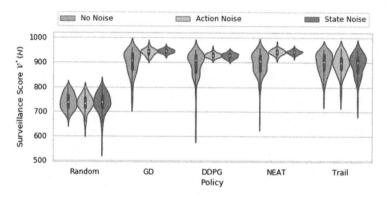

(b) 3 Agents

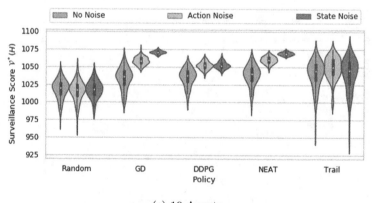

(c) 10 Agents

Fig. 8. Multi-Agent PSP $\mathcal{V}^*(H)$: Comparison of the effect of adding noise

5 Conclusion

This work was motivated by the idea of being able to design single-agent policies in isolation, and without the need for explicit cooperation or coordination still *successfully* deploy them to multi-agent scenarios. We used the multi-agent Persistent Surveillance Problem as a simple scenario to test our question. We outlined and demonstrated the results of five distinct single-agent policies designed to solve the single agent PSP: *Random*; *Gradient Descent*; *DDPG*; *NEAT*; and *Trail*. By deploying these single agent homogeneous policies to multiple agents we quickly observe a negative emergent property that we called the *Homogeneous-Policy Convergence Cycle* (HPCC). A property almost entirely the result of homogeneity and determinism. Whilst we demonstrated the existence of HPCC in MAPSP, one can imagine that this or a similar *class* of emergent properties could occur in other scenarios. Environments with similar action-state transitional properties of those depicted in Fig. 6a could be subject to similar undesirable effects. Importantly however, we showed that we are able to remove this property entirely, through the simple addition of noise. By adding a small amount of noise to each agent's action choice or state observation we were able to essentially create artificial heterogeneity from entirely homogeneous policies.

This shows that some degree of noise can be a desirable property within a system. This may appear somewhat reassuring as in many real world scenarios, the introduction of state and action noise will often arise inadvertently, through imperfections in aspects such as sensing, communication or computation. However, this also hints at the potential for a whole class of emergent properties such as HPCC which may exist in many complex systems but remain unnoticed.

Many future directions are of interest, including exploring the impact of *parameter space choices*, such as different reward and score functions along with different environments. However, of greatest interest is in understanding the impact of *system level choices*, such as the inclusion of different aspects of coordination and communcation, asking not just where, but also to what degree it is necessary.

Acknowledgments. This work was funded and delivered in partnership between the Thales Group and the University of Bristol, and with the support of the UK Engineering and Physical Sciences Research Council Grant Award EP/R004757/1 entitled 'Thales-Bristol Partnership in Hybrid Autonomous Systems Engineering (T-B PHASE)'.

References

1. Albani, D., Manoni, T., Nardi, D., Trianni, V.: Dynamic UAV swarm deployment for non-uniform coverage: robotics track. In: Proceedings of the International Joint Conference on Autonomous Agents and Multi-agent Systems, pp. 523–531. AAMAS (2018)
2. Arthur, W.B.: Complexity and the Economy. Science **284**(5411), 107–109 (1999). https://doi.org/10.1126/science.284.5411.107
3. Brockman, G., et al.: OpenAI Gym, pp. 1–4 (2016). http://arxiv.org/abs/1606.01540

4. Butterworth, J., Tuyls, K., Broecker, B., Paoletti, P.: Evolving coverage behaviours for MAVs using NEAT. In: Proceedings of the International Joint Conference on Autonomous Agents and Multi-agent Systems, Vol. 3, pp. 1886–1888. AAMAS (2018)

5. Cabreira, T., Brisolara, L., Ferreira Jr., P.R.: Survey on Coverage Path Planning with Unmanned Aerial Vehicles, Vol. 3 (2019). https://doi.org/10.3390/drones3010004

6. Hochreiter, S.: The vanishing gradient problem during learning recurrent neural nets and problem solutions. Int. J. Uncertain. Fuzz. Knowl. Based Syst. **06**(02), 107–116 (1998). https://doi.org/10.1142/S0218488598000094

7. LaValle, S.M.: Planning algorithms. Methods (2006). https://doi.org/10.1017/CBO9780511546877

8. Lillicrap, T.P., et al.: Continuous control with deep reinforcement learning, September 2015. http://arxiv.org/abs/1509.02971

9. Liu, Y., Nejat, G.: Robotic urban search and rescue: a survey from the control perspective. J. Intell. Robot. Syst. **72**(2), 147–165 (2013). https://doi.org/10.1007/s10846-013-9822-x

10. Mnih, V., et al.: Human-level control through deep reinforcement learning. Nature **518**(7540), 529–533 (2015). https://doi.org/10.1038/nature14236

11. Mogili, U.R., Deepak, B.B.: Review on application of drone systems in precision agriculture. Procedia Comput. Sci. **133**, 502–509 (2018). https://doi.org/10.1016/j.procs.2018.07.063

12. Nigam, N.: The multiple unmanned air vehicle persistent surveillance problem: a review. Machines **2**(1), 13–72 (2014). https://doi.org/10.3390/machines2010013

13. Nigam, N., Kroo, I.: Persistent surveillance using multiple unmanned air vehicles. In: IEEE Aerospace Conference Proceedings, pp. 1–15 (2008). https://doi.org/10.1109/AERO.2008.4526242

14. Peters, J.R., Wang, S.J., Surana, A., Bullo, F.: Asynchronous and dynamic coverage control scheme for persistent surveillance missions, pp. 1–12 (2016). http://arxiv.org/abs/1609.05264

15. Rummery, G.A., Niranjan, M.: On-line Q-learning using connectionist systems, vol. 37. University of Cambridge, Department of Engineering Cambridge, England (1994)

16. Stanley, K.O., Miikkulainen, R.: Evolving neural networks through augmenting topologies. Evolut. Comput. **10**(2), 99–127 (2002). https://doi.org/10.1162/106365602320169811

17. Stone, P., Veloso, M.: Multi-agent systems: a survey from a machine learning perspective. Autonom. Robots **8**(3), 345–383 (2000). https://doi.org/10.1023/A:1008942012299

18. Uhlenbeck, G.E., Ornstein, L.S.: On the theory of the Brownian motion. Phys. Rev. **36**(5), 823–841 (1930)

Explaining the Influence of Prior Knowledge on POMCP Policies

Alberto Castellini[(✉)], Enrico Marchesini, Giulio Mazzi,
and Alessandro Farinelli

Department of Computer Science, Verona University,
Strada Le Grazie 15, 37134 Verona, Italy
{alberto.castellini,enrico.marchesini,giulio.mazzi,
alessandro.farinelli}@univr.it

Abstract. Partially Observable Monte Carlo Planning is a recently proposed online planning algorithm which makes use of Monte Carlo Tree Search to solve Partially Observable Monte Carlo Decision Processes. This solver is very successful because of its capability to scale to large uncertain environments, a very important property for current real-world planning problems. In this work we propose three main contributions related to POMCP usage and interpretability. First, we introduce a new planning problem related to mobile robot collision avoidance in paths with uncertain segment difficulties, and we show how POMCP performance in this context can take advantage of prior knowledge about segment difficulty relationships. This problem has direct real-world applications, such as, safety management in industrial environments where human-robot interaction is a crucial issue. Then, we present an experimental analysis about the relationships between prior knowledge provided to the algorithm and performance improvement, showing that in our case study prior knowledge affects two main properties, namely, the distance between the belief and the real state, and the mutual information between segment difficulty and action taken in the segment. This analysis aims to improve POMCP explainability, following the line of recently proposed eXplainable AI and, in particular, eXplainable planning. Finally, we analyze results on a synthetic case study and show how the proposed measures can improve the understanding about internal planning mechanisms.

Keywords: Planning under uncertainty · POMCP · POMDP · Explainable artificial intelligence · XAI · eXplainable planning

1 Introduction

Planning is a central problem in robotics and artificial intelligence, and it is crucial in many real-world applications. Often the environments in which agents act are partially unknown and models of the interaction between agent and environment should consider this uncertainty to improve planning performance.

© Springer Nature Switzerland AG 2020
N. Bassiliades et al. (Eds.): EUMAS 2020/AT 2020, LNAI 12520, pp. 261–276, 2020.
https://doi.org/10.1007/978-3-030-66412-1_17

Partially Observable Markov Decision Processes (POMDPs) are a sound and complete framework for modeling dynamical processes in uncertain environments [23]. A key idea of this framework is to consider all possible configurations of the (partially unknown) states of the agent in the environment, and to assign to each of these states a probability value indicating the likelihood that the state is the true state. All these probabilities together form a probability distribution over states which is called *belief*. Then, policies are computed [30] considering beliefs (that deal with uncertainty) instead of single states, a transition model for the dynamics of the system and an observation model for the (probabilistic) relationships between observations and true state. Unfortunately, exact solutions for non-trivial POMDP instances are usually computationally infeasible [28], therefore many approximate solvers have been recently developed to generate good solutions in acceptable computational time and space.

One of the most recent and efficient approximation methods for POMDP policies is *Monte Carlo Tree Search (MCTS)* [4,17,25], an heuristic search algorithm that represents system states as nodes of a tree, and actions/observations as edges. The search of profitable actions in this tree is performed considering a weighted average of the reward gathered in different branches of the tree itself. The most influential solver for POMDPs which takes advantage of MCTS is *Partially Observable Monte Carlo Planning (POMCP)* [34]. It combines a Monte Carlo update of the agent's belief with a MCTS-based policy. This algorithm generates online a policy that can be used to solve large instances of planning problems using only a black-box simulator. This strategy is advantageous in many practical problems because precise transition and observation models (in strict POMDP style) are not required, while prior knowledge about the specific problem at hand can be exploited to improve the planning performance [11,12].

In this paper, we tackle a problem related to velocity control of a mobile robot following a pre-specified path in an environment with uncertain obstacle densities. The robot has to reach the end of the path in the shortest possible time and to avoid collisions, to preserve safety. Real-world applications of this case study concern, for instance, safety management in Industry 4.0, where human-robot interaction needs to be robust, reliable and long lasting, especially when robots interact with workers in highly uncertain environments. In our case study the path that must be traveled is divided into segments and subsegments, and every segment is characterized by a *difficulty* that considers the density of obstacles in the environment. The real difficulty of segments is unknown and the robot has to reach the end of the path quickly, hence it should move slowly in difficult segments to avoid collisions, and faster in simpler segments to minimize the travelling time. Since it is known a-priori that some pairs of segments can (probabilistically) have the same difficulty (e.g., because they have similar properties), the information about segment difficulties could be collected as the robot advances and used to improve the planning performance. In other words, if some information about the difficulty of a segment is collected while traversing (i.e., acting in and observing) it, then this information can be transferred to subsequent segments known (a-priori) to have the same difficulty. We represent difficulty relationships between pairs of segments by state-variable constraints in Markov Random Fields (MRF) form [12].

The problem here investigated has therefore a particular sequential structure, in which difficulties of previously traveled segments can be used to infer the difficulty of subsequent segments using MRF-based state-variable constraints to (probabilistically) propagate information. What we show in this work is how performance improvement is related to the prior knowledge introduced by state-variable constraints. In particular, we introduce two measures, namely, a distance between the real state and the belief, and the mutual information between segment difficulty and action taken in the segment, and we experimentally show that the performance improvement is related to a decrease in the distance between real state and belief, and to an increase in the mutual information between difficulty and action. The improved *explainability* of the planning process achieved in this way is important in applications involving human-robot interaction [8–10,13], in which understanding how intelligent agents select their actions is critical. This also positively affects the trust that humans have in plans, following recent trends related to *explainable planning* [20].

The contribution of this paper to the state-of-the-art is threefold:

- we present the formulation of a new planning problem (having real-world applications in Industry 4.0) related to mobile robot collision avoidance in paths with uncertain segment obstacle densities (i.e., difficulties), and show how planning performance in this context can take advantage of prior knowledge about obstacle density relationships;
- we introduce two measures to quantify the effect of the introduction of prior knowledge on *(i)* belief precision and *(ii)* correlation between segment difficulty and action;
- we analyze results on a simulated experiment by means of a newly developed visualization tool that supports POMCP explainability.

Hence, this work introduces some novel ways to analyze POMCP functioning when prior knowledge is available in a novel application domain related to mobile robot navigation, and it represents a preliminary step towards more sophisticated explainable planning approaches for POMCP.

The rest of the paper is structured as follows. Section 2 presents related works, Sect. 3 formalizes the problem of interest and describes the proposed methodology, Sect. 4 discusses the results of experimental tests, and Sect. 5 draws conclusion and directions for future works.

2   Related Work

This work has relationships with three main topics in the literature, namely, *(i)* planning under uncertainty and reinforcement learning, *(ii)* the POMCP solver and its extensions for dealing with prior knowledge, *(iii)* explainable planning. Planning under uncertainty dates back to the seventies [18,31] when aspects of mathematical decision theory started to be incorporated into the predominant symbolic problem-solving techniques. The interest in this topic has been kept very high in the years [3,23], since planning under uncertainty is a critical task for autonomous and intelligent agents based on current data-driven technologies. The most recent developments mainly concern the use of Monte Carlo Tree Search (MCTS) and deep Reinforcement Learning [32,33,38], respectively, to deal with very large state spaces and to learn from data also the environment model during the planning process. Among the recently developed approximate [22] and online [30,34] planning approaches, we found only few works [1,26] in which prior knowledge about specific problems is used to improve planning performance or to scale to large problem instances. What differentiates these approaches to our work is that, first, we use a different method to introduce prior knowledge [12]; second, we focus on an original problem related to robot obstacle avoidance [19,24,29,37] having strict sequential nature in the way in which the agent explores the environment and transfers the acquired knowledge to future exploration; third, our goal is to improve the explainability of POMCP-based decision-making strategies.

The methodology we use to introduce prior knowledge in POMCP [12] allows to define probabilistic relationships of equality between pairs of state-variables by means of Markov random fields. State variables in our application domain are segment difficulties and a relationship says that two segments have a certain relative "compatibility" to have the same difficulty. The MRF approach then allows to factorize the joint probability function of state-variable configurations and this probability is used to constrain the state space. In our application domain the state space is the space of all possible segment difficulty configurations and the constraints introduced by the MRF allow to (probabilistically) reduce the chance to explore states that have small probability to be the true state. The integration of MRF-based prior knowledge into POMCP is mainly performed in the particle filter initialization, in the belief update phase and in the reinvigoration phase, where the constraints are used to optimize the management of the particle filter representing the agent belief.

Explainable planning (XAIP) [7,20] is a branch of the recently introduced research topic called eXplainable Artificial Intelligence (XAI) [21], which aims at creating artificial intelligence systems whose models and decisions can be understood and appropriately trusted by end users. Three main challenges of XAI are the development of methods for learning more explainable models, the designation of effective explanation interfaces [14], and the understanding of psychologic requirements for effective explanations [21]. XAIP has a strong impact on safety-critical applications, wherein people accountable to authorize the execution of a plan need complete understanding of the plan itself. First approaches of XAIP [35] focus on human-aware planning and model reconciliation [16,36,39,40], and on data visualization [15]. One recent trend proposed in [20] is to answer questions that improve human understanding of planner decision, such as, "why does the planner chose action A rather than B?", which are referred to as *contrastive questions*. Providing alternative choices and *what-if* analyses has indeed psychological basis [6] and it seems to support the interpretability of decision models that otherwise would not be understandable by developers and users. In this context users are required to provide alternative actions, if they do not trust the proposed plan, and replanning is used to show that the alternative is effectively better or worse than the original plan. Among the technical challenges of XAIP, one concerns the ability to more naturally specify and utilize constraints on the planning process [35]. Ideally, constraints over models should be described using a rich language designed for specifying constraints on the form of a desired plan. Some recent works [5,27] focus specifically on this topic. The contribution of our work to explainable planning is related to the introduction of two measures and related data visualization tools that support to explain the influence of prior knowledge, defined by Markov Random Field constraints, on POMCP performance. To the best of our knowledge no other work in the literature provides this kind of results.

3   Materials and Methods

In this section we provide definitions of POMDPs and POMCP, and we formalize the problem of interest. Then we introduce the three extensions of the POMCP planner employed in our experiments, that make use of different levels of prior knowledge, and define the two measures used to explain the effect of prior knowledge on the POMCP policy.

3.1   Partially Observable Markov Decision Processes

A Partially Observable Markov Decision Process (POMDP) [23] is defined as a tuple $(S, A, O, T, Z, R, \gamma)$, where S is a finite set of partially observable *states*, A is a finite set of *actions*, Z is a finite set of *observations*, $T: S \times A \to \Pi(S)$ is the *state-transition model*, $O: S \times A \to \Pi(Z)$ is the *observation model*, $R: S \times A \to \mathbb{R}$ is the *reward function* and $\gamma \in [0, 1)$ is a *discount factor*. The goal of an agent operating a POMDP, is to maximize its expected total discounted reward (also called *discounted return*) $E[\sum_{t=0}^{\infty} \gamma^t R(s_t, a_t)]$, by choosing the best action a_t in each state s_t at time t; γ is used to reduce the weight of distant rewards and ensure the (infinite) sum's convergence. As mentioned above, the partial observability of the state is dealt with by considering at each time-step a probability distribution over states, called *belief*. The belief space is here represented by symbol B. We also notice that the term belief is sometimes exchanged with term *history* in the following, since an history h is a sequence of actions and observations that bring the agent from an initial belief b_0 to a certain belief b. POMDP *solvers* are algorithms that compute, in an exact or approximate way, a *policy* for POMDPs, namely a function $\pi: B \to A$ that provides an optimal action for each believe.

3.2   POMCP

Partially Observable Monte Carlo Planning (POMCP) [34] is an online Monte-Carlo based algorithm for solving POMDPs. It uses *Monte-Carlo Tree Search*

(MCTS) for selecting optimal actions at each time-step. The main elements of POMCP are a *particle filter*, which represents the belief state, and the *Upper Confidence Bound for Trees* (UCT) [25] search strategy, that allows to select actions from the Monte Carlo tree. The particle filter contains, at each time-step, a sampling of the agent's belief at that step (the belief evolves over time). In particular, it contains k particles, each representing a specific state. At the beginning the particle filter is usually initialized following a uniform random distribution over states, if no prior knowledge is available about the initial state. Then, at each time-step the Monte Carlo tree is generated performing $nSim$ simulations from the current belief. In other words, for $nSim$ times a particle is randomly chosen from the particle filter and the related state is used as initial state to perform a simulation. Each simulation is a sequence of action-observation pairs that collect a final return, where each action and observation brings to a new node in the tree. Rewards are then propagated upwards in the tree obtaining, for each action of the root node, an expected (approximated) value of the cumulative reward that this action can bring. The UCT strategy selects actions considering both their expected cumulative reward and the necessity to explore new actions from time to time. The belief is finally updated, after performing the selected action a and getting a related observation o from the environment, by considering only the particles (i.e., states) in the node (called hao) reached from current node h following edges a and o. New particles can be generated through a *particle reinvigoration* procedure based on local transformation of available states, if the particle filter gets empty. A big advantage of POMCP is that it does not require a complete matrix-based definition of transition model, observation model and reward, but it only needs a black-box simulator of the environment.

3.3   Problem Formalization

Here we formally define the problem we want to solve in this paper using different extensions of POMCP that consider different levels of prior knowledge. Let us assume to have a pre-defined path to be traversed by a mobile robot in an industrial environment. The path, of which one possible instance is displayed in Fig. 1, is made of segments s_i which are then split in subsegments s_{ij}. Each segment (and related subsegments) is characterized by a difficulty f_i, related to the average density of obstacles in it. The robot has to reach the end of the path in the shortest possible time, tuning its speed v in each subsegment to avoid obstacles, since the probability of collision depends on speed and segment difficulty, and each collision yields a time penalty. The robot cannot directly observe segment difficulties (which are hidden state variables) but only infer their values from (observable) variables o_i that provide information about the occupancy of each subsegment, based on the readings of a laser located on top of the agent.

This problem can be formalized as a POMDP. The *state* contains *(i)* the (hidden) true configuration of segment difficulties $(f_1, \ldots, f_n)$ where $f_j \in \{L, M, H\}$, L is low difficulty, M medium difficulty and H high difficulty, *(ii)* the position

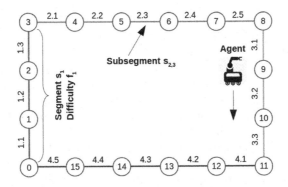

Fig. 1. Path travelled by the agent. Nodes are subsegment

Table 1. Main elements of our POMDP model for the collision avoidance problem. (a) Occupancy model $p(o \mid f)$: probability of subsegment occupancy given segment difficulty. (b) Action-time model: number of time units to traverse a subsegment given the action performed by the agent. (c) Collision model $p(c \mid f, a)$: collision probability given segment difficulty and action.

f	$p(o = 1 \mid f)$
L	0.0
M	0.5
H	1.0

(a)

a	dt
L	3
M	2
H	1

(b)

f	a	$p(c = 1 \mid f, a)$
L	L	0.0
L	M	0.0
L	H	0.0
M	L	0.0
M	M	0.5
M	H	0.9
H	L	0.0
H	M	1.0
H	H	1.0

(c)

$p = (i, j)$ of the robot in the path, where i is the index of the segment and j the index of the subsegment (saying that the agent is in position (i, j) we mean that it is at the beginning of subsegment $s_{i,j}$), (iii) the time t elapsed from the beginning of the path. *Actions* correspond to the speed the robot maintains in a subsegment, which may have three possible values, namely low (L), medium (M) or high (H). *Observations* are related to subsegment occupancy, where $o = 0$ means that the laser does not detect any obstacle in the current subsegment, and $o = 1$ means that it detects some obstacles (notice that observations are affected by uncertainty). The *observation model* hence corresponds to the *occupancy model* $p(o \mid f)$ which (probabilistically) relates segment difficulty to subsegment occupancy. The parameters of Table 1a concern the occupancy model used in our experiments.

The state transition model deals with the update of robot position and current time at each step. Position update is performed in a deterministic way since at each step the robot is assumed to reach the beginning of the next subsegment in the path. The current time is instead updated depending on both the action performed by the agent and the possibility to make collisions. The relationship between action and time elapsed to traverse a subsegment is displayed in Table 1b, namely the agent spends 1 time unit if the action is H (low speed), 2 time units if the action is M, and 3 time units if the action is L. The time penalty due to collision is instead governed by the probabilistic *collision model* $p(c \mid f, a)$ of Table 1c, where $c = 0$ means no collision and $c = 1$ means collision. Notice, that the probability of not making a collision is one minus the probability to make the collision, since the collision value is binary. The reward function here used is $R = -(t_1 + t_2)$, where t_1 is the time depending on agent's action and t_2 is the penalty due to collisions. We use $t_2 = 10$ in our experiments. Finally the discount factor is $\gamma = 0.95$.

3.4   Planning Strategies

Three planning strategies are used in our tests. The original implementation of POMCP [34], named *STD* in the following, is used as a baseline. An extended version of POMCP allowing the definition of state-variable constraints by Markov Random Fields [12], is named *MRF* in the following, and is used to introduce prior knowledge about segment difficulty relationships. For instance, in an instance of our problem we could know that the probability that segment s_0 and segment s_1 have same difficulty is 0.9. Planner *MRF* can use this information to improve the policy it generates and, consequently, the planning performance. The focus of this paper is, in particular, to identify the effects of prior knowledge on POMCP strategy and we perform this analysis considering the two measures introduced in Subsect. 3.6. Finally, we consider an oracle planner, named *ORC* in the following, in which perfect knowledge of segment difficulties is used. This planner performs the POMCP strategy using only the particle corresponding to the true state (i.e., configuration of segment difficulties).

3.5   Experimental Setup

We perform experiments to compare the three planning strategies described above. In planner MRF we introduce prior knowledge about the difficulty relationship of two segments actually having the same difficulty. In particular, we set to 0.9 the probability of these two segments to have same difficulty (meaning that we say to the planner that these two segments have probability 0.9 to have same difficulty). This high probability value allows the planner to consider also states not satisfying this constraint, but only with a small chance. Tests with inaccurate prior knowledge are reported in [12]. In each *run* the agent starts from node 0 in the path of Fig. 1 and has to reach the same node collecting the highest possible return. We perform 20 runs for each *test* in order to compute average returns and related standard errors. Different runs have different configurations of segment difficulties, for instance, one run could have a configuration (L, H, M, H) and another (M, H, L, L). Each test is performed using a fixed number of simulations $nSim$. We analyze results achieved using $nSim$ between 2^8 and 2^{15} with exponential step 2^x, $8 \leq x \leq 15$. As expected, runs performed using more simulations tend to reach better performance (we remind that $nSim$ simulations are performed each time the agent performs an action in the path, namely, for each subsegment).

3.6   Measures for Policy Explanation

To quantify the influence of prior knowledge on policy performance we introduce two measures about specific properties of the policy that support its explainability, namely, the *belief-state distance* and the *mutual information between difficulty and action*.

Belief-State Distance. We define the belief-state distance as the weighted averaged Manhattan distance between the configuration of segment difficulties in the true hidden state and the configurations of segment difficulties in the belief states. Mathematically, if we define the configuration of segment difficulties in the true state as $f_S = (f_1, \dots, f_n)$, where $f_j \in \{L, M, H\}$ and n is the number of segments, and we define the k configurations of segment difficulties in the belief as $f_B^i = (f_1^i, \dots, f_n^i)$, $i \in \{1, \dots, k\}$, $f_j^i \in \{L, M, H\}$ where the probability of each difficulty configuration f_B^i in the belief is p_B^i, then the belief-state distance is

$$d_{SB} = \sum_{i=1}^{k} \left(p_B^i \cdot \sum_{j=1}^{n} |f_j - f_j^i| \right). \tag{1}$$

Since the belief is updated at each time-step, this measure can be computed at each time-step too. This measure allows to quantify the discrepancy between what the agent believes about the real state of the environment and the real state of the environment, hence addiction of prior knowledge about segment difficulty relationships is expected to decrease this distance.

Mutual Information (MI) Between Segment Difficulty and Action. In the specific instance of the collision avoidance problem defined in Subsect. 3.3 it is expected that the agent takes particular actions if it has good knowledge about the true configuration of segment difficulties. In fact, analyzing the collision model in Table 1c we observe that high speed (i.e., $a = H$) should be selected in segments with low difficulty (i.e., $f = L$) because the collision probability is always 0.0 in that segment, hence high speed should be preferred to reach earlier the end of the path. On the other hand, in segments with high difficulty (i.e., $f = H$) the collision probability is 0.0 if low speed (i.e., $a = L$) is kept and it is 1.0 if medium or high speed (i.e., $a = M$ or $a = L$) is kept, hence low speed should be preferred. In case of medium difficulty the collision probability instead increases from 0.0 to 0.5 and to 0.9 when the speed increases from L to M and to H, thus the choice of the best action depends on collision penalty.

To check if the POMCP policy effectively generates actions related to segment difficulties we compute the mutual information between all actions taken in each run and corresponding segment difficulties. In other words, given a run we consider the sequence of actions $\mathcal{A} = (a_{i,j})$, where i is the index of a segment and j is the index of a subsegment, and the sequence of related subsegment difficulties $\mathcal{F} = (f_{i,j})$. The mutual information [2] between the two sequences, treated as random variables, is

$$I(\mathcal{A}, \mathcal{F}) = \sum_{a \in \mathcal{A}} \sum_{f \in \mathcal{F}} p_{(\mathcal{A}, \mathcal{F})}(a, f) log \left(\frac{p_{(\mathcal{A}, \mathcal{F})}(a, f)}{p_{\mathcal{A}}(a) p_{\mathcal{F}}(f)} \right), \tag{2}$$

where $p_{(\mathcal{A}, \mathcal{F})}(a, f)$ is the joint probability mass function of $\mathcal{A}$ and $\mathcal{F}$, and $p_{\mathcal{A}}$ and $p_{\mathcal{F}}$ are the marginal probability mass functions of $\mathcal{A}$ and $\mathcal{F}$, respectively. Average MI values are computed on sets of runs. We notice that selecting actions with high difficulty-action MI is not trivial since the true configuration of segment difficulties is hidden. In the next section we experimentally analyze the trend of this measure depending on the prior knowledge provided in different planners.

4   Results

In this section we present the results of the experiments described in Subsect. 3.5. The first observation we make is that the introduction of complete (ORC) and partial (MRF) prior knowledge about segment difficulty relationships yields performance improvement, in terms of discounted return. This effect is clear in Fig. 2a where the blue line (ORC performance) stands above the green line (MRF performance) which, in turns, stands above the red line (STD performance). Notice that the overtaking of MRF on STD for $nSim = 10$ is due only to an anomalous higher average difficulty value of the MRF runs w.r.t. the STD runs. In the following we analyze the reasons of this performance improvement, which is fundamental in real-world applications involving human-robot interaction because explainability supports safety preservation.

In Fig. 2b–e we decompose the effect on planning performance into its causes, and provide insight on the mechanisms that produce it. We first observe that the introduction of prior knowledge has a positive effect on both the average number of collisions (see Fig. 2b where the blue line stands below the green line, which stands below the red line) and the average action (see Fig. 2c where the blue line stands above the green line, which stands above the red line, at least for $nSim \geq 2^8$). This behavior is not obvious, since these two quantities have opposite effects. Namely, higher actions, i.e. higher speeds, usually cause higher number of collisions. If this is not the case, it means that planners using prior knowledge are able to select actions according to a (smart) strategy which improves average speed without increasing the collision rate.

Some explanation about the strategies implemented by planners ORC and MRF to reach this aim is displayed in Figs. 2d and e. Figure 2e shows that the mutual information between segment difficulties and related actions is much

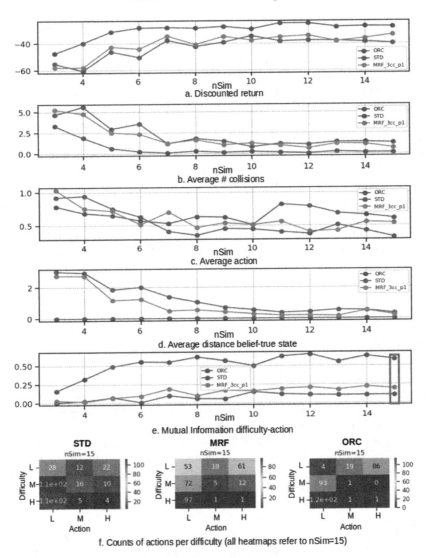

Fig. 2. Performance of the three planners ORC, MRF and STD, and explanation of the reasons of different performance. (Color figure online)

higher in the ORC planner than in the STD planner, and the MRF planner has intermediate MI values (see the blue line above the green line, and the green line above the red line in the chart). High MI between difficulty and action means that the planner is able to adapt the action to the (hidden) difficulty, which implies that the planner has some knowledge about true segment difficulties. The charts show that the (complete or partial) prior knowledge about segment difficulty relationships (see the distance between final belief and real state in

Fig. 2d) is correctly transferred to the policy, hence that knowledge about segment difficulties is actually used to better select actions.

Moving to deeper details, we discover (see Fig. 2f) that in the 20 runs performed with maximum number of simulations (i.e., $nSim = 2^{15}$) the ORC planner (on the right) selects 86 times (i.e., 79% of times) action H in subsegments with low difficulty (see the top-right cell in the heatmap), while it selects action M only 19 times (i.e., 17% of times) and action L only 4 times (i.e., 3.6% of times) (see other cells in the first row of the heatmap). As mentioned earlier, this strategy is correct since the collision probability is always 0.0 in segments with low difficulty, therefore high speed should be preferred in such segments. The STD planner, on the left of Fig. 2f, is unable to select the best action in segments with low difficulty. It selects 28 times (i.e., 45% of times) action L, 12 times (i.e., 20% of times) action M and 22 times (i.e., 35% of times) action H (see the first row of the heatmap in the left-hand side of Fig. 2f). Planner MRF performs better than STD but worse than ORC (see the first row of the heatmap in the center of Fig. 2f), selecting 61 times (i.e., 46% of times) action H, 18 times (i.e., 14% of times) action M and 53 times (i.e., 40% of times) action L. We stress that the differences between these strategies depend on the knowledge the planner has about the real difficulty of segments. In other words, planner STD sometimes does not provide best actions because its belief is not precise enough and actions are consequently affected by this uncertainty.

Analyzing planner behaviors in segments with high or medium difficulty, we observe that ORC selects almost 99% of times action L (see the second and third rows of the heatmap in the right hand side of Fig. 2f). STD instead selects action L respectively 78% (i.e., value 110) and 92% (i.e., value 110) of times in the same segments (see the second and third rows of the heatmap in the left hand side of Fig. 2f), and MRF selects action L respectively 80% (i.e., value 72) and 98% (i.e., value 97) of times in the same segments (see the last row of the heatmap in the center of Fig. 2f). Again, the ORC strategy is the best considering the collision model in Table 1), then comes MRF and finally STD. All the planners should learn the same strategy but the prior knowledge added to ORC and MRF let them learn it better.

To show how prior knowledge influences the belief evolution, we display in Fig. 3b and d the belief evolution for a run with hidden state (H, M, L, M) performed by the STD planner (on the left) and the MRF planner (on the right). The ORC planner is not displayed because it has fixed belief. Belief states are encoded by decimal numbers from 0 to 80, whose ternary encoding provides the difficulty configuration (e.g., decimal 64 corresponds to ternary 2101, namely difficulty configuration (H, M, L, M)). On top (see Figs. 3a and c) the evolution of difficulty, action, occupancy and belief-state distance over time (the time-step is in the x-axis). Red vertical lines delimit path segments and orange lines delimit subsegments. In the bottom (see Figs. 3b and d) the evolution of the belief over time (from top to bottom). Green horizontal lines delimit path segments (labels $SEG1, \ldots, SEG4$ in the central part of the figure).

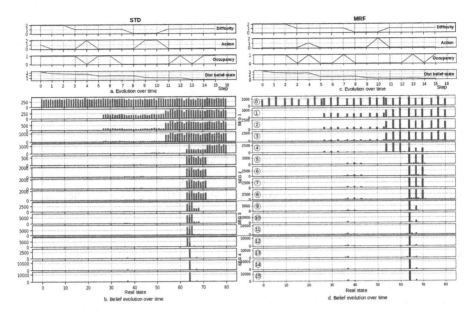

Fig. 3. Comparison of belief evolution in STD and a MRF runs with hidden state (H,M,L,M) and $nSim = 2^{15}$.

The prior knowledge used by the MRF planner constraints the second and the fourth segment to have the same difficulty with probability 0.9. The effect of this constraint on the belief evolution is evident in Fig. 3d. Namely, states with different difficulties in segments 2 and 4 are considered with smaller probability than states with same difficulty in those segments (see the sparse distribution of states in Fig. 3d). Then, interestingly enough, the belief about the difficulty of segment 4 is updated while the agent traverses segment 2, since these two segments are connected by a (probabilistic) constraint. In other words, when the agent discovers that segment 2 has medium difficulty, it updates also its belief about segment 4, accordingly. In this way, the information acquired by the agent in the current segment is forwarded to future segments and, when the agent will traverse those segments in the future, it will use this information to choose more efficient actions. This concept is clearly displayed in our experimental test of Fig. 3b and d where the belief of the MRF planner (on the right) at the end of segment 3 is almost completely peaked on the right state, while that of the STD planner (on the left) needs some steps in segment 4 to understand its difficulty. In this specific case the observation model is very informative and the agent needs only one step (i.e., step 13) to understand the true difficulty of the segment, but in real environments several steps could be required to gather the same information, yielding a further decrease of performance.

As a final remark we notice that the presented experiments are performed on a small path only to limit the belief space dimension and to allow the visualization of belief evolution in Fig. 3. However, the approach can easily scale to longer paths and in those cases even larger differences between the behavior (in terms of discounted return, # collisions, actions, belief-state distance and difficulty-action MI) of the three planners can be observed.

5   Conclusion and Ongoing Work

In this work we analyze the mechanisms by which prior knowledge is used by POMCP to improve planning performance in a collision avoidance problem. Although this is a first step towards full POMCP explainability, the approach has potential for several developments. Among them we are working on *(i)* the explanation of the Monte Carlo tree representing the policy, *(ii)* the application to real robotic platforms, *(iii)* the testing on longer paths and real-world environments.

Acknowledgments. The research has been partially supported by the projects "Dipartimenti di Eccellenza 2018–2022, funded by the Italian Ministry of Education, Universities and Research (MIUR), and "GHOTEM/CORE-WOOD, POR-FESR 2014–2020", funded by Regione del Veneto.

References

1. Amato, C., Oliehoek, F.A.: Scalable planning and learning for multi-agent POMDPs. In: Proceedings of AAAI 2015, pp. 1995–2002. AAAI Press (2015)
2. Bishop, C.M.: Pattern Recognition and Machine Learning. Springer-Verlag, New York (2006)
3. Boutilier, C., Dean, T., Hanks, S.: Decision-theoretic Planning: structural assumptions and computational leverage. JAIR **11**(1), 1–94 (1999)
4. Browne, C., et al.: A survey of Monte Carlo tree search methods. IEEE Trans. Comp. Intell. AI Games **4**(1), 1–43 (2012)
5. Byrne, R.M.J.: Constraints on counterfactuals. In: Proceedings of the Workshop of Explainable Artificial Intelligence, Twenty-Eighth International Joint Conference on Artificial Intelligence IJCAI 2019 (2019)
6. Byrne, R.M.J.: Counterfactuals in Explainable Artificial Intelligence (XAI): evidence from human reasoning. In: Proceedings of the Twenty-Eighth International Joint Conference on Artificial Intelligence, IJCAI 2019, Vol. 7, pp. 6276–6282. International Joint Conferences on Artificial Intelligence Organization (2019)
7. Cashmore, M., Collins, A., Krarup, B., Krivic, S., Magazzeni, D., Smith, D.: Towards Explainable AI Planning as a Service (2019). CoRR, abs/1908.05059
8. Castellini, A., et al.: Activity recognition for autonomous water drones based on unsupervised learning methods. In: Proceedings of 4th Italian Workshop on Artificial Intelligence and Robotics (AI*IA 2017), Vol. 2054, pp. 16–21 (2018)
9. Castellini, A., et al.: Subspace clustering for situation assessment in aquatic drones: a sensitivity analysis for state-model improvement. Cybern. Syst. **50**(8), 658–671 (2019)
10. Castellini, A., Bicego, M., Masillo, F., Zuccotto, M., Farinelli, A.: Time series segmentation for state-model generation of autonomous aquatic drones: a systematic framework. Eng. Appl. Artif. Intel. **90**, 103499 (2020)

11. Castellini, A., Blum, J., Bloisi, D., Farinelli, A.: Intelligent battery management for aquatic drones based on task difficulty driven POMDPs. In: Proceedings of the 5th Italian Workshop on Artificial Intelligence and Robotics, AIRO@AI*IA 2018, pp. 24–28, Trento, Italy (2018)
12. Castellini, A., Chalkiadakis, G., Farinelli, A.: Influence of state-variable constraints on partially observable monte carlo planning. In: Proceedings of 28th International Joint Conference on Artificial Intelligence (IJCAI 2019), pp. 5540–5546 (2019)
13. Castellini, A., Masillo, F., Bicego, M., Bloisi, D., Blum, J., Farinelli, A., Peigner, S.: Subspace clustering for situation assessment in aquatic drones. In: Proceedings of Symposium on Applied Computing, SAC 2019, pp. 930–937. ACM (2019)
14. Castellini, A., Masillo, F., Sartea, R., Farinelli, A.: eXplainable Modeling (XM): Data Analysis for Intelligent Agents. In: Proceedings of the 18th International Conference on Autonomous Agents and Multiagent Systems (AAMAS 2019), pp. 2342–2344. IFAAMAS (2019)
15. Chakraborti, T., et al.: Visualizations for an Explainable Planning Agent. In Proceedings of the Twenty-Seventh International Joint Conference on Artificial Intelligence, IJCAI-18, Vol. 7, pp. 5820–5822. International Joint Conferences on Artificial Intelligence Organization (2018)
16. Chakraborti, T., Sreedharan, S., Zhang, Y., Kambhampati, S.: Plan Explanations as Model Reconciliation: Moving Beyond Explanation as Soliloquy. In Proc. 26th Int. Joint Conference on Artificial Intelligence, IJCAI 2017, pp. 156–163 (2017)
17. Coulom, R.: Efficient selectivity and backup operators in Monte-Carlo tree search. In: van den Herik, H.J., Ciancarini, P., Donkers, H.H.L.M.J. (eds.) CG 2006. LNCS, vol. 4630, pp. 72–83. Springer, Heidelberg (2007). https://doi.org/10.1007/978-3-540-75538-8_7
18. Feldman, J.A., Sproull, R.F.: Decision theory and artificial intelligence II: the hungry monkey. Cogn. Sci. **1**(2), 158–192 (1977)
19. Foka, A., Trahanias, P.: Real-time hierarchical POMDPs for autonomous robot navigation. Robot. Autonom. Syst. **55**(7), 561–571 (2007)
20. Fox, M., Long, D., Magazzeni, D.: Explainable Planning (2017). CoRR, abs/1709.10256
21. Gunning, D., Aha, D.: DARPA's explainable artificial intelligence (XAI) program. AI Magazine **40**(2), 44–58 (2019)
22. Hauskrecht, M.: Value-function approximations for partially observable Markov Decision processes. JAIR **13**, 33–94 (2000)
23. Kaelbling, L., Littman, M., Cassandra, A.: Planning and acting in partially observable stochastic domains. Artif. Intell. **101**(1–2), 99–134 (1998)
24. Khatib, O.: Real-time obstacle avoidance for manipulators and mobile robots. In: Proceedings of 1985 IEEE International Conference on Robotics and Automation, Vol.2, pp. 500–505 (1985)
25. Kocsis, L., Szepesvári, C.: Bandit based Monte-Carlo planning. In: Fürnkranz, J., Scheffer, T., Spiliopoulou, M. (eds.) ECML 2006. LNCS (LNAI), vol. 4212, pp. 282–293. Springer, Heidelberg (2006). https://doi.org/10.1007/11871842_29
26. Lee, J., Kim, G.-H., Poupart, P., Kim, K.-E.: Monte-Carlo tree search for constrained POMDPs. In: NIPS 2018, pp. 1–17 (2018)
27. Mahajan, D., Tan, C., Sharma, A.: Preserving Causal Constraints in Counterfactual Explanations for Machine Learning Classifiers (2019)
28. Papadimitriou, C., Tsitsiklis, J.: The complexity of Markov decision processes. Math. Oper. Res. **12**(3), 441–450 (1987)

29. Potena, C., Nardi, D., Pretto, A.: Joint vision-based navigation, control and obstacle avoidance for UAVs in dynamic environments. In: 2019 European Conference on Mobile Robots (ECMR), pp. 1–7 (2019)
30. Ross, S., Pineau, J., Paquet, S., Chaib-draa, B.: Online planning algorithms for POMDPs. JAIR **32**, 663–704 (2008)
31. Russell, S., Norvig, P.: Artificial Intelligence: A Modern Approach, 2nd edn. Pearson Education, London (2003)
32. Silver, D., Huang, A., Maddison, C.J., et al.: Mastering the game of go with deep neural networks and tree search. Nature **529**(7587), 484–489 (2016)
33. Silver, D., Schrittwieser, J., Simonyan, K., et al.: Mastering the game of go without human knowledge. Nature **550**, 354–359 (2017)
34. Silver, D., Veness, J.: Monte-Carlo planning in large POMDPs. In: NIPS 2010, pp. 2164–2172 (2010)
35. Smith, D.E.: Planning as an iterative process. In: Proceedings of Twenty-Sixth AAAI Conference on Artificial Intelligence, AAAI 2012, pp. 2180–2185. AAAI Press (2012)
36. Sreedharan, S., Chakraborti, T., Kambhampati, S.: Handling model uncertainty and multiplicity in explanations via model reconciliation. In: Proceedings of International Conference on Automated Planning and Scheduling, ICAPS 2018, pp. 518–526 (2018)
37. Steccanella, L., Bloisi, D.D., Castellini, A., Farinelli, A.: Waterline and obstacle detection in images from low-cost autonomous boats for environmental monitoring. Robot. Autonom. Syst. **124**, 103346 (2020)
38. Lorenz, U.: Leitbilder in der Künstlichen Intelligenz. Reinforcement Learning, pp. 161–170. Springer, Heidelberg (2020). https://doi.org/10.1007/978-3-662-61651-2_6
39. Vanzo, A., Croce, D., Bastianelli, E., Basili, R., Nardi, D.: Grounded language interpretation of robotic commands through structured learning. Artif. Intell. **278**, 103181 (2020)
40. Zhang, Y., Sreedharan, S., Kulkarni, A., Chakraborti, T., Zhuo, H.H., Kambhampati, S.: Plan explicability and predictability for robot task planning. In: IEEE International Conferencce on Robotics and Automation (ICRA 2017), pp. 1313–1320 (2017)

EUMAS 2020 Best Papers Session

Approximating Voting Rules
from Truncated Ballots

Manel Ayadi[1,2(✉)], Nahla Ben Amor[1(✉)], and Jérôme Lang[2(✉)]

[1] Institut Supérieur de Gestion, LARODEC, Université de Tunis, Tunis, Tunisia
manel.ayadi@hotmail.com, nahla.benamor@gmx.fr
[2] LAMSADE, CNRS, PSL, Université Paris-Dauphine, Paris, France
lang@lamsade.dauphine.fr

Abstract. Classical voting rules assume that ballots are complete preference orders over candidates. However, when the number of candidates is large enough, it is too costly to ask the voters to rank all candidates. We suggest to fix a rank k, to ask all voters to specify their best k candidates, and then to consider "top-k approximations" of rules, which take only into account the *top-k* candidates of each ballot. We consider two measures of the quality of the approximation: the probability of selecting the same winner as the original rule, and the score ratio. We do a worst-case study (for the latter measure only), and for both measures, an average-case study and a study from real data sets.

Keywords: Voting rules · Truncated ballots · Approximations.

1 Introduction

The input of a voting rule is usually a collection of complete rankings over candidates (although there are exceptions, such as approval voting). However, requiring a voter to provide a complete ranking over the whole set of candidates can be difficult and costly in terms of time and cognitive effort. We suggest to ask voters to report only their *top-k* candidates, for some (small) fixed value of k (the obtained ballots are then said to be *top-k*). Not only it saves communication effort, but it is also often easier for a voter to find out the top part of their preference relation than the bottom part. However, this raises the issue of how usual voting rules should be adapted to top-k ballots. Reporting top-k ballots is a specific form of *voting with incomplete preferences*, and is highly related to *vote elicitation*. Work on these topics is reviewed in the recent handbook chapter [5]. Existing work on truncated ballots can be classified into two classes according to the type of interaction with the voters:

(i) Interactive elicitation
An interactive elicitation protocol asks voters to expand their truncated ballots in an incremental way, until the outcome of the vote is eventually determined. This line of research starts with Kalech et al. [14] who start by top-1 ballots,

© Springer Nature Switzerland AG 2020
N. Bassiliades et al. (Eds.): EUMAS 2020/AT 2020, LNAI 12520, pp. 279–298, 2020.
https://doi.org/10.1007/978-3-030-66412-1_18

then top-2, etc., until there is sufficient information for knowing the winner. Lu and Boutilier [16,17] propose an incremental elicitation process using *minimax regret* to predict the correct winner given partial information. A more general incremental elicitation framework, with more types of elicitation questions, is cost-effective elicitation [25]. Naamani Dery *et al.* [10] present two elicitation algorithms for finding a winner with little communication between voters.

(ii) Non-interactive elicitation

The central authority elicits the top-k ballots at once, for a fixed value of k, and outputs a winner without requiring voters to provide extra information. A possibility consists in computing possible winners given these truncated ballots: this is the path followed by Baumeister et al. [2] (who also consider double-truncated ballots where each voter ranks some of her top and bottom candidates). Another possibility – which is the one follow – consists in generalizing the definition of a voting rule so that it takes truncated ballots as input. In this line, Oren *et al.* [21] analyze *top-k* voting by assessing the values of k needed to ensure the true winner is found with high probability for specific preference distributions. Skowron *et al.* [23] use *top-k* voting as a way to approximate some multiwinner rules. Filmus and Oren [12] study the performance of top-k voting under the impartial culture distribution for the Borda, Harmonic and Copeland rules. They assess the values of k needed to find the true winner with high probability, and they report on numerical experiments that show that under the impartial culture, top-k ballots for reasonable small values of k give accurate results.

Bentert and Skowron [3] focus on top-k approximations of voting rules that are defined via the maximization of a score (positional scoring rules and maximin). They evaluate the quality of the approximation of a voting rule by a top-k rule by the worst-case ratio between the scores, with respect to the original profile, of the winner of the original rule and the winner of the approximate rule. They identify the top-k rules that best approximate positional scoring rules (we give more details in Sect. 5). Their theoretical analysis is completed by numerical experiments using profiles generated from different distributions over preferences: they show that for the Borda rule a small value of k is needed to achieve a high approximation guarantee while maximin needs more information from a sufficiently many voters to determine the winner.

Ayadi *et al.* [1] evaluate the extent to which STV with *top-k* ballots approximates STV with full information. They show that for small k, *top-k* ballots are enough to identify the correct winner quite frequently, especially for data taken from real elections. Finally, the recognition of singled-peaked *top-k* profiles is studied in [15] while the computational issues of manipulating rules with *top-k* profiles is addressed in [20].

Our contribution concerns non-interactive elicitation. We adapt different voting rules to truncated ballots: we define approximations of voting rules which take as input the *top-k* candidates of each ballot. The question is then, *are these approximations good predictors of the original rule?* We answer this question by considering two measures: the probability that the approximate rule selects the 'true' winner, and the ratio between the scores (for the original rule) of the true winner and the winner of the approximate rule. For the latter measure we give a worst-case theoretical analysis. For both measures we give an empirical study, based on randomly generated profiles and on real-world data. Our findings are that for several common voting rules, both for randomly generated profiles and real data, a very small k suffices.

Our research can be seen as a continuation of Filmus and Oren [12]. We go further on several points: we consider more voting rules; beyond impartial culture, we consider a large scope of distributions; we study score distortion; and we include experiments using real-world data sets. Our work is also closely related to [3], who have obtained related results independently (see Sects. 4 and 5 for a discussion).

Our interpretation of top-k ballots is *epistemic*: the central authority in charge of collecting the votes and computing the outcome ignores the voters' preferences below the *top-k* candidates of each voter, and has to cope with it as much as possible. Voters may very well have a complete preference order in their head (although it does not need to be the case), but they will simply not be asked to report it.

Section 2 gives some background. Section 3 defines top-k approximations of different voting rules. Section 4 analyses empirically the probability that approximate rules select the true winner. Section 5 analyses score distortion, theoretically and empirically.

2   Preliminaries

An election is a triple $E = \langle N, A, P \rangle$ where: $N = \{1, ..., n\}$ is the set of *voters*, A is the set of *candidates*, with $|A| = m$; and $P = (\succ_1, ..., \succ_n)$ is the *preference profile* of voters in N, where for each i, $\succ_i \in P$ is a linear order over A. $\mathcal{P}_m$ is the set of all profiles over m alternatives (for varying n).

Given a profile P, $N_P(a, b) = \#\{i, a \succ_i b\}$ is the number of voters who prefer a to b in P. The *majority graph* $M(P)$ is the graph whose set of vertices is the set of the candidates A and in which for all $a, b \in A$, there is a directed edge from a to b (denoted by $a \to b$) in $M(P)$ if $N_p(a, b) > \frac{n}{2}$.

A resolute voting rule is a function $f : E \to A$. Resolute rules are typically obtained from composing an irresolute rule (mapping an election into an non-empty subset of candidates, called co-winners) with a tie-breaking mechanism.

A *positional scoring rule* (PSR) f^s is defined by a non-negative vector $s = (s_1, ..., s_m)$ such that $s_1 \geq ... \geq s_m$ and $s_1 > 0$. Each candidate receives s_j points from each voter i who ranks her in the jth position, and the score of a candidate is the total number of points she receives from all voters i.e. $S(x) = \sum_{i=1}^{n} s_j$. The winner is the candidate with highest total score. Examples of scoring rules are the Borda and Harmonic rules, with $s_{Borda} = (m-1, m-2, ..., 0)$ and $s_{Harmonic} = (1, 1/2, ..., 1/m)$.

We now define three *pairwise comparison rules*.

The *Copeland* rule outputs the candidate maximizing the *Copeland score*, where the Copeland score of x is the number of candidates y with $x \to y$ in

$M(P)$, plus half the number of candidates $y \neq x$ with no edge between x and y in $M(P)$.

The *Ranked Pairs* (RP) rule proceeds by ranking all pairs of candidates (x, y) according to $N_P(x, y)$ (using tie-breaking when necessary); starting from an empty graph over A, it then considers all pairs in the described order and includes a pair in the graph if and only if it does not create a cycle in it. At the end of the process, the graph is a complete ranking, whose top element is the winner.

The *maximin* rule outputs the candidates that maximize $min_{x \in A(x \neq a)} N_P(a, x)$.

For the experiments using randomly generated profiles, we use the *Mallows* ϕ-*model* [18]. It is a (realistic) family of distributions over rankings, parametrized by a modal or reference ranking σ and a dispersion parameter $\phi \in [0, 1]$: $P(r; \sigma, \phi) = \frac{1}{Z} \phi^{d(r,\sigma)}$, where r is any ranking, d is the Kendall tau distance and $Z = \sum_{r'} \phi^{d(r,\sigma)} = 1 \cdot (1 + \phi) \cdot (1 + \phi + \phi^2) \cdot ... \cdot (1 + ... + \phi^{m-1})$ is a normalization constant. With small values of ϕ, the mass is concentrated around σ, while $\phi = 1$ gives the uniform distribution *Impartial Culture (IC)*, where all profiles are equiprobable.

3   Approximating Voting Rules from Truncated Ballots

Given $k \in \{1, ..., m-1\}$, a *top-k election* is a triple $E' = \langle N, A, R \rangle$ where N and A are as before, and $R = (\succ_1^k, ..., \succ_n^k)$, where each $\succ_i^k$ is a ranking of k out of m candidates in A. R is called a *top-k profile*. If P is a complete profile, $\succ_i^k$ is the top-k truncation of $\succ_i$ (i.e., the best k candidates, ranked as in $\succ_i$), and $P_k = (\succ_1^k, ..., \succ_n^k)$ is the top-k-profile induced from P and k. A *top-k (resolute) voting rule* is a function f_k that maps each *top-k election* E' to a candidate in A. We sometimes apply a top-k rule to a complete profile, with $f_k(P) = f_k(P_k)$. We now define several *top-k* rules.

3.1   Borda and Positional Scoring Rules

Definition 1. *A top-k PSR f_k^s is defined by a scoring vector $s = (s_1, s_2 ..., s_k, s^*)$ such that $s_1 \geq s_2 \geq ... \geq s_k \geq s^* \geq 0$ and $s_1 > s^*$. Each candidate in a top-k vote receives s_j points from each voter i who ranks her in the jth position. A non-ranked candidate gets s^* points. The winner is the candidate with highest total score.*

When starting from a specific *PSR* for complete ballots, defined by scoring vector $s = (s_1, ..., s_m)$, two choices of s^* particularly make sense:

- zero score: $s^* = 0$
- average score: $s^* = \frac{1}{m-k}(s_{k+1} + ... + s_m)$

We denote the corresponding approximate rules as f_k^0 and f_k^{av}. $Borda_k^{av}$ is known under the name *average score modified Borda Count* [8,13], while $Borda_k^0$ is known under the name *modified Borda Count* [11]). In the experiments we report only on $Borda_k^{av}$, as $Borda_k^0$ gives very similar results.

Young [24] characterized positional scoring rules by these four properties, which we describe informally (for resolute rules):

- *Neutrality*: all candidates are treated equally
- *Anonymity*: all voters are treated equally
- *Reinforcement*: if P and Q are two profiles (on disjoint electorates) and x is the winner for P and the winner for Q, then it is also the winner for $P \cup Q$.
- *Continuity*: if P and Q are two profiles and x is the winner for P but not for Q, adding sufficiently many votes of P to Q leads to elect x.

f is a *PSR* if and only if it satisfies neutrality, anonymity, reinforcement and continuity [24].

These four properties still make sense for truncated ballots. It is not difficult to generalize Young's result to *top-k* PSR:

Theorem 1. *A top-k voting rule is a top-k PSR if and only if it satisfies neutrality, anonymity, reinforcement, and continuity.*

Proof. The left-to-right direction is obvious. For the right-to-left direction, let us first define the *top-k-only* property: a standard voting rule is *top-k-only* if for any two complete profiles P, P', if $P_k = P'_k$, then $F(P) = F(P')$. Then (1) a positional scoring rule F is *top-k*-only if and only if $s_{k+1} = \ldots = s_m$ (if this equality is not satisfied, then it is easy to construct two profiles P, P' such that $P_k = P'_k$ and $F(P) \neq F(P')$). Now, assume F_k is a *top-k* rule satisfying neutrality, anonymity, reinforcement, and continuity. Let F be the standard voting rule defined by $F(P) = F_k(P_k)$. Clearly, F also satisfies neutrality, anonymity, reinforcement, and continuity, and due to Young's characterization result, F is a PSR, associated with some vector $(s_1, \ldots, s_m)$. Because F is also *top-k-only*, using (1) we have $s_{k+1} = \ldots = s_m$, therefore, F_k is a *top-k*-PSR.   □

3.2   Rules Based on Pairwise Comparisons

Given a truncated ballot $\succ_i^k$ and two candidates $a, b \in A$, we say that a dominates b in $\succ_i^k$, denoted by $a >_i^k b$, if one of these two conditions holds: (1) a and b are listed in $\succ_i^k$, and $a \succ_i^k b$; (2) a is listed in $\succ_i^k$, and b is not.

For instance, for $A = \{a, b, c, d\}$, $k = 2$, and $\succ_i^2 = (a \succ b)$, then a dominates b, both a and b dominate c and d, but c and d remain incomparable in $\succ_i^2$. Now, the notions of pairwise comparison and majority graph are extended to *top-k* truncated profiles in a straightforward way:

Definition 2. *Given a top-k profile R, $N_R(a, b) = \#\{i, a >_i^k b\}$ is the number of voters in R for whom a dominates b. The top-k majority graph $M_k(R)$ induced by R is the graph whose set of vertices is the set of the candidates A and in which there is a directed edge from a to b if $N_R(a, b) > N_R(b, a)$.*

The top-k rules $Copeland_k$, $Maximin_k$ and RP_k are defined exactly as their standard counterparts, but starting from the top-k pairwise comparisons and majority graph instead of the standard ones. Note that $f_{m-1} = f$, and (for all rules f we consider) f_1 coincides with plurality.

Example 1. *Let us consider this 62-voter profile: 20 votes $a \succ d \succ c \succ b$, 10 votes $b \succ c \succ d \succ a$, 15 votes $c \succ d \succ b \succ a$ and 17 votes: $d \succ c \succ a \succ b$.*

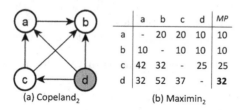

	a	b	c	d	MP
a	-	20	20	10	10
b	10	-	10	10	10
c	42	32	-	25	25
d	32	52	37	-	**32**

(a) Copeland$_2$ (b) Maximin$_2$

Fig. 1. Top-2 approximations of Copeland and Maximin

Figure 1 (a) shows the top-k majority graph and the Copeland winner for k = 2, and Fig. 1 (b) shows the top-k pairwise majority matrix and the Maximin$_k$ winner for k = 2. In both cases, the winner for k = 1 (resp. k = 3) is a (resp. d). For RP, the winner under RP$_k$ for k ∈ {1, 2, 3} is the same as the winner under Copeland$_k$ since the k-truncated majority graph does not create cycles.

4   Probability of Selecting the True Winner

The first way of measuring the quality of the *top-k* approximations is to determine the probability that they output the 'true winner'; that is, the winner of the original voting rule, under various distributions (Subsect. 4.1) and for real-world data (Subsect. 4.2). In both cases, the procedure is similar: given a voting rule f, we consider many profiles, and for each profile P we compare $f(P)$ to $f_k(P_k)$ for each $k = \{1, \ldots, m-2\}$. The difference between Subsects. 4.1 and 4.2 is that in the former we randomly draw profiles according to a given distribution, and for the latter, we draw a profile by selecting n votes at random in the database. We include in our experiments STV_k rule defined by Ayadi *et al.* [1], which takes *top-k* ballots as input; and we compared it to our truncated rules. STV_k proceeds as follows: in each round the candidate with the smallest number of votes is eliminated (using a tie breaking when necessary), if all ranked candidates are eliminated by STV, the vote is then 'exhausted' and ignored during further counting.

4.1   Experiments Using Mallows Model

Here we follow the research direction initiated by Filmus and Oren [12], but we consider more rules, and beyond *Impartial Culture* we also consider correlated distributions within the *Mallows* model. For each experiment we draw 1000 random preference profiles. In the first set of experiments, we take $m = 7$, we let n and ϕ vary, and we measure the accuracy of the approximate rule for $k = 1$ and $k = 2$. Results are reported on Table 1. Note that for $k = 1$, our results can be viewed as answering the question: *with which probability does the true winner with respect to the chosen rule coincide with the plurality winner?*

Table 1. Success rate, Mallows model: $m = 7$, varying n, k and ϕ.

ϕ	n=100	n=200	n=300	n=400	n=500	n=100	n=200	n=300	n=400	n=500
$Borda_1^{av}$						$Borda_2^{av}$				
0.7	0.902	0.958	0.986	0.992	**1.0**	0.951	0.98	0.992	**1.0**	1.0
0.8	0.77	0.855	0.9	0.94	0.963	0.853	0.913	0.956	0.972	0.986
0.9	0.588	0.694	0.685	0.718	**0.771**	0.772	0.805	0.827	0.846	0.873
1	0.434	0.445	0.424	0.422	**0.397**	0.576	0.56	0.586	0.598	**0.584**
$Copeland_1$						$Copeland_2$				
0.7	0.908	0.968	0.991	0.994	**1.0**	0.947	0.99	1.0	**1.0**	1.0
0.8	0.736	0.847	0.891	0.934	0.949	0.822	0.904	0.952	0.984	0.982
0.9	0.497	0.567	0.655	0.684	**0.726**	0.62	0.69	0.77	0.805	0.838
1	0.325	0.332	0.323	0.343	**0.319**	0.458	0.432	0.45	0.442	**0.425**
$Maximin_1$						$Maximin_2$				
0.7	0.908	0.969	0.986	0.99	**1.0**	0.968	0.991	1.0	**1.0**	1.0
0.8	0.787	0.856	0.915	0.939	0.955	0.872	0.934	0.961	0.976	0.977
0.9	0.57	0.633	0.691	0.717	**0.748**	0.735	0.76	0.794	0.838	0.869
1	0.415	0.4	0.423	0.393	**0.391**	0.52	0.532	0.544	0.545	**0.525**
$Harmonic_1$						$Harmonic_2$				
0.7	0.941	0.986	0.996	1.0	**1.0**	0.98	0.992	1.0	**1.0**	1.0
0.8	0.895	0.916	0.958	0.959	0.968	0.958	0.974	0.987	0.988	0.996
0.9	0.805	0.808	0.83	0.866	**0.863**	0.895	0.921	0.934	0.939	0.952
1	0.725	0.742	0.74	0.697	**0.737**	0.872	0.867	0.859	0.861	**0.859**
RP_1						RP_2				
0.7	0.926	0.972	0.995	0.995	**1.0**	0.963	0.994	1.0	**1.0**	1.0
0.8	0.778	0.856	0.908	0.939	0.957	0.871	0.928	0.967	0.983	0.989
0.9	0.587	0.64	0.674	0.718	**0.749**	0.725	0.765	0.777	0.838	0.862
1	0.426	0.405	0.416	0.375	**0.385**	0.558	0.524	0.557	0.498	**0.519**
STV_1						STV_2				
0.7	0.907	0.981	0.985	0.998	**1.0**	0.959	0.993	0.997	**1.0**	1.0
0.8	0.808	0.865	0.917	0.918	0.943	0.882	0.933	0.962	0.966	0.974
0.9	0.603	0.64	0.721	0.729	0.763	0.742	0.776	0.792	0.855	0.846
1	0.45	0.464	0.477	0.471	0.468	0.576	0.593	0.61	0.592	0.585

For $k = 1$: when $n \leq 100$ and $\phi \leq 0.7$, prediction reaches 90% for Borda, Copeland, Maximin and STV, 92% for RP, and 94% for Harmonic. When $n \geq$

500, the accuracy is perfect for all rules. For $\phi = 0.8$, the success rate decreases but results are still good with a large number of voters. For $\phi = 0.9$ and $n = 500$, the rate reaches 86% for Harmonic and 72% for Copeland, with intermediate (and similar) results for Borda, Maximin and RP and STV. For the IC, the rate decreases dramatically when k becomes small, except for Harmonic (73% when $n = 500$ against 46% for STV, 31% for Copeland and 40% for the remaining rules).

For $k = 2$: the probability of selecting the true winner reaches 100% (resp. 98%) when $\phi \leq 0.7$ (resp. $\phi \leq 0.8$) and $n \geq 400$ (resp. $n \geq 500$). With high values of ϕ, Harmonic still outperforms other rules followed by $Borda^{av}$ and STV then the other rules. Consistently with the results obtained by Bentert and Skowron [3] for the IC, approximating the maximin rule is harder than position scoring rules where maximin needs more information from the voters in order to obtain high approximation guarantees. In all cases, top-2 ballots seem to be always sufficient in practice to predict the winner with 100% accuracy with a low value of ϕ.

In the second set of experiments, we are interested in determining the value of k needed to predict the correct winner with large elections and with high value of ϕ. We take $k = \{1, ..., m\}$, $n = 2000$, $\phi = \{0.9, 1\}$ and $m = 20$. Figure 2 shows depicted results where 1000 random preference profiles are generated for each experiment. Results suggest that in large elections and unless ϕ is very high ($\phi = 0.9$), top-k rules are able to identify the true winner when $k = 6$ (resp. $k = 8$) for Harmonic (resp. the remaining rules) out of $m = 20$.

We can also observe the behavior of different truncated rules when $\phi = 0.9$: the best accuracy is obtained again by Harmonic and the accuracy of all other rules are very close, which we found surprising. When $\phi = 1$, the latter behavior changes: Harmonic still has the best results, followed by $Borda^{av}$ and STV, then the remaining rules. The good performance of Harmonic in all cases can be explained by the fact that the closer the scoring vector to plurality, the better the prediction.

Next, for each value of $n \in \{1000, 2000\}$, $\phi \in \{.7, .8, .9, 1\}$, and $m \in \{7, 10, 15, 20\}$, we generated 1000 random profiles, and for each of our rules, we determined the minimal value k (as a function of m) such that the winner is correctly determined from the top-k votes for all generated profiles. The results for $Borda^{av}$ are:

- for $\phi = 0.7$, $k = 1$ is always sufficient, whatever m.
- for $\phi = 0.8$, $k = 2$ (resp. $k = 1$) is always sufficient for $n = 1000$ (resp. $n = 2000$), whatever the value of m.
- for $\phi = 0.9$, we observe that the minimal value of k such that the correct winner is always correctly predicted is around $\frac{7}{10}m$ (for $n = 1000$) and $\frac{2}{5}m$ (for $n = 2000$).
- for $\phi = 1$, the minimal value of k is $m - 1$: we always find a generated profile for which we get an incorrect result if the profile is not complete.

The results for Copeland, maximin, RP and STV are similar to those for Borda. For Harmonic, we observe that $k = 1$ is always sufficient for $\phi \leq 0.8$ and

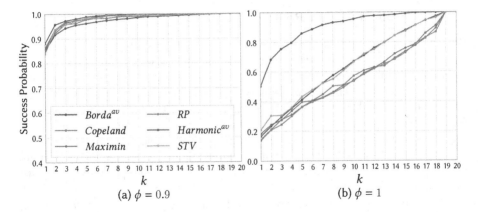

Fig. 2. Success rate, Mallows model: $n = 2000$, $m = 20$, varying ϕ and k.

$n = 2000$, and that for $\phi = 0.9$ (resp. $\phi = 1$), the value of k needed is around $\frac{1}{3}m$ (resp. $\frac{2}{3}m$).

In order to see how our approximations behave with small number of voters and a high dispersion parameter, we take $k = \{1, ..., m\}$, $n = 15$, $m = 7$, and $\phi \in \{0.9, 1\}$. The results are on Fig. 3. The worst performance is obtained with Copeland, while the other rules perform more or less equally well. These results are consistent with the results obtained by Skowron et al. [23] for multiwinner rules: elections with few voters and high dispersion appear to be the worst-case scenario for predicting the correct winner using top-truncated ballots. For Harmonic, even with few voters, winner prediction is almost perfect when $k = 4$ and $m = 7$.

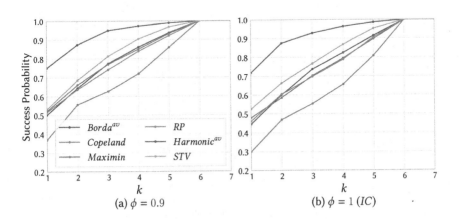

Fig. 3. Success rate, Mallows model: $m = 7$, $n = 15$, varying ϕ and k.

4.2   Experiments Using Real Data Sets

We now consider real data set from *Preflib* [19]: 2002 election for Dublin North constituency with 12 candidates and 3662 voters. We consider data where we randomly sample n^* voters among the n available votes ($n^* < n$). We start with $n^* = 10$ and increment n^* in steps of 10. In each experiment, 1000 random profiles are selected with n^* voters; then we consider the top-k ballots obtained from these profiles, with $k = \{1, 2, 3\}$ and we compute the probability of selecting the correct winner (the winner of the complete profile of then n^* sampled votes). Figure 4 shows results for Dublin with small elections ($n^* = \{10, ..., 100\}$) while Fig. 5 presents results for large elections ($n^* = \{100, ..., 2000\}$). Arrows indicate the number of voters from which the prediction is perfect.

Consistently with the results of Fig. 3, for small elections; the success rate is low when k is too small, except for Harmonic where it gives the best performance followed by STV (especially when $n^* < 60$) then the remaining rules, e.g. For Harmonic (resp. STV), 92% (resp. 82%) accuracy is reached with $k = 3$, $m = 12$ and $n^* = 50$ against around 75% for the remaining rules.

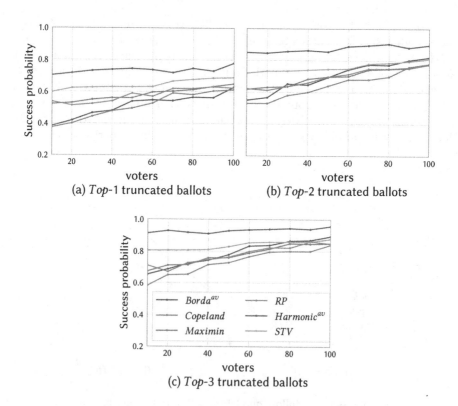

Fig. 4. Success rate, Dublin, varying k; $n^* = \{10, \ldots, 100\}$.

For large elections, when $k = 1$, the different approximations exhibit almost the same behavior except Harmonic, that performs better especially with few voters. Obviously, increasing the value of k leads to a decrease in the number of voters needed for correct winner selection. In general, the different approximations needs a sufficient number of voters to converge to the correct prediction. Scoring rules tend to require less voters.

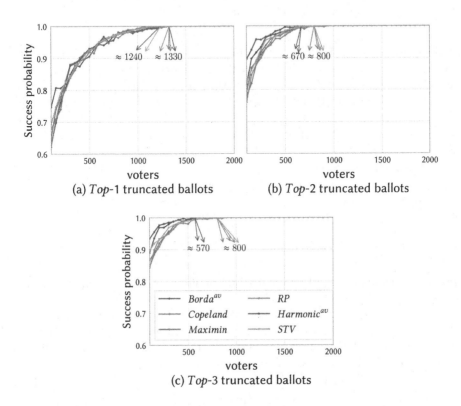

Fig. 5. Success rate, Dublin, varying k; $n^* = \{100, \ldots, 2000\}$.

5 Measuring the Approximation Ratio

5.1 Worst Case Study

In order to measure the quality of approximate voting rules whose definition is based on score maximization, a classical method consists in computing the worst-case approximation ratio between the scores (for the original rule) of the 'true' winner and of the winner of the approximate rule. Using worst-case score ratios is classical: they are defined for measuring the quality of approximate voting rules [7,22], for defining the price of anarchy of a voting rule [6] or for measuring the distortion of a voting rule [4].

Worst-case score ratios particularly make sense if the score of a candidate is meaningful beyond its use for determining the winner. This is definitely the case for Borda, as the Borda count is often seen as a measure of social welfare (see [9]). This worst-case score ratio is called the *price of top-k truncation*.

Definition 3. *Let f be a voting rule defined as the maximization of a score S, and f_k a top-k approximation of f. The* price of top-k-truncation *for f, f_k, m, and k, is defined as:* $R(f, f_k, m, k) = \max_{P \in \mathcal{P}_m} \frac{S(f(P))}{S(f_k(P_k))}$.

Positional Scoring Rules: Let f^s be a positional scoring rule defined with scoring vector s. Assume the tie-breaking priority favors x_1. Let $f_k^{\bar{s}}$ be a top-k approximation of f^s, associated with vector $\bar{s} = (s_1, \ldots, s_k, s^*)$, with the same tie-breaking priority. Let $s' = (s_1 - s^*, \ldots, s_k - s^*, 0) = (s_1', \ldots, s_k', 0)$, i.e., $s_i' = s_i - s^*$ for $i = 1, \ldots, k$. Obviously, $f_k^{\bar{s}} = f_k^{s'}$. For instance, if $f^{\bar{s}}$ is the average-score approximation of the Borda rule, then $\bar{s} = (m-1, \ldots, m-k, \frac{m-k-1}{2})$ and $s' = (m - 1 - \frac{m-k-1}{2}, \ldots, m - k - \frac{m-k-1}{2}, 0)$.

Let $S(x, P)$ be the score of x for P under f^s and $S_k'(x, P_k)$ be the score of x for P_k under $f_k^{s'}$. From now on when we write scores we omit P and P_k, i.e., we write $S(x)$ instead of $S(x, P)$, $S_k'(x)$ instead of $S_k'(x, P_k)$ etc. In the rest of Subsect. 5.1 we assume $k \geq 2$. Let $x_1 = f_k^{s'}(P_k)$ and $x_2 = f^s(P)$.

Lemma 1. $R(f^s, f_k^{s'}, m, k) \leq 1 - \frac{s_{k+1}}{s_1'} + \left(1 + \frac{s^*}{s_1'}\right) \frac{m s_{k+1}}{s_1' + \ldots + s_k'}$

Proof. The total number of points given to candidates under $f_k^{s'}$ is $n(s_1' + \ldots + s_k')$, therefore $S_k'(x_1) \geq \frac{n}{m}(s_1' + \ldots + s_k')$.

Let us write $S(x_2) = S_{1 \to k}(x_2) + S_{k+1 \to m}(x_2)$, where $S_{1 \to k}(x_2)$ (resp. $S_{k+1 \to m}(x_2)$) is the number of points that x_2 gets from the top k (resp. bottom $m - k$) positions of the ballots in P. Let γ be the number of ballots in which x_2 is not in the top k positions. Then $S_{k+1 \to m}(x_2) \leq \gamma s_{k+1}$.

As x_2 appears in at least $\frac{S_k'(x_2)}{s_1'}$ top-k ballots, we have $\gamma \leq n - \frac{S_k'(x_2)}{s_1'}$. Moreover we have $S(x_1) \geq S_{1 \to k}(x_1) = S_k'(x_1) + ns^* \geq S_k'(x_2) + ns^* = S_{1 \to k}(x_2)$. Now,

$$S(x_2) \leq S_{1 \to k}(x_2) + \left(n - \frac{S_k'(x_2)}{s_1'}\right) s_{k+1}$$

$$\leq S_{1 \to k}(x_2) + \left(n - \frac{S_k(x_2) - ns^*}{s_1'}\right) s_{k+1}$$

$$\leq (1 - \frac{s_{k+1}}{s_1'}) S_{1 \to k}(x_2) + ns_{k+1} + \frac{ns^* s_{k+1}}{s_1'}$$

$$\leq (1 - \frac{s_{k+1}}{s_1'}) S(x_1) + ns_{k+1} + \frac{ns^* s_{k+1}}{s_1'}$$

$$\frac{S(x_2)}{S(x_1)} \leq 1 - \frac{s_{k+1}}{s_1'} + ns_{k+1}(1 + \frac{s^*}{s_1'}) \frac{m}{n(s_1' + \ldots + s_k')}$$

$$\leq 1 - \frac{s_{k+1}}{s_1'} + s_{k+1}(1 + \frac{s^*}{s_1'}) \frac{m}{s_1' + \ldots + s_k'}$$

$\square$

We now focus on the lower bound. We build the following pathological complete profile P such that:

- the winner for P_k (resp. P) is x_1 (resp. x_2).
- in P_k, all candidates get the same number of points (x_1 wins thanks to tie-breaking), and x_1 and x_2 get all their points from top-1 positions.
- in P, the score of x_1 is minimized by ranking it last everywhere where it was not in the top k positions, and the score of x_2 is maximized by ranking it in position $k+1$ everywhere where it was not in the top k positions.
- P_k is symmetric in $\{x_3, \ldots, x_m\}$.

Formally, P_k is defined as follows:

1. for each ranked list L (resp. L') of $k-1$ (resp. k) candidates in $\{x_3, \ldots, x_m\}$:
   α votes $x_1 L$ and α votes $x_2 L$ (resp. β votes L'). α and β will be fixed later.
2. α and β are chosen in such a way that all candidates get the same score $S_k'(.)$.

Now, P is obtained by completing P_k as follows:

1. each top-k vote $x_1 L$ is completed into $x_1 L x_2-$. "$-$" means the remaining candidates are in an arbitrary order.
2. each top-k vote $x_2 L$ is completed into $x_2 L - x_1$.
3. each top-k vote L' is completed into $L' x_2 - x_1$.

For instance, for $m = 5$ and $k = 3$, P is as follows:

$$
\begin{array}{c|c|c}
\alpha \; x_1 x_3 x_4 x_2 x_5 & \alpha \; x_2 x_3 x_4 x_5 x_1 & \beta \; x_3 x_4 x_5 x_2 x_1 \\
\alpha \; x_1 x_3 x_5 x_2 x_4 & \alpha \; x_2 x_3 x_5 x_4 x_1 & \beta \; x_3 x_5 x_4 x_2 x_1 \\
\alpha \; x_1 x_4 x_3 x_2 x_5 & \alpha \; x_2 x_4 x_3 x_5 x_1 & \beta \; x_4 x_3 x_5 x_2 x_1 \\
\alpha \; x_1 x_4 x_5 x_2 x_3 & \alpha \; x_2 x_4 x_5 x_3 x_1 & \beta \; x_4 x_5 x_3 x_2 x_1 \\
\alpha \; x_1 x_5 x_3 x_2 x_4 & \alpha \; x_2 x_5 x_3 x_4 x_1 & \beta \; x_5 x_3 x_4 x_2 x_1 \\
\alpha \; x_1 x_5 x_4 x_2 x_3 & \alpha \; x_2 x_5 x_4 x_3 x_1 & \beta \; x_5 x_4 x_3 x_2 x_1
\end{array}
$$

Let $M = \dfrac{(m-3)!}{(m-k-1)!}$ and $Q = \dfrac{(m-2)!}{(m-k-1)!}$.

Lemma 2.
$$
S_k'(x_1) = S_k'(x_2) = \alpha(m-2)s_1' M
$$
and for $i \geq 3$, $S_k'(x_i) = 2\alpha(s_2' + \ldots + s_k')M + \beta(m-k-1)(s_1' + \ldots + s_k')M$

Proof. In P_k, x_1 and x_2 appear in top position in a number of votes equal to α times the number of different permutations (ordered lists) of $(k-1)$ candidates out of $(m-2)$, i.e. $\alpha \frac{(m-2)!}{(m-k-1)!}$ times. Thus $S_k'(x_1) = S_k'(x_2) = \alpha \frac{(m-2)!}{(m-k-1)!} s_1'$. For similar reasons, for each $i \geq 3$,

$$
S_k'(x_i) = 2\alpha \frac{(m-3)!}{(m-k-1)!}(s_2' + \cdots + s_k') + \beta \frac{(m-3)!}{(m-k-2)!}(s_1' + \cdots + s_k').
$$

$\square$

As a consequence, all candidates have the same score in P_k if and only if

$$\frac{\beta}{\alpha} = \frac{(m-2)s_1' - 2(s_2' + \ldots + s_k')}{(m-k-1)(s_1' + \ldots + s_k')}$$

We fix α and β such that this equality holds. Thanks to the tie-breaking priority, the winner in P_k is x_1. In P, the winner is x_2 and the scores of x_1 and x_2 are as follows:

Lemma 3.

$$S(x_1) = Q\alpha s_1$$
$$S(x_2) = Q\alpha s_1 + Q\alpha s_{k+1} + Q(m-k-1)\beta s_{k+1}$$

Proof. x_1 appears at the top of $\frac{(m-2)!}{(m-k-1)!}\alpha$ votes and at the bottom of all others, hence $S(x_1) = Q\alpha s_1$. x_2 appears $\alpha\frac{(m-2)!}{(m-k-1)!}$ times top position, and in position $(k+1)$ in the remaining votes, *i.e.*, $\alpha\frac{(m-2)!}{(m-k-1)!} + \beta\frac{(m-2)!}{(m-k-2)!}$. Thus

$$S(x_2) = \alpha\frac{(m-2)!}{(m-k-1)!}(s_1 + s_{k+1}) + \beta\frac{(m-2)!}{(m-k-2)!}s_{k+1}$$

$\square$

Lemma 4. $R(f^s, f_k^{s'}, m, k) \geq 1 - \frac{s_{k+1}}{s_1} + \frac{s_{k+1}}{s_1}\frac{ms_1'}{s_1' + \ldots + s_k'}$

Proof. From Lemma 3 we get $\frac{S(x_2)}{S(x_1)} \geq 1 + \frac{s_{k+1}}{s_1} + (m-k-1)\frac{s_{k+1}}{s_1}\frac{\beta}{\alpha}$.
Finally, using the expression of $\frac{\beta}{\alpha}$ we get

$$\frac{S(x_2)}{S(x_1)} \geq 1 + \frac{s_{k+1}}{s_1} + (m-k-1)\frac{s_{k+1}}{s_1}\frac{(m-2)s_1' - 2(s_2' + \ldots + s_k')}{(m-k-1)(s_1' + \ldots + s_k')}$$

From this we conclude:

$$R(f^s, f_k^{s'}, m, k) \geq 1 + \frac{s_{k+1}}{s_1} + \frac{s_{k+1}}{s_1}\frac{(m-2)s_1' - 2(s_2' + \ldots + s_k')}{s_1' + \ldots + s_k'}$$
$$\geq 1 + \frac{s_{k+1}}{s_1} + \frac{s_{k+1}}{s_1}\frac{(m-2)s_1' + 2s_1' - 2(s_1' + \ldots + s_k')}{s_1' + \ldots + s_k'}$$
$$\geq 1 + \frac{s_{k+1}}{s_1} + \frac{s_{k+1}}{s_1}\left(\frac{ms_1'}{s_1' + \ldots + s_k'} - 2\right)$$
$$\geq 1 - \frac{s_{k+1}}{s_1} + \frac{s_{k+1}}{s_1}\frac{ms_1'}{s_1' + \ldots + s_k'}$$

$\square$

Putting Lemmas 1 and 4 together we get

Proposition 1.

$$1 - \frac{s_{k+1}}{s_1} + \frac{s_{k+1}}{s_1}\frac{ms_1'}{s_1' + \ldots + s_k'} \leq R(f^s, f_k^{s'}, m, k) \leq 1 - \frac{s_{k+1}}{s_1} + \left(1 + \frac{s^*}{s_1'}\right)\frac{ms_{k+1}}{s_1' + \ldots + s_k'}$$

Note that the lower and upper bound coincide when $s^* = 0$, giving a tight worst-case approximation ratio for this class of approximations. This is however not guaranteed when $s^* > 0$ (the reason being that the pathological profile used in the proof of Lemma 1 may not be the worst). Moreover, when $s^* = 0$, our (lower and upper) bound coincides with the optimal ratio given in [3] (Theorem 1).[1] Since the ratio in [3] is shown to be the best possible ratio, this show that taking $s^* = 0$ gives an optimal top-k approximation of a positional scoring rule.[2]

In particular:

- for $Borda_k^0$ ($s_i = m - i, s^* = 0$), the lower and upper bounds coincide and are equal to $\frac{k}{m-1} + \frac{2m(m-k-1)}{k(2m-k-1)}$.
- for $Borda_k^{av}$ ($s_i = m - i, s^* = m-k-1/2$), the lower bound is $1 - \frac{m-k-1}{m-1} + \frac{(m-k-1)(m+k-1)}{k(m-1)}$ and the upper bound is $\frac{k(3k-m+1)+4(m-k-1)(m-1)}{k(m+k-1)}$.
- for $Harmonic_k^0$ ($s_i = 1/i, s^* = 0$), the lower and upper bounds are equal to $\frac{k}{k+1} + \frac{m}{(k+1)(1+\frac{1}{2}\cdots+\frac{1}{k})}$.

Also, note that for k'-approval with $k' > k$ and $s^* = 0$, the (exact) worst-case ratio $\frac{m}{k}$ does not depend on k'. As a corollary, we get the following order of magnitudes when m grows:

- $R(Borda, Borda_k^0, m, k) = \Theta\left(\frac{m}{k}\right)$.
- $R(Borda, Borda_k^{av}, m, k) = \Theta\left(\frac{m}{k}\right)$.
- $R(Harmonic, Harmonic_k^0, m, k) = \Theta\left(\frac{m}{k \log k}\right)$.

Maximin: Let $Maximin$ be the Maximin rule with tie-breaking priority $x_1 \dots x_m$, and $Maximin_k$ be the k-truncated version of the Maximin rule with the same tie-breaking priority order. Let $S_{Mm}(x_2, P)$ and $S_{Mm}(x_1, P_k)$ be the Maximin scores of x_2 and x_1 for P and P_k, respectively, with $S_{Mm}(x_2, P) = \min_{y \neq x_2} N_P(x_2, y)$ and similarly for P_k. Let P be a profile, and let $x_1 = Maximin_k(P_k)$ and $x_2 = Maximin(P)$. All candidates have the same Maximin score in P_k, therefore, by tie-breaking priority, $Maximin_k(P_k) = x_1$.

Lemma 5. $R(Maximin, Maximin_k, m, k) \leq m - k + 1$.

Proof. Because $x_1 = Maximin_k(P_k)$, we must have $S_{Mm}(x_1, P_k) \geq 1$ (otherwise we would have $S_{Mm}(x_1, P_k) \geq 0$, meaning that x_1 does not belong to any top-k ballot, and in this case we cannot have $x_1 = Maximin_k(P_k)$). Now, $S_{Mm}(x_2, P) \leq S_{Mm}(x_2, P_k) + (m - k) \leq S_{Mm}(x_1, P_k) + (m - k)$, therefore,

$$\frac{S_{Mm}(x_2, P)}{S_{Mm}(x_1, P)} \leq \frac{S_{Mm}(x_1, P_k) + (m-k)}{S_{Mm}(x_1, P_k)}$$
$$\leq m - k + 1$$

$\square$

Lemma 6. $R(Maximin, Maximin_k, m, k) \geq m - k$.

---

[1] Note that the ratios in our paper are the inverse of the ratios in [3]. That is, the inverse of the ratio given in Theorem 1 of [3] coincides with our ratio for $s^* = 0$.

[2] Interestingly, [3] give another optimal rule (thus with same worst-case ratio), which is much more complex, and which is not a top-k PSR. Comparing the average ratio of both rules is left for further study.

Proof. We consider the cyclic profile Cyc:

Cyc				$P\ (m = 5, k = 2)$
x_1 x_2	$\dots$	$m-1$	m	$x_1\ x_2\ x_3\ x_4\ x_5$
x_2 x_3	$\dots$	m	x_1	$x_2\ x_3\ x_4\ x_5\ x_1$
x_3 x_4	$\dots$	x_1	x_2	$x_3\ x_4\ x_2\ x_5\ x_1$
$\dots$	$\dots$	$\dots$	$\dots$	$x_4\ x_5\ x_2\ x_3\ x_1$
m x_1	$\dots$	$m-2$	$m-1$	$x_5\ x_1\ x_2\ x_3\ x_4$

Now, let P be obtained from Cyc by the following operations for every vote in Cyc:

– if x_1 is not in the top k positions in the vote, we move it to the last position (and move all candidates who were below x_1 one position upward)
– if x_2 is not in the top k positions in the vote, we move it to the $(k+1)^{th}$ position (and move all candidates who were between position $k + 1$ and 2's position one position downward).

For instance, for $m = 5$, $k = 2$, we get the profile P above.
$Maximin(P) = x_2$, and the Maximin scores of x_1 and x_2 in P are:

$$S_{Mm}(x_1, P) = 1 \text{ and } S_{Mm}(x_2, P) = m - k.$$

Hence $\frac{S_{Mm}(x_2, P)}{S_{Mm}(x_1, P)} = m - k.$ □

Proposition 2. $m - k \leq R(Maximin, Maximin_k, m, k) \leq m - k + 1.$

This worst-case ratio is quite bad, except if k is close to m. However, arguably, the maximin score makes less sense *per se* (i.e., as a measure of social welfare) than a positional score such as the Borda count.

Copeland: Again, for the Copeland rule, the ratio makes less sense, because the Copeland score is less meaningful as a measure of social welfare.[3] Still, for the sake of completeness we give the following result:

Proposition 3. $R(Copeland, Copeland_k, m, k) = \infty.$

Proof. Let P be the following profile:

– P_k contains two votes $x_1 x_2 \dots x_k$, and one vote L for each ordered list of k candidates among m.
– P is obtained by completing P_k by adding x_1 (resp. x_2) in last position (resp. in position $k + 1$) when it is not in the *top-k* positions.

In P_k, the winner for $Copeland_k$ is x_1. In P, the Copeland winner is x_2. Now, with respect to P, the Copeland score of x_1 (resp. x_2) is 0 (resp. $m - 1$), hence the result. □

---

[3] Moreover, there are several ways of defining the Copeland score, all leading to the same rule. However, this has no impact on the negative result below, as long as a Condorcet loser has score 0.

Discussion: The obtained worst-case bounds are rather negative: very negative for Copeland and maximin, less so for Borda, and even less so for Harmonic.[4] However, the maximin and Copeland scores make less sense as a measure of social welfare than positional scores. Note that for maximin rule the obtained lower bound matches the one given by Bentert and Skowron [3] (Sect. 4.3) which means that our top-k approximation of maximin is optimal.

Now, we may wonder whether these worst cases do occur frequently in practice or if they correspond to rare pathological profiles. The next two subsections show that the latter is the case.

5.2   Average Case Evaluation

We present the evaluation of the approximation ratio using data generated from Mallows ϕ model. For each experiment, we draw 10000 random profiles, with $m = 7$, $n = 15$, and let ϕ vary. Figure 6 presents the obtained results. Our results suggest that, in practice, results are much better than in the worst case where best results are obtained by Harmonic, followed by Borda and finally Maximin.

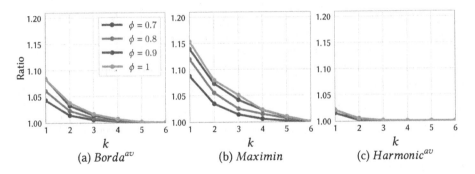

Fig. 6. Mallows model: approximation ratio when $n = 15$, $m = 7$ and varying ϕ.

5.3   Real Data Sets

Again we consider 2002 Dublin North data $(m = 12, n = 3662)$ with samples of n^* voters among n $(n^* < n)$ where $n^* = \{15, 100\}$. In each experiment 1000 random profiles are constructed with n^* voters; then we consider the top-k ballots obtained from these profiles with $k = \{1, \ldots, m - 1\}$. Again, the results are very positive (Fig. 7).

---

[4] As Ranked Pairs is not based on scores, it was not studied here.

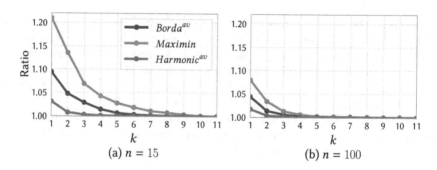

Fig. 7. Approximation ratio with Dublin North data set.

6   Conclusion

In this paper we have considered k-truncated approximations of rules which take only *top-k* ballots as input where we have considered two measures of the quality of the approximation: the probability of selecting the same winner as the original rule, and the score ratio. For the former, our empirical study show that a very small k suffices. For the latter, while the theoretical bounds are, at best; moderately encouraging, our experiments show that in practice the approximation ratio is much better than in the worst case: our results suggest that a very small value of k works very well in practice. Many issues remain open. Especially, it would be interesting to consider top-k approximations as voting rules on their own, and to study their normative properties.

Acknowledgement. This work was supported by Agence Nationale de la Recherche under the "Programme d'Investissements d'Avenir" ANR-19-P3IA-0001 (PRAIRIE).

References

1. Ayadi, M., Ben Amor, N., Lang, J., Peters, D.: Single transferable vote: incomplete knowledge and communication issues. In: Proceedings of the 18th International Conference on Autonomous Agents and Multi-Agent Systems, pp. 1288–1296. International Foundation for Autonomous Agents and Multi-agent Systems (2019)
2. Baumeister, D., Faliszewski, P., Lang, J., Rothe, J.: Campaigns for lazy voters: truncated ballots. In: Proceedings of the 11th International Conference on Autonomous Agents and Multi-agent Systems-Vol. 2, pp. 577–584. International Foundation for Autonomous Agents and Multi-agent Systems (2012)
3. Bentert, M., Skowron, P.: Comparing election methods where each voter ranks only few candidates. In: Proceedings of the AAAI Conference on Artificial Intelligence, vol. 34, no. 02, pp. 2218–2225 (2020). https://doi.org/10.1609/aaai.v34i02.5598
4. Boutilier, C., Caragiannis, I., Haber, S., Lu, T., Procaccia, A.D., Sheffet, O.: Optimal social choice functions: a utilitarian view. Artif. Intell. **227**, 190–213 (2015)
5. Boutilier, C., Rosenschein, J.S.: Incomplete information and communication in voting. In: Handbook of Computational Social Choice, pp. 223–258 (2016)

6. Brânzei, S., Caragiannis, I., Morgenstern, J., Procaccia, A.D.: How bad is selfish voting? AAAI. **13**, 138–144 (2013)
7. Caragiannis, I., Kaklamanis, C., Karanikolas, N., Procaccia, A.D.: Socially desirable approximations for Dodgson's voting rule. ACM Trans. Algorithms (TALG) **10**(2), 6 (2014)
8. Cullinan, J., Hsiao, S.K., Polett, D.: A borda count for partially ordered ballots. Soc. Choice Welf. **42**(4), 913–926 (2014)
9. d'Aspremont, C., Gevers, L.: Chapter 10 social welfare functional and interpersonal comparability. In: Handbook of Social Choice and Welfare, vol. 1, pp. 459–541. Elsevier (2002). https://doi.org/10.1016/S1574-0110(02)80014-5
10. Dery, L.N., Kalech, M., Rokach, L., Shapira, B.: Reaching a joint decision with minimal elicitation of voter preferences. Inform. Sci. **278**, 466–487 (2014). Elsevier
11. Emerson, P.J.: The Politics of Consensus: For The Resolution of Conflict and Reform of Majority Rule. De Borda Institute, Belfast (1994)
12. Filmus, Y., Oren, J.: Efficient voting via the top-k elicitation scheme: a probabilistic approach. In: Proceedings of the Fifteenth ACM Conference on Economics and Computation, pp. 295–312. ACM (2014)
13. Grandi, U., Loreggia, A., Rossi, F., Saraswat, V.: A Borda count for collective sentiment analysis. Ann. Math. Artif. Intell. **77**(3–4), 281–302 (2016). https://doi.org/10.1007/s10472-015-9488-0
14. Kalech, M., Kraus, S., Kaminka, G.A., Goldman, C.V.: Practical voting rules with partial information. Autonom. Agents Multi-Agent Syst. **22**, 151–182 (2011). Springer
15. Lackner, M.: Incomplete preferences in single-peaked electorates. In: Proceedings of the Twenty-Eighth AAAI Conference on Artificial Intelligence, July 27–31, 2014, Québec City, Québec, Canada, pp. 742–748 (2014)
16. Lu, T., Boutilier, C.: Robust approximation and incremental elicitation in voting protocols. Proceedings of IJCAI International Joint Conference on Artificial Intelligence. **22**, 287–293 (2011)
17. Lu, T., Boutilier, C.: Vote elicitation with probabilistic preference models: empirical estimation and cost tradeoffs. In: Brafman, R.I., Roberts, F.S., Tsoukiàs, A. (eds.) ADT 2011. LNCS (LNAI), vol. 6992, pp. 135–149. Springer, Heidelberg (2011). https://doi.org/10.1007/978-3-642-24873-3_11
18. Mallows, C.L.: Non-null ranking models. I. Biometrika, pp. 114–130 (1957)
19. Mattei, N., Walsh, T.: PREFLIB: a library for preferences HTTP://WWW.PREFLIB.ORG. In: Perny, P., Pirlot, M., Tsoukiàs, A. (eds.) ADT 2013. LNCS (LNAI), vol. 8176, pp. 259–270. Springer, Heidelberg (2013). https://doi.org/10.1007/978-3-642-41575-3_20
20. Narodytska, N., Walsh, T.: The computational impact of partial votes on strategic voting. In: ECAI 2014–21st European Conference on Artificial Intelligence, 18–22 August 2014, Prague, Czech Republic - Including Prestigious Applications of Intelligent Systems (PAIS 2014), pp. 657–662 (2014)
21. Oren, J., Filmus, Y., Boutilier, C.: Efficient vote elicitation under candidate uncertainty. In: Proceedings of the Twenty-Third International Joint Conference on Artificial Intelligence, pp. 309–316. AAAI Press (2013)
22. Service, T.C., Adams, J.A.: Communication complexity of approximating voting rules. Int. Conf. Autonom. Agents Multi-agent Syst. AAMAS **2012**, 593–602 (2012)

23. Skowron, P., Faliszewski, P., Slinko, A.: Achieving fully proportional representation: approximability results. Artif. Intell. **222**, 67–103 (2015)
24. Young, H.P.: Social choice scoring functions. SIAM J. Appl. Math. **28**(4), 824–838 (1975)
25. Zhao, Z., et al.: A cost-effective framework for preference elicitation and aggregation. In: Proceedings of the Thirty-Fourth Conference on Uncertainty in Artificial Intelligence, UAI 2018, Monterey, California, USA, August 6–10, 2018, pp. 446–456 (2018)

Privacy-Preserving Dialogues Between Agents: A Contract-Based Incentive Mechanism for Distributed Meeting Scheduling

Boya Di[(✉)] and Nicholas R. Jennings

Department of Computing, Imperial College London, London, UK
{b.di,n.jennings}@imeprial.ac.uk

Abstract. Meeting scheduling (MS) is a practical task in everyday life that involves independent agents with different calendars and preferences. In this paper, we consider the distributed MS problem where the host exchanges private information with each attendee separately. Since each agent aims to protect its own privacy and attend the meeting at a time slot that it prefers, it is necessary to design a distributed scheduling mechanism where the privacy leakage can be minimized and as many agents are satisfied with the outcome as possible. To achieve this, we propose an intelligent two-layer mechanism based on contract theory where the host motivates each agent to reveal its true preferences by providing different rewards without knowing the costs of each agent to attend the meeting. We first model the privacy leakage by measuring the difference between the revealed information of an agent's calendar and other agents' prior beliefs. An optimal control problem is then formulated such that the reward function and privacy leakage level can be jointly designed for each agent. Through theoretical analysis, we show that our proposed mechanism guarantees the incentive compatibility with respect to all agents. Compared to the state of the art, empirical evaluations show that our proposed mechanism achieves lower privacy leakage and higher social welfare within a small number of rounds.

Keywords: Meeting scheduling · Incentive mechanism · Privacy

1 Introduction

Many multi-agent systems involve reaching an agreement between self-interested agents that seek to minimize the amount of information revealed to their opponents. Examples include electronic commerce, computer games and meeting scheduling. In this paper, we focus on multi-agent meeting scheduling (MAMS) as a representative application. In this case, the host of a meeting is required to

This work was supported and funded by Samsung Electronics R&D Institute UK (SRUK).

© Springer Nature Switzerland AG 2020
N. Bassiliades et al. (Eds.): EUMAS 2020/AT 2020, LNAI 12520, pp. 299–315, 2020.
https://doi.org/10.1007/978-3-030-66412-1_19

arrange a staring time that is acceptable to all attendees. In practice, the MAMS problem is inherently a distributed one since the agents' calendars are different and private, meaning that they are unwilling to share them with others. Given this situation, there is a clear trade-off between maximizing social welfare and minimizing the amount of information revealed in this process [1].

Against this background, we study the distributed MAMS problem in a setting where the host proposes candidate time slots in each round and attendees respond to the proposals separately. Since all agents are self-interested, each of them desires the meeting to be scheduled at one of its preferable time slots while revealing as little private information as possible. In such cases, it is necessary to design an incentive mechanism with the following desirable features. *First*, the mechanism should be incentive compatible to avoid the case where a selfish agent can manipulate the scheduled meeting for its personal benefit. *Second*, privacy leakage should be minimized and the mechanism should have a fast convergence speed. *Third*, the social welfare should be maximized, meaning, as many agents as possible should be satisfied with the scheduled time slot.

A useful tool to handle the trade-off between incentive compatibility and privacy preservation is economic contract theory [2], in which agreements are designed to motivate agents with conflicting interests to accept mutually beneficial offers. This mathematical tool provides an efficient approach to incentivization by offering contracts to each type of agent (classified by the agents' private attributes). Here a contract consists of a required action and a corresponding reward. Given properly designed rewards, the agent only needs to choose the contract aligned with its own type to maximize its utility.

In this paper, we propose a distributed two-layer contract-based incentive mechanism where the host offers different rewards in the forms of tokens or credits to motivate attendees to reveal true preferences[1]. Such forms of rewards are widely used in on-line membership[3], resource trading [4], and blockchain systems [5]. Each attendee first selects one outer-layer contract from a candidate set provided by the host, which defines 1) a tailored set of rewards paid to each attendee corresponding to different preferences, and 2) the number of proposals each attendee is required to respond to at each round (i.e., the privacy leakage level). For each proposed time slot, the host provides attendees with multiple agent-specific inner-layer contracts, each of which consists of a reward along with the required action (e.g., attend/not attend the meeting, hold the offer, etc.).

As such, we advance the state-of-the-art in the following ways.

- We develop a novel metric to define the privacy leakage in a general way such that it can depict both privacy leakage and the amount of protected private information. By leveraging the probability distribution of an agent's availability, we measure privacy as the difference between other agents' prior belief and the agent's desired belief that it wishes to reveal to others.

---

[1] An agent's availability at each time slot reflects its preference over the time slots, which can be categorised as multiple types, such as 'free', 'OK with it', and 'busy'.

- We are the first to develop a privacy-preserving incentive mechanism in the context of MAMS where the privacy leakage level can be optimized based on each agent's calendar.
- We achieve a minimum incentive cost by properly designing the rewards and allowing the agents to have multiple types of responses. This is the first attempt to jointly optimize the reward functions and privacy leakage levels via an optimal control method.
- Simulation results show that the proposed mechanism saves 58.3% privacy leakage compared to the calendar-sharing scheme. Compared to current state-of-the-art negotiation mechanism, it also achieves a better trade-off between the privacy leakage and the convergence speed. To achieve the same convergence speed, the contract mechanism can reduce 26.2% privacy leakage; for a same level of privacy leakage, the contract mechanism saves 80% time costs for convergence. It achieves over 88.31% of the optimal social welfare obtained by a centralized method, and significantly outperforms existing works by up to 82% points. By allowing multiple types of responses, the mechanism reduces the incentive cost by up to 18%.

Existing literature on distributed MAMS problems explore various schemes such as negotiation-based methods, Max-Sum algorithms and its variants for distributed constraint optimization problems (DCOP), and incentive mechanisms for consensus. For instance, the works of [6,7] consider automated negotiation between the host and attendees. Agents' preferences were quantified and different negotiation strategies were developed to improve the social welfare. By formulating the MAMS problem as a DCOP, the Max-Sum algorithms proposed in [8] and local consistency reinforcement [9] can be utilized where the solution space is traversed indirectly via limited private information exchange among all agents. In the work of [10], the extended VCG mechanism finds the optimal strategy of each agent, which is aligned with the solution of social welfare maximization. Agents share all their calendar information with each other. However, these works have not linked privacy and incentive compatibility. The developed methods either rely on trust between agents [6–9] or agents' willingness to share their private information with others [8,10]. Neither of these extremes is suitable to solve our problem.

The mechanism we propose is also related to the literature on contract theory[2] and game theory where most works [11–13] focus on incentives in MAS with information asymmetry. For instance, the work of [11] concerns the task assignment problem where multiple contracts are offered to agents such that each agent only picks one that it is capable of to achieve the maximum utility. The work of [13] studies the privacy issue in multi-agent data collection. Privacy is considered as a type of service and assigned to agents for utility maximization. Nevertheless, this line of works assumes that the host is trustworthy and only cares about the incentive compatibility with respect to attendees.

---

[2] It is worth noting that contract theory is different from the contract network protocol. The latter is a type of negotiation-based mechanism for task assignment.

The rest of the paper is organized as below. In Sect. 2 we formulate the distributed MAMS problem where privacy leakage is modelled. In Sect. 3 we design a contract-based MAMS protocol to reach a consensus. The reward functions and privacy leakage level for each agent are jointly optimized via solving an optimal control problem in Sect. 4. Theoretical analysis on the proposed mechanism is also provided. In Sect. 5, we evaluate our proposed mechanism by simulations. Finally we conclude in Sect. 6.

2 Meeting Scheduling Problem Formulation

2.1 Problem Definition

The distributed MSP consists of multiple agents and a number of meetings to be scheduled. We consider a dynamic case where the need for new meetings arises randomly and is not known by the agents in advance. Given a set of meetings and a group of N agents $\mathcal{A}$, we define each meeting m by a tuple

$$m = \{\mathcal{A}_m, A_0, \mathcal{T}, l, t\}, \tag{1}$$

where $\mathcal{A}_m$ is the subset of agents to attend meeting m, A_0 is the agent who will host the meeting and propose candidate time slots to other agents, $\mathcal{T}$ is the set of time slots during which the meeting is expected to be held, and l is the length of meeting m (i.e., the number of time slots), t is the starting time of the meeting. In other words, the starting time t will be selected from $\mathcal{T}$ and l slots will be reserved for meeting m if scheduled.

A meeting is scheduled via the *propose-and-respond* process where in each round the host proposes multiple time slots to each attendee and receives responses. We classify the responses of each agent as three states[3] based on its availability: "I am free", "I am OK with this slot", or "I am busy". By replying OK, the attendee holds the offer temporally and expects the host to propose other time slots. It only accepts slot t if no other feasible solution to the MAMS problem is found. We denote the set of three possible states as $\mathcal{S} = [F, O, B]$. The real state and reported state of each attendee i with respect to time slot t are denoted as $r_i(t) \in \mathcal{S}$ and $s_i(t) \in \mathcal{S}$. We refer to one time slot as a free/OK/busy slot if the agent's real state is free/OK/busy at this slot.

If the meeting is scheduled at slot t, each attendee i's utility is given below

$$U_i\left(t, s_i(t), R_{r_i(t)}\right) = R_{r_i(t)} - C_i^{s_i(t), r_i(t)} - \alpha L_i\left(r_i(t)\right), \tag{2}$$

- $R_{r_i(t)}$ is the reward (in the forms of tokens or credits) paid by the host when the reported state of attendee i is $r_i(t)$;
- $C_i^{s_i(t), r_i(t)}$ is the cost of attendee i to report its state as $r_i(t)$ given its actual state $s_i(t)$. For example, $C_i^{O,F}$ is the cost of agent i to attend the meeting when it is OK with slot t.

---

[3] This can be extended to more types, but we use three to keep the example simple.

- $L_i(r_i(t))$ is the privacy leakage of attendee i, and α depicts its sensitivity towards privacy.

Similarly, the host's utility can be given by

$$U_0\left(t,(R_{r_i(t)})_{i\in\mathcal{A}}\right) = \begin{cases} \Gamma - \displaystyle\sum_{1\leq i\leq N} R_{r_i(t)} - C_0^{s_0(t),F} - \alpha L_0(r_0(t)), \forall r_i(t) \neq B \\ -\infty, \exists r_i(t) = B, \end{cases}$$

(3)

where Γ measures the satisfaction of the host for successfully scheduling a meeting. The above equation omits parameter m for convenience.

2.2 Agents' Preferences and Privacy Leakage

Agents' Preferences. Each agent i's preference over different time slots is related to its state. For example, agent i prefers slot t to t' if it is free at slot t and OK with slot t'. The cost function $C_i^{s_i(t),r_i(t)}$ is utilized to quantify each agent's preferences, which influences agent i's response strategy. The ordering of costs for each agent i is determined by the pair of states $(s_i(t), r_i(t))$:

$$C_i^{B,F} > C_i^{B,O} \gg C_i^{O,F} \gg C_i^{F,F} > C_i^{O,O} = C_i^{F,O} > C_i^{B,B} = C_i^{F,B} = C_i^{O,B} = 0.$$

(4)

- $C_i^{s,r} = 0, r = B$: When the agent reports it is busy at one slot, it does not need to attend the meeting. Thus, the cost is 0 regardless of its real state.
- $C_i^{O,O} = C_i^{F,O}$: The agent's cost of reporting OK is the same no matter whether it is actually free or OK at this time slot, since it is not necessary for the agent to attend the meeting in both cases.
- $C_i^{O,O} < C_i^{F,F}$: An agent's cost to tell the truth about an OK slot is lower than its cost of truth-telling with respect to a free slot, since it is required to guarantee the attendance at the OK slot.
- $C_i^{B,F} > C_i^{B,O} \gg C_i^{O,F} \gg C_i^{F,F}$: For agent i, its cost of attending the meeting at a busy slot is higher than that of claiming to be OK with this slot, which is also much higher than its cost at a free or OK slot regardless of its response. In other words, the fact that an agent cannot attend the meeting at a busy slot is represented by a high cost. Similarly, its cost of attending the meeting at an OK slot is higher than that at a free slot.

We assume that the cost of each agent i depends on how much availability it has throughout the calendar, i.e., the density of availability, which can be depicted by d_i. In other words, the busier an agent is, the higher its cost to attend a meeting. We define d_i by the number of free and OK time slots,

$$d_i = \left(\frac{N_{F,i}}{N}\right)^{\beta_1} + \left(\frac{N_{O,i}}{N}\right)^{\beta_2},$$

(5)

where $N_{F,i}$ and $N_{O,i}$ are the number of free and OK time slots, N is the total number of candidate slots, and β_1 and β_2 are scaling factors. We set $\beta_2 > \beta_1 > 0$ and $\beta_1, \beta_2 \notin \mathbb{Z}$ such that each pair of $(N_{F,i}, N_{O,i})$ is mapped to one unique density value d_i, which is considered as agent i's *type*. A general form of the cost function is then given by

$$C_i^{s,r}(d_i) = \frac{a_1^{s,r}}{(1+d_i)^{a_2^{s,r}}} + a_3^{s,r}, \tag{6}$$

where $a_k^{s,r} > 0$ is a parameter ($k = 1, 2, 3$). Following rule (4), the family of cost functions for each agent i can then be generated via (6).

Privacy Leakage. We consider the case where each attendee only communicates with the host and does not know any detail of other attendees. Therefore, the privacy information that each attendee (or the host) leaks is its calendar information revealed to the host (or the attendee).

Before the propose-and-respond process, the host and each attendee has a prior belief about the probability that the other is free at each time slot. As the process progresses, each attendee (or the host) gets new information from the host (or each attendee) and updates probability information based on the proposal (or the response). Note that each agent has different attitudes towards the privacy information. For those who tend to protect their calendar, they expect the host to believe that their probability of being free is 0.5 (i.e., not sure about its availability). In contrast, other agents might prefer others to have an impression that they are busy (or available) even if they are not.

To depict such diversity of agents' attitudes, we utilize the difference between one agent's expected probability distribution and other's belief, namely, *statistical distance*, to measure the privacy leakage. We denote the desired probability of being free at time slot t that agent j wishes others to believe and the prior belief that agent i has about agent j's availability at this slot as $p_{i \to j}^d(t)$ and $p_{i \to j}^b(t)$, respectively. After this time slot t is proposed, the updated probability is denoted by $p_{i \to j}^a(t, r_i(t))$. The privacy leakage $L_i(r_i(t))$ is given by

$$L_i(r_i(t)) = \left| p_{i \to j}^b(t) - p_{i \to j}^d(t) \right| - \left| p_{i \to j}^a(t, r_i(t)) - p_{i \to j}^d(t) \right|. \tag{7}$$

For $L_i(r_i(t)) > 0$ and $L_i(r_i(t)) < 0$, it measures leaked privacy and protected privacy, respectively.

Remark 1. The proposed privacy leakage metric can readily depict the agents' different attitudes towards their privacy information:

- $p_{i \to j}^d(t) = 0.5$: agent i is privacy-negative, i.e., it does not want others to know anything about its calendar;
- $p_{i \to j}^d(t) = 1$ (or $p_{i \to j}^d(t) = 0$): agent i is privacy-active, implying that it desires to leave others the impression that it has a clear/busy calendar;
- $p_{i \to j}^d(t)$ is set as the real probability of agent i: the agent is privacy-neutral, i.e., it does not care about how others view its calendar.

3   Contract-Based Meeting Scheduling Protocol

To motivate each attendee to reveal their availability at the proposed time slot, the host provides different rewards depending on the attendee's response. When a meeting is set at time slot t, an attendee is offered a high reward if it reports to be free and guarantees to attend the meeting. In contrast, it gets a medium reward if it reports to be OK and requires the host to spend more resources to explore other slots before finally accepting slot t. Given each attendee's cost functions, the rewards can be designed in a way that each attendee can only get the highest utility when it tells the truth.

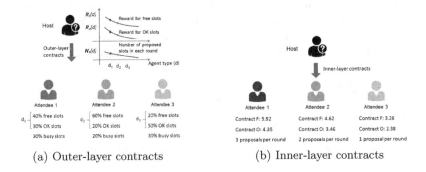

(a) Outer-layer contracts   (b) Inner-layer contracts

Fig. 1. Illustration of the contract-based mechanism

However, the cost functions are unknown to the host, which is determined by each agent's type, i.e., the density of availability as shown in (2). Examples of different types of agents are given in Fig. 1(a). The busier an attendee is (i.e., the value of d is smaller in Fig. 1(a), the higher its cost to attend the meeting, thereby requiring a higher reward. To avoid the attendee claiming to be busy to get high rewards, the host requires those busy attendees to respond to a larger number of proposed time slots in each round, leading to a higher privacy leakage level. Since each attendee is privacy-preserving[4], they are not willing to lie at the cost of higher privacy leakage. Following this insight, the reward function for each agent type, as well as the number of proposed slots, can be properly designed to keep them incentive compatible. For example, three red (or green) points on the three curves in Fig. 1(a) shows rewards and the number of proposed slots for an type-d_1 (or d_2) agent.

Based on the above intuitions, the detailed protocol is shown below.

1. When the need to schedule meeting m arrives, the host publishes the meeting information to the group of attendees.
2. Each attendee labels the valid starting time slots 'free', 'OK', and 'busy', and keeps it as private information along with its cost at each slot.

---

[4] Here we assume that every agent cares about its privacy to the same degree, which also makes sense in reality.

3. The host sends a menu of outer-layer contracts to each attendee, denoted by $\{(R_F(d), R_O(d), N_p(d))\}$, where d represents the type of an agent, identified by its density of availability as shown in (5). The menu is shown in Fig. 1(a). The number of contracts contained in the menu equals the number of agents' types. Each contract requires the agent to respond to on average $N_p(d)$ proposed time slots at each round, and will receive a reward $R_F(d)$ or $R_O(d)$ if the meeting is scheduled at a free or OK slot.

4. Each attendee i selects one outer-layer contract from the menu to maximize its expected utility received from the coming propose-and-respond process. For example, in Fig. 1(a) attendee 1 may select the outer-layer contract represented by three red circles.

5. According to the signed out-layer contract, the propose-and-respond process starts. In each round as shown in Fig. 1(b), the host proposes $N_p(d_i)$ time slots to each attendee. For each time slot t, the host offers three inner-layer contracts. 1) Contract F offers a high reward $R_F(d_i)$ and requires the attendee to attend the meeting. 2) Contract O offers a medium reward $R_O(d_i)$ and allows the attendee to attend the meeting at slot t only when there is no other options. 3) Contract B offers zero reward to the attendee who is busy at slot t. In Fig. 1(b), we omit the zero-reward contract B for simplicity.

6. Each attendee selects one inner-layer contract to maximize its utility shown in (2) and responds to the host. If an attendee reports to be OK with one slot, the host is required to explore at least one more slot in the next round.

7. Steps 5 and 6 are repeated until either one time slot is found in which at least N_t attendees are free or the maximum number of rounds M is reached. After M rounds, the host selects one slot t where the largest number of attendees is free, denoted by $N_f(t)$. The host then raises the rewards for $N_t - N_f(t)$ OK attendees so as to maintain its reputation.

The reasoning behind Step 7 will be illustrated in Sect. 4.2.

4   Two-Layer Contract Design

In this section, we first optimize the reward functions $(R_F(d), R_O(d))$ and privacy leakage level $N_p(d)$. Properties of the mechanisms are then analysed.

4.1   Joint Reward and Privacy Leakage Optimal Control

Attendee's Strategy

When each responder n selects the outer-layer contract, it does not know in which time slot the meeting will be scheduled yet. Therefore, it makes the decision by maximizing its expected utility. Attendee i's expected utility when a free/OK/busy slot is finalized for the meeting is given below.

$$E\left[U_e(\hat{d}, s_i)\right] = f_{s_i}(d_i) \cdot \max_{r_i \in S}\left[R_{r_i}(\hat{d}) - C^{s_i, r_i}(d_i) - \alpha N_p(\hat{d})L_i(r_i)\right], \qquad (8a)$$

$$= f_{s_i}(d_i) \cdot U_e(\hat{d}, s_i), \qquad (8b)$$

where $f_{s_i}(d_i) = N_{s_i,i}/N_i$ maps d_i to the density of free (or OK or busy) time slots as shown in Eq. (5), and $\alpha N_p(\hat{d})L_i(r_i)$ is the minimum accumulated privacy leakage. Note that α decreases with the increase of each attendee's calendar density, which can be depicted by a quadratic function. For convenience, we omit the subscript t here. Therefore, the expected utility of attendee i can be given by

$$E\left(\hat{d}; d_i\right) = \sum_{s_i \in \mathcal{S}} E\left[U_e(\hat{d}, s_i)\right], \tag{9}$$

and each attendee's strategy is to pick a type-$\hat{d}$ outer-layer contract to maximize the above expected utility.

Incentive Compatible Constraints of Attendees. To ensure that each attendee i selects the d_i-type outer-layer contract designed for it rather than other types, the following incentive compatible constraint should hold

$$\max_{\hat{d}} E\left(\hat{d}; d_i\right) = E\left(d_i; d_i\right), \forall i. \tag{10}$$

The sufficient conditions to satisfy this constraint can be given by

$$R_F(\hat{d}) - R_M(\hat{d}) > C^{F,F}(d_i) - C^{O,O}(d_i) + \alpha P_O \cdot N_p(\hat{d}), \tag{11a}$$

$$R_F(\hat{d}) - R_M(\hat{d}) < C^{O,F}(d_i) - C^{O,O}(d_i) + \alpha P_O \cdot N_p(\hat{d}), \tag{11b}$$

$$f_F(d_i) \cdot U_e(\hat{d}, F) + f_O(d_i) \cdot U_e(\hat{d}, O) \le f_F(d_i) \cdot U_e(d_i, F) + f_O(d_i) \cdot U_e(d_i, O), \tag{11c}$$

where P_O is the probability of an agent being free at an OK slot. The typical value is 0.5. We ignore $U_e(\hat{d}, F)$ here since it is usually rather small ($R_B = C^{B,B} = 0$).

When the outer-layer contract is selected, the propose-and-respond process starts. To motivate each attendee to report their true availability, the following constraint should be satisfied:

$$\max_{r_i(t) \in \mathcal{S}} U_i\left(t, s_i(t), R_{r_i(t)}\right) = U_i\left(t, s_i(t), R_{s_i(t)}\right). \tag{12}$$

We derive its equivalent conditions as

$$R_O(d) \ge C^{O,O}(d) + \alpha P_O + \epsilon, \tag{13a}$$

$$R_F(d) \ge R_O(d) + \max_d \left[C^{F,F}(d) - C^{O,O}(d)\right] + \alpha + \epsilon. \tag{13b}$$

where $\epsilon > 0$ is a number small enough, and $p_O \le 0.5$ is the probability of an attendee to be free at an OK time slot.

Optimal Control of the Host. The host offers a set of outer-layer contracts to attendees without knowing their types. Its objective is to find an optimal menu of contracts which minimizes the incentive cost and its own privacy leakage subject to all constraints listed above. The problem can be formulated below:

$$\min_{R(\cdot), N_p(\cdot)} \int_{\underline{d}}^{\overline{d}} [f_F(d)R_F(d) + f_O(d)R_O(d) + \alpha N_p(d) L_0(F)] g(d) dd \qquad (14a)$$

$$\text{s.t.} (11), (13), \qquad (14b)$$

where $g(d) = 1/N_{th}$ is the probability density function of d, following a uniform distribution and N_{th} is the number of possible values of d. The upper and lower bounds of d are given by $\overline{d}$ and $\underline{d}$. Though described with one simple inequality, (11c) actually implies a huge family of constraints, each of which corresponds to a certain pair of $\hat{d}$ and d_i. To identify the set of feasible solutions to the above problem, we simplify this constraint by its relaxed version shown in Proposition 1. The proof can be found in the Appendix A.

Proposition 1. *Constraint (11c) can be relaxed by the following constraints:*

$$\frac{dR_F(d)}{dd} \leq 0, \qquad (15a)$$

$$\frac{dR_O(d)}{dd} \leq 0, \qquad (15b)$$

$$\frac{1}{\alpha L(F)} \frac{dR_F(d)}{dd} = \frac{1}{\alpha L(O)} \frac{dR_O(d)}{dd} = \frac{dN_p(d)}{dd}, \qquad (15c)$$

The formulated problem is an optimal control problem to find an optimal function rather than a value. Based on the Pontryagin's maximum principle [14] as well as constraints (11a), (11b), and (13), the numerical forms of both reward and privacy leakage functions can be obtained.

4.2 Properties of the Mechanism

Privacy Preservation. As shown in (8) and (14a), an optimal privacy leakage level exists for each agent to reach a balance between the amount of leaked information and its social welfare.

Incentive Compatibility. We investigate the behaviours of attendees and the host separately to show the incentive compatibility of the proposed mechanism.

Definition 1. *In the MAMS setting, an incentive compatible mechanism motivates attendee i to always reveals its true preference over the proposed time slots to maximize its utility, i.e.,*

- *When selecting the outer-layer contracts, attendee i selects the type-d_i contract to maximize its expected utility, as shown in (10).*
- *In the propose-and-response process, if the meeting is scheduled at slot t, attendee i can only obtain the maximum utility when they tell the truth, i.e.,*

$$\arg \max_{r_i(t) \in S} U_i(t, s_i(t), R_{r_i(t)}) = s_i(t). \qquad (16)$$

– In the propose-and-response process, the attendee has no incentive to manipulate the meeting to be scheduled at time slot t' by lying about its availability at slot t, i.e.,

$$E\left[U_i^{lie}\left(t', s_i(t'), R_{s_i(t')}|r_i(t) \neq s_i(t)\right)\right] \neq E\left[U_i^{tru}\left(t, s_i(t), R_{s_i(t)}\right)\right]. \quad (17)$$

Based on Definition 1, we present Proposition 2 as proved in Appendix B.

Proposition 2. *The proposed mechanism is incentive compatible with respect to all attendees.*

For the host, there might exist a conflict between its own preference and others' social welfare, leading to unfaithful behaviours. For example, when the host is free at the proposed time slot t' while all attendees report to be either free or OK, it may claim that it is busy at all other time slots so as to schedule the meeting at time slot t' by ignoring those OK attendees' will.

Definition 2. *An mechanism is incentive compatible with respect to the host if it cannot get higher expected utility by lying about its availability at time slot t^* in meeting m, i.e.,*

$$U_0\left(m, t', R_{r_i(t')}|r_0(t^*) \neq s_0(t^*)\right) + E_{m'}\left[U_0\left(m', t, R_{r_i(t)}|m, r_0(t^*) \neq s_0(t^*)\right)\right] \leq$$
$$U_0\left(m, t, R_{r_i(t)}|r_0(t^*) = s_0(t^*)\right) + E_{m'}\left[U_0\left(m', t, R_{r_i(t)}|m, r_0(t^*) = s_0(t^*)\right)\right]$$
$$(18)$$

where t' is the time slot that the host prefers to hold the meeting m. This implies that the host's expected utility will reduce in future meetings $\{m'\}$.

Observation 1. An attendee who reports OK at slot t expects the host to propose other time slots. If the attendee does not trust the host to do so, it reports it is busy. This leads to a higher probability of scheduling failure, which brings negative utility to the host.

Observation 2. Once the attendees do not trust the host, the host needs to provide a new inner-layer contract F' with a higher reward R'_F below to motivate the OK attendee to attend the meeting.

$$R'_F(d) \geq C^{O,F}(d) + \alpha P_O - \alpha + \epsilon. \quad (19)$$

This guarantees the meeting to be scheduled successfully at the host's preferred time slot at an expense of a higher incentive cost.

The above observations imply that once an OK attendee finds the host not trust-worthy, it lies about its availability and has less chance to be scheduled at a free slot, i.e., its social welfare is degraded. The host then needs to offer higher rewards to successfully schedule the meeting.

Remark 2. The interaction between the host and an attendee OK with time slot t in the propose-and-respond process can be formulated as a non-cooperative repeated game. Only when they both tell the truth, they each gets the maximum utility. Since we have a dynamic setting that new meetings arrive randomly and are not known to agents, this is an infinite repeated game.

Proposition 3. *In an infinite repeated game of MAMS, the optimal strategy for both the host and attendees is to tell the truth in order to obtain the maximum utility.*

We design Step 7 as shown in the contract-based protocol in Sect. 3 for attendees to evaluate whether the host is trustworthy. For each meeting, the host is required to guarantee at least M attendees are satisfied with the scheduled time slot either by providing them a free time slot or by offering reward R'_F to compensate their loss. In this way, the host's reputation is kept and attendees will continue to trust it in future meetings.

5   Simulation Results

We conduct empirical studies to evaluate our proposed mechanism based on a set of metrics including 1) privacy leakage, 2) social welfare measured by the number of agents free at the scheduled slot, 3) the number of rounds for convergence, 4) incentive cost which is the total rewards paid by the host.

For experiment setups, we look into a period of 5 days, 9 a.m. to 5 p.m. The whole period is split into 80 time slots of length 30 min. The meetings to be scheduled have different scales ranging from 6 to 12 agents. Each agent's calendar is generated with different preferences. Different cost functions are tested in the experiments and all results are averaged over 20000 cases. We compare our proposed mechanism with the following benchmarks:

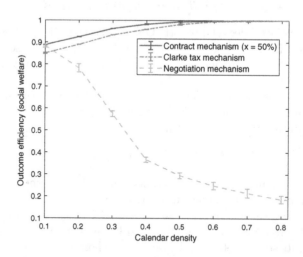

Fig. 2. Social welfare with respect to agents' average density of availability.

- *Centralized meeting scheduling*: a central controller is aware of all the agents' calendars and schedules the meeting in a way that the social welfare is maximized. This serves as an upper bound of the social welfare.

- *Clarke-Tax based mechanism* [10]: this is a typical incentive mechanism without privacy preservation. Each responder reports its availability at all time slots at the first round of negotiation. We evaluate how much privacy leakage can be saved compared to it.
- *Negotiation-based distributed mechanism* [7]: this line of work represents the commonly used meeting scheduling scheme without any incentive compatible guarantees. By comparing with it, we show how incentive compatibility can help to improve the performance.

We evaluate the social welfare of different mechanisms, measured by the ratio of the social welfare in the proposed scheme to the optimal social welfare in the centralized scheme, i.e., the outcome efficiency. Unlike the IC contract-based mechanism where all selfish agents are motivated to tell the truth about their preferences, the benchmarks cannot guarantee the IC property. The Clarke Tax mechanism can motivate all selfish responders to tell the truth about their preferences, but cannot do the same with an selfish initiator. The negotiation mechanism does not even consider IC at all.

In Fig. 2, the outcome efficiency grows with the calendar density in the contract-based and Clarke Tax mechanisms. This is because as the density increases, the number of feasible time slots becomes smaller. Thus, the initiator is more likely to select a time slot which is also the outcome of the centralized scheme, bringing a higher social welfare. For the negotiation mechanism, the outcome efficiency decreases with the increase of the calendar density. When more agents have dense calendars, it is harder for the initiator to find a feasible time slot since selfish responders keep turning down the OK time slots (as illustrated in Observation 1) which could be the output of the centralized scheme. Therefore, the social welfare decreases.

We observe that the contract mechanism serving selfish agents can achieve at least 88.31% outcome efficiency compared to the centralized scheme, which outperforms the Clarke Tax one by 3.31% points, implying that the IC constraint of the initiator helps improve the social welfare. Compared to the negotiation mechanism, the outcome efficiency of the contract mechanism is significantly higher by up to 82% points.

We also report on the balance between the average privacy leakage and the convergence speed as shown in Fig. 3(a). This figure presents the accumulated privacy leakage varying with the ID number of rounds starting from round 0 until convergence. Since the Clarke Tax mechanism requires all responders to report their costs of each time slot at the beginning, each agent leaks all its private information in the first round. It depicts the upper bound of privacy leakage and the lower bound of time complexity. Compared to the Clarke Tax mechanism, The contract one saves privacy leakage by 58.3%. Compared with the negotiation mechanism, the contract-based mechanism can achieve the same level of privacy leakage with a significantly smaller number of rounds, saving 80% time costs. For the same number of rounds to converge, our mechanism efficiently reduces the privacy leakage by 26.2%. This is because the contract mechanism intelligently adjusts the number of proposed time slots based on each responder's

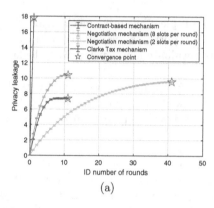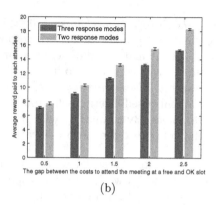

(a)   (b)

Fig. 3. a) Privacy leakage with respect to number of rounds; b) Average reward paid to each attendee with respect to the gap between cost functions $C^{F,F}$ and $C^{O,O}$

calendar density, which is different from the negotiation mechanism where only the same number of time slots are proposed to all responders regardless of their calendar densities. Benefited from this flexible propose-and-respond manner, the contract-based mechanism can achieve a better balance between privacy leakage and time complexity.

In Fig. 3(b) we evaluate the incentive cost of the contract-based mechanism, i.e., the average reward paid to each attendee, for two response modes[5]. In the first one, each attendee can report it is free/OK/busy. In the second mode, each attendee can only reply free or busy information. As discussed in Sect. 4.2, the host has to raise rewards to incentivize attendees to attend the meeting. Results in Fig. 3(b) verify our analysis and show that the average required reward in the second mode is up to 19.6% higher than that in the first mode. The gap between these cases enlarges with the gap between the cost functions $C^{F,F} - C^{O,O}$.

6   Conclusions

We have studied the MAMS problem where the host is required to schedule meetings via information exchange with each attendee. By optimizing the rewards and privacy leakage level, we develop a distributed incentive mechanism based on contract theory to achieve a balance between incentive compatibility, social welfare, and privacy-preservation. Through both theoretical analysis and simulation results, the following features of the proposed mechanism are verified. 1) The mechanism is guaranteed to be incentive compatible with respect to all agents. 2) Multiple types of responses are designed for each attendee such that the incentive costs are largely saved. 3) The contract mechanism can achieve a better trade-off between the privacy leakage and the convergence speed. Given the same convergence speed, the privacy leakage is reduced by 26.2% compared

---

[5] We do not compare with other works here since each of them has a different metric of incentive costs, which is not compatible to ours.

to a state-of-the-art negotiation mechanism; while at the same level of privacy leakage, the contract mechanism can save 80% time costs for convergence. 4) Compared to the Clarke Tax mechanism, the contract one reduces the privacy leakage by 58.3%. 5) Social welfare approaches the upper bound by at least 88.31%, and significantly surpasses that of the Clarke Tax mechanism the negotiation one by up to 3.31 and 82% points, respectively.

Although we deliver this work in the domain of meeting scheduling, the mechanism we design contains various merits which enable other multi-agent applications that involve information exchange among agents who have privacy concerns. For future works, we will extend the constructed framework to explore its applicability to other scenarios such as e-Commerce platforms where multiple agents trade with each other to reach a consensus while protecting their own private information.

A   Appendix: Proof of Proposition 1

According to (11c), for any $(d, \hat{d})$, the following inequalities hold:

$$
\begin{aligned}
&f_F\,(d)\left(R_F(\hat{d}) - \alpha N_p(\hat{d})L(F)\right) + f_O\,(d)\left(R_O(\hat{d}) - \alpha N_p(\hat{d})L(O)\right) \le \\
&f_F\,(d)\,(R_F(d) - \alpha N_p(d)L(F)) + f_O\,(d)\,(R_O(d) - \alpha N_p(d)L(O))\,, \quad\quad (20a)
\end{aligned}
$$

$$
\begin{aligned}
&f_F\left(\hat{d}\right)(R_F(d) - \alpha N_p(d)L(F)) + f_O\left(\hat{d}\right)(R_O(d) - \alpha N_p(d)L(O)) \le \\
&f_F\left(\hat{d}\right)\left(R_F(\hat{d}) - \alpha N_p(\hat{d})L(F)\right) + f_O\left(\hat{d}\right)\left(R_O(\hat{d}) - \alpha N_p(\hat{d})L(O)\right). \quad\quad (20b)
\end{aligned}
$$

When $f_O\,(d) = f_O(\hat{d})$, adding (20a) and (20b) yields

$$
\left(\hat{d} - d\right)\left(R_F\,(d) - R_F\left(\hat{d}\right)\right) + \alpha L_F\left(\hat{d} - d\right)\left(N_p\,(d) - N_p\left(\hat{d}\right)\right) \le 0. \quad\quad (21)
$$

The sufficient conditions to satisfy (21) are that both $R_F\,(d)$ and $N_p\,(d)$ are non-increasing functions. Similarly, by fixing $f_F\,(d) = f_F(\hat{d})$, we can learn that $R_O\,(d)$ is also a non-increasing one, which verifies (15a) and (15b) .

Given d, (20a) implies that the function $y(\hat{d}) = f_F\,(d)\left(R_F(\hat{d}) - \alpha N_p(\hat{d})\right.$ $\left. L(F)\right) + f_O\,(d)\left(R_O(\hat{d}) - \alpha N_p(\hat{d})L(O)\right)$ reaches its maximum at $\hat{d} = d$. We have

$$
f_F(d)\cdot\left[\frac{dR_F\,(d)}{dd} - \alpha L(F)\cdot\frac{dN_p\,(d)}{dd}\right] + f_O(d)\cdot\left[\frac{dR_O\,(d)}{dd} - \alpha L(O)\cdot\frac{dN_p\,(d)}{dd}\right] = 0. \quad\quad (22)
$$

Since it holds for all $f_F(d), f_O(d) > 0$, we have (15c).

B   Appendix: Proof of Proposition 2

The first and second conditions stated in Definition 1 are guaranteed by constraints (11) and (13) . We now look into whether the third condition holds.

An attendee i may claim to be busy at an OK time slot t so as to mislead the host to schedule the meeting at time slot t' in which it is free. In this case, the desired probability that attendee i wishes others to believe is $p_{0 \to i}^d (t) = 0$. Note that slot t' is a time slot that has not been proposed yet. We consider one case that slot t' is a time slot that has not been proposed yet. The expected utility of responder i when lying and telling the truth are separately given by

$$U_i^{lie} = \left(1 - p^{lie}\right) \left[R_F - C^{F,F} + \alpha \left(p_b - 1\right) + \alpha \left(2P_O - p_b\right)\right] \tag{23a}$$

$$U_i^{tr} = \left(1 - p^{tr}\right) \left[R_O - C^{O,O} + \alpha \left(p_b - P_O\right) + \alpha \left(1 - p_b\right)\right], \tag{23b}$$

where p^{lie} and p^{tr} are the probability that the meeting can not be successfully scheduled in two cases, respectively. p_b is the host's prior belief of the free probability of the attendee. In (23a), $\alpha \left(p_b - 1\right)$ represents the privacy leakage reporting to be free at time slot t', and $\alpha \left(2p_O - p_b\right)$ represents the protected privacy information by lying. In (23b), $\alpha \left(p_b - p_O\right)$ is the privacy leakage at time slot t, and $\theta \left(1 - p_b\right)$ is the protected privacy information of slot t'.

Since $p_O \leq 0.5$ and $p^{lie} > p^{tr}$, we have $E\left[U_i^{tru}\right] > E\left[U_i^{lie}\right]$. Therefore, the attendee has no motivation to lie, which verifies the third condition.

References

1. Sen, S., Durfee, E.H.: A formal study of distributed meeting scheduling. Group Decis. Negot. **7**(3), 265–289 (1998)
2. Bolton, P., Dewatripont, M.: Contract Theory. MIT Press, Cambridge (2005)
3. Lee, Y.: Online Membership Incentive System & Method. U.S. Patent Application No. 13/503,831 (2012)
4. Li, Z., Yang, Z., Xie, S., Chen, W., Liu, K.: Credit-based payments for fast computing resource trading in edge-assisted Internet of Things. IEEE Internet Things J. **6**(4), 6606–6617 (2019)
5. Wang, J., Li, M., He, Y., Li, H., Xiao, K., Wang, C.: A blockchain based privacy-preserving incentive mechanism in crowdsensing applications. IEEE Access **6**, 17545–17556 (2018)
6. Jennings, N.R., Jackson, A.J.: Agent based meeting scheduling: a design and implementation. IEEE Electron. Lett. **31**(5), 350–352 (1995)
7. Crawford, E., Veloso, M.: Learning to select negotiation strategies in multi-agent meeting scheduling. In: Bento, C., Cardoso, A., Dias, G. (eds.) EPIA 2005. LNCS (LNAI), vol. 3808, pp. 584–595. Springer, Heidelberg (2005). https://doi.org/10.1007/11595014_57
8. Farinelli, A., Rogers, A., Petcu, A., Jennings, N.R.: Decentralised coordination of low-power embedded devices using the Max-Sum algorithm. In: Seventh International Conference on Autonomous Agents and Multi-Agent Systems (AAMAS-08), pp. 639–646 (2008)
9. Hassine, A.B., Ho, T.B., Ito, T.: Meetings scheduling solver enhancement with local consistency reinforcement. Appl. Intell. **24**(2), 143–154 (2006)
10. Tanaka, T., Farokhi, F., Langbort, C.: A faithful distributed implementation of dual decomposition and average consensus algorithms. In: 52nd IEEE Conference on Decision and Control (2013)

11. Itoh, H.: Incentives to help in multi-agent situations. Econometrica **59**(3), 611–636 (1999)
12. Di, B., Wang, T., Han, Z., Song, L.: Collaborative smartphone sensing using overlapping coalition formation games. IEEE Trans. Mob. Comput. **16**(1), 30–43 (2017)
13. Xu, L., Jiang, C., Chen, Y., Ren, Y., Liu. K.J.: Privacy or utility in data collection? A contract theoretic approach. IEEE J. Sel. Top. Signal Process. **9**(7), 1256–1269 (2015)
14. Bryon, A.E.: Applied Optimal Control: Optimization, Estimation and Control, 1st edn. Taylor & Francis Group, New York (1975)

EUMAS-AT 2020 Joint Session

An Argumentation-Based Approach to Generate Domain-Specific Explanations

Nadin Kökciyan[1]([⊠]), Simon Parsons[2], Isabel Sassoon[3], Elizabeth Sklar[2], and Sanjay Modgil[4]

[1] University of Edinburgh, Edinburgh, UK
nadin.kokciyan@ed.ac.uk
[2] University of Lincoln, Lincoln, UK
{sparsons,esklar}@lincoln.ac.uk
[3] Brunel University, London, UK
isabel.sassoon@brunel.ac.uk
[4] King's College London, London, UK
sanjay.modgil@kcl.ac.uk

Abstract. In argumentation theory, argument schemes are constructs to generalise common patterns of reasoning; whereas critical questions (CQs) capture the reasons why argument schemes might not generate arguments. Argument schemes together with CQs are widely used to instantiate arguments; however when it comes to making decisions, much less attention has been paid to the attacks among arguments. This paper provides a high-level description of the key elements necessary for the formalisation of argumentation frameworks such as argument schemes and CQs. Attack schemes are then introduced to represent attacks among arguments, which enable the definition of domain-specific attacks. One algorithm is articulated to operationalise the use of schemes to generate an argumentation framework, and another algorithm to support decision making by generating domain-specific explanations. Such algorithms can then be used by agents to make recommendations and to provide explanations for humans. The applicability of this approach is demonstrated within the context of a medical case study.

Keywords: Computational argumentation · Explainability · Human-agent systems

1 Introduction

In recent years, artificial intelligence (AI) has made an increasing impact on decisions taken in day to day life. Many AI systems involve black-box models that make decisions on behalf of humans often without providing any explanations. This is problematic since AI does not always make fair or correct decisions [14]. There is an increasing focus on developing techniques to help humans to make

© Springer Nature Switzerland AG 2020
N. Bassiliades et al. (Eds.): EUMAS 2020/AT 2020, LNAI 12520, pp. 319–337, 2020.
https://doi.org/10.1007/978-3-030-66412-1_20

better decisions while being assisted by AI models [20]. In situations where there are multiple recommendations and the decision as to what action to take depends on a human, then being able to reason with the justifications for the recommendations becomes crucial.

Computational argumentation [26], a well-founded logic methodology with roots in philosophy, has been applied in AI and multi-agent systems as a (structured) technique for reasoning in which conclusions are drawn from evidence that supports the conclusions. Users find examining the arguments behind a recommendation to be helpful [28]. This makes a strong case for basing decision-support systems around argumentation to assist humans in making informed decisions. The fact that the General Data Protection Regulation [6] requires transparency for any automated decisions, further strengthens this case.

In existing argumentation-based approaches, an agent constructs an argumentation framework based on the information in its knowledge base; and computes a set of acceptable arguments. Most of the times, an acceptable argument does not provide any additional information such as why it was deemed to be acceptable. Furthermore, there is little information about the defeated arguments [7,32]. To provide such information requires a representation for attacks among arguments. Such a representation can give a better understanding of why certain decisions are made by agents.

On the other hand, it is common to carry out knowledge acquisition using argument schemes (AS) and critical questions (CQs) [1,17,29]. Argument schemes are a means to compactly represent all the arguments that may be generated in different situations; whereas CQs are a way of capturing all the reasons why argument schemes might not generate arguments, either as pre-conditions to the construction of arguments, or as a way of formulating counter-arguments. Despite the popularity of the argument schemes and critical questions approach, there is no consensus on a formal representation of these elements, nor on an approach to construct an argumentation framework (AF), in the sense of [4], and there is no clear method to use these elements to create explanations, what we term "explainability by design".

In this paper, we make the following contributions: (i) we propose a formal representation of arguments through their respective argument schemes and critical questions; (ii) we introduce the notion of *attack schemes* to account for the conflicts between arguments in a given domain; (iii) we propose one algorithm to construct an argumentation framework for decision support; and another algorithm to provide explanations for acceptable arguments and attacks by the use of explanation templates. Such algorithms can help agents to reason about (possibly conflicting) information, make a decision and explain this to humans. The rest of the paper is as follows. Section 2 discusses related work. In Sect. 3, we introduce a high-level description of AFs that support explainability; and we propose algorithms to construct AFs and explanations automatically. Sections 4 and 5 introduce a medical scenario from the hypertension domain to show the applicability of our approach. Section 6 concludes and details future directions.

2 Related Work

Argumentation has been applied to many domains including medicine [8,10,17], multi-agent systems [1,18,28] and legal reasoning [11,24]. We now focus on the application of argumentation to support decision making.

Argument schemes and their associated critical questions are often modelled as defeasible inference rules. Prakken *et al.* model legal cases as argument schemes together with their associated undercutting attacks within the ASPIC+ framework [24]. Similar to us, they model CQs as argument schemes that can be challenged by other CQs. Atkinson *et al.* propose an argumentation-based approach to reason with defeasible arguments [2]. Unlike us, the above authors do not provide a formal representation for the CQs, but they use CQs to manually construct arguments in natural language.

Various argumentation-based approaches focus on the medical domain and determining treatment options. Tolchinsky *et al.* propose an agent-based architecture, Carrel+, to help transplant physicians in deliberating over organ viability [29]. Gordon and Walton generalise Dung's abstract argumentation frameworks [4] such that the arguments have weights to help one to choose among alternative options [12]. Similar to us, they provide a formal model of a structured argument. However, in addition, we model different types of attacks through attack schemes and use explanation templates to explain the decisions that agents make in a specified domain. Glasspool *et al.* [9] construct and evaluate pro and con arguments on different treatment options independently. ArguEIRA [13] is an ASPIC based clinical decision support system aimed at detecting a patient's anomalous reaction to a medication.

Some work combines argumentation with explanations. Kakas, Moraitis and Spanoudakis propose an approach to take scenario-based preferences in a tabular format, and to translate these preferences into a *Gorgias* argumentation theory and code automatically [15]. Rago, Cocarascu and Toni propose an application of Tripolar argumentation frameworks to support argumentation based explanations in recommender systems [25]. The method relies on visual representations of the argumentation frameworks, which includes supporting and attacking arguments, and allows users to tweak the recommendations. Unlike our work, neither of these approaches provides a natural language explanation. In addition, we believe that whilst arguments can encapsulate premises and claims, even in the case where these are instantiated through the use of argument schemes, simply putting forward extensions or collections of arguments falls short of constituting an explanation [20]. We believe that our approach of using explanation templates to translate the contents of an argument and attack into a structured form of natural language is a promising step towards creating good explanations [27].

In [21], Modgil and Bench-Capon explore the idea of attacking the attacks in AFs at the meta-level. Here, we focus on reasoning in the object-level. In both approaches, we can include arguments that represent human preferences and values to attack the attacks. We plan on exploring a comparison of different approaches in future work.

3   A Formal Model to Represent Argumentation Frameworks

This section contains the main contribution of this paper, which is a high-level formal representation of an argumentation framework. This representation can: (i) be implemented in various ways (e.g. logic-based systems, in any programming language), (ii) enable the sharing of domain-specific knowledge across domains, (iii) add explainability by design, where explanation templates are part of the model to generate domain-specific explanations. We then articulate algorithms so that agents can construct argumentation frameworks and generate explanations.

3.1   Formal Model

We capture the semantics of an argument scheme in Definition 1. The premises and the conclusion are sentences, which can be represented in a logical language $\mathcal{L}$. Each of these sentences includes variables, which are then instantiated with elements of this language. We give an example of an argument scheme from the medical domain, Argument Scheme for a Proposed Treatment (ASPT) [17], in Table 1. ASPT represents an argument in support of each possible treatment TR within the current treatment step S, given the patient's treatment goal G to be realised. In the remaining of the paper, we will use the auxiliary function $\text{Var}(AS)$ to refer to the set of variables used in AS.

Definition 1 (Argument Scheme). $AS = \langle P, c, V \rangle$ *denotes an argument scheme, where* P *is a set of premises,* c *is the conclusion, and* $P \cup \{c\} \subseteq \mathcal{L}$. V *is the set of variables used in the argument scheme.*

Table 1. Argument Scheme for a Proposed Treatment (ASPT) [17]

$\mathbf{ASPT} = \langle \{p_1, p_2, p_3\}, c, \{G, TR, S\} \rangle$
p_1: Bringing about G is the goal
p_2: Treatment TR promotes the goal G
p_3: Treatment TR is indicated at step S
c: Treatment TR should be offered

An argument scheme can be associated with a set of critical questions (CQs) which provide reasons why that argument scheme might not generate arguments. We define CQs to themselves be argument schemes as suggested in [24, 29]. We do not consider CQs to be part of a given argument scheme since this allows a CQ to be used by multiple argument schemes. We capture this structure in Definition 2.

Definition 2 (ASCQ). $ASCQ : AS \to 2^{AS}$, is a function mapping an argument scheme to a set of argument schemes that represent the CQs of the original argument scheme.

A knowledge base (KB) is the information store of an agent that includes premises, rules and the relationships between schemes, as captured in Definition 3. R is the set of rules written using the elements of the logical language. Rules and premises can be *strict*, in which case they admit no exceptions (we call strict premises "axioms"). For example, factual information about a patient may be considered to be axioms. Rules and premises can also be *defeasible*, in which case they allow exceptions. Thus defeasible rules and facts can be falsified based on evidence. For example, argument schemes can be represented as defeasible rules, as we do in this paper, so that they represent tentative inferences that can be overturned. KB also has information about CQ relations among argument schemes as described via the $ASCQ$ function.

Definition 3 (Knowledge Base). $KB = \langle P, R, ASCQ \rangle$ denotes a knowledge base; where P is the set of premises (e.g. facts), R is the set of rules and $ASCQ$ is the function as described in Definition 2.

Arguments are constructed by instantiating each argument scheme according to ground terms that exist in the KB (i.e. terms that do not contain any free variables) (Definition 4). All the variables in AS are replaced with the ground terms to construct an argument (Definition 5). The notation $[X]$ will be used to denote the name of the scheme X (e.g. type of an argument).

Definition 4 (Argument Scheme Instantiation). $AS_i = \langle AS, G, KB \rangle$ denotes an instantiation of the AS with $G \subseteq \mathcal{L}$ in the knowledge base KB, $AS\{v_i \mapsto g_i\}$ for all $i = 1, .., k$ where k is the size of $\mathsf{Var}(AS)$, v_i is the *i*th element in $\mathsf{Var}(AS)$ and g_i is the *i*th element in G. $\mathsf{Prem}(AS_i)$ returns the set of instantiated premises $AS.P$; $\mathsf{Conc}(AS_i)$ returns the instantiated conclusion $AS.c$; $\mathsf{Gr}(AS_i)$ returns the set of pairs (v_i,g_i); and $\mathsf{Gr}(AS_i)(v_i)$ returns g_i.

Definition 5 (Argument). $[AS]arg_i = \langle \mathsf{Prem}(AS_i), \mathsf{Conc}(AS_i) \rangle$ is an argument, which is derived from the argument scheme instantiation AS_i.

Attacks among arguments are critical components of argumentation. In early works, attacks were defined syntactically, with an attack being between a formula and its negation. The well-known argumentation system ASPIC+ generalises this idea with the notion of a contrary function, which defines the set of formulae that conflict with a formula [22]. There are three forms of attacks among arguments: (i) a fallible premise of an argument can be attacked (*undermining*), (ii) the conclusion of a defeasible rule can be attacked (*rebuttal*), and (iii) a defeasible rule can be attacked as a whole (*undercutting*), for example denying its applicability in a particular setting.

While modelling well-known attacks is important, we introduce attack schemes (Definition 6) to: (i) provide flexibility to capture all the ways in which an attack may arise between two arguments, and (ii) explain the existence of

Table 2. The attack schemes T_{cq} and ALT

(a) An undercutting attack
$T_{cq} = \langle \{p_1, p_2, p_3\}, c, \mathsf{Var}(X) \cup \mathsf{Var}(Y) \rangle$
p_1: An argument of type X.
p_2: An argument of type Y.
p_3: X challenges Y (i.e. $X \in ASCQ(\mathsf{Y})$).
c: p_1 attacks p_2.

(b) Attack between ASPT Arguments
ALT=$\langle \{p_1\text{-}p_5\}, c, \{A.TR, B.TR, S\} \rangle$
p_1: A is an argument of $ASPT$
p_2: B is an argument of $ASPT$
p_3: A.TR is offered at step S.
p_4: B.TR is offered at step S.
p_5: A.TR is an alternative to B.TR.
c: A attacks B.

attacks among arguments. This new representation allows for specific, domain dependent, forms of attack, such as drug contra-indications or the guideline conflicts of [31], as well as domain-independent attacks, such as undercuts.

Definition 6 (Attack Scheme). $ATS = \langle \{p_1, p_2\} \cup P, c, V \rangle$ *denotes an attack scheme with* $P \cup \{c\} \subseteq \mathcal{L}$; *where* p_1 *is an argument of type X,* p_2 *is an argument of type Y, P is a set of premises, c is the conclusion of the form 'p_1 attacks p_2' and* $V = \mathsf{Var}(X) \cup \mathsf{Var}(Y)$. *X and Y can be same type.*

Table 2 shows two different attack types. In Table 2a, we provide the attack scheme T_{cq} to represent an undercutting attack between two arguments, where the argument scheme X is a critical question of Y. Note that each argument scheme can be represented as a defeasible rule in the knowledge base. Therefore, challenging one argument through a critical question would mean an undercutting attack. Table 2b gives an example of a domain-specific attack scheme, where an attack exists between two arguments because two treatments promoting the same goal are alternatives to each other. Definition 7 captures the idea of an attack, which is constructed when an attack scheme is initialised.

Definition 7 (Attack). $[ATS]att_i = \langle \mathsf{Prem}(ATS_i), \mathsf{Conc}(ATS_i) \rangle$ *is an attack, which is derived from the attack scheme instantiation* ATS_i.

We make use of Dung's abstract argumentation framework [4], captured in Definition 8, to evaluate the arguments and attacks generated by the schemes in a KB. In a Dung AF, the idea is represent arguments as nodes, and attacks among them with arrows in a directed graph; it is abstract in the sense that the internal structure of arguments and attacks is not defined.

Definition 8 (Dung Argumentation Framework, Dung AF). *A Dung AF is a tuple* $\langle \mathcal{A}', \mathcal{R}' \rangle$, *where* $\mathcal{A}'$ *is the set of arguments and* $\mathcal{R}' \subseteq \mathcal{A}' \times \mathcal{A}'$ *is a relation such that for arguments a and b,* $(a, b) \in \mathcal{R}'$ *iff* $\{a, b\} \subseteq \mathcal{A}'$ *and a attacks b.*

Having defined the notions of argument and attack in a structured way previously, we can map these concepts into a Dung AF (Definition 9). The aim of this translation will be to compute acceptable arguments in the structured AF that we construct. Note that $\mathsf{Prem}(x)[i]$ returns the ith premise of x, where x is a scheme instantiation.

Definition 9 (Argumentation Framework, AF). *An argumentation frame-work is a tuple* $\langle \mathcal{A}, \mathcal{R} \rangle$, *where* $\mathcal{A}$ *and* $\mathcal{R}$ *are, respectively, the set of arguments (Definition 5) and the set of attacks (Definition 7). The mapping to a Dung AF* $\langle \mathcal{A}', \mathcal{R}' \rangle$ *is as follows:* $\mathcal{A}' = \mathcal{A}$; $\mathcal{R}' = \{(\mathsf{Prem}(r)[0], \mathsf{Prem}(r)[1]) \mid r \in \mathcal{R}\}$.

Given a Dung AF, it is typical to evaluate it by computing the *acceptable* arguments according to the chosen Dung semantics [3,4]. For example we might use the *grounded* or the *preferred* semantics. The grounded semantics is sceptical in the sense that one can only accept arguments that cannot be rejected for any reason; whereas one can accept mutually exclusive alternative arguments (each set represented in different *extensions*) while using preferred semantics. Under the chosen semantics, the acceptable arguments are the ones that can be considered to hold for that AF. In this paper, we introduce the idea of an *acceptable attack* in Definition 10.

Definition 10 (Acceptable attack). *An attack is acceptable, if* $\forall r \in \mathcal{R}$, $\mathsf{Prem}(r)[0]$ *is an acceptable argument in Dung AF,* $\mathcal{R}$ *being the set of attacks.*

We distinguish such attacks because we believe that they are key to understand-ing, and *explaining* why a particular set of arguments is acceptable. More than one extension may hold when evaluating an AF under the chosen semantics such as the preferred semantics. Therefore, each extension will consist of a pair of acceptable arguments and attacks. Definition 11 captures this.

Definition 11 (Acceptability). $ACC = \langle AF, \mathcal{S} \rangle$ *denotes the set of* $(A_{arg}, A_{att})_i$ *where:* $\mathcal{S}$ *is the chosen semantics to evaluate* AF, $(A_{arg}, A_{att})_i$ *is the pair of acceptable arguments and attacks in the ith extension of* AF.

Now that we have the sets of acceptable arguments and attacks, we can use argument and attack schemes to give rationales behind the existence of arguments and attacks within the argumentation framework. The basic idea is to map the acceptable arguments and attacks into the *explanation templates* that we introduced in [27]. Definition 12 captures the idea of an explanation template for an argument scheme. An explanation template for the ASPT scheme can be described as: $e_1 = \langle ASPT,$ *"Treatment* $\{TR\}$ *should be considered at step* $\{S\}$ *as it promotes the goal of* $\{G\}$."$\rangle$. The variables are shown in curly brackets in textual representation, and the template includes all the variables (TR, S, G) that exist in ASPT scheme. The explanation definitions below are similar for attacks, where AS and $[AS]arg_i$ are replaced by ATS and $[ATS]att_i$ respectively.

Definition 12 (Explanation template). *An explanation template is a tuple* $E = \langle AS, t \rangle$, *where* AS *is an argument scheme, and* t *is a text in natural language that can include variables* V *such that* $V \subseteq \mathsf{Var}(AS)$.

We build explanations from explanation templates by instantiating them with acceptable arguments (and attacks). Each variable in the explanation text ($E.t$)

is replaced by a ground term found in the argument (attack) scheme instantiation, giving us Definition 13. An explanation for an ASPT argument can be represented as: $\langle e_1, \langle \{goal(rbp), promotes(d, rbp), indicatedAt(d, s1)\}, offer(d) \rangle \rangle$. In this case, $e_1.t$ will become *"Treatment d should be considered at step 1 as it promotes the goal of reducing blood pressure."*

Definition 13 (Explanation). *An explanation is a tuple $\langle E, [AS]arg_i \rangle$, where E is an explanation template of the argument scheme AS, $[AS]arg_i$ is an acceptable argument (Definition 11); and for each variable $v \in E.t$, $E.t\{v \mapsto Gr(AS_i)(v)\}$.*

A given argument scheme might have different explanations in different contexts [19,32]. For example, patients and healthcare professionals may see different explanations for the same set of acceptable arguments and attacks concerning a medical decision. For now, however, we assume that each scheme is associated with a single explanation template, leaving the question of handling context-specific explanations for future work.

3.2   Mapping ASPIC+ Theory into Our Formal Model

In this section, we show how an existing argumentation theory, the well-known ASPIC+, can be mapped into our formal model. We do this to demonstrate the expressibility of our approach. Our formal model includes explainability features by design, which cannot be represented in existing approaches directly. Therefore, we only define mappings for arguments and attacks.

Proposition 1. *An ASPIC+ argument can be represented as an argument constructed according to Definition 5.*

Proof sketch. Assume that we have a defeasible rule r, where the conjunction of predicates implies the conclusion $(p_1, ..., p_n \Rightarrow c)$ and $r \in \mathcal{R}_d$, where $\mathcal{R}_d$ is the set of defeasible rules in an ASPIC+ argumentation theory. In this theory, the knowledge base K includes all the predicates p_i, where $i=1, .., n$. *Prem, Conc, Sub, DefRules,* and *TopRule* are functions defined in the theory; where *Prem* is the set of premises and *Conc* is the conclusion of the argument, *Sub* returns all sub-arguments, *DefRules* returns all the defeasible rules and *TopRule* returns the last rule to construct the argument. Assume that A is an argument on the basis of this theory such that $Sub(A) = \{A\}$, $DefRules(A) = r$, $TopRule(A) = r$. Hence, the corresponding ASPIC+ argument is '$A : p_1, ..., p_n \Rightarrow c$'.

With our formal model, we can represent r as the argument scheme $as = \langle\{p_1, ..., p_n\}, c, \{\}\rangle$, the scheme instantiation as $as_1 = \langle as, \{\}, KB\rangle$; where the knowledge base KB includes all the predicates p_i and the argument scheme as. The mapping from an ASPIC+ argument to our formal model is then straightforward: $Prem(A) = \mathsf{Prem}(as_1)$, $Conc(A) = \mathsf{Conc}(as_1)$. The ASPIC+ argument A can then be represented as $\langle\{p_1, ..., p_n\}, c\rangle$.

Proposition 2. *ASPIC+ attack types (undermining, rebuttal and undercutting) can be represented as attack schemes according to Definition 6.*

Algorithm 1. EVALAF $(\mathcal{X}, \mathcal{S})$

Input: $\mathcal{X}$, the set of schemes of interest
Input: $\mathcal{S}$, chosen semantics
Output: ACC, the sets of acceptable arguments and attacks

Require: KB, the knowledge base
1: $\mathcal{A} \leftarrow \{\}, \mathcal{R} \leftarrow \{\}$
2: $I \leftarrow$ instantiateSchemes$(\mathcal{X}, KB)$
3: **for all** i in I **do**
4:     $x \leftarrow$ arg$(i.sname, \mathsf{Prem}(i), \mathsf{Conc}(i))$
5:     $\mathcal{A} \leftarrow$ EXTENDARG$(x, \mathcal{A})$
6: $K \leftarrow$ instantiateAttSchemes$(\mathcal{A}, KB)$
7: **for all** k in K **do**
8:     $at \leftarrow$ att$(k.sname, \mathsf{Prem}(k), \mathsf{Conc}(k))$
9:     $\mathcal{R} \leftarrow \mathcal{R} \cup \{at\}$
10: $AF \leftarrow$ computeAF$(\mathcal{A}, \mathcal{R})$
11: $ACC \leftarrow$ getAccepted$(AF, \mathcal{S})$
12: **return** ACC
13: **function** EXTENDARG$(arg, \mathcal{A})$
14:     $Q \leftarrow$ getCQs$(arg.sname)$
15:     **for all** q in Q **do**
16:        $J \leftarrow$ instantiateScheme$(q.name, KB)$
17:        **for all** j in J **do**
18:           $a \leftarrow$ arg$(j.sname, \mathsf{Prem}(j), \mathsf{Conc}(j))$
19:           $\mathcal{A} \leftarrow \mathcal{A} \cup \{a\}$
20:           $\mathcal{A} \leftarrow$ EXTENDARG$(a, \mathcal{A})$
21:     **return** $\mathcal{A}$

Proof sketch. Assume that A and B are two ASPIC+ arguments. A premise in argument A can be a contrary of the conclusion of an argument B (rebuttal), or a premise in argument A can be a contrary of a premise in argument B (undermining). All these attack types are represented by the use of the contrary function in ASPIC+. Proposition 1 ensures that ASPIC+ arguments can be represented as arguments in our formal model. Table 2a shows an undercutting attack; whereas other attack types can be represented through the use of additional predicates in attack schemes as well. However, domain-specific attacks, such as the one in Table 2b, can only be represented with our formal model.

3.3 The EvalAF Algorithm

Having introduced our representation, we propose the EVALAF algorithm. An agent can employ this algorithm to: (i) generate an argumentation framework from a knowledge base, and (ii) compute extensions under a chosen semantics. EVALAF thus provides an operational semantics for our system of schemes and critical questions, showing how they translate into arguments and attacks that conform to the proposed formal model.

The EVALAF algorithm requires two inputs: the set of schemes of interest ($\mathcal{X}$) to initialise arguments and a semantics ($\mathcal{S}$) to compute the extensions in the argumentation framework. In other words, $\mathcal{X}$ includes the scheme set to initialise the construction of an AF; therefore, only relevant arguments are constructed. The output of the algorithm is the sets of acceptable arguments and acceptable attacks. KB is the knowledge base that includes domain-specific content such as schemes, critical questions, facts and rules (Definition 3). The set of arguments ($\mathcal{A}$) and the set of attacks ($\mathcal{R}$) are initialised as empty sets (line 1). The function instantiateSchemes is used to instantiate the schemes in $\mathcal{X}$ (Definition 4) (line 2). Each instantiation is translated into an argument x (Definition 5), and the set of arguments is updated to include more arguments as a result of applying critical questions (line 5). So far, all possible arguments are constructed regarding argument schemes; in line 6, the attack schemes are instantiated to generate attacks among arguments. For each of these instantiations, an attack relation is formed and added to the set of attacks (lines 8–9). The auxiliary function computeAF generates an argumentation framework by using the sets of arguments and attacks (Definition 9). At this point, the AF can be used to make a decision under the chosen semantics $\mathcal{S}$. getAccepted returns the sets of acceptable arguments and attacks (line 11) (Definition 11).

The function EXTENDARG is described between the lines 13 and 21. The inputs are an argument arg, and the current set $\mathcal{A}$. Since each argument is constructed according to an argument scheme, the set of CQs are collected in order to challenge the current argument arg (Definition 2)(line 14). Each CQ is a scheme to be initialised (line 16), and an argument is generated accordingly (line 18). The set of arguments is updated (line 19). Each new CQ argument can be challenged by other CQs as well, hence EXTENDARG is invoked recursively (line 20). Note that at this point the order in which we ask critical questions is not important, because KB does not change but the argumentation framework is updated by the construction of new arguments and attacks.

It is easy to show that the algorithm is sound in the sense that it only returns arguments that are acceptable:

Proposition 3 (Soundness). *Given a set of argument schemes and a semantics, the set of arguments returned by* EVALAF *are acceptable arguments.*

Proof sketch. getAccepted ensures the mapping into a Dung AF (Definitions 8 and 9). Existing reasoning tools, such as *Aspartix* [5], can be used to compute acceptable arguments. Therefore, EVALAF returns acceptable arguments as well.

Note that EVALAF will always construct all the arguments and attacks given an initial set of argument schemes:

Proposition 4 (Completeness/AF). EVALAF *returns the complete AF when arguments are instantiated from an argument scheme in* $\mathcal{X}$.

Proof sketch. Assume that $\mathcal{F}_1$ is the complete Dung AF that can be constructed given a specific $\mathcal{X}$ (Definition 8); i.e, $\mathcal{F}_1$ will include all the possible arguments and attacks. When an agent invokes EVALAF each argument scheme in $\mathcal{X}$ will be instantiated to construct an argument (Definition 5). EXTENDARG is then invoked recursively to instantiate all the argument schemes and add the resulting arguments to the set of arguments. Hence, all possible arguments will be constructed. instantiateAttSchemes will initialise all possible attacks. computeAF will then construct an AF, which can then mapped into the Dung AF, $\mathcal{F}_2$ (Definition 9). Since there can only exist one Dung AF, $\mathcal{F}_1$ and $\mathcal{F}_2$ should be the same. Therefore, EVALAF constructs the complete AF given a specific $\mathcal{X}$.

Proposition 5 (Completeness/Acceptability). EVALAF *returns all the acceptable arguments that are instantiated from an argument scheme in $\mathcal{X}$. EVALAF returns all the acceptable attacks that are instantiated from acceptable arguments.*

Proof sketch. EVALAF returns all acceptable arguments in a complete AF (follows from Propositions 3 and 4). Definition 10 ensures that there is an acceptable attack when an argument is acceptable. Hence, EVALAF returns all the acceptable arguments and attacks in an argumentation framework.

3.4   The ExpAF Algorithm

The next important step is to map acceptable arguments and attacks into explanations in natural language. In this section, we propose EXPAF algorithm that conforms to Definitions 12 and 13. The algorithm requires two inputs the set of acceptable arguments ($\mathcal{A}'$) and the set of acceptable attacks ($\mathcal{R}'$). KB is the knowledge base that includes domain-specific information as before. EVALAF ensures that only relevant arguments and attacks will be constructed. In other words, the agent will not try to initialise all the schemes in its KB but it will start constructing the argumentation framework with the ones specified in $\mathcal{X}$. Hence, when an agent provides outputs of EVALAF algorithm as inputs to EXPAF algorithm, it will get explanations that are relevant to the problem instance.

In line 1, the sets of explanations for arguments and attacks are initialised as empty sets. *objects* keeps a set of all the inputs. For each object o, getSchemeName returns the scheme name (line 4), getExpTemplate returns the explanation template e (Definition 12) (line 5); and the explanation tuple exp (Definition 13) is generated by the generateExp (line 6). The explanation tuple is added to E_{arg} if o is an acceptable argument; otherwise, exp is added to E_{att}. The algorithm returns the explanation sets for each object (line 11).

Proposition 6. EXPAF *always returns explanations for acceptable arguments and attacks.*

Proof sketch. The input $\mathcal{A}'$ includes acceptable arguments; for each argument, there will be an instantiated scheme. If there is an instantiated scheme, an explanation template will exist; and this template will have an instance initialised

---

Algorithm 2. EXPAF $(\mathcal{A}', \mathcal{R}')$

Input: $\mathcal{A}'$, the set of acceptable arguments
Input: $\mathcal{R}'$, the set of acceptable attacks
Output: E_{arg}, E_{att}, sets of explanations for arguments and attacks
Require: KB, the knowledge base
 1: $E_{arg} \leftarrow \{\}, E_{att} \leftarrow \{\}$
 2: $objects \leftarrow \mathcal{A}' \cup \mathcal{R}'$
 3: **for all** o in $objects$ **do**
 4:     $sname \leftarrow o.\mathsf{getSchemeName}(KB)$
 5:     $e \leftarrow \mathsf{getExpTemplate}(sname, KB)$
 6:     $exp \leftarrow \mathsf{generateExp}(e, o)$
 7:     **if** $o \in \mathcal{A}'$ **then**   ▷ o is an acceptable argument
 8:         $E_{arg} \leftarrow E_{arg} \cup exp$
 9:     **else**   ▷ o is an acceptable attack
10:         $E_{att} \leftarrow E_{att} \cup exp$
11: **return** E_{arg}, E_{att}

---

with ground terms, which will constitute an explanation (follows from Definitions 4, 5, 12 and 13). EXPAF conforms to these definitions; hence, it provides an explanation for any acceptable argument. Similar reasoning holds for attacks.

The output of EXPAF can then be used by tools to provide explanations for acceptable arguments and/or attacks.

4 Arguments and Attacks

The formal model introduced above can be used in order to describe a particular domain. We represent the hypertension domain via first-order language predicates as in our previous work [17]. This language consists of predicates of different arities. Variables are denoted as capital letters, the predicates are written in italic text and the constants are in lower case. The knowledge base (KB) includes information such as the clinical guidelines, patient information, argument and attack schemes in terms of facts and rules.

4.1 Guideline Representation

In the domain and example that follow we refer to the NICE hypertension guidelines [23]. NICE[1] has a set of guidelines to help healthcare professionals in diagnosing and treating primary hypertension. The guideline includes treatment steps, such that a patient progresses to the next step and takes a new drug if their blood pressure control does not improve in the previous step. It provides guidance on which of the treatments or treatment combinations should be considered at each step. For example, c (Calcium-Channel Blocker) and d

---

[1] https://www.nice.org.uk/.

(Thiazide-like Diuretic) are two treatment options that may be offered if the patient facts indicate a goal of blood pressure reduction. A treatment that *promotes* a *goal*, can be offered or not offered (predicates are *offer* and *notoffer* respectively). Moreover, a treatment can be marked as *offered* at a specific time. A treatment can be *indicatedAt* a specific step according to guidelines. *greater* is used to define an ordering between different time points. A treatment that is previously prescribed *may_cause* a side effect.

4.2 Patient Information

The choice of a treatment may depend on the *facts* about a patient. In the hypertension domain; *age*, *ethnic_origin*, the current treatment *step* in the treatment process and an *observation* about the patient are important facts to consider before recommending a particular treatment. Observations include information such as if any side-effect has been reported or the desired goal (e.g. reduction in blood pressure) has been achieved. Such information can dynamically be added to the knowledge base. For example, in our previous work, we showed that the knowledge base can be populated with patient facts collected via wellness sensors [16].

4.3 Argument Schemes

We use the ASPT scheme in order to construct arguments in support of different treatment options (Table 1). There are different reasons precluding a treatment from being an option for a specific patient, so there are multiple critical questions associated with ASPT–we just show one in the following. SE scheme ascertains that no treatment will be offered if a side effect is observed (i.e. $ASCQ(\text{ASPT}) = \{\text{SE}\}$). SE is challenged by SEF scheme in situations where the treatment is effective so should not be excluded as an option despite the side effect (i.e. $ASCQ(\text{SE}) = \{\text{SEF}\}$). In Table 3, the first frame shows these schemes in a first-order language.

4.4 Attack Schemes

In Sect. 3, we have discussed different types of attacks that could exist among arguments, and Table 2a gives an example of an undercutting attack between arguments. Now, we give an example of an attack scheme that is domain-specific and describes the rationale behind an attack in terms of domain-specific premises. Table 2b shows the attack scheme, ALT, belonging to the hypertension domain. The ALT scheme defines an attack between two ASPT arguments when two treatments promoting the same goal are offered at a specific step. ALT has a similar intuition as *Argument from Alternative* scheme proposed by Walton [30]. The instantiation of this attack scheme will result in attacks among alternative treatment arguments in the argumentation framework.

Table 3. Arguments schemes and arguments used in the running example

Schemes	
ASPT	$\langle\{goal(\text{G}),\ promotes(\text{TR,G}),$ $indicatedAt(\text{TR,S})\},\ offer(\text{TR}),$ $\{\text{G,TR,S}\}\rangle$
SE	$\langle\{greater(\text{T,T'}),\ offered(\text{TR,T'}),$ $may\_cause(\text{TR,S})\},\ notoffer(\text{TR}),$ $\{\text{T,T',TR,S}\}\rangle$
SEF	$\langle\{greater(\text{T,T'}),\ effective(\text{TR,T'})\},$ $offer(\text{TR}),\ \{\text{T,T',TR}\}\rangle$
Arguments	
$[ASPT]arg_1$:	$\langle\{goal(\text{rbp}),\ promotes(c,\text{rbp}),$ $indicatedAt(c,\text{s1})\},\ offer(c)\rangle$
$[ASPT]arg_2$:	$\langle\{goal(\text{rbp}),\ promotes(d,\text{rbp}),$ $indicatedAt(d,\text{s1})\},\ offer(d)\rangle$
$[SE]arg_{1.1}$:	$\langle\{greater(t_2,t_1),\ offered(c,t_1),$ $caused(c,\text{swollen-ankles},t_1)\},$ $notoffer(c)\rangle$
$[SEF]arg_{1.1.1}$:	$\langle\{greater(t_2,t_1),\ effective(c,t_1)\},$ $offer(c)\rangle$

5 A Stroke Survivor: Baula

We will work through the case of Baula a 32-year-old person of African origin. Baula suffered a stroke and has hypertension. In order to prevent secondary stroke, Baula's blood pressure (BP) needs to be controlled. Baula has started using a new medication c to control blood pressure as suggested by a GP. During a follow up visit, Baula's BP is 130/90 (indicating the treatment is having the desired BP lowering effect) but there is a side effect (swollen ankles). In the light of this information, *what* are the treatment options to consider and *why*?

We now illustrate the use of EVALAf algorithm on the example. The two inputs provided to the algorithm are *ASPT* and *preferred*, respectively. In our running example, the goal is set to reducing blood pressure (*rbp*) by default. The construction of the arguments will start by initialising *ASPT* according to the information available in the knowledge base. The use of *preferred* semantics will ensure that there can be multiple acceptable sets of arguments and attacks. The human user (e.g. Baula's GP) will make a final decision in the light of the suggested possible solutions. The bottom part of Table 3 includes all the arguments generated by the algorithm.

The arguments arg_1 and arg_2 are constructed as a result of the instantiation of ASPT. The CQs for each scheme are considered in the following steps. SE is relevant only to arg_1, and given the side effects there is an attack generated on arg_1 from $arg_{1.1}$. Even if Baula reports side effects, c is still effective in *rbp*.

Therefore, $arg_{1.1.1}$ attacks $arg_{1.1}$ as well. Figure 1 depicts the resulting AF; where arguments are displayed as boxes, the solid arrows represent attacks instantiated by T_{cq}, and the dashed arrows show attacks instantiated by the ALT scheme. For simplicity, the attacks are annotated without scheme names. Each attack has a unique label att_i. att_4, which conforms to the attack scheme T_{cq}, is instantiated as: $\langle \{[SEF]arg_{1.1.1}, [SE]arg_{1.1}, challenges(SEF, SE)\}, attacks(arg_{1.1.1}, arg_1) \rangle$. att_1, which conforms to the attack scheme ALT, is instantiated as: $\langle \{[ASPT]arg_2, [ASPT]arg_1, alt(c, d), indicatedAt(c, s1), indicatedAt(d, s1)\}, attacks(arg_2, arg_1) \rangle$. att_2 and att_4 are instantiated similarly.

The EVALAF algorithm returns the set of acceptable arguments and attacks (Definition 11). Under the preferred semantics, there are two extensions: $(\{arg_1, arg_{1.1.1}\}, \{att_2, att_4\})$ and $(\{arg_2, arg_{1.1.1}\}, \{att_1, att_4\})$.

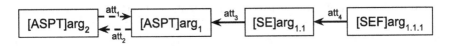

Fig. 1. Argumentation framework constructed by EVALAF algorithm.

5.1 Explanations

As argument and attack schemes are associated with explanation templates (Definition 12), agents can instantiate them with an algorithm like EXPAF to generate explanations in natural language (Definition 13). In Sect. 3, we introduced e_1 as an explanation template for ASPT. In a similar way, we can describe an explanation template for the ALT scheme as: $\langle ALT$, *"Since $\{A.TR\}$ and $\{B.TR\}$ promote the same goal at step $\{S\}$, $\{A.TR\}$ is an alternative to $\{B.TR\}$; hence, they should not be offered together."* $\rangle$.

When we consider the following extension $(\{arg_2, arg_{1.1.1}\}, \{att_1, att_4\})$, EXPAF will generate an explanation for each acceptable argument and attack. For example, an explanation for arg_2 will be *"Treatment d should be considered at step 1 as it promotes the goal of reducing blood pressure."*; and an explanation for att_1 will be *"Since d and c promote the same goal at step 1, d is an alternative to c; hence, they should not be offered together."*, applying the explanation templates described above. The remaining explanations are generated in a similar way by the use of explanation templates. $arg_{1.1.1}$ can be explained as *"Treatment ccb can be considered as it was an effective treatment at time t1."*; and att_4 can be explained as *"The scheme sef is a critical question of the scheme se"*.

Given the suggested treatments and explanations, one option is to continue the current treatment c as it is effective, another option is to offer a new treatment such as d. At this point, the GP should also consider Baula's preferences when making a decision.

5.2 Demonstration of the Proposed Approach

We provide an example implementation of the proposed approach in our GitLab repository[2]. Baula's example is also provided to demonstrate the applicability of the proposed algorithms. By running the code, one can get the textual explanations for acceptable arguments and attacks as described in this paper. In our implementation, we make use of *Aspartix*, an answer set programming approach to find the justified arguments of an argumentation framework [5]. In a first-order language, we describe the knowledge base, the argument and attack schemes, and data about Baula in terms of facts and rules. More use cases can be described in a similar manner. We also make our Python-based implementation public; we share an implementation of the proposed algorithms that use explanation templates to generate textual explanations. Moreover, our implementation provides means to export the generated Dung AF as a graph, which is useful in providing a visual explanation of the constructed arguments and attacks.

Figure 2 depicts one extension as a Dung AF where the recommended action is offering a new treatment d (thiazide). Each box represents an argument constructed using argument schemes, each arrow represents an attack between arguments constructed using attack schemes. The acceptable arguments are highlighted with a green color. Note that since we are using preferred semantics in this example, there is also another extension (i.e. another graph) supporting the idea of using the current treatment c (ccb).

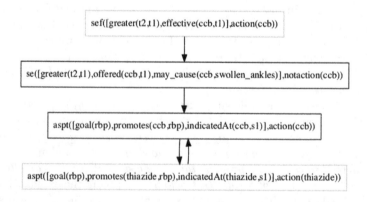

Fig. 2. One extension recommends offering a new treatment thiazide (d)

6 Discussion and Conclusion

We proposed a formalism to describe arguments and attacks in a given domain through the use of schemes. We introduced the notion of attack schemes to capture domain-specific conflicts between two arguments. We articulated an

---

[2] https://git.ecdf.ed.ac.uk/nkokciya/explainable-argumentation/.

algorithm that generates an AF from a set of schemes to establish the set of acceptable arguments and attacks and provided soundness and completeness proof sketches. We also introduced another algorithm for generating explanations, and illustrated our approach through an example. We showed that further explanations can be generated by extending the acceptable set of arguments with the acceptable attacks. Intuitively, this enables the explainability of both accepted and defeated arguments through the instantiation of argument schemes and attack schemes respectively. We shared a prototype implementation to demonstrate how our approach works in practice. In this work, the initialisation of arguments and attacks is performed according to the information available in the knowledge base. In this paper, the description of schemes or guideline rules is static; however, such information can be automatically learned from data.

There are two important steps to achieve explainability by design. First, we need a formal model that captures the essential components of a decision, and we propose the use of argument and attack schemes in this paper. Second, we need methods to deliver explanations for end-users. In this paper, we propose a simple algorithm to generate textual explanations based on explanation templates. However, machine learning techniques could be used to construct explanations in a dynamic way, something which is out of the scope of this paper. In future work, we will extend the explainability definitions to cover cases such as how an attack affects the status of an argument in an AF. We are planning to develop user interfaces where we will show graphs and explanations together, similar to [28]. Moreover, we will evaluate the quality of generated explanations by conducting user studies. Finally, we will extend our theoretical results to fully explain the translation of existing argumentation frameworks into our proposed approach.

Acknowledgements. This work was supported by the UK Engineering & Physical Sciences Research Council (EPSRC) under grant #EP/P010105/1.

References

1. Atkinson, K., Bench-Capon, T.: Practical reasoning as presumptive argumentation using action based alternating transition systems. Artif. Intell. **171**(10–15), 855–874 (2007)
2. Atkinson, K., Bench-Capon, T., Modgil, S.: Argumentation for decision support. In: Bressan, S., Küng, J., Wagner, R. (eds.) DEXA 2006. LNCS, vol. 4080, pp. 822–831. Springer, Heidelberg (2006). https://doi.org/10.1007/11827405_80
3. Baroni, P., Caminada, M., Giacomin, M.: An introduction to argumentation semantics. Knowl. Eng. Rev. **26**(4), 365–410 (2011)
4. Dung, P.M.: On the acceptability of arguments and its fundamental role in nonmonotonic reasoning, logic programming and n-person games. Artif. Intell. **77**(2), 321–358 (1995)
5. Egly, U., Gaggl, S.A., Woltran, S.: ASPARTIX: implementing argumentation frameworks using answer-set programming. In: Garcia de la Banda, M., Pontelli, E. (eds.) ICLP 2008. LNCS, vol. 5366, pp. 734–738. Springer, Heidelberg (2008). https://doi.org/10.1007/978-3-540-89982-2_67

6. European Parliament and Council of the European Union: General Data Protection Regulation (GDPR) (2016). https://gdpr-info.eu. Accessed 12 Feb 2020

7. Fan, X., Toni, F.: On explanations for non-acceptable arguments. In: Black, E., Modgil, S., Oren, N. (eds.) TAFA 2015. LNCS (LNAI), vol. 9524, pp. 112–127. Springer, Cham (2015). https://doi.org/10.1007/978-3-319-28460-6_7

8. Fox, J., Glasspool, D., Grecu, D., Modgil, S., South, M., Patkar, V.: Argumentation-based inference and decision making-a medical perspective. IEEE Intell. Syst. **22**(6), 34–41 (2007)

9. Glasspool, D., Fox, J., Oettinger, A., Smith-Spark, J.: Argumentation in decision support for medical care planning for patients and clinicians. In: AAAI Spring Symposium: Argumentation for Consumers of Healthcare, pp. 58–63 (2006)

10. Glasspool, D., Oettinger, A., Smith-Spark, J., Castillo, F., Monaghan, V., Fox, J., et al.: Supporting medical planning by mitigating cognitive load. Methods Inf. Med. **46**(6), 636–640 (2007)

11. Gordon, T.F., Walton, D.: Legal reasoning with argumentation schemes. In: Proceedings of the 12th International Conference on Artificial Intelligence and Law, pp. 137–146. ACM (2009)

12. Gordon, T.F., Walton, D.: Formalizing balancing arguments. In: Proceedings of the Conference on Computational Models of Argument, pp. 327–338 (2016)

13. Grando, M.A., Moss, L., Sleeman, D., Kinsella, J.: Argumentation-logic for creating and explaining medical hypotheses. Artif. Intell. Med. **58**(1), 1–13 (2013)

14. Guidotti, R., Monreale, A., Ruggieri, S., Turini, F., Giannotti, F., Pedreschi, D.: A survey of methods for explaining black box models. ACM Comput. Surv. **51**(5), 1–42 (2019)

15. Kakas, A.C., Moraitis, P., Spanoudakis, N.I.: Gorgias: applying argumentation. Argument Comput. **10**(1), 55–81 (2019)

16. Kökciyan, N., et al.: A collaborative decision support tool for managing chronic conditions. In: MEDINFO 2019: Health and Wellbeing e-Networks for All, vol. 264, pp. 644–648 (2019)

17. Kökciyan, N., et al.: Towards an argumentation system for supporting patients in self-managing their chronic conditions. In: AAAI Joint Workshop on Health Intelligence (2018)

18. Kökciyan, N., Yaglikci, N., Yolum, P.: An argumentation approach for resolving privacy disputes in online social networks. ACM Trans. Internet Technol. **17**(3), 27:1–27:22 (2017)

19. Kökciyan, N., Yolum, P.: Context-based reasoning on privacy in internet of things. In: Proceedings of the Twenty-Sixth International Joint Conference on Artificial Intelligence, pp. 4738–4744 (2017)

20. Miller, T.: Explanation in artificial intelligence: insights from the social sciences. Artif. Intell. **267**, 1–38 (2019)

21. Modgil, S., Bench-Capon, T.: Metalevel argumentation. J. Logic Comput. **21**(6), 959–1003 (2011)

22. Modgil, S., Prakken, H.: A general account of argumentation with preferences. Artif. Intell. **195**, 361–397 (2013)

23. NICE: Hypertension in adults: diagnosis and management (2016). https://www.nice.org.uk/guidance/cg127. Accessed 12 Feb 2020

24. Prakken, H., Wyner, A., Bench-Capon, T., Atkinson, K.: A formalization of argumentation schemes for legal case-based reasoning in ASPIC+. J. Logic Comput. **25**(5), 1141–1166 (2013)

25. Rago, A., Cocarascu, O., Toni, F.: Argumentation-based recommendations: fantastic explanations and how to find them. In: Proceedings of the 27th International Joint Conference on Artificial Intelligence, pp. 1949–1955. AAAI Press (2018)
26. Rahwan, I., Simari, G.R.: Argumentation in Artificial Intelligence. Springer, Boston (2009). https://doi.org/10.1007/978-0-387-98197-0
27. Sassoon, I., Kökciyan, N., Sklar, E., Parsons, S.: Explainable argumentation for wellness consultation. In: Calvaresi, D., Najjar, A., Schumacher, M., Främling, K. (eds.) EXTRAAMAS 2019. LNCS (LNAI), vol. 11763, pp. 186–202. Springer, Cham (2019). https://doi.org/10.1007/978-3-030-30391-4_11
28. Sklar, E., Parsons, S., Li, Z., Salvit, J., Wall, H., Mangels, J.: Evaluation of a trust-modulated argumentation-based interactive decision-making tool. J. Auton. Multi Agent Syst. 30(1), 136–173 (2016)
29. Tolchinsky, P., Cortes, U., Modgil, S., Caballero, F., Lopez-Navidad, A.: Increasing human-organ transplant availability: argumentation-based agent deliberation. IEEE Intell. Syst. 21(6), 30–37 (2006)
30. Walton, D., Reed, C., Macagno, F.: Argumentation Schemes. Cambridge University Press, New York (2008)
31. Zamborlini, V., et al.: Analyzing interactions on combining multiple clinical guidelines. Artif. Intell. Med. 81, 78–93 (2017)
32. Zeng, Z., Fan, X., Miao, C., Leung, C., Jih, C.J., Soon, O.Y.: Context-based and explainable decision making with argumentation. In: Proceedings of the 17th International Conference on Autonomous Agents and MultiAgent Systems, pp. 1114–1122 (2018)

Distributed Multi-issue Multi-lateral Negotiation Using a Divide and Rule Approach

Ndeye Arame Diago[1($\boxtimes$)] ![ORCID], Samir Aknine[2], Sarvapali Ramchurn[3],
and El hadji Ibrahima Diago[2]

[1] CY Cergy Paris University, Cergy, France
aramesdiago@yahoo.fr
[2] Université de Lyon1, Lyon, France
samir.aknine@univ-lyon1.fr, elibrahimadiago@gmail.com
[3] University of Southampton, Southampton, UK
sdr1@soton.ac.uk

Abstract. In this paper, we consider the problem of multi-issue multi-lateral negotiation. We assume that each agent may be interested only in a subset of issues at stake. They nevertheless have to make a collective choice that addresses all issues. We propose a heuristics-based negotiation model where the agents'reasoning mechanisms may be very complex as a result of multiple issues being negotiated. Given this complexity, we propose a distributed negotiation mechanism drawn on divide and rule. The proposed protocol consists of two iterative steps: the partitioning of the agents into groups and the negotiation step where the agents in each group interact without a central controller (no mediator). Our negotiation protocol converges and leads to efficient outcomes, as demonstrated by our empirical results.

Keywords: Collective decision-making · Negotiation · Hierarchical clustering

1 Introduction

Negotiation complexity significantly grows when self-interested agents must make a choice involving several issues and when each agent may be interested only in a subset of the issues at stake. Previous studies [1,3–5] propose multi-lateral negotiation protocols, but they typically rely on a mediator that facilitates the negotiation by suggesting contracts or by preventing fraud. Those solutions are centralised and suffer from a single point of failure. Additionally, designing a mediator with such skill may be computationally prohibitive. In the alternating affers protocol [2], the agents negotiate without mediator they sequentially take a turn. The first agent submits an offer, the next evaluates it and makes a decision by accepting, counter-offering or walking. However, in a context where agents may have (non) overlapping subsets of issues they are interested in, each agent makes offers which concern its issues of interest and it could happen that the agent who's turn it is to evaluate an offer may have to evaluate issues it is not interested in. Thus, this may affect the negotiation convergence and the agents' order turn-taking has a major influence on the negotiation outcome. Our solution aims to

ⓒ Springer Nature Switzerland AG 2020
N. Bassiliades et al. (Eds.): EUMAS 2020/AT 2020, LNAI 12520, pp. 338–350, 2020.
https://doi.org/10.1007/978-3-030-66412-1_21

overcome these limitations by structuring the process in terms of the multi-agent organisation and agents' tactics to make offers [6]. In decentralized negotiation settings of the sort we study, agent communication and reasoning may be prohibitively complex. We relax this complexity via careful design of organizational aspects of the multi-agent system, as organisational relationships may have a significant effect on complexity, flexibility and reactivity, and impose computation and communication overheads [7,8].

We propose a novel negotiation model based on a multi-step approach that fully distributes the negotiation and facilitates the search for agreements. The underlying approach is based on the "divide and rule" approach. It consists of two iterative steps: Firstly, we partition agents into groups based on their overlapping subsets of issues (not the values of the issues) and this is done in a centralized way. We search through this decomposition to gather the agents which share the maximum number of issues. In this way, they can construct partial solutions by focusing on their common issues. Each agent can evaluate an offer from its group's member. So we explicitly decompose the agents into groups and implicitly the issues, in contrast to existing works which focus only on decomposing the issues into groups [1,9]. Secondly, after the partitioning, agents in each group negotiate in a fully decentralized way (with no mediator) to find partial solutions over their overlapping issues. The motivation of our approach is to limit the scope of the agents' interactions and hence to reduce agent reasoning complexity. The agents progressively build a solution by merging their solutions throughout their interactions and form alliances.

2   Negotiation Framework

We focus on self-interested agents that negotiate over multiple issues[1]. To illustrate the problem at hand, we consider a scenario where a set of households decide to join a bundled offer to reduce their energy costs. So they must agree upon the energy contract, they will subscribe for. Issues for an energy contract could be energy type, energy provider, contract duration, tariff type, conditions for retracting, and so on. Each of these issues is effectively an attribute of the collective contract. The energy consumers may wish to focus only on a subset of the issues above, depending on their consumption profiles and their needs and preferences.

Let $\mathcal{A} = \{a_1, ..., a_n\}$ be the set of agents and E the set of issues at stake. Each agent a_i chooses the attributes it wants to negotiate; we denote these by E_i. Let D_e^i be a subset of values for e which are acceptable for a_i. Each agent a_i assigns a weight $w_e^i \in]0, 1]$ to each attribute $e \in E_i$ which represents its importance in the negotiation. The value of each attribute's weight is defined such that $\sum_{e \in E_i} w_e^i = 1$.

An agent assigns a score to a value of an attribute according to its evaluation criteria. For example, a household may evaluate an energy provider according to its reliability and its service levels. Before the negotiation, a_i sets for each attribute $e \in E_i$ a range of acceptable score values denoted by $[minV_e^i, maxV_e^i]$. So D_e^i matches to the set of values for e such that the score values belong to this interval. $minV_e^i$, $maxV_e^i$ are,

---

[1] Here, the negotiated issues match the attributes of the solution. Thus we may use these concepts interchangeably.

respectively, the minimal and maximal expected scores agent wants to obtain for e during the negotiation. Thus, a_i could offer or accept over time every value of attribute e whose the score is between $[minV_e^i, maxV_e^i]$.

EXAMPLE 1. *We consider a set of households which negotiate to decide upon the energy provider (attribute e). Let $\{p_1, p_2, p_3, p_4, p_5\}$ be the set of energy providers and $(0.9, 0.7, 0.8, 0.3, 0.5)$ be, respectively, the scores that a_i assigns to each energy provider. For example, an agent a_i aims to contract with a provider whose the score value is between $minV_e^i = 0.5$ and $maxV_e^i = 0.9$. Its $D_e^i = \{p_1, p_2, p_3, p_5\}$. Thus, the value that a_i offers at each time depends on the score it wants to get for this attribute at this time. The first value a_i proposes when the negotiation starts is $p1$ and the last value (reservation value) a_i proposes when the deadline is almost reached is p_5.*

At the beginning of the negotiation process, each agent forms a singleton alliance and defines for each attribute $e \in E_i$ a negotiation tactic [6]. A negotiation tactic is a decision function which allows to determine the values of an attribute e to be offered when negotiation progresses. This value can be computed by considering multiple criteria such as time and resource [6]. Here, we focus on a time-dependent tactic. It consists of deciding for each attribute $e \in E_i$ an acceptable value in D_e^i to be offered according to the remaining negotiation time.

3   Negotiation Protocol

Our solution approach draws on hierarchical agglomerative clustering [10] and allows the agents to progressively build an agreement while limiting their reasoning complexity. The proposed protocol is a multi-step process. At each round, it clusters pairs of alliances. Pairing is based on similarity among the alliances over their issues. Specifically, alliances whose subsets of issues of interest overlap are paired in order to allow them to progress the negotiation. Agents in each cluster negotiate in order to build a solution about their common attributes. They form a new alliance when they reach an agreement for each negotiated attribute. The protocol builds incrementally, over multiple steps, the grand alliance (including all or the majority of the agents) that supports a proposal that addresses all issues, i.e complete proposal (Fig. 1). The negotiation terminates with an agreement or a disagreement over the set of issues at stake. In summary, the proposed protocol involves two key steps that are executed iteratively: clustering phase and negotiation phase.

3.1   Clustering Phase

This phase consists of clustering pairs of alliances. The partitioning is done by the system based on the subsets of issues from the agents. We define similarity functions over overlapping issues which are used to identify candidates for clustering. Each alliance is characterised by the number of agents and the number of attributes it holds. We present two similarity functions named Sim_L and Sim_{L_+}.

- Sim_L is based on a simple Jaccard index, named Sim_L. Let L_x, L_y be two alliances, E_{L_x}, E_{L_y} represent, respectively, their sets of attributes they hold. The similarity

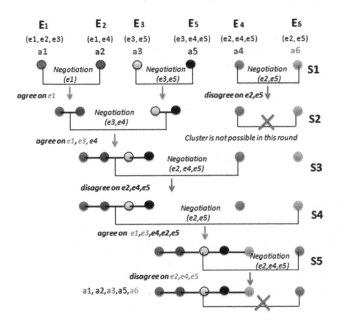

Fig. 1. 6 agents a_1 to a_6 negotiate over the issues e_1 to e_5. s_1 to s_5 are the different rounds.

function between alliances is defined as follows:

$$Sim_L = J(E_{L_x}, E_{L_y}) = \frac{E_{L_x} \cap E_{L_y}}{E_{L_x} \cup E_{L_y}}.$$

- Sim_{L_+} takes into account additional criteria, e.g.., the fact that each alliance aims to get the maximum number of agents via an offer that addresses a maximal number of attributes. We define a gain function $gain$ which gives a real value representing the gain obtained by cluster's alliances when they merge.

$$Sim_{L_+} = Sim_L + gain \quad gain(L_x, L_y) = \frac{|E_{L_x} \cup E_{L_y}|}{k} \times \frac{|L_x \cup L_y|}{n}$$

n, k represent, respectively, the number of agents in the system and the number of all attributes at stake.

Alliances are clustered according to the following rules:

- R_1: only the alliances that have overlapping attributes are clustered.
- R_2: when an alliance does not find another with which it forms a cluster, it will not participate in the negotiation at this round. But at the next round, it will be considered to generate new clusters.

These rules facilitate efficient negotiation and help limit the negotiation time.

EXAMPLE 2. *Consider the agents in Fig. 1. Tables in Fig. 2 show, respectively, the set of attributes chosen by each agent (Table 1) and their similarity matrix computed according to Sim_L (Table 2) and Sim_{L+} (Table 3). These agents form clusters $g_1 = \{a_4, a_6\}, g_2 = \{a_3, a_5\}, g_3 = \{a_1, a_2\}$.*

Agent	E_i
a_1	e_1, e_2, e_3
a_2	e_1, e_4
a_3	e_3, e_5
a_4	e_2, e_4, e_5
a_5	e_3, e_4, e_5
a_6	e_2, e_5

Table 1

	a_1	a_2	a_3	a_4	a_5	a_6
a_1		0,25	0,25	0,2	0,2	0,25
a_2			0	0,25	0,25	0
a_3				0,25	0,67	0,33
a_4					0,5	0,67
a_5						0,25
a_6						

Table 2

	a_1	a_2	a_3	a_4	a_5	a_6
a_1		0,52	0,52	0,53	0,53	0,52
a_2			0.27	0,52	0,52	0,27
a_3				0,52	0,87	0,53
a_4					0,77	0,87
a_5						0,52
a_6						

Table 3

Fig. 2. Similarity matrix

3.2   Negotiation Phase

We denote by $S = \{S_1, ..., S_Q\}$ the set of negotiation rounds. At each S_q, alliances are paired into several clusters in which negotiations take place simultaneously. We denote by $G_{s_q} = \{g_x\}$ the set of clusters at the round S_q. Agents in each cluster g_x negotiate to reach a partial agreement over their common issues named E_{g_x}. To make more flexible the negotiation and to facilitate the research of agreements, the proposed protocol allows the agents to have more flexibility about the offers they submit.

Offer Types: An attribute may be negotiated in a cluster holding either all agents or a part of the agents which are interested in this attribute. Thus, for these both cases, we distinguish two offer types. In each cluster, the set of attributes E_{g_x} is divided into two subsets $E_{g_x}^f$, $E_{g_x}^d$ which represent, respectively, the attributes for which all of the agents which are interested in this attribute belong to this cluster and the attributes for which a part of these agents belong to this cluster.

- When an attribute is negotiated in a cluster which holds all agents which are interested in this attribute, these latter must find a final solution. This is because this attribute will not be negotiated in future rounds when an agreement is found. We denote by $\mathcal{O}^f$ a *fixed offer* which consists of assigning a single value to each attribute in $E_{g_x}^f$.
- When an attribute is negotiated in a cluster which holds a part of the agents which are interested in this attribute, these latter must find a partial solution since this attribute interests other agents outside this cluster. We denote by $\mathcal{O}^d$ a *partial offer* which consists of assigning a range of values over the attributes in $E_{g_x}^d$.

The range of values of attributes supported by different alliances may overlap and this may facilitate agreements among the alliances.

The decomposition of E_{g_x} into $E_{g_x}^f$ and $E_{g_x}^d$ may be performed by every agent in the cluster since the subset of issues for each agent is a public information. Each agent a_i knows the set of agents whose subset of issues overlap with theirs. In a cluster, for each attribute in E_{g_x} an agent may verify if all of the agents with which it shares this attribute are present in the cluster. If so, then there exists no agent outside the cluster which is interested in this attribute. Otherwise, this attribute is susceptible to be negotiated outside the cluster.

Making an Offer: Alliances in a cluster g_x exchange offers in a round-robin way. They make offers about the attributes in E_{g_x}. For each attribute e, each alliance must compute either a point value or a range of values to be proposed. For the example in Fig. 1, let $L_{1,2}, L_{3,5}$ be the alliances formed, respectively, by $\{a_1, a_2\}$ and $\{a_3, a_5\}$ during the round S_1. $E_{L_{1,2}} = \{e_1, e_2, e_3, e_4\}$ $E_{L_{3,5}} = \{e_3, e_4, e_5\}$. $L_{1,2}, L_{3,5}$ are clustered during the round S_2 and they negotiate over their common attributes $E_{L_{1,2}} \cap E_{L_{3,5}} = \{e_4, e_5\}$. Before the negotiation in the round S_2 : alliance $\{a_1, a_2\}$ has already agreed on a final solution (fixed value) for e_1 but $\{e_2, e_3, e_4\}$ have not been negotiated in the previous round. Alliance $\{a_3, a_5\}$ has already agreed on partial solutions for $\{e_3, e_5\}$ and the agents have defined a common negotiation tactic for these attributes. Attribute e_4 has not been negotiated in the previous round.

- *When an alliance holds an attribute not negotiated, this attribute interests only one agent in this alliance. This is because a cluster holds two alliances which become one alliance when they agree on all of their common attributes.*

When an alliance submits an offer in a cluster g_x:

- for each attribute $e \in E_{g_x}$ already negotiated, the value or range of values to be offered is computed by using the common negotiation tactic they defined.
- for each attribute $e \in E_{g_x}$ not negotiated, the value or range of values is proposed by the agent which holds this attribute. It uses its own negotiation tactic.

Decision-Making: Alliances interact between them by using speech acts: *Propose, Accept and Refuse.* Each a_i uses its utility function u_i to evaluate an offer and to make a decision. When an alliance receives an offer, each agent in this alliance evaluates it.

Accepting an Offer: An alliance L_k accepts an offer $O_{L_r, t}$ made by an alliance L_r at time t, if every agent in L_k accepts this offer. An agent accepts an offer if its utility is superior or equal to the utility of its alliance's offer at time $t + 1$, $u_i(O_{L_k, t+1}) \leq u_i(O_{L_r, t})$ otherwise the offer is refused.

Merging Alliances: When in a cluster, the pairs of alliances agree on an offer they merge and become a new alliance formed by the agents of this cluster. For each attribute $e \in E_{g_x}^d$ whose range of values has been negotiated, they define a common negotiation tactic they use in the next round. For each attribute $e \in E_{g_x}^f$, a final solution has been found and it will not be negotiated in the next round.

4   Negotiation Tactics

In the beginning, each agent tries to reach a maximum score value for each attribute it negotiates. The proposed protocol allows the agents to make concessions. This consists of reducing its maximal expected score values over time in order to facilitate the search of agreements.

A negotiation tactic defined by an agent a_i for an attribute e is a function $V_e^i(t)$ which determines at time t the expected score value a_i wants to get at this time.

$$V_e^i(t) = minV_e^i + (1-\alpha_e^i(t)) \times [maxV_e^i - minV_e^i].$$

$\alpha_e^i(t)$ is a time-dependent function. [6] describes a range of time-dependent functions which can be defined by varying the strategies to compute $\alpha_e^i(t)$.

$\alpha_e^i(t)$ is defined such that:

$$0 \le \alpha_e^i(t) \le 1, \quad \alpha_e^i(0) = k_e^i, \quad \alpha_e^i(t_{max}^i) = 1$$

t_{max}^i is the deadline at which the reservation value is proposed, d_l is the negotiation deadline. $0 \le t \le t_{max}^i \le d_l$.

Each a_i chooses a constant $k_e^i \in [0,1]$ for each of its attributes. This constant k_e^i determines the first score value the agent wants to get and hence the first value of the attribute e it will propose or accept. $\alpha_e^i(t)$ may be a polynomial or exponential function parameterized by a value $\beta_e^i \in \mathcal{R}^+$ which determines the convexity degree of V_e^i curve. Polynomial and exponential functions are significantly different in the way they model concessions according to the value of β_e^i [6]. As part of this paper, we work on a range of families of functions with arbitrary values for $\beta_e^i \in [0,50]$. This covers different ways to concede, showing significant differences.

- The case of $\beta_e^i < 1$ is denoted the *Boulware tactic*. It maintains the initially offered value until the time is almost exhausted, where it concedes by proposing the reservation value.
- The case of $\beta_e^i > 1$ is denoted *Conceder tactic*, in which case the agent will offer very quickly its reservation value.

We present below polynomial and exponential functions we consider.

$$\alpha_e^i(t) = k_e^i + (1 - k_e^i)(\frac{min(t, t_{max}^i)}{t_{max}^i})^{\frac{1}{\beta_e^i}}$$

$$\alpha_e^i(t) = e^{(1-\frac{min(t,t_{max}^i)}{t_{max}^i})^{\beta_e^i} \ln k_e^i}$$

In our framework, we propose some methods to compute the β_e^i parameter according to the weight of attribute e. Intuitively, a higher weight is associated with lower agent willingness to compromise its initial value; a lower weight indicates the opposite. For each of its issues of interest, an agent holds a negotiation tactic according to the weight it assigns to that issue.

4.1 Methods to Compute β_e^i

Let β_{min}, β_{max} the domain of β_e^i. Here, we set $\beta_{min} = 0, \beta_{max} = 50$.

We present below some ways to compute β_e^i according to the weight of the attribute w_e^i:

- Method A: $\beta_e^i = \beta_{min} + (\beta_{max} - \beta_{min}) \times (1 - w_e^i), \quad 0 < w_e^i \le 1$

Agent	Methods	w_e^i	k_e^i	k^i	β_e^{im}	β_e^{iM}	$minV_e^i$	$maxV_e^i$	V_e^{im} and V_e^{iM}
a_1	A and A'	0.9	0.001	0.5	0.51	22.25	0.3	1	see Fig.3
a_2	B and B'	0.9	0.001	0.5	0.29	0.5	0.3	1	see Fig.3
a_3	A and A'	0.9	0.5	0.5	5.01	27.5	0.3	0.65	see Fig.4
a_4	B and B'	0.9	0.5	0.5	0.2	0.6	0.3	0.65	see Fig.4

Fig. 3. agents a_1, a_2, a_3, a_4 negotiate over an attribute e. They assign a same weight equal to 0.9 to e but they use different methods and parameters (k_e^i, k^i) to define their negotiation tactic. This table presents the parameters for each agent.

- Method B: $\beta_e^i = \begin{cases} 1 + (\beta_{max} - 1) \times (1 - 2w_e^i), & 0 < w_e^i \le 0.5 \\ 1 + (1 - \beta_{min}) \times (1 - 2w_e^i), & 0.5 \le w_e^i \le 1 \end{cases}$

The difference between strategies A and B is such that in B the range of weight $[0, 1]$ is split into two ranges $[0, 0.5]$, $[0.5, 1]$ and it assigns them, respectively, a family of tactics with $\beta_e^i > 1$ and family of tactics with $\beta_e^i < 1$. This means that the agent assigns a *Boulware tactic* [14] to the attributes whose the weight is in $[0.5, 1]$ and a *Conceder* [15] to the attributes whose the weight is in $[0, 0.5]$.

4.2 Methods to Compute a Range of Values for an Attribute

Making a *partial offer* consists of proposing for each concerned attribute a range of values to be offered. However, a negotiation tactic produces a single value. Hence, for each attribute e, we define a couple of parameters $(\beta_e^{im}, \beta_e^{iM})$ to define a couple of time-depending functions $\alpha_e^{im}(t), \alpha_e^{iM}(t)$ and hence a couple of functions $V_e^{im}(t), V_e^{iM}(t)$ which allow to compute a range of score values a_i wants to get at time t.

$$V_e^{im}(t) = minV_e + (1 - \alpha_e^{im}(t)) \times [maxV_e - minV_e]$$

$$V_e^{iM}(t) = min_{v_e} + (1 - \alpha_e^{iM}(t)) \times [maxV_e - minV_e]$$

. The values of $\beta_e^{im}, \beta_e^{iM}$ for an attribute e are determined according to β_e^i:

- Method A': $\beta_e^{im} = \beta_e^i$, $\beta_e^{iM} = \beta_e^i + k^i(\beta_{max} - \beta_e^i)$, $\beta_{min} \le \beta_e^i \le \beta_{max}$
- Method B': $\beta_e^{im} = \beta_e$, $\beta_e^{iM} = \begin{cases} \beta_e^i + k^i(1 - \beta_e^i)), & \beta_e^i \le 1 \\ \beta_e^i + k^i(\beta_{max} - \beta_e^i), & \beta_e^i \ge 1 \end{cases}$

k^i is a constant in $]0, 1]$ defined by each agent.

$V_e^{im}(t) \ge V_e^{iM}(t)$ because β_e^{iM} leads to concession more quickly than β_e^{im}. Thus the range of values to be offered at time t is the set of attribute's values such that the score values are between V_e^{iM} and $V_e^{im}(t)$ (Fig. 3).

4.3 Common Tactic Defined by an Alliance

When the alliances in g_x agree on an offer and form a new alliance L_k, they establish common negotiation tactics to be used at the next round. This is done by computing the average weight across all agents belonging to this alliance. Specifically, β_e^L is computed according to w_e^L with $w_e^L = \dfrac{\sum\limits_{i \in L} w_e^i}{2}$. The couple of parameters $(\beta_e^{Lm}, \beta_e^{LM})$ to be used when they must negotiate a partial solution for e is determined according to β_e^L.

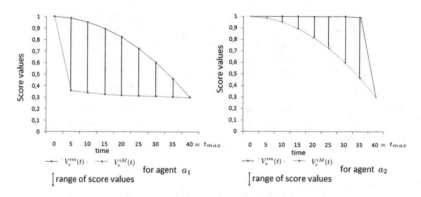

Fig. 4. a_1, a_2 use, respectively, methods A, A' and B, B' to compute, respectively, parameters $\beta_e^1, \beta_e^{1m}, \beta_e^{1M}$ and $\beta_e^2, \beta_e^{2m}, \beta_e^{2M}$ for attribute e. a_1 will concede faster than a_2.

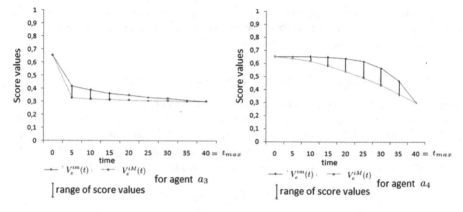

Fig. 5. a_3, a_4 use, respectively, methods A, A' and B, B' to compute, respectively, parameters $\beta_e^1, \beta_e^{1m}, \beta_e^{1M}$ and $\beta_e^2, \beta_e^{2m}, \beta_e^{2M}$ for attribute e. They use, respectively, $k_e^3 = 0.5$ and $k_e^4 = 0.5$. Thus, they first expected score value is equal to 0.63. a_1 will concede faster than a_2.

4.4 Negotiation Outcome

At the end of the negotiation, it could happen that several alliances are formed. These alliances may share attributes of which values may be different. To determine the negotiation outcome, only alliances that share no attributes are merged. There may exist several alternatives to merge alliances. The merging process we propose aims to determine the alliances to be merged in order to get an effective and fair solution. A solution is acceptable when it is supported by more than 50% of the agents (i.e. the majority) and holds all of the attributes at stake. In Fig. 1, the solution supported by $\{a_1, a_2, a_3, a_5, a_6\}$ is acceptable. The merging process may generate several acceptable solutions which are compared in order to determine a unique effective solution.

5 Theoretical Analyse

To analyse the complexity of our negotiation mechanism, we focus on evaluating the number of formed clusters during the negotiation process. Each attribute at stake may interest one or more agents. We denote by n_e the number of agents which negotiate over the attribute e. To reach a final solution for this attribute, all of the n_e agents must meet to exchange in different clusters when the negotiation progresses. Each agent must negotiate with all of the agents with which it shares its attributes. We analysed the number of clusters in which attribute e is negotiated. We consider two situations: the negotiation in both best and worst cases (Fig. 5).

5.1 Negotiation in the Best Case

The best case: whenever the agents in a cluster negotiate, they find an agreement and become one alliance (see Fig. 6).

- In the best case, the number of clusters to be formed to reach a final solution for e is the sum of geometrical sequence's terms with a common ratio $\frac{1}{2}$ and a first term equal to $\lfloor \frac{1}{2} \times n_e \rfloor$.

At round S_1 of the negotiation, the number of formed clusters is: $U_{S_1} = \lfloor \frac{1}{2} \times n_e \rfloor$.

$$U_{S_q} = \lfloor \frac{1}{2^q} \times n_e \rfloor \quad if \quad \frac{1}{2^q} \times n_e - \lfloor \frac{1}{2^q} \times n_e \rfloor \leq 0.5 \quad with \quad 1 \leq q \leq Q$$

$$U_{S_q} = \lceil \frac{1}{2^q} \times n_e \rceil \quad if \quad \frac{1}{2^q} \times n_e - \lfloor \frac{1}{2^q} \times n_e \rfloor > 0.5 \quad with \quad 1 \leq q \leq Q$$

Q is the number of negotiation rounds. U_{S_q} is the number of clusters to be formed at the round S_q. The expression of U_{S_q} allows taking into account the case where the number of alliances to be clustered is an odd number. The total number of clusters to be formed during all of the negotiation rounds is the sum of the Q first terms of the geometrical sequence. Q is such that $U_{S_{Q+1}} = 0$.

5.2 Negotiation in the Worst Case

The worst case: whenever the agents in a cluster negotiate no agreement is found. The cluster will be split (see Fig. 6).

- In the worst case, the number of formed clusters is the number of 2-combinations that can be formed from the n_e. More formally, the number of 2-combinations is equal to the binomial coefficient. $\binom{n_e}{2} = \frac{n_e!}{2!(n_e-2)!}$.

- For each attribute e, the number of clusters where it is negotiated is limited. This number is between $\sum_{q=1}^{Q} U_{S_q}$ and $\frac{n_e!}{2!(n_e-2)!}$.

In our protocol, several attributes may be negotiated in a cluster.

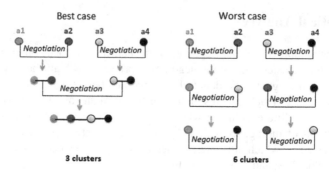

Fig. 6. Example of a negotiation between 4 agents over an attribute e.

- *When all of the attributes interest all of the agents the number of clusters in which these attributes are negotiated is limited. This number is between $\sum_{q=1}^{Q} U_{S_q}$ and $\frac{n_e!}{2!(n_e-2)!}$.*

In each round, the agents in each cluster negotiate over the set of attributes at stake. So the number of clusters to be formed does not depend on the number of attributes but it depends on the number of agents.

- *When each agent is interested in a part of the attributes at stake and their subset of attributes are disjoint no cluster will be formed. This case is not interesting because there is no negotiation.*
- *When each agent is interested in a part of the attributes at stake and the subsets of attributes from these agents overlap, the number of clusters to be formed depends on the degree of the similarity of the agents according to their subsets of attributes.*

6   Experimental Results

We have implemented our model in Java/Jade. We considered a set of agents $\mathcal{A}$ which negotiate over multiple attributes E. Each agent a_i selects randomly its attributes in E and randomly assigns a weight to each one. It computes, for each chosen attribute e, the parameters $\beta_e^i, \beta_e^{im}, \beta_e^{iM}$. Each agent selects randomly the criteria that it uses to generate its offers. We tested our protocol with each of these strategies and we analyse their effect on the results of the negotiation. To evaluate the convergence of our protocol we performed several tests by varying negotiation parameters such as the deadline and the strategies used to compute the negotiation tactics.

We performed several tests by varying the number of agents and the strategies they use to compute negotiation tactics. We tested our protocol with up to 50 agents. We compared our protocol with a negotiation model where all of the agents form only one group to negotiate. We ran the protocol several times and computed the average of the obtained convergence rates for each execution. In these tests, the number of issues at stake was not varied. The graphs in Fig. 7 show the convergence rate obtained for each

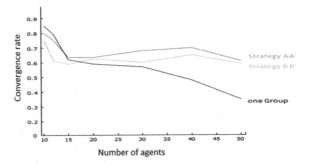

Fig. 7. Comparison between our model and the centralized model (all of the agents form one group) according to agreement rate. In our model the agents use with strategies A,A' and B,B'.

Issues \ Agents	20	40	50
5	0.6%	**0.75%**	**0.6%**
10	0.9%	0.8%	0.76%
15	0.9%	0.75%	0.87%
20	**0.57%**	0.92%	0.89%

Fig. 8. The rate of agreement reached by varying number of agents and issues. Text in grey and bold represent, respectively, the best rate of agreement and the worst rate of agreement. This table shows the rate of agreement reached by agents after three negotiation rounds. Columns 2 to 4 represent, respectively, the results for 20 agents, 40 agents and 50 agents while varying the number of issues from 5 to 20.

pair of strategies A,A' and B,B' used to compute the negotiation tactics. The empirical results in Fig. 4 show that agents concede more quickly when they use A,A' than when B,B' are used. The graph in Fig. 7 proves that when the agents concede, this facilitates the convergence of the negotiation. We observe that our protocol converges faster when strategies A,A' are used. Figure 7 shows also the convergence rate obtained when a centralized model is used (where all of the agents form one group to negotiate) by varying the number of agents. Our protocol allows the agents to reach more agreements when the number of agents grows. The results show that our protocol allows the agents to reach more agreements than the centralized mechanism as the number of agents and issues grow. We also observe that when the ratio between the number of agents and the number issues grows the number of agreements reached is lower (Fig. 8).

7 Conclusion

This paper presented a multi-lateral negotiation model over multiple issues. Our approach allows the agents to progressively build a collective solution addressing all of the issues at stake. We present various negotiation tactics that enable the agents to determine the offers to be proposed and to make concessions. In our empirical analysis, we tested the influence of the negotiation tactics on the negotiation outcome. We have additionally evaluated the convergence of the negotiation under various settings and have demonstrated promising convergence rates.

References

1. Fujita, K., Ito, T., Klein, M.: An approach to scalable multi-issue negotiation: decomposing the contract space. Comput. Intell. **30**(1), 30–47 (2014)
2. Aydoğan, R., Festen, D., Hindriks, K.V., Jonker, C.M.: Alternating offers protocols for multilateral negotiation. In: Fujita, K., et al. (eds.) Modern Approaches to Agent-based Complex Automated Negotiation. SCI, vol. 674, pp. 153–167. Springer, Cham (2017). https://doi.org/10.1007/978-3-319-51563-2_10
3. Aydoğan, R., Hindriks, K.V., Jonker, C.M.: Multilateral mediated negotiation protocols with feedback. In: Marsa-Maestre, I., Lopez-Carmona, M.A., Ito, T., Zhang, M., Bai, Q., Fujita, K. (eds.) Novel Insights in Agent-based Complex Automated Negotiation. SCI, vol. 535, pp. 43–59. Springer, Tokyo (2014). https://doi.org/10.1007/978-4-431-54758-7_3
4. Ito, T., Hattori, H., Klein, M.: Multi-issue negotiation protocol for agents: exploring nonlinear utility spaces. In: IJCAI, pp. 1347–1352 (2007)
5. Ito, T., Klein, M., Hattori, H.: A multi-issue negotiation protocol among agents with nonlinear utility functions. Multiagent Grid Syst. **4**(1), 67–83 (2008)
6. Faratin, P., Sierra, C., Jennings, N.R.: Negotiation decision functions for autonomous agents. Robot. Auton. Syst. **24**(3–4), 159–182 (1998)
7. Horling, B., Lesser, V.: A survey of multiagent organizational paradigms. Knowl. Eng. Rev. **19**(4), 281–316 (2004)
8. Schuldt, A., Berndt, J.O., Herzog, O.: The interaction effort in autonomous logistics processes: potential and limitations for cooperation. In: Hülsmann, M., Scholz-Reiter, B., Windt, K. (eds.) Autonomous Cooperation and Control in Logistics, pp. 77–90. Springer, Heidelberg (2011). https://doi.org/10.1007/978-3-642-19469-6_7
9. Meir, R., Polukarov, M., Rosenschein, J.S., Jennings, N.R.: Convergence to equilibria in plurality voting. AAAI **10**, 823–828 (2010)
10. Farinelli, A., Bicego, M., Bistaffa, F., Ramchurn, S.D.: A hierarchical clustering approach to large-scale near-optimal coalition formation with quality guarantees. Eng. Appl. Artif. Intell. **59**, 170–185 (2017)
11. Jennings, N.R., Faratin, P., Lomuscio, A.R., Parsons, S., Wooldridge, M.J., Sierra, C.: Automated negotiation: prospects, methods and challenges. Group Decis. Negot. **10**(2), 199–215 (2001)
12. Thompson, L.L., Fox, C.R.: Negotiation within and between groups in organizations: levels of analysis. Groups at Work: Theory and Research, pp. 221–266 (2001)
13. Sanchez-Anguix, V., Botti, V., Julian, V., Garcıa-Fornes, A.: Analyzing intra-team strategies for agent-based negotiation teams. In: Proceedings of the 10th International Conference on Autonomous Agents and Multiagent Systems, vol. 3, pp. 929–936 (2011)
14. Raiffa, H.: The Art and Science of Negotiation. Harvard University Press, Combridge (1982)
15. Pruitt, D.G.: Negotiation Behavior. Academic Press, New York (1981)
16. Adair, P.: La theorie de la justice de John Rawls: contrat social versus utilitarisme. Rev. Fr. Sci. Politique **41**, 81–96 (1991)

Increasing Negotiation Performance
at the Edge of the Network

Sam Vente[1], Angelika Kimmig[2], Alun Preece[1],
and Federico Cerutti[1,3(✉)]

[1] Cardiff University, Cardiff CF10 3AT, UK
{VenteDA,PreeceAD,CeruttiF}@cardiff.ac.uk
[2] Department of Computer Science, KU Leuven, Leuven, Belgium
angelika.kimmig@kuleuven.be
[3] Department of Information Engineering, University of Brescia, Brescia, Italy
federico.cerutti@unibs.it

Abstract. Automated negotiation has been used in a variety of distributed settings, such as privacy in the Internet of Things (IoT) devices and power distribution in Smart Grids. The most common protocol under which these agents negotiate is the Alternating Offers Protocol (AOP). Under this protocol, agents cannot express any additional information to each other besides a counter offer. This can lead to unnecessarily long negotiations when, for example, negotiations are impossible, risking to waste bandwidth that is a precious resource at the edge of the network. While alternative protocols exist which alleviate this problem, these solutions are too complex for low power devices, such as IoT sensors operating at the edge of the network. To improve this bottleneck, we introduce an extension to AOP called Alternating Constrained Offers Protocol (ACOP), in which agents can also express constraints to each other. This allows agents to both search the possibility space more efficiently and recognise impossible situations sooner. We empirically show that agents using ACOP can significantly reduce the number of messages a negotiation takes, independently of the strategy agents choose. In particular, we show our method significantly reduces the number of messages when an agreement is not possible. Furthermore, when an agreement is possible it reaches this agreement sooner with no negative effect on the utility.

Keywords: Automated negotiation · Multi-agent systems · Constraints

This research was sponsored by the U.S. Army Research Laboratory and the U.K. Ministry of Defence under Agreement Number W911NF-16-3-0001. The views and conclusions contained in this document are those of the authors and should not be interpreted as representing the official policies, either expressed or implied, of the U.S. Army Research Laboratory, the U.S. Government, the U.K. Ministry of Defence or the U.K. Government. The U.S. and U.K. Governments are authorized to reproduce and distribute reprints for Government purposes notwithstanding any copyright notation hereon.

© Springer Nature Switzerland AG 2020
N. Bassiliades et al. (Eds.): EUMAS 2020/AT 2020, LNAI 12520, pp. 351–365, 2020.
https://doi.org/10.1007/978-3-030-66412-1_22

1   Introduction

Autonomous agents, in particular those at the edge of the network—near to the source of the data like single or cooperative sensors—often need to coordinate actions to achieve a shared goal: for instance, they might need to negotiate either access to local data to learn a shared model; or access to a shared resource like bandwidth; or joint actions for complex activities such as patrolling an area against wildfires (cf. Sect. 2).

Automated negotiation can provide a solution, by allowing agents to reach a mutual consensus on what should and what should not be shared. However, the standard method of negotiation under the Alternating Offers Protocol (AOP, Sect. 3) [1] can be resource intensive and in particular bandwidth intensive due to the number of messages that need to be exchanged before an outcome can be determined. This might be particularly wasteful when considering autonomous agents at the edge of the network, which have limited bandwidth resources. At the same time, because such agents are often deployed on low-power devices, they cannot be equipped with extremely complex reasoning capabilities able to learn and predict other agents' behaviour.

In Sect. 4 we present a novel extension of AOP called Alternating Constrained Offers Protocol (ACOP), that provides a suitable trade-off between reasoning capabilities and bandwidth usage, allowing agents to express constraints on any possible solution along with the proposals they generate. This allows agents to search more effectively for proposals that have a higher probability of being accepted by the adversary. To measure the impact of this on the length and outcomes of negotiations, we perform empirical analysis on a dataset of simulated negotiations (Sect. 5). To summarise, in this work we will address the following questions:

Q1. Do negotiations operating under ACOP exchange fewer messages than negotiations operating under AOP in similar scenarios?
Q2. Does adopting ACOP negatively impact the outcome of negotiations when compared to negotiations using AOP?

Results summarised in Sect. 6 provide evidence that negotiations operating under ACOP require substantially fewer messages than negotiations operating under AOP, without negatively affecting the utility of the outcome.

2   Context and Motivating Examples

Automated negotiation [5] is a wide field: while our focus is much narrower, it encompasses a substantial number of application domains such as but not limited to, resource allocation, traffic flow direction, e-commerce, and directing Unmanned Vehicles (UxVs) [13,20,21]. As mentioned before, the most commonly used protocol for automated negotiation, AOP, can require large amounts of messages to be communicated before an outcome can be determined. While more sophisticated methods that alleviate communication bottlenecks by using, for example, fully-fledged constraint satisfaction solvers [6] exist, these can include very complex reasoning that is not appropriate for agents deployed on low-power devices that operate at the edge of a network. Additionally, many of these solutions require a neutral third party to act as a mediator, which is not always possible in distributed or adversarial settings. Below we will explore three examples to illustrate some of these applications.

Firstly, autonomous agents can share the burden of learning a model. Federated Learning is a machine learning setting where the goal is to train a high-quality model with training data distributed over a large number of agents, each possibly with unreliable and relatively slow network connections [12] and with constraints such as limited battery power. For instance, in [17] the authors introduce an incentive mechanism using auction-like strategies to negotiate with bidding in a format similar to [18].

A second domain concerns the negotiation of wireless spectrum allocation [9,18]. For instance, due to the low cost of IP-based cameras, wireless surveillance sensor networks are now able to monitor large areas. These networks thus require frequency channels to be assigned in a clever way: to this end, in [9] the authors propose to use a text mediation protocol [11].

Consider now our third case, that involves a fully distributed and autonomous surveillance system such as using Unmanned Aerial Vehicles (UAVs) to patrol an area at high risk of wildfires. Each UAV is fully autonomous and equipped with processing capability for analysing their sensor streams and detect early signs of wildfire. The uplink to the command control centre is via a slow and unreliable satellite connection. However, each UAV is aware of the existence of other UAVs via low-bandwidth wireless connections. Each UAV has access to commercial-grade GPS. All UAVs are programmed to jointly cover a given area, and have access to high-quality maps of the area which includes detailed level curves. For simplicity, let us assume that the area is divided into sectors, and each UAV announces the sector where it is, and the sector where it intends to proceed.

Each UAV begins its mission randomly choosing a direction, and hence the next sector it will visit. Its main goal is to preserve its own integrity—after all it is worth several hundreds thousands dollars—while collaborating towards the achievement of the shared goal. It is therefore allowed to return to base, even if this will entail that the shared goal will not be achieved. Examples of this include, when its battery cell level is too low, when adverse weather conditions affect the efficiency of the UAV rotors, or when it has been damaged by in-flight collision or some other unpredictable situation. In the case two UAVs announce that they are moving towards the same sector, a negotiation between them needs to take place in order to achieve coverage of the sector, while avoiding unnecessary report duplication.

Let us suppose UAV1 receives an update that UAV2 can visit sector Sierra, the same sector it was also aiming at. It can then send a negotiation offer to UAV2 asking to be responsible for Sierra. UAV2 most likely will at first reply that it should take care of Sierra, while UAV1 can take care of the nearby Tango:

after all, it announced it first, it is already en route, and it needs to protect its own integrity. Let us suppose that UAV1 knows that with its current power level and/or performance of its 18 rotors, it cannot visit sector Tango as it would require a substantial lifting. It would then be useful for it to communicate such a constraint, so to shorten the negotiation phase and proceed towards an agreement (or a certification of a disagreement) in a short time frame. Indeed, knowing of UAV1's constraint, UAV2 can accept to visit Tango, or maybe not, due to other constraints. In the latter case, UAV1 can then quickly proceed to search for other sectors to visit, or, alternatively, to return to base.

This last example illustrates potential uses of being able to communicate constraints to other agents. In the next section we will set up the necessary theory to discuss our proposed solution.

3   Background in Alternating Offers Protocol

Firstly we will give a brief overview of the basic negotiation theory used in this work. Here all negotiations are assumed to be *bilateral*, meaning between only two agents, referred to as A and B respectively. The *negotiation space*, which is denoted Ω, represents the space of allowable proposals. This consists of the product of several sets called *issues*, each containing a finite number of elements called *values*. So, to reiterate, when we write $\Omega = \prod_{i=0}^{N} \Lambda_i$ with $|\Lambda_i| = M_i$ that means that the negotiation consists of N issues consisting of M_i values. In the case that $\forall i, j \in \{1, \ldots, N\} : \Lambda_i = \Lambda_j$ we may also write $\Omega = \Lambda^N$. Each agent is also assumed to have a *utility function* $u_A, u_B : \Omega \to \mathbb{R}$ which each induce a total preorder $\succeq_A$ and $\succeq_B$ on Ω via the following relation

$$\forall \omega, \zeta \in \Omega : \omega \succeq_A \zeta \iff u_A(\omega) \geq u_A(\zeta)$$

and analogous for B, allowing the agents to decide whether they prefer one proposal to another, vice versa or are indifferent towards them. Each agent also has a *reservation value* ρ_A, ρ_B respectively, which is the minimum utility an offer must have to an agent to be acceptable. A utility function u is called *linearly additive* when the following identity holds:

$$\forall \omega \in \Omega : u(\omega) = \sum_{i=1}^{n} w_i e_i(\omega_i) \tag{1}$$

Here $\sum_{i=0}^{N} w_i = 1$ and $\forall i \in \{1, \ldots, N\} : w_i \in [0, 1]$. Here the w_i represents the relative importance of the ith issue. This makes explicit that the assignment of any issue does not influence the utility of any of the other issues.

The way in which the agents communicate is detailed by the *protocol*. This is a technical specification of the modes of communication and what types of communication are allowed. The most commonly used protocol is called the Alternating Offers Protocol (AOP). In this protocol, the agents have only three options: make a proposal, accept the previous proposal or terminate the interaction without coming to an agreement. Here we use ω^t to denote the offer made at time-step t. Note that t is discrete.

Finally, agents explore the negotiation space according to their *strategy*. Two well known examples, known as *zero intelligence* and *concession* [3]. The zero intelligence strategy is also referred to as a *random sampling* strategy. Agents using a random sampling strategy generate offers by simply defining a uniform distribution over the values of each issue, and constructs offers by sampling from those distributions until they find one that is acceptable to them. Agents using a concession strategy might just simply enumerate the offers in the negotiation space in descending order of preference, either until the other accepts or until they are unable to find offers that they find acceptable. We will use these two strategies in our empirical analysis below. Both these strategies are well known in the literature [2,4,7,8,14,16,19]. Zero Intelligence agents are often used as a baseline for benchmarks and concession strategies in various forms are well studied [3]. We therefore use them here as a proof of concept.

4   Our Proposal: Alternating Constrained Offers Protocol

Almost any negotiation is subject to certain constraints. For example, a good faith agent will never be able to agree to sell something they do not have. When constraints are incompatible, this can dramatically increase the length of the negotiation, since under AOP there is no way to communicate boundaries of acceptable offers. In an effort to alleviate this problem, without introducing too much complexity, we propose an extension of AOP called Alternating Constrained Offers Protocol (ACOP). Using this protocol agents have the opportunity to express a constraint to the opponent when they propose a counter offer. This constraint makes evident that any proposal not satisfying this constraint will be rejected apriori.

In this way, agents can express more information to the opponent about which part of the negotiation space would be useful to explore without having to reveal too much information about their utility function. This can even present some strategic options. Cooperative agents could express all their constraints as fast as possible to give the opponent more information to come up with efficient proposals. On the other hand, more conservative agents can express constraints only as they become relevant, which might lead to expose fewer information in the case the negotiation terminates with an agreement before exposing *red lines*. In this work we focus on the use of *atomic constraints*. These are constraints that express which one of single particular issue value assignments is unacceptable. These constraints can either be given to the agent apriori, or they can be deduced by the agent themselves. Especially in the discrete case with linear utility functions, a simple branch and bound search algorithm can be enough to deduce where certain constraints can be created, which we illustrate with the following example.

Example 1. Let A, B both be negotiation agents having the reservation value $\frac{1}{3}$ and linear additive utility functions u_A, u_B respectively, using uniform importance weights. Furthermore, let $\Omega = \Lambda^3$ with $\Lambda = \{v_1, \ldots, v_6\}$. Therefore we have 3 issues, with 6 values each. In this setup we can represent u_A and u_B as matrices which are depicted in Fig. 1, with the rows representing the issues and the columns possible values. For example the offer $\omega = (v_1, v_1, v_1)$ would have 0 utility for A and thus be unacceptable but utility 1 for B and be acceptable. Due to the scale of the potential losses A can deduce using branch and bound that $\omega_2 = v_2$ can never be part of a solution they could accept. Therefore they can record this constraint, and express this to B according to their strategy. An example of a negotiation under ACOP of this scenario can be seen in Fig. 2.

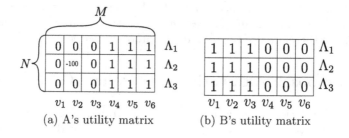

(a) A's utility matrix   (b) B's utility matrix

Fig. 1. Utility matrices for A and B respectively for example 1

This kind of reasoning is simple enough that it could be evaluated in response to new information, such as an opponent ruling out a crucial option during a negotiation. These constraints can help agents find acceptable options more efficiently, but are also useful to help agents terminate faster by letting them realise that a negotiation has no chance of succeeding. For example, when each possible value of a particular issue is ruled out by at least one of the participants, agreement is impossible and the agents can terminate early.

5   Experimental Methodology

Our empirical analysis provides evidence that ACOP improves over AOP in terms of negotiation length and does not negatively impact utility. We simulated a variety of negotiations with randomly generated problems and agents using either a random sampling or concession strategy as defined earlier, both under AOP and ACOP. At the end of a simulation we recorded metrics such as length of the negotiation and the outcome. In this section we will first detail how the problems were generated and how the simulations were run. Then we will discuss the results in more detail in the next section.

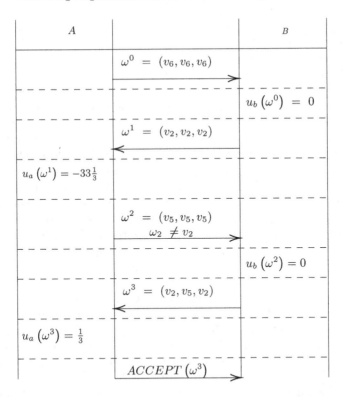

Fig. 2. A schematic representation of an example negotiation under ACOP in the setting set out in Example 1 assuming both agents use uniform weights

5.1 Problem Generation

To run a simulation of a negotiation, four things are required:

1. A negotiation space.
2. The utility functions for the two agents.
3. The reservation value for both agents.
4. The strategy and protocol the agents will use (in this case they are always equal for both agents).

To make the results easier to compare, the negotiation space remained constant, consisting of 5 issues each with 5 values across all negotiations. The utility function and the reservation value determine which part of the negotiation space is acceptable to which of the agents, whereas an agent's strategy determines how they explore the possibility space. We refer to an offer which is acceptable to both participants of a negotiation as a *solution* to that negotiation. Furthermore we call a negotiation *possible* if there exists at least one solution, and otherwise *impossible*. We use *configuration* to refer to a pair of utility functions and a pair of reservation values. A pair of utility functions is referred to as a *scenario*. Note that for any configuration, the number of solutions can be calculated to any outside observer with perfect information, since this is deterministic given the parameters. In total 261, 225 configurations were generated, for each of which 4 negotiations were simulated, each corresponding to one of the strategy and protocol pairs. This means that in total 1, 044, 900 negotiations were simulated and for each of them the length of the negotiation and the utility the agents achieved at the end were recorded.

Initially 300 unique pairs of utility functions were generated by drawing from uniform distributions on either $\{0, 1, \ldots, 100\}$ or $\{0, 1, \ldots, 25\}$. The scenarios were drawn from two possible distributions to ensure that both sufficient impossible and possible configurations would be tested. Whether there are many, if any, mutually agreeable options in a configuration can be quite sensitive to randomness in the utility functions, and the reservation values the agents adopt, especially when the utility functions have a wide range. For each of the 300 base scenarios, several variants were created by adding an equal number of constraints in both utility functions, up to a maximum of 12 per agent. Note that if we were to create a constraint in a value assignment where the opponent has very low utility, the constraint is unlikely to make a difference, since the opponent is not likely to make an offer that violates that constraint, meaning that the additional information doesn't get utilised. To avoid this problem we applied what we call *constraint injection*. This means that if we want to introduce n constraints in the utility function of agent A, we do this by determining the n most favourable assignments for B and overwrite the utilities for those assignments in A's utility function with a value that is low enough to create a constraint. If A has a maximum utility of u_{maxA} then a value lower than $-u_{maxA}$ is enough to ensure a constraint will be created. In this scenario, the theoretical best utility possible is 100. Therefore we used -1000 as our constraint value, to avoid potential boundary issues. An example of a generated scenario sampled from $[0, 100]$ before and after injecting 1 constraint in each utility function can be seen in Fig. 3.

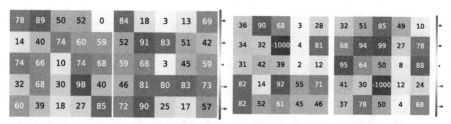

(a) Scenario as originally generated

(b) Scenario after injecting 1 constraint in each utility function. Note that the colour of the constrained cells is not to scale to preserve differentiability of the other colours

Fig. 3. Examples of generated utility matrices before and after injecting 1 constraint

We express reservation values as a percentage of the agent's maximum possible utility: an agent with a reservation value of $\frac{1}{2}$ will only accept offers that have at least half the utility of the best possible outcome. Firstly let $R_{lin} = \{\frac{1}{2} + \frac{i}{20} | i \in \{0, 1, \ldots, 9\}\}$, i.e. 10 points spaced equally apart on $[\frac{1}{2}, 1]$. Furthermore let $R_{log} = \left\{10^{\log_{10}(\frac{1}{2}) - \frac{i \log_{10}(\frac{1}{2})}{10}} | i \in \{0, 1, \ldots, 9\}\right\}$, i.e. 10 points in $[\frac{1}{2}, 1]$ such that they are equally spaced in log-space. Pairs of reservation values were taken from either $(R_{lin})^2$ or $(R_{log})^2$. Again, taking pairs from these two sets was to ensure that enough possible and impossible configurations would be explored.

5.2   Running the Simulations

We introduced the two strategies used in this work—random sampling and concession—and how they work under AOP back in Sect. 3. We will now first explain how the agents adapt these strategies to function under ACOP.

The constraint-aware version of the random sampling agent will adjust the distribution it samples from, when a new constraint is introduced so that any assignment that has been ruled out is given probability 0. Since base random sampling agents construct offers by independently sampling from the possible values for each issue, an agents using ACOP can simply assign probability 0 to the values that were ruled out, and renormalise the distribution.

The concession agent explores the negotiation space using breadth-first search with the utility function as a heuristic. When the constraint aware version of this agent receives a constraint, they adjust their utility function, but overwriting the utility of the value that is being ruled out by a value that is smaller than negative their best utility. This ensures that all offers not satisfying it will fall below the reservation value, ensuring that they will never generate an offer that violates a known constraint.

To summarise, for each of the configurations generated, as discussed in the last section, 4 simulations were run, corresponding to one of the following strategy and protocol pairs:

1. Random sampling using AOP.
2. Concession using AOP.
3. Random sampling using ACOP.
4. Concession using ACOP.

To ensure that the negotiations would terminate, even if the configuration was impossible, a timeout of 400 rounds was introduced, meaning that each agent is allowed to make at most 200 offers. After this number of offers, agents would simply terminate the negotiation without reaching an agreement. In addition, the random sampling agent also terminates if it cannot discover an offer that is acceptable to themselves after 1000 samples, and the concession agent would terminate as soon as it cannot find new offers that have a utility above the reservation value. We chose these values as they were deemed to provide generous upper bounds for agents on the edge of a network. At the end of the negotiation three variables were collected:

1. Whether the negotiation was successful.
2. How many messages were exchanged during the entire negotiation.
3. The utility achieved at the end of the negotiation by both agents.

Here the utility achieved by each of the agents was equal to the utility of the offer that was accepted or 0 if no agreement was reached.

6   Results

6.1   Impact of Adopting ACOP on Negotiation Length

In this section, we study the impact that changing protocols, i.e., using constraints, has on negotiation length, keeping everything else fixed. Figure 4 plots for each strategy the frequency of different negotiation lengths, in a logarithmic scale.

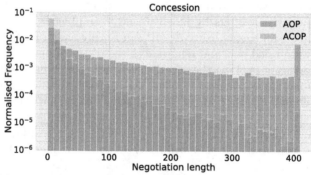

(a) Distribution of the length of the negotiations using concession

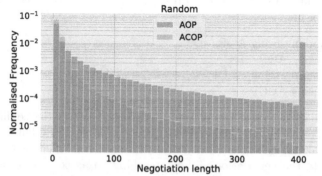

(b) Distribution of the length of the negotiations using random

Fig. 4. A distribution plot of the length of all the negotiations simulated. Note the logarithmic scale.

This shows that ACOP requires substantially fewer messages than AOP on average, evidenced by the fact that much more of the mass of the ACOP bars is concentrated near the left in both graphs. It is worth noting that the peak at the right of the graphs is mostly due to impossible negotiations. This solidifies the idea that no matter the 'difficulty' of a negotiation, ACOP will on average terminate faster than AOP. We will investigate whether this means that ACOP achieves lower outcomes than AOP in the next section.

We can get a more detailed understanding of the impact of using ACOP compared to AOP by looking at the box-plot in Fig. 5. This figure depicts the number of messages saved by using ACOP instead of AOP in an identical configuration. Here we have broken down the data by two categories: The strategy used, and whether the configuration had a solution or not.

For the agents using a random strategy, by far the most gains were made in the impossible configurations. Note that there are some configurations for which ACOP performed worse than AOP, as evidenced by the lower whisker. However, this is due to the randomness of the bidding. In these cases, the agents using AOP were simply unable to find an offer they found acceptable themselves, and thus terminated, while the constraints allowed the agents using ACOP to find proposals that were acceptable to themselves and thus kept negotiating. However we can deduce from the box plot that this is actually a relatively rare case. Even in cases where ACOP did not save a large number of messages, it almost never prolonged the negotiation by much if at all.

For concession agents, ACOP saved more messages when the configurations did have a solution, meaning that ACOP allowed the concession agents to search the negotiation space much more effectively. In the case where the configurations were impossible, ACOP still decreased the number of messages used even if fewer messages were saved. This is due to the fact that a lot of the impossible negotiations still have large sets of offers that are acceptable to just one of the agents that have to be ruled out. When considering all simulations run, we see that ACOP saves an average of 75 messages and with a median of 8 messages saved. Considering that the distribution of negotiation lengths is heavily skewed towards the lower end, we consider this to be a very favourable result. With these observations we conclude that ACOP performs at least as well as AOP and improves upon AOP substantially in the majority of cases when considering the length of a negotiation.

6.2 Impact of Adopting ACOP on Competitive Advantage

Before analysing the outcome of a negotiation in terms of utility two key observations need to be made. First of all, these results are highly dependent on the range of the utility functions. Secondly, the cost that agents incur by ending a negotiation without agreement can have a big impact on the results. The impact of having different non-agreement costs or very different utility functions is outside of the scope of this work. Therefore the agents in this work did not receive an additional penalty for failing to reach an agreement (i.e., a non-agreement was given utility 0 for both agents) and they were all given similar utility functions as discussed previously.

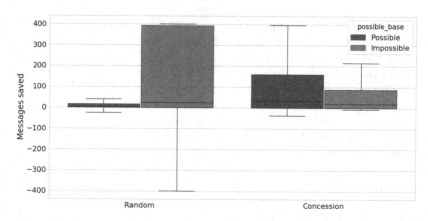

Fig. 5. A box plot detailing the messages saved by using ACOP compared to AOP with identical configurations.

Here we will investigate whether adopting ACOP negatively impacts the outcome of identical negotiations in which agents use AOP. To this end we compared the utility of the negotiations using ACOP to that of the negotiations of the same configuration but using AOP. In Table 1 a per-strategy-breakdown can be seen of what percentage of the negotiations using ACOP had a much better, better, equal, worse or much worse outcome than negotiations of equal configurations using AOP. If ACOP has a higher utility, the configuration was classified as better. If ACOP had a utility of at least 10 higher (10% of the theoretical maximum utility) it was classified as much better, with worse and much worse being defined similarly in the other direction.

In this table, we can see that for the concession agent, the vast majority of negotiations using ACOP (81.68%) had the exact same utility at the end as a negotiation of an identical configuration using AOP. While there were some cases in which ACOP performed slower, this happened in only roughly 3% of all cases, and in only 0.55% was the difference in utility bigger than 10. Conversely, in about 15% of the cases ACOP achieved a higher utility at the end of a negotiation, and in roughly 9% did it gain more than 10 utility above what AOP achieved.

Looking at the percentages for the random agent, we see that while there are more negotiations where ACOP achieves a lower utility than AOP. This was to be expected, since agents will immediately accept any offer from the adversary they find acceptable. Furthermore, we can see that the frequencies are symmetrically distributed, meaning there are roughly equal numbers of configurations that achieved a higher utility using ACOP as there are configurations that achieved a lower utility using ACOP. This pattern can be easily explained by the randomness of the bidding of the agents.

With all of these observations, we conclude that using ACOP does not negatively affect the outcome of the negotiations in any systematic way.

Table 1. Table detailing the percentages of configurations broken down by strategy and how the utility of the outcome of ACOP compared to that of AOP. Configurations for which the difference in utility was greater than 10 would be classified as either much better (if ACOP did better), or much worse (if AOP did better)

Strategy	ACOP compared to AOP	Percentage of total
Concession	Much better	9.06
	Better	5.88
	Equal	81.68
	Worse	2.82
	Much worse	0.55
Random	Much better	3.40
	Better	27.83
	Equal	38.44
	Worse	27.62
	Much worse	2.70

7 Conclusion

In this paper we proposed a novel extension to the Alternating Offers Protocol (AOP) called Alternating Constrained Offers Protocol (ACOP) which allows agents to express constraints to the adversary along with offering counter proposals. These constraints can be given to an agent apriori, or discovered using branch-and-bound algorithms. This protocol allows agents—especially agents deployed on low-power devices at the edge of a network—to terminate negotiations faster without consistently negatively impacting the utility of the outcome, allowing them to save bandwidth without the need to equip them with sophisticated reasoning capabilities. We explored the impact that this extension has on the length of the negotiations as well as on the utility achieved at the end of the negotiation. We empirically showed that this extension substantially reduces the number of messages agents have to exchange during a negotiation. When agreement is possible, using ACOP helps agents to come to an agreement faster, and when agreement is impossible, agents using ACOP terminate much faster than agents using AOP both when agents adopt a probabilistic or a deterministic search method. In addition, we showed that using ACOP has no systematic negative impact on the quality of the outcome in terms of utility when compared to the same strategies using AOP.

While the results of this work were promising, the scenarios and strategies used to produce them were not very complex. Future work will include investigating the performance of ACOP under non-linear utility functions, and with more sophisticated strategies and opponent models, comparing also with other approaches for dealing for instance with fuzzy constraints [15], and with also much larger large, non-linear agreement spaces [10]. Another avenue will be to understand the impact of using soft constraints rather than hard ones.

References

1. Aydoğan, R., Festen, D., Hindriks, K.V., Jonker, C.M.: Alternating offers protocols for multilateral negotiation. In: Fujita, K., et al. (eds.) Modern Approaches to Agent-based Complex Automated Negotiation. SCI, vol. 674, pp. 153–167. Springer, Cham (2017). https://doi.org/10.1007/978-3-319-51563-2_10

2. Azar, A.G., Nazaripouya, H., Khaki, B., Chu, C., Gadh, R., Jacobsen, R.H.: A non-cooperative framework for coordinating a neighborhood of distributed prosumers. IEEE Trans. Ind. Inform. **15**(5), 2523–2534 (2019). https://doi.org/10.1109/TII.2018.2867748

3. Baarslag, T., Hendrikx, M.J.C., Hindriks, K.V., Jonker, C.M.: Learning about the opponent in automated bilateral negotiation: a comprehensive survey of opponent modeling techniques. Auton. Agent. Multi-Agent Syst. **30**(5), 849–898 (2016). https://doi.org/10.1007/s10458-015-9309-1

4. Baarslag, T., Hindriks, K.V.: Accepting optimally in automated negotiation with incomplete information. In: Proceedings of the 2013 International Conference on Autonomous Agents and Multi-Agent Systems, AAMAS 2013, International Foundation for Autonomous Agents and Multiagent Systems, Richland, SC, pp. 715–722 (2013)

5. Fatima, S., Kraus, S., Wooldridge, M.: Principles of Automated Negotiation. Cambridge University Press, New York (2014)

6. Gaciarz, M., Aknine, S., Bhouri, N.: Constraint-based negotiation model for traffic regulation. In: Proceedings of the IEEE/WIC/ACM International Conference on Web Intelligence and Intelligent Agent Technology (WI-IAT 2015), vol. 2, pp. 320–327. IEEE, Singapore (2015). https://doi.org/10.1109/WI-IAT.2015.72

7. Gode, D.K., Sunder, S.: Allocative efficiency of markets with zero-intelligence traders: market as a partial substitute for individual rationality. J. Polit. Econ. **101**(1), 119–137 (1993). https://doi.org/10.1086/261868

8. Hindriks, K., Jonker, C., Tykhonov, D.: Using opponent models for efficient negotiation. In: Proceedings of the 8th International Conference on Autonomous Agents and Multiagent Systems, AAMAS 2009, International Foundation for Autonomous Agents and Multiagent Systems, Richland, SC, vol. 2, pp. 1243–1244 (2009)

9. de la Hoz, E., Gimenez-Guzman, J.M., Marsa-Maestre, I., Orden, D.: Automated negotiation for resource assignment in wireless surveillance sensor networks. Sensors **15**(11), 29547–29568 (2015). https://doi.org/10.3390/s151129547, https://www.ncbi.nlm.nih.gov/pubmed/26610512, 26610512[pmid]

10. Jonge, D., Sierra, C.: NB³: a multilateral negotiation algorithm for large, non-linear agreement spaces with limited time. Auton. Agent. Multi-Agent Syst. **29**(5), 896–942 (2015). https://doi.org/10.1007/s10458-014-9271-3

11. Klein, M., Faratin, P., Sayama, H., Bar-Yam, Y.: Negotiating complex contracts. Group Decis. Negot. **12**(2), 111–125 (2003)

12. Konečný, J., McMahan, H.B., Yu, F.X., Richtarik, P., Suresh, A.T., Bacon, D.: Federated learning: strategies for improving communication efficiency. In: NIPS Workshop on Private Multi-Party Machine Learning (2016). https://arxiv.org/abs/1610.05492

13. Lamparter, S., Becher, S., Fischer, J.G.: An agent-based market platform for smart grids. In: Proceedings of the 9th International Conference on Autonomous Agents and Multiagent Systems: Industry Track, AAMAS 2010, International Foundation for Autonomous Agents and Multiagent Systems, Richland, SC, pp. 1689–1696 (2010)

14. Lopes, F., Coelho, H.: Concession strategies for negotiating bilateral contracts in multi-agent electricity markets. In: Proceedings of the 2012 23rd International Workshop on Database and Expert Systems Applications, pp. 321–325 (2012). https://doi.org/10.1109/DEXA.2012.24

15. Luo, X., Jennings, N.R., Shadbolt, N., Leung, H., Lee, J.H.: A fuzzy constraint based model for bilateral, multi-issue negotiations in semi-competitive environments. Artif. Intell. **148**(1), 53–102 (2003). https://doi.org/10.1016/S0004-3702(03)00041-9

16. Wang, Z., Wang, L.: Intelligent negotiation agent with learning capability for energy trading between building and utility grid. In: IEEE PES Innovative Smart Grid Technologies, pp. 1–6 (2012). https://doi.org/10.1109/ISGT-Asia.2012.6303167

17. Xu, Z., Li, L., Zou, W.: Exploring federated learning on battery-powered devices. In: Proceedings of the ACM Turing Celebration Conference - China, ACM TURC 2019, pp. 6:1–6:6. ACM, New York (2019). https://doi.org/10.1145/3321408.3323080, http://doi.acm.org/10.1145/3321408.3323080

18. Yang, S., Peng, D., Meng, T., Wu, F., Chen, G., Tang, S., Li, Z., Luo, T.: On designing distributed auction mechanisms for wireless spectrum allocation. IEEE Trans. Mob. Comput. **18**(9), 2129–2146 (2019). https://doi.org/10.1109/TMC.2018.2869863

19. Yang, Y., Luo, X.: A multi-demand negotiation model with fuzzy concession strategies. In: Rutkowski, L., Scherer, R., Korytkowski, M., Pedrycz, W., Tadeusiewicz, R., Zurada, J.M. (eds.) Artificial Intelligence and Soft Computing, pp. 689–707. Springer International Publishing, Lecture Notes in Computer Science (2019)

20. Yassine, A., Hossain, M.S., Muhammad, G., Guizani, M.: Double auction mechanisms for dynamic autonomous electric vehicles energy trading. IEEE Trans. Veh. Technol. **68**(8), 7466–7476 (2019). https://doi.org/10.1109/TVT.2019.2920531

21. Zhang, G., Jiang, G.R., Huang, T.Y.: Design of argumentation-based multi-agent negotiation system oriented to E-commerce. In: Proceedings of the International Conference on Internet Technology and Applications, ITAP 2010, pp. 1–6 (2010). https://doi.org/10.1109/ITAPP.2010.5566198

Challenges and Main Results of the Automated Negotiating Agents Competition (ANAC) 2019

Reyhan Aydoğan[1,2](✉), Tim Baarslag[3,4], Katsuhide Fujita[5,9],
Johnathan Mell[6], Jonathan Gratch[6], Dave de Jonge[7], Yasser Mohammad[8,9],
Shinji Nakadai[8,9], Satoshi Morinaga[8,9], Hirotaka Osawa[10], Claus Aranha[10],
and Catholijn M. Jonker[2]

[1] Özyeğin University, Istanbul, Turkey
reyhan.aydogan@ozyegin.edu.tr
[2] Delft University of Technology, Delft, The Netherlands
[3] Centrum Wiskunde & Informatica, Amsterdam, The Netherlands
[4] Utrecht University, Utrecht, The Netherlands
[5] Tokyo University of Agriculture and Technology, Fuchu, Japan
[6] USC Institute for Creative Technologies, Los Angeles, USA
[7] IIIA-CSIC, Bellaterra, Spain
[8] NEC Corporation, Minato City, Japan
[9] National Institute of Advanced Industrial Science and Technology, Tsukuba, Japan
[10] University of Tsukuba, Tsukuba, Japan

Abstract. The Automated Negotiating Agents Competition (ANAC) is a yearly-organized international contest in which participants from all over the world develop intelligent negotiating agents for a variety of negotiation problems. To facilitate the research on agent-based negotiation, the organizers introduce new research challenges every year. ANAC 2019 posed five negotiation challenges: automated negotiation with partial preferences, repeated human-agent negotiation, negotiation in supply-chain management, negotiating in the strategic game of Diplomacy, and in the Werewolf game. This paper introduces the challenges and discusses the main findings and lessons learnt per league.

1 Introduction

Negotiation has become a well-established research field within the area of Artificial Intelligence and multi-agent systems. The research has focused on formalization of negotiation process (i.e., domain and preference representation, and protocols) and the design of intelligent negotiating agents (i.e., bidding strategies, opponent models, and acceptance strategies) in order to automate this complex process. Automated negotiation dates back to the 1980's when e-commerce took flight, see e.g., [29,37]. The field was formalized in the 1990's (see e.g., [34,36,38]). Over the years negotiating agents have been developed for automated negotiation, human-agent negotiation, and negotiation support.

N. Bassiliades et al. (Eds.): EUMAS 2020/AT 2020, LNAI 12520, pp. 366–381, 2020.
https://doi.org/10.1007/978-3-030-66412-1_23

In automated negotiation all negotiation parties are automated agents, while in human-agent negotiation, some of them are human [31]. Negotiation support agents form a team with one or more humans to play together as one negotiation party in any kind of negotiation (automated, human-human, or human-agent) [18].

With the growing number of proposed negotiation agents, the need for comparison and rigorous evaluation of the quality of the negotiating agents increases as well. This led to formal evaluation metrics [12,14,21,23], the open-source negotiation platform GENIUS to enable benchmarking [20], and in 2010 it initiated the annual ANAC (Automated Negotiation Agents Competition) [5].

The competition turned into a mechanism for the field to organize itself as the researchers use the yearly meetings to jointly set the research agenda. Over the years, the negotiation problems studied in the context of ANAC [3] span bilateral [5], non-linear [2], multilateral [11], and repeated [1] negotiations. As an added advantage, by now GENIUS holds a host of agents, negotiation domains and preference profiles.

Since 2017, ANAC has added two new leagues: a Human-Agent league and a league for the game Diplomacy. In the Human-Agent league, which is based on the IAGO framework [24], agents exchange partial offers, preferential information and through emoji's some emotional information with their human opponents, see e.g., [26]. In the game Diplomacy the agents have to negotiate on the basis of heuristics, as there is no explicit utility function available [15]. In 2019, two more leagues were added: the Supply Chain Management league (SCM) [28] and the Werewolf League [30]. The SCM league allows researchers to study negotiation and partner selection in a recurring setting of trade. In the Werewolf game the essence of negotiation studied is that agents need to assess the utility functions of the other players and convince others to play a successful voting strategy. The challenges for the ANAC 2019 competition were as follows (organised per league):

- **Automated Negotiation Main League: preference uncertainty.** Human negotiators do not necessarily know their own utility function explicitly, and there are practical limits on the preference elicitation process. Therefore, the challenge is to design an agent that can do bilateral negotiations receiving only partial qualitative preference information.
- **Human-Agent League: building cooperation.** The challenge is to establish a cooperative relationship with the human participant in repeated negotiations with the same human opponent. Successful agent strategies capture human behavior. While an aggressive strategy in the first negotiation may prove effective, it could have such a backfire effect by the last negotiation that it is not the right choice overall.
- **Diplomacy: beat the basic agent.** Like last year, the challenge was to beat the standard agent provided by the BANDANA framework. No participating agent managed this in 2018.
- **Supply Chain Management: recurrent chain negotiations.** The challenges are to decide on their own utility function, when and with whom to

negotiate and how to negotiate in a supply chain in order to maximize their overall profit.
- **The Werewolf game.** The challenge for the agents is to estimate possible allies and deceivers (estimated utility), to communicate strategy and information to other agents, and to negotiate a voting pattern that is beneficial to one's own team.

This paper consists of sections for each league in which the challenges and main competition results are discussed. The last section presents some of the upcoming challenges.

2   Automated Negotiation Main League

There are still many open challenges for automated negotiation [6,7], such as strategy learning, opponent recognition, domain learning, preference elicitation and reasoning. The Automated Negotiation league in 2019, informally known as the GENIUS league, focused on negotiating agents that receive partial preference information. This challenge is part of the larger research problem of domain learning and preference elicitation. The motivating idea is that when a negotiating agent represents a user in a negotiation, it cannot know exactly what the user wants due to practical limits on the preference elicitation process [4].

For ANAC 2019, the preferences of the agent were given in the form of a ranking of a limited number of possible agreements ω_i; i.e. $\omega_1 \leq \cdots \leq \omega_d$. The rankings were generated randomly from existing negotiation scenarios in which full utility information was available from a standard additive utility function u. Intuitively, the number of rankings d that the agent receives is inversely correlated to the preference uncertainty of the agent. The agent has to negotiate based on these ordinal preference information, and if it manages to reach a certain outcome ω^*, then the score the agent receives for this agreement is based on the original utility function, i.e., $u(\omega^*)$. An overview of this procedure is presented in Fig. 1. In short, the agent receives ordinal information only, but is evaluated based on the underlying cardinal ground-truth.

Table 1 shows the average individual utility and the average product of utilities gained by all participants in a tournament in which each agent negotiated with all other agents five times for each negotiation scenario. When evaluating on individual utility, AgentGG won the competition with an average of 0.76, the agents KakeSoba and SAGA were awarded second and third place. When evaluating on fairness (i.e. the product of the utilities of the negotiated agreements), winkyAgent won the competition with an average utility of 0.56, and agents FSEGA2019 and AgentGP were awarded second and third place respectively.

As intended, the key to win this league is for agents to predict both their own and their opponent's utility accurately from uncertain information. The top agents were able to obtain high individual utilities even under high preference certainty, using a variety of preference estimation techniques. In estimating the preferences, the top ranking agents used techniques such as batch gradient

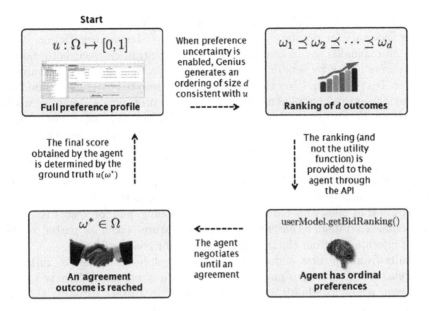

Fig. 1. Uncertainty challenge in ANAC 2019

descent (e.g. `winkyAgent`), genetic algorithms using spearman's rank correlation (e.g. `SAGA`), and statistical frequency modelling (e.g. `AgentGG`).

The performance of the top ranking agents suggests that it is possible to reconstruct enough of the true utility function based on partial information about the ranking of a number of bids. The next question is of course, *how much* partial information is required. Therefore, the ANAC community decided to formulate the next challenge, which incentivizes agent designers to use as little information as possible to still get good performance: next year, the agents initially will receive very sparse preference data, and will be allowed to ask for more preference information against an elicitation cost.

3   Human-Agent League

The human-agent league focuses on the myriad social effects present in mixed human-agent interactions. Indeed, understanding how humans negotiate has been a key question in business and psychological literature for many years—it is a complex social task [19,25,32,33]. But as automated agents are used more frequently in real-life applications (e.g., chatbots), we should design agents that are capable of interacting with humans in social settings. As human-agent negotiation is fundamentally different from agent-agent negotiation, the Human-Agent League (HAL) was added in 2017 to promote research into this promising area.

HAL utilizes the IAGO Negotiation platform, which was proposed and designed by Mell et al. [24]. IAGO provides a front-facing GUI for the human participants. This feature allows subjects to be recruited using online platforms, such as Amazon's Mechanical Turk (MTurk). Additionally, IAGO provides the features necessary for simulating the characteristics of human negotiation. These include an expanded set of channels for communication between both sides of negotiation, such as by sending text, expressing preferences, and transmitting emotions. Text is transmitted through a set of pre-selected utterances, and emotions are transmitted by selecting from a variety of prototypical "emojis" within the interface. Furthermore, IAGO allows "partial offers" (i.e., offers not containing values for all negotiation issues) and implements a flexible, human-inspired protocol: few enforcement mechanisms for incomplete deals, and no explicit turn-taking.

These features of IAGO mean that it provides a platform to address the basic features that intelligent agents require to negotiate with humans. It provides information that allows for human-opponent modeling, and for agents to pursue more complex strategies that require specific features (such as partial offers), and the information from the multiple channels for communication.

Results from the first and second human-agent leagues (see [25,26]) show that while certain strategies may be effective in the short term, there is a trade-off between agent likeability and agent success. To further examine this, the structure of the repeated negotiations were changed.

In this year's competition, three back-to-back negotiations were conducted. Similar to previous competitions, the negotiation involved a 4-issue bargaining task. Each issue could take from 4 to 8 items, e.g., offering 4 to 8 bananas. Each of the three negotiations took up to 7 min, and a BATNA was available for those who could not reach an agreement. Each agent negotiated against at least 25 human participants using Amazon's Mechanical Turk subject pool, and those participants were subject to *attention checks and filtering*. All participants were US-residing, and English-speaking. Per standard practice, incentives were scaled with performance, so participants were encouraged to do well. Data was collected on demographics, performance metrics, and subject-reported likeability measures of the agent. All procedures were approved by University of Southern California's Institutional Review Board, including the informed consent process.

In contrast to previous years, the negotiations were not identical in structure. Instead, while there were integrative opportunities to "grow the pie" within each negotiation, there was a larger, cross-negotiation possibility to find integrative potential between negotiations #1 and #3. This higher performance opportunity is reflected in negotiation #3, where agents generally have more points due to structural differences.

Regardless of this effect, we did find a variety of performance differences across the submitted agents. In particular, we had two standout agents in terms of performance: agents **Dona** and **Draft** (See Fig. 2). The **Draft Agent** was submitted by Bohan Xu, Shadow Pritchard, James Hale, & Sandip Sen from the University of Tulsa, while the **Dona Agent** was submitted by Eden Shalom Erez, Inon Zuckerman, and Galit Haim of Ariel University and The College of Management Academic Studies. These agents took unique approaches to the challenges of negotiation by making agents be guided by the "meta-rules" of negotiation.

Table 1. Results of automated negotiation league

Agent	Individual utility		Nash product	
	♮	Mean	♮	Mean
AgentGG	1	**0.7574**	5	0.5398
AgentGP	10	0.6948	3	0.546
AgentLarry	15	0.5984	11	0.5082
AgentPeraltaV2	18	0.5528	17	0.4012
AuthenticAgent	20	0.3882	20	0.1947
dandikAgent	9	0.6995	13	0.4628
EAgent	14	0.6553	16	0.4286
FSEGA2019	8	0.7002	2	0.5495
GaravelAgent	13	0.6571	15	0.4365
Gravity	17	0.5782	18	0.361
Group1_BOA	11	0.6927	6	0.5392
HardDealer	5	0.7245	9	0.5172
IBasic	21	0.32	21	0.136
KAgent	16	0.5943	14	0.4569
KakeSoba	2	0.7433	7	0.5259
MINF	4	0.728	10	0.5133
SACRA	19	0.4901	19	0.3166
SAGA	3	0.7315	4	0.5423
SolverAgent	6	0.7126	8	0.5257
TheNewDeal	12	0.6863	12	0.4873
winkyAgent	7	0.7093	1	**0.5625**

Dona agent customized the interface to instruct the user to answer questions using the emoji buttons. Draft agent enforced strict protocols for the humans to follow; it required human participants to describe their preferences in a set order. The success of these agents speaks to the importance of setting a clear protocol in negotiations that cannot be manipulated by the agents. Furthermore, we learned that humans are inclined to adhere to changes in protocol made by their automated counterparts.

For the next Human-Agent competition, we have decided to adapt the task beyond the 2019 competition. Firstly, while the novelty of the agents that modified the interface led to some unexpected yet interesting results, we will be returning to a competition in which the interface protocols are set at the beginning of the interaction. The lessons learned from this competition have led to new insights in UI design which have been integrated into the IAGO platform. Secondly, we will be allowing the human users to set their own preferences in the negotiation. This is both more realistic to the real world, and will also ensure that the agent designers have to contend with a set of potential negotiation structures. We hope that this next competition will continue to push the envelope in designing more realistic and useful social agents.

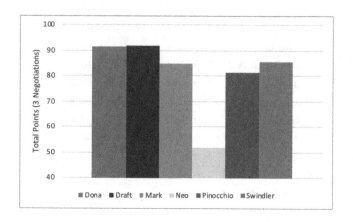

Fig. 2. Total agent score (summed over all negotiations)

4   The Diplomacy League

Diplomacy [9] is a deterministic board game for seven players, with no hidden information. It is designed such that players need to form coalitions and negotiate with each other. The interesting aspect of Diplomacy as a test case for Automated Negotiations is that there is no explicit formula to calculate utility values. Just as in games like Chess or Go, it is simply too complex to calculate such values exactly, so agents have to apply heuristics to estimate the values of their deals. Although Diplomacy has been under attention of the Automated Negotiations community for a long time [8,10,17,22,35], to date few successful negotiating Diplomacy players have been developed.

In the previous two editions of the ANAC Diplomacy League ANAC [15] none of the submitted agents was able to beat the challenge and outperform even a non-negotiating agent. Therefore, we decided to make the challenge slightly easier by making sure that negotiating agents were always assigned to 'Powers' that are known to work well together [15]. Other than this, the setup of the 2019 competition was kept practically identical to the previous years.

Participants had to implement a negotiation algorithm on top of the existing D-Brane agent [17], which by itself does not negotiate. Negotiations took place under the Unstructured Negotiation Protocol [16]. The competition consisted of two rounds. In Round 1, each agent only played against three copies of itself and three non-negotiating instances of D-Brane, while in Round 2, all submitted agents played against each other. In order to *beat the challenge*, an agent had to satisfy two criteria: it would have to outperform the non-negotiating D-Branes in Round 1, as well as beat all opponents in Round 2. In case no agent was able to beat the challenge (as in previous years) the *Backup Rule* would come into effect, which states that the agent that made the most proposals in Round 2 that were eventually accepted by other agents would be declared the winner.

The competition received five submissions. Unfortunately, none of them was able to outperform `D-Brane` in Round 1 (Table 2). This suggests that the agents were not cooperative enough to be able to strike a good deal even when their opponents are identical to themselves. On the plus side, in Round 2 we did see that for the first time in the history of the ANAC Diplomacy league one agent, namely `Oslo_A`, by Liora Zaidner *et al.*, was able to clearly outperform all other agents (Table 3). However, according to the rules of the competition it was `Saitama`, by Ryohei Kawata that was declared to be the winner, by virtue of the Backup Rule (Table 4).

Table 2. Results of round 1. None of the agents outperformed `D-Brane`

Agent	Score	Result
D-Brane	15.15	
Saitama	14.75	FAIL
Oslo_A	14.62	FAIL
DipBrain	14.56	FAIL
Biu3141	14.48	FAIL
BackstabAgent	14.47	FAIL

Table 3. Results of round 2. `Oslo_A` outperforms all other agents, and is the only one that outperforms the non-negotiating `D-Brane`. `Biu3141` could not participate in this round because it was too slow. `GamlBot` and `M@stermind` are submissions from previous years that were added to complete the field.

	Agent	Score
1	**Oslo_A**	6.68 ± 0.31
	D-Brane	5.56 ± 0.27
2	**DipBrain**	5.06 ± 0.24
3	**Saitama**	4.88 ± 0.23
	GamlBot	4.79 ± 0.21
4	**BackstabAgent**	4.20 ± 0.25
	M@sterMind	2.83 ± 0.17

Analyzing the source code of `Oslo_A` we noticed that its bidding strategy was surprisingly simple. At the beginning of each round it simply asks the underlying `D-Brane` module which moves it would make if no agreements are made. Then, for each of these moves, it asks the other players to support those moves. The authors

Table 4. Results according to the Backup Rule. This table displays the number of proposals proposed by each agent in Round 2 that were eventually accepted by the other agents. `Saitama` was declared the winner.

	Agent	Accepted proposals
1	**Saitama**	9091
2	**BackstabAgent**	6585
3	**Oslo_A**	4393
4	**DipBrain**	4373

also intended their agent to react to incoming proposals by either accepting them or making counter proposals, but due to bugs in the code, these components did not work. This also explains why `Oslo_A` failed in Round 1: if all players are copies of `Oslo_A` then no proposal is ever accepted, so no deals are made at all.

From this competition (as well as its predecessors in 2017 and 2018) we learn that it is still very hard to implement successful negotiation algorithms for domains as complex as Diplomacy. So far, no submission has been able to beat the challenge. Specifically, we make the following observations:

1. Most agents never make any proposals for any of the future turns. They only make proposals for the current turn.
2. Many agents do not outperform the non-negotiating `D-Brane`, or even score worse. This means that the deals they make often have a detrimental effect.
3. Many of the agents seem to have bugs in their code.

Regarding the first point, we remark that in Diplomacy it is essential to plan several steps ahead, because it does not often occur that two players can both directly benefit from cooperation. Players should therefore be willing to help another player while only expecting the favor to be returned at a later stage. However, most submissions do not seem to exhibit this behavior. The second point might explain the success of `Oslo_A`. After all, this agent only asked the other agents to support the orders that it was already going to make anyway. Therefore, its agreements can never have any detrimental effect. Furthermore, these observations suggest that Diplomacy is so complex that it requires a long time to design sophisticated agents for the game. This may explain that within the design time given in the ANAC competition, none of the participating teams managed to develop an agent that can beat `D-Brane`.

5 The Werewolf League

Werewolf, also known as *Mafia*, is a communication game where an uninformed majority team (the village) plays against an informed minority team (the werewolves). The goal of the game is to eliminate all players from the opposing team through a voting process: at each turn, the players must agree on one player to eliminate. This takes the shape of a discussion, followed by a vote, and a simple majority eliminates one player from the game.

From an Automated Negotiation point of view, the challenge for an agent in Werewolf is to successfully engage in coalition-building. In other words, the agent must identify other players in the game that share the same utility values as itself, at the same time that it must avoid deceitful agents. This requires the agent to communicate its own utility to the other agents, and engage in discussion to obtain the necessary information.

In the past six years, the AIWolf Project has proposed the Werewolf game as a benchmark for AI research [39] and organized four national competitions on the game. Compared to other AI benchmark games such as Go, Starcraft or Poker, Werewolf is unique in that the communication between agents is the key skill that must be mastered to obtain high levels of play. A successful Werewolf agent must be able to build a model of the other players' beliefs, identify allied players, and exchange this information through communication [13].

The 2019 Automated Negotiating Agents Competition was the first time that the AIWolf Project competition was held for an international audience. The participants were tasked to implement an agent capable of playing the Werewolf game against other automated players. The interaction of the agents is governed by a communication protocol[1]. This protocol uses a formal grammar, a fixed set of keywords, basic logic and causal expressions [30]. The keywords enable the players to express intent, beliefs about the game state, requests for information, and requests for action. For example, to express the following sentence:
"I vote for agent 3 because agent 3 did not vote for agent 4, and agent 4 was a werewolf",
An agent would have to use the following protocol sentence:
```
BECAUSE (AND (NOT <agent3> VOTE <agent4>)
             (COMINGOUT <agent4> <werewolf>))
(VOTE <agent3>)
```
The competition happens in two stages. In the *preliminary* stage, all agents play in a large number of trials. Each trial is composed of one hundred 15-player games, where the players are chosen randomly from the competition pool, and the roles are also distributed randomly. These trials are repeated until all agents have played a minimum number of games. The agents are ranked by their victory rate, and the 15 highest agents advance to the next stage. In the *finalist* stage, the participating design teams are allowed to modify their agents and submit source code and a description document. Then, the agents play several games against each other in 15-player games. The agent with the highest victory rate is declared the winner of the competition.

A total of 94 people registered to the competition, and 74 submitted agents. Out of those agents, 43 were disqualified due to bugs. Many of these disqualified competitors submitted a single version of their agents, which indicates that they did not review their agent based on the feedback from the testing server. Among the 15 finalists, 8 submitted agents in Java, 6 in Python, and 1 in C-Sharp. The

---

[1] AIWolf Protocol Version 3.6.

winning agent, "Takeda", had a 0.6 overall win rate, and a 0.68 villager win rate. Two of the finalists had to be disqualified due to bugs in their code.

Most of the finalist agents were forks of the agents that won the 4th Japanese AIWolf competition. Here we highlight the "Fisherman" agent, which used three different winners from the previous competition as basis, and chose which winner to play based on a multi-armed bandit strategy. Five agents, including the grand winner "Takeda", used some form of machine learning to estimate the team allegiance of the other players. The other nine agents used hand-crafted scripts to define the actions of the agents. Among these hand crafted rules, we highlight trying to remove agents with the highest or lowest winning rate on previous game, and rules for estimating the best timing for revealing role information.

We were satisfied with the high number of participants in this competition. However, the large number of disqualified agents shows that there is still a lot of work necessary in providing good quality English translations of the reference materials in Japanese, as well as better guidance on the use of the training server. In fact, all of the 15 finalists were from Japanese institutions, indicating that much work needs to be done for the internationalization of the Werewolf competition.

Regarding the strategies of the finalist agents, this year's protocol had many new features compared to last year's competition, in particular the introduction of logical and causal statements to the communication protocol. However, none of the winning agents made heavy use of these new features. In fact, it seems that the current winning strategy is to fine tune the ability of the agent to estimate the role of the other players based on their output, with very little back and forth happening between the players. This indicates that the best agents in werewolf are stuck in "wait and detect" local optima for their strategy. We hope that participants in future competition will find ways to exploit this fixed strategy.

With this in mind, the ANAC 2020 werewolf challenge will focus on refining the development environment by providing more documentation, example code, and tools, so that the participants can spend less time finding bugs in their agents, and more time developing interesting and diverse strategies for the Werewolf game.

6 Supply Chain Management

The SCM league models a real-world scenario characterized by profit-maximizing agents that inhabit a complex, dynamic, negotiation environment [28]. A distinguishing feature of the SCM league is the fact that agents' utility functions are endogenous. The agents are responsible for devising their utilities for various possible agreements, given their unique production capabilities, and then to negotiate with other agents to contract those that are most favorable to them.

The world modeled by SCML2019 consists of four types of entities: factories, miners, consumers, and an insurance company. In more detail:

Factories. Entities that convert raw materials and intermediate products into intermediate and final products by running their manufacturing processes.

Different factories are endowed with different capabilities, specified as *private production profiles*, known only to the factory's manager.

Miners. Facilities capable of mining raw materials as needed to satisfy their negotiated contracts. Miners act only as sellers in the SCM world.

Consumers. Companies interested in consuming a subset of the final products to satisfy some predefined consumption schedule. Consumers act only as buyers in the SCM world.

Insurance Company. A single insurance company that can insure buyers against *breaches of contract* committed by sellers, and vice versa.

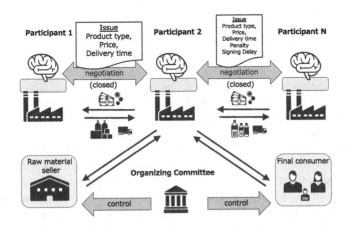

Fig. 3. SCML Organization. Factory managers controlled by participants negotiate with each other and the organization-committee provided miners, consumers and factory mangers.

In the SCM world, each type of entity is run by a *manager* agent. The organizing committee provided manager agents for miners, consumers, and the insurance company. Figure 3 shows the organization of SCML. The organizing committee provided a description of the behavior of these agents, including the miners' and consumers' (exact) utility functions, the factory managers' scheduling algorithm, and an estimation method for the factory managers' utility functions to all participants [28]. The simulation used NegMAS as the negotiation platform [27].

The committee also provided a default agent: i.e., a *greedy factory manager*, instances of which participated in the competition to ensure sufficiently many trading opportunities. The goal of each factory manager agent is to accrue as much wealth (i.e., profit) as possible.

Participants needed to write and submit code (in Java or Python) for an autonomous agent that acts as a factory manager trying to maximize its total profit on multiple simulations with varying world configurations.

The competition was conducted in three tracks: basic, collusion and sabotage. In the basic and collusion tracks, agents were tasked with maximizing their own profit. In the sabotage track, they were tasked with *minimizing* everyone else's profits. The difference between the basic and collusion tracks is that in the former at most one instance of every submitted agent was running in any simulation. In the collusion tracks, participants were encouraged to find ways for their agents to collude together to maximize their profit (e.g. by cornering the market). The sabotage track was introduced to find problems in the league design that could be exploited to block trade in the market.

After disqualifying agents that did not conform to the rules of the competition, six agents ran in the basic and collusion tracks and two agents ran in the sabotage competition.

7   Future Directions

This paper presents the challenges and discusses the results of the competition leagues. Future directions for research are determined by the participants in ANAC's leagues after the lessons learned have been shared. These directions per league are as follows.

For the Automated Negotiation Main league, the challenge for 2020 is to design a negotiating agent that can elicit preference information from a user during the negotiation. The idea is that when a negotiating agent represents a user in a negotiation, it does not know exactly what the user wants, and therefore the agent needs to actively improve its user model through a preference elicitation process. To improve the user model, the agent may elicit further information about the ranking against an elicitation cost.

For Diplomacy, we have concluded that the challenge requires a long-time effort beyond the possibilities for the current competitors, which may also explain the low number of competitors. Therefore, we decide to discontinue this league for the time being.

For the Werewolf league, we will focus in providing a more complete suite of manuals and sample code to participants, and extend the communication with organizers during the initial agent testing phase, with the objective of reducing the number of agents rejected due to bugs and crashes.

For the next Human-Agent competition, we have decided to continue to expand the problem by allowing human users to specify their own preferences. We hope this may help increase participant investment in the scenario, as well as encourage agent designers to respond to a variety of negotiation structures.

For the SCM league, we plan to strengthen the competition while reducing its complexity. This will be achieved by removing the insurance company, avoiding any sources of external funds from being inducted into the system, removing built-in agents from the simulation, having a larger variety of built-in agents and decomposing the agent into easy to manage components allowing participants to focus all of their efforts on the main challenge of situated negotiation.

Acknowledgements. This work is part of the Veni research programme with project number 639.021.751, which is financed by the The Dutch Research Council (NWO). This work was partially funded by project LOGISTAR, under the E.U. Horizon 2020 research and innovation programme, Grant Agreement No. 769142. This research was also sponsored by the U.S. Army Research Office and was accomplished under Cooperative Agreement Number W911NF-20-2-0053. The views and conclusions contained in this document are those of the authors and should not be interpreted as representing the official policies, either expressed or implied, of the Army Research Office or the U.S. Government. The U.S. Government is authorized to reproduce and distribute reprints for Government purposes notwithstanding any copyright notation herein.

References

1. Aydogan, R., Fujita, K., Baarslag, T., Jonker, C.M., Ito, T.: ANAC 2018: repeated multilateral negotiation league. In: The 33rd Annual Conference of the Japanese Society for Artificial Intelligence, Japan (2019)
2. Aydoğan, R., et al.: A baseline for non-linear bilateral negotiations: the full results of the agents competing in ANAC 2014 (2016)
3. Baarslag, T., Aydoğan, R., Hindriks, K.V., Fuijita, K., Ito, K., Jonker, C.M.: The automated negotiating agents competition, 2010–2015. AI Mag. **36**(4), 115–118 (2015)
4. Baarslag, T., Gerding, E.H.: Optimal incremental preference elicitation during negotiation. In: Proceedings of the Twenty-fourth International Joint Conference on Artificial Intelligence, IJCAI 2015, pp. 3–9. AAAI Press (2015)
5. Baarslag, T., Hindriks, K., Jonker, C., Kraus, S., Lin, R.: The first automated negotiating agents competition (ANAC 2010). In: Ito, T., Zhang, M., Robu, V., Fatima, S., Matsuo, T. (eds.) New Trends in Agent-Based Complex Automated Negotiations, vol. 383, pp. 113–135. Springer, Heidelberg (2012). https://doi.org/10.1007/978-3-642-24696-8_7
6. Baarslag, T., Kaisers, M., Gerding, E.H., Jonker, C.M., Gratch, J.: Computers that negotiate on our behalf: major challenges for self-sufficient, self-directed, and interdependent negotiating agents. In: Sukthankar, G., Rodriguez-Aguilar, J.A. (eds.) AAMAS 2017. LNCS (LNAI), vol. 10643, pp. 143–163. Springer, Cham (2017). https://doi.org/10.1007/978-3-319-71679-4_10
7. Baarslag, T., Kaisers, M., Gerding, E.H., Jonker, C.M., Gratch, J.: When will negotiation agents be able to represent us? The challenges and opportunities for autonomous negotiators. In: Proceedings of the Twenty-sixth International Joint Conference on Artificial Intelligence, IJCAI 2017, pp. 4684–4690 (2017)
8. Fabregues, A.: Facing the challenge of automated negotiations with humans. PhD thesis, Universitat Autònoma de Barcelona (2012)
9. Fabregues, A., Sierra, C.: DipGame: a challenging negotiation testbed. Eng. Appl. Artif. Intell. **24**, 1137–1146 (2011)
10. Ferreira, A., Cardoso, H.L., Reis, L.P.: DipBlue: a diplomacy agent with strategic and trust reasoning. In: Proceedings of the 7th International Conference on Agents and Artificial Intelligence (ICAART 2015), pp. 398–405 (2015)
11. Fujita, K., Aydoğan, R., Baarslag, T., Hindriks, K., Ito, T., Jonker, C.: The sixth automated negotiating agents competition (ANAC 2015). In: Fujita, K., Bai, Q., Ito, T., Zhang, M., Ren, F., Aydoğan, R., Hadfi, R. (eds.) Modern Approaches to Agent-based Complex Automated Negotiation. SCI, vol. 674, pp. 139–151. Springer, Cham (2017). https://doi.org/10.1007/978-3-319-51563-2_9

12. Hindriks, K., Jonker, C.M., Tykhonov, D.: Let's dans! an analytic framework of negotiation dynamics and strategies. Web Intell. Agent Syst. Int. J. **9**(4), 319–335 (2011)

13. Hirata, Y., et al.: Werewolf game modeling using action probabilities based on play log analysis. In: Plaat, A., Kosters, W., van den Herik, J. (eds.) CG 2016. LNCS, vol. 10068, pp. 103–114. Springer, Cham (2016). https://doi.org/10.1007/978-3-319-50935-8_10

14. Jennings, N.R., Faratin, P., Lomuscio, A.R., Parsons, S., Sierra, C., Wooldridge, M.: Automated negotiation: prospects, methods and challenges. Int. J. Group Decis. Negot. **10**(2), 199–215 (2001)

15. de Jonge, D., Baarslag, T., Aydoğan, R., Jonker, C., Fujita, K., Ito, T.: The challenge of negotiation in the game of diplomacy. In: Lujak, M. (ed.) AT 2018. LNCS (LNAI), vol. 11327, pp. 100–114. Springer, Cham (2019). https://doi.org/10.1007/978-3-030-17294-7_8

16. de Jonge, D., Sierra, C.: NB3: a multilateral negotiation algorithm for large, nonlinear agreement spaces with limited time. Auton. Agent. Multi-Agent Syst. **29**(5), 896–942 (2015)

17. de Jonge, D., Sierra, C.: D-brane: a diplomacy playing agent for automated negotiations research. Appl. Intell. **47**, 1–20 (2017)

18. Jonker, C.M., et al.: An introduction to the pocket negotiator: a general purpose negotiation support system. In: Criado Pacheco, N., Carrascosa, C., Osman, N., Julián Inglada, V. (eds.) EUMAS/AT -2016. LNCS (LNAI), vol. 10207, pp. 13–27. Springer, Cham (2017). https://doi.org/10.1007/978-3-319-59294-7_2

19. Kelley, H.H.: A classroom study of the dilemmas in interpersonal negotiations. In: Strategic Interaction and Conflict, p. 49 (1966)

20. Lin, R., Kraus, S., Baarslag, T., Tykhonov, D., Hindriks, K., Jonker, C.M.: Genius: an integrated environment for supporting the design of generic automated negotiators. Comput. Intell. **30**(1), 48–70 (2014)

21. Lomuscio, A.R., Wooldridge, M., Jennings, N.R.: A classification scheme for negotiation in electronic commerce. Group Decis. Negot. **12**(1), 31–56 (2003)

22. Marinheiro, J., Lopes Cardoso, H.: Towards general cooperative game playing. In: Nguyen, N.T., Kowalczyk, R., van den Herik, J., Rocha, A.P., Filipe, J. (eds.) Transactions on Computational Collective Intelligence XXVIII. LNCS, vol. 10780, pp. 164–192. Springer, Cham (2018). https://doi.org/10.1007/978-3-319-78301-7_8

23. Marsa-Maestre, I., Klein, M., Jonker, C.M., Aydoğan, R.: From problems to protocols: towards a negotiation handbook. Decis. Support Syst. **60**, 39–54 (2014)

24. Mell, J., Gratch, J.: IAGO: interactive arbitration guide online. In: Proceedings of the 2016 International Conference on Autonomous Agents and Multiagent Systems, pp. 1510–1512. International Foundation for Autonomous Agents and Multiagent Systems (2016)

25. Mell, J., Gratch, J., Aydoğan, R., Baarslag, T., Jonker, C.M.: The likeability-success tradeoff: results of the 2nd annual human-agent automated negotiating agents competition. In: Proceedings of the 8th International Conference on Affective Computing and Intelligent Interaction (ACII 2019), pp. 1–7. IEEE (2019)

26. Mell, J., Gratch, J., Baarslag, T., Aydoğan, R., Jonker, C.M.: Results of the first annual human-agent league of the automated negotiating agents competition. In: Proceedings of the 18th International Conference on Intelligent Virtual Agents, pp. 23–28. ACM (2018)

27. Mohammad, Y., Greenwald, A., Nakadai, S.: NegMAS: a platform for situated negotiations. In: Twelfth International Workshop on Agent-based Complex Automated Negotiations (ACAN 2019) in Conjunction with IJCAI (2019)

28. Mohammad, Y., Viqueira, E.A., Ayerza, N.A., Greenwald, A., Nakadai, S., Morinaga, S.: Supply chain management world. In: Baldoni, M., Dastani, M., Liao, B., Sakurai, Y., Zalila Wenkstern, R. (eds.) PRIMA 2019. LNCS (LNAI), vol. 11873, pp. 153–169. Springer, Cham (2019). https://doi.org/10.1007/978-3-030-33792-6_10
29. Narayanan, V., Jennings, N.R.: An adaptive bilateral negotiation model for e-commerce settings. Econometrica **50**, 97–110 (1982)
30. Osawa, H., Otsuki, T., Aranha, C., Toriumi, F.: Negotiation in hidden identity: designing protocol for werewolf game. In: Agent-Based Complex Automated Negotiation Workshop (2019)
31. Oshrat, Y., Lin, R., Kraus, S.: Facing the challenge of human-agent negotiations via effective general opponent modeling. In: AAMAS (1), pp. 377–384. IFAAMAS (2009)
32. Patton, B.: Negotiation. In: The Handbook of Dispute Resolution, pp. 279–303 (2005)
33. Raiffa, H.: The Art and Science of Negotiation. Harvard University Press, Cambridge (1982)
34. Rosenschein, J.S., Zlotkin, G.: Rules of Encounter: Designing Conventions for Automated Negotiation Among Computers. MIT Press, Cambridge (1994)
35. Ephrati, E., Kraus, S., Lehman, D.: An automated diplomacy player. In: Levy, D., Beal, D. (eds.) Heuristic Programming in Artificial Intelligence: The 1st Computer Olympia, pp. 134–153. Ellis Horwood Limited (1989)
36. Sandholm, T.: Automated negotiation. Commun. ACM **42**(3), 84–85 (1999)
37. Sycara, K.P.: Resolving goal conflicts via negotiation. In: AAAI, vol. 88, pp. 21–26 (1988)
38. Sycara, K.P.: Negotiation planning: an AI approach. Eur. J. Oper. Res. **46**(2), 216–234 (1990)
39. Toriumi, F., Osawa, H., Inaba, M., Katagami, D., Shinoda, K., Matsubara, H.: AI wolf contest — Development of game AI using collective intelligence —. In: Cazenave, T., Winands, M.H.M., Edelkamp, S., Schiffel, S., Thielscher, M., Togelius, J. (eds.) CGW/GIGA -2016. CCIS, vol. 705, pp. 101–115. Springer, Cham (2017). https://doi.org/10.1007/978-3-319-57969-6_8

Optimal Majority Rule Versus Simple Majority Rule

Vitaly Malyshev[1,2,3(✉)] [iD]

[1] Trapeznikov Institute of Control Sciences, Russian Academy of Sciences,
Moscow, Russia
vit312@gmail.com
[2] Kotelnikov Institute of Radioengineering and Electronics,
Russian Academy of Sciences, Moscow, Russia
[3] Moscow Institute of Physics and Technology, Moscow, Russia

Abstract. We consider social dynamics determined by voting in a stochastic environment with qualified majority rules for homogeneous society consisting of classically rational economic agents. Proposals are generated by means of random variables in accordance with the ViSE model. In this case, there is an optimal, in terms of maximizing the agents' expected utility, majority threshold for any specific environment parameters. We obtain analytical expression for this optimal threshold as a function of the parameters of the environment and specialize this expression for several distributions. Furthermore, we compare the relative effectiveness of the optimal and simple (with the threshold of 0.5) majority rule.

Keywords: Social dynamics · Voting · Pit of losses · Stochastic environment · ViSE model

1 Introduction

Collective decisions are often made based on a simple majority rule or qualified majority rules. A certain proportion of voters (more than 0.5 in case of the simple majority rule) must support an alternative for its approval. Society chooses from two alternatives (status quo and reform) in the simplest case. We focus on the iterated game where reforms may be beneficial for some participants and disadvantageous for others in order to reveal whether qualified majority rules surpass the simple one in dynamics. The study may be applicable to optimize the work of local governments, senates, councils, etc.

1.1 The Model

We use the ViSE (Voting in a Stochastic Environment) model proposed in [5]. It describes a society that consists of n economic *agents*. Each agent is characterized by the current value of individual *utility*. A *proposal* of the environment

N. Bassiliades et al. (Eds.): EUMAS 2020/AT 2020, LNAI 12520, pp. 382–395, 2020.
https://doi.org/10.1007/978-3-030-66412-1_24

is a vector of proposed utility increments of the agents. It is stochastically generated by independent identically distributed random variables. The society can accept or reject each proposal by voting. If the proportion of the society supporting this proposal is greater than a *strict relative voting threshold* $\alpha \in [0, 1]$, then the proposal is accepted and the participants' utilities are incremented in accordance with this proposal. Otherwise, all utilities remain unchanged[1]. The voting threshold (quota) α can also be called the *majority threshold* or the *acceptance threshold*, since $\alpha < 0.5$ (minority) is allowed and sometimes more effective. After accepting/rejecting the proposal, the environment generates a next one and puts it to a general vote over and over again.

Each agent chooses some cooperative or non-cooperative strategy. An agent that maximizes his/her individual utility in every act of choice will be called an *egoist*. Each egoist votes for those and only those proposals that increase their individual utility. Cooperative strategies where each member of a group votes "for" if and only if the group gains from the realization of this proposal (the so-called *group strategies*) are considered in [5]. The key theorems showing how the utility increment of an agent depends on the mentioned strategies and environmental parameters are obtained in [6]. The case of gradual dissemination of group strategy to all egoists is presented in [7]. In [13], a modification of the group strategy by introducing a "claims threshold," i.e., the minimum profitability of proposals the group considers acceptable for it, is examined. The agents that support the poorest strata of society or the whole society are called *altruists* (they were considered in [9]).

1.2   Related Work and Contribution

The subject of the study is the dynamics of the agents' utilities as a result of repeated voting.

There are several comparable voting models. Firsts, a similar dynamic model with individual utilities and majority voting has been proposed by A. Malishevski and presented in [14], Subsection 1.3 of Chap. 2. It allows one to show that a series of democratic decisions may (counterintuitively) systematically lead the society to the states unacceptable to all the voters.

Another model with randomly generated proposals and voting was presented in [10]. The main specificity of this model is in a discount factor that reduces utility increment for every rejection. This factor makes the optimal quota lower to speed up decision-making.

Unanimity and simple majority rule (which are special cases of majority rule) are considered in [3]. In this paper agents are characterized by competence (the likelihood of choosing a proposal that is beneficial to all agents). Earlier in [2] the validity of the optimal qualified majority rule under subjective probabilities was studied within the same model.

An interesting model with voting and random agent types was studied in [1]. If we consider environment proposals (in the ViSE model) as agent types in the

---

[1] This voting procedure called "α-majority" is also considered in [11,15–17].

model of [1] and are limited to qualified majority rules, then we get the same models.

Another model whose simplest version is very close to the simplest version of the ViSE model was studied in [4]. The "countries" of n agents with representatives and two-stage voting (a representative aggregates agents' opinions and representatives' choices are aggregated on the second stage) is considered. If each country consists of 1 agent, the agent's strategy is the first voting, and the second voting is "α-majority", then the models coincide.

On other connections between the ViSE model and comparable models, we refer to [9].

In this paper, we show that when all agents are classically rational, then there is an optimal, in terms of maximizing the agents' expected utility, acceptance threshold (quota) for any specific stochastic environment. Furthermore, we focus on four families of distributions: continuous uniform distributions, normal distributions (cf. [8]), symmetrized Pareto distributions (see [9]), and Laplace distributions.

Each distribution is characterized by its mathematical expectation, μ, and standard deviation, σ. The ratio σ/μ is called the coefficient of variation of a random variable. The inverse coefficient of variation $\rho = \mu/\sigma$, which we call the *adjusted mean of the environment*, measures the relative favorability of the environment. If $\rho > 0$, then the environment is favorable on average; if $\rho < 0$, then the environment is unfavorable. We investigate the dependence of the optimal acceptance threshold on ρ for several types of distributions and compare the expected utility increase of an agent when society uses the simple majority rule and the optimal one.

2   Optimal Acceptance Threshold

2.1   A General Result

The optimal acceptance threshold solves one serious problem of simple majority rule that can be revealed from the dependence of the expected utility increment of an agent on the adjusted mean ρ of the environment [8].

Consider an example. The dependence of the expected utility increment on $\rho = \mu/\sigma$ for 21 participants and $\alpha = 0.5$ is presented in Fig. 1, where proposals are generated by the normal distribution.

Figure 1 shows that for $\rho \in (-0.85, -0.266)$, the expected utility increment is a negative value, i.e., proposals approved by the majority are unprofitable for the society on average. This part of the curve is called a *"pit of losses."* For $\rho < -0.85$, the negative mean increment is very close to zero, since the proposals are extremely rarely accepted.

Let $\boldsymbol{\zeta} = (\zeta_1, \ldots, \zeta_n)$ denote a random proposal on some step. Its component ζ_i is the proposed utility increment of agent i. The components $\zeta_1, \ldots, \zeta_n$ are independent identically distributed random variables. ζ will denote a similar scalar variable without reference to a specific agent. Similarly, let $\boldsymbol{\eta} = (\eta_1, \ldots, \eta_n)$ be

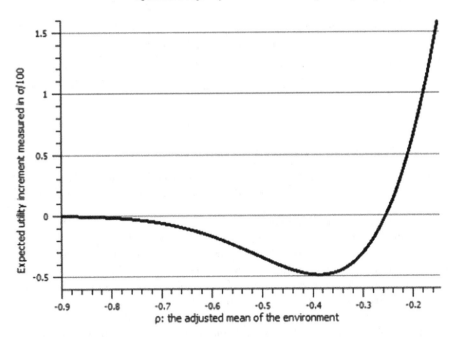

Fig. 1. Expected utility increment of an agent: 21 agents; $\alpha = 0.5$; normal distribution.

the random vector of *actual* increments of the agents on the same step. If $\boldsymbol{\zeta}$ is adopted, then $\boldsymbol{\eta} = \boldsymbol{\zeta}$; otherwise $\boldsymbol{\eta} = (0, \dots, 0)$. Consequently,

$$\boldsymbol{\eta} = \boldsymbol{\zeta} I(\boldsymbol{\zeta}, \alpha n), \tag{1}$$

where[2]

$$I(\boldsymbol{\zeta}, \alpha n) = \begin{cases} 1, & \#\{k : \zeta_k > 0, k = 1, ..., n\} > \alpha n \\ 0, & \text{otherwise.} \end{cases} \tag{2}$$

Equation (1) follows from the assumption that each agent votes for those and only those proposals that increase his/her individual utility.

Let η be a random variable similar to every η_i, but having no reference to a specific agent. We are interested in the expected utility increment of an agent, i.e. $E(\eta)$, where $E(\cdot)$ is the mathematical expectation.

For each specific environment, there is an *optimal acceptance threshold*[3] α_0 that provides the highest possible expected utility increment $E(\eta)$ of an agent.

The optimal acceptance threshold for the normal distribution as a function of the environment parameters has been studied in [8]. This threshold turns out to be independent of the size of the society n.

---

[2] $\#X$ denotes the number of elements in the finite set X.

[3] See [1,15] on other approaches to optimizing the majority threshold and [18,19] for a discussion of the case of multiple voting in this context.

The following theorem, proved in [12], provides a general expression for the optimal voting threshold, which holds for any distribution that has a mathematical expectation.

Theorem 1. *In a society consisting of egoists, the optimal acceptance threshold is*

$$\alpha_0 = \left(1 + \frac{E^+}{E^-}\right)^{-1}, \tag{3}$$

where $E^- = \left|E(\zeta \mid \zeta \le 0)\right|, E^+ = E(\zeta \mid \zeta > 0)$, *and* ζ *is the random variable that determines the utility increment of any agent in a random proposal.*

Voting with the optimal acceptance thresholds always yields positive expected utility increments and so it is devoid of "pits of losses."

Let $\bar{\alpha}_0$ be the center of the half-interval of optimal acceptance thresholds for fixed n, σ, and μ. Then this half-interval is $[\bar{\alpha}_0 - \frac{1}{2n}, \bar{\alpha}_0 + \frac{1}{2n})$. Figures 2 and 3 show the dependence of $\bar{\alpha}_0$ on $\rho = \mu/\sigma$ for normal and symmetrized Pareto distributions used for the generation of proposals.

For various distributions, outside the segment $\rho \in [-0.7, 0.7]$, if an acceptance threshold is close to the optimal one and the number of participants is appreciable, then the proposals are almost always accepted (to the right of the segment) or almost always rejected (to the left of this segment). Therefore, in these cases, the issue of determining the exact optimal threshold loses its practical value.

2.2 Proposals Generated by Continuous Uniform Distributions

Let $-a < 0$ and $b > 0$ be the minimum and maximum values of a continuous uniformly distributed random variable, respectively.

Corollary 1. *The optimal majority/acceptance threshold in the case of proposals generated by the continuous uniform distribution on the segment* $[-a, b]$ *with* $-a < 0$ *and* $b > 0$ *is*

$$\alpha_0 = \left(1 + \frac{b}{a}\right)^{-1}. \tag{4}$$

Indeed, in this case, $E^- = \frac{a}{2}, E^+ = \frac{b}{2}$, and $R = \frac{b}{a}$, hence, (3) provides (4).

If b approaches 0 from above, then α_0 approaches 1 from below, and the optimal voting procedure is unanimity. Indeed, positive proposed utility increments become much smaller in absolute value than negative ones, therefore, each participant should be able to reject a proposal.

As $-a$ approaches 0 from below, negative proposed utility increments become much smaller in absolute value than positive ones. Therefore, a "coalition" consisting of any single voter should be able to accept a proposal. In accordance with this, the optimal relative threshold α_0 decreases to 0.

Corollary 2. *In terms of the adjusted mean of the environment* $\rho = \mu/\sigma$, *it holds that for the continuous uniform distribution,*

$$\alpha_0 = \begin{cases} 1, & \rho \leq -\sqrt{3}, \\ \frac{1}{2}\left(1 - \frac{\rho}{\sqrt{3}}\right), & -\sqrt{3} < \rho < \sqrt{3}, \\ 0, & \rho \geq \sqrt{3}. \end{cases} \tag{5}$$

This follows from (4) and the expressions $\mu = \frac{-a+b}{2}$ and $\sigma = \frac{b+a}{2\sqrt{3}}$. It is worth mentioning that the dependence of α_0 on ρ is linear, as distinct from (4).

2.3   Proposals Generated by Normal Distributions

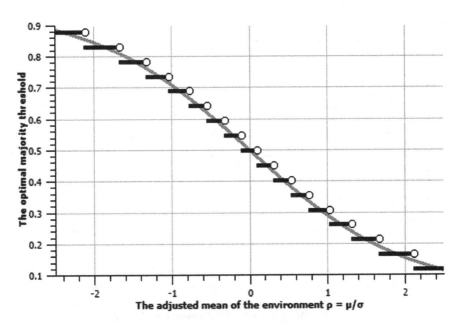

Fig. 2. The center $\bar{a}_0$ of the half-interval of optimal majority/acceptance thresholds (a "ladder") for $n = 21$ and the optimal threshold (6) as functions of ρ for normal distributions.

For normal distributions, the following corollary holds.

Corollary 3. *The optimal majority/acceptance threshold in the case of proposals generated by the normal distribution with parameters μ and σ is*

$$\alpha_0 = F(\rho)\left(1 - \frac{\rho F(-\rho)}{f(\rho)}\right), \tag{6}$$

where $\rho = \mu/\sigma$, while $F(\cdot)$ and $f(\cdot)$ are the standard normal cumulative distribution function and density, respectively.

Corollary 3 follows from Theorem 1 and the facts that $E^- = -\sigma \left(\rho - \frac{f(\rho)}{F(-\rho)} \right)$ and $E^+ = \sigma \left(\rho + \frac{f(\rho)}{F(\rho)} \right)$, which can be easily found by integration. Note that Corollary 3 strengthens the first statement of Theorem 1 in [8].

Figure 2 illustrates the dependence of the center of the half-interval of optimal majority/acceptance thresholds versus $\rho = \mu/\sigma$ for normal distributions in the segment $\rho \in [-2.5, 2.5]$.

We refer to [8] for some additional properties (e.g., the rate of change of the optimal voting threshold as a function of ρ).

2.4   Proposals Generated by Symmetrized Pareto Distributions

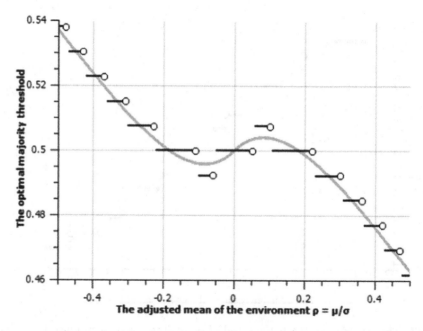

Fig. 3. The center $\bar{a}_0$ of the half-interval of optimal majority/acceptance thresholds (a "ladder") for $n = 131$ (odd) and the optimal threshold (7) as functions of ρ for symmetrized Pareto distributions with $k = 8$.

Pareto distributions are widely used for modeling social, linguistic, geophysical, financial, and some other types of data. The Pareto distribution with positive parameters k and a can be defined by means of the function $P\{\xi > x\} = \left(\frac{a}{x} \right)^k$, where $\xi \in [a, \infty)$ is a random variable.

The ViSE model normally involves distributions that allow both positive and negative values. Consider the *symmetrized Pareto distributions* (see [9] for more details). For its construction, the density function $f(x) = \frac{k}{x} \left(\frac{a}{x} \right)^k$ of the

Pareto distribution is divided by 2 and combined with its reflection w.r.t. the line $x = a$.

The density of the resulting distribution with mode (and median) μ is

$$f(x) = \frac{k}{2a} \left(\frac{|x - \mu|}{a} + 1 \right)^{-(k+1)}.$$

For symmetrized Pareto distributions with $k > 2$, the following result holds true.

Corollary 4. *The optimal majority/acceptance threshold in the case of proposals generated by the symmetrized Pareto distribution with parameters μ, σ, and $k > 2$ is*

$$\alpha_0 = \frac{1}{2} \left(1 + \text{sign}(\rho) \frac{1 - (k-2)\hat{\rho} - (1+\hat{\rho})^{-k+1}}{1 + k\hat{\rho}} \right) \tag{7}$$

where $\rho = \frac{\mu}{\sigma}$, $C = \sqrt{\frac{(k-1)(k-2)}{2}} = \frac{a}{\sigma}$, *and* $\hat{\rho} = |\rho/C| = |\mu/a|$.

Corollary 4 follows from Theorem 1 and the facts (their proof is given below) that:

$$E^- = \sigma \left(\frac{C+\rho}{k-1} \right), \quad E^+ = \frac{\sigma}{1 - \frac{1}{2}\left(\frac{C}{C+\rho}\right)^k} \left(\rho + \left(\frac{C}{C+\rho} \right)^k \frac{C+\rho}{2(k-1)} \right) \quad \text{whenever } \mu > 0;$$

$$E^- = -\frac{\sigma}{1 - \frac{1}{2}\left(\frac{C}{C-\rho}\right)^k} \left(\rho - \left(\frac{C}{C-\rho} \right)^k \frac{C-\rho}{2(k-1)} \right), \quad E^+ = \sigma \left(\frac{C-\rho}{k-1} \right) \quad \text{whenever } \mu \leq 0.$$

The "ladder" and the optimal acceptance threshold curve for symmetrized Pareto distributions are fundamentally different from the corresponding graphs for the normal and continuous uniform distributions. Namely, $\alpha_0(\rho)$ increases in some neighborhood of $\rho = 0$.

As a result, $\alpha_0(\rho)$ has two extremes. This is caused by the following peculiarities of the symmetrized Pareto distribution: an increase of ρ from negative to positive values decreases E^+ and increases E^-. By virtue of (3), this causes an increase of α_0.

This means that the plausible hypothesis about the profitability of the voting threshold raising when the environment becomes less favorable (while the type of distribution and σ are preserved) is not generally true. In contrast, for symmetrized Pareto distributions, it is advantageous to lower the threshold whenever a decreasing ρ remains close to zero (an abnormal part of the graph).

Figure 3 illustrate the dependence of the center of the half-interval of optimal voting thresholds versus $\rho = \mu/\sigma$ for symmetrized Pareto distributions with $k = 8$.

2.5   Proposals Generated by Laplace Distributions

The density of the Laplace distribution with parameters μ (location parameter) and $\lambda > 0$ (rate parameter) is

$$f(x) = \frac{\lambda}{2} \exp\left(-\lambda |x - \mu| \right).$$

For Laplace distributions, the following corollary holds.

Corollary 5. *The optimal majority/acceptance threshold in the case of proposals generated by the Laplace distribution with parameters μ and λ is*

$$\alpha_0 = \frac{1}{2}\left(1 + \text{sign}(\rho)\frac{1 - \beta - \exp(-\beta)}{1 + \beta}\right), \tag{8}$$

where $\beta = |\lambda\mu| = |\lambda\sigma\rho| = |\sqrt{2}\rho|$.

Corollary 5 follows from Theorem 1 and the facts (their proof is similar to the proof of Corollary 4) that:

$E^- = \frac{1}{\lambda}$, $E^+ = \frac{2\mu + \frac{e^{-\lambda\mu}}{\lambda}}{2 - e^{-\lambda\mu}}$ whenever $\mu > 0$;

$E^- = -\frac{2\mu - \frac{e^{\lambda\mu}}{\lambda}}{2 - e^{\lambda\mu}}$, $E^+ = \frac{1}{\lambda}$ whenever $\mu \le 0$.

In Lemma 3 of [9], it was proved that the symmetrized Pareto distribution with parameters k, μ, and σ tends, as $k \to \infty$, to the Laplace distribution with the same mean and standard deviation.

2.6 Proposals Generated by Logistic Distributions

The density of the logistic distribution with parameters μ (location parameter) and $s > 0$ (scale parameter) is

$$f(x) = \frac{1}{4s}\text{sech}^2\left(\frac{x - \mu}{2s}\right).$$

For logistic distributions, the following corollary holds.

Corollary 6. *The optimal majority/acceptance threshold in the case of proposals generated by the logistic distribution with parameters μ and s is*

$$\alpha_0 = \frac{\left(\frac{1}{2} + \frac{1}{2}\tanh\left(\frac{\mu}{2s}\right)\right)\left(s\ln 2 + s\ln\left(\cosh\left(\frac{\mu}{2s}\right)\right) - \frac{\mu}{2}\right)}{s\ln 2 + s\ln\left(\cosh\left(\frac{\mu}{2s}\right)\right) - \frac{\mu}{2}\tanh\left(\frac{\mu}{2s}\right)}. \tag{9}$$

Corollary 6 follows from Theorem 1 and the facts, which can be easily found by integration, that:

$$E^- = \frac{s\ln 2 + s\ln\left(\cosh\left(\frac{\mu}{2s}\right)\right) - \frac{\mu}{2}}{\left(\frac{1}{2} - \frac{1}{2}\tanh\left(\frac{\mu}{2s}\right)\right)}, \quad E^+ = \frac{s\ln 2 + s\ln\left(\cosh\left(\frac{\mu}{2s}\right)\right) + \frac{\mu}{2}}{\left(\frac{1}{2} + \frac{1}{2}\tanh\left(\frac{\mu}{2s}\right)\right)}.$$

We summarize the results of the above corollaries in Tables 1 and 2.

3   Comparison of the Expected Utility Increments

By a *"voting sample"* of size n with absolute voting threshold n_0 we mean the vector of random variables $(\zeta_1 I(\zeta, n_0), \ldots, \zeta_n I(\zeta, n_0))$, where $\zeta = (\zeta_1, \ldots, \zeta_n)$ is a sample from some distribution and $I(\zeta, n_0)$ is defined by (2).

According to this definition, a voting sample vanishes whenever the number of positive elements of sample ζ does not exceed the threshold n_0.

The lemma on "normal voting samples" obtained in [6] can be generalized as follows.

Table 1. Probabilities of positive and negative proposals for several distributions.

Distribution	Parameters	p	q
Continuous uniform distribution	$-a < 0, b > 0$	$\frac{b}{a+b}$	$\frac{a}{a+b}$
Normal distribution	μ, σ	$F(\rho)$	$F(-\rho)$
Symmetrized Pareto distr. ($\mu > 0$)	$k > 2, \mu, \sigma$	$1 - \frac{1}{2}\left(\frac{C}{C+\rho}\right)^k$	$\frac{1}{2}\left(\frac{C}{C+\rho}\right)^k$
Symmetrized Pareto distr. ($\mu \leq 0$)	$k > 2, \mu, \sigma$	$\frac{1}{2}\left(\frac{C}{C-\rho}\right)^k$	$1 - \frac{1}{2}\left(\frac{C}{C-\rho}\right)^k$
Laplace distribution ($\mu > 0$)	μ, λ	$1 - \frac{1}{2}e^{-\lambda\mu}$	$\frac{1}{2}e^{-\lambda\mu}$
Laplace distribution ($\mu \leq 0$)	μ, λ	$\frac{1}{2}e^{\lambda\mu}$	$1 - \frac{1}{2}e^{\lambda\mu}$
Logistic distribution	μ, s	$\frac{1}{2} + \frac{1}{2}\tanh\left(\frac{\mu}{2s}\right)$	$\frac{1}{2} - \frac{1}{2}\tanh\left(\frac{\mu}{2s}\right)$

where $C = \sqrt{\frac{(k-1)(k-2)}{2}}$, $\rho = \mu/\sigma$, while $F(\cdot)$ is the standard normal cumulative distribution function.

Table 2. Expected win and loss for several distributions.

Distribution	Parameters	E^+	E^-
Continuous uniform distribution	$-a < 0, b > 0$	$\frac{b}{2}$	$\frac{a}{2}$
Normal distribution	μ, σ	$\mu + \sigma\frac{f(\rho)}{F(\rho)}$	$-\mu + \sigma\frac{f(\rho)}{F(-\rho)}$
Symmetrized Pareto distr. ($\mu > 0$)	$k > 2, \mu, \sigma$	$\frac{\sigma}{p}\left(\rho + q\frac{C+\rho}{k-1}\right)$	$\sigma\left(\frac{C+\rho}{k-1}\right)$
Symmetrized Pareto distr. ($\mu \leq 0$)	$k > 2, \mu, \sigma$	$\sigma\left(\frac{C-\rho}{k-1}\right)$	$-\frac{\sigma}{q}\left(\rho - p\frac{C-\rho}{k-1}\right)$
Laplace distribution ($\mu > 0$)	μ, λ	$\frac{1}{p}\left(\mu + \frac{e^{-\lambda\mu}}{2\lambda}\right)$	$\frac{1}{\lambda}$
Laplace distribution ($\mu \leq 0$)	μ, λ	$\frac{1}{\lambda}$	$-\frac{1}{q}\left(\mu - \frac{e^{\lambda\mu}}{2\lambda}\right)$
Logistic distribution	μ, s	$\frac{s\ln 2 + s\ln\left(\cosh\left(\frac{\mu}{2s}\right)\right) + \frac{\mu}{2}}{p}$	$\frac{s\ln 2 + s\ln\left(\cosh\left(\frac{\mu}{2s}\right)\right) - \frac{\mu}{2}}{q}$

where $C = \sqrt{\frac{(k-1)(k-2)}{2}}$, $\rho = \mu/\sigma$, while $F(\cdot)$ and $f(\cdot)$ are the standard normal cumulative distribution function and density, respectively; p and q are presented in the corresponding rows of Table 1.

Lemma 1. *Let $\eta = (\eta_1, \ldots, \eta_n)$ be a voting sample from some distribution with an absolute voting threshold n_0. Then, for any $k = 1, ..., n$,*

$$\mathrm{E}(\eta_k) = \sum_{x=n_0+1}^{n} \left((E^+ + E^-)\frac{x}{n} - E^-\right)\binom{n}{x}p^x q^{n-x}, \tag{10}$$

where $E^- = \left|\mathrm{E}(\zeta \mid \zeta \leq 0)\right|, E^+ = \mathrm{E}(\zeta \mid \zeta > 0), p = P\{\zeta > 0\} = 1 - F(0), q = P\{\zeta \leq 0\} = F(0)$, ζ is the random variable that determines the utility incre-

ment of any agent in a random proposal, and $F(\cdot)$ is the cumulative distribution function of ζ.

In [9], the issue of correct location-and-scale standardization of distributions for the analysis of the ViSE model has been discussed. An alternative (compared to using the same mean and variance) approach to standardizing continuous symmetric distributions was proposed. Namely, distributions similar in position and scale must have the same μ and the same interval (centered at μ) containing a certain essential proportion of probability. Such a standardization provides more similarity in the central region and the same weight of tails outside this region.

In what follows, we apply this approach for the comparison of the expected utility for several distributions. Namely, for each distribution, we find the variance such that the first quartiles (and thus, all quartiles because the distributions are symmetric) coincide for zero mean distributions, where the first quartile, Q_1, splits off the "left" 25% of probability from the "right" 75%.

For the normal distribution, $Q_1 \approx -0.6745\sigma_N$, where σ_N is the standard deviation.

For the continuous uniform distribution, $Q_1 = -\frac{\sqrt{3}}{2}\sigma_U$, where σ_U is its standard deviation.

For the symmetrized Pareto distribution, $Q_1 = C(1 - 2^{\frac{1}{k}})\sigma_P$, where σ_P is the standard deviation and $C = \sqrt{\frac{(k-1)(k-2)}{2}}$. This follows from the equation

$$F_P(Q_1) = \frac{1}{2}\left(\frac{C}{C - \frac{Q_1}{\sigma_P}}\right)^k = \frac{1}{4},$$

where $F_P(\cdot)$ is the corresponding cumulative distribution function.

For the Laplace distribution, $Q_1 = \frac{-\ln 2}{\lambda} = -\sigma_L \frac{\ln 2}{\sqrt{2}}$, where σ_L is the standard deviation.

For the logistic distribution, $Q_1 = \frac{-2\sqrt{3}}{\pi} \tanh^{-1}\left(\frac{1}{2}\right)\sigma_{Log}$, where σ_{Log} is the standard deviation.

Consequently, $\sigma_U \approx 0.7788\sigma_N$, $\sigma_P \approx 1.6262\sigma_N$ for $k = 8$, $\sigma_L \approx 1.3762\sigma_N$ and $\sigma_{Log} \approx 1.1136\sigma_N$.

Figures 4 and 5 show the dependence of the expected utility increment of an agent on the mean μ of the proposal distribution for several distributions (normal, continuous uniform, symmetrized Pareto, Laplace and logistic) for the majority threshold $\alpha = \frac{1}{2}$ and difference in expected utility increment of an agent as a function of μ between the optimal majority/acceptance thresholds and $\alpha = \frac{1}{2}$ cases for several distributions, respectively. They are obtained by substituting the parameters of the environments into (10), (5), (6), (7), and (8). Obviously, the optimal acceptance threshold excludes "pits of losses" because the society has the option to take insuperable threshold of 1 and reject all proposals.

Figure 6 illustrates the dependence of the optimal majority threshold on μ for the same list of distributions. It helps to explain why for $\alpha = \frac{1}{2}$, the continuous uniform distribution has the deepest pit of losses (because of the biggest difference between the actual and optimal thresholds), and why the symmetrized

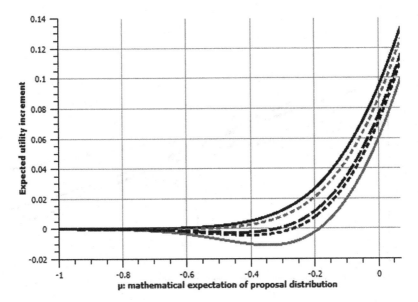

Fig. 4. Expected utility increment of an agent as a function of μ with a majority/acceptance threshold of $\alpha = \frac{1}{2}$ for several distributions: black line denotes the symmetrized Pareto distribution, black dotted line the normal distribution (with $\sigma_N = 1$), black dashed line the logistic distribution, gray line the continuous uniform distribution, and gray dotted line the Laplace distribution.

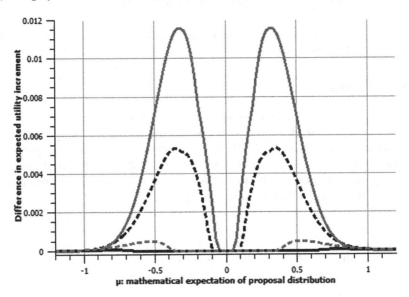

Fig. 5. Difference in expected utility increment of an agent as a function of μ between the optimal majority/acceptance thresholds and $\alpha = \frac{1}{2}$ cases for several distributions: black line denotes the symmetrized Pareto distribution, black dotted line the normal distribution (with $\sigma_N = 1$), black dashed line the logistic distribution, gray line the continuous uniform distribution, and gray dotted line the Laplace distribution.

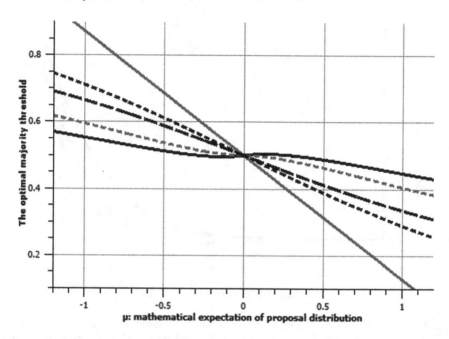

Fig. 6. The optimal majority/acceptance threshold as function of μ for several distributions: black line denotes the symmetrized Pareto distribution, black dotted line the normal distribution, black dashed line the logistic distribution, gray line the continuous uniform distribution, and gray dotted line the Laplace distribution.

Pareto and Laplace distributions have no discernible pit of losses (because those differences are the smallest).

4   Conclusion

In this paper, we used closed-form expressions for the expected utility increase and the optimal voting threshold (i.e., the threshold that maximizes social and individual welfare), as functions of the parameters of the stochastic proposal generator in the assumptions of the ViSE model, to calculate difference in expected utility increment of an agent between the optimal majority/acceptance thresholds and simple majority voting rule cases for several distributions. These expressions were given more specific forms for several types of distributions.

Estimation of the optimal acceptance threshold seems to be a solvable problem. If the model is at least approximately adequate and one can estimate the type of distribution and $\rho = \mu/\sigma$ by means of experiments, then it is possible to obtain an estimate for the optimal acceptance threshold using the formulas provided in this paper.

We found that for some distributions of proposals, the plausible hypothesis that it is beneficial to increase the voting threshold when the environment becomes less favorable is not generally true. A deeper study of this issue should be the subject of future research.

References

1. Azrieli, Y., Kim, S.: Pareto efficiency and weighted majority rules. Int. Econom. Rev. **55**(4), 1067–1088 (2014)
2. Baharad, E., Ben-Yashar, R.: The robustness of the optimal weighted majority rule to probabilities distortion. Public Choice **139**, 53–59 (2009). https://doi.org/10.1007/s11127-008-9378-7
3. Baharad, E., Ben-Yashar, R., Nitzan, S.: Variable competence and collective performance: unanimity versus simple majority rule. Group Decis. Negot. (2019). https://doi.org/10.1007/s10726-019-09644-3
4. BarberÁ , S., Jackson, M.O.: On the weights of nations: assigning voting weights in a heterogeneous union. J. Polit. Economy **114**(2), 317–339 (2006)
5. Borzenko, V.I., Lezina, Z.M., Loginov, A.K., Tsodikova, Y.Y., Chebotarev, P.Y.: Strategies of voting in stochastic environment: egoism and collectivism. Autom. Remote Control **67**(2), 311–328 (2006)
6. Chebotarev, P.Y.: Analytical expression of the expected values of capital at voting in the stochastic environment. Autom. Remote Control **67**(3), 480–492 (2006)
7. Chebotarev, P.Y., Loginov, A.K., Tsodikova, Y.Y., Lezina, Z.M., Borzenko, V.I.: Snowball of cooperation and snowball communism. In: Proceedings of the Fourth International Conference on Control Sciences, pp. 687–699 (2009)
8. Chebotarev, P.Y., Malyshev, V.A., Tsodikova, Y.Y., Loginov, A.K., Lezina, Z.M., Afonkin, V.A.: The optimal majority threshold as a function of the variation coefficient of the environment. Autom. Remote Control **79**(4), 725–736 (2018a)
9. Chebotarev, P.Y., Tsodikova, Y.Y., Loginov, A.K., Lezina, Z.M., Afonkin, V.A., Malyshev, V.A.: Comparative efficiency of altruism and egoism as voting strategies in stochastic environment. Autom. Remote Control **79**(11), 2052–2072 (2018b)
10. Compte, O., Jehiel, P.: On the optimal majority rule. CEPR Discussion Paper (12492) (2017)
11. Felsenthal, D., Machover, M.: The treaty of nice and qualified majority voting. Soc. Choice Welfare **18**(3), 431–464 (2001)
12. Malyshev, V.: Optimal majority threshold in a stochastic environment (2019). https://arxiv.org/abs/1901.09233
13. Malyshev, V.A., Chebotarev, P.Y.: On optimal group claims at voting in a stochastic environment. Autom. Remote Control **78**(6), 1087–1100 (2017). https://doi.org/10.1134/S0005117917060091
14. Mirkin, B.G.: Group choice. In: Fishburn, P.C. (ed.) V.H. Winston [Russian edition: Mirkin BG (1974) Problema Gruppovogo Vybora. Nauka, Moscow] (1979)
15. Nitzan, S., Paroush, J.: Optimal decision rules in uncertain dichotomous choice situations. Int. Econ. Rev. **23**(2), 289–297 (1982)
16. Nitzan, S., Paroush, J.: Are qualified majority rules special? Public Choice **42**(3), 257–272 (1984)
17. O'Boyle, E.J.: The origins of homo economicus: a note. Storia del Pensiero Economico **6**, 1–8 (2009)
18. Rae, D.: Decision-rules and individual values in constitutional choice. Am. Polit. Sci. Rev. **63**(1), 40–56 (1969)
19. Sekiguchi, T., Ohtsuki, H.: Effective group size of majority vote accuracy in sequential decision-making. Jpn. J. Ind. Appl. Math. **32**(3), 595–614 (2015). https://doi.org/10.1007/s13160-015-0192-6

Evaluating Crowdshipping Systems with Agent-Based Simulation

Jeremias Dötterl[1]([envelope]), Ralf Bruns[1], Jürgen Dunkel[1], and Sascha Ossowski[2]

[1] Department of Computer Science, Hannover University of Applied Sciences and Arts, Hannover, Germany
{jeremias.doetterl,ralf.bruns,juergen.dunkel}@hs-hannover.de
[2] CETINIA, University Rey Juan Carlos, Madrid, Spain
sascha.ossowski@urjc.es

Abstract. Due to e-commerce growth and urbanization, delivery companies are facing a rising demand for home deliveries, which makes it increasingly challenging to provide parcel delivery that is cheap, sustainable, and on time. This challenge has motivated recent interest in crowdshipping. In crowdshipping systems, private citizens are incentivized to contribute to parcel delivery by making small detours in their daily lives. To advance crowdshipping as a new delivery paradigm, new crowdshipping concepts have to be developed, tested, and evaluated. One way to test and evaluate new crowdshipping concepts is agent-based simulation. In this paper, we present a crowdshipping simulator where the crowd workers are modeled as agents who decide autonomously whether they want to accept a delivery task. The agents' decisions can be modeled based on shipping plans, which allow to easily implement the most common behavior assumptions found in the crowdshipping literature. We perform simulation experiments for different scenarios, which demonstrate the capabilities of our simulator.

Keywords: Crowdsourced delivery · Agent-based simulation · Agent-based models

1 Introduction

Parcel delivery companies are currently facing a high demand of home deliveries. Thereby, the so called "last mile" is one of the most costly and time-demanding delivery legs [11,13,24]: the delivery of parcels from hubs to the recipients' homes is served with dedicated trips by professional drivers. These dedicated trips lead to high costs [11] and contribute to increased traffic and air pollution.

These challenges have lead to increased interest in crowdshipping [3,18,19, 23]. Crowdshipping systems rely on the help of private citizens (the crowd) who are willing to make small modifications to their daily trips to contribute to parcel delivery. A person on their way to the supermarket or workplace can accept a delivery task in exchange for a small monetary compensation. While

© Springer Nature Switzerland AG 2020
N. Bassiliades et al. (Eds.): EUMAS 2020/AT 2020, LNAI 12520, pp. 396–411, 2020.
https://doi.org/10.1007/978-3-030-66412-1_25

professional drivers probably still are going to deliver parcels that require large detours, the crowd can help with those deliveries that require only minor detours and that can be completed quickly, which makes them attractive for the crowd. With the support of the crowd, the need for dedicated trips can be reduced, which decreases the burden from the professional drivers and helps to fight air pollution.

Crowdshipping systems are an interesting problem area for agent-based systems [27] and agreement technologies [17]. As the crowd workers are self-interested volunteers rather than permanent employees, they can best be modeled as *autonomous* agents. Furthermore, multiple agents can possibly avoid costly and environment-unfriendly trips more efficiently together if they can *agree to cooperate*. A group of agents that can find agreements to form a "delivery chain" could deliver a parcel over a larger distance than a single agent. In fact, first agent-based contributions in this direction have been put forward [8,12,21,22].

Research on crowdshipping needs testing environments to evaluate new crowdshipping proposals. Simulation is an established method for exploring and evaluating new ideas prior to costly real-world deployment. New crowdshipping concepts – such as new task assignment strategies, compensation schemes, or cooperation approaches – could be evaluated with agent-based simulation.

In this paper, we present a crowdshipping simulator where crowd workers are modeled as autonomous agents. While various general-purpose agent-based simulators [16,25] exist, they provide no explicit support for simulating the particular characteristics of crowdshipping systems. In contrast to general-purpose simulators, our crowdshipping simulator is not only able to simulate the agents' physical movements, but also their cognitive decision making. For example, our simulator provides explicit support for modeling the agents' task acceptance decisions. Additionally, it supports customized task assignment strategies.

The rest of the paper is structured as follows. First, we provide an overview of related work on crowdshipping (Sect. 2) with special focus on the different crowd behavior assumptions. In Sect. 3, we describe a model of the crowdshipping system we want to simulate. In Sect. 4, we present the architecture of our simulator and its configuration options based on strategies. Then, we present the concept of shipping plans that allow to easily implement behavior assumptions (Sect. 5). In Sect. 6, we report some experiments with our simulator. Finally, in Sect. 7 we close with our conclusions.

2 Related Work

Crowdshipping is a relatively new research topic with the first wave of publications having appeared in 2016 (see, e.g., [2,18,26]). Crowdshipping belongs to the family of crowdsourced systems [9], i.e., systems that operate based on contributions by workers who participate spontaneously and on their own schedule. In contrast to these "classical" crowdsourcing systems, crowdshipping requires the contributors to perform tasks that are spatially distributed. Such crowd-sourced systems are known under the names location-based crowdsourcing [1] and mobile crowdsourcing [28].

Research on crowdshipping, the crowdsourced delivery of parcels, focuses on several different research topics. Some works study the motivations of people to use the system for shipping their goods and their motivations to participate as crowd workers [15,19,20]. Other works focus on task assignment and route planning, mostly with some optimization objective, e.g., to minimize costs [2,3, 6]. Other works focus on sustainability [5,12] and cooperative task fulfillment [6, 21,22]. The crowd workers can be modeled as autonomous agents.

In agent-based modeling [4,14], the actors of a system are modeled as autonomous decision makers; the interaction of the different agents leads to a system-level behavior. In the context of crowdshipping, the agents are the autonomous couriers who decide whether they want to accept a delivery task. To simulate crowdshipping systems, not only the physical movement of the couriers has to be simulated, but also the cognitive decision making process of the couriers. In the crowdshipping literature, many different models can be found for the couriers' task acceptance decisions. In Table 1 we summarize the models and provide references to publications that use them.

Table 1. Task acceptance models

Model	Couriers accept delivery tasks...
Detour threshold [2,6]	...if the required detour does not exceed a certain fraction of the length of their original route
Coverage area [7]	...if the delivery destination lies in the courier's personal coverage area, e.g., within a certain radius of the courier's destination
Capacity-based [26]	...if accepting the task does not exceed their personal capacity. (This model is typically used together with other constraints)
Stochastic [10]	...at a certain probability. The agents' decision making is not modeled explicitly; no assumptions are made about the agents' internal reasoning
Utility-based [8,22]	...if they provide positive utilities. The agents are modeled as utility maximizers that include economic criteria into their decisions, such as delivery reward and costs for fuel, vehicle maintenance, travel distance, and lost time

The choice of behavior model determines the agent behavior and thus affects the simulation outcome. To observe the effects of different models, the simulation should support the models of Table 1. Additionally, the simulation should make it easy to adapt existing models or implement completely new ones.

While there are several agent-based simulation tools available, such as Repast Symphony [16] or NetLogo [25], they provide no explicit support for the simulation of crowdshipping. These simulators aim to be general and adaptable to a wide range of simulation settings. Being generic, in those simulators there is no explicit notion of delivery tasks, shipping plans, etc. Therefore, the aim of these simulators differs from ours. Our simulator is specific to crowdshipping and conveniently supports crowdshipping-specific features. To the best of our knowledge no simulator exists that provides explicit support for the specific characteristics of crowdshipping.

3   Crowdshipping Model

In this section, we introduce a model of the crowdshipping systems that we want to simulate.

The crowdshipping system consists of the parcel delivery company, the couriers, and the crowdshipping platform. The crowdshipping system is operated by the *parcel delivery company*, which wants to deliver parcels with the help of the crowd. The crowd consists of *couriers*, who are registered at the crowdshipping platform and principally interested in delivering parcels. The *crowdshipping platform* is a web platform where interested individuals can register to receive delivery tasks; the platform manages the payment of delivery rewards and is responsible for task assignment.

During the day, the delivery company receives requests for parcels to be delivered between two locations. The delivery company operates in an *operation area* and accepts parcels whose location and destination lie within this area. Delivery requests are converted to delivery tasks that can be delegated to couriers.

A *delivery task* requires the delivery of a parcel from its location to the desired destination. A delivery task is associated with a delivery reward, which is paid to the courier who completes the task. When a new task is created, it is assigned to one of the couriers who is currently present and active in the operation area.

Task assignment is performed by an algorithm, which receives as input the available couriers and decides who should perform the delivery. Thereby the task assignment decision is constrained by the courier autonomy.

The couriers are usually autonomous and self-interested agents who are allowed to reject task assignments. If a courier is not interested in a delivery task, e.g., because its reward is too low or the required effort too high, the courier can reject the task. If a courier accepts a delivery task, the courier becomes responsible for the delivery of the parcel. The courier travels to the parcel location, picks the parcel up, carries it to its destination and receives the delivery reward.

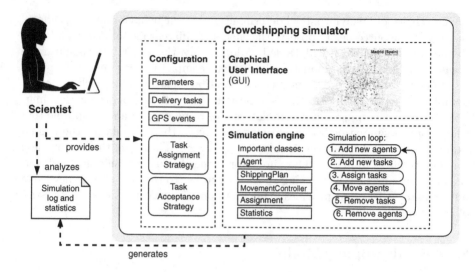

Fig. 1. Architecture of the crowdshipping simulator

4   Crowdshipping Simulator

The model of Sect. 3 is implemented by our simulator, which we describe in this section together with its most important components and configuration.

Figure 1 shows the simulation environment, which consists of the crowdshipping simulator and the scientist who interacts with the simulator. The crowdshipping simulator consists of three top-level modules: the graphical user interface (GUI), the simulation engine, and the configuration. The configuration files are provided by the scientist and are used by the simulator to control the execution. The execution is controlled by the simulation engine, which, when it terminates, generates a simulation log and statistics. This output is analyzed by the scientist to gain new insights.

In the following sections, we discuss the most important components of the simulator: the simulation engine and the configuration.

4.1   Simulation Engine

The simulation engine is the core component of the simulator. The simulation engine implements a simulation loop consisting of six steps.

1. *Add new agents*: The simulation simulates the appearance of new agents.
2. *Add new tasks*: The simulation simulates the appearance of new delivery tasks.
3. *Assign tasks*: The simulation tries to assign tasks that are currently unassigned to agents who are currently active in the simulation. Agents are autonomous and can reject assignments. Hence, it is possible that some tasks keep unassigned and an assignment is re-attempted in a future cycle.

4. *Move agents*: The simulation moves the active agents. Initially, an agent's movement is given by GPS data that is read from a configuration file. When an agent accepts a delivery task, the agent has to make a detour from their original route. In this case, the simulator simulates an artificial route at runtime.
5. *Remove tasks*: The simulation checks which parcels have been delivered to their destinations and removes the associated tasks.
6. *Remove agents*: The simulation checks which agents have arrived at their destinations and removes them from the simulation.

The most important classes of the simulation engine are the Agent, the ShippingPlan, the MovementController, the Assignment, and the Statistics class.

- The *Agent* class represents the individual deliverers. Each agent object holds information about a deliverer's current location, destination, and task acceptance behavior. The agent's movement and task acceptance behavior are influenced by its shipping plan.
- The *ShippingPlan* class consists of the locations on the map that the agent has to visit to pick up and deliver parcels. In Sect. 5, we discuss shipping plans in detail since they are an important concept of our simulator.
- The *MovementController* moves the agents on the map.
- The *Assignment* class is responsible for the assignment of new delivery tasks to interested agents. Whenever a new delivery task occurs in the simulation, this class searches for an agent that is willing to accept the task.
- The *Statistics* class uses the simulation events to generate a log and to compute performance measures, such as delivery times and their mean, median, minimum, maximum, standard deviation, and variance.

4.2 Simulator Configuration

The simulation behavior can be configured in various ways.

- *Parameters*: define values that are used during simulation, e.g., the default reward that is paid for parcel delivery.
- *Delivery tasks*: define when a task occurs, its initial location, and its destination.
- *GPS events*: provide the couriers' GPS data. For each courier, there exists a sequence of GPS events. Each GPS event consists of a timestamp, the courier ID, and a geographic location (latitude, longitude). The simulator can use real or artificial GPS data provided as CSV files.
- *Task Assignment Strategy*: determines how tasks are assigned to the available agents.
- *Task Acceptance Strategy*: implements the agents' decision making regarding task acceptance.

In the remainder of this section, we explain the task assignment strategy and the task acceptance strategy.

Task Assignment Strategy. The task assignment strategy determines how new tasks are assigned to the available couriers. The strategy receives the unassigned task and the set of couriers W who are currently active. From W, the strategy selects one $w \in W$ who shall perform the task. If w accepts the task, the assignment takes place. If w rejects the task, the strategy is queried again, now with $W \setminus \{w\}$. This procedure is repeated until the task gets assigned or W is empty. If W is empty, the assignment fails and has to be re-attempted later.

A simple example of assignment strategies is distance-based assignment, where the task is assigned to the nearest courier who accepts it.

Task Acceptance Strategy. The task acceptance strategy determines whether an agent accepts a task. The strategy receives the unassigned task and the agent with their shipping plan. Based on the task properties (pickup location, destination, reward) and the agent's shipping plan, the strategy responds with acceptance or rejection.

The shipping plan includes already accepted tasks and allows to compute necessary detours. With shipping plans, it is easy to implement the most common strategies of the crowdshipping literature (see Sect. 2), e.g., acceptance based on detour thresholds. How these strategies can be implemented is shown in Sect. 5.3.

5   Modeling Agent Behavior with Shipping Plans

In this section, we describe how the agents' task acceptance decisions can be modeled and implemented with shipping plans.

5.1   Model

A parcel delivery task p is a tuple (l_p, d_p) where l_p is the current location of the parcel and d_p is its destination.

Each agent $a \in A$ consists of the following information: (l_a, d_a, ϕ_a) where l_a is the agent's current location, d_a is the agent's destination, and ϕ_a is the agent's shipping plan. The agent's destination d_a is fixed. The agent's current location l_a changes over time. The agent's shipping plan ϕ_a is a sequence of waypoints that the agent has to visit to deliver their assigned tasks. Many common assumptions about the agents' acceptance behavior can be modeled with shipping plans.

A shipping plan ϕ_a is an ordered sequence of waypoints that agent a intends to visit to pickup and deliver parcels. For each parcel, the agent has to visit two waypoints: one for pickup and one for dropoff. Whenever the agent accepts a new delivery task, the two waypoints are inserted into the agent's shipping plan such that pickup takes place before dropoff and the additionally required travel distance is minimal.

More formally, a waypoint w is a tuple (l_w, p_w, x_w) where l_w denotes the location of the waypoint and p_w is the parcel on which action x_w is performed. Let action x_w be element of the set $\{\text{pickup}, \text{dropoff}\}$. For each parcel p, the two waypoints are initialized as follows: (l_p, p, pickup) and $(d_p, p, \text{dropoff})$.

The agent always moves towards the first waypoint of the shipping plan. As soon as this waypoint w is reached, the agent performs action x_w on parcel p_w and w is removed from the shipping plan. Then, the agent continues the journey towards the new first waypoint. When the shipping plan is empty, the agent moves towards their destination.

5.2 Methods of Shipping Plans

Shipping plans have different methods, which are listed in Table 2. While most of them are self-explanatory, the agent's detour requires some explanation.

Table 2. Methods of shipping plans

Operation	Description
Insert waypoints for delivery task p	Adds waypoints for p to the shipping plan such that the required detour is minimal
Remove waypoints of delivery task p	Removes the waypoints that are associated with task p
Number of waypoints	Returns the number of waypoints included in the shipping plan
Length of shipping plan	Returns the number of delivery tasks associated with the shipping plan
Length of detour	Computes the total detour that has to be made by an agent to visit the waypoints in comparison to traveling from l_a to d_a directly

Detour of Shipping Plans. The $planDetour(\phi_a)$ is the additional distance that agent a has to cover to visit the waypoints in the given order compared to the shortest route between the agent's current location l_a and destination d_a. As mentioned, we assume that agents choose the order of waypoints that implies the minimal necessary travel distance and that agents always travel on the shortest route between waypoints. When ϕ_a is empty, $planDetour(\phi_a)$ is zero.

Figure 2 visualizes the detour computation for an agent a who wants to travel from l_a to d_a. The shortest route has a distance $d = D(l_a, d_a)$. If a accepts the delivery task p, the agent has to visit the pickup location l_p and the dropoff location d_p before traveling to destination d_a. The length of this route is $d' = D(l_a, l_p) + D(l_p, d_p) + D(d_p, d_a)$. The $planDetour(\phi_a) = d' - d$.

Knowing the detour, the agent can reject tasks that require travels beyond their personal detour threshold or that are too costly in terms of required effort to be compensated by the promised delivery reward.

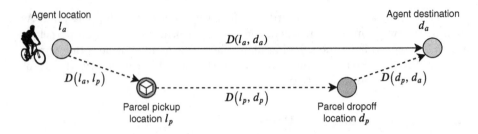

Fig. 2. Shipping plan with two waypoints

5.3   Implementing Task Acceptance Strategies with Shipping Plans

We show how the assumptions identified in Sect. 2 can be implemented with shipping plans.

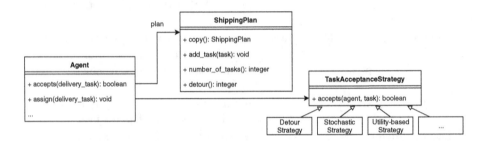

Fig. 3. Class diagram

Figure 3 shows the class diagram of the most important classes that are involved in the acceptance decision. The `Agent` class has methods to check whether the agent is willing to accept a delivery task and to assign the task to the agent. Each agent has a `ShippingPlan`, which has different methods to copy an existing plan, to add tasks to the plan, to obtain the number of tasks included in the plan, and to obtain the detour that is caused by the shipping plan. To decide whether to accept a delivery task, the agent uses a `TaskAcceptanceStrategy`. The strategy provides an `accepts` methods, that given the agent and the task returns whether the agent accepts the task. The concrete strategies are implemented as subclasses of `TaskAcceptanceStrategy`. We use Python code to demonstrate how different strategies can be implemented. Stochastic acceptance and acceptance based on coverage areas can be implemented without shipping plans. We show code for the acceptance based on capacities, detour thresholds, and utilities.

Capacity-Based. The capacity-based acceptance can be implemented with the following lines of code:

```
def accepts(agent, task):
    return agent.plan.number_of_tasks() + 1 <= CAPACITY_LIMIT
```

The given agent accepts the given task if, by adding one more task, the plan does not exceed the capacity limit. `CAPACITY_LIMIT` is a constant value that is defined somewhere else and used for all agents.

Detour Threshold

```
def accepts(agent, task):
    plan_with_task = agent.plan.copy()
    plan_with_task.add_task(task)
    detour = plan_with_task.detour()
    return detour < DETOUR_THRESHOLD
```

The required detour is computed by adding the task to a copy of the agent's current plan. The agent accepts the task if the detour does not exceed a certain detour threshold.

Utility-Based Acceptance. To compute the agent's utility, the detour can be computed as in the detour strategy above. Then the costs of the required detour can be compared with the delivery reward.

```
def accepts(agent, task):
    detour = compute_detour(agent.plan, task)
    detour_cost = detour * COSTS_PER_METER_OF_DETOUR
    utility = task.reward - detour_cost
    return utility > 0
```

The agent accepts the task if the task yields a positive utility.

6   Simulation Experiments

We performed explorative experiments with our simulator[1] to demonstrate its capabilities. Even though it is hard to show whether a deployed crowdshipping system would behave exactly like in our simulation, we will show that our simulator produces plausible results. We demonstrate the plausibility of the simulation results by running the simulation with different parameter values and observing their effects. For instance, if agents are willing to accept larger detours, it can be expected that it is easier to find agents willing to deliver parcels and that therefore parcels arrive at their destinations faster. We demonstrate such dependencies for three input-output pairs: detour and delivery time, required reward and delivery time, and acceptance probability and delivery time.

---

[1] The simulator is available online:
sw-architecture.inform.hs-hannover.de/en/files/crowdsim.

6.1 BiciMAD GPS Dataset

Our simulator can use real GPS data to simulate the agents' movements. Unfortunately, there is no open data set of crowdshipping GPS data that we could use as input for simulation. Therefore, we used GPS data from BiciMAD, the Bike Sharing System of Madrid[2]. The users of BiciMAD rent a bike at one of the bike stations, ride the bike, and then return it at any of the stations. The data set contains the trips performed by the users and the GPS events that were gathered during each trip. For each trip, the data set contains the start timestamp (with some artificial noise for privacy), the start location, the end location, and the GPS traces. We used data from two dates (15 January 2019 and 16 January 2019) with around 17,000 users and 175,000 GPS events in total.

We used this data as bike sharing systems are conceptually similar to crowdshipping systems. There are users that log into the system, move in the city, and log out of the system.

Table 3. Simulation parameters

Parameter	Value
Operating area	Radius of 1.5 km
Delivery tasks	50 per hour (600 total)
Delivery reward	€5
Default agent speed	5 m/s
Task assignment	Assign to nearest
Task acceptance	Detour model | Utility-based model | Stochastic model

6.2 Simulation Setup

We simulated parcel delivery in the urban center of Madrid in an operating area with a radius of 1.5 km. The occurrence, start location, and destination of the couriers were derived from the BiciMAD data set. We generated 50 tasks for each hour between 8:00 and 20:00 o'clock (600 tasks in total). The 50 tasks were uniformly distributed over the hour. The tasks have random origins and destinations within the operating area. Each task completion is rewarded with €5. Tasks are assigned to the nearest agent who accepts. After task acceptance, the agents move with 5 m/s (18 km/h) on a straight line to the parcel location, the parcel destination, and eventually to their personal destination.

We performed experiments with three different task acceptance models: the detour model, the utility-based model, and the stochastic model. The simulation setup is summarized in Table 3.

---

[2] opendata.emtmadrid.es/Datos-estaticos/Datos-generales-(1) (Accessed: 2020-03-12).

For each simulation scenario, we measured the mean and median delivery time. By delivery time, we refer to the time that passed between the occurrence of a parcel and the arrival at its destination. We will show that changing the values of the simulation parameters has the expected effect on the measured delivery time.

6.3   Simulation Results

In this section, we discuss the simulation results under the three different models.

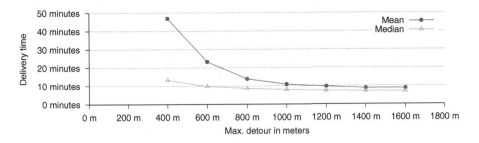

Fig. 4. Delivery times using the detour model

Detour Model. Figure 4 shows the delivery times for different instantiations of the detour model. When all agents accepted a detour of at most 400 m, the *median delivery time* was about 13 min. As expected, the median delivery time decreased when agents accepted larger detours. When agents accepted a detour of up to 1600 m, the median delivery time was about 7 min.

The *mean delivery times* follow a similar curve. However, while most tasks find a willing agent reasonably quickly, there are some that require larger detours and therefore a lot of time to get delivered. When agents accepted detours of at most 400 m, the longest delivery time was 32 h. This causes the difference between the median and mean delivery times. Such parcels should be delivered by professional drivers or by a group of cooperating agents.

Utility-Based Model. Figure 5 shows the delivery times for different instantiations of the utility-based model. All tasks were compensated with a reward of €5. When the agents demanded at least €1 for each kilometer of detour, the *median delivery time* was about 6 min. As expected, when agents demanded higher compensations, the median delivery times increased. When all agents demand more, it takes generally longer to find an agent for whom the detour is small enough to be acceptable. When agents demanded at least €8 for each kilometer of detour, the median delivery time was about 10 min.

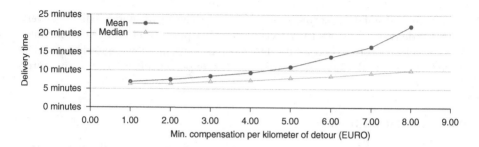

Fig. 5. Delivery times using the utility-based model and a reward of €5

The *mean delivery times* also increased when agents demanded higher compensation. In comparison with the median delivery times, the mean delivery times increased faster. Again, this is caused by a small number of parcels that require large detours. In one case, the parcel could only be delivered after 23 h.

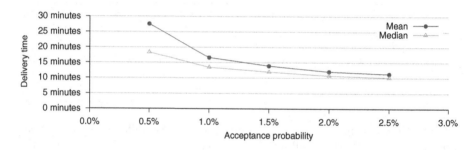

Fig. 6. Delivery times using the stochastic model

Stochastic Model. Figure 6 shows the delivery times for the stochastic model. When agents accepted tasks with a probability of 0.5%, the *median delivery time* was 18 min. By increasing the acceptance probability, the median delivery time decreased, as was expected. For an acceptance probability of 2.5%, the median delivery time was about 10 min.

As in the other models, the *median delivery time* is affected by a small fraction of parcels whose delivery takes very long. In the worst case, the delivery took 2 h and 38 min.

In summary, we observed the expected behavior for all of the three behavior models. Delivery times decreased when agents were willing to make larger detours, when agents were satisfied with lower rewards, and when the acceptance probability was increased. Even though it is unlikely that the simulation outcomes correspond exactly to the outcomes that would be observed in a deployed crowdshipping system, the behavior of our simulator responds plausibly to changes of the simulation parameters. While realistic values would require careful calibration, ideally guided by real-world observations, with our simulator different assignment and acceptance strategies can be tested and the tendencies of their effects can be observed.

7   Conclusion

Crowdshipping is a promising paradigm to face the challenges of last-mile delivery and is an interesting application area for agent-based systems and agreement technologies. To test and evaluate new crowdshipping concepts prior to deployment, a crowdshipping simulator is required. In this paper, we have presented an agent-based crowdshipping simulator, in which the individuals of the crowd are modeled as autonomous agents that take decisions based on shipping plans. Shipping plans allow modeling a wide range of agent behaviors that can be found in the crowdshipping literature. The runtime behavior of the simulator can be adapted and extended via strategies. Our experiments demonstrated the capabilities of our simulator and showed that plausible results can be obtained.

References

1. Alt, F., Shirazi, A.S., Schmidt, A., Kramer, U., Nawaz, Z.: Location-based crowdsourcing: extending crowdsourcing to the real world. In: Proceedings of the 6th Nordic Conference on Human-Computer Interaction: Extending Boundaries, NordiCHI 2010, pp. 13–22. ACM, New York (2010). https://doi.org/10.1145/1868914.1868921
2. Archetti, C., Savelsbergh, M., Speranza, M.G.: The vehicle routing problem with occasional drivers. Eur. J. Oper. Res. **254**(2), 472–480 (2016). https://doi.org/10.1016/j.ejor.2016.03.049
3. Arslan, A.M., Agatz, N., Kroon, L., Zuidwijk, R.: Crowdsourced delivery–a dynamic pickup and delivery problem with ad hoc drivers. Transp. Sci. **53**(1), 222–235 (2019). https://doi.org/10.1287/trsc.2017.0803
4. Bonabeau, E.: Agent-based modeling: Methods and techniques for simulating human systems. Proc. Natl. Acad. Sci. **99**(suppl 3), 7280–7287 (2002). https://doi.org/10.1073/pnas.082080899
5. Buldeo Rai, H., Verlinde, S., Merckx, J., Macharis, C.: Crowd logistics: an opportunity for more sustainable urban freight transport? Eur. Transp. Res. Rev. **9**(3), 1–13 (2017). https://doi.org/10.1007/s12544-017-0256-6
6. Chen, W., Mes, M., Schutten, M.: Multi-hop driver-parcel matching problem with time windows. Flex. Serv. Manuf. J. **30**(3), 517–553 (2017). https://doi.org/10.1007/s10696-016-9273-3
7. Dayarian, I., Savelsbergh, M.: Crowdshipping and same-day delivery: employing in-store customers to deliver online orders (2017)
8. Dötterl, J., Bruns, R., Dunkel, J., Ossowski, S.: On-time delivery in crowdshipping systems: an agent-based approach using streaming data. In: Frontiers in Artificial Intelligence and Applications, ECAI 2020, vol. 325, pp. 51–58. IOS Press Ebooks (2020). https://doi.org/10.3233/FAIA200075
9. Estellés-Arolas, E., de Guevara, F.G.L.: Towards an integrated crowdsourcing definition. J. Inf. Sci. **38**(2), 189–200 (2012). https://doi.org/10.1177/0165551512437638

10. Gdowska, K., Viana, A., Pedroso, J.P.: Stochastic last-mile delivery with crowd-shipping. Transp. Res. Procedia **30**, 90–100 (2018). https://doi.org/10.1016/j.trpro.2018.09.011

11. Gevaers, R., de Voorde, E.V., Vanelslander, T.: Cost modelling and simulation of last-mile characteristics in an innovative b2c supply chain environment with implications on urban areas and cities. Procedia Soc. Behav. Sci. **125**, 398–411 (2014). https://doi.org/10.1016/j.sbspro.2014.01.1483, eighth International Conference on City Logistics 17-19 June 2013, Bali, Indonesia

12. Giret, A., Carrascosa, C., Julian, V., Rebollo, M., Botti, V.: A crowdsourcing approach for sustainable last mile delivery. Sustainability **10**(12) (2018). https://doi.org/10.3390/su10124563

13. Lee, H.L., Whang, S.: Winning the last mile of e-commerce. MIT Sloan Manage. Rev. **42**(4), 54–62 (2001)

14. Macal, C.M., North, M.J.: Tutorial on agent-based modeling and simulation. In: Proceedings of the Winter Simulation Conference, p. 14 pp. (2005). https://doi.org/10.1109/WSC.2005.1574234

15. Marcucci, E., Le Pira, M., Carrocci, C.S., Gatta, V., Pieralice, E.: Connected shared mobility for passengers and freight: investigating the potential of crowd-shipping in urban areas. In: 2017 5th IEEE International Conference on Models and Technologies for Intelligent Transportation Systems (MT-ITS), pp. 839–843, June 2017. https://doi.org/10.1109/MTITS.2017.8005629

16. North, M.J., et al.: Complex adaptive systems modeling with repast simphony. Complex Adapt. Syst. Model. **1**(1), 3 (2013). https://doi.org/10.1186/2194-3206-1-3

17. Ossowski, S. (ed.) Agreement Technologies. Springer, Heidelberg (2013). https://doi.org/10.1007/978-94-007-5583-3

18. Paloheimo, H., Lettenmeier, M., Waris, H.: Transport reduction by crowdsourced deliveries - a library case in Finland. J. Clean. Prod. **132**, 240–251 (2016). https://doi.org/10.1016/j.jclepro.2015.04.103

19. Punel, A., Ermagun, A., Stathopoulos, A.: Studying determinants of crowd-shipping use. Travel Behav. Soc. **12**, 30–40 (2018). https://doi.org/10.1016/j.tbs.2018.03.005

20. Punel, A., Stathopoulos, A.: Modeling the acceptability of crowdsourced goods deliveries: role of context and experience effects. Transp. Res. Part E Logist. Transp. Rev. **105**, 18–38 (2017). https://doi.org/10.1016/j.tre.2017.06.007

21. Rebollo, M., Giret, A., Carrascosa, C., Julian, V.: The multi-agent layer of CALMeD SURF. In: Belardinelli, F., Argente, E. (eds.) EUMAS/AT -2017. LNCS (LNAI), vol. 10767, pp. 446–460. Springer, Cham (2018). https://doi.org/10.1007/978-3-030-01713-2_31

22. Rodríguez-García, M.Á., Fernández, A., Billhardt, H.: Dynamic delivery plan adaptation in open systems. In: Lujak, M. (ed.) AT 2018. LNCS (LNAI), vol. 11327, pp. 190–198. Springer, Cham (2019). https://doi.org/10.1007/978-3-030-17294-7_14

23. Sadilek, A., Krumm, J., Horvitz, E.: Crowdphysics: planned and opportunistic crowdsourcing for physical tasks. SEA **21**(10,424), 125–620 (2013)

24. Savelsbergh, M., van Woensel, T.: City logistics: challenges and opportunities. Transp. Sci. **50**(2), 579–590 (2016). https://doi.org/10.1287/trsc.2016.0675

25. Tisue, S., Wilensky, U.: Netlogo: a simple environment for modeling complexity. In: International Conference on Complex Systems (2004)

26. Wang, Y., Zhang, D., Liu, Q., Shen, F., Lee, L.H.: Towards enhancing the last-mile delivery: an effective crowd-tasking model with scalable solutions. Transp. Res. Part E Logist. Transp. Rev. **93**, 279–293 (2016). https://doi.org/10.1016/j.tre.2016.06.002
27. Wooldridge, M., Jennings, N.R.: Intelligent agents: theory and practice. Knowl. Eng. Rev. **10**(2), 115–152 (1995). https://doi.org/10.1017/S0269888900008122
28. Yan, T., Marzilli, M., Holmes, R., Ganesan, D., Corner, M.: mCrowd: a platform for mobile crowdsourcing. In: Proceedings of the 7th ACM Conference on Embedded Networked Sensor Systems, SenSys 2009, pp. 347–348. ACM, New York (2009). https://doi.org/10.1145/1644038.1644094

EUMAS 2020 Session 4: Agent-Based Models, Social Choice, Argumentation, Model-Checking

Measuring the Strength of Rhetorical Arguments

Mariela Morveli-Espinoza[1]([✉]) [iD], Juan Carlos Nieves[2] [iD],
and Cesar Augusto Tacla[1] [iD]

[1] Program in Electrical and Computer Engineering (CPGEI), Federal University
of Technology of Parana (UTFPR), Curitiba, Brazil
`morveli.espinoza@gmail.com, tacla@utfpr.edu.br`
[2] Department of Computing Science of Umeå University, Umeå, Sweden
`jcnieves@cs.umu.se`

Abstract. Rhetorical arguments are used in negotiation dialogues when a proponent agent tries to persuade his opponent to accept a proposal more readily. When more than one argument is generated, the proponent must compare them in order to select the most adequate for his interests. A way of comparing them is by means of their strength values. Related articles propose a calculation based only on the components of the rhetorical arguments, i.e., the importance of the opponent's goal and the certainty level of the beliefs that make up the argument. This article aims to propose a model for the measurement of the strength of rhetorical arguments, which is inspired on the pre-conditions of credibility and preferability stated by Guerini and Castelfranchi. Thus, we suggest the use of two new criteria to the strength calculation: the credibility of the proponent and the status of the opponent's goal in the goal processing cycle. The model is empirically evaluated and the results demonstrate that the proposed model is more efficient than previous works of the state of the art in terms of number of exchanged arguments and number of reached agreements.

Keywords: Rhetorical arguments · Strength calculation · Persuasive negotiation

1 Introduction

Negotiation is a key form of interaction, among agents, that is used for resolving conflicts and reaching agreements. Arguments used in negotiation dialogues are generally explanatory ones and allow agents to argue about their beliefs or other mental attitudes during the negotiation process [16]. Nevertheless, there are other types of arguments that may act as persuasive elements. These ones are called rhetorical arguments[1] and are the following:

---

[1] When an agent uses rhetorical arguments to back their proposals, the negotiation is called persuasive negotiation [17].

© Springer Nature Switzerland AG 2020
N. Bassiliades et al. (Eds.): EUMAS 2020/AT 2020, LNAI 12520, pp. 415–430, 2020.
https://doi.org/10.1007/978-3-030-66412-1_26

- **Threats** carry out sanctions when the opponent does not accept the proposal sent by the proponent.
- **Rewards** are used when the proponent wants to entice an opponent to do a certain action by offering to do another action as a reward or by offering something that the opponent needs.
- **Appeals** try to persuade the opponent by offering a reward; however, this recompense is not a consequence of an action of the proponent. If the proponent does not have a recompense to offer, he can appeal to one goal of the opponent that does not need the proponent's intervention. Appeals can be seen as self-rewards [3].

Let us consider a scenario of a Consumer Complaint Website whose goal is to try to resolve a conflict between consumers and companies. In this scenario, a software agent (denoted by CONS) complains about a service on behalf of a human user and another software agent acts in behalf of a company (denoted by COMP), offers possible solutions. In the following example, the user of CONS missed an international flight due to a schedule change and he wants the airline company to reimburses him the total price of the ticket; however, the airline company only wants to refund the 20% of the total price of the ticket. At this point, CONS tries to force COMP to accept his proposal and decides to send a threat. The following are two threats that CONS can generate:

- th_1 : *You should refund the total price of the ticket, otherwise I will never buy a ticket in your company anymore, so you will not reach your financial goals.*
- th_2 : *You should refund the total price of the ticket, otherwise I will destroy your reputation in social networks, so you will not gain the award to the Best Airline Frequent Flier Loyalty Program (BAFFLP).*

The question is: which of these threats (arguments) will CONS choose to try to persuade COMP to accept his proposal? According to Guerini and Castelfranchi [9], a rhetorical argument has to meet some pre-conditions in order for the proponent to reach a negotiation favorable to him; therefore, the chosen argument has to be in the set of arguments that meet such pre-conditions. However, before the proponent decides what argument to send, he needs to have a way of differentiating the arguments of that set. A way of doing it is by measuring their strengths [17]. Thus, the research question of this article is: *What criteria should an agent take into account in order to measure the strength of a rhetorical argument and how should this measurement be done?*

Some studies about rhetorical arguments strength take into account the importance of the opponent's goal and the certainty level of the beliefs that make up the argument [3,5]. However, there exist situations in which other criteria are needed in order to perform a more exact measurement of the arguments strength. To make this discussion more concrete, consider the following situations:

- CONS knows that "reaching the financial goals" (denoted by go_1) and "gaining the award to the BAFFLP" (denoted by go_2) are two goals of COMP –the opponent– that have the same importance. If CONS only considers the importance of the opponent's goal to calculate the strength of the threats built with these goals, he cannot decide which threat to send because all of them have the same strength. Thus, there exist the need of another criterion –related to the COMP's goals– that helps CONS to break the ti.e. In order to achieve a goal, it has to pass for some states before be considered achieved. For instance, assume that go_1 has already been achieved; hence, threatening this goal would not be useful for CONS. On the other hand, COMP has not achieved go_2 yet; hence, attacking it can make COMP lose the award; and consequently, he will not achieve go_2.

– CONS has already threaten other companies before and rarely he has fulfilled his threats, and agent COMP knows about it. In this case, the strength of a threat sent by CONS is also influenced by his credibility.

In the first case, notice that besides importance, there is another criterion to evaluate the worth of an opponent's goal, because it does not matter how important a goal is if it is far from being achieved or if it is already achieved. In the second case, the credibility of the proponent should also be considered, since even when the an opponent's goal is very important and/or achievable, a low level of credibility could impact on the strength value of an argument. Thus, the new suggested criteria for the measurement of the strength of rhetorical arguments are the proponent's credibility and the status of the opponent's goal.

To determine the possible statuses of a goal, we base on the Belief-based Goal Processing (BBGP) model [8]. In this model, the processing of goals is divided in four stages: (i) activation, (ii) evaluation, (iii) deliberation, and (iv) checking; and the status a goal can adopt are: (i) active (=desire), (ii) pursuable, (iii) chosen, and (iv) executive (=intention). The status of a goal changes when it passes from one stage to the next. Thus, when it passes the activation stage it becomes active, when it passes the evaluation stage it becomes pursuable, and so on. A goal is closer to be achieved when it is closer of passing the last stage. Besides, we consider the cancelled status. A goal is cancelled when it is not pursued anymore.

Next Section presents the knowledge representation and the architecture of BBGP-based agent. Section 3 is devoted to the logical definition of rhetorical arguments. Section 4 presents the strength calculation model. It includes the analysis of the criteria that will be considered and the steps of the model. Section 5 presents the empirical evaluation of the proposed model. In Sect. 6, we discuss the related work. Finally, Sect. 7 summarizes this article and outlines future work.

2   Knowledge Representation and Negotiating Agents

We use rule-based systems to represent the mental states of the agent. Thus, let $\mathcal{L}$ be a set of finite literals[2] $l, l_1, ..., l_n$ in first order logical language and $\mathcal{C}$

---

[2] Literals are atoms or negation of atoms (the negation of an atom A is denoted $\neg A$).

a set of finite constant symbols. Facts are elements of $\mathcal{L}$, strict rules are of the form $r = l_1, ..., l_n \rightarrow l$, and defeasible rules are of the form $r = l_1, ..., l_n \Rightarrow l$. $\mathtt{HEAD}(r) = l$ denotes the head of a rule and $\mathtt{BODY}(r) = \{l_1, ..., l_n\}$ denotes the body of the rule. We assume that the body of every strict/defeasible rule is finite and not empty. We now define a theory as a triple $\mathcal{T} = \langle \mathcal{F}, \mathcal{S}, \mathcal{D} \rangle$ where $\mathcal{F} \subseteq \mathcal{L}$ is a set of facts, $\mathcal{S}$ is a set of strict rules, and $\mathcal{D}$ is a set of defeasible rules. As consequence operator, we use derivation schemas.

Definition 1 (Derivation schema [2]). *Let $\mathcal{T} = \langle \mathcal{F}, \mathcal{S}, \mathcal{D} \rangle$ be a theory and $l \in \mathcal{L}$. A derivation schema for l from $\mathcal{T}$ is a finite sequence $T = \{(l_1, r_1), ..., (l_n, r_n)\}$ such that:*
- *$l_n = l$, for $i = 1...n$, $l_i \in \mathcal{F}$ and $r_i = \emptyset$, or $r_i \in \mathcal{S} \cup \mathcal{D}$ and $\mathtt{HEAD}(r_i) = l_i$ and $\mathtt{BODY}(r_i) \subseteq \{l_1, ..., l_{i-1}\}$*
- *$\mathtt{SEQ}(T) = \{l_1, ..., l_n\}$, $\mathtt{FACTS}(T) = \{l_i \mid i \in \{1, ..., n\}, r_i = \emptyset\}$*
- *$\mathtt{STRICT}(T) = \{r_i \mid i \in \{1, ..., n\}, r_i \in \mathcal{S}\}$, $\mathtt{DEFE}(T) = \{r_i \mid i \in \{1, ..., n\}, r_i \in \mathcal{D}\}$*
- *$\mathtt{CN}(\mathcal{T})$ denotes the set of all literals that have a derivation schema from $\mathcal{T}$, i.e., the consequences drawn from $\mathcal{T}$.*

T is *minimal* when $\nexists T' \subset (\mathtt{FACTS}(T), \mathtt{STRICT}(T), \mathtt{DEFE}(T))$ such that $l \in \mathtt{CN}(T')$. A set $\mathcal{L}' \subseteq \mathcal{L}$ is *consistent* iff $\nexists l, l' \in \mathcal{L}'$ such that $l = \neg l'$; otherwise, it is inconsistent.

Definition 2. *A **negotiating BBGP-based agent** is a tuple $\langle \mathcal{T}, \mathcal{G}, \mathcal{O}pp, \mathcal{GO}, \mathcal{S}_{\mathcal{O}pp}, \mathcal{S}_{\mathcal{GO}}, \mathcal{A}, \mathcal{AO}, \mathtt{REP} \rangle$ such that:*

- *$\mathcal{T}$ is the theory of the agent;*
- *$\mathcal{G}$ is the set of goals of the agent, whose elements are ground atoms of $\mathcal{L}$;*
- *$\mathcal{O}pp$ is the opponents base, whose elements are constants of $\mathcal{C}$;*
- *$\mathcal{GO} = \mathcal{GO}_a \cup \mathcal{GO}_p \cup \mathcal{GO}_c \cup \mathcal{GO}_e \cup \mathcal{GO}_{canc}$ is the set of the opponent's goals. $\mathcal{GO}_a$ is the set of the active opponent's goals, $\mathcal{GO}_p$ the set of the pursuable ones, $\mathcal{GO}_c$ the set of the chosen ones, $\mathcal{G}_e$ is the set of the executive ones, and $\mathcal{GO}_{canc}$ is the set of the cancelled ones. These sets are pairwise disjoint. Finally, elements of $\mathcal{GO}$ are ground atoms of $\mathcal{L}$;*
- *$\mathcal{S}_{\mathcal{O}pp}$ is a set of tuples $(op, \mathtt{THRES}, L_{\mathcal{GO}})$ where $op \in \mathcal{O}pp$, $\mathtt{THRES} \in [0, 1]$ is the value of the threshold of the opponent[3], and $L_{\mathcal{GO}} = TH_{\mathcal{GO}} \cup RW_{\mathcal{GO}} \cup AP_{\mathcal{GO}}$ is the set of goals of opponent op such that these goals can be threatanable ($go \in TH_{\mathcal{GO}}$), rewardable ($go \in RW_{\mathcal{GO}}$), or appealable ($go \in AP_{\mathcal{GO}}$). It holds that $\forall go \in L_{\mathcal{GO}}, go \in \mathcal{GO}$, this means that if a goal is in the goals list of an opponent – $L_{\mathcal{GO}}$ – it is also in the opponent's goal set $\mathcal{GO}$. It also holds that $TH_{\mathcal{GO}}, RW_{\mathcal{GO}}$, and $AP_{\mathcal{GO}}$ are pairwise disjoint. Finally, let $\mathtt{TH\_GO}(op) = TH_{\mathcal{GO}}, \mathtt{RW\_GO}(op) = RW_{\mathcal{GO}}$, and $\mathtt{AP\_GO}(op) = AP_{\mathcal{GO}}$ be three functions that return the sets of threatanable, rewardable, and appealable goals of op, respectively;*
- *$\mathcal{S}_{\mathcal{GO}}$ is a set of pairs $(go, \mathtt{IMP})$ such that $go \in \mathcal{GO}$ and $\mathtt{IMP} \in [0, 1]$ represents the importance value of go;*

---

[3] The threshold is a value used in the strength calculation model. This is better explained in Sect. 4.

– $\mathcal{A}$ *(resp.* $\mathcal{AO}$*) is the base of the proponent's actions (resp. opponent's actions). The elements of both bases are ground atoms. The role of action in our calculation model will be further explained in next section;*

– $\mathcal{A}_{val}$ *is a set of pairs* (ac, val) *such that* $ac \in \mathcal{A}$ *or* $ac \in \mathcal{AO}$ *is an action and* $val \in [0, 1]$ *is a real number that represents the value of action* ac *where zero means that* ac *is not valuable at all whereas one is the maximum value of an action.* VALUE$(ac) = val$ *is a function that returns* ac*;*

– REP *is the reputation value of the proponent, which is visible for any other agent.*

Furthermore, goals in $\mathcal{G}$ are divided in (i) goals that the agent himself has to perform actions to achieve them, and (ii) goals that need the opponent involvement to be achieved. For example, the goal of CONS is that COMP refunds the total price of the ticket. For this goal to be achieved, it is necessary that COMP executes the required action. We call this type of goal *outsourced*.

Definition 3 *(Outsourced goal). An outsourced goal* g *is an expression of the form* $g(op, ac)$*, such that,* $op \in \mathcal{O}pp$ *and* $ac \in \mathcal{AO}$ *represents an action that* op *has to perform. Let* OPPO$(g) = op$ *and* ACT$(g) = ac$ *be the functions that return each component of the outsourced goal* g*, respectively.*

We assume that a negotiating agent has in advance the necessary information for generating rhetorical arguments and for calculating their strengths. This information is related to the opponent's goals, the status of these goals, the opponent's actions, and the values of these actions. In order to obtain such information, the agent can gather information about his opponent(s). This approach is known as opponent modelling[4].

3   Threats, Rewards, and Appeals

In this section, we present the logical definitions of the rhetorical arguments that are being studied in this article.

Based on the example presented in Introduction, we can say that a threat (and a reward or appeal) is mainly made up of two goals: (i) an **opponent's goal**, which is the goal of the opponent that is being threatened by the proponent. It is a goal that the opponent wants to achieve. For example, *"reaching the financial goals"* and (ii) an **outsourced goal of the proponent**, which is the goal of the proponent that needs the opponent involvement to be achieved. For example, *"getting that* COMP *refunds the ticket's money"*. Following, we present the formal definition of a threat, reward, and appeal. These definitions are based on the definition given in [3], with some modifications that consider the mental states of the negotiating BBGP-based agent and the rule-based approach.

---

[4] Baarslag et al. [6] present a survey about some techniques of opponent modeling that are based on learning. Other works about opponent modelling with focus on argumentation are [10–12,18].

Definition 4 (Threat). *Let T be the theory of a negotiating BBGP-based agent, G his goals base, and GO his opponent's goals base. A threat constructed from T, G and GO is a triple $th = \langle T, g, go \rangle$, where:*

- *$go \in GO$ such that $go \in \text{TH\_GO}(\text{OPPO}(g))$,*
- *$g \in G$,*
- *$T \cup \neg\text{ACT}(g)$ is a derivation schema for $\neg go$ from T,*
- *$\text{SEQ}(T)$ is consistent and T is minimal.*

Let us call T the support of the threat, g its conclusion and go the threatened goal.

Example 1. Let us formalize one of the threats of CONS. Consider the following mental state of agent CONS:

$S = \{\neg ref(ticket) \rightarrow \neg buy(ticket), \neg buy(ticket) \rightarrow \neg reach(fin\_goa)\}$

$Opp = \{\text{COMP}\}$, $G = \{g\}$ such that $g = get(\text{COMP}, \text{'}ref(ticket)\text{'})$ $GO = \{go_1\}$ such that $go_1 = reach(fin\_goa)$ $S_{Opp} = (\text{COMP}, \text{THRES}, \{go_1\})$ such that $go_1 \in TH_{GO}$

The following threat can be generated:

$th_1 = \langle T_1, g, go_1 \rangle$ such that

$T_1 \cup \neg\text{ACT}(g) = \{(\neg \ ref(ticket), \emptyset),$

$(\neg buy(ticket), \neg \ ref(ticket) \rightarrow \neg buy(ticket)),$

$(\neg reach(fin\_goa), \neg buy(ticket) \rightarrow \neg reach(fin\_goa)\}$

Definition 5 (Reward/Appeal). *Let T be the theory of a negotiating BBGP-based agent, G his goals base, and GO his opponent's goals base. A reward/appeal constructed from T, G, and GO is a triple $re/ap = \langle T, g, go \rangle$, where:*

- *$g \in G$, $go \in GO$,*
- *For rewards: $go \in \text{RW\_GO}(\text{OPPO}(g))$ and for appeals: $go \in \text{AP\_GO}(\text{OPPO}(g))$,*
- *$T \cup \text{ACT}(g)$ is a derivation schema for go from T,*
- *$\text{SEQ}(T)$ is consistent and T is minimal*

Let us call T the support of the reward/appeal, g its conclusion and go is the rewardable/appealable goal. Furthermore, let RHETARG denote the set of threats, rewards, and appeals that an agent can construct from his theory T.

4 Strength Measurement Model

In this section, we start by analysing the pre-conditions for considering a rhetorical argument convincing. Then we detail the steps of the measurement model, including the formula for calculating the arguments' strength.

4.1 Pre-conditions: Credibility and Preferability

Guerini and Castelfranchi [9] claim that a rhetorical argument can be considered **convincing** when it is both credible and preferable. Consequently, the rhetorical argument that will be sent to the opponent has to belong to the set of rhetorical arguments that meet such pre-conditions. Next, we analyze each pre-condition and establish how each of them will be evaluated.

4.1.1 Credibility

When a proponent P utters an influencing sentence to an opponent O, there exists a goal cognitive structure [7,9]. Thus, when P utters a sentence for O about his intention of performing an action, his first goal is that O believes that P is indeed going to benefit or damage O. We can note that this first goal of the proponent is related to his credibility. In other words, when a proponent wants to persuade an opponent, the opponent has to believe that the proponent is credible.

In this work, in order to evaluate the credibility of the proponent, we take into account the following concepts:

1. **The Proponent's Reputation:** Reputation can be defined as a social notion associated with how trustworthy an individual is within a society[5].
   In this work, reputation can be seen as the "social" notion – within an agents society – about how trustworthy the proponent is with respect to fulfil his threats, rewards, and appeals. In other words, it is an evidence of the proponent's past behavior with respect to his opponents. We assume that this value is already estimated and it is not private information. Thus, reputation value of the proponent is known by any other agent. It means that when the proponent begins a negotiation with other agent (his opponent), this one is conscious of the reputation of the proponent. We also assume that the proponent has only one reputation value for the three kinds of rhetorical arguments. The reputation value of a proponent agent P is represented by a real number: $REP(P) \in [0,1]$ where zero represents the minimum reputation value and one the maximum reputation value.

2. **The Opponent's Credibility Threshold:** It is used to indicate the lowest value of the proponent's reputation so that the opponent considers a rhetorical argument credible. Thus, the credibility threshold of an opponent agent O is represented by a real number: $THRES(O) \in [0,1]$ where zero represents the minimum threshold value and one the maximum threshold value. A low threshold denotes a trusting (or easier to be persuaded) opponent whereas a high threshold denotes a mistrustful opponent, i.e., more difficult to be persuaded. We assume that the proponent knows the values of the thresholds of his possible opponents.

The proponent evaluates his credibility by comparing both values: his reputation and the opponent's threshold.

---

[5] The estimate value of reputation is formed and updated over time with the help of different sources of information. Several computational models of reputation consider that reputation can be estimated based on two different sources: (i) the direct interactions and (ii) the information provided by other members of the society about experiences they had in the past (e.g., [15,19,20]).

Definition 6 *(Proponent's credibility).* *Let P be a proponent agent,* REP(P) *his reputation, and* THRES(O) *the threshold of his opponent O. P is credible if* REP$(P) \geqslant$ THRES(O); *otherwise, P is not credible.*

4.1.2 Preferability

The second pre-condition a rhetorical argument has to meet is the *preferability*. This pre-condition is based on the relation between the opponent's goal and the action that the opponent is required to perform. Thus, the opponent's goal must be more valuable for him (the opponent) than performing the required action [9]. If the value of the opponent's goal is greater than the value of the required action then, the argument that uses that goal is considered *preferable*. Let us explain it with human examples. During an assault, a thief (the proponent) threatens the victim (the opponent) with the following sentence: *"If do not give me your bag, I hurt you"*. In this situation, it is rational to think that the physical well-being is more valuable than the required action (*giving the bag*). In another scenario, a boss (the proponent) tries to convince one of his employees (the opponent) to work on Saturdays with the following reward: *"If you work every Saturday, then I will give you a Panettone in Christmas"*. In this situation, it is reasonable to believe that that the value of the opponent's goal (*receiving a Panettone*) is not grater than the value of the required action (*working every Saturday*).

Next, we present the criteria that will be evaluated in order to estimate the value or worth of an opponent's goal.

1. **Importance of the Opponent's Goal:** It is related to how meaningful the goal is for the opponent. The value of the importance of a given goal go is a real number represented by IMP$(go) \in [0,1]$ where zero means that the goal is not important at all, and one is the maximum importance of the goal. The more important a goal is for the opponent, the more threatenable, rewardable, or appealable this goal is.

2. **Effectiveness of the Opponent's Goal:** It is related to the degree to which an opponent's goal is successful for persuasion and it is based on the status of the goal in the goal processing cycle. Let us recall that we are working with BBGP-based agents; therefore, the goals base of the opponent is divided in five sub-sets: active, pursuable, chosen, executive, and cancelled goals. A goal is close of be achieved when its status is chosen or executive and it is far of be achieved when its status is active or pursuable. Thus, depending on its status, a goal can be considered more or less threatenable, rewardable, or appealable. Let us analyse each case:

   – **Threatenable Goal:** Recall that threats have a negative nature. In terms of the status of a goal it means that a threat may make a goal go back to a previous status. In this work, we assume that every threatened goal will become cancelled; so a goal is more threatenable when its status is executive and less threatenable when its status is active. This is because an agent has more to lose when an executive goal is threaten than when an active goal is threaten. Regarding a cancelled goal, it is not threatenable at all.

– **Rewardable/appealable Goal:** In this case, both rewards and appeals have a positive nature. In terms of the status of a goal it means that a reward/appeal may make a goal go forward to an advanced status. In this work, we assume that every rewarded/appealed goal will become executive. Therefore, a goal is considered more rewardable/appealable when its status is cancelled and less rewardable/appealable when its status is chosen. This is because an agent has more to win when a cancelled goal is rewarded/appealed than when a chosen goal is rewarded/appealed. Executive goals cannot be rewarded/appealed because the proponent has nothing to offer that makes them go forward. Therefore, executive goals are not rewardable/appealable at all.

The value of the effectiveness of a goal go depends on the argument that is built using it. We denote by $\mathbf{arg}(go) \in \{th, rw, ap\}$ the type of argument that can be built where th means that the argument is a threat, rw means that it is a reward, and ap means that it is an appeal. The effectiveness of an opponent's goal go is represented by $\mathtt{EFF}(go) \in \{0, 0.25, 0.5, 0.75, 1\}$ such that zero means that go is not effective at all and one means that go is completely effective. The effectiveness is evaluated as follows:

$$
\mathtt{EFF}(go) = \begin{cases}
0 & \begin{array}{l} \text{if } \mathbf{arg}(go) = th \text{ and } go \in \mathcal{GO}_{canc}, \text{ or} \\ \text{if } \mathbf{arg}(go) = rw/ap \text{ and } go \in \mathcal{GO}_e \end{array} \\[2ex]
0.25 & \begin{array}{l} \text{if } \mathbf{arg}(go) = th \text{ and } go \in \mathcal{GO}_a, \text{ or} \\ \text{if } \mathbf{arg}(go) = rw/ap \text{ and } go \in \mathcal{GO}_c \end{array} \\[2ex]
0.5 & \begin{array}{l} \text{if } \mathbf{arg}(go) = th \text{ and } go \in \mathcal{GO}_p, \text{ or} \\ \text{if } \mathbf{arg}(go) = rw/ap \text{ and } go \in \mathcal{GO}_p \end{array} \\[2ex]
0.75 & \begin{array}{l} \text{if } \mathbf{arg}(go) = th \text{ and } go \in \mathcal{GO}_c, \text{ or} \\ \text{if } \mathbf{arg}(go) = rw/ap \text{ and } go \in \mathcal{GO}_a \end{array} \\[2ex]
1 & \begin{array}{l} \text{if } \mathbf{arg}(go) = th \text{ and } go \in \mathcal{GO}_e, \text{ or} \\ \text{if } \mathbf{arg}(go) = rw/ap \text{ and } go \in \mathcal{GO}_{canc} \end{array}
\end{cases}
$$

Based on the importance and the effectiveness of a opponent's goal, we estimate how valuable the goal is. Thus, the worth of an opponent's goal is a function $\mathtt{WORTH} : \mathcal{GO} \to [0, 1]$ and it is estimated as follows.

Definition 7 (Worth of the opponent's goal). *Let go be an opponent's goal, $\mathtt{IMP}(go)$ its importance, and $\mathtt{EFF}(go)$ its effectiveness. The equation for calculating the worth of go is:*

$$
\mathtt{WORTH}(go) = \frac{\mathtt{IMP}(go) + \mathtt{EFF}(go)}{2} \tag{1}
$$

We use the average value because we consider that both criteria are equally significant to make the calculation and they do not overlap each other, since each of them characterizes a different aspect of the goal.

So far, we have analysed the criteria to estimate how valuable an opponent's goal is. In order to evaluate the pre-condition preferability, the proponent has to compare this value with the value the opponent gives to the required action.

Definition 8 (Preferability of an opponent's goal). *Let $go \in \mathcal{GO}$ be an opponent's goal and $ac \in \mathcal{AO}$ an opponent's action. Goal go is preferable if* WORTH$(go) >$ VALUE(ac); *otherwise, it is not preferable.*

4.2   Steps of the Model

During a dialogue, an agent may generate more than one convincing rhetorical argument, so he needs a way to compare such arguments. Thus, the strength value of each argument is necessary to make such comparison. In this sub-section, we study how the previously studied pre-conditions are part of the measurement model and how to obtain the strength values. The output of this model is a set of rhetorical arguments along with their respective strength values.

Before presenting the measuring model, let us analyse de following situation, which will allow to understand the formula for calculating the arguments strength value. Let P be a proponent agent and O his opponent, let REP$(P) = 0.6$ be the reputation of P and THRES$_1(O) = 0.5$ and THRES$_2(O) = 0.2$ be two possible thresholds of O. We can notice that THRES$_1$ reflects a less credulous attitude than THRES$_2$; thus, although P is credible in both cases, the "accurate" value of P's credibility is different for each case since the difference between REP(P) and THRES$_1$ is less than the difference between REP(P) and THRES$_2$. Therefore, the credibility value of P has a different impact on the calculation of the strength of the arguments because the higher the difference between the threshold value and the reputation value is, the higher the credibility of the proponent is. We use next Equation to calculate the **"accurate" value of the credibility** of P with respect to an opponent O, whose threshold is THRES(O).

$$\text{ACCUR\_CRED}(P, O) = \text{REP}(P) - \text{THRES}(O) \tag{2}$$

This value is used to obtain the strength value of the arguments. Thus, the strength of an argument depends on the worth of the opponent's goal and the "accurate" value of the proponent's credibility.

Definition 9 (Strength Value). *Let $A = \langle T, g, go \rangle$ be a rhetorical argument and $O \in \mathcal{O}pp$ be an opponent whose threatened/rewarded/appealed goal is go. The strength of A is obtained by applying:*

$$\text{STRENGTH}(A) = \text{WORTH}(go) \times \text{ACCUR\_CRED}(P, O) \tag{3}$$

We can now show the steps of our proposed model. Figure 1 depicts these steps in a work-flow fashion.

5   Empirical Evaluation

In this section, we present an experiment that aims to evaluate our proposal. For this evaluation, we compare our proposal with its closest alternative approach (i.e., [1,3]), which is based on the importance of the opponent's goal. The

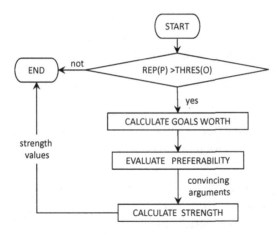

Fig. 1. Work-flow of the proposed strength measurement model.

environment is an abstract one involving just two agents. The experiment was implemented in C++ and the values of the importance and the effectiveness of each argument were generated randomly in the interval [0,1] and in the set $\{0, 0.25, 0.5, 0.75, 1\}$, respectively. These values were always different for each individual negotiation encounter. We use an elementary protocol, where the two agents make moves alternately. The nature of the rhetorical argument is not taken into account, which means that the agents may use any type of argument to defend their interests. An agent sends an argument if he has a stronger argument than the one sent previously by his opponent; otherwise, he accepts the proposal of his opponent.

In our experiment, a single simulation run involves 1000 separate negotiation encounters between two agents. For all the negotiations, the agents were paired against agents that use the same mechanism of strength calculation. We call "BBGP-based agents" the agents that use the strength evaluation model proposed in this article and "IMP-based agents" the agents that use the strength evaluation model based on the importance of the opponent's goal. We performed negotiations where agents generate 10, 25, 50, and 100 rhetorical arguments. This means that an agent has at most 10, 25, 50, or 100 arguments to defend his position. We make the experiments with different amounts of arguments in order to analyse the bias of the efficiency of our proposal. For each setting of number of arguments, the simulation was repeated 10 times. This makes a total of 10000 encounters for each setting. Finally, the experimental variables that were measured are: (i) the number of reached agreements made and (ii) the number of arguments (threats, rewards, appeals) used.

Considering that BBGP-based agents evaluate the credibility before engaging in a negotiation, this leads to three possible situations:

1. Both the proponent and the opponent agents are credible. In this case, a negotiation dialogue begins.

2. The proponent agent is credible, whereas the opponent agent is not credible. In this case, any argument used by the opponent will be evaluated by the proponent due to the opponent low credibility. This means that, the proponent does not believe that any of his goals can be threatened/rewarded/appealed. On the other hand, the arguments used by the proponent can impact on the goals of the opponent. Thus, we settled that the opponent has to accept to do the required action.
3. The proponent agent is not credible, whereas the opponent agent is credible. In this case, the negotiation does not even begin, because the proponent will never convince the opponent.

Figures 2 and 3 show the behavior of the variables *number of exchanged arguments* and *number of reached agreements*, respectively. Recall that for each experiment, we run 1000 negotiation encounters; however, BBGP-based agents only engage in a negotiation when either both are credible or the proponent is credible. We run experiments taking into account different reputation values for the agents and we have noticed that the less the reputation value is the less the number of negotiation encounters is. This is quite rational because low reputation values mean that it is more difficult that agents engage in a negotiation. For the results presented in this experiment, we used a reputation value of 0.8 for both agents and the thresholds are generated randomly in the interval [0, 1] before each negotiation encounter.

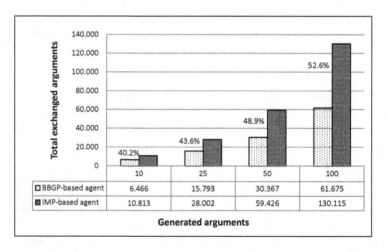

Fig. 2. Comparison of the variable *number of exchanged arguments*. The labels of each group denote the percentage difference between both values represented by the bars.

In summary, we can notice that our mechanism fares better than the other mechanism. This means that when both the worth of the opponent's goal and the proponent's credibility are taken into account, our proposal has better results than the approach based only on the importance of the opponent's goal.

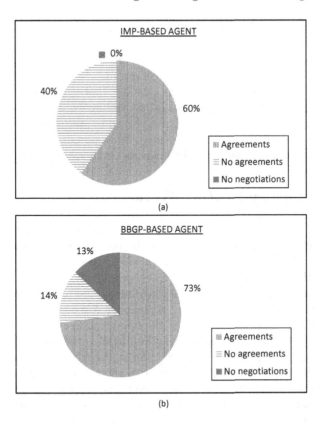

Fig. 3. Percentage of negotiations that end in an agreement versus percentage of negotiations that do not end in an agreement. (a) For IMP-based agents. (b) For BBGP-based agents.

6   Related Work

Ramchurn et al. [17] propose a model where the strength value of rhetorical arguments varies during the negotiation depending on the environmental conditions. For calculating the strength value of an argument, it is taken into account a set of world states an agent can be carried to if he uses such argument. The intensity of the strength values depends on the desirability of each of these states. For a fair calculation, an average over all possible states is used.

Amgoud and Besnard [3–5] present a formal definition of rhetorical arguments and a strength evaluation system. For the evaluation of the strength, the certainty of the beliefs that are used for the generation of the argument and the importance of the opponent's goal are considered.

In previous articles, Morveli-Espinoza et al. [13, 14] employ the criteria status of the opponent's goal and proponent's credibility; however, the pre-conditions that define convincing arguments were not taken into account. Therefore, the proponent's credibility and the preferability of the arguments were not evaluated.

Although the proponent's credibility is considered, the accurate credibility value is not defined, which is important for the strength calculation.

Comparing with the above related work, this article proposes more than a way of calculating the strength of rhetorical arguments, in terms of arithmetical operations. Thus, this article proposes a model that guides the agent during the strength measurement process as can be seen in Fig. 1. The fact of using a criterion related to the participant agents gives to the measure one more dimension and is also useful for avoiding agreements that possibly will not be fulfilled, which may happen when low-credibility agents reach agreements.

7   Conclusions and Future Work

In this article, we have first presented a formalization of a negotiating agent, which is based on the BBGP model. For the measurement of the strength of rhetorical arguments, we base on the proposal of Guerini and Castelfranchi [9], which states that (1) the credibility of the proponent and (2) the preference of the opponent's goal with respect to the value of the required action are two pre-conditions to consider an argument convincing. We use the reputation of the proponent and the threshold of trust of the opponent to evaluate the credibility of the proponent and the opponent's goal importance and its status to evaluate the preferability. We do not use directly the status of an opponent's goal but we judge its effectiveness based on the type of rhetorical argument it makes up and the its status. Based on these pre-conditions, we have proposed a model for evaluating and measure the strength value of the rhetorical arguments. The model starts evaluating the credibility of the proponent agent. The proponent agent can continue to the calculation of the rhetorical arguments only if he is considered credible by his opponent; otherwise, the process ends. We consider that this model is the main contribution of this article.

While it is true that our approach has a better performance, it is also true that it is necessary to model further knowledge about the opponent. This need of further modelling may be seen as a weakness of the model; however, we can notice that in the evaluated variables, the model is always more efficient than the compared approach. Specifically, BBGP-based agents achieved more agreements with fewer exchanged arguments than the IMP-based agents.

We have worked under the premise that the proponent agent knows in advance the information about his opponent. An interesting future work is to complement this model with the study of an adequate opponent modelling approach. We can also consider that the information of the opponent is uncertain, which may directly impact on the strength calculation. Furthermore, in the proposed approach, there is no a model of the environment or the context where the negotiation occurs, especially in terms of organizational structure. We believe that this information can influence on the strength of the arguments and therefore on the persuasion power of the agents, specifically it can influence on the credibility of the agent. Finally, defeasible rules are part of the theory of the agent; however, they were not explored in the article. Another direction of future work will be endow the agents with the ability of generating attacks, such that, during the persuasive negotiation the agents may exchange both arguments and counter-arguments. Such attacks can be directed to the defeasible rules.

Acknowledgements. Mariela Morveli-Espinoza is financed by the Coordenação de Aperfeiçoamento de Pessoal de Nível Superior (CAPES), Brazil. Juan Carlos Nieves was partially supported by the European Union's Horizon 2020 research and innovation programme under grant agreement n° 825619 (AI4EU project).

References

1. Amgoud, L.: A formal framework for handling conflicting desires. In: Nielsen, T.D., Zhang, N.L. (eds.) ECSQARU 2003. LNCS (LNAI), vol. 2711, pp. 552–563. Springer, Heidelberg (2003). https://doi.org/10.1007/978-3-540-45062-7_45

2. Amgoud, L., Besnard, P.: A formal characterization of the outcomes of rule-based argumentation systems. In: Liu, W., Subrahmanian, V.S., Wijsen, J. (eds.) SUM 2013. LNCS (LNAI), vol. 8078, pp. 78–91. Springer, Heidelberg (2013). https://doi.org/10.1007/978-3-642-40381-1_7

3. Amgoud, L., Prade, H.: Threat, reward and explanatory arguments: generation and evaluation. In: Proceedings of the 4th Workshop on Computational Models of Natural Argument, pp. 73–76 (2004)

4. Amgoud, L., Prade, H.: Handling threats, rewards, and explanatory arguments in a unified setting. Int. J. Intell. Syst. **20**(12), 1195–1218 (2005)

5. Amgoud, L., Prade, H.: Formal handling of threats and rewards in a negotiation dialogue. In: Parsons, S., Maudet, N., Moraitis, P., Rahwan, I. (eds.) ArgMAS 2005. LNCS (LNAI), vol. 4049, pp. 88–103. Springer, Heidelberg (2006). https://doi.org/10.1007/11794578_6

6. Baarslag, T., Hendrikx, M.J.C., Hindriks, K.V., Jonker, C.M.: Learning about the opponent in automated bilateral negotiation: a comprehensive survey of opponent modeling techniques. Auton. Agents Multi Agent Syst. **30**(5), 849–898 (2015). https://doi.org/10.1007/s10458-015-9309-1

7. Castelfranchi, C., Guerini, M.: Is it a promise or a threat? Pragmatics Cogn. **15**(2), 277–311 (2007)

8. Castelfranchi, C., Paglieri, F.: The role of beliefs in goal dynamics: prolegomena to a constructive theory of intentions. Synthese **155**(2), 237–263 (2007)

9. Guerini, M., Castelfranchi, C.: Promises and threats in persuasion. In: 6th Workshop on Computational Models of Natural Argument, pp. 14–21 (2006)

10. Hadjinikolis, C., Modgil, S., Black, E.: Building support-based opponent models in persuasion dialogues. In: Black, E., Modgil, S., Oren, N. (eds.) TAFA 2015. LNCS (LNAI), vol. 9524, pp. 128–145. Springer, Cham (2015). https://doi.org/10.1007/978-3-319-28460-6_8

11. Hadjinikolis, C., Siantos, Y., Modgil, S., Black, E., McBurney, P.: Opponent modelling in persuasion dialogues. In: Proceedings of the 23th International Joint Conference on Artificial Intelligence, pp. 164–170 (2013)

12. Hunter, A.: Modelling the persuadee in asymmetric argumentation dialogues for persuasion. In: Proceedings of the 24th International Joint Conference on Artificial Intelligence, pp. 3055–3061 (2015)

13. Morveli-Espinoza, M., Possebom, A.T., Tacla, C.A.: Construction and strength calculation of threats. In: Proceedings of the 6th International Conference on Computational Models of Argument (COMMA 2016), pp. 403–410 (2016)

14. Morveli-Espinoza, M., Possebom, A.T., Tacla, C.A.: Strength calculation of rewards. In: Proceedings of the 16th Workshop on Computational Models of Natural Arguments (CMNA 2016), pp. 8–13 (2016)
15. Pinyol, I., Sabater-Mir, J.: Computational trust and reputation models for open multi-agent systems: a review. Artif. Intell. Rev. **40**(1), 1–25 (2013)
16. Rahwan, I., Ramchurn, S.D., Jennings, N.R., Mcburney, P., Parsons, S., Sonenberg, L.: Argumentation-based negotiation. Knowl. Eng. Rev. **18**(04), 343–375 (2003)
17. Ramchurn, S.D., Jennings, N.R., Sierra, C.: Persuasive negotiation for autonomous agents: a rhetorical approach (2003)
18. Rienstra, T., Thimm, M., Oren, N.: Opponent models with uncertainty for strategic argumentation. In: Proceedings of the 23th International Joint Conference on Artificial Intelligence, pp. 332–338 (2013)
19. Sabater, J., Sierra, C.: Regret: a reputation model for gregarious societies. In: Proceedings of the 4th Workshop on Deception Fraud and Trust in Agent Societies, vol. 70, pp. 61–69 (2001)
20. Yu, B., Singh, M.P.: A social mechanism of reputation management in electronic communities. In: Klusch, M., Kerschberg, L. (eds.) CIA 2000. LNCS (LNAI), vol. 1860, pp. 154–165. Springer, Heidelberg (2000). https://doi.org/10.1007/978-3-540-45012-2_15

Understanding the Role of Values and Norms in Practical Reasoning

Jazon Szabo$^{(\boxtimes)}$, Jose M. Such, and Natalia Criado

King's College London, London, UK
{jazon.szabo,jose.such,natalia.criado}@kcl.ac.uk

Abstract. Mistrust poses a significant threat to the widespread adoption of intelligent agents. Guarantees about the behaviour of intelligent systems could help foster trust. In this paper, we investigate mechanisms to integrate value-based reasoning in practical reasoning as a way to ensure that agents actions align not only with society norms but also with user's values. In particular, we expand a normative BDI agent architecture with an explicit representation of values.

Keywords: Norms · Values · BDI · Responsible AI

1 Introduction

There is a social need to offer guarantees about the behaviour of artificial agents. Endowing agents with the ability to reason about norms and values could enhance not only safety but also trustworthiness of these agents. Values are what we find important in life and they can be used, for example, in explanations about agent behaviour [14]. Furthermore, values can anchor agents to certain behaviours [10] and more generally, values can align the behaviour of agents with our own values, for example in cases of moral reasoning [2]. In fact, value alignment has emerged as one of the basic principles that should govern agents and is an important part of responsible AI [13]. Norms are regulative mechanisms in a society [12] and any responsible agent should be able to behave in a norm-conforming way [9]. Hence, both norms and values are needed to ensure that agents behave in a human-aligned manner [2].

In this paper we will use the following motivational example: Jay is at a restaurant and is using a software assistant to handle the payment. However, Jay is having trouble financially, and so would prefer to tip as little as possible. What should the software assistant consider to find the ideal amount to pay? There are social norms such that tipping 12.5% is ideal, but tipping at least a certain amount, say 5%, is expected. Furthermore, Jay values the happiness of the waiter, conforming to social norms and his financial security; these values

This work was supported by UK Research and Innovation (EP/S023356/1), in the UKRI Centre for Doctoral Training in Safe and Trusted Artificial Intelligence; and the Engineering and Physical Sciences Research Council (EP/R033188/1).

N. Bassiliades et al. (Eds.): EUMAS 2020/AT 2020, LNAI 12520, pp. 431–439, 2020.
https://doi.org/10.1007/978-3-030-66412-1_27

conflict, making the decision non-trivial. Thus, the software assistant should recommend an amount based on Jay's desire to pay as little as possible, the norms about tipping and Jay's values.

In this paper, we argue that the best way to incorporate values to a cognitive agent architecture is to make values basic mental attitude. In particular, we will augment a normative BDI agent [6] with values to create an agent architecture whose behaviour is aligned with societal norms and user's values. We give a way of doing this and identify key properties of this representation of values. We also show how our architecture leads to the correct suggestion in Jay's case. Finally, we discuss related work, limitations and future work.

2   Background

2.1   Preliminaries

We focus on the integration of values and norms in practical reasoning. For this purpose, we use a normative multi-context BDI agent architecture [6] to address the different mental, ethical and normative attitudes in a modular way. A context in a normative BDI agent contains a partial theory of the world. In particular, there are contexts for beliefs, desires, intentions and norms. Reasoning in one context may affect reasoning in other contexts, which is represented by across-context inference rules, named *bridge rules*.

Let $\mathcal{L}$ be a classical propositional language (built from a countable set of propositional variables with connectives $\rightarrow$ and $\neg$). A normative BDI Agent [6] is defined by a tuple $\langle B, D, I, N \rangle$, where:

- B is the belief context, which language is formed by (γ, ρ) expressions, where γ is a grounded formula of $\mathcal{L}$; and $\rho \in [0, 1]$ represents the certainty degree associated to this proposition. The logical connective $\rightarrow$ is used to represent explanation and contradiction relationships between propositions.
- D is the desire context, which language is formed by (γ, ρ) expressions, where γ is a grounded formula of $\mathcal{L}$; and $\rho \in [0, 1]$ represents the desirability degree associated to this proposition.
- I is intention context, which language is formed by expressions such as (γ, ρ) expressions, where γ is a grounded formula of $\mathcal{L}$; and $\rho \in [0, 1]$ is the intentionality degree of proposition γ.
- N is the set of norms that affect the agent. Its language is composed of $(\langle D, C \rangle, \rho)$ expressions, where D is the deontic modality of a norm (i.e., $\mathcal{O}$bligation or $\mathcal{P}$rohibition), C is a literal of $\mathcal{L}$ representing the situations that the agent needs to bring about or avoid according to the norm, and $\rho \in [0, 1]$ is a real value that assigns a relevance to the norm. This relevance represents the degree in which the norm concerns the agent.

In normative BDI agents the information flows from perception to action according to three main steps (see Fig. 1). Here, we briefly describe these steps[1], and explain those processes affected by the incorporation of values:

1. The agent *perceives* the environment and updates its beliefs, and norms.
2. In the *deliberation* step, the desire set is revised. New desires may be created from the user preferences as formulae according to the following bridge rule:

$$\frac{B : (desire(\alpha), \rho)}{D : (\alpha, \rho)} \tag{1}$$

meaning that if $(desire(\alpha), \rho)$ is deduced in context B, then (α, ρ) is inferred in D. Similarly, desires that have been achieved must be dropped. At this step the agent considers the norms and makes a decision about which ones it wants to obey. As a result, new desires are created for fulfilling norms. If the agent is willing to comply with an obligation, then a desire for reaching the state imposed by the obligation is created by the following bridge rule:

$$\frac{N : (\langle \mathcal{O}, C \rangle, \rho), w(C) > \delta}{D : (C, c(\rho, w(C)))} \tag{2}$$

where w calculates the agent willingness to comply with a given norm:

$$w(C) = \frac{\underset{B:(C \to \gamma, \rho_B), D:(\gamma, \rho_D)}{\sum} \rho_B \times \rho_D}{\underset{B:(C \to \gamma, \rho_B)}{\sum} \rho_B} - \frac{\underset{B:(\neg C \to \gamma, \rho_B), D:(\gamma, \rho_D)}{\sum} \rho_B \times \rho_D}{\underset{B:(\neg C \to \gamma, \rho_B)}{\sum} \rho_B} \tag{3}$$

This function considers the desirability of the consequences of fulfilling and violating the norm together with the plausibility of these consequences to calculate the agent willingness to comply with the norm. When the willingness is greater than δ, it means that the agent is willing to comply with the obligation. The degree assigned to the new desire is calculated by the compliance function (c) that considers the relevance of the norm and the willingness to comply with it. For prohibition norms there is an analogous bridge rule creating desires to avoid forbidden states.

3. In the *decision making* step, desires help the agent to select the most suitable plan to be intended. This is implemented by the following bridge rule:

$$\frac{D : (\varphi, \delta), B : ([\alpha]\varphi, \rho), P : plan(\varphi, \alpha, c_\alpha)}{I : (\alpha_\varphi, h(\rho \times (u(\delta) - c_\alpha)))} \tag{4}$$

A formula $([\alpha]\varphi, \rho)$ is interpreted as the probability that φ satisfies the user by executing α. Then, the intention degree to reach a desire φ by means of a plan α is taken as a trade-off between the benefit of reaching this desire (calculated by u, which is a mapping that transforms desire degrees into benefits); and the cost of the plan (c_α), weighted by the belief degree ρ. h is a transformation that maps global benefits back to normalized utility degrees.

---

[1] Neither normative nor practical reasoning is the focus of this paper. We use a simple normative definition to illustrate the interplay between norms and values. For a detailed description of normative and practical reasoning see [6] and [3], respectively.

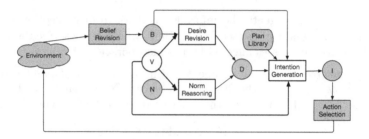

Fig. 1. Reasoning Phases in a normative BDI Agent. Context are represented as circles and bridge rules are represented as boxes. Note white boxes and circles correspond to the inclusion of values into the normative BDI architecture.

2.2 Values

Values are "what is important to us in life" [11] and play a critical role in how people behave. The most widely accepted system of values is the Schwartz Theory of Basic Values [11], which identifies 10 different basic values shared by everyone: self-direction, stimulation, hedonism, achievement, power, security, conformity, tradition, benevolence and universalism. However, how people order values can be different from person to person. For example, in the scenario Jay considers universalism, security and comformity important, in that order[2]. Universalism means to value the welfare of all people and nature. In the scenario to care for the wealth of a waiter would be valued by universalism and so universalism would imply giving a good tip. Security means to value stability in relationships, society and one's self. In the scenario security means to value not wasting money on optional expenses (because in this scenario even such small expenses could cause financial instability) and so would imply giving a low tip or no tip at all. Conformity means to value behaving according to society's rules and expectations. In the scenario conformity values behaving according to the norm that one should tip 12.5%. As we can see values can be aligned with each other or in conflict with each other and humans make decisions considering the relative importance of multiple values. Assuming that universalism, security, conformity is the order of Jay's values, we can intuitively conclude that Jay should leave a good tip.

3   Integrating Values in Normative BDI Agents

Values are fundamentally different from beliefs, desires, intentions and norms [11]: beliefs refer to the subjective probability that something is true, not to the importance of goals as a guiding principles in life; similarly, desires, intentions and norms are about specific situations, whereas values transcend specific situations. Hence, we propose to include a new value context (see Fig. 1).

---

[2] We are using a subset of the ten basic values for brevity.

Our definition of this new context is inspired by Schwartz's theory of values and the 4 key properties necessary for a representation of values [11]: (i) *comparability*, it should be possible to assess values in specific situations and to compare these different situations with respect to a specific value; (ii) *orderability*, values should be ordered by importance; (iii) *practicality*, the agent should consider multiple values and their relative importance when selecting a course of action; and (iv) *normativity*, values influence whether the agent (or person) accepts or rejects a norm.

3.1 Value Language

Syntax. V_C is a set formed by 10 constants, one per each Schwartz value. The language of the value context, denoted by V, is formed by three predicates. Predicates $promote(v, \gamma, \rho)$ and $demote(v, \gamma, \rho)$ —where $v \in V_C$, γ is a propositional variable of $\mathcal{L}$, and $\rho \in [0, 1]$— represent to what degree a state of the world promotes or demotes a value. For example, the statement $demote(security, bigtip, 0.8)$ expresses that leaving a big tip demotes the value of security. Predicate $weight(v, \rho)$ —where $v \in V_C$, and $\rho \in [0, 1]$— represents the extent the agent holds a value important. For example, the statement $weight(security, 0.7)$ expresses that the agent holds the value of security fairly important.

Semantics. For every $v \in V_C$ and propositional variable γ, there is exactly one ρ such that $promote(v, \gamma, \rho)$ holds (and respectively for $demote$). Note that if a proposition doesn't promote a value, it is expressed by $promote(v, \gamma, 0)$ (and respectively for $demote$)[3]. For every $v \in V_C$, there is exactly one ρ such that $weight(v, \rho)$ holds.

3.2 Value-Based Reasoning

The value context endows agents with an explicit representation of values and their importance, and knowledge about which situations promote or demote some values. This representation will allow values to influence the actions taken by agents. To this aim, we need to associate each propositional variable γ of $\mathcal{L}$ with its valuing: i.e., a numerical value representing to what degree states of the world satisfying γ promote the agent's values:

$$val(\gamma) = \frac{\sum\limits_{v \in V_C} (\rho_{promoted} - \rho_{demoted}) \times \rho_{weight}}{\sum\limits_{v \in V_C} \rho_{weight}}$$

where $promote(v, \gamma, \rho_{promoted})$, $demote(v, \gamma, \rho_{demoted})$ and $weight(v, \rho_{weight})$ hold in context V. Note the above function will calculate the valuation as a

---

[3] Depending on the particular domain of application, a constraint to ensure that one of $promote(v, \gamma, 0)$ or $demote(v, \gamma, 0)$ holds could be added to the V context.

value within the $[-1, 1]$ interval, the normalized valuation is defined as:

$$\overline{val}(\gamma) = \frac{val(\gamma) + 1}{2}$$

Desire Revision Bridge Rules. The desire revision bridge rules are modified to avoid the generation of any desire incompatible with the agent's values. For example, the desire generation bridge rule is modified as follows:

$$\frac{B : (desire(\varphi), \rho), \overline{val}(\varphi) > \delta_v}{D : (\varphi, \rho)} \qquad (1^*)$$

A desire to achieve φ is generated if $\overline{val}(\varphi) > \delta_v$, where δ_v is a domain-dependent threshold determining the trade-off between the user goals and desires.

Norm Compliance Bridge Rules. Values guide the selection or evaluation of norms and, hence, it is necessary to update the Norm Compliance Bridge Rules to account for values. In particular, we propose here to modify the willingness function w to include the valuation of each consequence of a norm:

$$w(C) = \frac{\sum\limits_{B:(C \to \gamma, \rho_B), D:(\gamma, \rho_D)} (\rho_B \times \rho_D) \oplus \overline{val}(\gamma)}{\sum\limits_{B:(C \to \gamma, \rho_B)} \rho_B} - \frac{\sum\limits_{B:(\neg C \to \gamma, \rho_B), D:(\gamma, \rho_D)} (\rho_B \times \rho_D) \oplus \overline{val}(\gamma)}{\sum\limits_{B:(\neg C \to \gamma, \rho_B)} \rho_B} \qquad (3^*)$$

where $\oplus$ is a operator that combines the desirability and probability of a consequence with their valuation as a real value within the $[0, 1]$ interval. $\oplus$ is a function such that: $\oplus(1, 1) = 1$, $\oplus$ has as null element 0, and $\oplus$ is increasing with respect to both arguments and is continuous.

Intention Generation Bridge Rule. This rule is modified to consider how intentions affect values. In particular, each plan is assessed not only in terms of cost and benefit but also in terms of the valuation of its consequences:

$$\frac{D : (\varphi, \delta), B : ([\alpha]\varphi, \rho), P : plan(\varphi, \alpha, c_\alpha)}{I(\alpha_\varphi, h((r \times (u(d) - c_\alpha)) \oplus \biguplus\limits_{\gamma \in postcond(\alpha)} \overline{val}(\gamma)))} \qquad (4^*)$$

where *postcond* maps each plan into its postconditions and $\biguplus$ combines different normalized valuation values into a single value within the $[0, 1]$ interval.

In our tipping example, there is a social norm of tipping 12.5% represented in context N. When the agent considers this norm, the agent creates a desire to adhere to the norm (through the norm compliance bridge rules and the willingness function) because the high importance of universalism and conformity values. From this normative desire, an intention is created. Although the plan to pay an ideal tip compromises the financial security of Jay (i.e. the value of security), this negative impact is drowned out by the positive impact the plan has on the values of universalism and comformity. Finally, the agent acts on its intention to leave an ideal tip and recommends it to its user.

3.3   Value Properties

Once the language and rules for representing and reasoning about values have been proposed we will formally discuss the ways in which this formalization satisfies the key 4 key properties of values:

- *Comparability*, predicates *promote* and *demote* allows to compare different situations with respect to a specific value.
- *Orderability*, the *weight* predicate defines an ordering on values. Associating each value with a weight is more general than an ordering on the set of values.
- *Practicality*, actions available to the agent are shaped by their desires and intentions, which themselves are generated and filtered based on values.
- *Normativity*, the modified willingness function considers not only the desirability of each norm consequence but also their impact on the agent's values, thus allowing the agent to reason about which norms to adhere to based on the relative importance of multiple values.

Note that none of these properties would be satisfied in the absence of an explicit representation of values.

4   Discussion

Recent research has looked at ways to integrate values and norms into practical reasoning. For example, Mercuur et al. [10] have incorporated values and norms into social simulations. In their work, agents can act in accordance with values or norms, but they do not consider the interplay between norms and values. However, several authors have claimed that agents should use value-based arguments to decide which action to take, including whether to comply with or violate norms [2,12]. Cranefield et al. [5] have studied how to consider values in plan selection algorithm used by a BDI agent, choosing the plan that is most consistent with the agent's values to achieve a given goal. However, other aspects of value-based reasoning, such as the interplay between values and goals and norms are not considered.

In our work we state that values and norms play a more fundamental role in the functioning of a BDI agent, and a combination of these two mental attitudes enable agents behave in a way that is more aligned with human expectations. In particular, we have made a first attempt to expand a normative BDI architecture [6] with an explicit representation of values and identified 3 key ways in which values influence behaviour: (i) determining which norms should be complied with; (ii) determining which goals are worth pursuing; and (iii) determining the course of action to achieve a goal.

In this paper, we have proposed ways to integrate value-based reasoning in a normative BDI agent by focusing on the quantitative aspects of value promotion and demotion. However, values are usually the object of deliberations of a different nature:

- Values rarely play an explicit role in common decisions. Value-based reasoning is more frequent when humans are faced with new dilemmas usually having conflicting implications for different values [11].
- Situations with respect to a value can not only differ in the degree that the value is promoted or demoted but also in what quality of the value is being promoted or demoted: consider the difference between the relaxing and luxurious pleasure one gets from lying in the sun and the intense and sharp pleasure one gets from quenching a thirst [4]. Even though both actions promote pleasure, they do it in a way that differs not only in how much pleasure is being promoted but also in what kind of pleasure is being promoted.
- Research suggest that humans have an ordering among values. However, it is not clear that humans can state quantitatively value importance or assess in absolute terms how particular situations promote and demote values.

As future work we will work on how to incorporate quantitative reasoning with forms of reasoning that more adequate for value-based reasoning; e.g., severity-based approach [8], coherence maximisation [7] or argumentation [1].

References

1. Atkinson, K., Bench-Capon, T.J.M.: Taking account of the actions of others in value-based reasoning. Artif. Intell. **254**, 1–20 (2018)
2. Bench-Capon, T., Modgil, S.: Norms and value based reasoning: justifying compliance and violation. Artif. Intell. Law **25**(1), 29–64 (2017). https://doi.org/10.1007/s10506-017-9194-9
3. Casali, A., Godo, L., Sierra, C.: A graded BDI agent model to represent and reason about preferences. Artif. Intell. **175**(7–8), 1468–1478 (2011)
4. Chang, R.: Value pluralism. In: International Encyclopedia of the Social & Behavioral Sciences: Second Edition, pp. 21–26. Elsevier Inc. (2015)
5. Cranefield, S., Winikoff, M., Dignum, V., Dignum, F.: No pizza for you: Value-based plan selection in BDI agents. In: Proceedings of IJCAI, pp. 178–184 (2017)
6. Criado, N., Argente, E., Noriega, P., Botti, V.J.: Reasoning about norms under uncertainty in dynamic environments. Int. J. Approx. Reason. **55**(9), 2049–2070 (2014)
7. Criado, N., Black, E., Luck, M.: A coherence maximisation process for solving normative inconsistencies. Auton. Agents Multi Agent Syst. **30**(4), 640–680 (2015). https://doi.org/10.1007/s10458-015-9300-x
8. Gasparini, L., Norman, T.J., Kollingbaum, M.J.: Severity-sensitive norm-governed multi-agent planning. Auton. Agents Multi Agent Syst. **32**(1), 26–58 (2017). https://doi.org/10.1007/s10458-017-9372-x
9. Malle, B.F., Bello, P., Scheutz, M.: Requirements for an artificial agent with norm competence. In: Proceedings of AIES, pp. 21–27 (2019)

10. Mercuur, R., Dignum, V., Jonker, C.: The value of values and norms in social simulation. J. Artif. Soc. Soc. Simul. **22**(1) (2019)
11. Schwartz, S.H.: An overview of the schwartz theory of basic values. Online Read. Psychol. Cult. **2**(1), 11 (2012)
12. Serramia, M., López-Sánchez, M., Rodríguez-Aguilar, J.A., Morales, J., Wooldridge, M.J., Ansótegui, C.: Exploiting moral values to choose the right norms. In: Proceedings of AIES, pp. 264–270 (2018)
13. Sierra, C., Osman, N., Noriega, P., Sabater-Mir, J., Perello-Moragues, A.: Value alignment: a formal approach. In: Responsible Artificial Intelligence Agents Workshop (RAIA) in AAMAS 2019 (2019)
14. Winikoff, M., Dignum, V., Dignum, F.: Why bad coffee? Explaining agent plans with valuings. In: Proceedings of SAFECOMP, pp. 521–534 (2018)

Predicting the Winners of Borda, Kemeny and Dodgson Elections with Supervised Machine Learning

Hanna Kujawska$^{(\boxtimes)}$, Marija Slavkovik, and Jan-Joachim Rückmann

University of Bergen, Bergen, Norway
Han.Kujawska@gmail.com, {marija.slavkovik,Jan-Joachim.Ruckmann}@uib.no

Abstract. Voting methods are widely used in collective decision making, not only among people but also for the purposes of artificial agents. Computing the winners of voting for some voting methods like Borda count is computationally easy, while for others, like Kemeny and Dodgson, this is a computationally hard problem. The question we explore here is can winners of Kemeny and Dodgson elections be predicted using supervised machine learning methods? We explore this question empirically using common machine learning methods like XGBoost, Linear Support Vector Machines, Multilayer Perceptron and regularized linear classifiers with stochastic gradient descent. We analyze elections of 20 alternatives and 25 voters and build models that predict the winners of the Borda, Kemeny and Dodgson methods. We find that, as expected, Borda winners are predictable with high accuracy (99%), while for Kemeny and Dodgson the best accuracy we could obtain is 85% for Kemeny and 89% for Dodgson.

Keywords: Computational social choice · Voting · Machine learning application

1 Introduction

Voting theory is concerned with the design and analysis of methods that choose a winner for elections. An election is a pair (C, V) where C is a finite set of candidates (also called options or alternatives) and V is a set of voters, each represented as a total, strict, asymmetric order $\succ_i$ over C. As a collective decision making method, voting theory finds its implementation not only in politics, but also in automated decision making [22]. One of the computationally simplest methods is, for example, plurality where the winner is the alternative top ranked by the highest number of voters. It is well documented that with some voting methods, such as Kemeny and Dodgson computing the winners is computationally hard, winner determination in the case of both voting methods is Θ_2^p [2,11,12].

Efficient computing of a representative rank of alternatives is also of interest to recommender systems, specifically in collaborative filtering [20]. Unlike voting theory, which has extensively studied what it means for a collective rank

© Springer Nature Switzerland AG 2020
N. Bassiliades et al. (Eds.): EUMAS 2020/AT 2020, LNAI 12520, pp. 440–458, 2020.
https://doi.org/10.1007/978-3-030-66412-1_28

to be representative of individual ranks, in collaborative filtering, the representativeness of a "collective" rank is measured by user satisfaction, which is not always available. Social choice methods, like the Kemeny and Dodgson methods, may have valuable properties [16][1], but it is the high computational complexity that deters from their use. It is therefore interesting to explore whether some "precision" can be "traded off" for computing time. Clearly this is not of interest where exactly the Kemeny/Dodgson winners are sought, but for situations, such as collaborative filtering, where imprecision can be afforded while gaining "representability" of the collective rank in a classic social choice sense.

We ask whether machine learning, specifically classification with supervised learning, can be used to predict the winners of Dodgson and Kemeny elections.

Classification is the problem of assigning a label to a given data point, using a set of labeled data points as examples, called a *training set*. A data point is a vector of values, where each value is associated with a *feature*. Features are used to build a factorized representation of an entity or event. A label, or class, of a data point is the feature we are trying to predict. Training the classifier over a dataset is the process of building a model that when presented with feature values of an unknown instance (example or datapoint) on input, outputs a classification (or a label) for that instance.

We are motivated by the work of Devlin and O'Sullivan [7] who treat satisfiability (SAT) of a Boolean formula[2] as a classification problem. They do this by labeling examples of formulas as satisfiable or unsatisfiable (by having calculated them) and using then these examples as a training data set to build a model that predicts the satisfiability of a formula. They accomplish 99% accuracy for hard 3-SAT problems, and accuracy in excess of 90% for "large industrial benchmarks".

For a given set of candidates C and number of voters $|V|$, it is possible to calculate all the profiles of voters that can occur, that is combinations (with repetition) of strict, total, asymmetric orders over C. For a nontrivially large C and $|V|$ this number can be very big. Can we then, calculate the election winners for some of these profiles, use the so calculated winners as a label for the profile, and use these labeled profiles as a training data set to build a winner prediction model? This is the question we address here. We use a data set of 12360 profiles for 20 candidates and 25 voters and for each of this profiles we calculate the Borda, Kemeny and Dodgson winners.

We hypothesize that the Borda winners can be predicted with high accuracy and use Borda as a kind of "benchmark". We test the predictability of Kemeny and Dodgson winners, as these are computationally hard to calculate. We would like to point out that, it was shown in [18] that the class of scoring rules, of which the Borda method is a member, is efficiently probably approximately correct (PAC) learnable.

---

[1] To be fair, the value of the properties that Dodgson satisfies has been disputed [3].

[2] The satisfiability problem SAT is the problem of deciding whether a given a Boolean formula is admits a truth assignment to each of its variables such that the formula evaluates true.

The first problem of feeding profiles as training examples to a machine learning algorithm is to represent the voting profiles as data points, i.e., use factorized representation of collections of preference orders. There are different ways in which the *factorization* of profiles can be accomplished and the way a profile is factorized can affect the classifier performance. We consider three different factorizations and analyze their fitness for Borda, Kemeny and Dodgson respectively.

Voting rules often are irresolute, namely, for some elections they identify more than one winner in a ti.e. We intend to use the winner as a label that needs to be predicted, however to do this we need to address the problem of ties. We break ties using a lexicographic tie-breaking, which is common in the voting literature, to choose a label for an irresolute profile. However we find out that ties do matter in the accuracy of predicting winners.

To find the right methods for classification, we explored the large pool of all available machine learning classification methods in the scikit-learn library[3] through a process of trial and error. We lastly settled using on ten different classifiers and compared their performance.

Code and datasets for this paper are given at https://github.com/hanolda/learning-election-winners.

This paper is structured as follows. In Sect. 2 we introduce the basic concepts and definitions from voting and machine learning. In Sect. 3 we give an overview of the data sets we used in our experiments. In Sect. 4 we present how profiles can be represented as data sets for supervised machine learning. In Sect. 5 we describe our experiments, results and evaluation methods, while in Sect. 6 we discuss the experiments' outcomes. Related work is discussed in Sect. 7. Lastly, in Sect. 8 we make our conclusions and outline directions for future work.

Our contribution is twofold. Our results in predicting Kemeny and Dodgson winners are promising, but admittedly explorative. We have established feasibility of the approach and are thus opening the possibility to use machine learning for predicting winners in voting and social choice theory. Once learned, a model for a particular size of candidate set and voter set, can be reused for any election of that "size". Predicting the outcomes of functions that can be computed, however computationally inefficient, allows us to check at any point how well the predictor is performing which opens exciting opportunities for predicting instead of calculating voting outcomes when precision is not critical, for example, for the purposes of collaborative filtering, or in pre-election estimation of election results in politics.

2   Background

We first introduce the basic definitions and concepts from voting theory and supervised machine learning.

2.1   Voting Theory

An election is a pair (C, V) where C is a finite set of alternatives (or candidates) $C = \{c_1, c_2, \ldots, c_m\}$ and V is a finite collection of agents or voters. Each voter i

---

[3] https://scikit-learn.org/stable/.

is represented with her *preference relation* i.e., a strict, complete, transitive and antisymmetric order $\succ_i$ over the set C of alternatives. The top-ranked candidate of $\succ$ is at position 1, the successor at position 2, while the last-ranked candidate is at position m. A collection of preference orders $V = (\succ_1, \ldots, \succ_n)$ is called a preference *profile*. A voter i prefers candidate c over candidate c' iff $c \succ_i c'$. A voting rule F is a mapping from an election E to a non-empty subset of C called winners of the election.

The Borda method, or Borda count, is *a positional scoring rule*. Each candidate in C is associated with a score that is obtained by the position that candidate has in the preference orders of the profile. A candidate $c \in C$ receives $m-1$ points from each $\succ_i$ where it is top ranked, $m-2$ points from all $\succ_i$ where it is second ranked, and so on, receiving 0 points when it is the last ranked alternative. Borda winners are the candidates that have a maximal sum of points, which is called Borda score.

The Kemeny method is a *distance-based rule*. For two preference orders $\succ_i$ and $\succ_j$ we can define the *swap* distance, also called Kendall Tau distance, as the minimal number of pairwise swaps required to make the two orders the same. Formally we can define the swap distance d between two orders $\succ$ and $\succ'$ over a set of candidates C with $c_i, c_j \in C$:

$$d(\succ, \succ') = |\{(c_i, c_j) : (c_i \succ c_j \wedge c_j \succ' c_i) \vee (c_j \succ c_i \wedge c_i \succ' c_j)\}|. \qquad (1)$$

The collective preference order of a profile V is the order $\succ$ for which the sum of swap distances from $\succ$ to each $\succ_i \in V$ is minimal. This collective preference order is called a Kemeny ranking of election E. Kemeny winners are the top-ranked alternatives in a Kemeny rank (there could be more than one rank "tied"). Formally we can define the Kemeny method as follows. Let $\mathcal{C}$ be the set of all total, strict and antisymmetric orders that can be constructed over a set of alternatives C.

$$\text{Kemeny}(V) = \underset{\succ \in \mathcal{C}}{\text{argmin}} \sum_{\succ_i \in V} d(\succ, \succ_i) \qquad (2)$$

Before defining the Dodgson method, we need to introduce the concept of Condorcet winner. The Condorcet winner of an election E is the candidate that defeats all other candidates in a pair-wise comparison. Condorcet winners do not exist for every election, but when they do exist, they are unique. Let $\mathcal{V}$ be the set of all profiles for $|V|$ agents that can be formed from $\mathcal{C}$. The Dodgson winner of a profile V is either its Condorcet winner when it exists, or the Condorcet winner of a profile V' which is obtained from V by a minimal number of adjacent swaps. Formally

$$\text{Dodgson}(V) = \text{Condorcet}(\underset{V' \in \mathcal{V}}{\text{argmin}} \sum_{\substack{\succ_i \in V \\ \succ_i' \in V'}} d(\succ_i, \succ_i')), \qquad (3)$$

where V is the set of profiles that have a Condorcet winner and d is the swap distance defined in (2).

Example 1. Let us consider an election E with four candidates $C = \{a; b; c; d\}$ ($|C| = 4$) and $|V| = 7$ voters. Table 1 presents the preference profile of the V voters. Each row represents the preference order of a subset of voters, where the first column is the number who voted with this preference order, and the following column is the order of the vote. For instance, 3 voters have the preference order: $a \succ b \succ c \succ d$.

Table 1. Preference profile example.

Number of voters	Preference order
3 voters	$a \succ b \succ c \succ d$
1 voter	$d \succ b \succ a \succ c$
1 voter	$d \succ c \succ a \succ b$
1 voter	$b \succ d \succ c \succ a$
1 voter	$c \succ d \succ b \succ a$

The Borda winner is b, the Kemeny winner is a, and the Dodgson winner is b. This profile does not have a Condorcet winner because a defeats b and c but not d; b defeats only d, c defeats only d and d defeats only a, in a pairwise comparison.

2.2 Machine Learning

We now introduce the machine learning methods we use in our experiments. These are: XGBoost, Linear Support Vector Machines (SVM), Multilayer Perceptron and regularized linear classifiers with stochastic gradient descent (SGD). These approaches were chosen through a process of trial and error that considered all available machine learning classification methods in the scikit-learn library[4].

Support Vector Machines (SVM). Conceptually, a data point, for which all feature values are real numbers, can be seen as a point in hyperspace. Binary classification would then be the problem of finding a hyper-plane that separates the points from one class from the points of the other class. SVM's find this hyper-plane by considering the two closest data points from each class. Since not all datasets can be separated with a hyper-plane, SVM's use *kernels* to transform the dataset into one that can be split by a hyper-plane. Both linear and nonlinear kernels can be used. The efficiency of a machine learning method can be improved by tuning the so called hyper-parameters of an SVM classifier. The SVM we used provides one hyper-parameter to tune: cost of miss-classification of the data on the training process.

Gradient Boosted Decision Trees (GB) are among the most powerful and widely used models for supervised learning. Predicting a label can be done with

---

[4] https://scikit-learn.org/stable/.

a decision tree built using the training data. To increase the prediction performance, GB builds an ensemble of decision trees in a serial manner: each new tree is built to correct the mistakes of the previous one. GB's offers a wide range of hyper-parameters that can be tuned to improve prediction performance, among else the number of trees ($n\_estimators$) and $learing\_rate$, which controls the degree to which each tree is allowed to correct the mistakes of the previous trees.

Multilayer Perceptrons (MLP) are feed-forward neural networks. MLPs are often applied to supervised learning problems: they learn to model the correlation (or dependencies) in two phases process: *forward* pass - the training data flow moves from the input layer through the hidden layers to the output layer (also called the visible layer). There, the prediction of the output layer is measured against the target labels. The error can be measured in a variety of ways, e.g. root mean squared error (RMSE). In the *backward* pass, *backpropagation* is used to make model parameters, i.e. *weigh* and *bias* adjustments relative to the error. That act of differentiation, based on any gradient-based optimization algorithm, gives us a landscape of error. During the convergence state, the parameters are adjusted along the gradient, which minimize the error of the model.

Regularized Linear Classifiers with Stochastic Gradient Descent (SGD). SGD is very efficient approach in the context of large-scale learning. For classification purposes, regularized linear classifiers use a plain stochastic gradient descent learning routine which supports different regression *loss functions*, that measures the model (mis)fit and the *penalties*, regularization term that penalizes model complexity. SGD is fitted with the training samples and the target values (class labels) for the training samples and for each observation updates the model parameters: *weights* and *bias* (also called offset or intercept). A common choice to find the model parameters is by minimizing the regularized training error.

3   Datasets and Preprocessing

We originally intended to use datasets from the `preflib.org`, however we found them unsuitable for various reasons such as there were too few candidates, or too few profiles in the data set. We used a dataset of 361 profiles of ranked lists of music tracks (songs) from Spotify[5] as a basis to generate a high-dimensional dataset of 12360 profiles. The such obtained datasets consist of profiles for $|C| = 20$ candidates with $|V| = 25$ voters per profile.

The Spotify dataset consists of daily top-200 music rankings for 63 countries in 2017. Ranked are 20 music tracks (songs) described by *position, track name, artist, streams* and *URL*. *A single voter's* preference order represents one ranking for one day in one country. We considered 25 countries on 361 days, as some days had to be removed due to preference order incompleteness. We also only considered profiles that have a unique winner under the three voting methods we studied, as is was our intention to not consider ties.

---

[5] https://spotifycharts.com/regional.

Analyzing the Spotify dataset, however, we observed that the profiles' labels are not uniformly distributed, namely not all candidates are winners of an approximately equal number of the profiles in the dataset. Specifically, the Spotify dataset contains many profiles where the winner is candidate number 16 or candidate 18. We handled this issue by generating a synthetic dataset with the same number of candidates $|C|$ and voters $|V|$ as in Spotify. In the newly built dataset, we kept only those profiles that ensured class-balanced output, i.e., the same number of profiles for each possible winner. The synthetic dataset extends the Spotify dataset into a total of 12360 profiles, which were generated by creating permutations of $|C| = 20$ alternatives and joining them into $|V| = 25$ combinations with repetitions.

For the synthetic dataset we further created three datasets: separately for Borda, Kemeny and Dodgson winners. Each dataset consists of preference ranks (the same for all voting methods) along with labels denoting the winner, as per voting method. For Borda we used all of the 12360 labeled profiles, synthetic and from Spotify. To label the profiles with Kemeny and Dodgson winners, we calculated the winners using DEMOCRATIX[6][5]. DEMOCRATIX was not able to process all of our 12360 profiles. For Kemeny we were able to label 10653 profiles, and for Dodgson we had 11754 labeled profiles.

We split the dataset into a training, validation and testing sets $(70/15/15[\%])$, using the *Stratified ShuffleSplit* cross-validator from the Model Selection module

Table 2. No. profiles for training, validation and test.

Dataset	Training set	Validation set	Test set
Borda	6666	1429	1429
Kemeny	6921	1484	1483
Dodgson	7362	1578	1578

Table 3. Borda, Kemeny and Dodgson winner distribution.

Candidate	As Borda winner	In training	As Kemeny winner	In training	As Dodgson winner	In training
1	483	338	597	418	483	338
10	358	250	299	209	551	386
11	481	337	419	293	511	358
12	307	215	322	225	460	322
13	491	344	397	278	542	379
14	544	381	401	281	519	363
15	522	365	387	271	499	349
16	404	283	381	267	1156	809
17	387	271	360	252	206	144
18	479	335	496	347	513	359
19	513	359	585	409	522	365
2	497	348	613	429	515	361
20	553	387	598	419	500	350
3	494	346	563	394	502	352
4	550	385	612	428	489	342
5	453	317	565	396	501	351
6	475	332	522	365	535	375
7	508	355	633	443	512	358
8	484	339	590	413	513	359
9	541	379	548	384	489	342

---

[6] http://democratix.dbai.tuwien.ac.at/index.php.

of *scikit-learn* library[7], which creates a single training/testing set having equally balanced (stratified) classes. Table 2 presents the train, validation and test split of profiles in the generated dataset. The detailed final distribution of total and training samples per candidate is presented in Table 3.

4 Factorization of Profiles

A profile of votes is a list of total orders, typically encoded as a nested list of ordered lists representing the voters. To be able to use profiles as training data in ML algorithms, we need to find a way to model the profiles using factorized representation. There are several ways in which this can be done and the choice of representation can have a substantial impact on the winner prediction. We explored three different approaches. The approaches differ in what is considered a *feature* of a voting profile.

4.1 Labeling Profiles

Each of the voting methods we consider, Borda, Kemeny and Dodgson, admit non-unique election winners. Namely, more than one candidate can appear in a tie as a winner. We use supervised learning with the profile of votes as a data point and the winner for a given election as the class or label for that profile.

Typically, voting methods are accompanied by tie-breaking mechanisms. There are numerous approaches to tie-breaking including randomly choosing one among the winners or pre-fixing an order over C that will be used for breaking ties. The tie-breaking mechanism does have an impact on the election outcome and the properties of the method [1,15]. We here applied a *lexicographic tie-breaking* and used this winner to label the profiles in the training set.

Other possible approaches we could take, which we leave for future work, is to use the whole set of winners as a label. In this case the set of possible labels for a profile would be the power set of C rather than C as is the case now. Allowing a datapoint to be labeled as a member of more than one class is a subject of study of multi-label classification methods [21]. Both of these approaches pose considerable challenges. Using subsets of C as labels makes the feature engineering and data pre-processing task more elaborate, while multi-class classification methods are not as off-the-shelf wide spread as classification methods.

Observe that the Borda winners can be exactly computed from all three representations, the Kemeny winners from Representation 3, while the Dodgson winners cannot be exactly computed from any of the three.

4.2 Representation 1

In this representation the set of features is the set of candidates C and the value for each feature is the Borda score of the feature. The profile from Example 1 is given in Table 4.

---

[7] The seed for the random number generator during the split is equal to 42.

Table 4. The profile from Example 1 in Representation 1.

f-a	f-b	f-c	f-d	Label
11	12	9	10	b

The shape of the new representation is:

$$(\#profiles, \#candidates).$$

Here, the shape of the Spotify model is $(361, 20)$ and of our generated model is $(12360, 20)$.

The main drawback of this factorization is that it forces anonymity on the profile. Namely the factorized representation loses the information about who voted for whom. The main advantage is that the original profiles don't have to be the same size (number of voters) to transform the dataset to this feature representation. That means that once learned, the prediction model can be used for winner prediction of any new election.

4.3   Representation 2

In this representation there is one feature for each candidate-possible_rank pair. The value of the feature is the number of voters ranking the candidate at the featured position. In other words, we count the number of times each of the candidates is ranked at each position. This is the so called *positional information* of a profile. For example, if the set of candidates has four candidates, we obtain 16 features. The profile from Example 1 is given in Table 5.

Table 5. The profile from Example 1 in Representation 2.

f-a1	f-a2	f-a3	f-a4	f-b1	f-b2	f-b3	f-b4	f-c1	f-c2	f-c3	f-c4	f-d1	f-d2	f-d3	f-d4	label
3	0	2	2	1	4	1	1	1	1	4	1	2	2	0	3	b

The shape of the new representation is:

$$(\#profiles, |C| \cdot |C|).$$

Thus, for given $N = 20$ candidates and length of each vote (ranking) equal to 20 positions, we obtain 400 features. Here, the shape of the Spotify model is $(361, 400)$ and of the generated model: $(12360, 400)$.

The main drawback of this transformation is that we lose the information about the sequence of individual preferences. Although time efficiency was not something we directly were interested in increasing, this representation was observed to lead to a significant reduction in model training time, in particular in when predicting Kemeny winners.

4.4   Representation 3

As a third way to factorize profiles we consider the set of features to be the set of unique pairs of candidates. The value of the feature then is the number of voters that prefer the first candidate to the second in the pair. This is the so called *pairwise majority matrix*. The profile from Example 1 is given in Table 6.

Table 6. The profile from Example 1 in Representation 3.

ab	ac	ad	ba	bc	bd	ca	cb	cd	da	db	dc	label
4	4	3	3	5	4	3	2	5	4	2	3	b

For given $N = 20$ candidates we have 380 possible combinations (without repetition, order matters). The shape of the representation is:

$$(\#profiles, \binom{|C|}{2}).$$

The shape of the Spotify model is: $(361, 380)$ and the generated model: $(12360, 380)$.

5   Experiments and Testing

The three different profile representations yielded nine dataset, three for each voting methods. We considered ten different classifiers. We tested the performance of the classifiers on each representation using cross-validation testing. As evaluation metrics to assess the performance of the ten classifiers we used accuracy and F1-score. Accuracy is the proportion of correctly classified instances from the total number of instances. The F1-score is calculated for each class (category) separately and the average is taken as the final F1-score. For each class the F1-Score is $2 * \frac{precision \cdot recall}{precision + recall}$, where $precision = \frac{t_p}{t_p + f_p}$, $recall = \frac{t_p}{t_p + f_n}$, t_p is the number of true positive, namely the number of samples correctly predicted as positive and f_p is the number of false positive, namely number of samples wrongly predicted as positive.

5.1   Borda Results

Table 7 summaries the performance of the classifiers using Representation 1. We obtain the best accuracy by using the Gaussian Naive Bayes classifier (100%) and XGBclassifier (99,5%). We noticed that the top-performing classification models are those generated by the group of algorithms capable of generating probability predictions. These also had the highest F1-scores. The 100% accuracy of the Naive Bayes classifier could be the result of overfitting, however we did not succeed in underfitting without reducing the size of the training dataset.

To understand better the "behavior" of the models we also considered wether the miss-predictions are actually other winners that were in a tie which were not used for labeling due to the lexicographic tie-breaking we used. If the predicted winner was a true winner in a tie we counted that datapoint as true positive. That improved the accuracy results by 0–6%. It is interesting to mention that we noticed that GaussianNaiveBayes tended to push probabilities of the likelihood of a candidate being a winner to 0 or 1. The reason for it is because it assumes that features are conditionally independent given the class, which is the case in this dataset in Representation 1 containing not redundant features.

Table 7. Representation 1: Borda predictions after hyper-parameter tuning.

	Accuracy [%]	Precision [%]	Recall [%]	F1score [%]	# In ties [# samples]	ties [%]	Acc. with ties [%]
GaussianNB	100	100	100	100	0	0	100
XGBClassifier	99.5	66.56	66.37	66.47	4	0.22	99.79
RandomForestClassifier	90.29	33.34	31.88	32.52	2	0.11	90.4
SGDClassifier	85.6	49.58	46.82	47.92	26	1.4	87
SVC(kernel = 'linear')	76.86	27	23.05	24.79	20	1.08	77.94
RidgeClassifier	70.01	26.25	21.1	21.95	5	0.27	70.28
DecisionTreeClassifier	66.07	49.94	57.14	52.33	0	0	66.07
RandomForestClassifier	4.91	25.04	17.54	19.37	44	2.37	57.28
LinearSVC (C = 1.0)	52.32	25.82	16.05	16.64	38	2.05	54.37
AdaBoostClassifier	48.33	33.21	42.86	35.58	0	0	48.33
MLPClassifier	43.37	19.18	13	15.16	111	5.99	49.36
SVC (C = 1, kernel = 'rbf')	22.55	86.3	22.49	15.87	0	0	22.55

Table 8. Representation 2: Borda predictions after hyper-parameter tuning.

	Accuracy [%]	Precision [%]	Recall [%]	F1score [%]	# In ties [# samples]	ties [%]	Acc. with ties [%]
XGBClassifier	100	100	100	100	0	0	100
GaussianNB	100	100	100	100	0	0	100
DecisionTreeClassifier	66.07	49.94	57.14	52.33	0	0	66.07
SVC(kernel =' linear')	64.72	33.04	29.97	30.75	0	0	64.72
AdaBoostClassifier	48.33	33.21	42.86	35.58	0	0	48.33
LinearSVC	41.96	19.57	13.33	15.58	2	0.11	42.07
SGDClassifier	40.45	20.3	14.38	16.18	0	0	40.45
RidgeClassifier	30.04	17.12	9.09	11.45	52	2.8	32.84
MLPClassifier	29.29	11.43	9.74	9.87	1	0.05	29.34
SVC(kernel = 'rbf')	22.55	86.3	22.49	15.87	0	0	22.55
RandomForestClassifier	17.31	9.4	5.2	6.4	151	8.14	25.45

Table 8 and Table 6 respectively summarize the ML performance under Representations 2 and 3. We also observed best performance for the ML methods that performed well with Representation 1 (Table 9).

Table 9. Representation 3:Borda predictions after hyper-parameter tuning.

	Accuracy [%]	Precision [%]	Recall [%]	F1score [%]	# In ties [# samples]	ties [%]	Acc. with ties [%]
XGBClassifier	100	100	100	100	0	0	100
GaussianNB	100	100	100	100	0	0	100
SVC(kernel='linear')	81.55	26.87	24.49	25.57	2	0.11	81.66
LinearSVC	70.12	26.04	21.07	23.2	9	0.49	70.61
DecisionTreeClassifier	66.07	49.94	57.14	52.33	0	0	66.07
SGDClassifier	60.46	29.33	19.66	19.67	20	1.08	61.54
AdaBoostClassifier	48.33	33.21	42.86	35.58	0	0	48.33
MLPClassifier	46.44	18.87	13.92	15.74	72	3.88	50.32
RandomForest(depth = 5)	45.47	19.74	13.66	15.47	76	4.1	49.57
RidgeClassifier	38.78	20.57	11.65	14.16	36	1.94	40.72
RandomForestClassifier	31.45	17.29	9.4	11.17	76	4.1	35.55
SVC(kernel = 'rbf')	22.55	86.3	22.49	15.87	0	0	22.55

Table 10. Representation 1: Kemeny predictions.

	Accuracy [%]	Precision [%]	Recall [%]	F1score [%]	# In ties [# samples]	ties [%]	Acc. with ties [%]
XGBClassifier	51.81	38.96	37.51	37.4	101	6.32	58.13
GaussianNB	44.43	35.39	36.51	34.88	95	5.94	50.37
RandomForestClassifier	42.55	34.31	35.42	33.47	138	8.64	51.19
SVC(kernel = 'linear')	40.43	32.57	31.91	31.08	136	8.51	48.94
RidgeClassifier	35.48	36.96	33.36	28.43	205	12.83	48.31
LinearSVC	35.33	40.51	27.36	24.62	97	6.07	41.3
RandomForest(depth = 5)	34.61	31.47	27.64	28.26	130	8.14	42.75
SGDClassifier	25.34	30.38	23.42	20.94	93	5.82	31.16
AdaBoostClassifier	24.97	21.48	18.59	17.7	472	29.54	54.51
MLPClassifier	18.46	19.86	19	15.02	253	15.83	34.29
SVC(kernel = 'rbf')	8.94	90.14	10.46	10.42	151	9.45	18.09
DecisionTreeClassifier	5.94	16.57	12.84	6.88	109	6.82	12.76

5.2   Kemeny Results

Tables 10, 11 and 12 respectively, summarize the performance of the classifiers on predicting Kemeny winners. All the measures are calculated after hyper-parameter tuning. Here the results are discouraging compared with the Borda winner predictions. We obtained the best results for SVC(kernel='rbf') and the RandomForestClassifier when using Representation 3. However, after analyzing the miss-predictions and comparing them with the tied winners, we observed that the SGDClassifier actually has an accuracy of 85%, which is still low, but a considerable improvement. The percentage of the correctly predicted winner involved in the ties varied considerably across classifiers.

Table 11. Representation 2: Kemeny predictions.

	Accuracy [%]	Precision [%]	Recall [%]	F1score [%]	# In ties [# samples]	ties [%]	Acc. with ties [%]
XGBClassifier	21.53	24.42	21.8	18.02	188	11.78	33.29
LinearSVC	19.27	19.80	19.28	16.71	149	9.32	28.59
SVC(kernel = 'linear')	19.21	21.67	19.19	16.49	201	12.58	31.79
SGDClassifier	17.63	24.42	18.43	16.14	91	5.69	23.82
RidgeClassifier	17.65	19.48	17.6	16.23	151	9.45	27.1
GaussianNB	16.21	22.71	18.24	14.7	189	11.83	28.04
RandomForestClassifier	9.64	15.38	10.79	9.09	278	17.4	27.04
SVC(kernel = 'rbf')	8.64	90.14	10.46	10.42	151	9.45	18.09
MLPClassifier	7.32	11.25	8.93	6.38	241	15.08	22.4
AdaBoostClassifier	6.7	13.65	7.98	5.46	402	25.16	31.86
DecisionTreeClassifier	3.5	7.04	5.41	2.88	189	11.83	15.33

Table 12. Representation 3: Kemeny predictions.

	Accuracy [%]	Precision [%]	Recall [%]	F1score [%]	# In ties [# samples]	ties [%]	Acc. with ties [%]
SGDClassifier	2.44	0.12	5.0	0.24	1771	83.11	85.55
RandomForestClassifier	60.85	57.18	61.32	55.78	128	6.01	66.87
SVC(kernel = 'rbf')	60.58	95.26	61.82	71.49	82	3.85	64.43
GradientBoostingClassifier	59.5	55.43	58.66	54.09	79	3.71	63.21
XGBClassifier	34.94	33.13	38.27	28.07	175	8.21	35.15
RandomForest(depth = 5)	7.74	37.15	14.93	8.26	348	16.33	34.07
AdaBoostClassifier	6.39	7.04	7.32	5.04	232	10.89	17.18
DecisionTreeClassifier	5.02	10.71	6.5	3.65	252	11.83	16.85
GaussianNB()	6.34	8.28	7.72	5.37	219	10.28	16.62
RidgeClassifier	4.27	8.11	6.99	3.09	245	11.5	15.77
MLPClassifier	4.41	3.54	4.71	1.7	118	5.4	9.81
LinearSVC	6.62	0.53	5.0	0.62	15	0.7	7.32

5.3 Dodgson Results

Surprisingly, we obtained better results predicting Dodgson winners than Kemeny winners, but still with a relatively lower accuracy than Borda winners: 87% with the GradientBoostingClassifier under Representations 1 and 3. Tables 13, 14 and 15 respectively summarize our results. Again, all the measures are calculated after hyper-parameter tuning. Here again, after analyzing the miss-predictions, we observe that the GradientBoostingClassifier actually correctly predicts winners that are among ties.

Table 13. Representation 1: Dodgson prediction.

	Accuracy [%]	Precision [%]	Recall [%]	F1score [%]	# In ties [# samples]	ties [%]	Acc. with ties [%]
GradientBoostingClassifier	87.2	81.37	75.34	77.96	51	2.17	89.37
RandomForestClassifier	84.22	79.05	73.69	73.87	54	2.3	86.52
XGBClassifier	77.62	65.96	48.08	53.13	90	3.83	81.46
GaussianNB	66.31	42.34	41.84	41.63	120	5.1	71.41
RandomForest(depth = 5)	66.57	55.43	36.24	39.28	88	3.74	70.31
SVC(kernel = 'rbf')	68.06	97.07	61.14	73.34	10	0.43	68.49
RidgeClassifier	63.16	40.37	38.84	38.73	114	4.85	68.01
MLPClassifier	57.64	43.33	44.4	38.79	113	4.81	62.45
AdaBoostClassifier	55.98	35.27	36.61	35.32	117	4.98	60.96
SGDClassifier	50.91	27.14	30.64	23.01	129	5.49	56.4
LinearSVC	34.11	34.02	25.55	19.77	116	4.93	39.04
DecisionTreeClassifier	23.52	17.17	12.22	8.5	25	1.06	24.58

Table 14. Representation 2: Dodgson predictions.

	Accuracy [%]	Precision [%]	Recall [%]	F1score [%]	# In ties [# samples]	ties [%]	Acc. with ties [%]
GradientBoostingClassifier	80.77	68.75	73.07	70.46	59	2.51	83.28
MLPClassifier	77.16	63.44	71.96	66.57	68	2.89	90.05
XGBClassifier	69.72	53.67	57.13	54.12	97	4.13	73.85
SVC(kernel = 'rbf')	68.06	97.07	61.14	73.34	10	0.43	68.49
LinearSVC	62.91	51.52	55.26	50.02	125	5.32	69.23
RandomForestClassifier	61.93	52.59	62.03	52.96	141	6.0	67.98
RidgeClassifier	63.16	46.39	51.67	47.73	102	4.34	67.5
GaussianNB	57.59	42.61	51.95	44.99	120	5.1	62.69
SGDClassifier	52.21	48.54	60.58	37.82	93	3.96	57.17
AdaBoostClassifier	25.1	12.59	22.26	18.23	196	8.29	33.39
DecisionTreeClassifier	21.23	9.1	8.0	5.52	66	2.81	24.04
RandomForest(depth = 5)	22.59	1.13	5.0	1.84	19	0.81	23.4

Table 15. Representation 3: Dodgson predictions.

	Accuracy [%]	Precision [%]	Recall [%]	F1score [%]	# In ties [# samples]	ties [%]	Acc. with ties [%]
GradientBoostingClassifier	87.28	80.85	77.62	78.91	50	2.13	89.41
XGBClassifier	85.92	77.83	78.41	77.9	66	2.81	88.73
RandomForestClassifier	71.08	59.15	69.32	60.71	105	4.47	75.55
GaussianNB	65.76	50.52	45.52	45.62	115	4.89	70.65
SVC(kernel = 'rbf')	68.06	97.07	61.14	73.34	10	0.43	68.491
RidgeClassifier	62.14	42.01	43.51	41.85	113	4.81	66.95
MLPClassifier	54.4	39.04	42.54	38.8	110	4.68	59.08
SGDClassifier	50.87	36.31	29.72	22.74	128	5.44	56.31
LinearSVC	41.56	46.0	19.17	20.69	51	2.17	43.73
RandomForest(depth = 5)	26.8	62.52	10.2	10.87	23	0.98	27.78
DecisionTreeClassifier	17.31	10.01	18.27	9.93	192	8.17	25.48
AdaBoostClassifier	15.06	11.9	14.83	9.21	172	7.32	22.38

6   Discussion

A learning curve is a graphical representation of model's learning performance[8] over 'experience' or time. We used learning curves here as an ML diagnostic tool

---

[8] Algorithms that learn from a training dataset incrementally.

for the behavior (underfitting, overfitting or good fit) of ML models and as a diagnosis tool to evaluate if the datasets (training and validation) are representative of the problem domain. We omit including all the learning curve graphs due to space restrictions and only highlight the most interesting observations.

Borda Model Behavior. We identified underfitting in the following models: SVM with RBF kernel and Random Forest, where the training loss remains flat regardless of experience. We identify under-fitted models by analyzing the learning curve of the training loss. A learning curve shows under-fitting if : (i) the training loss continues to increase until the end of the training, i.e. premature halt occurs or (ii) the training loss remains flat regardless of training. Some of the ML methods showed over-fitting in their learning curves. A learning curve shows over-fitting if: (i) the training loss continues to increase until the end of training, i.e. premature halt occurs, which we observed with the MLP and SGD classifiers; or (ii) validation loss increases in order to decrease again, which we observed with the Random Forest classifier at its late state. The learning curves' plot showed a good fit for XGBoost, linear SVM and the AdaBoost classifiers, where we observed (i) the training loss decreases to the point of stability and (ii) the validation loss increases to a stability point but there remained a small gap with the training loss. Here, the suitable model fit was presented by the XGBoost, Linear SVM with SGD classifiers. The Representation 2 training set was easier to learn compared to Representation 1, namely more algorithms achieved 100% accuracy for the training set while at the same time increasing accuracy for the test set. Figure 1 presents an example of the train and validation learning curves for models learned in Representation 2.

Kemeny and Dodgson Miss-predictions

We observed that in the case of predicting Kemeny winners, a model using Representation 3 was very well learnable by the SGD classifier. Here, however, the accuracy of the original dataset was very low ca. 2% and the number of miss-prediction was very high – ca. 83 % were wrongly classified (false positive). After checking the miss-classified profiles, we found that 83% of the original miss-predictions were found in ties, meaning a true winner was predicted, but not the winner that was selected by the lexicographic tie-breaking. That analysis revealed that the model accuracy is actually ca. 85%. Figures 2 and 3 (in the Appendix) present an example of the train and validation learning curves for models learned in Representation 3. For predicting Dodgson winners, we obtained the best accuracy with the Gradient Boost classifier learned using Representations 1 and 3. Curiously, here although some winners were correctly classified, but not used as labels due to the tie-breaking rule, their numbers did not make for such a drastic difference as with Kemeny winner predictions. Figures 4, 5 and 6 presents an example of the train and validation learning curves for models using Representations 1, 2 and 3 respectively.

7   Related Work

Machine learning, in the context of social choice, has been used to predict the missing components of preference orders (ballots) in [8]. Machine learning has also been used to do political sentiment analysis, namely predict winners of elections given Twitter data (not preference rankings) in [19]. Data science techniques for handling large elections have been used in [6].

Most similar to our work is perhaps Neural networks are used in [4] where the authors train the network to classify profiles with their unanimity winner, their Condorcet winners and unique Borda winner (only profiles that have such a respective winner are used). Burka et al. use, what we call representation 3 and profiles in which the number of voters equals 7, 9 or 11, while the number of alternatives equals 3, 4 or 5. Their best Borda accuracy is 92.60%, while their best Condorcet winner accuracy is 98.42%.

Procaccia et al. [18] consider the problem of PAC-learnability of scoring methods. We present methods in which the winners of a scoring method, Borda, can be predicted.

Apart from the work we already discussed [7], machine learning, specifically neural networks, have been applied to solve NP-complete problems, specifically the traveling salesman problem [17]. Prates et al. accomplish 80% accuracy with their approach.

8   Conclusions

We asked if winners of computationally hard to compute voting methods can be predicted using machine learning classification. We considered two voting methods for which it can be hard to compute the winners: Kemeny and Dodgson and also one method, Borda, for which winners can be efficiently computed. We considered ten different machine learning classifiers. We constructed considered elections with 20 alternatives for 25 voters. For training machine learning classifiers, we constructed 12360 profiles which we factorized three different ways and for which we computed the Borda, Kemeny and Dodgson winners. Predicting election winners is a robust approach. Once a model is created for an election of a particular size, it can be reused for any election of that size regardless of what the options or who the voters are.

Our answers are, as expected, Borda winners can be predicted with high accuracy. Kemeny and Dodgson winners can be predicted with relative accuracy of 85%-89%. It is important to emphasize that the 12360 profiles we used in training comprise less than 0.01% of all possible profiles for 20 alternatives and 25 agents. The total number of all possible profiles for $|C|$ alternatives and $|V|$ voters is: $\frac{(|V|+|C|!-1)!}{|C|!(|V|-1)!}$. Better accuracies can be obtained with a higher percentage of labeled profiles for training. Further experiments are needed, with different sets of candidates and voters (sets of different sizes that is) to explore the impact of the data set dimensions on the performance of classifiers.

Surprisingly, the Kemeny winners, which in the worst case are computationally easier to compute that the Dodgson winners, are predictable with a lower accuracy than the Dodgson winners. Also surprisingly, our models were able to predict the correct winners for elections when the winners were in a tie (and not used to label a profile because the lexicographic tie-breaking mechanism did not select them).

It would be interesting to see where the miss-predictions occur in the aggregated preference order of Kemeny and Dodgson, are they from among the top ranked or low ranked alternatives or whether there is no correlation between the prediction and a specific position in the Kemeny/Dodgson rank. DEMOCRATIX calculates just the winner(s) not a full preference order, so we were not able to do this analysis at present. In the future we will consider building prediction models for smaller profiles for which the full Kemeny and Dodgson ranks can be computed for analysis.

An interesting avenue to explore is the learnability of collective judgment sets in judgment aggregation. Judgment aggregation studies how the opinions of different individuals on the truth value of a issues can be aggregated into a collective judgment set when the issues that need to be decided upon are possibly logically interconnected [9,14]. Judgment aggregation is known to generalize voting, namely the problem of finding winners for an election can be represented as the problem of finding collective judgment sets [9,14]. Furthermore, Borda, Kemeny and Dodgson are generalizable to judgment aggregation methods [10,13]. The complexity of finding collective judgements using these generalized "voting" methods is typically higher than that of calculating election winners. Furthermore, while the models that predict election winners can be reused for elections of same size of candidate and voter sets, the logic relations between the issues on which opinions are given, would prevent this re-usability in judgment aggregation.

Acknowledgements. The research was partly supported by the project "Better Video workflows via Real-Time Collaboration and AI-Techniques in TV and New Media", funded by the Research Council of Norway under Grant No.: 269790.

Appendix -Figures

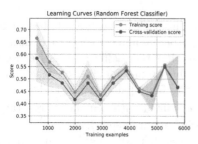
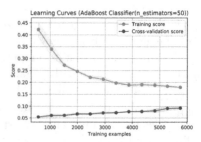

Fig. 1. Train and validation learning curves for Borda models learned in Repres. 2.

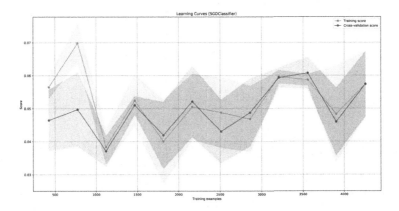

Fig. 2. Train and validation learning curves for Kemeny using Repres. 3., SDG classifier.

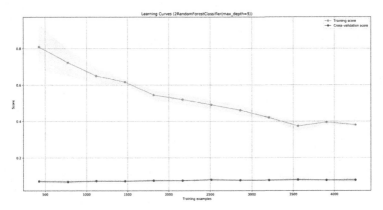

Fig. 3. Train and validation learning curves for Kemeny using Repres. 3., SDG classifier top, 2Random Forest classifier bottom.

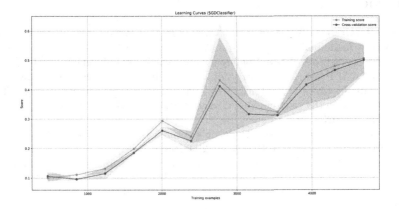

Fig. 4. Learning curve for Dodgson using Representation 1

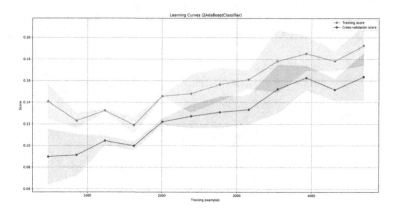

Fig. 5. Learning curve for Dodgson using Representation 2

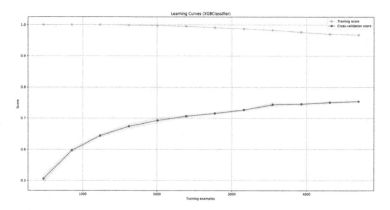

Fig. 6. Learning curve for Dodgson using Repres. 3

References

1. Aziz, H., Gaspers, S., Mattei, N., Narodytska, N., Walsh, T.: Ties matter: complexity of manipulation when tie-breaking with a random vote. In: Proceedings of the Twenty-Seventh AAAI Conference on Artificial Intelligence, AAAI 2013, pp. 74–80. AAAI Press (2013). http://dl.acm.org/citation.cfm?id=2891460.2891471
2. Bartholdi, J., Tovey, C.A., Trick, M.A.: Voting schemes for which it can be difficult to tell who won the election. Soc. Choice Welf. **6**, 157–165 (1989). https://doi.org/10.1007/BF00303169
3. Brandt, F.: Some remarks on Dodgson's voting rule. Math. Log. Q. **55**(4), 60–463 (2009). https://doi.org/10.1002/malq.200810017
4. Burka, D., Puppe, C., Szepesvary, L., Tasnadi, A.: Neural networks would 'vote' according to borda's rule. Technical report, Karlsruher Institut für Technologie (KIT) (2016). https://doi.org/10.5445/IR/1000062014
5. Charwat, G., Pfandler, A.: Democratix: a declarative approach to winner determination. In: Walsh, T. (ed.) ADT 2015. LNCS (LNAI), vol. 9346, pp. 253–269. Springer, Cham (2015). https://doi.org/10.1007/978-3-319-23114-3_16

6. Csar, T., Lackner, M., Pichler, R., Sallinger, E.: Winner determination in huge elections with mapreduce. In: Proceedings of the Thirty-First AAAI Conference on Artificial Intelligence, 4–9 February 2017, San Francisco, California, USA, pp. 451–458 (2017). http://aaai.org/ocs/index.php/AAAI/AAAI17/paper/view/14894

7. Devlin, D., O'Sullivan, B.: Satisfiability as a classification problem. In: Proceedings of the 19th Irish Conference on Artificial Intelligence and Cognitive Science (2008). http://www.cs.ucc.ie/osullb/pubs/classification.pdf

8. Doucette, J.A., Larson, K., Cohen, R.: Conventional machine learning for social choice. In: Proceedings of the Twenty-Ninth AAAI Conference on Artificial Intelligence, 25–30 January 2015, Austin, Texas, USA, pp. 858–864 (2015). http://www.aaai.org/ocs/index.php/AAAI/AAAI15/paper/view/9340

9. Endriss, U.: Judgment aggregation. In: Brandt, F., Conitzer, V., Endriss, U., Lang, J., Procaccia, A.D. (eds.) Handbook of Computational Social Choice. Cambridge University Press (2016)

10. Endriss, U.: Judgment aggregation with rationality and feasibility constraints. In: Proceedings of the 17th International Conference on Autonomous Agents and MultiAgent Systems, AAMAS 2018, Stockholm, Sweden, 10–15 July 2018, pp. 946–954 (2018). http://dl.acm.org/citation.cfm?id=3237840

11. Hemaspaandra, E., Hemaspaandra, L.A., Rothe, J.: Exact analysis of Dodgson elections: Lewis Carroll's 1876 voting system is complete for parallel access to NP. J. ACM **44**(6), 806–825 (1997). https://doi.org/10.1145/268999.269002

12. Hemaspaandra, E., Spakowski, H., Vogel, J.: The complexity of Kemeny elections. Theoret. Comput. Sci. **349**(3), 382–391 (2005). https://doi.org/10.1016/j.tcs.2005.08.031. http://www.sciencedirect.com/science/article/pii/S0304397505005785

13. Lang, J., Slavkovik, M.: Judgment aggregation rules and voting rules. In: Algorithmic Decision Theory - Third International Conference, ADT 2013, Bruxelles, Belgium, 12–14 November 2013, Proceedings, pp. 230–243 (2013). https://doi.org/10.1007/978-3-642-41575-3_18

14. List, C., Polak, B.: Introduction to judgment aggregation. J. Econ. Theor. **145**(2), 441–466 (2010)

15. Mattei, N., Narodytska, N., Walsh, T.: How hard is it to control an election by breaking ties? In: ECAI 2014–21st European Conference on Artificial Intelligence, 18–22 August 2014, Prague, Czech Republic - Including Prestigious Applications of Intelligent Systems (PAIS 2014), pp. 1067–1068 (2014). https://doi.org/10.3233/978-1-61499-419-0-1067

16. Nurmi, H.: Voting procedures: a summary analysis. Br. J. Polit. Sci. **13**(2), 181–208 (1983). http://www.jstor.org/stable/193949

17. Prates, M.O.R., Avelar, P.H.C., Lemos, H., Lamb, L.C., Vardi, M.Y.: Learning to solve np-complete problems: a graph neural network for decision TSP. In: The Thirty-Third AAAI Conference on Artificial Intelligence, AAAI 2019, The Thirty-First Innovative Applications of Artificial Intelligence Conference, IAAI 2019, The Ninth AAAI Symposium on Educational Advances in Artificial Intelligence, EAAI 2019, Honolulu, Hawaii, USA, 27 January–1 February 2019, pp. 4731–4738 (2019). https://doi.org/10.1609/aaai.v33i01.33014731

18. Procaccia, A.D., Zohar, A., Peleg, Y., Rosenschein, J.S.: The learnability of voting rules. Artif. Intell. **173**(12-13), 1133–1149 (2009). https://doi.org/10.1016/j.artint.2009.03.003

19. Rodríguez, S., Allende-Cid, H., Palma, W., Alfaro, R., Gonzalez, C., Elortegui, C., Santander, P.: Forecasting the chilean electoral year: using twitter to predict the presidential elections of 2017. In: Meiselwitz, G. (ed.) SCSM 2018. LNCS, vol. 10914, pp. 298–314. Springer, Cham (2018). https://doi.org/10.1007/978-3-319-91485-5_23
20. Shakirova, E.: Collaborative filtering for music recommender system. In: 2017 IEEE Conference of Russian Young Researchers in Electrical and Electronic Engineering (EIConRus), pp. 548–550 (2017). https://doi.org/10.1109/EIConRus.2017.7910613
21. Tsoumakas, G., Katakis, I.: Multi-label classification: an overview. Int. J. Data Warehouse. Min. **2007**, 1–13 (2007)
22. Zwicker, W.S.: Introduction to the theory of voting. In: Handbook of Computational Social Choice, pp. 23–56. Cambridge University Press (2016). https://doi.org/10.1017/CBO9781107446984.003

From Virtual Worlds to Mirror Worlds: A Model and Platform for Building Agent-Based eXtended Realities

Angelo Croatti$^{(\boxtimes)}$ and Alessandro Ricci

Computer Science and Engineering Department (DISI), Alma Mater Studiorum –
Università di Bologna, via dell'Università, 50, Cesena, Italy
{a.croatti,a.ricci}@unibo.it

Abstract. Extended Reality (XR) refers to applications that blend the digital and the physical worlds in different ways: both by situating *virtual worlds* into physical environments by means of Augmented and Mixed Reality Technologies, and by exploiting smart things and devices in the physical environment connected to the Virtual World, in a pervasive computing perspective. Like in the case of Virtual Worlds and Intelligent Virtual Environments, XR applications are a relevant application domain for multi-agent systems and AI—for instance, for designing XR-based smart environments. The research question addressed by this paper is about the definition of a model for conceiving and designing agent-based XR applications, effective enough to capture essential aspects in spite of the specific implementing technologies. To this purpose, the paper describes a model based on the Mirror World conceptual framework and a concrete platform used to evaluate its strengths and weaknesses.

Keywords: eXtended Reality · Mirror worlds · Agents · BDI · Virtual worlds

1 Introduction

Since their appearance, *virtual worlds* [14,16] have been considered an interesting application context for agents, multi-agent systems and AI in general, to develop the so called Intelligent Virtual Environments (IVEs) [15]. Virtual worlds and IVEs typically do not consider the physical world: every interaction occurs in the virtual world. The physical environment plays an essential role instead in Augmented and Mixed Reality (AR, MR), where the virtual world is overlaid onto the physical reality [1,6]. In AR/MR, human users can interact with virtual objects (*holograms*) that are situated in their physical environment—either indoor or outdoor. The last decade has witnessed a remarkable development of AR/MR technologies. Examples of commercial technologies range from MR based on head-mounted displays such as Microsoft Hololens and Magic Leap up to smartphone solutions based on technologies such as Google ARCore, Apple ARKit.

© Springer Nature Switzerland AG 2020
N. Bassiliades et al. (Eds.): EUMAS 2020/AT 2020, LNAI 12520, pp. 459–474, 2020.
https://doi.org/10.1007/978-3-030-66412-1_29

eXtended Reality systems (XR) [9] further extend this view by devising an even more deeper blending between the virtual and the physical worlds, involving pervasive computing/IoT (Internet of Things) technologies, aside to Virtual Worlds and MR. In XR applications, the physical environment is augmented, on the one hand, by computing devices equipped with sensors and actuators embedded in things, tools in the environment; on the other hand, by holograms situated in the same environment, enriching the functionalities beyond the limits imposed by the physical reality.

The research question addressed by this paper is about the definition of a general model that would make it possible to think about and design agent-based XR applications. Like IVEs, agent-based XR is about virtual worlds, eventually distributed, where multiple users can interact with both agents and virtual objects. Like in the case of MR/AR, such virtual worlds are situated in the physical reality. Like in the case of pervasive computing, such virtual worlds can be understood as a digital layer augmenting the functionality of physical objects and environment, being coupled to smart things.

In this paper we propose an approach for modelling and building agent-based XR based on *mirror worlds* (MW). The basic concepts and vision about MWs have been already introduced elsewhere in literature [10,20]. As a further development of previous work, in this paper:

- we introduce a concrete model for mirror worlds as a blueprint for designing agent-based XR (Sect. 3). The value of the model is to be the first formalisation in literature of mirror worlds, useful for rigorously defining the structure and behaviour abstracting from specific implementations;
- we introduce an open-source platform implementing the model (Sect. 4). The value of the platform is both to be used for validating the model and as a practical tool developing and exploring agent-based XR applications in different application domains. The platform can be easily integrated with existing agent programming languages, tools and technologies for developing individual agents.

Before introducing the model, in next section (Sect. 2) we provide a background of our work, including also a discussion of related works.

2   Background and Related

In this section we first provide a background about Mirror Worlds, used in this paper as reference conceptual model. Then, before get into the main contribution of the paper, we provide an overview of main related research works, in the context of Intelligent Virtual Environments, Intelligent Virtual Agents and agent-based Mixed Reality/Augmented Reality.

2.1   Mirror Worlds

The term *Mirror World* (MW) has been introduced by D. Gelernter to define *software models of some chunk of reality* [10]. Using his words, a MW represents *a*

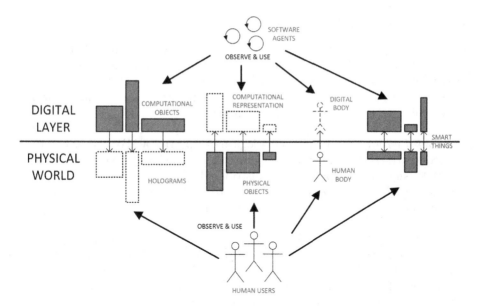

Fig. 1. A conceptual representation of a Mirror World.

true-to-life mirror image trapped inside a computer, which can be then viewed, zoomed, analysed by real-world inhabitants with the help of proper software (autonomous) assistant agents.

Inspired by the Gelernter's vision, a concrete research work on mirror worlds has been carried on in the context of agents and multi-agents systems [20]. In this work, a mirror world is conceived as an open society/organisation of cognitive software agents spatially layered upon some physical environment, augmenting its functionalities [18]. Mirroring occurs when physical things, which can be perceived and acted upon by humans in the physical world, have a digital counterpart (or extension) in the mirror world so that they can be observed and acted upon by agents. Vice versa, an entity in the mirror world that can be perceived and acted upon by software agents can have a physical appearance (or extension) in the physical world – for example, through augmented reality – so that it can be observed and acted upon by humans. See Fig. 1 for a conceptual representation of a Mirror World.

The coupling between the physical world and the corresponding mirror digital layer could have a deep impact on humans and their sociality, with different levels of *augmentations* [22]—social, cognitive, temporal. In [21], a toy practical framework based on the JaCaMo platform [4] to design and simulate mirror worlds is introduced. There, the CArtAgO framework [19] has been extended to support situated workspaces and situated artifacts as extensions of regular ones.

2.2   Features and Challenges

From an engineering point-of-view, MWs expose several technical challenges. Generally speaking, a MW is a hybrid environment where both humans and proactive autonomous entities can interact and cooperate through the digital layer. Among others, the following paragraphs reports main technical features (and challenges) considered by mirror worlds.

Distributed nature. Although from a logical perspective a MW can be observed as a concentrated system, consider its nature, is obviously that each instance of a MW should be deployed as a distributed software system. This requires considering all of the issues exposed by distributed software systems about time and temporal synchronization, information and event propagation, causal consistency, etc.

Real-time constraint. The execution and propagation of information among a mirror world instance should be done in real time. This feature is important at any level. From the users perspective, since the current state of the world's entities is shared by all, each update to this state performed by a user should be instantly available to other users taking in account concurrency issues coming from concurrency actions performed by different users on the same entity. Also from agents perspective, the constraint of real-time is mandatory if these entities need to reason on and act upon the current state of the digital world. Finally, because the digital layer is strongly coupled with the physical world (see next proposed feature for details), the digital state must be rapidly informed and updated according to real-time changes of the physical world.

Cooperative environments. A mirror world is a context where multiple human users could be concurrently involved. Each user, equipped with a proper computational device, must be allowed by the system to enter in the extended reality mainly for both observe and interact with digital entities. The system has to perceive the presence of each user, allowing to all of them to cooperate and collaborate exploiting provided functionalities.

2.3   Related Work

Besides Mirror Worlds, we report here a selection of research works proposed in the agents and MAS literature related to the purposes of our contribution.

Intelligent Virtual Environments. A first interesting related work can be found in the literature on Intelligent Virtual Environments (IVEs) [15]. In particular, considering those contributions extending the basic IVEs definition towards the integration in their models of the physical environment (e.g., [23]). IVEs are the result of the combination between autonomous agents – equipped with intelligent techniques and tools provided by Artificial Intelligence (AI) – with significant graphical representation for both agents and digital environment [3].

The primary objective of an IVE is to provide a context where simulate a physical/real environment with autonomous software entities as inhabitants, interacting with the simulated environment as they were the real entities (e.g., humans) of the simulated real world.

Intelligent Virtual Agents. Intelligent Virtual Agents (IVAs) can be defined as embodied digital characters situated in a mixed reality environment that look, communicate, and act like real creatures. A primary feature of IVAs is that their behaviour should exhibit some aspects of human intelligence. Examples of IVAs are: non-player characters in computer games, virtual tutors in educational software, virtual assistants or chat-bots, virtual guides in digital heritage environments, and so on. Intelligent virtual agents software has improved with advances in AI and cognitive computing. Current conversational technology allows virtual agents to go far beyond interactive voice response (IVR) systems; virtual agents understand users intent and can provide personalised answers to customer questions in a human-like manner. An avatar is often used to provide a visual representation of the virtual agent.

Mixed and Augmented Reality Cognitive Agents. In agents literature, concepts of MiRA (Mixed Reality Agents) [13] and AuRAs (Augmented Reality Agents) [5] offers a full description about the role of agents and MAS in MR and AR contexts. The main aim of MiRA and AuRAs is about agents having a representation in an AR/MR environment, making them perceivable by human users and enabling interaction both with them and with other agents. Avoiding entering in details – even though both works referring to similar concepts – we can consider MiRA as the broadest concept, used to delineate *an agent living in a mixed reality context*. Vice versa, AuRAs identify those mixed reality agents that can both sense and act in the virtual component of their reality but can only sense in the physical.

3   A Model for Mirror Worlds

In this section we describe a model for mirror worlds, first describing the MW structure and then the *laws* that govern that structure. The main point about the model is capturing the *bidirectional coupling* that occurs between the digital layer and physical layer. By virtue of that coupling, from the agents perspective, a mirror world is a distributed environment composed by virtual objects (called *mirror objects*) that are the *digital twins* of physical entities situated in the physical world. These physical entities include physical things, as well as processes, phenomena, activities occurring in the physical reality – anything that can be perceived and acted upon by human users. This includes also *holograms* as defined in mixed reality. In our case, a hologram is modelled as a physical manifestation of mirror objects living in the mirror world.

3.1 Structure

A mirror world ($\mathcal{MW}$) can be represented by a 5-tuple $\langle \mathcal{A}, \mathcal{U}, \mathcal{M}_{obj}, \mathcal{P}_e, \mathcal{S_S} \rangle$ where:

- $\mathcal{A} = \{a_1, a_2, \ldots, a_N\}$ is the set of agents that operate in the mirror world;
- $\mathcal{U} = \{u_1, u_2, \ldots, u_N\}$ is the set of users (i.e. human users) that interact with and within the mirror world;
- $\mathcal{M}_{obj} = \{m_{obj1}, m_{obj2}, \ldots, m_{objN}\}$ is the agents' environment composed by a set of *mirror objects*, as digital entities that – on the one hand – can be perceived/acted upon by agents, and – on the other hand – are the *digital twin* of some entity $pe \in \mathcal{P}_e$ situated in the physical environment.
- $\mathcal{P}_e$ is a set of entities situated in a physical environment that can be perceived/acted upon by users, including both physical objects – each one coupled with a corresponding mirror object – and *holograms* as defined in MR, as physical manifestation of mirror objects.
- $\mathcal{S_S}$ – referred as *shared space* – defines the *spatial model* of mirror world and its mapping on the spatial structure of the physical environment and reality where the MW is situated.

Agents. Each element of $\mathcal{A}$ is an autonomous computational entity acting in the extended reality shaped by the mirror world. Examples could be personal assistant agents of human users working in the mirror, or intelligent agents encapsulating smart functionalities of the environment. MW is not bound to any specific model for agents. Nevertheless, it is useful in the following to consider a cognitive model so we can talk about agent beliefs and goals. To achieve their goals, agents in MW have the ability to perceive the *properties* exposed by mirror objects, mapped into beliefs about the state of the MW, and act through the actions provided by mirror objects.

Agents, in this model, do not have and can not have percepts from the physical world directly: in order to perceive some state or event from any physical entity or phenomenon, there should be a corresponding mirror object m_{obj} among $\mathcal{M}_{obj}$ modelling it. Dually, the only way to affect the physical world is through actions provided by a mirror object.

The perception of mirror objects by agents can occur either by intentionally observing/tracking individual mirror objects, or by specifying some *observable region* of the shared space to track, perceiving any event about any mirror object – including appearance and disappearance – situated there. Observable regions are modelled here as part of the shared space, described later.

For the purpose of this paper an agent $a \in \mathcal{A}$ can be represented by a 4-tuple $\langle a_{id}, B, Obs_m, Obs_R \rangle$ where a_{id} is the agent identifier, B is the belief base, Obs_m and Obs_R are the set of identifiers of, respectively, mirror objects and observable regions observed by the agent.

Users. Users refer to the human users that are working and cooperating in same MW, equipped with proper MR devices (e.g., MR visors, smartglasses or MR-enabled smartphones). Users are meant to be physically situated in the physical environment bound to the MW. Users can interact with the MW by acting upon and observing the physical entities $\mathcal{P}_e$, including holograms, which are bound to some mirror object in $\mathcal{M}_{obj}$.

Mirror Objects and Physical Entities. Mirror objects are used to explicitly model and represent in the mirror any *asset* of the physical world that can be relevant to observe, to reason about, to act upon from the agent point of view. A mirror object can be conceived as the *digital twin* [11] of some physical entity situated in the physical world, possibly extending its functionalities. As a digital twin, a mirror object reflects the dynamic state (or, a model of) of the physical counterpart, to which it is coupled. Such a state can be observed and tracked by agents living in the MW.

Physical entities here are not limited to physical things or objects, but may include also physical phenomena (e.g., the wind) and physical manifestation, such as holograms. In MW a hologram is the physical manifestation of mirror object, as a kind of *view* that can be perceived by human users equipped by proper MR devices. Besides, even activities occurring in the physical reality (e.g., an ongoing rescue) can be coupled to a mirror object, in order to be tracked by agents. Physical entities include also the users' physical bodies, that are then modelled by proper mirror objects in the mirror: for each user $u \in \mathcal{U}$, it exists a mirror object $m_u \in \mathcal{M}_{obj}$ that makes it observable relevant information – both static and dynamic – about the user, including her position and gaze direction. We refer to these mirror objects as *user avatars.*

In our model, a mirror object $m_{obj} \in \mathcal{M}_{obj}$ is represented by a 5-tuple $\langle mo_{id}, mo_s, obsp, acts, pe_{id} \rangle$ where mo_{id} represents a unique identifier, mo_s the internal (non observable) state, $props = \{p_1, p_2, \ldots, p_n\}$ is the set of observable properties exposed by the object and $actions = \{a_1, a_2, \ldots, a_n\}$ is the set of actions that be invoked by agents. An observable property $o \in props$ can be represented as a couple $(key, value)$. Each mirror object is coupled to a physical entity $pe \in \mathcal{P}_e$, identified by the pe_{id} identifier. In user avatars, the physical entity is the user (body) itself.

Shared Space. Every mirror object is coupled to a physical entity which is located in some *position*[1] of the physical world. Such a position is included among the observable properties of the mirror object, to be observable by agents. To give a meaning to that concept, a shared *spatial reference system* is needed, defining a coordinate space in the mirror which could be a meaningful mapping of the one adopted in the physical space, in order to represent locations as well as the geometry and extension of objects, and for computing distances. In the model, this is captured by the shared space component $\mathcal{S}_\mathcal{S}$. The shared space is coupled with the physical space through a mapping function $\mathcal{M}$ responsible of the conversion of the coordinates of the physical space into the ones of the digital layer and viceversa. Every mirror object $m_{obj} \in \mathcal{M}_{obj}$ has a position

---

[1] Note that with the term *position* referred to a particular element, we refer both to its location and its orientation.

defined by $\mathcal{S}_S$, modelled as built-in observable property pos (a 3D point). All mirror objects that represent user avatars track also user gaze, modelled by a further observable property $gaze$ (a 3D vector).

In a mirror world, agents may want to observe what happens in any spatial regions of the physical environment on which the MW is mapped. For instance: tracking if/what mirror objects are going to appear in that region. An example of a region could be some part of a room (e.g., a corner), but also a sphere around a human user moving inside the room. To that purpose, the concept of *observable region* is introduced in the model, as part of the shared state component. An observable region $r \in Regs$ is modelled here by a 2-tuple $\langle reg_{id}, ext \rangle$, where reg_{id} is the identifier of the region, and ext is a representation of its (geometrical) extension, that can change dynamically.

3.2   Mirror World General Laws

In this section, we describe a core set of laws that capture the key aspects related to the dynamics of a MW. Such laws can be expressed by means of *transitions* that define the MW dynamics, that is: the MW is modelled as a transition system in which the state – represented by a tuple as defined in previous section – evolves, atomically.

Coupling laws. These laws define the bidirectional coupling between a mirror object and a corresponding physical entity. Given a mirror object $m_{obj} \in \mathcal{M}_{obj}$ and a physical entity $pe \in \mathcal{P}_e$ that are coupled, i.e.:

$$m_{obj} = \langle mo_{id}, mo_s, props, acts, pe_{id} \rangle, \quad pe = \langle pe_{id}, pe_s, mo_{id} \rangle$$

then, a change of the state of the physical entity pe_s (either because of human users actions or because of the internal behaviour of the objects e.g. a clock) triggers a transition of the MW in which also the full state of the corresponding mirror object is updated:

$$pe \rightarrow \langle pe_{id}, pe'_s, mo_{id} \rangle, \quad m_{obj} \rightarrow \langle mo_{id}, mo'_s, props', acts, pe_{id} \rangle$$

This holds also dually, that is: any state changes of the mirror object m_{obj} (either because of agents' actions or internal object mechanics) cause a transition of the MW in which the state of the coupled physical entity pe is updated correspondingly, according to the coupling relationship.

These laws concern also physical entities that are holograms, as part of the mixed reality level. So a human user interacting with an hologram can lead to state changes of the hologram itself, that are then propagated to the corresponding mirror object and can be eventually perceived by interested agents, observing the mirror object. Viceversa, a human user can observe changes to the hologram that are caused by agents acting in the mirror on the corresponding mirror object.

In this model, transitions are atomic, in spite of the fact the coupled entities (the mirror object and the physical entity) are distributed. This implies that any action done either by agent(s) on a mirror object or by user(s) on the coupled physical entity (including holograms) must be performed *transactionally* with respect the two entities. This is a strong requirement to guarantee the consistency of the state of mirror objects and physical entities. At the implementation level, this implies that e.g. any actions performed by agents on a mirror object are actually transactions involving also the physical entities, and viceversa any physical actions performed by a human user on a physical entity are transactions as well, involving the mirror object. At the implementation level such a strong consistency has a price in terms of latency and availability. Actually, this strong requirement can be relaxed when either the mirror object or the physical entity do not provide actions, but only an observable state: in this case the state of the "observe-only" element can be eventually updated by events generated by the coupled element, preserving the order of events but without the need of using transactions.

A further related remark – which is important from an implementation point of view, in particular – is that holograms, as well as physical entities and mirror objects, could have a part of their state not coupled with the corresponding twin, so that changes that that part *do not* require synchronisation. A typical example in the practice is given by the animation of holograms, that typically needs to be executed with real-time constraints that would make it prohibited a synchronisation with the corresponding distributed mirror object.

Agent observation laws. These laws define how agents can be aware of what happens in a MW. If a mirror object $m_{obj} = \langle mo_{id}, mo_s, props, acts, pe_{id} \rangle$ is observed by an agent $a \in \mathcal{A}$, that is:

$$a = \langle a_{id}, B, Obs_m, Obs_r \rangle, mo_{id} \in Obs_m$$

then the agent beliefs B include a subset of beliefs that are about the observable properties *props*. Then, a change of the observable state of mirror object (because of e.g. the execution of an action by some agent) causes a transition of the MW in which the beliefs of any agents observing the mirror object are updated accordingly:

$$m_{obj} \rightarrow \langle mo_{id}, s', props', acts, pe_{id} \rangle$$

$$a \rightarrow \langle a_{id}, B'', Obs_m, Obs_r \rangle, B'' = buf(B, props')$$

where buf is a belief update function, updating the belief base with the updated value of the observable properties.

Besides individual mirror objects, agents can track also observable regions. In that case, if a region $reg = \langle reg_{id}, ext \rangle$, part of the observable regions *Regs* defined in $\mathcal{S}_S$, is observed by an agent $a \in \mathcal{A}$, that is:

$$a = \langle a_{id}, B, Obs_m, Obs_R \rangle, reg_{id} \in Obs_R$$

then, the agent has beliefs about all mirror objects that are situated in that region, according to the shared space model/geometry and the extension of the region. In this case, a change of the state of the observable region – either because of mirror object appears/enters or disappears/exits as effect of agent actions or the observable state of mirror objects in the region changes, like in the previous case – involves a transition of the MW:

$$a \rightarrow \langle a_{id}, B', Obs_m, Obs_R \rangle$$

in which the belief base B of the agent observing the region gets updated.

4   A Platform for Agent-Based XR Based on Mirror Worlds

In this section, we discuss a software platform that implements the mirror worlds formal model presented in the previous section.

A first proposal for a platform to design and develop mirror worlds was proposed in [21] where JaCaMo [4] was extended with several features and concepts to deal with mirror worlds main elements. Nevertheless, this solution can not be considered as a real platform for building robust agent-based extended realities. It does not offer concrete support for dealing with mixed reality issues and challenges, and also the support for agents technologies is limited to Jason programming languages and, potentially, to others able to interact with CArtAgO [19] environments.

The platform that we discuss in this paper, instead, extends and refactors the first version of a software platform proposed by us in [8] called MiRAgE (acronym for Mixed Reality Agent-based Environments) that is a general-purpose framework for building software systems where agents can live and interact in a mixed reality environment where the physical and the digital layer are deeply coupled through the software layer. The refactoring mainly consists in injecting into MiRAgE the mirror world formal model with its abstractions in place of the ad-hoc model upon which it was originally built, redesigning abstraction for agent interaction with the mirror world.

4.1   Platform Architecture

Figure 2 depicts the logical architecture of the MiRAgE framework, showing its main components. Following paragraph enter into details.

The Platform Runtime. The main core of the platform is encapsulated by the MW-Runtime, representing the *virtual machine* supporting the execution of an instance of a MW and the creation and the evolution of all mirror objects. In other words, the MW-Runtime is responsible (1) to keep updated the state of each involved mirror object, (2) to allow to each mirror object to obtain the required resources to evolve their internal state, and (3) to provide a standard and interoperable interface for agents to interact with the MW and its entities. The MW-Runtime can be alternatively hosted on a single server node or can be

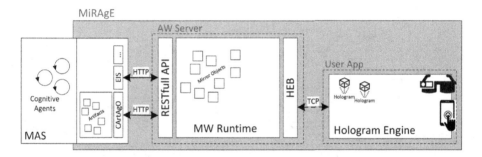

Fig. 2. The MiRAgE logical architecture and main components.

distributed on several machines. In any case, from the agent perspective, the runtime is always access with a single reference.

The access to the running instance of a MW, to its mirror objects – to observe them or to invoke their operations – is mediated by a RESTful API to maximize interoperability. In fact, this API is the only way to access to mirror objects from external active entities, e.g. agents. The API is based on self-descriptive messages, HTTP operations and event-oriented mechanisms (e.g. web-socket) [7]. Observable properties defining the observable state of each mirror object are naturally mapped onto Web-of-Things (WoT) [12] properties and, analogously, actions (operations) are naturally mapped onto actions of the WoT model. Moreover, like WoT, to support event-oriented interactions, in the MiRAgE RESTful API mirror object can be subscribed both at the resource level and the property/action level.

The Hologram Engine The platform architecture introduces the component called Hologram Engine to support the interaction of human users and allow them to perceive the mixed reality. It is a part of the platform running on the user's device and responsible both to generate and show holograms in relation with the user reference system and to keep them updated according to the evolving state of the mirror world. The hologram engine exploits a dedicated/infrastructural bidirectional TCP-based channel to communicate with the platform runtime through a dedicated bridge (HEB, Hologam Engine Bridge). This represents an important feature of the platform because ensures a real-time, effective and reliable experience to users observing and interacting with holograms.

4.2 The Platform Model and APIs

The mirror worlds model has been developed into MiRAgE as a set of first-class concepts summarized in Fig. 3. The structure and the laws previously discussed have been mapped into MiRAgE to govern each running instance of a mirror world. Agents deal with such concepts to join and manage mirror objects composing the extended reality represented by the mirror world.

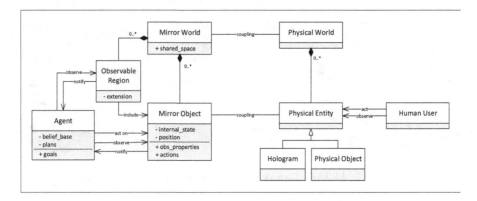

Fig. 3. A UML diagram representing MW concepts.

```
@HOLOGRAM(geometry = "CubeHologram") class Cube extends MirrorObject {

  @PROPERTY String color = "white";

  @ACTION void changeColor(String color) {
    customProperty("color", color);
  }

  @ACTION void rotate(Double degrees) {
    Orientation o = this.orientation();
    this.orientation(new Orientation(
      o.roll(), (o.pitch() + degrees) % 360, o.yaw()));
  }
}
```

Fig. 4. The cube mirror object implementation.

To give a taste of how the model can be used in MiRAgE to design mirror worlds, consider an instance of a MW with just one mirror object: a cube coupled with a hologram, created by an agent and active within the digital reality. Let assume that the cube has a state represented by two observable properties referring to its rotation and its color. Moreover, let assume the availability of an action for rotating the cube and another one for changing its color. The mirror object structure can be coded in MiRAgE through an annotate Java class using a specific syntax built upon the OOP model (see Fig. 4). It can declare both operations (fields annotated with @OPERATION) and actions (methods annotated with @ACTION). Each instance of a mirror object is in execution on the node where the platform runtime runs. Exploiting specific APIs, remote agents can interact with the runtime to join the mirror world and act within it. To guarantee a wide level of interoperability for agents interaction, the architecture of MiRAgE provides web-based APIs to observe and act on mirror object. Nonetheless, assuming BDI

```
!test.

+!test
  <- observe("cube");
     changeColor("red").

+color("green")
  <- .println("done!").

+rotation(Degrees) : Degrees < 45
  <- rotate(Degrees + 1).

+rotation(Degrees) : Degrees >= 45
  <- changeColor("green").
```

Fig. 5. An agent using the generated artifact.

cognitive agents in the A&A [17] perspective as the way for implementing agents, through a dedicated library developed in CArtAgO, MiRAgE offers to agents the possibility to see mirror objects as artifacts. In other words, although the state of the shared mirror world is kept within the platform runtime, each agent can count on a proper local representation in terms of artifacts of the interesting subset of mirror object allowing the agent for a more smooth-less interaction with them. It is in charge of the platform to create, dismiss and keep updated local artifacts considering the global state of the running system.

The snippet of code reported in Fig. 5 is a portion of the agent code reacting to changes of observable properties and using operations of the artifact representing, locally to the agent, the cube mirror object real instance.

4.3   Evaluation in a Real Context

A first real test-bed for the MiRAgE platform is provided by a project[2] developed in the context of cultural heritage enhancement. The case study allowed us to test main MiRAgE features and to conduct a first qualitative and technical evaluation considering a real complex running instance of a mirror world.

We built a mirror world within the internal courtyard of an ancient fortress to offer visitors a memory of a medieval scenario in shared mixed reality where they can also interact with digital entities (see Fig. 6). Exploiting Android Tablets, visitors can share, see and interact with the medieval holograms. Agents control the environments and digital entities encapsulated into mirror objects. As this case study shows, agents can focus their behaviours in managing mirror objects, reasoning considering beliefs about the whole mirror world state (including human users current state) and acts within the extended reality. The complete process

---

[2] In collaboration with "Rocca delle Caminate", Meldola, Italy.

Fig. 6. A picture of holograms composing the Mirror World developed within the fortress courtyard.

to build the shared, cooperative, agent-based extended reality environment is in charge of the MiRAgE platform.

5   Concluding Remarks

In this paper we described a model for mirror worlds used as conceptual reference for designing agent-based XR applications. The main value of the model is to provide a simple set of concepts and laws that makes it possible to capture key points of XR applications, integrating aspects from virtual worlds, AR/MR and pervasive computing, in spite of specific implementing technologies. Besides, we introduced also a concrete platform, implementing the model. The platform makes it possible to evaluate the effectiveness of the model by developing concrete agent-based XR applications, eventually using different agent technologies.

So far, the platform has been used to develop simple case studies, as the ones described in [8]—not discussed in this paper for lack of space. Nevertheless, a very important part of ongoing and future work is about tackling the development of more complex real-world case studies, both to stress the effectiveness of the underlying mirror world model defined in this paper and to stress platform robustness and performances. The main application domains that we are considering for this purpose concern smart environments in the context of Pervasive Healthcare and Hospital 4.0 [2], modelled as mirror worlds.

References

1. Azuma, R.T.: A survey of augmented reality. Presence: Teleoper. Virtual Environ. **6**(4), 355–385 (1997)

2. Bardram, J.E., Baldus, H., Favela, J.: Pervasive computing in hospitals. In: Pervasive Computing in Healthcare, pp. 75–104. CRC Press (2006)
3. Barella, A., Carrascosa, C., Botti, V.J., Martí, M.: Multi-agent systems applied to virtual environments: a case study. In: Proceedings of the ACM Symposium on Virtual Reality Software and Technology, VRST 2007, Newport Beach, California, USA, November 5–7, 2007, pp. 237–238 (2007)
4. Boissier, O., Bordini, R.H., Hübner, J.F., Ricci, A., Santi, A.: Multi-agent oriented programming with JaCaMo. Sci. Comput. Program. **78**(6), 747–761 (2013)
5. Campbell, A.G., Stafford, J.W., Holz, T., O'hare, G.M.: Why, when and how to use augmented reality agents (auras). Virtual Real **18**(2), 139–159 (2014)
6. Costanza, E., Kunz, A., Fjeld, M.: Mixed reality: a survey. In: Lalanne, D., Kohlas, J. (eds.) Human Machine Interaction. LNCS, vol. 5440, pp. 47–68. Springer, Heidelberg (2009). https://doi.org/10.1007/978-3-642-00437-7_3
7. Croatti, A., Ricci, A.: Mashing up the physical and augmented reality: the web of augmented things idea. In: Proceedings of the Eighth International Workshop on the Web of Things, pp. 4–7. WoT 2017, ACM, New York, NY, USA (2017)
8. Croatti, A., Ricci, A.: A model and platform for building agent-based pervasive mixed reality systems. In: Demazeau, Y., An, B., Bajo, J., Fernández-Caballero, A. (eds.) Advances in Practical Applications of Agents, Multi-Agent Systems, and Complexity: The PAAMS Collection, pp. 127–139. Springer, Cham (2018)
9. Devereaux, A.: Is the singularity the new wild west? on social entrepreneurship in extended reality. SSRN Electron. J. (2019)
10. Gelernter, D.: Mirror Worlds or the Day Software Puts the Universe in a Shoebox: How Will It Happen and What It Will Mean. Oxford University Press Inc, New York, NY, USA (1991)
11. Grieves, M., Vickers, J.: Digital twin: mitigating unpredictable, undesirable emergent behavior in complex systems. In: Kahlen, F.-J., Flumerfelt, S., Alves, A. (eds.) Transdisciplinary Perspectives on Complex Systems, pp. 85–113. Springer, Cham (2017). https://doi.org/10.1007/978-3-319-38756-7_4
12. Guinard, D., Trifa, V.: Building the Web of Things: With Examples in Node.Js and Raspberry Pi, 1st edn. Manning Publications Co., Greenwich, CT, USA (2016)
13. Holz, T., Campbell, A.G., O'Hare, G.M.P., Stafford, J.W., Martin, A., Dragone, M.: Mira-mixed reality agents. Int. J. Hum.-Comput. Stud. **69**(4), 251–268 (2011)
14. Liu, H., Bowman, M., Chang, F.: Survey of state melding in virtual worlds. ACM Comput. Surv. **44**(4), 21:1–21:25 (2012)
15. Luck, M., Aylett, R.: Applying artificial intelligence to virtual reality: intelligent virtual environments. Appl. Artif. Intell. **14**(1), 3–32 (2000)
16. Nevelsteen, K.J.L.: Virtual world, defined from a technological perspective and applied to video games, mixed reality, and the metaverse. Comput. Animation Virtual Worlds **29**(1), e1752 (2018)
17. Omicini, A., Ricci, A., Viroli, M.: Artifacts in the A&A meta-model for multi-agent systems. Auton. Agent. Multi-Agent Syst. **17**(3), 432–456 (2008)
18. Ricci, A., Tummolini, L., Piunti, M., Boissier, O., Castelfranchi, C.: Mirror worlds as agent societies situated in mixed reality environments. In: Ghose, A., Oren, N., Telang, P., Thangarajah, J. (eds.) COIN 2014. LNCS (LNAI), vol. 9372, pp. 197–212. Springer, Cham (2015). https://doi.org/10.1007/978-3-319-25420-3_13
19. Ricci, A., Viroli, M., Omicini, A.: CArtA gO: a framework for prototyping artifact-based environments in MAS. In: Weyns, D., Parunak, H.V.D., Michel, F. (eds.) E4MAS 2006. LNCS (LNAI), vol. 4389, pp. 67–86. Springer, Heidelberg (2007). https://doi.org/10.1007/978-3-540-71103-2_4

20. Ricci, A., Piunti, M., Tummolini, L., Castelfranchi, C.: The mirror world: preparing for mixed-reality living. IEEE Pervasive Comput. **14**(2), 60–63 (2015)
21. Ricci, A., Croatti, A., Brunetti, P., Viroli, M.: Programming mirror worlds: an agent-oriented programming perspective. In: Baldoni, M., Baresi, L., Dastani, M. (eds.) Eng. Multi-Agent Syst., pp. 191–211. Springer, Cham (2015)
22. Ricci, A., Tummolini, L., Castelfranchi, C.: Augmented societies with mirror worlds. AI & Soc. **34**(4), 745–752 (2017). https://doi.org/10.1007/s00146-017-0788-2
23. Rincon, J.A., Poza-Lujan, J.L., Julian, V., Posadas-Yague, J.L., Carrascosa, C.: Extending mam5 meta-model and JaCalIVE framework to integrate smart devices from real environments. PLOS ONE **11**(2), 1–27 (2016)

Model-Checking Information Diffusion in Social Networks with PRISM

Louise A. Dennis[1] and Marija Slavkovik[2(✉)]

[1] University of Liverpool, Liverpool, UK
L.A.Dennis@liverpool.ac.uk
[2] University of Bergen, Bergen, Norway
marija.slavkovik@uib.no

Abstract. In this paper we present an agent-based approach to formalising information diffusion using Markov models which attempts to account for the internal informational state of the agent and investigate the use of probabilistic model-checking for analysing these models. We model information diffusion as both continuous and discrete time Markov chains, using the latter to provide an agent-centred perspective. We present a negative result - we conclude that current model-checking technology is inadequate for analysing such systems in an interesting way.

Keywords: Verification of agent behaviour in a social network ·
Information diffusion

1 Introduction

Interest in social networks research is increasing, following the rise of *social network services* in the last decade. Various aspects of networks have been studied, see *e.g.,* [13].

Social network analysis is concerned with the structures of social relations and the graph they form, as well as how that structure influences, and is influenced by, the spread of information in the networks *e.g.,* [12,27]. Recently we see also see work that brings together social network research and logic. Informational and motivational states of the agents in the network are modelled, not just the relations between agents, *e.g.,* [4,11,21,25,28]. Network phenomena are also being given formal models and specifications *e.g.,* [4,20,21].

Diffusion is the process of spreading information through a network of agents. A social network is given as a graph of agents (vertices) and there exists an edge between two agents if they communicate/share information with each other. Depending upon a number of factors, an agent that has received information might be socially influenced to adopt it as true (believe it) and share it further in the network. There are several social influence models proposed in the literature, each describing different conditions under which the agent spreads the received information. An example of a question typically studied in diffusion is:

N. Bassiliades et al. (Eds.): EUMAS 2020/AT 2020, LNAI 12520, pp. 475–492, 2020.
https://doi.org/10.1007/978-3-030-66412-1_30

will a point be reached where the information is adopted by all agents? Following early work studying social networks as part of epidemiology, this is referred to as full contagion. We are particularly interested in how the internal informational state of the agent affects its decisions to spread information, and so have developed an agent-based model for information diffusion which explicitly uses this information. We adopted a Markov chain formalisation for this model since we were secondarily interested in using formal verification to analyse the network.

Formal verification involves proving or disproving that a system is compliant with a formally specified property [10]. Arguably the most practical method of formal verification is model-checking [7], in which all possible executions of a system can be examined automatically based on a model of the system.

Diffusion has been extensively studied in the social network analysis literature, see for example [13,19] for an overview, in particular the impact of the social network graph on the diffusion process has been studied. Social networks of communication have physically changed. In particular aspects of these networks, such as the distance between two nodes, and the speed of communication, have changed drastically. This observation has revived interest in the study of information diffusion, including work that represents the phenomena using Markov chains (*e.g.*, [3]) as we do here.

In our work we have built formal specifications of social networks and diffusion properties using the input language of a probabilistic model-checker (PRISM). Unfortunately even simple models that take account of both network structure and an agent's informational state proved largely intractable for model-checking on networks of any significant size. This essentially gives us a negative result for the use of probabilistic model-checking for information diffusion on social networks. However the formal Markov chain framework for studying the effect of an agent's informational state on information diffusion should also be amenable to study using simulation based techniques which we leave for further work.

Contribution. We provide a framework for formalising information diffusion in a way that takes account of an agent's internal informational state as Markov chains which focuses on the broadcasting of opinions as a key feature of study.

Model-checkers can be used as simulation systems, but their value is in their ability to exhaustively explore all possible system states and produce highly accurate results, exploring best and worst outcomes. Their weakness is that such exploration is computationally expensive and necessarily limits the size of the systems that can be examined. We determine experimentally that the PRISM model-checker – arguably the state of the art in terms of probabilistic model-checkers can not be used to analyse networks of any significant size – a negative result and a challenge to the developers of such tools.

2   Information Diffusion in Social Networks

Several models of information diffusion through influence have been proposed, although the task of finding a good model remains challenging [6]. The social influence models used to define processes of diffusion can broadly be classified into two classes: infection models and threshold models, with the possible exception of the recent Simmelian model [25]. In an infection model, each node is assigned a probability of being influenced [20]. In threshold models, an agent is influenced when the number of her influenced neighbours passes a certain threshold [29].

The SIS model. One of the classic infection models is the SIS model [1]. In this infection model each of the nodes in the graph can be in one of two states: infected or susceptible to infection. At time t, $s(t)$ represents the susceptible proportion of the total population N, $i(t)$ represents the infected proportion, and λ represents the daily contact rate, which means the proportion of the susceptible users infected by infected users in the total population, where $s(t) + i(t) = 1$. There will be $\lambda s(t)$ susceptible users infected at time t. At time $t = 0$ the proportion of infected nodes is i_0.

The SIS model assumes that μ represents the daily rates of the "cured" nodes (a mode can now become uninfected). The SIS model can be described by

$$\frac{di}{dt} = \lambda i(1 - i) - \mu i$$
$$i(0) = i_0.$$

Threshold influence models. Threshold influence models define the choice of whether a node will become infected or not as a function of the degree (or set of neighbours) of the node in question. Given an agent (node) x, let $n(x)$ be the set of agents that are directly connected to x in the social graph. Threshold models define a threshold q. The agent x will become infected if $|n(x)| \geq q$.

Other influence models. In the Simmelian model [25] of influence x gets infected if x is in a clique in which all other nodes are infected.

We will use the SIS model and threshold influence model as our starting point for introducing an agent's information state into models of information diffusion.

3   PRISM Background and Theory

PRISM [17] is a probabilistic symbolic model-checker in continuous development since 1999, primarily at the Universities of Birmingham and Oxford. Typically a model of a system is supplied to PRISM in the form of a probabilistic automata. This can then be exhaustively checked against a property written in PRISM's own probabilistic property specification language, which subsumes several well-known probabilistic logics including PCTL, probabilistic LTL, CTL, and PCTL*. PRISM has been used to formally verify a variety of systems in which reliability and uncertainty play a role, including communication protocols and biological systems [9,18].

In our models we use discrete-time and continuous-time Markov Chains as our probabilistic automata.

Definition 1. *[16] (Discrete-time Markov chain (DTMC)). A discrete-time Markov chain (DTMC) is a tuple $D = (S, s_i, P, L)$, where is S a finite set of states, $s_i \in S$ is a distinguished initial state, $P : S \times S \rightarrow [0, 1]$ is a transition probability matrix such that $\sum s' \in S. P(s, s') = 1$ for all $s \in S$, and $L(s) \subseteq AP$ is labelling with atomic propositions.*

A discrete-time Markov Chain describes a set of execution paths through the state space S where P gives the probability of one state moving to the next and L describes propositions that are true in any given state. PRISM explores the state space and can calculate the probability that various logical properties are always true, sometimes true, or true at some time t and so on in the model.

Definition 2. *[16] (Continuous-time Markov chain (CTMC)). A continuous-time Markov chain (CTMC) is $C = (S, s_i, R, L)$ where:*

- *S, s_i and L are defined as for DTMCs*
- *$R : (S \times S) \rightarrow \mathbb{R}_{\geq 0}$ is the rates matrix.*

Intuitively a CTMC describes a set of states and the rate at which one state moves to another. It is possible that for any state s there are several states s' such that $R(s, s') > 0$ and whichever state it transitions to first will determine the resulting behaviour of the system. Given a set of rates, $R(s, s')$ for some state s it is possible to infer the probability with which it will transition to each s' for any given time step t. PRISM can then explore this state space.

As well as calculating probabilities, PRISM is able to calculate the *expected reward* in some system. We can specify a rewards function, $\rho : S \rightarrow \mathbb{R}$ which assigns some reward value to the states in S. Among other things, this allows us to investigate the expected reward at some time step, t, in the system. This proves a particularly powerful tool in the study of information diffusion since we can model the number of agents adopting some idea as a reward.

4   Model-Checking Infection Models

4.1   Classic SIS Model

We choose as a first example the classic *SIS* infection model. This model takes neither the network structure nor the informational state of the agents into account, beyond the infection and recovery rates. We model this as a continuous time Markov Chain (CTMC). Our main aim in presenting this model is to illustrate the kinds of questions that can be asked and answered using a probabilistic model-checker.

Model 1. *We consider a network with m_a agents. This network contains $m_a + 1$ states, $s_i, 0 \leq i \leq m_a$. There are $m_a + 1$ propositional variables $p_i, 0 \leq i \leq m_a$ where p_i means that i agents in the model are infected. The labelling function is $L(s_i) = p_i$ (i.e., i agents are infected in state s_i). The initial state is s_1 (1 agent is infected at the start).*

λ and μ are the infection and recovery rates from the SIS infection model and these give us the following rate matrix:

$$R(s_i, s_{i+1}) = \lambda(m_a - i) \qquad\qquad if\ 0 < i < m_a \qquad (1)$$
$$R(s_i, s_{i-1}) = \mu(i) \qquad\qquad\qquad if\ 0 < i \qquad\qquad\quad (2)$$

We use PRISM to explore the behaviour of this model for different values of λ, μ, m_a and so on. For instance, Fig. 1 shows the probability of full contagion for all values of μ given $\lambda = 0.5$ and $m_a = 20$. We can see that where $\mu < \lambda$ there is a high probability that all agents will adopt some information while as soon as $\mu \geq \lambda$ this probability drops.

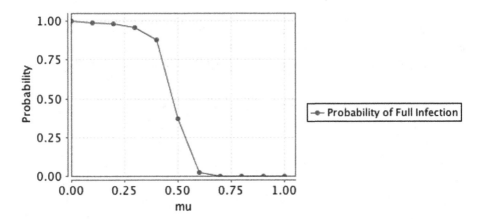

Fig. 1. Probability that all agents are infected in model 1 where $\lambda = 0.5$ and $m_a = 20$

This result doesn't hold for all network sizes. As the network grows the probability of full infection increases. Figure 2 shows that even when $\mu = 1$ the probability of full infection occurring at some point is over 0.9 once there are more than 30 agents.

Figure 3 shows the probability that all agents will be infected before time t (for $t < 100,000$) given various values of μ when $m_a = 20$. From this we can see that when $\mu = 0$ (i.e., when there is no possibility of recovery) or $\mu = 0.2$ the model rapidly reaches a point where the probability that all agents are infected is close to 1. However with $\mu = 0.4$ it takes in the region of 65,000 time steps for the probability of full infection to converge (to a value of 0.92). For higher values of μ the probability of full infection remains very low.

However as the network size increases (to numbers where we know the overall probability of full infection at some point is high for all μ) then this difference disappears. It becomes a more interesting question to ask how many people do we expect to be infected at any point in time. Figure 4 shows the expected number of infected agents at time T for various values of μ in a network of 200 agents.

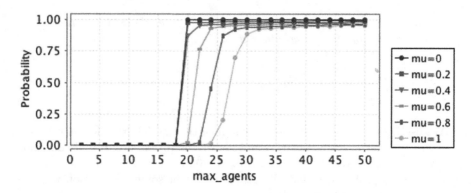

Fig. 2. Probability that all agents are infected in model 1 for $\lambda = 0.5$

As can be seen this value stabilizes quite rapidly and then remains steady, but as the value of μ increases the expected number of infected agents decreases (as the rate at which agents are recovering from infection has increased).

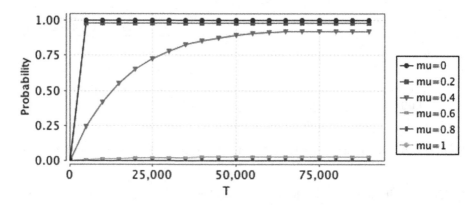

Fig. 3. Probability that all agents are infected by time T in model 1 for $\lambda = 0.5$ and $m_a = 20$

4.2 Taking the Agent View: Informational State and Opinion Broadcast

As has been noted in the literature [4,5] the transmission of information around a social networks may depend both on the features of the specific agents in the network and on the structure of the social network itself. We are interested in the possibility of using model-checking to explore traditional social analysis aspects of how network structure affects the spread of ideas. Further we want to see how agent properties contribute to the global effect (and ultimately in how actions by a mediating platform in a network service may contribute).

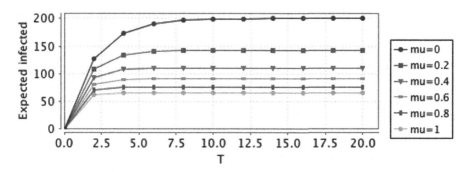

Fig. 4. The expected number of infected agents at time T in model 1 for $\lambda = 0.5$ and $m_a = 200$

As an example of an agent feature that might influence contagion we consider how one idea may be associated with an "anti-idea" which might either cause an idea to be abandoned (analogous to recovering from infection in traditional model) or might cause other behaviour (e.g., greater adherence to the original idea, modifications to network structure and so on). Taking this example, which to the best of our knowledge has not been considered in social network analysis, is motivated by the insight from psychology that "once formed impressions are remarkably perseverant" [22]. In this case we use the current informational state of the agent to inform both how likely it is to adopt an opinion. Once adopted it will broadcast the opinion to its network.

It is natural, in such a case, to consider the transition system of our model in terms of the transitions of the individual agents. PRISM provides support for constructing a DTMC from a specification of a transition relation on individual modules within a system were the state s of the system is the product of the states, s_{m_i}, of each module, $s = (s_{m_1}, \ldots, s_{m_n})$. This support uses a labelling on transitions within modules which synchronizes across all modules. Each module specifies the probability that the module will transition to some new state when a particular labelled transition, say l, occurs within the system. From this PRISM can calculate the probability distribution for the next state of the whole system given transition l. PRISM then assigns an equal probability that any transition that can occur will occur to derive the transition probability matrix over all possible transitions[1].

In order to take an agent view of a social network, we will model each agent as a PRISM module and use the notation $s^{a_i} \xrightarrow{l} p_1 : s_1^{a_i} \wedge \ldots \wedge p_n : s_n^{a_i}$ to indicate that agent, a_i in state, s^{a_i} transitions to state $s_j^{a_i}$ with probability p_j where $\sum_{i=1}^{n} p_i = 1$ when the transition labelled l occurs.

Model 2. *We will use a DTMC to model a network of agents. Each agent, a_i, in the network is a PRISM module and can be in one of three states. Either the agent agrees with some idea ϕ (written as state $s_\phi^{a_i}$) or it disagrees with the*

---

idea ($s^{a_i}_{\neg\phi}$) or it is indifferent to ϕ (written as $s^{a_i}_{\perp}$)). If there are n agents in the network, there are 3^n states in S.

An agent will broadcast a message in favour of ϕ (respectively $\neg\phi$) to all of its connections if it agrees with ϕ. We treat this as a transition labelled $a_i\_says_\phi$. On receiving a message in favour of ϕ (respectively $\neg\phi$) there is a probability of λ that the agent will adopt the idea ϕ (abandoning the idea $\neg\phi$ if necessary).

$$s^{a_i}_\phi \xrightarrow{a_i\text{-}says_\phi} \qquad 1 : s^{a_i}_\phi \qquad\qquad\qquad\qquad (3)$$

$$s^{a_i}_\phi \xrightarrow{a_j\text{-}says_\phi} \qquad 1 : s^{a_i}_\phi \qquad\qquad\qquad \text{if } cn(i,j) \quad (4)$$

$$s^{a_i}_\phi \xrightarrow{a_j\text{-}says_{\neg\phi}} \qquad \lambda : s^{a_i}_{\neg\phi} \wedge (1-\lambda) : s^{a_i}_\phi \qquad \text{if } cn(i,j) \quad (5)$$

$$s^{a_i}_{\neg\phi} \xrightarrow{a_i\text{-}says_{\neg\phi}} \qquad 1 : s^{a_i}_{\neg\phi} \qquad\qquad\qquad\qquad (6)$$

$$s^{a_i}_{\neg\phi} \xrightarrow{a_j\text{-}says_{\neg\phi}} \qquad 1 : s^{a_i}_{\neg\phi} \qquad\qquad\qquad \text{if } cn(i,j) \quad (7)$$

$$s^{a_i}_{\neg\phi} \xrightarrow{a_j\text{-}says_\phi} \qquad \lambda : s^{a_i}_\phi \wedge (1-\lambda) : s^{a_i}_{\neg\phi} \qquad \text{if } cn(i,j) \quad (8)$$

$$s^{a_i}_{\perp} \xrightarrow{a_j\text{-}says_\phi} \qquad \lambda : s^{a_i}_\phi \wedge (1-\lambda) : s^{a_i}_{\perp} \qquad \text{if } cn(i,j) \quad (9)$$

$$s^{a_i}_{\perp} \xrightarrow{a_j\text{-}says_{\neg\phi}} \qquad \lambda : s^{a_i}_{\neg\phi} \wedge (1-\lambda) : s^{a_i}_{\perp} \qquad \text{if } cn(i,j) \quad (10)$$

Fig. 5. Transition System for agent a_i in model 2

Figure 5 shows the transition system for agent a_i where $cn(i,j)$ means i is connected to j in the network. Where a transition isn't specified (i.e., for all the agents i is not connected to) then PRISM assumes a_i's state is unchanged by that transition (after all a_i is unaware of what a_j is saying). Where a transition is specified for only some of a_i's states (e.g., $a_i\_says_\phi$ is specified only for state $s^{a_i}_\phi$) then that transition can only occur when a_i is in one of those states (a_i can not broadcast ϕ unless it agrees with ϕ).

To start with we considered a fully connected network (FCN) of 10 agents. We seeded the network with one agent believing ϕ and one agent believing $\neg\phi$ and set the probability of infection, λ to 0.5. We created a reward function $\rho(s) = \sum_{i=0}^{n} : s^{a_i} = s^{a_i}_\phi$ (i.e., the reward for a state s is the number of agents who believe ϕ in that state). Figure 6 shows that this network as quickly converges to a state where the expectation is that half the agents believe ϕ – the expected reward is 5.

We are not very interested in FCNs. Research in the information diffusion under the SIS model from early on has shown that the structure of the network has a big influence on the effectiveness of the contagion [26]. Mathematical analysis shows that the diffusion likelihood increases with the number of connections [19].

We want to have a "higher detail" insight into the impact a particular graph has on the spread of information. We generated a random network that satisfies

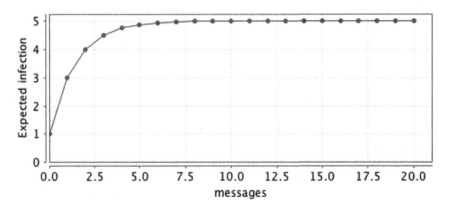

Fig. 6. Expected number of infected agents per message sent for model 2 on a FCN

the criteria for modelling a social network as a random graph as outlined in [23]: the maximal degree of separation is low, the probability of an edge between two agents is higher if they have mutual neighbours, and the network has a skewed degree distribution. This network contained 10 agent nodes, some with a minimum of 2 connections within the network and one with 8 connections. We initially studied the spread of ideas within this network with an λ of 0.5 and ϕ and $\neg\phi$ inserted in poorly connected agents (i.e., agents with only two connections within the network), well-connected agents (i.e., agents with six connections) and when the agent with idea ϕ had 8 connections while the agent with idea $\neg\phi$ had only 2 connections. The results are shown in Fig. 7.

As it can be seen in the case where the initial agents have similar numbers of connections, the expected number of infected agents converges to 5 (converging more rapidly in the case where the initial agents have more connections). However in the case where the agent initially wishing to disseminate ϕ has more connections than the agent wishing to disseminate $\neg\phi$ then the number of agents believing ϕ converges to just under 6 – showing that the **initial advantage had a long term effect**. This result came as a surprise to us and, as far as we are aware, is not one that has been studied in the context of diffusion in the literature. We generated a further 9 networks (for a total of 10) and observed the same effect in all of them. However we were unable to investigate whether the same effect held for larger network sizes using PRISM.

We also investigated the probability that all agents in the network would become infected with the idea ϕ – i.e., that its opposite idea was completely eradicated from the network. In the case of the unbalanced starting position the probability was 0.58 while in the balanced starting conditions the probability was 0.5.

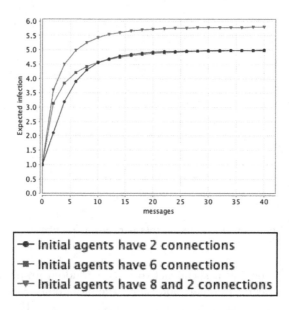

Fig. 7. Expected number of infected agents per message sent for model 2 on a randomly generated network

5   Model-Checking Threshold Influence Models

We now consider threshold influence models. In these models it is not the receipt of a message bearing the idea ϕ that causes an agent to adopt the idea, but the perception that most of the agent's connections agree with ϕ.

We start with a FCN, as before.

Model 3. *We assume that an agent, a_i, can be in one of two states, $s_\phi^{a_i}$ (the agent publicly supports ϕ) or $s_\perp^{a_i}$ (the agent does not publicly support ϕ). All agents that publicly support ϕ broadcast the fact to all their neighbours, but we don't represent this as a transition in the network. Instead we have a joint transition, think, on all agents where they update a decision on whether or not they believe (or at least publicly support) ϕ themselves. Here the probability that they will adopt ϕ is proportional to the number of their connections who publicly support ϕ. n^{c_i} is the number of connections a_i has in the network and $n_\phi^{c_i}$ is the number of their connections who are broadcasting messages in support of ϕ so the chance of an agent deciding to espouse ϕ is $\lambda.\frac{n_\phi^{c_i}}{n^{c_i}}$ for some λ.*

This gives us the following transition system for agent a_i:

$$s_\perp^{a_i} \xrightarrow{think} \lambda.\frac{n_\phi^c}{n^c} : s_\phi^{a_i} \wedge (1 - \lambda.\frac{n_\phi^c}{n^c}) : s_\perp^{a_i} \tag{11}$$

$$s_\phi^{a_i} \xrightarrow{think} 1 : s_\phi^{a_i} \tag{12}$$

Figure 8 shows the expected number of agents who support ϕ, in a fully connected network of 10 agents, after T think transitions, given an influence probability of $\lambda = 0.5$. As can be seen this network converges to a state where we expect all 10 agents to support ϕ after 17 transitions.

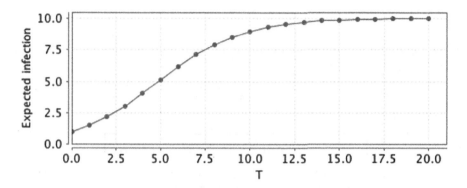

Fig. 8. Expected number of agents expressing ϕ after T transitions in model 3 on a FCN

Figure 9 shows the spread of ϕ on our more realistic network in the case where ϕ is first adopted by an agent with only 2 connections and in the case when ϕ is first is first adopted by an agent with 8 connections.

As in infection models, we can also add $\neg\phi$ into our influence model – with the chance that an agent expresses the opinion ϕ or $\neg\phi$ depending upon their perception of how many of their connections believe ϕ or $\neg\phi$.

Model 4. *We extend our transition system from model 3 with an agent state, $s_{\neg\phi}^{a_i}$ (the agent is expressing support for $\neg\phi$) and the variable $n_{\neg\phi}^{c_i}$ (the number of a_i's connections expressing support for $\neg\phi$). Therefore an agent's transitions become:*

$$s_{\perp}^{a_i} \xrightarrow{think} \lambda.\frac{n_{\phi}^{c_i}}{n^{c_i}} : s_{\phi}^{a_i} \wedge \lambda.\frac{n_{\neg\phi}^{c_i}}{n^{c_i}} : s_{\neg\phi}^{a_i} \wedge$$

$$(1 - \lambda.\frac{n_{\phi}^{c_i} + n_{\neg\phi}^{c_i}}{n^{c_i}}) : s_{\perp}^{a_i} \tag{13}$$

$$s_{\phi}^{a_i} \xrightarrow{think} \lambda.\frac{n_{\neg\phi}^{c_i}}{n^{c_i}} : s_{\neg\phi}^{a_i} \wedge (1 - \lambda.\frac{n_{\neg\phi}^{c_i}}{n^{c_i}}) : s_{\phi}^{a_i} \tag{14}$$

$$s_{\neg\phi}^{a_i} \xrightarrow{think} \lambda.\frac{n_{\phi}^{c_i}}{n^{c_i}} : s_{\phi}^{a_i} \wedge (1 - \lambda.\frac{n_{\phi}^{c_i}}{n^{c_i}}) : s_{\neg\phi}^{a_i} \tag{15}$$

As before we start with a fully connected model the results of which are shown in Fig. 10. Here, instead of all agent eventually expressing ϕ, we expected to reach a state where half the agents express ϕ (and by extension half are expressing $\neg\phi$).

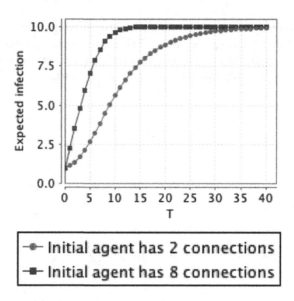

Fig. 9. Expected number of agents expressing ϕ after T transitions in model 3 on a randomly generated network

Now we turn to our randomly generated model and examine the effect on the expected spread of ϕ, given the connectivity of the initial agents expressing ϕ and $\neg\phi$. The results are shown in Fig. 11. In the infection models (Fig. 7) the models converged to a state where half the agents adopted ϕ when both ϕ and $\neg\phi$ had similar starting states while it converged to a state where roughly 60% of the agents adopted ϕ when ϕ had an advantage over $\neg\phi$ at the start. In the case of influence models we see that the advantage conveyed by a better initial state is larger than it is in infection models, with the network converging to a state where we expect over 8 agents to be expressing ϕ.

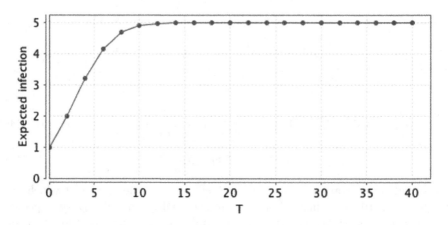

Fig. 10. Expected number of agents expressing ϕ after T transitions for model 4 on a FCN

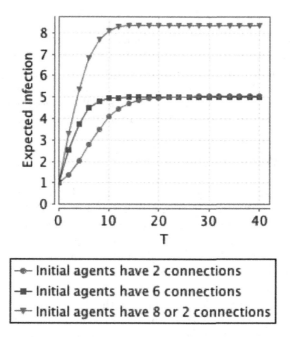

Fig. 11. Expected number of agents expressing ϕ after T transitions for model 4 on a randomly generated network

6   Analysing Larger Networks

Clearly networks of 10 agents are inadequate models of behaviour over large social networks. Unfortunately PRISM proved incapable of analysing larger models. In some cases PRISM couldn't even construct a larger model rendering even its simulation capabilities out of reach. Figure 12 shows the time taken to build a model of a FCN and to use PRISM model-checking to find the probability that the entire network would be fully infected with ϕ after 10 time steps for both model 2 and model 4.

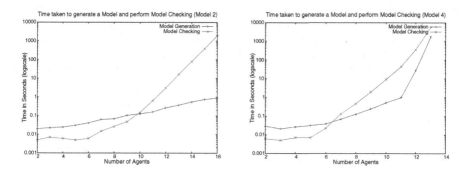

Fig. 12. Times taken to build a model and perform model checking for fully connected networks

The reasons for these problems are unclear[2]. While we did not expect to be able to model networks containing hundreds of agents in PRISM we had expected to model networks of more than ten. We have been invited to submit the social network models as challenge problems.

This does mean, however, that for the time being the use of model-checking as a tool for analysing information diffusion in social networks is limited although the same formalism can be used for simulation based analysis.

7   Related Work

The influence of network structure on diffusion has been extensively studied in economics, see *e.g.,* [19] for an extensive literature list and [14] for a more general overview of the impact of social network structure on behaviour.

The methodology used to study network structure impact on diffusion throughout the literature is numerical analysis, simulation and experiments. Both micro and macro aspects of the network structure have been considered, but in both cases these aspects refer to statistical properties of the network. For example, a macro network aspect example is the degree distribution in the network, while a micro network aspect example is the average distance between two agents in the network and network component diameters. In nearly all diffusion models, the likelihood of adopting new information or behaviour increases with the increase of adjacent agents who have adopted it and a higher agent degree leads to higher contagion [19]. We also observe this here.

Bolzern et al.'s [3] approach is most similar to our own, using Markov chain models to capture network structure and to show how opinions among the agents in the network may vary among a fixed set of opinions (a generalisation of the idea of an idea, an "anti-idea", and indifference that we use here). However in their model the chance an agent will change its opinion does not depend upon its existing opinion, only upon the opinions of its neighbours. They use both formal analysis to generate results about the behaviour of the general system and monte-carlo simulation to analyse a specific system consisting of a fully connected network and two possible opinions.

Model-checking information in social networks has been studied from a theoretical perspective in [24] and [8]. Pardo and Schneider [24] consider the problem of verifying knowledge properties over social network models (SNM's) and shows that the model checking problem for epistemic properties over SNMs is decidable. Dennis et al. [8] introduce a formal specification for SNM's and privacy properties that can be established to hold using model-checking using PRISM. Belardinelli and Grossi [2] present a model-checking algorithm and property specification logic for studying contagion-type models in open dynamic networks. This takes an agent view but does not explicitly consider the informational states of the agents. The proposed model-checking algorithm has not been implemented. Kouvaros and Lomuscio [15] use parameterised model-checking in the MCMAS system

---

[2] Ernst Moritz Hahn, private communication.

to study opinion formation protocols for swarm robotics. These protocols are similar to threshold models and involve agents in a swarm switching their opinion to the majority opinion of their neighbours. The interest in this work was primarily on answering whether the protocol guaranteed convergence to an opinion, not on analysing the behaviour of information diffusion itself and probabilistic aspects were not studied. Lastly, Zonghao et al. [30] use PRISM to evaluate the efficacy of methods for controlling harmful network propagation using different protection strategies for individual nodes. Although Zonghao et al. [30] are interested in security an protecting networks from e-viruses, the approach and methodology can be seen as related to ours in the case of information diffusion.

8   Discussion

While we have successfully made steps to account for internal informational states of agents in models of information diffusion. We have not successfully managed to use formal verification to analyse these models.

Clearly, there is no free lunch and, at least for now, there are technical limitations to the number of agents we can model. While we did not expect to model networks containing thousands of agents we had hoped that model-checking would provide a useful tool for exploration of networks of sufficiently large size to allow reasonable variation in network structure to be studied. This has not proved to be the case.

There are two approaches to overcoming this problem both of which we intend to pursue. We intend to continue using Markov chain models to study information diffusion in social networks – in particular we wish to study networks where an agent's informational state, its decision to broadcast a particular opinion and the decision of the network itself to propagate a broadcast to particular other agents all interact. While we could not use PRISM to simulate on our models we hope to either adopt or build a suitable alternative tool that can be used in this way.

Secondly, it is common in model-checking to develop abstractions of the problem which allow systems of realistic size to be studied. Work on parameterised model checking in swarm scenarios is also a promising avenue of research and, indeed, this is the approach taken in [15].

9   Summary

We have developed an initial framework for modelling information diffusion in social networks which takes an agent-centred view that includes an account of the agent's informational state when considering changes in the network. This framework uses Markov chain models to represent the agents within the network and their relationships to each other. Unfortunately even comparatively simple models proved intractable for analysing models of interesting size in PRISM, a current state-of-the-art tool for probabilistic model-checking.

Open Data

The PRISMmodels, network graphs, output and timing data reported in this paper can all be found in the University of Liverpool Data Catalogue DOI: https://doi.org/10.17638/datacat.liverpool.ac.uk/909.

Acknowledgements. The research was partly supported by the project "Better Video workflows via Real-Time Collaboration and AI-Techniques in TV and New Media", funded by the Research Council of Norway under Grant No.:269790.

References

1. Bailey, N.: The Mathematical theory of Infectious Diseases and its applications. Charles Griffin and Company Ltd., London (1975)
2. Belardinelli, F., Grossi, D.: On the formal verification of diffusion phenomena in open dynamic agent networks. In: Proceedings of the 2015 International Conference on Autonomous Agents and Multiagent Systems, pp. 237–245. AAMAS 2015, International Foundation for Autonomous Agents and Multiagent Systems, Richland, SC (2015). http://dl.acm.org/citation.cfm?id=2772879.2772912
3. Bolzern, P., Colaneri, P., Nicolao, G.D.: Opinion influence and evolution in social networks: a markovian agents model. Automatica **100**, 219–230 (2019). https://doi.org/https://doi.org/10.1016/j.automatica.2018.11.023, http://www.sciencedirect.com/science/article/pii/S0005109818305557
4. Christoff, Z., Hansen, J.U.: A two-tiered formalization of social influence. In: Grossi, D., Roy, O., Huang, H. (eds.) LORI 2013. LNCS, vol. 8196, pp. 68–81. Springer, Heidelberg (2013). https://doi.org/10.1007/978-3-642-40948-6_6
5. Christoff, Z., Hansen, J.U.: A logic for diffusion in social networks. J. Appl. Logic **13**(1), 48–77 (2015). https://doi.org/10.1016/j.jal.2014.11.011
6. Christoff, Z., Hansen, J.U., Proietti, C.: Reflecting on social influence in networks. J. Logic Lang. Inform. **25**(3), 299–333 (2016). https://doi.org/10.1007/s10849-016-9242-y
7. Clarke, E.M., Grumberg, O., Peled, D.: Model Checking. MIT Press, Cambridge (1999)
8. Dennis, L.A., Slavkovik, M., Fisher, M.: "How Did They Know?"—model-checking for analysis of information leakage in social networks. In: Cranefield, S., Mahmoud, S., Padget, J., Rocha, A.P. (eds.) COIN -2016. LNCS (LNAI), vol. 10315, pp. 42–59. Springer, Cham (2017). https://doi.org/10.1007/978-3-319-66595-5_3
9. Duflot, M., et al.: Practical applications of probabilistic model checking to communication protocols. In: Gnesi, S., Margaria, T. (eds.) FMICS Handbook on Industrial Critical Systems, pp. 133–150. IEEE Computer Society Press, Los Alamitos (2010)
10. Fisher, M., Dennis, L.A., Webster, M.: Verifying autonomous systems. Commun. ACM **56**(9), 84–93 (2013)
11. Grandi, U., Lorini, E., Novaro, A., Perrussel, L.: Strategic disclosure of opinions on a social network. In: Proceedings of the 16th International Joint Conference on Autonomous Agents and Multiagent Systems (AAMAS-2017) (2017)
12. Granovetter, M.: Threshold models of collective behavior. Am. J. Sociol. **83**(6), 1420–1443 (1978). https://doi.org/10.1086/226707

13. Jackson, M.O.: Social and Economic Networks. Princeton University Press, Princeton, NJ, USA (2008)
14. Jackson, M.O., Rogers, B.W., Zenou, Y.: The economic consequences of social-network structure. J. Econ. Lit. **55**(1), 49–95 (2017). https://doi.org/10.1257/jel.20150694
15. Kouvaros, P., Lomuscio, A.: Formal verification of opinion formation in swarms. In: Proceedings of the 2016 International Conference on Autonomous Agents & #38; Multiagent Systems, pp. 1200–1208. AAMAS 2016, International Foundation for Autonomous Agents and Multiagent Systems, Richland, SC (2016). http://dl.acm.org/citation.cfm?id=2936924.2937099
16. Kwiatkowska, M., Norman, G., Parker, D.: Stochastic model checking. In: Bernardo, M., Hillston, J. (eds.) SFM 2007. LNCS, vol. 4486, pp. 220–270. Springer, Heidelberg (2007). https://doi.org/10.1007/978-3-540-72522-0_6
17. Kwiatkowska, M., Norman, G., Parker, D.: PRISM 4.0: verification of probabilistic real-time systems. In: Gopalakrishnan, G., Qadeer, S. (eds.) CAV 2011. LNCS, vol. 6806, pp. 585–591. Springer, Heidelberg (2011). https://doi.org/10.1007/978-3-642-22110-1_47
18. Kwiatkowska, M., Thachuk, C.: Probabilistic model checking for biology. In: Software Safety and Security. NATO Science for Peace and Security Series - D: Information and Communication Security, IOS Press (2014), to appear
19. Lamberson, P.J.: Linking network structure and diffusion through stochastic dominance. In: Complex Adaptive Systems and the Threshold Effect, Papers from the 2009 AAAI Fall Symposium, Arlington, Virginia, USA, November 5–7, 2009 (2009)
20. Li, M., Wang, X., Gao, K., Zhang, S.: A survey on information diffusion in online social networks: models and methods. Information **8**(4), 118 (2017). https://doi.org/10.3390/info8040118
21. Liu, F., Seligman, J., Girard, P.: Logical dynamics of belief change in the community. Synthese **191**(11), 2403–2431 (2014). https://doi.org/10.1007/s11229-014-0432-3
22. Mercier, H., Sperber, D.: The Enigma of Reason. Harvard University Press, London, UK (2017)
23. Newman, M.E.J., Watts, D.J., Strogatz, S.H.: Random graph models of social networks. Proc. Nat. Acad. Sci. **99**(suppl 1), 2566–2572 (2002). https://doi.org/10.1073/pnas.012582999
24. Pardo, R., Schneider, G.: Model checking social network models. In: Proceedings Eighth International Symposium on Games, Automata, Logics and Formal Verification, GandALF 2017, Roma, Italy, 20–22 September 2017, pp. 238–252 (2017). https://doi.org/10.4204/EPTCS.256.17, https://doi.org/10.4204/EPTCS.256.17
25. Pedersen, T., Slavkovik, M.: Formal models of conflicting social influence. In: An, B., Bazzan, A., Leite, J., Villata, S., van der Torre, L. (eds.) PRIMA 2017. LNCS (LNAI), vol. 10621, pp. 349–365. Springer, Cham (2017). https://doi.org/10.1007/978-3-319-69131-2_21
26. Rapoport, A.: Spread of information through a population with socio-structural bias: I. assumption of transitivity. Bull. Math. Biophys. **15**(4), 523–533 (1953). https://doi.org/10.1007/BF02476440, https://doi.org/10.1007/BF02476440
27. Schelling, T.C.: Dynamic models of segregation. J. Math. Sociol. **1**(2), 143–186 (1971)
28. Smets, S., Velázquez-Quesada, F.R.: How to make friends: a logical approach to social group creation. In: Baltag, A., Seligman, J., Yamada, T. (eds.) LORI 2017. LNCS, vol. 10455, pp. 377–390. Springer, Heidelberg (2017). https://doi.org/10.1007/978-3-662-55665-8_26

29. Winship, C.: Threshold models of social influence. In: Bearman, P., Hedström, P. (eds.) The Oxford Handbook of Analytical Sociology. Oxford University Press, Oxford (2011). https://doi.org/10.1093/oxfordhb/9780199215362.013.20
30. Zonghao, G., Ou, W., Peng, Y., Lansheng, H., Weiming, W.: Model checking probabilistic network propagation protection strategies. In: 2016 IEEE Trustcom/BigDataSE/ISPA, pp. 354–361 (August 2016). https://doi.org/10.1109/TrustCom.2016.0084

"Roads? Where We're Going We Don't Need Roads." Using Agent-Based Modeling to Analyze the Economic Impact of Hyperloop Introduction on a Supply Chain

Francesco Bertolotti[✉] and Riccardo Occa

Università Cattaneo – LIUC, Corso G. Matteotti 22, 21053 Castellanza, (VA), Italy
{fbertolotti,rocca}@liuc.it

Abstract. The opportunity to connect distant areas in quick and economical ways has always been a critical element for trade and economic development. Significant progress is often accompanied by the emergence of new transport models, as it happened in 21st century China with high-speed railways, a driving force for its economic growth. In 2013, the Hyperloop Alpha white paper publication presented the opportunity for a significant innovation in transportation, which could have an even more disruptive effect. In this paper, we will estimate the possible impact on a Supply Chain of constructing a Hyperloop line for goods transportation. We develop an agent-based model of a simple Supply Chain system to simulate the introduction of a faster transport line. We observed that a positive relationship exists between the introduction of a faster line and the performance of the firms near the cities connected by the new line. We conclude that the adoption of a Hyperloop could significantly affect the region in which it is implemented. Since the technology is in its infancy, there is still room for further research.

Keywords: Agent-based modeling · Hyperloop · Economic models · Supply chain · Regional development · Infrastructure development

1 Introduction

Individuals' desire to travel has led to some of humanity's most amazing creations, like ships, cars, and airplanes, which now have an enormous influence on our life. The more the technologies advance, the more the quantity of goods and products transported becomes vital for the world's development. In 2013, Elon Musk presented a first proposal for the Hyperloop, a new technology that could radically revolutionize the transportation of goods and people. It consists of capsules traveling inside airless tubes, reaching speeds over 1200 km per hour [13]. This innovation could offer many advantages over traditional travel methods. For example, it could reduce travel time, ticket costs, and construction costs compared to a conventional high-speed line [5, 19]. In the field of freight transport, it can lead to the development of on-demand freight services in a short time frame, reducing the need for high advance planning and increasing transport reliability and flexibility for

© Springer Nature Switzerland AG 2020
N. Bassiliades et al. (Eds.): EUMAS 2020/AT 2020, LNAI 12520, pp. 493–500, 2020.
https://doi.org/10.1007/978-3-030-66412-1_31

companies [11]. This preliminary research aims to understand if the practical application of Hyperloop technology could lead to improvements in freight transport and supply chain performance, and in which kind of regions would be better to implement it. The methodology we adopt is agent-based modeling, a well-known technique for modeling real-world dynamical systems in a wide set of applications [1]. We developed an agent model of a trading system based on a simple supply chain, and we analyzed the impact of a new single fast line, which stands for the Hyperloop, on the firms in the connected areas. First, we found a positive correlation between the introduction of a Hyperloop and the performances of the firms nearby it. Second, we concluded that the first Hyperloop line should be introduced in a region already economically and infrastructurally developed. Third, we proposed a list of some possible developments and future research that are needed to be addressed. The remaining of the paper is structured as follows: in Sect. 2, we introduce previous research on the topic; in Sect. 3, we show the model and the methodology adopted; in Sect. 4, we show the results and discuss them. Finally, in Sect. 5, we conclude and define future possible research trajectories.

2 Literature Analysis

2.1 Hyperloop

Although Hyperloop has begun to spread through newspapers and companies reports, scientific production on the subject is still limited. We performed a literature search on Scopus to find scientific works available on the topic, finding only 16 documents. The query was asked on February 1st 2020, with the next research key: ((TITLE (hyperloop*) AND KEY (hyperloop*)) AND (LIMIT-TO (DOCTYPE, "ar") OR LIMIT TO (DOC-TYPE, "cp")) AND (LIMIT-TO (SRCTYPE, "j") OR LIMIT-TO (SRCTYPE, "p"))). All the results were recent. The first document on this topic was published in 2017 [22]. However, the number of papers published is also growing over the years, suggesting increasing interest in the field. The majority of the papers regarded the different areas of design and construction of a Hyperloop system. The main topics were magnetic levitation systems [3, 12] and testing activities [11, 14]. Some papers [6, 16] focused on safety and the possible physical impacts on passenger's transportation of the use of Hyperloop technology. There was also a work related to the modeling and analysis of the possible performances of the Hyperloop technology [18], comparing it with high-speed rail and air transport. However, the analysis only concerned passenger transport, without considering the possible effects of the Hyperloop introduction on freight transport.

2.2 Impact of High-Speed Trains

In the previous paragraph, it is clear that, to the best of our knowledge, there isn't in the literature any work related to the possible impact of a Hyperloop on the development of a region. Hence, we collected information on the impact of high-speed trains, the latest technologies introduced for the rapid transport of goods. This choice was made to have a clearer image of the phenomenon we wanted to analyze. The research was carried out with Scopus on February 1st 2020, with the following key: (TITLE ("railway*"

OR " high speed trains" OR " High* Rail*" OR "Transport Development") AND KEY ("Development" OR "accessibility" OR "economic growth" OR "Urban growth")). The following thematic areas have been excluded because they are not congruent with the aims of the research: "EART, PHYS, MATE, ARTS, MEDI, CHEM, CENG, BIOC, HEAL, PHAR, PSYC, IMMU, VETE." The main results are reported in Table 1.

Table 1. Main results of bibliographic research about high-speed trains.

Finding	Sources
There was a positive relationship between rail transport and GDP growth, a relationship not necessary present with passenger transport. This was especially true for high capacity lines	Weidong 2008, Hang 2011, Sun 2012, Wang et al. 2009
The evolution of the railway network was also capable of changing the pace and development paths of urban areas	Wang et al. 2009, Huang et al. 2016
Accessibility of stations is a key element for attractiveness of high-speed lines, since it influenced the total travel time. With lower accessibility (or reduced interconnections), total travel time was stable and there were not significant benefits	Wang et al. 2013, Brezina and Knoflacher 2014
For passenger transport, high-speed trains had no advantages over traditional lines under 150 km, while they are particularly effective between 400 and 800 km	Gleave 2004, Chen & Hall 2011

3 Model Presentation

The proposed model allows to observe how the introduction of a higher speed transportation line dedicated to goods between two urban centers impact the performance of the firms around them. To achieve this goal, we simulated the behavior of a simple supply chain composed of different levels, in which a single kind of good is produced, exchanged in a single direction, and consumed.

The model scenario is a squared territory on which are distributed two kinds of agents, Cities, and Suppliers. In every simulation, Cities are uniformly randomly distributed in the territory, and Suppliers are uniformly randomly distributed around the Cities. Each Supplier is connected to his City by "roads," while the Cities are connected to each other by "railroads." The link breeds differ from each other in travel time and the travel cost per unit of space, which is higher for the "roads" connection. It stands by the higher cost and lower speed of local transport. The supply chain is divided into different tiers. Suppliers with a tier equal to one are directly supplying the Cities, the final market of the model, and the final destination of goods. At the same time, suppliers with the highest tier are producers. Each tier has the same number of Suppliers. In every tier, Suppliers define their selling price by applying a mark-up to their average cost of the stock, which includes buying and transportation cost. Agents have some commerce constraints. First, they can only commerce with agents with an adjacent tier (plus or minus one). Second, agents can receive goods only from Suppliers with a higher tier. Third, agents can ask for products only to a limited set of suppliers, which is selected through an evaluation score (from now on ES). ES is the mean of normalized values of travel time to the Supplier, travel cost to the Supplier, quality of Supplier goods, and cost of Supplier goods. Selected Suppliers are ranked by the ES. Except for producers, every agent has the same number of selected Suppliers. Cities' demand is generated by a pseudo-random continuing uniform distribution and depends on the City's population level, a constant parameter defined at the beginning of the simulation. At each time step, Cities have an incoming demand and ask the Suppliers in their network to fulfill it. If a Supplier has enough stock, the demand is satisfied. Otherwise, the City receives all the stock of the first Supplier and ask another Supplier for goods. This process keeps on until the demand is satisfied or available Suppliers finish. Suppliers with higher ES would be chosen before Suppliers with lower ES. The same supplying process is also repeated for every non-producing Supplier. So, at each time step, the demand of the City goes upstream on the supply chain until it arrives to producers, which generates a number of goods equal to the minimum value between the production constraint and the incoming demand. There is no limit in the quantity of goods an agent can sell in a single time step (except for a non-negative constraint for sold goods and stock level). Thus, at every time step, some goods are still in transit. To conclude, each agent starts the simulation with the same amount of cash. Every time step, it will earn cash for selling goods, spend cash for buying goods, and for covering fixed costs, equal for every agent in the market.

4 Model Analysis

4.1 Methods

We executed an experiment on the model to observe the effect of the introduction of a single Hyperloop line on the supply chain. We analyzed the impact on a ten-year time frame (520 steps of one week), introduced the new connection after five years, and observed if it implied a higher differential performance of the Suppliers around the Cities connected by the Hyperloop compared to the others. We implemented both the model and experiment with NetLogo, a well-known agent-based simulation platform. We especially exploited BehaviourSpace, a tool for performing multiple experiments at the same time with different parameters. We executed 128000 simulations overall to have highly reliable results [17]. The measure we used to evaluate the relative effect of a faster line for the Suppliers near the connected Cities is the difference between the average percentual increase of cash level of Suppliers near the connected Cities and the average percentual increase of cash level of the other Suppliers (from now on REFL). The increase is calculated when the fast line is introduced to the last time step of the simulation. The idea behind this measure is to detect the effect of the fast line without interferences since the supply chain had already stabilized before. The higher the REFL, the higher the impact of the new line on Suppliers' performances in the simulated model. Furthermore, the measure is a proxy of the differential performance of Suppliers connected with the new link.

4.2 Results

In our analysis, we focused on five parameters: the number of Cities in the model, the number of connections for every City, the number of Suppliers in the model, the number of tiers in the supply chain, and the transportation cost per unit of space. We chose these parameters because they were the ones that could give us better insights about where and how a Hyperloop connection should be developed.

From Table 2, it is possible to observe that the average impact of the introduction of a high-speed line is positive (a global performance better by 284,4%). Additionally, RELF decreased with the number of Cities and increased with the number of Cities connected to each City. A single line's impact is diluted with a bigger number of Cities because a random Supplier is more probable to have a nearer Supplier from another City. On the other side, more connections between Cities meant more possible paths in the network to go from one City to another. The consequence was that, with the same number of agents, on average, each Supplier was easier to reach than before, and then the part of ES related to distance was more sensitive to small variations. With the introduction of a new line, it was more likely than before that the increase of the track's performance changed the previous equilibrium in the selection process of Suppliers.

Table 2. REFL per different number of Cities and connections between Cities.

# Cities	# Cities connections (per City)		
	2	4	Total
5	322,8%	351,6%	337,2%
20	171,0%	262,0%	216,5%
Total	256,5%	312,4%	284,4%

From Table 3, we learned that the RELF increased with the number of Suppliers in the model and decreased with the number of tiers in the supply chain. Ceteris paribus, there were more Suppliers in the area influenced by the new connections, and we expected them to select more often Suppliers from the new connected Cities with high frequency than others. So, the first relation was justified by the presence of an aggregation phenomenon. The other could be explained analogously to the relation with the number of Cities.

In Table 4, we observed a negative correlation between the transport cost per unit of space of the new fast line and the REFL. The explanation of this negative correlation is related with the fact that the more the line cost, the less likely it was for Suppliers around the Cities to be selected because the ES would be lower.

Table 3. REFL per different number of Suppliers and tier of the supply chain.

	# tiers of supply chain		
# Suppliers	2	4	Total
40	373,6%	89,1%	229,2%
80	498,8%	182,6%	337,8%
Total	437,2%	136,7%	284,4%

Table 4. REFL per different level of transport cost.

Transport cost	REFL
0.02	424,0%
0.08	153,8%
Total	284,4%

4.3 Discussion

From the analysis of experiments, we got four main insights. First, to have a higher marginal benefit, the positive relationship between RELF and the increment of connections between Cities could suggest that the first Hyperloop lines should be developed in regions with already a higher infrastructural development. This was confirmed by the negative correlation between RELF and the number of Cities in the model, and by the higher connections/Cities ratio. Second, the positive association between the number of Suppliers and RELF indicated that a Hyperloop line would bring higher benefits if it would be developed in regions with a higher index of competitiveness. Third, the presence of higher travel costs of the goods time implied lower values of REFL. It hinted that the effect of Hyperloop on a supply chain system would depend on the technology's performance. Also, there would be a threshold in the performance/cost ratio under which it would not be convenient to invest in a Hyperloop line. This was relevant for policymakers and also for the firms that are developing the technology and their stakeholders. They could know in advance the technological standards they had to achieve to sell their transportation systems and have a positive return from the investment. Fourth and last, in our experiment, the RELF decreased when the supply chain's number of tiers increased. This meant that a line's development could be more efficient if the supply chain would be shorter.

5　Conclusions and Future Research

In conclusion, we can confirm the idea present in literature that faster transport lines could positively affects on the area in which they would be developed. To analyze the global benefit of the investment, it would still be necessary on one side to also quantify and study the impact on the transportation of people, and on the other to have more information about the performances and costs of a Hyperloop. Regardless, our study concluded that the development of a Hyperloop line for transporting goods would be positive, especially for regions with a high number of firms and a high level of infrastructure development.

Still, this is preliminary work, and there is space for further development. For example, it is possible to expand the actual model in order to replicate better real scenarios. It could also be interesting to add multiple goods in the supply by introducing a sort of circular economy. In this simulation, the Cities could be bought from the producers, introducing maximum transport capacity for each transport line, or implementing a more sophisticated decision making for both Cities and Suppliers. Another remarkable advance could be to simulate the introduction on a Hyperloop line directly on a real-world case, with real data, to give new highlights to investors and policymakers. In conclusion, it would also be interesting to change the subject of study and analyze the impact of a Hyperloop on tourism and economic growth of different regions through an agent-based model.

References

1. Bonabeau, E.: Agent-based modeling: methods and techniques for simulating human systems. Proc. Natl. Acad. Sci. U.S.A. **99**, 7280–7287 (2002). https://doi.org/10.1073/pnas.082080899
2. Brezina, T., Knoflacher, H.: Railway trip speeds and areal coverage. the emperor's new clothes of effectivity? J. Transp. Geogr. **39**(17), 121–130. https://doi.org/10.1016/j.jtrangeo.2014. 06.024. Author, F., Author, S., Author, T.: Book title. 2nd edn. Publisher, Location (1999)
3. Chaidez, E., Bhattacharyya, S.P., Karpetis, A.N.: Levitation methods for use in the hyperloop high-speed transportation system. Energies **12**(21) (2019). https://doi.org/10.3390/en1221 4190
4. Chen, C.L., Hall, P.: The impacts of high-speed trains on British economic geography: a study of the UK's intercity 125/225 and its effects. J. Transp. Geogr. **19**(4), 689–704 (2011). https:// doi.org/10.1016/j.jtrangeo.2010.08.010
5. Dudnikov, E.E.: Advantages of a new hyperloop transport technology. In: Proceedings of 2017 10th International Conference Management of Large-Scale System Development, MLSD 2017, pp. 1–4 (2017). https://doi.org/10.1109/MLSD.2017.8109613, http://www.springer. com/lncs. Accessed 21 Nov 2016
6. Dudnikov, E.E.: The problem of ensuring the tightness in hyperloop passenger systems. In: Proceedings of 2018 11th International Conference & quot; Management of Large-Scale System Development & quot; MLSD 2018, pp. 1–4 (2018). https://doi.org/10.1109/MLSD. 2018.8551881
7. Dudnikov, E.E.: Structure of hyperloop systems with intermediate station. In: Proceedings of 2019 12th International Conference & amp; Amp; Quot; Management of Large-Scale System Development & amp; Amp; Quot; MLSD 2019, pp. 1–3 (2019). https://doi.org/10. 1109/MLSD.2019.8911040
8. Gleave, S.D.: High Speed Rail: International Comparisons – Final Report. Commission for Integrated Transport, London (2004)
9. Huang, C., Lv, Y., Liu, S.: Research on the measurement and adaptability of intercity railway network scale of urban agglomeration. J. Railway Eng. Soc. **33**(2), 17 (2016)
10. https://www.dpworld.com/en/smart-trade/cargospeed

11. Jayakumar, V., et al.: Verification and validation for a finite element model of a hyperloop pod space frame. In: Barthorpe, R. (ed.) Model Validation and Uncertainty Quantification, Volume 3. CPSEMS, pp. 33–40. Springer, Cham (2020). https://doi.org/10.1007/978-3-030-12075-7_4

12. Ji, W.Y., Jeong, G., Park, C.B., Jo, I.H., Lee, H.W.: A Study of non-symmetric double-sided linear induction motor for hyperloop all-in-one system (Propulsion, Levitation, and Guidance). IEEE Trans. Magn. **54**(11), 1–4 (2018). https://doi.org/10.1109/TMAG.2018.2848292

13. Musk, E.: Hyperloop Alpha. Space X (2013)

14. Oh, J.S., et al.: Numerical analysis of aerodynamic characteristics of hyperloop system. Energies **12**(3) (2019). https://doi.org/10.3390/en12030518

15. Sun, S.: Strategy research of high-speed railway promoting liaoning regional economy development. Lecture Notes Electr. Eng. (2012). https://doi.org/10.1007/978-3-642-27963-8_10

16. Sutton, I.: Process safety and the hyperloop. In: Institution of Chemical Engineers Symposium Series, Volume 2019-May, no. 166 (2019)

17. Thiele, J.C., Kurth, W., Grimm, V.: Facilitating parameter estimation and sensitivity analysis of agent-based models: A cookbook using NetLogo and R. *JASSS* (2014). https://doi.org/10.18564/jasss.2503

18. van Goeverden, K., Milakis, D., Janic, M., Konings, R.: Analysis and modelling of performances of the HL (Hyperloop) transport system. Eur. Transp. Res. Rev. **10**(2), 1–17 (2018). https://doi.org/10.1186/s12544-018-0312-x

19. Voltes-Dorta, A., Becker, E.: The potential short-term impact of a hyperloop service between San Francisco and Los Angeles on airport competition in California. Transp. Pol. **71**(February 2017), 45–56 (2018). https://doi.org/10.1016/j.tranpol.2018.07.013D

20. Wang, J.J., Xu, J., He, J.: Spatial impacts of high-speed railways in China: a total-travel-time approach. Environ. Plann. A **45**(9), 2261–2280 (2013). https://doi.org/10.1068/a45289

21. Wang, J., Jin, F., Mo, H., Wang, F.: Spatiotemporal evolution of China's railway network in the 20th century: an accessibility approach. Transp. Res. Part A: Pol. Pract. **43**(8), 765–778 (2009). https://doi.org/10.1016/j.tra.2009.07.003

22. Wang, H., Yang, Y., Coleman, D., Benedict, M.: Aerodynamic simulation of high-speed capsule in the hyperloop system. In: 35th AIAA Applied Aerodynamics Conference, 2017, June 2017. https://doi.org/10.2514/6.2017-3741

23. Weidong, L.: Research on the quantitative relationship between china's railway transportation industry and national economic development. In: Proceedings - 2008 International Seminar on Future Information Technology and Management Engineering, FITME 2008 (2008). https://doi.org/10.1109/FITME.2008.89

Sensitivity to Initial Conditions in Agent-Based Models

Francesco Bertolotti[✉], Angela Locoro, and Luca Mari

Università Carlo Cattaneo - LIUC, Corso G. Matteotti, 22, 21053 Castellanza, VA, Italy
{fbertolotti,alocoro,lmari}@liuc.it

Abstract. In the last thirty years, agent-based modelling has become a well-known technique for studying and simulating dynamical systems. Still, there are some open issues to be addressed. One of these is the substantial absence of studies about the sensitivity to initial conditions, that is the effect of small variations at the beginning of simulation on the macro-level behaviour of the model. The goal of this preliminary work is to explore how a single modification on one agent affects the evolution of the simulation. Through the analysis of two deterministic models (a simple market model and Reynolds' flocking model), we obtain two main results. First, we observe that the impact of the variation of a single initial condition on the simulation behaviour is high in both models. Second, there is evidence of an at least qualitative relation between some general agent-based model settings (numerosity of agents in the model and rate of connections between agents) and the sensitivity to the modified initial condition. We conclude that at least some significant classes of agent-based models are affected by a high sensitivity to initial conditions that have a negative effect on the predictive power of simulations.

Keywords: Agent-based modeling · Initial conditions · Sensitivity analysis

1 Introduction and Motivations

Agent-based modelling is a well-known technique for "describing and simulating a system composed of 'behavioral' entities" [3]. Unlike in other kinds of dynamic systems models, what is observed in agent-based simulations is not only a behavior of some kind but also the behaving subjects (ibidem). These subjects may be studied in their interaction topologies and behavioral heterogeneity [5], and with the aim of predicting specific outcomes. For these reasons, initial settings such as the topology of the model and all of those "conditioning assumptions imposed or implicit in the model" [4] may influence the predictive power and accuracy of the simulation.

Although sensitivity analysis is generally considered a fundamental element of the analysis of agent-based models [9, 13], to the best of our knowledge the effect of the sensitivity to initial conditions was never investigated in a systematic way [6–8], with the exception for spatial conditions in geosimulation models [10]. With this study, we propose to fill a gap in the direction of the research questions whether and how the sensitivity to initial conditions in agent-based models impacts their prediction power.

© Springer Nature Switzerland AG 2020
N. Bassiliades et al. (Eds.): EUMAS 2020/AT 2020, LNAI 12520, pp. 501–508, 2020.
https://doi.org/10.1007/978-3-030-66412-1_32

To this goal, we analyzed two simple agent-based models, of a simple market and of a simple swarm [11], and we tested the effects of two small changes in the initial conditions: the small increase of a single parameter of one of the agents and the removal of one agent from the model. We show that, in both cases, there is a high impact on the macro-behavior of the system, and a negative relationship between the numerosity of the agents in the model and the sensitivity to the initial condition.

The remaining of the paper is structured as follows: in Sect. 2 we introduce the two models exploited in the experiments; Sect. 3 presents the methodology adopted; Sect. 4 shows the results and discusses them; Sect. 5 concludes and outlines future research directions.

2 Models and Methods

In this work, we analyzed a simple market model and a variation of traditional Reynolds' flocking, to get information related to their sensitivity to the variation of a single initial condition. The model selection follows the following criteria:

1. the models should be simple so that it is easier to detect the effect of the modification of an initial condition;
2. the models should be natively deterministic, or at least it should be possible to remove the stochasticity without modifying neither their macro- nor their micro-behavior so that the effect of a single variation can be analyzed independently of the presence of noise;
3. the models should differ from each other in topology, rules of interaction and domain, to confer genericity to the results.

In what follows, we introduce the two models and show the methodology used to obtain the results.

2.1 A Simple Market Model

To the best of our knowledge, no classic simple agent-based model of a generic market exists in the literature, so we developed one. The purpose of the model is to simulate an elementary dynamical trading system in which heterogeneous individuals produce, exchange and trade one kind of good over time. The agents are connected through each other with a Scale-Free distributed network [2], representing the structure of the market. Hence, the spatial distribution is irrelevant.

Each agent follows the same set of rules in each time step. First, it produces goods. Second, it trades them under these conditions:

- if the level of goods is below a "security threshold" and some of the neighbors has a level of goods beyond a "plenty threshold" (push trading);
- if the level of goods is beyond a "plenty threshold" and some of the neighbors has a level of goods below a "security threshold" (pull trading).

The number of goods exchanged in every transaction is equal to a "trading quantum" set at the beginning of the simulation. Third, each agent consumes goods at an individual consume rate. If the level of goods is lower than that consume rate, the agent consumes everything. Agents can not die of starvation. The rate of production and consumption are individual parameters, independent one to each other and randomly generated at the beginning of the simulation.

2.2   The Reynold's Flocking Model

The flocking model is a traditional agent-based model developed by Reynolds [11]. Its purpose is to show how a collective swarm behavior can emerge from a set of "bird-oid objects" (from now on "boids") that interact according to three simple rules:

- separation from other boids;
- cohesion with other boids;
- alignment of the heading with the direction of nearby boids.

We adapted the implementation by Wilensky [15], by removing all the stochasticity. In this version separation is the overriding rule, which means that cohesion and alignment are taken into consideration only if a minimum separation threshold is exceeded. Furthermore, all boids flock on a toroidal surface with the same constant speed.

3   Methods

To the best of our knowledge, in agent-based modelling there is not a well-established method to analyze the sensitivity to the variation of a single initial condition related to a single agent. Therefore, we developed a workflow on three steps: model implementation, measure development, and simulation cycle.

First, we developed a deterministic implementation of the simulation models under study. We wrote the market model from scratch, while we slightly modified the Reynolds' flocking model from NetLogo library (Wilensky 1998). Both models are implemented in NetLogo, a well-known agent-based simulation platform [1, 14]. Second, we defined some functions to evaluate the sensitivity to initial conditions. In the market model, we calculated the percentage difference between the average goods level of each agent at the final step of two simulations with the same seed of the pseudo-random number generator ("seed" from now on), one with the initial modification and one without. In Reynolds' flocking model, we defined how the initial condition variation impacts on the position of each boid by computing the average distance of the position (in the percentage of the size of the world) of the same boid at the end of two different simulations with the same seed, one with the initial variation and one without.

Third, we translated into code the simulation process shown in Fig. 1.

The entire simulation (both agents and global variables) was initialized in the "Setup" phase. Then there was a four steps cycle made by two simulation runs ("Go" phases) and two special setup processes: "Setup2" and "Setup3". In "Setup2", the model was reset without changing the seed, agents were created, and the target initial condition modified.

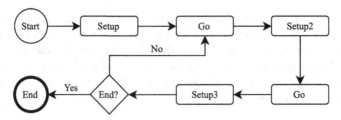

Fig. 1. Simulation process developed for testing the sensitivity of a model to the variation of a single initial condition on a sole agent.

In "Setup3" the difference between the two simulations (from the "Go" phases) was calculated and saved on an external file with the progressive number of the simulation, the seed and the setup general parameters. Then, the model was initialized with a new seed and the whole model was reset, with exception of global variables designed to take track of the experiment. For every experiment, we executed 75000 pairs of simulations, after which the gate "End?" opens. The number of repetitions was chosen to have reliable results [12].

4   Results and Discussion

4.1   Simple Market Model

We performed a total of 150000 simulations on this model, using two kinds of variation of the initial conditions:

1. A 1% increment in the production rate parameter of one of the agents ("IPR experiment" from now on);
2. the removal of one of the agents.

The test was performed on different general parameters of the model, to discover possible relations between them and the sensitivity to the variation of the initial condition. The analyzed parameters were the numerosity of the agents in the model and the minimum degree of the scale-free network generator algorithm.

Table 1 and Table 2 show that the average value is high, due to a strong sensitivity to the variation of the initial condition. In the IPS experiment, the total and subtotals average percent differences were lower than in the removal experiment. This could be a consequence of the more invasiveness of the second experiment: we expected that deleting a single agent from the model had a greater impact than increasing a single parameter. Furthermore, it was possible to see qualitative relations between the characteristic of the model and the sensitivity to the initial condition.

In both experiments, a greater number of agents implied a lower sensitivity to the initial condition, which could be a consequence of the dilution of the impact in a bigger model. It hinted that it could be possible to lower this phenomenon by developing simulated models with more agents. Besides, in the first experiment, a higher minimum degree in the network topology of agents brought to a lower effect of the modification

Table 1. Absolute percentage difference of the mean of good level of each agent at the end of the simulation in the IPR experiment.

# Agents	Min degree %					Total
	2	3	4	5	6	
15	152.9	95.5	87.4	84.8	87.8	101.5
45	105.1	39.0	33.2	33.9	30.9	48.4
135	71.2	19.3	17.0	17.5	17.2	29.7
405	47.1	12.0	10.0	10.1	9.8	17.8
1205	26.5	7.3	5.9	5.8	5.5	10.2
Total	84.1	36.7	33.0	33.0	32.8	44.1

Table 2. Absolute percent difference of the mean of good level of each agent at the end of simulation in the removal experiment

# Agents	Min degree %					Total
	2	3	4	5	6	
15	121.0	107.0	113.5	108.0	109.6	111.8
45	93.2	92.8	95.6	96.2	96.8	94.9
135	72.3	80.7	90.6	94.7	96.0	86.9
405	55.0	52.4	61.2	72.3	81.9	64.5
1205	36.8	26.9	28.8	33.3	38.4	32.8
Total	75.5	71.9	77.9	80.9	84.5	78.1

of the initial parameters. We suggest that a higher level of connectivity between the agents could have brought to a better compensation of production rate from the market, and then to a lower effect on the macro-behaviour of the model. This relationship was reversed in the second experiment, since the more the network was connected the more increased the probability that an agent lost a trading partner. Also, higher connectivity implied also that a greater number of agents were indirectly connected by the removed agent, and since all these links were ended, we awaited a positive relationship between the increment of connection rate and the variation of macro-behaviour. In conclusion, the kind of connection between sensitivity to initial condition and the level of connectivity depended on the kind of modification.

4.2 Reynolds' Flocking Model

As in the previous model, two experiments were performed, each with 75000 simulation runs:

1. a 1% increment of pace of one of the boids ("IPP experiment" from now on);
2. the removal of one of the boids (Tables 3 and 4).

Table 3. Average of percentage distance of each boid at the end of the two simulations in IPP experiment.

# Agents	Vision radius (in patches) %					Total
	2	3	4	5	6	
15	33.5	36.9	37.0	37.0	36.6	36.2
45	37.4	37.8	37.6	37.1	37.0	37.4
135	38.0	37.9	37.3	36.8	35.9	37.2
405	38.0	37.4	36.9	36.1	35.5	36.8
1205	38.0	37.5	37.0	36.6	36.3	37.1
Total	37.0	37.5	37.2	36.7	36.3	36.9

Table 4. Average of percentage distance of each boid at the end of the two simulations in removal experiment.

# Agents	Vision radius (in patches) %					Total
	2	3	4	5	6	
15	28.5	31.7	32.2	32.6	32.5	31.5
45	35.9	36.2	36.2	36.2	36.0	36.1
135	37.5	37.4	37.2	36.9	37.0	37.2
405	37.9	37.6	37.2	36.8	36.6	37.2
1205	38.0	37.6	37.3	37.1	36.9	37.4
Total	35.6	36.1	36.1	35.9	35.8	35.9

In both cases, the average percentage distance between boids was near 38%, which is the expected distance between two random points on a torus. It means that in both the experiment the modification was enough to completely shuffle the boids' topology during the simulation. As a consequence, in this second model, it was not possible to highlight any qualitative relationship between the sensitivity to the initial condition and the general parameters of the model. We suppose that this was due to the measure we chose. Since in the majority of the observed cases the impact was near the expected value for a random distribution, it was not possible to observe any clear trend.

5 Conclusions, Limitations and Future Works

Evidence suggests that small variations in single initial conditions strongly influence the global behavior of agent-based simulations. This is relevant because it could have a negative effect on the forecasting power of the technique, which is considered one of the main reasons to develop an agent-based model [6, 7]. Furthermore, the results in the market model imply that there could be a negative correlation between the impact of variation and the numerosity of the agents in the model. It suggests that it is possible to mitigate the effect of the sensitivity to initial conditions by performing simulations with a higher number of agents. Still, this is a preliminary study: a statistical analysis of data taken from a wider variety of models is required before to confirm this hypothesis and generalize the results.

Future research could lead to different directions. First, to individuate a class of models for which these findings are valid. Second, to define general rules that link the sensitivity to initial conditions of different model parameters. These rules could depend also by the typology and the size of modification. Third, appraise the relationship between sensitivity to initial conditions and the topology of the agents' network.

References

1. Abar, S., Theodoropoulos, G.K., Lemarinier, P., O'Hare, G.M.P.: Agent based modelling and simulation tools: a review of the state-of-art software. Comput. Sci. Rev. **24**, 13–33 (2017). https://doi.org/10.1016/j.cosrev.2017.03.001
2. Barabási, A.L., Albert, R.: Emergence of scaling in random networks. Science **286**, 509–512 (1999). https://doi.org/10.1126/science.286.5439.509
3. Bonabeau, E.: Agent-based modeling: Methods and techniques for simulating human systems. Proc. Natl. Acad. Sci. U.S.A. **99**, 7280–7287 (2002). https://doi.org/10.1073/pnas.082080899
4. Boschetti, F., Grigg, N.J., Enting, I.: Modelling = conditional prediction. Ecol. Complex. **8**, 86–91 (2011). https://doi.org/10.1016/j.ecocom.2010.06.001
5. Castellano, C., Fortunato, S., Loreto, V.: Statistical physics of social dynamics. Rev. Mod. Phys. **81**, 591 (2009). https://doi.org/10.1103/RevModPhys.81.591
6. Edmonds, B.: Different modelling purposes. In: Edmonds, B., Meyer, R. (eds.) Simulating Social Complexity. UCS, pp. 39–58. Springer, Cham (2017). https://doi.org/10.1007/978-3-319-66948-9_4
7. Epstein, J.M.: Why model? JASSS (2008). https://doi.org/10.1016/s0168-9525(01)02382-4
8. Klein, D., Marx, J., Fischbach, K.: Agent-based modeling in social science, history, and philosophy. An introduction. Hist. Soc. Res. (2018). https://doi.org/10.12759/hsr.43.2018.1.7-27
9. Railsback, S., Grimm, V.: Agent-Based and Individual-Based Modeling: A Practical Introduction. Princeton University Press (2011)
10. Raimbault, J., Cottineau, C., Le Texier, M., Le Néchet, F., Reuillon, R.: Space matters: extending sensitivity analysis to initial spatial conditions in geosimulation models. JASSS (2019). https://doi.org/10.18564/jasss.4136
11. Reynolds, C.W.: Flocks, herds, and schools. In: Computers & Graphics (1987)
12. Thiele, J.C., Kurth, W., Grimm, V.: Facilitating parameter estimation and sensitivity analysis of agent-based models: a cookbook using NetLogo and R. JASSS (2014). https://doi.org/10.18564/jasss.2503

13. Wilensky, U., Rand, W.: An Introduction to Agent-Based Modeling: Modeling Natural, Social, and Engineered Complex Systems with NetLogo. MIT Press (2015)
14. Wilensky, U.: NetLogo (1999). http://ccl.northwestern.edu/netlogo/. Center for Connected Learning and Computer-Based Modeling, Northwestern University, Evanston, IL
15. Wilensky, U.: NetLogo Flocking model (1998). http://ccl.northwestern.edu/netlogo/models/ Flocking. Center for Connected Learning and Computer-Based Modeling, Northwestern University, Evanston, IL

EUMAS 2020 Session 5: Agent-Oriented Software Engineering, Game Theory, Task Allocation, Learning

Statecharts and Agent Technology: The Past and Future

Nikolaos I. Spanoudakis(⊠)

Applied Mathematics and Computers Laboratory,
School of Production Engineering and Management,
Technical University of Crete, 73100 Chania, Greece
nikos@amcl.tuc.gr

Abstract. This work aims to bring forward the intersection between the world of statecharts and that of agent technology. We begin by disambiguating the different terms related to statecharts, i.e. state machines and finite state automata/machines. Subsequently we review their impact to agent technology, mainly in the area of Agent-Oriented Software Engineering. Our findings are that multi-agent systems modeling has used and, some times, extended the language of statecharts, mainly for modeling agent interaction protocols and for coordinating the different modules of an agent. We conclude with some future directions related to the use of statecharts by the Multi-agent Systems community in the coming years.

Keywords: Agent oriented software engineering · Statecharts · Finite state machines · Agent interaction protocols · Agent control · Engineering multi-agent systems

1 Introduction

Agent Technology and Statecharts technology are two worlds that started almost at the same time, in the eighties, the first as Distributed Artificial Intelligence [30] and the second as a method for engineering complex and reactive systems [19]. Since then, a lot has happened, this work will focus in their intersection.

Agent-oriented Software Engineering (AOSE) has long used statecharts. Initially, they were employed for modeling agent interactions [27,35] but also agent plans [10,31,32]. Agent interaction modeling is mainly concerned with defining protocols that govern an interaction. Such models have also been referred to as *inter-agent control* models [10,42]. Later, statecharts were used by AOSE methodologies for the coordination of the different agent modules, and such models are also referred to as *intra-agent control* models [10,41]. Moreover, agent platforms like the popular Java Agent Development Framework (JADE [2,3]) base complex agent behaviour to the definition of state machines.

This paper aims to collect the experience of using statecharts for agent-related research and propose some future directions based on the modern development for statecharts but also the needs of the agents community.

© Springer Nature Switzerland AG 2020
N. Bassiliades et al. (Eds.): EUMAS 2020/AT 2020, LNAI 12520, pp. 511–528, 2020.
https://doi.org/10.1007/978-3-030-66412-1_33

Section two provides a background on statecharts and finite state machines, also trying to disambiguate these terms. Then, section three provides an overview of the use of the language of statecharts in AOSE and generally in multi-agent systems (MAS) research. Section four discusses these findings. Section five proposes several research directions, and, finally, section six concludes.

2 Background on Statecharts

Statecharts are often confused with automata [12], finite state automata, or finite state machines (FSMs [4]). Let's try to give a formalism that will aid us throughout this paper.

Definition 1. *An FSM-like statechart can be defined as a tuple (L, δ) where:*

- $L = (S, Name)$ *is a set representing the states of the statechart, and:*
  - $S \subseteq \mathbb{N}^*$
  - *Name is a mapping from nodes to their names*
- $\delta \subseteq S \times TE \times S$ *is the set of state transitions, where TE is a set of transition expressions*

Harel proposed statecharts for modeling software systems [20]. According to that work, statecharts are based on an activity-chart that is a hierarchical data-flow diagram, where the functional capabilities of the system are captured by activities and the data elements and signals can flow between them. The behavioral aspects of these activities (what activity, when and under what conditions it will be active) are specified in statecharts.

While in FSMs states represent different states of the world and actions take place in the transitions, in statecharts states represent activities. Actions are still possible in transition expressions, however, these are instant actions that modify variable values and generally affect the data structures of the modeled system. On the other hand, the ability of the transition expressions to allow for events makes them compatible with FSMs in the sense that the outcomes of activities can be sensed and lead to the next state of the world. Moreover, activities can occur concurrently, or can be complex, i.e. can be analyzed to more "basic" ones.

In a sense an FSM is a restricted case of a statechart, where there is no explicit activity associated with a state, there is no hierarchy of states, there are no history connectors, and, finally, the orthogonality feature is missing. Nevertheless, there are researchers that have proposed hierarchical FSMs [6,17].

In this paper, when we refer to statecharts we imply the formalism given by Harel [19,20]. Based on that we can extend Definition 1 with regard to nodes (L) [41] (see Definition 2).

Harel defines several state types. Three are the main types of states in a statechart, i.e. *OR-states*, *AND-states*, and *basic* states. OR-states have sub-states that are related to each other by "exclusive-or", i.e. only one can be active at any given time, and AND-states have orthogonal components that are related by "and", they are active at the same time. Basic states are those at the bottom of the state hierarchy, i.e., those that have no sub-states. The state at the highest level, i.e., the one with no parent state, is called the root. There are some more states types, such as *start* and *end*. These are nodes without activity, which exist so that execution can start and end inside OR-states. A *condition* state allows for branching a transition. *Shallow_history* and *history* allow for "remembering" the last active state in an OR-state or a whole branch of L respectively. All these auxillary state types, i.e. *start*, *end*, *basic*, *shallow_history*, *history* and *condition* are leaves of L.

Definition 2. *A Statechart can be defined as a tuple (L, δ) where:*

- $L = (S, \lambda, Name, Activity)$ *is an ordered rooted tree structure representing the states of the statechart, and:*
  - $S \subseteq \mathbb{N}^*$
  - *Name is a mapping from nodes to their names.*
  - $\lambda : S \rightarrow \{and, or, basic, start, end, shallow\_history, history, condition\}$, *is a mapping from the set of nodes to labels giving the type of each node.*
  - *Activity is a mapping from nodes to their algorithms in text format implementing the processes of the respective states.*
- $\delta \subseteq S \times TE \times S$ *is the set of state transitions, where TE is a set of transition expressions*

Each transition from one state (source) to another (target) is labeled by a Transition Expression (TE), whose general syntax is $e[c]/a$, where e is the event that triggers the transition; c is a condition that must be true in order for the transition to be taken when e occurs; and a is an action that takes place when the transition is taken. All elements of the transition expression are optional.

Moreover, there can also be compound transitions (CT), that can have more than one source or target states. We will not refer to that level of detail in this work. The scope of a transition is the lowest level OR-state that is a common ancestor of both the source and target states.

The statechart formalism also defines execution semantics. We will give a brief overview, for the details the reader is referred to Harel and Naamad [20]. The execution of a statechart is a sequence of steps. After each step we view a snapshot of the statechart. Execution starts at *start* states. When a step is taken, the events that have happened are sensed, including retrospection events (such as the entering of a state at the previous step). When the step finishes the statechart is in a valid configuration, i.e. specific *basic* states are active and the respective OR- and AND-states up to the root. Other types of states cannot be included in the configuration (e.g. the a *start* state cannot be active in a snapshot).

When a transition occurs all states in its scope are exited and the target states are entered. Multiple concurrently active statecharts are considered to be orthogonal components at the highest level of a single statechart. If one of the statecharts becomes non-active (e.g. when the activity it controls is stopped) the other charts continue to be active and that statechart enters an idle state until it is restarted.

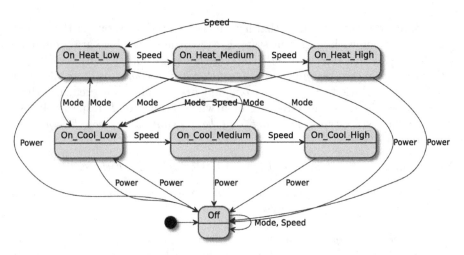

Fig. 1. FSM representation of an air conditioner. The figure was generated using the PlantText free tool, https://www.planttext.com/

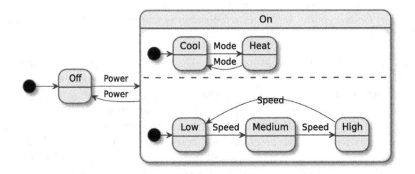

Fig. 2. Statechart representation of an air conditioner.

To illustrate the difference between a statechart and an FSM, a basic representation of an air-conditioner is provided using both formalisms, see Fig. 1 and Fig. 2. The reader will notice that using OR and AND states the statechart formalism prevents the explosion of states that takes place in FSMs as one combines contexts (in this case the context of the air-conditioner fan speed and its mode). The depicted events correspond to pressing the power, fan and mode buttons on the air-conditioner remote control.

In the Unified Modeling Language (UML), which is the mainstream language for defining object-oriented software and a standard supported by the Object Management Group (OMG), https://www.uml.org/, statecharts have been used to model the dynamic behavior of a class instance (object).

3   Statecharts and Agent Oriented Software Engineering

Statecharts were proposed by Harel for modeling reactive systems [19] and researchers in AOSE and agent interaction protocols modeling communities were quick to adopt them and propose formalisms, extentions, languages and semantics for use in agent-based systems engineering.

One of the pioneers, Moore [27], proposed an agent interactions protocol formalism based on statecharts and the Formal Language for Business Communication (FLBC), an Agent Communication Language (ACL). Usually, the message types of ACLs (or performatives) are understood as speech acts. A speech act is an act that a speaker performs when making an utterance [1]. Performatives express the intent of an agent when it sends a message to another agent. Thus, a message has four parts, a) the sender, b) the receiver, c) the performative and d) the message content (what is said). For example, the performative "inform" may be interpreted as a request that the receiving agent adds the message content to its knowledge-base. Thus, an ACL message can be defined as: *performative(sender, receiver, content)*.

For his work on conversation policies, Moore makes the assumption that developers that adopt his models can understand a formal specification and implement it in whatever way they see fit. In the FLBC, Moore defines, for example, that the message *request(sender, receiver, action)* can express that:

a. The receiver believes that the sender wants him to do the action
b. The receiver believes that the sender wants the receiver to want to do the action

According to the work of Moore, a *conversation policy* (CP) defines a) how one or more conversation partners respond to messages they receive, b) what messages a partner expects in response to a message it sends, and, c) the rules for choosing among competing courses of action.

Moore introduces the idea of modeling the activities of the participants in a conversation as orthogonal components of a statechart. The transition expressions contain the actions of sending and receiving a message. Moore's conversation policies allow for exceptions when a conversation is interrupted by assuming that an agent has stored all allowed CPs in a kind of repository where he can browse a new policy to handle the exception in the form of a sub-dialog to the original one. When this sub-dialog terminates the original one can resume.

Statecharts were introduced in AOSE methodologies by the Multiagent Systems Engineering methodology (MaSE [9,10]). In the MaSE design phase, the first activity is about creating agent classes and then agent classes can connect to other classes indicating the possible interactions or conversations. The latter are defined in the communication class diagram, which is in the form of a finite state machine. MaSE defines a system goal oriented MAS development methodology. The authors define for the first time inter and intra-agent interactions that must be integrated.

Recognizing the fact that a protocol should have both a graphical and formal representation, Paurobally et al. [35] combined the language of statecharts and a language based on Propositional Dynamic Logic (PDL), the Agent Negotiation Meta-Language (ANML). PDL blends the ideas behind propositional logic and dynamic logic by adding actions while omitting data; hence the terms of PDL are actions and propositions. Then, the authors defined templates for transforming the ANML formulas to statecharts, extending the statecharts language in the process. The representation of all computation is in transitions, while states just describe a situation (where specific conditions hold). The representation can be general, or specialized for a specific agent participant. The expressions in the transitions are ANML formulas. The proposal of Paurobally et al. [35] and later by Dunn-Davies et al. [11] did not employ the orthogonality feature of the statecharts because they considered that the agents are not subsystems and, thus, execute on their own. If they were combined as orthogonal components for execution they would have to combine parts of interactions between temporally autonomous agents into a pseudo whole.

At the same time, König [23] presented a new possibility in inter-agent protocols definition. He used the state transition diagrams (STD) formalism to model protocols, but also decision activities, thus, using for both the same formalism. An STD is a special case of a Finite State Machine (FSM) that allows transitions between states either when an external or an internal event occurs to the system (according to his work, transitions in FSMs can only contain external events).

König defined a protocol as a structured exchange of messages. Then, he compared three approaches to modeling conversation policies, i.e. those based on STDs, FSMs and Petri nets. He observed that all approaches modeling conversations from the viewpoint of an observer are using either STD or petri nets, in contrast to those using FSM (or statecharts) that are representing the conversation from the viewpoint of a participating agent. For modeling a conversation from the point of view of a participating agent who receives and sends messages, König argued that a model supporting input and output operations is more suitable. When a conversation should be modeled from an observer's view, it is sufficient to use a model which is able to express that a message has been transmitted from one agent to another, like a transition in a STD or in a petri net. He chose STD aiming to model both activities and protocols, allowing also for object-oriented development.

König made the assumption that only two agents are involved in a protocol, i.e. the primary (who initiates the interaction) and the secondary. Moreover, the messages exchange is always synchronous, when one of them sends a message the other one is in a state of receiving a message (they cannot both be sending at the same time). Then, he defines an FSM for the observer and from it he derives the FSMs of the participants. In a next level (higher level of abstraction) he defines communication acts that can make use of the protocols in the form of STDs. Finally, in a third level he defines the activities of the agents that can invoke one or more communication acts and assume a wait state until the acts finish. The acts themselves can choose to execute one or more protocols and enter a wait state until they are finished. All these can only happen sequentially.

One of the most influential methodologies for AOSE also appeared at that time. The Gaia methodology [46,47] emphasized the need for new abstractions in order to model agent-based systems and supported both the levels of the individual agent structure and the agent society in the multi-agent (MAS) development process. Gaia added the notion of situatedness to the agent concept. According to this notion, the agents perform their actions while situated in a particular environment. The latter can be a computational environment (e.g. a website) or a physical one (a room) and the agent can sense and act in the environment.

MAS, according to Gaia, are viewed as being composed of a number of autonomous interactive agents that live in an organized society in which each agent plays one or more specific roles. Gaia defined the structure of a MAS in terms of a role model. The model identifies the roles that agents have to play within the MAS and the interaction protocols between the different roles.

The objective of the Gaia analysis phase is the identification of the roles and the modelling of interactions between the roles found. Roles consist of four attributes: responsibilities, permissions, activities and protocols. Responsibilities are the key attribute related to a role since they determine the functionality. Responsibilities are of two types: liveness properties – the role has to add something good to the system, and safety properties – the role must prevent something bad from happening to the system. Liveness describes the tasks that an agent must fulfil given certain environmental conditions and safety ensures that an acceptable state of affairs is maintained during the execution cycle. In order to realize responsibilities, a role has a set of permissions. Permissions represent what the role is allowed to do and, in particular, which information resources it is allowed to access. The activities are tasks that an agent performs without interacting with other agents. Finally, protocols are the specific patterns of interaction, e.g. a seller role can support different auction protocols. Gaia defined operators and templates for representing roles and their attributes and schemas for the abstract representation of interactions between the various roles in a system.

The Gaia2JADE process appeared in 2003 [28,29] and was concerned with the way to implement a multi-agent system with the emerging JADE framework using the Gaia methodology for analysis and design purposes. This process used the Gaia models and provided a roadmap for transforming Gaia liveness formulas to Finite State Machine diagrams. The JADE framework provided an object-oriented solution to building MAS and it became the most celebrated framework for building real-world software agents applications [3].

In 2004 there was also a proposal for the use of distilled statecharts (DSCs) for modeling mobile agents [16]. The proposal came along an object oriented implementation based on UML modeling. DSCs define some limitations to the language of Statecharts, e.g. only the OR-state decomposition is used, states do not have properties such as activities, therefore activities are only carried out under the form of atomic actions attached to transitions. If their source is not *start* and *history* states, transitions always include an *event*. In a later work, Fortino et al. [14] proposed a JADE implementation for DSC.

An important work on statecharts based agent development was that of Murray [31]. The latter, working for defining Robocup soccer player agents, explained that statecharts is a natural formalism for expressing multi-agent plans, as a player usually assumes a role, e.g. defender, attacker, goalkeeper, and the role's plan can be modeled as a sequence of states an agent passes through. A passing of a state can be the result of an (external) event or the completion of an activity, e.g. passing the ball. Moreover, as team players work together towards a common goal, they need to synchronize their actions and this can be modelled with one agent waiting for another agent to finish an action. Murray proposed a methodology and tool (StatEdit) for capturing this behavior based on a three layered approach:

- In the top level the different roles (*modes*) that the player can assume when active are represented as states and the transitions indicate a change of role
- In a middle level an agent chooses among a set of plans adding detail at each mode of the previous level. The states here capture the agent general activity and show where the player synchronizes its actions with other roles (e.g. wait for the center player to pass the ball and then shoot to score).
- On a bottom level of the hierarchy each activity of the role is detailed to specifc actions (e.g. acquire the ball and then kick towards the goal)

A similar layered approach was used later [22] for modeling the behavior of non-player characters in computer games. Murray also proposed an extension to statecharts with *synch* states for synchronizing the actions of different agents. His work, along with the previous one of Obst [33] both supported semi-automatic code generation for Robolog, a robot programming language based on Prolog.

Later, ASEME [40,43], uniquely among AOSE methodologies, used the statecharts formalism both for inter- and intra-agent control modeling. Moreover, it extended the statechart formalism by adding state-dependent variables. Thus, each state is associated with variables that it can monitor and change/update. To propose this extension, the authors were motivated by the Gaia methodology and the role's access to data structures with the read or write/update permissions [46]. Thus, ASEME proposed the addition of the *Var* property to the statechart nodes. The different states can be connected with variables that can be used for exchanging information.

Definition 3. *The tuple (L, δ) defined in Definition 2 is extended by adding Var to L:*

- *$L = (S, \lambda, Name, Activity, Var)$ is an ordered rooted tree structure representing the states of the statechart, where:*
  - *Var is a mapping from nodes to sets of variables. var(l) stands for the subset of local variables of a particular node l.*

According to ASEME, a state name that starts with the string "send" implies an inter-agent message sending behavior for the state's activity. A send state has only one exiting transition and its event describes the message(s) sent. Similarly, a state name that starts with the string "receive" implies that the activity of the state should wait for the receipt of one or more inter-agent messages. The type and quantity of the expected messages can be implied by the events monitored by the transition expressions that have this state as source. The events that can be used in the transition expressions can be:

- a sent or received (or perceived, in general) inter-agent message,
- a change in one of the executing state's variables (also referred to as an intra-agent message),
- a timeout, and,
- the ending of the executing state activity (empty event).

This formalism allows also for environment-based communication by defining state activities that monitor for a specific effect in the environment. This effect can be expected to be caused by any other agent or a particular agent. Such activities can be, for example, "wait for someone to appear" or "wait until my counterpart lifts the object" respectively.

ASEME defines protocols as statecharts where the participating roles are defined as orthogonal components. See Fig. 3 as an example. Two roles are connected to this protocol, the service requester (sr) and the service provider (sp). The reader will notice these two roles as orthogonal components in the *Request-ForServices* protocol state. The requester sends a request *message* using the *Request* performative whose variables are the sending and receiving agents (we use the abbreviation sr for service requester and sp for service provider) and the *request*, which can be an object for object oriented implementations or a query for logic-based implementations. On the other hand, the service provider waits to receive this message, then processes the request and either replies with a *Refuse* (the service is refused for this agent), *Failure* (failed to reply), or *Inform* (with the results of the computation) performative. Note that the protocol terminates for both roles after a timeout of 10000 ms. A similar model also appears in the work of Seo et al. [39] for buying products.

The work of Moore [27] supported the possibility of an agent getting involved in a *sub-dialog* when in a dialog. In ASEME, the model for describing such dialogs is the inter-agent control model. Moore supposed that the agent has access to a repository of dialogs and dynamically selects a sub-dialog model whenever an incoming message is not permitted by the existing dialog but is permitted by another in the repository. In the intra-agent control model, ASEME allows for this possibility as all roles the agent can participate in can be instantiated as orthogonal components. Information between orthogonal components can be exchanged through the use of common variables and their usage in transition expressions, thus, a given protocol can remain in a given state until some information becomes available (an implicit intra-agent message).

Another feature of ASEME is the catering for *embedded dialogs* in an agent's design, i.e. in its intra-agent control model. Dialogs occur when an agent participates in an agent interaction protocol. Instances of dialogs contained entirely within other dialogs are said to be embedded [25]. ASEME defines that when a

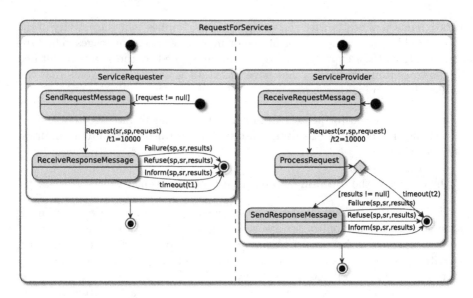

Fig. 3. Statechart representation of a protocol for requesting a service. The diamond shape represents a condition state.

role in a protocol model is integrated in an intra-agent control model, the protocol role OR-state is inserted as-is in the intra-agent control. Then, the designer is free to define the activities of the basic states. The designer can even select to expand a basic state and turn it to an OR-state.

Thus, the reader can see a broker agent in Fig. 4 realizing the protocol defined in Fig. 3. The broker agent realizes the service provider role of the service request protocol. However, for defining the process request state activity, the designer decided that the broker will initially perform a service matching activity and then either invoke a web service, or employ an embedded dialog, i.e. the service request protocol, this time as a service requester. Note that the transition expressions have been omitted in Fig. 4 so as not to clutter the diagram.

Recently, researchers explored the translation of agent models defined using the Distilled StateCharts (DSC) [13,16] into a Belief-Desires-Intentions (BDI) framework [15], including a BDI-like code generation feature. BDI is an example of an agent architecture including an execution paradigm besides ontological features [36]. BDI advocates the fact that an agent first senses its environment and updates its *beliefs*, then it searches possible *desires*, i.e. goals that are valid in this environment state, and, finally, selects some of these desires to actively pursue. The latter are now its *intentions*.

Statecharts can be used for modelling the dynamic behaviour of a BDI agent. See for example the execution model followed by 3APL [8], a BDI-based agent development language, modelled as a statechart in Fig. 5. The lifecycle of this agent starts in the *ReceiveMessage* state. Then, as soon as a message arrives, or another monitored for event occurs, the BDI agent enters the

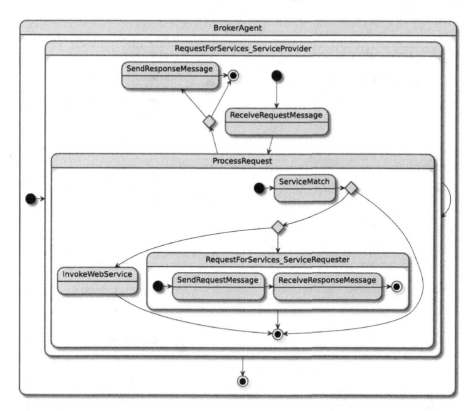

Fig. 4. Statechart representation of a Broker agent embedding a dialog in another dialog.

ApplyGoalPlanningRules OR state. Within that OR state, more specific activities match the goals with rules, select rules matching the agent's beliefs and apply a goal planning rule. The next OR state, i.e. *ApplyPlanRevisionRules*, and its substates find rules matching to the plans, select rules matching the agent's beliefs and apply the selected plan revision rule. Finally, the agent reaches the *ExecutePlan* state that, depending on the selected plan, may send a message, take an external action or an internal (or mental) action, or do nothing. After finishing the plan execution the agent returns to his message receiving state. This is an example of how someone can use statecharts to coordinate the agent's capabilities and to accommodate a well-known type of architecture in a platform independent manner, i.e. the way to implement this model is not yet chosen at this time.

In another work, researchers provided the Kouretes Statechart Editor (KSE) CASE tool for authoring robotic behaviours [44]. Given existing bottom level functionalities [31], e.g. kick the ball, the modeler could define a robotic behaviour visually and immediately generate the code and upload it to a humanoid (Nao) robot.

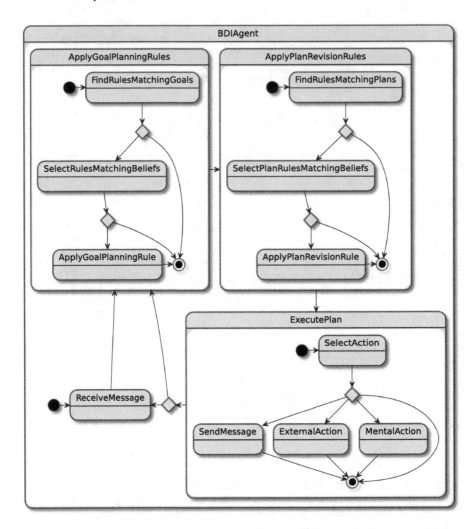

Fig. 5. Statechart representation of a BDI agent [41].

4   Discussion

The statecharts main added value is the capability of the language to capture both the static (activities and variables) and dynamic aspect of a system [19,20]. Thus, one can have a unique design model and use it to generate code for diverse platforms.

AOSE researchers have argued on other pros and cons of statecharts. Mainly inspired by the work of Paurobally et al. [35] we present some of their advantages (+) and disadvantages (-):

+ States and processes can be treated equally allowing an agent to refer and reason about the state of an interaction
+ Statechart notation is more amendable for extension thanks to their simple semantics
+ Visual models are easier to conceive and display [16]
+ Engineers familiar with UML can start working with them immediately [37]
- Participating roles are not shown explicitly
- Compound transitions are not shown in detail
- There is a question of completeness

One of our findings by working with statecharts is that agent behavior specification is not a trivial task. The development of the simplest possible player in Robocup took a statechart with 99 states in a hierarchy with a depth of 17 [34,44]. This demonstrated the added value of the ASEME methodology as it allows for the automatic transformation of Gaia liveness formulas to a statechart [42], which is at least a "good start", as opposed to starting the design directly with a statechart CASE tool, as was the case of StatEdit [31], or using a flat statechart model with no hierarchy, such as the plan diagrams of MaSE [10].

Proposing radical extensions to the language of statecharts may seem to facilitate or enable new features, e.g. as in the case of ANML, however, it renders them incompatible with existing CASE tools and they may become difficult for mainstream software engineers to learn and use [37].

Some times, and especially in works that do not adopt the orthogonal components of statecharts (i.e. AND-states), it is not obvious how one develops an agent realising more than one protocols simultaneously, and/or how to combine them with other agent capabilities.

The ASEME inter and intra-agent control models, being derived by Gaia formulas, do not use the possibility of the state transitions to traverse levels or the history connectors. If the developers, however, choose to introduce these features to the statechart they lose the connection of the design phase models (the statecharts) to the analysis phase models (i.e. the role model and the Gaia formulas). This situation can impact the tracing of software features to their requirements and has been reported as the "round-trip" problem [38]. The acquired experience after modeling a number of systems for software and robotic agents shows that the choice to not use state transitions traversing levels or the history connectors does not hinder the possibility to model complex systems, on the other hand, important engineering concepts, such as comprehension, modularity and reusability, are enhanced. The same has been reported by the more recent work on Armax statecharts for modeling robotic behaviour [45].

5 Future Directions

The future holds many challenges. Regarding the use of statecharts, agents and autonomous systems continuously face the possibility of an unexpected (at design time) event to happen while they are in operation. Unexpected means that either a known event happens that the system is unable to handle at its current state (unexpected at that time), although it is related to its operation, or an unknown event happens (totally unexpected), see Marron et al. [24] for a detailed definition. Although there are some hacks for ad-hoc catering for this issue, such as having a default handler for incoming messages not handled by a defined behaviour that replies with information about the services offered by the agent, this is a valid research direction.

In the area of design for autonomy (empowerment, self-management and self-regulation) it is very interesting to research how an inter- or intra-agent control can self-evolve over time. Evolution may be triggered through introspection or through the desire to maximize or fine-tune an agent's performance. For example, a robot may have a failing limb, it may need to fine tune its grasp to manage its best with the available functionality. Another example is related to the previously presented broker agent. What happens if, while usually its service matching activity successfully matches 99% of the requests, suddenly, and for a significant period, it matches only 30% of the requests. Now the agent needs a strategy to mitigate, e.g. to reboot its system, or update its services repository. Another kind of evolution is to evolve the statechart itself. Researchers are already delving into this area with results only for flat statecharts until now [18].

Recently, researchers proposed the concept of the property statecharts [26] for expressing and enforcing safety criteria in statecharts. Safety properties have been defined in AOSE, and the Gaia methodology's role model [46], however, statechart-based design models have not yet fully realised this feature, especially those leading to object-oriented implementations. Property statecharts are monitoring the events generated by the execution of normal statecharts and safeguard conditions. For example, and in the area of *smart contracts*, Mens et al. [26] have given an example, where an agent A signs a Service Level Agreement (SLA) with agent B. The SLA dictates that whenever A receives a request from B, then A must reply within 1 h. The property statechart gets in the monitoring state whenever A receives a request from B. If the A's state for sending a reply to B is not exited within 1 h the contract is considered violated. It would be very interesting to adapt this idea to safety properties of agents.

To realize implementations of agents in the modern open systems [21], agents need to use predefined protocols to interact. However, when diverse stakeholders come in, they need to work the protocols with their own algorithms and/or goals. Currently, protocols focus on defining sequences of exchanged messages. Adopting the point of view of the ASEME methodology [40,43], where protocols are regarded not as simple communication protocols that determine how data is transmitted (as in telecommunications and computer networking), but as their higher level abstractions used by humans, where protocols define *codes of behaviour* (or *procedural methods*), we can use statecharts for defining them. Thus, a protocol does not only answer the question of what messages are allowed but also what actions the participants need to do within the protocol. In this context, an important direction is towards defining new design patterns, that on the one hand will allow the developers to re-use existing protocol parts and logic defined in the open system; and on the other hand to customize key functionality or capabilities according to their needs and/or goals.

Thus, when defining open systems, or even proprietary systems, the use of statechart repositories would lead to the simplification of the statechart-based agent development. Consider for example, the Robocup Player agent that we referred to in the discussion above. It would be much easier to develop this agent if some parts of its statechart or intra-agent control model were reused from local or public repositories.

For example, 28 students taking the Autonomous Agents class at an Electrical and Computer Engineering school of the Technical University of Crete were asked to develop a robocup player in one of the 2-h laboratory sessions of the class. The students worked in small teams of two or three people per team. The students first went through a quick tutorial on using the ASEME CASE tool, which demonstrated the development of a Goalie behavior for the Nao robot. This included the Gaia formulas for the goalie role, and its IAC model. Then, they were asked to use the existing functionalities of the Goalie (scan for the ball, kick the ball, approach the ball, etc) to develop an *attacker* behavior using KSE. Thus, the students did not have to develop the robot functionalities. They defined the attacker role's liveness and then edited the generated statechart, i.e. they defined variables and transition expressions. All student teams were able to deliver the requested Attacker behavior and enjoyed watching their players in a game (for more information the reader can consult [43,44]).

A step forward would be to have the developers not reuse just activities of states (as they did in the above experiment) but whole statechart components (including transition expressions) as modules. Modules have also been referred to as capabilities in the AOSE community [5,43]. Modular programming has been identified as the ultimate aim of agent programming languages and developing frameworks be they declarative or imperative [7].

6   Conclusion

Statecharts and agent technology are quite close, as the reader may have already found out. The future holds more prospects for both areas but also for their cooperation. Statechart-based agent modeling has been used for developing software and physical agents, object-oriented or logic-based agents, agents communicating through message exchanging or through a blackboard.

We presented several future directions, mainly for the intra-agent's control, on one hand monitoring events that are essential for the agent's successful operation and detecting failing capabilities, and on the other hand safeguarding restrictions and contracts. Statecharts are a still evolving paradigm [6,24,26,45] and modern AOSE works use it [15,43].

In the future, this work can be expanded by adding a survey on the real-world multi-agent systems that have been developed using statechart-based designs. This is interesting as it will flesh out the relevant application domains and gather the experience that goes along with developing real-world systems. Moreover, more related work from the statechart research community can be added, as the present work was concerned with the works from the autonomous agents and MAS community.

References

1. Austin, J.L.: How To Do Things With Words. Harvard University Press, Cambridge (1975)
2. Bellifemine, F.L., Caire, G., Greenwood, D.: Developing Multi-Agent Systems with JADE. Wiley Series in Agent Technology. Wiley, Hoboken (2007)
3. Bordini, R.H., et al.: A survey of programming languages and platforms for multi-agent systems. Informatica **30**(1) (2006)
4. Brand, D., Zafiropulo, P.: On communicating finite-state machines. J. ACM (JACM) **30**(2), 323–342 (1983)
5. Braubach, L., Pokahr, A., Lamersdorf, W.: Extending the capability concept for flexible BDI agent modularization. In: Bordini, R.H., Dastani, M.M., Dix, J., El Fallah Seghrouchni, A. (eds.) ProMAS 2005. LNCS (LNAI), vol. 3862, pp. 139–155. Springer, Heidelberg (2006). https://doi.org/10.1007/11678823_9
6. Broad, A., Argall, B.: Path planning under interface-based constraints for assistive robotics. In: Proceedings of the 26th International Conference on Automated Planning and Scheduling, ICAPS 2016, pp. 450–458. AAAI Press (2016)
7. Dastani, M.: Programming multi-agent systems. Knowl. Eng. Rev. **30**(4), 394–418 (2015). https://doi.org/10.1017/S0269888915000077
8. Dastani, M., van Birna Riemsdijk, M., Meyer, J.-J.C.: Programming multi-agent systems in 3APL. In: Bordini, R.H., Dastani, M., Dix, J., El Fallah Seghrouchni, A. (eds.) Multi-Agent Programming. MSASSO, vol. 15, pp. 39–67. Springer, Boston, MA (2005). https://doi.org/10.1007/0-387-26350-0_2
9. DeLoach, S.A., Garcia-Ojeda, J.C.: O-MaSE: a customisable approach to designing and building complex, adaptive multi-agent systems. Int. J. Agent-Oriented Softw. Eng. **4**(3), 244–280 (2010)
10. DeLoach, S.A., Wood, M.F., Sparkman, C.H.: Multiagent systems engineering. Int. J. Softw. Eng. Knowl. Eng. **11**(03), 231–258 (2001)
11. Dunn-Davies, H., Cunningham, R., Paurobally, S.: Propositional statecharts for agent interaction protocols. Electron. Notes Theor. Comput. Sci. **134**, 55–75 (2005)
12. Eilenberg, S.: Automata, Languages, and Machines. Academic Press (1974)
13. Fortino, G., Garro, A., Mascillaro, S., Russo, W.: Using event-driven lightweight DSC-based agents for MAS modelling. Int. J. Agent-Oriented Softw. Eng. **4**(2), 113–140 (2010)
14. Fortino, G., Rango, F., Russo, W.: Statecharts-based JADE agents and tools for engineering multi-agent systems. In: Setchi, R., Jordanov, I., Howlett, R.J., Jain, L.C. (eds.) KES 2010. LNCS (LNAI), vol. 6276, pp. 240–250. Springer, Heidelberg (2010). https://doi.org/10.1007/978-3-642-15387-7_28
15. Fortino, G., Rango, F., Russo, W., Santoro, C.: Translation of statechart agents into a BDI framework for MAS engineering. Eng. Appl. Artif. Intell. **41**, 287–297 (2015)
16. Fortino, G., Russo, W., Zimeo, E.: A statecharts-based software development process for mobile agents. Inf. Softw. Technol. **46**(13), 907–921 (2004)
17. Girault, A., Lee, B., Lee, E.A.: Hierarchical finite state machines with multiple concurrency models. IEEE Trans. Comput. Aided Des. Integr. Circuits Syst. **18**(6), 742–760 (1999)

18. Goldsby, H.J., Cheng, B.H., McKinley, P.K., Knoester, D.B., Ofria, C.A.: Digital evolution of behavioral models for autonomic systems. In: Proceedings of the 5th IEEE International Conference on Autonomic Computing (ICAC 2008), pp. 87–96. IEEE Computer Society, Los Alamitos (2008)
19. Harel, D.: Statecharts: a visual formalism for complex systems. Sci. Comput. Program. **8**(3), 231–274 (1987)
20. Harel, D., Naamad, A.: The statemate semantics of statecharts. ACM Trans. Softw. Eng. Methodol. (TOSEM) **5**(4), 293–333 (1996)
21. Huynh, T.D., Jennings, N.R., Shadbolt, N.R.: An integrated trust and reputation model for open multi-agent systems. Auton. Agents Multi-Agent Syst. **13**(2), 119–154 (2006)
22. Kienzle, J., Denault, A., Vangheluwe, H.: Model-based design of computer-controlled game character behavior. In: Engels, G., Opdyke, B., Schmidt, D.C., Weil, F. (eds.) MODELS 2007. LNCS, vol. 4735, pp. 650–665. Springer, Heidelberg (2007). https://doi.org/10.1007/978-3-540-75209-7_44
23. König, R.: State-based modeling method for multiagent conversation protocols and decision activities. In: Carbonell, J.G., Siekmann, J., Kowalczyk, R., Müller, J.P., Tianfield, H., Unland, R. (eds.) NODe 2002. LNCS (LNAI), vol. 2592, pp. 151–166. Springer, Heidelberg (2003). https://doi.org/10.1007/3-540-36559-1_13
24. Marron, A., Limonad, L., Pollack, S., Harel, D.: Expecting the unexpected: developing autonomous-system design principles for reacting to unpredicted events and conditions (2020)
25. McBurney, P., Parsons, S.: Dialogue games for agent argumentation. In: Simari, G., Rahwan, I. (eds.) Argumentation in Artificial Intelligence, pp. 261–280. Springer, US, Boston (2009). https://doi.org/10.1007/978-0-387-98197-0_13
26. Mens, T., Decan, A., Spanoudakis, N.I.: A method for testing and validating executable statechart models. Softw. Syst. Model. **18**(2), 837–863 (2018). https://doi.org/10.1007/s10270-018-0676-3
27. Moore, S.A.: On conversation policies and the need for exceptions. In: Dignum, F., Greaves, M. (eds.) Issues in Agent Communication. LNCS (LNAI), vol. 1916, pp. 144–159. Springer, Heidelberg (2000). https://doi.org/10.1007/10722777_10
28. Moraïtis, P., Petraki, E., Spanoudakis, N.I.: Engineering JADE agents with the Gaia methodology. In: Carbonell, J.G., Siekmann, J., Kowalczyk, R., Müller, J.P., Tianfield, H., Unland, R. (eds.) NODe 2002. LNCS (LNAI), vol. 2592, pp. 77–91. Springer, Heidelberg (2003). https://doi.org/10.1007/3-540-36559-1_8
29. Moraitis, P., Spanoudakis, N.: The GAIA2JADE process for multi-agent systems development. Appl. Artif. Intell. **20**(2–4), 251–273 (2006). https://doi.org/10.1080/08839510500484249
30. Moulin, B., Chaib-Draa, B.: An overview of distributed artificial intelligence. In: O'Hare, G.M., Jennings, N.R. (eds.) Foundations of Distributed Artificial Intelligence. Wiley (1996)
31. Murray, J.: Specifying agent behaviors with UML statecharts and StatEdit. In: Polani, D., Browning, B., Bonarini, A., Yoshida, K. (eds.) RoboCup 2003. LNCS (LNAI), vol. 3020, pp. 145–156. Springer, Heidelberg (2004). https://doi.org/10.1007/978-3-540-25940-4_13
32. Nwana, H.S., Ndumu, D.T., Lee, L.C., Collis, J.C.: Zeus: a toolkit for building distributed multiagent systems. Appl. Artif. Intell. **13**(1–2), 129–185 (1999)
33. Obst, O.: Specifying rational agents with statecharts and utility functions. In: Birk, A., Coradeschi, S., Tadokoro, S. (eds.) RoboCup 2001. LNCS (LNAI), vol. 2377, pp. 173–182. Springer, Heidelberg (2002). https://doi.org/10.1007/3-540-45603-1_18

34. Paraschos, A., Spanoudakis, N.I., Lagoudakis, M.G.: Model-driven behavior specification for robotic teams. In: Proceedings of the 11th International Conference on Autonomous Agents and Multiagent Systems, vol. 1, pp. 171–178. International Foundation for Autonomous Agents and Multiagent Systems (2012)

35. Paurobally, S., Cunningham, J., Jennings, N.R.: Developing agent interaction protocols using graphical and logical methodologies. In: Dastani, M.M., Dix, J., El Fallah-Seghrouchni, A. (eds.) ProMAS 2003. LNCS (LNAI), vol. 3067, pp. 149–168. Springer, Heidelberg (2004). https://doi.org/10.1007/978-3-540-25936-7_8

36. Rao, A.S., Georgeff, M.P.: Modeling rational agents within a BDI-architecture. In: KR, pp. 473–484 (1991)

37. Riemenschneider, C.K., Hardgrave, B.C., Davis, F.D.: Explaining software developer acceptance of methodologies: a comparison of five theoretical models. IEEE Trans. Softw. Eng. **28**(12), 1135–1145 (2002)

38. Selic, B.: The pragmatics of model-driven development. IEEE Softw. **20**(5), 19–25 (2003)

39. Seo, H.-S., Araragi, T., Kwon, Y.R.: Modeling and testing agent systems based on statecharts. In: Núñez, M., Maamar, Z., Pelayo, F.L., Pousttchi, K., Rubio, F. (eds.) FORTE 2004. LNCS, vol. 3236, pp. 308–321. Springer, Heidelberg (2004). https://doi.org/10.1007/978-3-540-30233-9_23

40. Spanoudakis, N., Moraitis, P.: An agent modeling language implementing protocols through capabilities. In: Proceedings of the 2008 IEEE/WIC/ACM International Conference on Web Intelligence and Intelligent Agent Technology, vol. 02, pp. 578–582. IEEE Computer Society (2008)

41. Spanoudakis, N.: The agent systems engineering methodology (ASEME). Ph.D. thesis, Paris Descartes University (2009)

42. Spanoudakis, N., Moraitis, P.: Gaia agents implementation through models transformation. In: Yang, J.-J., Yokoo, M., Ito, T., Jin, Z., Scerri, P. (eds.) PRIMA 2009. LNCS (LNAI), vol. 5925, pp. 127–142. Springer, Heidelberg (2009). https://doi.org/10.1007/978-3-642-11161-7_9

43. Spanoudakis, N.I., Moraitis, P.: The ASEME methodology. Int. J. Agent-Oriented Softw. Eng. (in press)

44. Topalidou-Kyniazopoulou, A., Spanoudakis, N.I., Lagoudakis, M.G.: A CASE tool for robot behavior development. In: Chen, X., Stone, P., Sucar, L.E., van der Zant, T. (eds.) RoboCup 2012. LNCS (LNAI), vol. 7500, pp. 225–236. Springer, Heidelberg (2013). https://doi.org/10.1007/978-3-642-39250-4_21

45. Wächter, M., Ottenhaus, S., Kröhnert, M., Vahrenkamp, N., Asfour, T.: The ArmarX statechart concept: graphical programing of robot behavior. Front. Robot. AI **3**, 33 (2016)

46. Wooldridge, M., Jennings, N.R., Kinny, D.: The Gaia methodology for agent-oriented analysis and design. Auton. Agents Multi-Agent Syst. **3**(3), 285–312 (2000)

47. Zambonelli, F., Jennings, N.R., Wooldridge, M.: Developing multiagent systems: the Gaia methodology. ACM Trans. Softw. Eng. Methodol. **12**(3), 317–370 (2003). https://doi.org/10.1145/958961.958963

A Game of Double Agents: Repeated Stackelberg Games with Role Switch

Matteo Murari[(✉)], Alessandro Farinelli, and Riccardo Sartea

Department of Computer Science, University of Verona,
Strada le Grazie 15, 37134 Verona, Italy
{matteo.murari,alessandro.farinelli,riccardo.sartea}@univr.it

Abstract. We introduce a novel variation of the widely used 2-player Stackelberg game formalism. In our variation, a master player can decide to act as a leader or as a follower across the iterations of the game. This model naturally arises in many real-world applications and particularly in cyber-security scenarios, where an analyzer agent can arbitrarily decide which role to play in each iteration. We propose a first solution approach for this model assuming bounded rationality for the players and adopting a Monte Carlo Tree Search approach to devise the analyzer's strategy. We empirically show the effectiveness of our method in two experimental domains, i.e. synthetic game instances (using randomly generated games) and malware analysis (using real malware samples).

Keywords: Stackelberg game · Active malware analysis

1 Introduction

In recent years, Stackelberg Security Games (SSG) have been widely employed as theoretical models to address many safety-critical domains, such as the deployment of checkpoints in the Los Angeles Airport (LAX) [15], the organization of US Coast Guard patrols [1] and the detection of illegal fishing and poaching activities in protected natural reserves [4,18]. Such security games build upon the formalism of Stackelberg games, which involves two agents, i.e. a leader and a follower (a.k.a. defender and attacker in security scenarios). Every Stackelberg game divides in two phases: in the first step, the leader publicly commits to a strategy; once this operation terminates, the follower player can observe such strategy and then select a pure strategy in response [5].

Unfortunately, the optimality guarantees associated to the leader solution rely on some strict hypothesis that rarely occur in real scenarios. One important assumption is to perfectly know a priori the utility value obtained by any strategy profile composed of the joint actions of the leader and the follower agents. However, this information is often not available in practical scenarios and is approximated with an estimation procedure affected by a degree of uncertainty. Considering such cases, the studies conducted in [10] and [11] point out the need for the leader agent to use learning methods to profile the follower policy and

© Springer Nature Switzerland AG 2020
N. Bassiliades et al. (Eds.): EUMAS 2020/AT 2020, LNAI 12520, pp. 529–545, 2020.
https://doi.org/10.1007/978-3-030-66412-1_34

therefore incrementally refine such estimate in a repeated Stackelberg game, i.e. performing multiple rounds of interaction. Other works propose to embed the uncertainty in the utility function by defining intervals of potential payoffs [8].

Another critical point is represented by the rationality of the players: since the methods constructing the best leader strategy suppose that the follower selects an optimal response, a follower which deviates from such assumption may cause a loss for the leader. The main causes of such deviations are the uncertainty over the agent self-preferences, the partial knowledge about the environment and the non observability of the rewards. Previous works approach this problem by proposing bounded rational agent models which exploit subjective utility functions and the distribution of the follower responses [2,13]. Recently these methods have been improved adding features to reason about the success/failure of the opponent actions in preceding interactions and on the similarity between targets [6]. Finally, even though both agents behave as fully rational, the computational costs required to execute the algorithms to find the optimal solution are often prohibitive, hence agents are unable to compute an optimal strategy in a reasonable amount of time, even for relatively small problems.

More importantly, in many real interactive systems, the players do not have a clear, pre-determined role (i.e., always act either as leader or follower). Rather, they alternate behavioral patterns typical of a leader to others compliant to a follower, and viceversa. For instance, in the context of Active Malware Analysis (AMA) [17,20], an analyzer agent selects specific actions (triggers) to induce the malware sample into showing core behavioral patterns that otherwise would remain undetected, so as to correctly classify the sample; in this interaction setting the analyzer agent has a follower role since it first monitors the initial transparent (i.e. non concealed) operations performed by the malware and then executes a suitable trigger. However, to tackle the problem of anti-emulation mechanisms[1] implemented by many malware samples, the analyzer agent must commit a deceitful policy defining the outputs in response to malware checks, aiming to mask the true configuration of the analysis environment to trick the malware into showing its core functionalities [16]. In this second analyzer-malware dynamics, the analyzer assumes the leader role, because it needs to choose which deceitful policy to use before the malware does anything, otherwise the analysis would be ineffective. Such interactive techniques are related because they may interweave in subsequent analysis steps to achieve a common goal.

This key observation led us to the definition of a novel type of repeated Stackelberg games where the leader-follower roles assumed by the interacting agents can be exchanged along the iterations of the process. We apply such formalism to two case studies: in the first experiment, we aim at validating our method on synthetic games showing that it allows to optimize the cumulated reward obtained by the analyzer, while in the second we test our technique in the

---

[1] When using anti-emulation mechanisms, a malware sample starts by querying the running system to check if it is being executed inside a simulated environment (sandbox): if this is the case, it does not reveal any malicious behaviors.

scenario of Android AMA to prove that it can be used to conduct an exhaustive behavioral profiling of the policy implemented in real malware samples.

In summary, our contributions are the following:

1. We define Stackelberg Switch-Role Game (SSRG), a novel repeated Stackelberg game such that, between each round of the game, the agents can switch the leader-follower roles.
2. We show that computing optimal strategies for a SSRG is intractable. Hence, we propose a technique to compute an agent policy based on Monte Carlo Tree Search (MCTS) and a heuristic determining when it is convenient to switch roles.
3. We empirically evaluate the proposed method on synthetic game instances and real malware samples. In the former we highlight benefits and limitations of our approach in terms of achievable reward; in the latter we test the effectiveness of our method in a practical case study.

2   Background

2.1   Bayesian Stackelberg Game

The definition of a Stackelberg game assumes that payoffs of the players are perfectly known. In order to relax such constraint, the variant called Bayesian Stackelberg Game (BSG) has been proposed to model the uncertainty in payoff functions [15]. A BSG is constructed as a Stackelberg game in which a set Θ of possible types for the follower is defined[2]. The utility function associated to the follower $u_f : \Theta \times A_l \times A_f \to \mathbb{R}$ depends on the specific type θ characterizing the follower. Hence, the follower type contributes to determine the reward achieved by the follower together with the joint action profile of leader and follower, producing in general different outcomes for distinct types. In BSGs the leader is not aware about the chosen follower type, knowing only the probability distribution $P(\Theta)$ concerning the elements belonging to the type set Θ.

2.2   Monte Carlo Tree Search (MCTS)

We leverage on MCTS as a technique to implement the policy of our agent in the proposed framework. MCTS can estimate the most rewarding action for an agent to execute in a given domain by taking random samples in the agent's action space. The algorithm is based on the construction of a tree structure that is asymmetrically expanded so to explore the space of possible actions by focusing on the most convenient ones. The tree is initially empty and the procedure repeatedly performs the 4 phases depicted in Fig. 1: *selection* aims at descending the tree to reach the most promising node using a *tree policy* which mathematically estimates the attractiveness of the vertices; *expansion* attaches a new node to the previously selected vertex; a *simulation* is therefore run from

---

[2] There might be also a leader type set, but it is usually assumed to be a unit set.

the expanded node in order to evaluate the reward obtained by executing such action; finally, in *backpropagation*, the obtained reward is propagated up to the root, updating the statistics of the parent nodes.

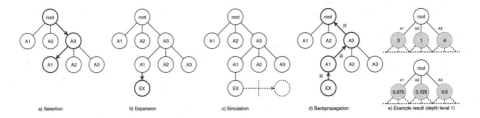

a) Selection   b) Expansion   c) Simulation   d) Backpropagation   e) Example result (depth level 1)

Fig. 1. Monte Carlo Tree Search scheme

The application of MCTS has been tested successfully both as a solution procedure for Stackelberg games [11] and for active malware analysis [17]. Indeed, assuming a proper choice of tree and default policies [9], the failure probability, namely the likelihood to return as output a non-optimal explored action, converges to zero at a polynomial rate as the number of simulations grows linearly.

3 Proposed Methodology

The Stackelberg game model can naturally encode many real world scenarios where agent interactions are not simultaneous and one agent can decide which actions to perform after observing the other agent's actions. However, there are cases in which such model may not accurately represent the dynamics of the interactions for the agents. In particular, we notice that there is a special class of scenarios where the agents involved in the interaction can decide to be either leader or follower, hence switching roles during the game. To capture these scenarios we propose the Stackelberg Switch Role Game (SSRG) model, that we define as follows:

Definition 1 (Stackelberg Switch-Role Game (SSRG)). *Let p_1, p_2 be a couple of agents and $R = \{(p_1 \leftarrow lead, p_2 \leftarrow follow), (p_1 \leftarrow follow, p_2 \leftarrow lead)\}$ the set of possible leader-follower role assignments. Suppose that the agent p_1 can arbitrarily select a role allocation $r \in R$. A SSRG is defined as a repeated Stackelberg game $s = (s_1, s_2, \ldots, s_n)$ of length $n \in \mathbb{N}$, where each $s_i = (r, A_l, A_f, u_l, u_f)$ is a single Stackelberg game such that:*

- *$r \in R$ is the role assignment chosen by p_1 for the i-th stage*
- *A_l is the set of pure strategies of the leader*
- *A_f is the set of pure strategies of the follower*
- *$u_l : A_l \times A_f \to \mathbb{R}$ is the leader's utility function*
- *$u_f : A_l \times A_f \to \mathbb{R}$ is the follower's utility function*

We call the agent that controls the role switch (i.e., p_1) the *master* and the procedure it uses to choose in each round the role allocation *Role Switch Policy (RSP)*[3]. In our scenarios, the master agent is decided a priori, without any chance for the involved agents to affect such choice. We decided to make this assumption because it captures well the malware analysis domain we are interested in. The definition above implies that whenever an agent p_j switches between leader and follower, the achievable payoffs may change accordingly, since the u_l and u_f are related to the role assumed by p_j. In our SSRG model, the aim for the agents is to maximize the global average reward achievable at the end of the process.

3.1   Assumptions and Complexity Results

We assume that the payoffs for leader and follower are initially unknown to the agents: players maintain an estimation about the rewards induced by the action profiles that is updated as the game progresses. This core assumption is justified by the characteristics related to real-world multi-agent systems, as players typically are affected by incomplete knowledge due to the lack of information about strategies and revenues of other agents and the incapability to accurately evaluate a reliable reward function for themselves.

Corollaries 1 and 2 demonstrate that for any SSRG instance such that there is at least a not uniquely defined payoff value, the problem of selecting the optimal policy for the master agent in each SSRG round is NP-hard. In order to prove such statement we leverage on the theorems 5 and 7 given in [3] which refer to BSG. Indeed, we show that a similar result holds in our setting by giving a procedure to reduce a SSRG round to an equivalent instance of BSG.

Corollary 1. *Finding an optimal mixed strategy to commit to in a round of a 2-player SSRG is NP-hard if the leader agent is uncertain about the follower rewards and the follower has at least two actions, even when the leader is fully aware about its rewards.*

Proof. We show that an instance of single round a SSRG can be reduced to a corresponding instance of a BSG. Accomplishing such goal, we leverage on theorems 7 reported in [3] to prove corollary 1.

Suppose w.l.o.g. that we are given an instance of a 2-player SSRG where the leader is uncertain between two different payoff values for a given joint leader-follower action profile. Then we can formulate equivalently this uncertainty over the outcome of such action profile by splitting explicitly into two distinct payoff matrices. The two created matrices can be interpreted as two behavioral types of follower. Therefore we obtain an instance of BSG where the leader has a single type and follower has two types. Hence theorem 7 of [3] applies.

Corollary 2. *Finding an optimal mixed strategy to commit to in a round of a 2-player SSRG is NP-hard if the leader agent is uncertain about its rewards, even when the leader perfectly knows the follower rewards.*

---

[3] In general, the choice about the employed RSP might be not determined by one agent, since it can be affected by environmental aspects or multiple agents.

Proof. Since we can obtain a transformation of any SSRG round to an equivalent BSG instance where we have at least two types (payoff functions) defined for the leader, the obtained BSG matches the hypothesis of theorem 5 shown in [3], which states the NP-hardness of committing an optimal pure strategy: since the pure strategies of the leader represent a subset of the possible mixed strategies, such NP-hardness result applies also generally to mixed strategies.

Whenever an agent behaves as follower, there are no complexity limitations in computing the optimal response to a committed mixed strategy, since such task requires a polynomial time for the resolution. However, if the master decides to address an SSRG interpreting the follower in every round to play optimally (and avoiding the burden of finding optimal mixed strategies), it may miss the opportunity to achieve a greater reward, since the leader sub-game might present more attractive payoffs. Thus the master would not obtain optimal overall results.

In the next section, we focus on a sub-optimal solution approach assuming that the agent we design is the master in the SSRG.

3.2   Solution Method: SAFE

The main elements to devise a solution procedure for a SSRG are the following: *a)* a routine to determine, at the beginning of each round, which leader-follower assignment is more profitable for the master; *b)* a method to compute the master strategy for both the roles; *c)* a procedure to update the estimated rewards w.r.t. the actual reward achieved in previous rounds. In Fig. 2, we show a scheme of Switching Agent FramEwork (SAFE), the framework we design to handle SSRG: first, a routine chooses the role assumed by each player in the next round; then a Stackelberg game round is performed between two bounded rational agents, producing expected and actual payoffs that update respectively the behavioral model of the adversary the master maintains and the reward estimation of the master for the chosen joint action profile.

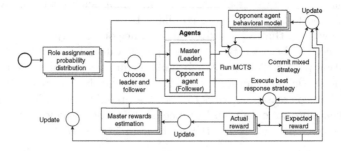

Fig. 2. Overview of SAFE (master acting as leader)

Role Switch Policy (RSP). As it can be seen from Fig. 2, the keystone of the framework is represented by the block that assigns, at each round of the SSRG, the leader and follower roles to the agents. The implementation of this routine shapes the evolution of the game, affecting the potential reward score that both players can achieve and the kind of interaction that takes place[4].

We propose a first RSP heuristic that analyzes past rounds of the SSRG to return in output a probability distribution defined over the possible leader-follower allocations for the agents. Once the RSP generates such distribution, it is used to select the role assignment leading the next round accordingly.

In order to explain the RSP modeling features, we sketch an example scenario. Let's assume that the SSRG is at iteration n and that in the previous round $n - 1$ the master has received a high payoff. Then our speculation would be to encourage for the round n the same role assignment decided for $n - 1$, since it has previously produced a good result. Conversely, we would aim at switching the roles if at step $n - 1$ the master obtained a poor reward, expecting that such change might improve the master revenue. In other words, we state that it is worth to exchange the roles only when the master gains a payoff that it does not consider sufficient. Moreover, there is another additional property that we want to insert in the RSP: the output distribution should never present 0 likelihoods, unless such role assignments are proven to be detrimental for our agent.

Algorithm 1. ROLE SWITCH POLICY (RSP)

Require:
   r - expected reward obtained at step $n - 1$
   a - leader-follower assignment at step $n - 1$
   c - constant value
Ensure:
   A leader-follower allocation for round n

1: **if** $n > 0$ **then**
2:     $update \leftarrow \frac{c \cdot \log{(r+1)}}{1 + c \cdot \log{(r+1)}}$
3:     $a \leftarrow update, \bar{a} \leftarrow (1 - update)$
4: **else**   ▷ 1st SSRG round
5:     $a \leftarrow 0.5, \bar{a} \leftarrow (1 - a)$ ▷ Use uniform distribution
6: **return** RANDOM$(a, \bar{a})$

We propose Algorithm 1 to implement the RSP for SSRGs we described in Subsect. 3.1, considering the previous requirements. The heuristic is based only on the expected reward r obtained in the last round, since we assume that it is the most reliable estimation of the actual payoff obtainable playing the sub-game specified by role allocation a. In contrast, if SSRG is at the starting iteration,

---

[4] The leader can have a different action set w.r.t. the follower. Similarly the reward function of an agent can vary if it plays as a leader or as a follower.

we just sample the uniform distribution defined over the set of possible leader-follower assignments (line 5). In the non-trivial case (lines 2–3), the fundamental point is given in line 2, where a probability value to associate to a is computed, representing how attractive it appears for the master agent to maintain the a role in the next round. The formula we suggest fits the features we described, since it incentives a if it has induced a high reward in the previous round, whilst penalizes it in the opposite case[5]. Moreover, the likelihoods associated to the two possible role assignments will never be equal to 0, no matter how large or small r is, thus preventing 0 probabilities for any allocation. Once the update value for a is computed, the probability coupled to $\bar{a}$, the other possible allocation, is defined as its complement. Finally, line 6 randomly selects the next role according to the probability distribution between a and $\bar{a}$.

Monte Carlo Tree Search (MCTS). The playing strategy for the master agent has been realized adopting the MCTS. Our implementation of the MCTS searches among the set of pure strategies (actions) defined for the role held by the master. The selection, expansion and backpropagation steps are based on the Upper Confidence Bound for Trees (UCT) [9]. The tree policy proposed with UCT addresses the exploration-exploitation dilemma to balance between the selection of actions that have not been well sampled yet and the promising ones already executed in previous iterations. Since the master incrementally refines a behavioral model of the adversary expressing the relationship between joint action profiles issued and the associated rewards, the simulation step of MCTS uses the information contained in such model to predict the response of the opponent agent. We implement such routine with the same approach presented in [17], both to shape the agent model and to perform the simulation.

When the MCTS terminates, we obtain a tree where at depth 1 there are all the nodes belonging to the action set of the master: we employ the simulated rewards embedded in such vertices to construct the master strategy. If the master plays as leader in this round, then the mixed strategy committed is built normalizing to 1 the rewards accumulated in such nodes. This procedure converts the set of considered simulated unbounded rewards into a corresponding probability distribution, which results to be the mixed strategy for the master. Otherwise, if the master decides to play as follower, it will choose as pure strategy the action with highest simulated reward among the same subset of the nodes. For example, in Fig. 1e the blue nodes are children of the root used to compute the master policy. If the master is the leader, we convert the rewards (upper image) normalizing to 1, obtaining the depicted mixed strategy (lower image); otherwise, it issues the pure strategy $A3$ since it achieved the highest reward.

If the agent running the MCTS is aware about all the information needed (no uncertainty or noise) then the MCTS would lead to the optimal mixed strategy asymptotically (see Subsect. 2.2). However, due to the limited amount of time

---

[5] The logarithm has been employed because it has a smooth trend; r is summed to 1 in the logarithm to avoid undefined results.

the MCTS executes and the incomplete/noisy information available to our agent, it produces approximated strategies. It is worth to underline that we divided the RSP and the algorithm generating the strategy of the master because, whenever the master plays as follower, these two steps are inherently separated by the observation of the leader committed policy.

Reward Estimation. As mentioned earlier, both players begin an SSRG without knowing any true payoff for any action profile. Therefore, the agents need to maintain estimates of the actual rewards for themselves and for the opponents to devise a proper strategy. Initially the agents fix the reward estimation for all action combinations to an uninformative constant: since all the actions produce the same value w.r.t. such estimation, they are evaluated likewise. However, as the SSRG progresses, the players receive reward signals that are useful to revise such estimation and to learn the actual game payoffs.

In order to implement such refinement process of the agent reward estimation, we rely on the widely used concept of moving average [7]. In particular we employ the exponential moving average to update the reward estimation as the tradeoff obtained balancing the actual reward received by the master at the end of game iteration n and the estimation computed at the previous round $n - 1$. Such update function weights the first mentioned term most in the early stages of the SSRG, since the reward estimation held by the master is considered inaccurate. However, as the game advances, the agent reward estimation tends to converge to the actual reward set for the SSRG instance.

4   Empirical Evaluation

We consider two sets of experiments to show the most important features of our approach. In the former we are interested in studying the results obtained with SAFE in normal form Stackelberg game scenarios. For this set of experiments we use synthetic games built by randomly creating the payoff matrices of the players. This setting has a double objective: *1.* demonstrating that our method provides key insights increasing the initial knowledge about players' payoffs and behavioral policies; *2.* proving that modeling a problem as a SSRG is outperforming whenever we do not perfectly know the opponent we face, having a degree of uncertainty over such agent. In the latter evaluation, we apply our method to a practical case study, namely the behavioral analysis of real Android malware. In this context our aim is to investigate whether our methods can provide more information on the malware samples that we are analyzing.

4.1   Synthetic Games

We start our evaluation creating a set of 2-player normal form game instances, each one representing the ground truth payoff matrices for a SSRG. For each game, we are interested in constructing two distinct couples of reward matrices, i.e. two sub-games: the first couple represents the payoff matrices for leader and follower whenever the master holds the leader role, while the second applies when the master is the follower[6]. We allow to have asymmetric couples, i.e. the leader matrices in the two sub-games can differ, as well as the follower ones. As it is common in the relevant literature, we assume that the payoffs remain constant for leader and follower in every game iteration.

In order to generate such games, we make use of the GAMUT tool [14]. We build 100 SSRG instances as random games having payoffs sampled in the interval $[0, 100]$. The action space assigned to each player is composed by 4 pure strategies. The mixed strategies issued by the leader, be it the master or the other agent, are subject to a 0.01 discretization to limit the cardinality of the possible mixed policies. Moreover, we set the length of each SSRG to 20 as, based on our empirical tests, going beyond it results do not change.

Once the games are generated, we compare the performance of SAFE with the results gained with: *a)* SAFE adopting a fixed uniform switch-role probability distribution; *b)* SAFE where the master is always the leader; *c)* SAFE where the master is always the follower. Points *b)* and *c)* are just SSRG issuing a constant role assignment. In every setting described, our agent relies on the same implementation of the MCTS to devise the players' strategy. Figure 3 shows the main results obtained running the described approaches on a SSRG instance, while in Fig. 4 we track how the master weights leader and follower roles, thus sub-games, during the game rounds using our RSP.

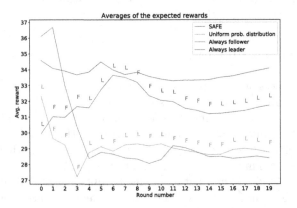

Fig. 3. Average of the expected rewards obtained across the rounds of a single instance SSRG considering 4 RSP implementations (L and F indicate the role chosen by the master)

The instance we consider is interesting because leader and follower roles have similar payoff matrices. The leader sub-game presents a mean payoff equals to 33, a slightly higher value than the follower sub-game mean reward, set to 29. Both master payoff matrices are characterized by a high standard deviation,

---

[6] We refer to them respectively as leader and follower sub-games.

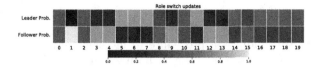

Fig. 4. The heat map representing how RSP changes the probability distribution of role assignment as the SSRG referred by Fig. 3 progresses

since they store sparse utility values (respectively 27.96 and 27.07). Thus the first sub-game results more profitable than the second for the master. In the plot of Fig. 3 the key point is that, after an initial confused phase due to the high estimation error on rewards, our RSP performs better than the ones using a fixed uniform switch probability distribution and the "only follower" policy. In particular, the comparison with the uniform distribution case underlines that a trivial RSP implementation brings no benefits. In this experiment, the SAFE master tends to exchange roles whenever it detects a not significant improvement in the reward obtained in consecutive rounds: this policy is needed by the master in the first steps of the SSRG to evaluate the responses achieved with different roles and action profiles[7]. For this reason we obtain an average reward that is lower than the one for the "only leader" strategy: since our RSP is a stochastic procedure, the master is induced to play as a follower for a given fraction of steps even if it is less rewarding (on average), reducing the overall mean expected reward. Nevertheless it allows to achieve a reward result that progressively gets closer to the average payoffs of the leader sub-game, since on the long term our agent significantly reduces the initial uncertainty by incrementally acquiring information and hence plays choosing the most advantageous sub-game, i.e. role.

This instance is a good representation of the general behaviors observed in all the synthetic game scenario: SAFE achieves a higher reward with respect to the constant selection of the less profitable role (in Fig. 3 the follower role) and to the use of a random uniform RSP. Clearly SAFE achieves a lower reward with respect to the RSP that always selects the most profitable role, as this information is not available to our algorithm[8].

Such result demonstrates two key insights. Whenever the ground truth payoffs remain fixed during all rounds of the SSRG, for both leader and follower sub-games, it is optimal for the master to choose in each round the most advantageous role assignment. In other terms, once the master identifies which sub-game is preferable (i.e. most rewarding), it shall opt constantly for the associated role allocation, avoiding any switch: such policy allows the agent to maximize its goal and therefore the role switch would deteriorate the overall reward (converging into playing the optimal role). However, there are many application cases in which SAFE outperforms the fixed role allocation to the players. Indeed, as a

---

[7] Estimating at the same time the behavioral patterns issued by the adversary.

[8] We decided to focus on this particular one because its payoff structure emphasizes the capability of SAFE to learn the rewards and drive the master effectively in spite of the high similarity of the leader and the follower sub-games.

second observation, if we assume that the master does not have a priori information (or a limited amount) about the rewards set for the players, the role switch provided by a SSRG induces a procedure to incrementally acquire knowledge about the actual game payoffs specific for both leader and follower. As the characterization of game payoffs and opponent behavioral model refines, the RSP provides role probability distributions that are gradually more stable, indicating that the master has learned a reliable ranking of the sub-game (i.e. role assignment) that is aligned with the real one. Such property allows to identify the most beneficial role assignment for the master after a proper amount of steps and, therefore, to play from that point onward with such chosen leader-follower allocation. Such feature is clearly observable in Fig. 4 where in the final stages of the game the heat map of the master role probability distribution becomes stable, showing a higher evaluation for the leader role. Another interesting point of Fig. 4 is that the probability difference between the two roles reflects roughly the gap between the mean utilities of the two sub-games. Indeed, as mentioned earlier, in this case the leader sub-game returns only slightly higher payoffs to the master w.r.t. the follower role: this small difference is highlighted in the last couple of tiles in the heat map, where we have the distribution $(0.55, 0.45)$.

Moreover the SAFE approach brings another key advantage: if we admit a scenario where the payoff matrices can vary across the rounds, lowering payoffs in profitable sub-games and increasing in less rewarding sub-games, then role switch provided by SSRG definition is a fundamental operation to maximize the reward of the master.

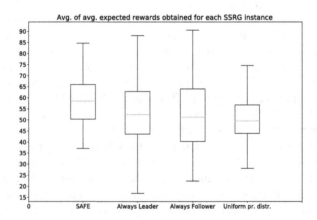

Fig. 5. For each RSP method, the box plot reports the average of the averages expected rewards obtained from the 100 SSRG instances faced

In order to support such consideration, we compute the average of the mean reward produced by each SSRG instance we created. Such results are represented in Fig. 5, where we can see that SAFE outperforms all the other methods. Indeed, the generated SSRGs are roughly divided into instances favoring the leader role and others fostering the follower: SAFE shows the highest average and a limited standard deviation due to the capability to recognize sub-games issuing potential good rewards and hence adapting to the most beneficial role assignment; conversely, the other naive heuristics blindly select role allocations, without reasoning on reward signals previously received. Moreover, the long fliers of "only leader" and "only follower" cases shows that payoffs varies significantly across the SSRGs population. In other words, SAFE allows to effectively identify after n repetitions of the game, both the role allocation and the action profile which induce the best result for the master agent and hence to play such configuration. Conversely, the other methods perform worse on average because the agent does not adapt its behavioral policy to the information gained in each interaction, even though such information may be used to infer that it would be more profitable to change role. The mean value of SAFE shown in Fig. 5 is statistically different for a T-test with 5% significance level.

4.2 Malware Analysis

Malware analysis is a crucial element to deploy effective countermeasures to ensure safe operations of cyber-systems. A key point of such analysis consists in determining the malware family, i.e. verify if the considered program shares common behavioral patterns with already studied malware.

However, advanced malware use two main methods to hinder the analysis: environment querying (a.k.a. anti-detection or anti-emulation) and active triggering. The former refers to the ability of the malicious software to infer if it is running in a simulated environment, e.g. an emulator, or in a real one; in the first case, the malware stops its execution or behaves as a harmless application to mislead the analysis. The latter technique consists in the malware requirement to be stimulated to perform its payload. For example, an SMS spyware needs the user to send or receive messages to perform data stealing actions. In order to thwart such mechanisms, proposed solutions suggest respectively to set a deceitful environment configuration [16] and executing user actions to induce the malware to unveil its dynamics [17]. The techniques combining triggering and deception are studied in a branch of malware analysis called AMA. Our aim is to prove that SAFE is a suitable method to address an AMA.

We model both in a single SSRG where our analyzer agent (master) acts as leader when it submits a deceptive configuration of the environment, while it becomes a follower when performing a triggering action. In fact, as a leader the analyzer must commit a deceitful configuration of the simulated environment before the malware starts its execution in order to counter the malicious query checks returning to the malware a fake result[9]. If the analyzer succeeds in its deception attempt, the malware is induced to issue an informative execution trace as response. On the other hand, triggering the malware is a follower behavior for the analyzer, since usually the malware executes first a sequence of

---

[9] If the analyzer makes this step later, the malware would perceive to be running in a simulated environment and hence stop.

setup operations (e.g. the initialization of event listeners) which are not necessarily exhaustive for the analysis but can guide the analyzer in choosing which trigger is most suitable to stimulate a significant malicious reaction. After the observation of such actions, the analyzer executes a user action as pure strategy. Deception and triggering can be considered sub-games composing the same SSRG.

The goal of our experiment with malware samples is to empirically prove that the application of SAFE brings a notable improvement in the amount of recorded malicious behaviors w.r.t. other analysis which only focus either on triggering or deception. We adapt the tool proposed in [17] with the design principles of SAFE and we compare its results with SSRGs fixing the analyzer action set to either triggering or deceptive actions. The analyzer thus is provided with the following triggers: send/receive SMS, make/receive call, add/delete contact, enable/disable GPS position. The analyzer action space defined for the deception sub-game cannot be extensively reported due to the huge amount of space it would require. However, we construct first a naive deceitful configuration as the composition of the values returned by the Android emulator in response to the most common routines employed by malware to query the system. In other terms, such configuration represents the environment not subject to any deception measure. The other 3 configurations are obtained modifying such basic configuration congruently to the anti-analysis method documented for the malicious families we took into account in our experiment.

Relying on the dataset built in [19], we select 46 malware samples belonging to 5 different families containing spyware and ransomware that integrate both the mentioned anti-analysis techniques. The action set used by the master for the triggering sub-game is composed by 8 different actions that mimic a standard user's behavior. In parallel we define the action set relative to the deception sub-game with 4 possible configurations for the emulator encapsulating the malware: when the master (leader) commits to a mixed strategy over such action set, the analyzer provides to make visible each given configuration for a fraction of time proportional to the associated probability value. At the end of the SSRG, the APIs composing the collected malicious execution traces are abstracted as done in [12] to group similar API calls into the same abstract API and the observed execution trace is handled by the analyzer to update the behavioral model of the malware. Similar to the work of [17], the utility function adopted to determine the analyzer payoffs for such SSRGs corresponds to the entropy of the malicious execution traces. It is worth to highlight that the entropy represents only an estimation measure of the real payoff: we used it since there is not any clear and accepted reward function ranking the malware-analyzer interactions.

Table 1 reports the results obtained by performing the described analysis modeled as SSRG composed of 20 rounds. The table reports for each malicious family the number of different execution traces extracted using the different methods. In particular, for every malware family we compare the behaviors recorded by "only triggering" and "only deceive" with the ones obtained with SAFE using a substring matching algorithm: if a trace belonging to the

Table 1. Discovered malicious behaviors comparison

Family	SAFE	Only triggering	Only deception
BankBot	74	19 – 0.26	46 – 0.62
Svpeng	64	52 – 0.81	25 – 0.39
Gumen	120	99 – 0.83	79 – 0.66
Koler	4	2 – 0.5	2 – 0.5
Bankun	26	14 – 0.54	15 – 0.60
Overall	288	186 – 0.64	167 – 0.58

outcome set of the triggering/deception sub-game is contained as substring in any of SAFE set, then we infer that such behavior has been detected by SAFE too. Considering such rule, we notice that every execution trace generated with both "only triggering" and "only deceive" is included in the trace set associated to SAFE. Nevertheless, SAFE retrieved execution traces characterized by a greater amount of detail about malicious patterns. For a clear comparison, we provide in table 1 the absolute number of different malware execution traces extracted with each method and, for triggering and deception, we add their relative code coverage w.r.t. SAFE, i.e. the portion of malware behaviors obtained with SAFE that is also recorded by "only triggering" and "only deception". The coverage values reported confirm that the problem modeling and the solution approach we propose significantly improves the amount of information achieved.

From a high level perspective, our framework proves to be effective due to the inherent reward function underlying the SSRG. The payoff function depends from the past interactions occurred between the agents: in an analysis context, once we received a specific information, we are not interested in getting the same again; rather, we aim to capture novel undisclosed behaviors. This key point implicitly suggests that the reward function varies as the SSRG progresses showing that a proper switching of analyzer roles is crucial to achieve high rewards.

5   Conclusions

We propose the Stackelberg Switch-Role Game, a novel Stackelberg formalism where agents involved in the game can switch between leader-follower roles. In order to study the features of SSRG, we developed a solution approach tested on synthetic game instances and on Android malware. Our method is based on a MCTS, it learns the agents payoffs online and it employs a heuristic routine to manage the role switching process. Our empirical evaluation verifies the validity of the approach showing benefits in the achieved reward. In particular in the case of malware analysis, our method induces a greater coverage of the detected malicious behaviors w.r.t. other state-of-the-art analysis techniques, unveiling execution patterns that would have remained hidden otherwise.

Many future lines of research can arise from our work. Since we suppose the a priori determination of the master agent, a first extension may consider relaxations of this constraint. In each stage, we could study SSRG where there is not a unique master affecting the role switch or in which there is a competition among the players to decide which one will be the master.

References

1. An, B., et al.: A deployed quantal response-based patrol planning system for the U.S. coast guard. Interfaces **43**, 400–420 (2013). https://doi.org/10.1287/inte.2013. 0700
2. Brown, M., Haskell, W.B., Tambe, M.: Addressing scalability and robustness in security games with multiple boundedly rational adversaries. In: Poovendran, R., Saad, W. (eds.) GameSec 2014. LNCS, vol. 8840, pp. 23–42. Springer, Cham (2014). https://doi.org/10.1007/978-3-319-12601-2_2
3. Conitzer, V., Sandholm, T.: Computing the optimal strategy to commit to. In: Proceedings of the 7th ACM Conference on Electronic Commerce, EC 2006, pp. 82–90. ACM, New York (2006). https://doi.org/10.1145/1134707.1134717
4. Fang, F., Stone, P., Tambe, M.: When security games go green: designing defender strategies to prevent poaching and illegal fishing. In: Proceedings of the 24th International Conference on Artificial Intelligence, IJCAI 2015, pp. 2589–2595. AAAI Press (2015)
5. Fudenberg, D., Tirole, J.: Game Theory. MIT Press, Cambridge (1991)
6. Kar, D., Fang, F., Delle Fave, F., Sintov, N., Tambe, M.: "a game of thrones": When human behavior models compete in repeated stackelberg security games. In: Proceedings of the 2015 International Conference on Autonomous Agents and Multiagent Systems, AAMAS 2015, pp. 1381–1390. International Foundation for Autonomous Agents and Multiagent Systems, Richland (2015)
7. Kenney, J.F.: Mathematics of Statistics, vol. 1, 3rd edn. Van Nostrand, New York (1964)
8. Kiekintveld, C., Islam, T., Kreinovich, V.: Security games with interval uncertainty. In: Proceedings of the 2013 International Conference on Autonomous Agents and Multi-agent Systems, AAMAS 2013, pp. 231–238. International Foundation for Autonomous Agents and Multiagent Systems, Richland (2013)
9. Kocsis, L., Szepesvári, C.: Bandit based monte-carlo planning. In: Fürnkranz, J., Scheffer, T., Spiliopoulou, M. (eds.) ECML 2006. LNCS (LNAI), vol. 4212, pp. 282–293. Springer, Heidelberg (2006). https://doi.org/10.1007/11871842_29
10. Letchford, J., Conitzer, V., Munagala, K.: Learning and approximating the optimal strategy to commit to. In: Mavronicolas, M., Papadopoulou, V.G. (eds.) SAGT 2009. LNCS, vol. 5814, pp. 250–262. Springer, Heidelberg (2009). https://doi.org/10.1007/978-3-642-04645-2_23
11. Marecki, J., Tesauro, G., Segal, R.: Playing repeated stackelberg games with unknown opponents. In: Proceedings of the 11th International Conference on Autonomous Agents and Multiagent Systems - Volume 2, AAMAS 2012, pp. 821–828. International Foundation for Autonomous Agents and Multiagent Systems, Richland (2012)
12. Martín, A., Rodríguez-Fernández, V., Camacho, D.: Candyman: classifying android malware families by modelling dynamic traces with markov chains. Eng. Appl. Artif. Intell. **74**, 121–133 (2018). https://doi.org/10.1016/j.engappai.2018.06.006

13. Nguyen, T.H., Yang, R., Azaria, A., Kraus, S., Tambe, M.: Analyzing the effectiveness of adversary modeling in security games. In: Proceedings of the Twenty-Seventh AAAI Conference on Artificial Intelligence, AAAI 20, . 718–724. AAAI Press (2013)
14. Nudelman, E., Wortman, J., Shoham, Y., Leyton-Brown, K.: Run the gamut: a comprehensive approach to evaluating game-theoretic algorithms. In: Proceedings of the Third International Joint Conference on Autonomous Agents and Multiagent Systems - Volume 2, AAMAS 2004, pp. 880–887. IEEE Computer Society, Washington DC (2004). https://doi.org/10.1109/AAMAS.2004.238
15. Pita, J., et al.: Deployed armor protection: the application of a game theoretic model for security at the Los Angeles international airport. In: Proceedings of the 7th International Joint Conference on Autonomous Agents and Multiagent Systems: Industrial Track, AAMAS 2008, pp. 125–132. International Foundation for Autonomous Agents and Multiagent Systems, Richland (2008)
16. Raffetseder, T., Kruegel, C., Kirda, E.: Detecting system emulators. In: Garay, J.A., Lenstra, A.K., Mambo, M., Peralta, R. (eds.) ISC 2007. LNCS, vol. 4779, pp. 1–18. Springer, Heidelberg (2007). https://doi.org/10.1007/978-3-540-75496-1_1
17. Sartea, R., Farinelli, A.: A monte carlo tree search approach to active malware analysis. In: Proceedings of the Twenty-Sixth International Joint Conference on Artificial Intelligence, IJCAI-17, pp. 3831–3837 (2017). https://doi.org/10.24963/ijcai.2017/535
18. Wang, B., Zhang, Y., Zhou, Z.-H., Zhong, S.: On repeated stackelberg security game with the cooperative human behavior model for wildlife protection. Appl. Intell. 49(3), 1002–1015 (2018). https://doi.org/10.1007/s10489-018-1307-y
19. Wei, F., Li, Y., Roy, S., Ou, X., Zhou, W.: Deep ground truth analysis of current android malware. In: Polychronakis, M., Meier, M. (eds.) DIMVA 2017. LNCS, vol. 10327, pp. 252–276. Springer, Cham (2017). https://doi.org/10.1007/978-3-319-60876-1_12
20. Williamson, S.A., Varakantham, P., Hui, O.C., Gao, D.: Active malware analysis using stochastic games. In: Proceedings of the 11th International Conference on Autonomous Agents and Multiagent Systems - Volume 1, AAMAS 2012, pp. 29–3. International Foundation for Autonomous Agents and Multiagent Systems, Richland (2012)

Learning Summarised Messaging Through Mediated Differentiable Inter-Agent Learning

Sharan Gopal, Rishabh Mathur, Shaunak Deshwal,
and Anil Singh Parihar[(✉)] [ID]

Delhi Technological University, Delhi, India
{sharangopal_bt2k16,rishabh_bt2k16,shaunak_bt2k16}@dtu.ac.in,
parihar.anil@gmail.com

Abstract. In recent years, notable research has been done in the area of communication in multi-agent systems. When agents have a partial view of the environment, communication becomes essential for collaboration. We propose a Deep Q-Learning based multi-agent communication approach: Mediated Differentiable Inter-Agent Learning (M-DIAL), where messages produced by individual agents are sent to a mediator that encodes all the messages into a global embedding. The mediator essentially summarises the crux of the messages it receives into a single global message that is then broadcasted to all the participating agents. The proposed technique allows the agents to receive only essential abstracted information and also reduces the overall bandwidth required for communication. We analyze and evaluate the performance of our approach over several collaborative multi-agent environments.

Keywords: Multi-agent systems · Multi-agent communication · Deep Q-learning · Deep reinforcement learning

1 Introduction

Proficient communication between individual agents be it natural, human or artificial is paramount for success in a collaborative environment [2,7,20]. It is prevalent among most intelligent species and the sophistication of the language used is often indicative of the overall competence at any given collaborative task. Communicating meaningful information and the inferences derived, helps the agents to coordinate and cooperate towards achieving a common goal. Thus, learning to communicate becomes inevitable in conditions where agents only have access to a partial view of the environment but need to work in unison.

Deep Reinforcement Learning (DRL) has seen considerable success in complex single-agent games such as chess, shogi and go [15] and has immense scope in real-life applications like robotics [9] and self-driving cars [22]. However, owing

---

S. Gopal, R. Mathur and S. Deshwal—Contributed equally to this work.

© Springer Nature Switzerland AG 2020
N. Bassiliades et al. (Eds.): EUMAS 2020/AT 2020, LNAI 12520, pp. 546–557, 2020.
https://doi.org/10.1007/978-3-030-66412-1_35

to factors such as ineffective credit assignment, partial observability, and the non-stationarity of the environment, they tend to underperform in multi-agent scenarios [13]. The introduction of communication channels between agents alleviates the problem of partial observability and non-stationarity as the agents can communicate observations and intentions which could be crucial information for another agent.

Initial attempts at communication in Multi-Agent Systems (MAS) used predetermined discrete symbols to give the agents a language structure to communicate upon. DIAL [3] and CommNet [17] suggested the use of differentiable message channels which allows these networks to learn communication protocols by passing gradients through backpropagation to optimize a downstream task. We hypothesize that in order to scale up well the agents must receive an intelligent summary rather than a myriad of individual messages.

To this end, we propose a cooperative Multi-Agent Deep Reinforcement Learning (MADRL) system - Mediated Differentiable Inter-Agent Learning (M-DIAL). We introduce a mediator network, which receives messages from each agent on every timestep and summarizes them into a global embedding. This embedding is then forwarded to every agent in the next timestep as a global message. Each agent then uses this global message and observations from the environment to take the next action. The mediator network renders control over the global message dimensions, such that a lesser bandwidth can be used despite an increase in the number of agents. The reward structures are designed to incentivize cooperative behavior amongst agents.

The rest of the paper is organised as follows : Sect. 2 discusses the related literature and the motivation for our work. Section 3 gives the necessary background of the Deep Q-learning algorithm. Section 4 lays out our proposed approach and the M-DIAL architecture. Section 5 presents the experimental findings and finally, Sect. 6 presents the conclusion and future work.

2   Related Work

MAS have a rich literature with their own set of unique hurdles [5,11,12]. The straightforward approach is to use independent Q-Learning agents [20] or its variants like Deep Q-Learning [10] or Deep Recurrent Q-Learning [4], that treat the other agents as a part of the environment. A drawback to this is the non-stationarity of the environment, since each agent experiences changes in its policy during training. This limits the use of experience replay, thereby not guaranteeing convergence. One of the methods to mitigate this problem is the introduction of inter-agent communication methods.

Differentiable Inter-Agent Learning (DIAL) [3] was the first to introduce a differentiable message channel between deep Q-agents to enable learnable communication. The agents are allowed to send messages through these channels to facilitate a downstream task in the next timestep. During backpropagation gradients are pushed through these channels, thus making the entire network end-to-end trainable.

CommNet [17] proposed the cooperation of agents through an aggregated continuous vector communication channel that carries the mean transmission from each other agents to the next timestep. The model also allowed for real time change in the type and number of agents. Vertex Attention Interaction Networks (VAIN) [6] extended this with an attention mechanism that determines the weights with which an agent gets a share in the final message.

However, CommNet does not scale well in cases when the state-action space of the games increases exponentially with an increase in the number of agents. BiCNet [14] addressed this problem by introducing Bidirectional Coordinated Network (BicNet), it is modeled using bi-directional RNN's to allow parameter sharing amongst agents.

Das et. al. [1] proposed an actor-critic based targeted multi-agent communication approach wherein the agents decide on what message to send as well as whom to send it. Each agent sends the communication message to every other agent along with an additional signature which encodes agent specific information. The receiving agents then calculate the relevance of this message using this signature.

3   Background: DQN

Deep Q-networks are employed to approximate the maximum cumulative reward function, i.e. the maximum total reward that can be received from the current state, doing a particular action, till the end of the episode (or forever into the future for non-terminating tasks), given the current state s and the action a selected for the current step. Using an ϵ-greedy approach, we can sample random actions with probability ϵ and select the action that yields the maximum reward, as per the current Q function with probability $1 - \epsilon$. We aim to carry out updates using the following equation:

$$Q(s,a) = E[r|s,a] + \gamma \sum_{s'} P(s'|s,a) \arg\max_{a'} Q(s',a') \qquad (1)$$

which is approximated by sampling as

$$Q(s,a) = r + \gamma \arg\max_{a'} Q(s',a') \qquad (2)$$

where γ is the discount factor, typically chosen to be in the range $[0, 1]$. This factor exponentially reduces the weight given to future rewards and is useful in mathematically establishing that the Q function will converge, given that the reward sequence is bounded [18]. Using a target network, we compute the right hand side and improve the Q outputs of the main network by reducing the L_2 distance between the target y_t^i and proposed Q outputs.

4   Proposed Approach

In this section, we discuss our approach for achieving communication in MAS. Neural networks are effective feature extractors and are often used to compress information [21]. To this end, we introduce a mediating deep network that intakes sparse, redundant messages from all the agents and amalgamates them into a compressed encoding.

4.1 M-DIAL Architecture

We present the architecture of the proposed setup as in Fig. 1. For every time step t, each agent A_i, parameterised by θ (shared between all agents), is a deep Q-network. Every agent A_i is given a partial observation o_t^i of the underlying environment at time t and the global message m_{t-1}^g of the previous temporal layer as the input. Each agent generates the Q-values and a message that is forwarded to the mediator. The action a_t^i for timestep t is selected in an ϵ-greedy manner based on the generated Q-value.

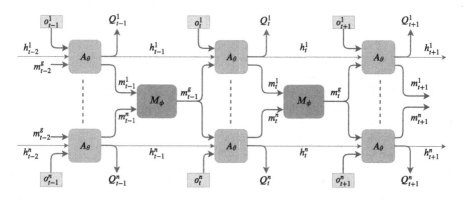

Fig. 1. The proposed architecture shows for every timestep t, each agent A_i, with parameters θ and mediator with parameters ϕ. The messages m_t^i produced by the individual agents are fed into the mediator, whose output, m_t^g is given to each agent for the next timestep.

The mediator network M parameterized by ϕ is a multi-layer neural network, which receives messages of dimensions $|m^a|$ from each of the participating agents. The messages are concatenated and fed into the mediator, which produces a global encoding of dimensions $|m^g|$ that is forwarded to each of the agents in the next timestep. The mediator doesn't have any specific loss functions associated with itself, but is part of the end-to-end training setup and receives gradient updates from the message channels as described in Sect. 4.2.

The advantage here is that instead of each agent relaying a number of messages to communicate with each other, the global message is produced as an optimal encoding of relevant information, transferring processing load to an external entity. Further, since the mediator concentrates the knowledge gathered by distributed agents into one encoding, it is easier to interpret and explain the behaviour of the multi-agent system (Fig. 2).

Algorithm 1: Mediated Differentiable Inter-Agent Learning

Result: Trained parameters θ and ϕ for the Mediator and Agent Networks
Initialize θ, ϕ, target parameters θ^-, ϕ^-;
for *each episode e* **do**
    Initialize initial messages and network states $m_0^g, m_0^{g-}, h_0^i, h_0^{i-} \leftarrow 0$;
    for *each agent i* **do**
        $m_1^{i-}, h_1^{i-}, Q_1^{i-} \leftarrow A(m_0^{g-}, h_0^{i-}, o_1^{i-}; \phi^-)$;
    end
    $m_1^{g-} \leftarrow M(..., m_1^{i-}, ...; \theta^-)$ //... represents iteration over agents [i];
    for $t \leftarrow 1$ *to* T **do**
        for *each agent i* **do**
            $m_t^i, h_t^i, Q_t^i \leftarrow A(m_{t-1}^g, h_{t-1}^i, o_t^i; \theta)$;
            $a_t^i \leftarrow \varepsilon\text{-greedy-action-select}(Q_t^i)$;
        end
        $m_t^g \leftarrow M(..., m_t^i, ...; \phi)$;
        $(..., r_t^i, ...), (..., o_t^i, ...) \leftarrow \text{env.move}(..., a_t^i, ...)$;
        if *e is done* **then**
            $(..., y_t^i, ...) \leftarrow (..., r_t^i, ...)$;
        else
            for *each agent i* **do**
                $m_{t+1}^{i-}, h_{t+1}^{i-}, Q_{t+1}^{i-} \leftarrow A(m_t^{g-}, h_t^{i-}, o_{t+1}^{i-}; \theta^-)$;
                $y_t^i \leftarrow r_t^i + \gamma \max_a Q_{t+1}^{i-}[a]$;
            end
            $m_{t+1}^{g-} \leftarrow M(..., m_{t+1}^{i-}, ...; \phi^-)$;
        end
    end
    $\nabla\theta, \nabla\phi \leftarrow 0$;
    for $t \leftarrow T$ *downto* 1 **do**
        Compute Gradients and find $\nabla\theta_t^i, \nabla\phi_t^i$ for agent i, using equations (3) to (10);
        for *each agent i* **do**
            $\nabla\theta \leftarrow \nabla\theta + \nabla\theta_t^i$;
            $\nabla\phi \leftarrow \nabla\phi + \nabla\phi_t^i$;
        end
    end
    $(\theta, \phi) \leftarrow (\theta, \phi) + \eta(\nabla\theta, \nabla\phi)$;
    Every τ timesteps, update $(\theta^-, \phi^-) \leftarrow (\theta, \phi)$;
end

4.2   Training

Gradients pass through the message channels as well, hence we need to sum the gradients through those channels. The following equations are used to find out gradients while traversing back in time. We have given equations pertaining

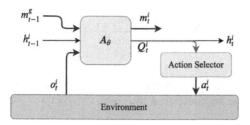

Fig. 2. A single agent A_i's interaction with the environment. It is given an observation o_t^i and the global message from the previous step m_{t-1}^i. The Q values produced are used to select an action signal that is passed to the environment and a message vector m_t^i is sent to the mediator.

to one-dimensional agent and global messages for simplicity, and equations for higher dimensional messages can be obtained simply by using transpose operations and matrix multiplications.

Updates to the Agent's Network Parameters θ: The updates to θ, denoted by $\nabla\theta$ can be computed as the gradient of the squared distance between the target value y_t^i and the current output over θ, as:

$$\nabla\theta = 2\sum_i \sum_{t=1}^T (Q_t^i - y_t^i)(\nabla\theta_i^t) \tag{3}$$

where $\nabla\theta_i^t$ is the gradient term for the agent i at timestep t. We sum over the gradients through the internal states h_t^i and the messages m_t^i, each of which can be computed using the product rule:

$$\nabla\theta_i^t = \sum_{i'}\sum_{t'<t} \frac{\partial Q_t^i[a_t^i]}{\partial h_{t'}^{i'}}\frac{\partial h_{t'}^{i'}}{\partial\theta} + \frac{\partial Q_t^i[a_t^i]}{\partial m_{t'}^{i'}}\frac{\partial m_{t'}^{i'}}{\partial\theta} \tag{4}$$

$\frac{\partial Q_t^i[a_t^i]}{\partial h_{t'}^{i'}}$ and $\frac{\partial Q_t^i[a_t^i]}{\partial m_{t'}^{i'}}$ can be computed using the following equations, moving back in time. During backpropagation, we can use the gradients computed for timesteps $t+1$, for computing gradients for timestep t. For the internal state h_t^i, this can be done as:

$$\frac{\partial Q_t^i[a_t^i]}{\partial h_{t'}^{i'}} = \frac{\partial Q_t^i[a_t^i]}{\partial h_{t'+1}^{i'}}\frac{\partial h_{t'+1}^{i'}}{\partial h_{t'}^{i'}} + \frac{\partial Q_t^i[a_t^i]}{\partial m_{t'+1}^{i'}}\frac{\partial m_{t'+1}^{i'}}{\partial h_{t'}^{i'}} \tag{5}$$

For the message channel m_t^i, this can be computed as:

$$\frac{\partial Q_t^i[a_t^i]}{\partial m_{t'}^{i'}} = \frac{\partial Q_t^i[a_t^i]}{\partial m_{t'}^g}\frac{\partial m_{t'}^g}{\partial m_{t'}^{i'}} \tag{6}$$

$$\frac{\partial Q_t^i[a_t^i]}{\partial m_{t'}^g} = \sum_{i''} \frac{\partial Q_t^i[a_t^i]}{\partial m_{t'+1}^{i''}} \frac{\partial m_{t'+1}^{i''}}{\partial m_{t'}^g} + \frac{\partial Q_t^i[a_t^i]}{\partial h_{t'+1}^{i''}} \frac{\partial h_{t'+1}^{i''}}{\partial m_{t'}^g} \tag{7}$$

Updates to the Mediator's Network Parameters ϕ: Similarly updates to ϕ, denoted by $\nabla \phi$ can be computed as:

$$\nabla \phi = 2 \sum_i \sum_{t=1}^T (Q_t^i - y_t^i)(\nabla \phi_t^i) \tag{8}$$

where $\nabla \phi_t^i$ is the gradient term for agent i at timestep t

$$\nabla \phi_t^i = \sum_{t' < t} \frac{\partial Q_t^i[a_t^i]}{\partial m_{t'}^g} \frac{\partial m_{t'}^g}{\partial \phi} \tag{9}$$

$\frac{\partial Q_t^i[a_t^i]}{\partial m_{t'}^g}$ can be computed as we did for θ, utilizing the gradients computed for timestep $t + 1$:

$$\frac{\partial Q_t^i[a_t^i]}{\partial m_{t'}^g} = \sum_{i'} \frac{\partial Q_t^i[a_t^i]}{\partial m_{t'+1}^{i'}} \frac{\partial m_{t'+1}^{i'}}{\partial m_{t'}^g} + \frac{\partial Q_t^i[a_t^i]}{\partial h_{t'+1}^{i'}} \frac{\partial h_{t'+1}^{i'}}{\partial m_{t'}^g} \tag{10}$$

5   Experimental Results

We evaluate our model on multi-agent tasks, hidden reward in Sect. 5.1 and a modified pong environment described in Sect. 5.2. Each agent is fully cooperative, receives global rewards, and has a partial view of the environment to trigger communication among the agents. Comparisons are made on varying message dimensions and an analysis of the content of the messages is done for the pong environment.

We use the following parameters in all our experiments unless stated otherwise. The optimizer used is Adam [8] with a learning rate $\eta = 0.0005$ and discount factor gamma $\gamma = 0.95$. The network trains using an ϵ-greedy approach with epsilon $= 0.05$. Each agent A_i is modeled using a DRQN with Gated Recurrent Networks (GRU) and tanh activations. But this may be modified to a stateless DQN when the environment calls for it. Here, mathematically the hidden state h_t^i can be set to zero and the remaining terms in the equations will remain the same (Fig. 3).

5.1   Hidden Reward

The hidden reward [16] is a partially observable multi-agent environment where the task is to find the location of the reward zone within a stipulated time limit. This limit is decided such that a single agent cannot randomly explore the entire

(a) Hidden Reward: The agents (black) need to explore the map to find the reward area (red), they then need to broadcast messages to help the other agents find it as well.

(b) Pong Game: The agents (paddles) can only see the ball when it is in their half of the court. They must communicate to collaborate and keep the ball in play for the longest duration.

Fig. 3. Environments used to test our approach.

map. At every time-step, each agent receives the following information from the environment - a binary value indicating whether or not they have found the reward and coordinates for all the agents. Each agent can either go up, down, left, right, or stay to explore its surroundings and a reward is given only to those agents who have successfully found the reward zone.

We use four stateless agents to evaluate this task. M-DIAL agents are seen to coordinate among themselves to search in different areas of the overall space to find the reward zone. Once it is found, the agents tend to quickly converge to the zone indicating that the communication mechanism is working effectively. On the other hand, it is seen that in the case of no communication, each agent tries to individually search its surroundings to find the reward zone. No satisfactory policy is found as the agents cannot communicate vital information such as the location of the found reward.

Figure 4 shows the progression of the cumulative rewards received by the team during training epochs, where each epoch consists of 100 training episodes. The reward for our best model converges at 92 which is significantly higher than the convergence value of 30 when there is no communication. Figure 4a shows a comparison between varying sizes of agent message dimensions while keeping a constant size for the global message. A performance increase is seen with an increase in the dimensions of the agent message, while the input to the agents remains constant in size. This maintains the computational cost at the input layer of the agent and offloads it to the mediator, while still having the computational cost increase linearly with the agent message dimensions at the output layer of the agent. Figure 4b shows a comparison between varying global message dimensions. A similar convergence value across dimensions indicates

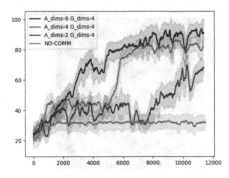
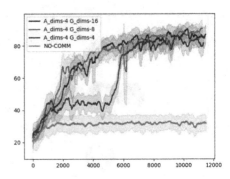

(a) Comparison of varying the size of the Agent message channels.

(b) Comparison of varying the size of the Global message channels.

Fig. 4. Results on the Hidden Rewards Environment, where the curves are a plot between the cumulative rewards received by the agents and the epochs. G_dims represents the size of the Global message channel and A_dims represents the size of the individual Agent message channel.

that the mediator is effective at performing compression while retaining essential information.

5.2 Pong

We also demonstrate our approach on our version of the Pong game which is explicitly tweaked to provoke communication to collaborate. The goal of the game is to maximize the total number of paddle hits and global rewards [19] are awarded to promote collaboration. Each paddle is controlled by an independent agent with partial visibility of their half of the screen along the y axis. The velocity of the ball increases exponentially at every frame at the rate of $\nu = 1.0012$. The increase in velocity makes it infeasible for the agents to merely react when the ball becomes visible to them, this drives the agents to develop strategic communication protocols to overcome the visibility handicap.

To avoid trivial solutions to the game such as playing the game adjacent to a wall so as to minimize the overall distance that needs to be traveled [19], we introduce a variable rebound that varies depending on the point of impact on the paddle with high deviation.

Figure 5 shows the progression of the average number of paddle hits per episode during training. In both cases, our model outperforms the model without communication, with a slight increase seen with an increase in the broadcast dimensions. The paddles were seen to be moving in the direction of the ball even when it was outside their visibility zone, indicating the messages were effective. Most of the missed balls were due to the fact that beyond a point (approximately 12 hits) the velocity of the ball increases to the extent that it would be impossible for the paddles to keep up even at with an optimal strategy.

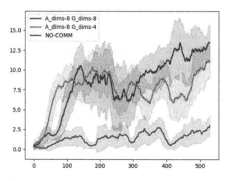

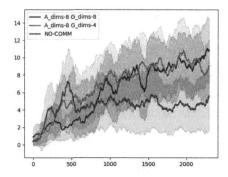

(a) Individual agents modelled as DRQN with varying message dimensions

(b) Individual agents modelled as DQN with varying message dimensions

Fig. 5. Results on the Pong Environment, where the curves are a plot between the average paddle hits and the test episodes. G_dims represents the size of the Global message channel and A_dims represents the size of the individual Agent message channel.

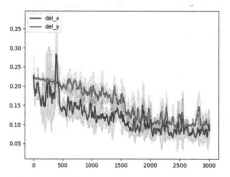

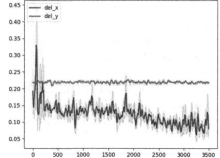

(a) Analysis of the agent message m^a. The message contains information about both coordinates of the ball.

(b) Analysis of the global message m^g. The message only contains information about x coordinates.

Fig. 6. Analysis of the contents of agent messages m^a and global message m^g in the Pong environment, where the curves are a plot between the fraction of the screen by which the coordinate prediction is off and the epochs. del_x and del_y represent the difference between the predicted and actual value of the ball for the x and y axes respectively.

We further carry out an analysis of the content of the agent and global messages. We train a shallow neural network that takes the messages and predicts an aspect of the underlying environment: the position of the ball. Figure 6 show training epochs of this network while plotting the differences between the predicted coordinates and the ground truth coordinates of the ball as a fraction of the screen size. In Fig. 6a, while predicting the location of the ball using the agent messages, the difference of the actual and predicted values of the x and y coordinates of the ball decreases as our model is trained and converges at a

0.1 fraction of the screen size. This shows that the agent messages contain information about both coordinates of the ball. An interesting counter observation is seen in Fig. 6b for the global message where the x-coordinate is predicted correctly but the information for the y-coordinate is not being communicated and the network always predicts the mean value. This implies that the mediator explicitly excludes the y-coordinate information. This is logically explainable since the agents (paddles) primarily depend on the x-coordinate of the ball to decide their next actions.

6 Conclusion

In this paper, we have introduced a new multi-agent communication learning architecture that uses a mediator network to summarise the crux of the input messages of the agents and produces a global message which is then passed on to each agent. Our approach uses less overall bandwidth since there is no direct agent to agent communication and all the communication happens through the mediator. Our results show that M-DIAL's protocol of communication performs significantly better than non communicating agents and we analyze the results by varying input message dimensions and output message dimensions. Further, we train a shallow neural network to analyze the content of the agent and global message and show how the messages accurately predict the actual coordinates of the ball in Pong.

Future work would entail the use of an attention mechanism to customize the global message of each agent. We also believe that our approach is a step towards distributed neural architectural schemes for reinforcement learning.

References

1. Das, A., et al.: TarMAC: targeted multi-agent communication. In: Proceedings of the 36th International Conference on Machine Learning. Proceedings of Machine Learning Research, vol. 97, pp. 1538–1546. PMLR, 09–15 Jun 2019
2. Ferber, J.: Multi-Agent Systems: An Introduction to Distributed Artificial Intelligence, 1st edn. Addison-Wesley Longman Publishing Co., Inc., Boston (1999)
3. Foerster, J., Assael, I.A., de Freitas, N., Whiteson, S.: Learning to communicate with deep multi-agent reinforcement learning. In: Lee, D.D., Sugiyama, M., Luxburg, U.V., Guyon, I., Garnett, R. (eds.) Advances in Neural Information Processing Systems, vol. 29, pp. 2137–2145. Curran Associates, Inc. (2016)
4. Hausknecht, M.J., Stone, P.: Deep recurrent q-learning for partially observable MDPs. In: AAAI Fall Symposia (2015)
5. Hernandez-Leal, P., Kartal, B., Taylor, M.E.: A survey and critique of multiagent deep reinforcement learning. Auton. Agents Multi-Agent Syst. **33**(6), 750–797 (2019)
6. Hoshen, Y.: Vain: attentional multi-agent predictive modeling. In: Guyon, I., et al. (eds.) Advances in Neural Information Processing Systems, vol. 30, pp. 2701–2711. Curran Associates, Inc. (2017)
7. Jackson, D., Ratnieks, F.: Communication in ants. Curr. Biol. **16**, R570–R574 (2006)

8. Kingma, D.P., Ba, J.: Adam: a method for stochastic optimization. In: International Conference on Learning Representations, December 2014

9. Long, P., Fan, T., Liao, X., Liu, W., Zhang, H., Pan, J.: Towards optimally decentralized multi-robot collision avoidance via deep reinforcement learning. In: 2018 IEEE International Conference on Robotics and Automation (ICRA), pp. 6252–6259, May 2018

10. Mnih, V., et al.: Playing atari with deep reinforcement learning. In: NIPS Deep Learning Workshop (2013)

11. Nguyen, T.T., Nguyen, N.D., Nahavandi, S.: Deep reinforcement learning for multi-agent systems: A review of challenges, solutions and applications. CoRR abs/1812.11794 (2018). http://arxiv.org/abs/1812.11794

12. Oroojlooyjadid, A., Hajinezhad, D.: A review of cooperative multi-agent deep reinforcement learning. ArXiv abs/1908.03963 (2019)

13. Papoudakis, G., Christianos, F., Rahman, A., Albrecht, S.V.: Dealing with nonstationarity in multi-agent deep reinforcement learning. CoRR abs/1906.04737 (2019). http://arxiv.org/abs/1906.04737

14. Peng, P., et al.: Multiagent bidirectionally-coordinated nets for learning to play starcraft combat games. CoRR abs/1703.10069 (2017). http://arxiv.org/abs/1703.10069

15. Silver, D., et al.: A general reinforcement learning algorithm that masters chess, shogi, and go through self-play. Science **362**(6419), 1140–1144 (2018)

16. Simões, D., Lau, N., Reis, L.P.: Multi-agent deep reinforcement learning with emergent communication. In: 2019 International Joint Conference on Neural Networks (IJCNN), pp. 1–8, July 2019

17. Sukhbaatar, S., Szlam, A., Fergus, R.: Learning multiagent communication with backpropagation. In: Proceedings of the 30th International Conference on Neural Information Processing Systems, NIPS 2016, pp. 2252–2260. Curran Associates Inc., Red Hook (2016)

18. Sutton, R.S., Barto, A.G.: Reinforcement Learning: An Introduction. A Bradford Book, Cambridge (2018)

19. Tampuu, A., et al.: Multiagent cooperation and competition with deep reinforcement learning. PLOS ONE **12**(4), 1–15 (2017). https://doi.org/10.1371/journal.pone.0172395

20. Tan, M.: Multi-agent reinforcement learning: independent vs. cooperative agents. In: In Proceedings of the Tenth International Conference on Machine Learning, pp. 330–337. Morgan Kaufmann (1993)

21. Theis, L., Shi, W., Cunningham, A., Huszár, F.: Lossy image compression with compressive autoencoders (2017)

22. Valogianni, K., Ketter, W., Collins, J.: A multiagent approach to variable-rate electric vehicle charging coordination. In: Proceedings of the 2015 International Conference on Autonomous Agents and Multiagent Systems, AAMAS 2015, pp. 1131–1139 (2015)

Integrating Deep Learning and Non-monotonic Logical Reasoning for Explainable Visual Question Answering

Mohan Sridharan[1]([⊠]) [ID] and Heather Riley[2]

[1] School of Computer Science, University of Birmingham, Birmingham, UK
m.sridharan@bham.ac.uk
[2] Electrical and Computer Engineering, The University of Auckland,
Auckland, New Zealand
hri1230@aucklanduni.ac.nz

Abstract. Deep learning algorithms represent the state of the art for many problems in robotics and AI. However, they require a large labeled dataset, are computationally expensive, and the learned models are difficult to understand. Our architecture draws inspiration from research in cognitive systems to address these limitations. In the context of answering explanatory questions about scenes and an underlying classification task, our architecture uses non-monotonic logical reasoning with incomplete commonsense domain knowledge, and the features extracted from input images, to answer the input queries. Features from images not processed by such reasoning are mapped to the desired answers using a learned deep network model. In addition, previously unknown state constraints of the domain are learned incrementally and used for subsequent reasoning. Experimental results show that in comparison with an "end to end" deep architecture, our architecture significantly improves accuracy and efficiency of decision making.

1 Introduction

Deep networks represent the state of the art for many problems in robotics and AI. However, training these data-driven models requires many labeled training examples and considerable computational resources, which are not available in many domains. Also, it is difficult to interpret the behavior of the learned models, whereas humans may want to understand the decisions made by an automated reasoning or learning system. This "explainability" also helps designers improve the underlying algorithms[1].

In this paper, we consider Visual Question Answering (VQA) as a motivating example of a complex task requiring explainable reasoning and learning.

---

[1] A journal article based on this work was published in the *Frontiers in AI and Robotics* [15].

© Springer Nature Switzerland AG 2020
N. Bassiliades et al. (Eds.): EUMAS 2020/AT 2020, LNAI 12520, pp. 558–570, 2020.
https://doi.org/10.1007/978-3-030-66412-1_36

Given an image of a scene, the objective is to answer explanatory questions, e.g., about objects and their relationships, or the outcomes of executing actions. Deep networks represent the state of the art for VQA, but exhibit the limitations described above. To address these limitations, we draw inspiration from research in cognitive systems, which indicates that explainable reasoning and learning can be achieved by jointly reasoning with incomplete domain knowledge and learning from experience. For VQA, our architecture uses Convolutional Neural Networks (CNNs) to extract concise visual features from image(s) of any given scene. It first attempts to answer the questions about the scene and an underlying classification problem using non-monotonic logical reasoning with the extracted features and incomplete commonsense domain knowledge. Feature vectors not classified by such reasoning train a decision tree classifier that is then used to answer questions about the classification. The decision tree's output and the feature vectors then train a Recurrent Neural Network (RNN) to answer the questions. Furthermore, feature vectors that are misclassified (or not classified) are used to learn constraints for subsequent reasoning.

For evaluation, we consider VQA while: (i) estimating the stability of configurations of simulated blocks; and (ii) recognizing traffic signs in a benchmark image dataset. We also consider a simulated robot computing and executing plans. We do not consider benchmark datasets and algorithms for VQA that focus on generalizing across domains, and do not support our architecture's capabilities. Our focus is very different; we want to explore the interplay between commonsense reasoning and learning for *explainable, reliable, and efficient scene understanding in any given domain*, especially when a large labeled dataset is not available. Experimental results show a significant improvement in accuracy, efficiency, and the ability to compute correct plans, in comparison with an architecture based only on deep networks. For a more detailed description of this work and additional experimental results, please see [15].

2   Related Work

Although deep networks represent state of the art for VQA [9] and other pattern recognition tasks, they are computationally expensive, require large, labeled datasets, and make it difficult to understand the internal representations, transfer knowledge, or identify bias. Methods have been developed to understand the operation of deep networks, e.g., by computing the contribution of each neuron in a CNN to the decision [12], or using captions to explain answers to questions [8]. Methods have also been developed to understand the predictions of learning algorithms, e.g., by tracing predictions back to data [6].

The training data requirements (or data bias) of a deep network can be reduced by focusing on data relevant to the task(s) at hand. Examples for VQA include a stacked attention network that prioritizes relevant features [19], or a method that reduces data bias by associating questions with images that require different answers [5]. Learning for VQA has also been made more efficient by answering common questions using domain knowledge [18], and using physics engines that simulate domain knowledge [17].

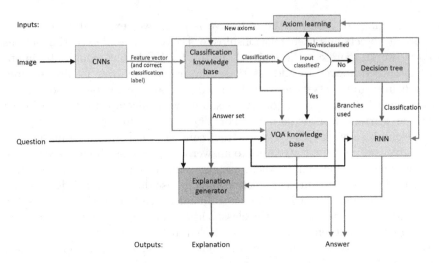

Fig. 1. Overview of our architecture's components.

Cognitive systems research indicates that reliable, efficient, and explainable reasoning and learning can be achieved by jointly reasoning with domain knowledge and learning from experience. Methods that refine first-order logic representations of action operators do not support commonsense reasoning or merging of new, unreliable information [4]. Non-monotonic logics such as Answer Set Prolog (ASP) address these limitations in different applications [2]. ASP has been combined with inductive learning to acquire domain knowledge [7], and combined with probabilistic representations for reasoning [1]. Approaches based on classical first-order logic are not expressive enough, e.g., modeling uncertainty by attaching probabilities to logic statements is not always meaningful. Logic programming methods, by themselves, do not support all desired capabilities such as efficient incremental learning of knowledge and real-time reasoning with large probabilistic components. Frameworks have ben developed to address these problems using principles of step-wise refinement, e.g., reasoning with tightly-coupled transition diagrams at different resolutions [13], or combining commonsense reasoning with active learning and relational reinforcement learning to acquire knowledge [14].

Using VQA as a motivating example, and building on work in cognitive systems and our prior work [10], our architecture combines the complementary strengths of reasoning with commonsense knowledge, inductive learning of knowledge, and deep learning. For more details, please see [15].

3   Architecture

Figure 1 is an overview of our VQA architecture, which embeds commonsense reasoning with incomplete knowledge, and inductive learning, in a deep network architecture. CNN-based feature extractors are trained to extract feature vectors from images of scenes. For each feature vector, an attempt is first made to classify it and explain the decision using non-monotonic logical reasoning. If this method fails, a decision tree is trained to classify the feature vector and explain the outcome. If logical reasoning is used for classification, it is also used to answer explanatory questions about the scene. If a decision tree is used for classification, an RNN is trained to map the decision tree output, image features, and the query, to the answer. Furthermore, decision-tree induction with training data and existing knowledge identifies previously unknown state constraints used for subsequent reasoning. We hypothesize that this architecture will make learning more time and sample efficient, and make decisions more interpretable. Due to space limitations, we briefly describe the components below.

We use three domains for evaluation. The **Structure Stability (SS)** domain (top left, Fig. 2) has 2500 images of structures of simulated blocks from a physics-based simulator; the objective ois to classify structures as being stable or unstable, and to answer explanatory questions, e.g., "why is this structure unstable?" and "what should be done to make this structure stable?". The **Traffic Sign (TS)** domain (bottom left, Fig. 2) uses the BelgiumTS benchmark dataset [16] with ≈ 7000 real-world images of 62 traffic signs. The objective is to classify the signs and answers questions such as "what is the sign's message?" and "how should the driver respond to this sign?". The third domain (used for planning) is introduced later.

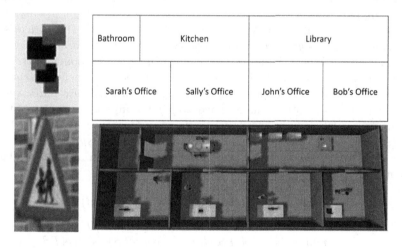

Fig. 2. Illustrative domains: (top left) blocks in SS domain; (bottom left) traffic sign in TS domain; (right) simulated scenario in the RA domain.

3.1   Feature Extraction Using CNNs

Input images are mapped to concise features. The selection of features is based on domain expertise, e.g., features of the SS domain include number of blocks in structure, whether the structure is on a lean etc, and features of the TS domain include primary and secondary colors and symbols, shape of the sign etc. For each feature, a simple CNN was trained and additional layers added until training accuracy converged. For more complex features, previously trained CNN models can be fine-tuned. The code for this component is in our online repository [11].

3.2   Classification Using Non-monotonic Logical Reasoning or Decision Trees

A class label is assigned to the extracted feature vector using one of two methods: (i) non-monotonic logical reasoning; or (ii) a learned decision tree.

ASP Reasoning with Commonsense Knowledge: ASP is a declarative language based on stable model semantics. Each literal can be true, false or unknown, and the agent reasoning with domain knowledge does not believe anything that it is not forced to believe. ASP can represent recursive definitions, defaults, causal relations, and language constructs difficult to express in classical logic formalisms [3]. ASP supports *default negation*, *epistemic disjunction*, and non-monotonic logical reasoning, i.e., it can revise previously held conclusions based on new evidence, which aids in the recovery from errors made by reasoning with incomplete knowledge.

A domain description in ASP has a *system description* $\mathcal{D}$ and a *history* $\mathcal{H}$. $\mathcal{D}$ has a *sorted signature* Σ and axioms. Σ has *basic sorts*, *statics*, i.e., domain attributes whose values do not change, *fluents*, i.e., domain attributes whose values can change over time, and *actions*. Basic sorts include *structure*, *color*, and *size* for SS domain; and *main_color*, *other_color*, *main_symbol* etc for TS domain; both domains have *step* for temporal reasoning. Statics and fluents model domain attributes, e.g., *num_blocks(structure, num)* and *stable(structure)* in SS domain, and the relations *primary_symbol(sign, main_symbol)* and *primary_color(sign, main_color)* in TS domain. Axioms of $\mathcal{D}$ govern dynamics; in our domains, they include:

$$stable(S) \leftarrow num\_blocks(S, 2), \neg structure\_type(S, lean)$$
$$sign\_type(TS, no\_parking) \leftarrow primary\_color(TS, blue),$$
$$primary\_symbol(TS, blank), \; cross(TS), \; shape(TS, circle)$$

History $\mathcal{H}$ is usually a record of fluents observed to be true or false at a particular time step, and the occurrence of an action at a particular time step. This notion is expanded to include default statements that are true in all but certain exceptional circumstances. e.g., "structures with two blocks of the same size are usually stable". For robotics examples, please see [13].

Reasoning is achieved by translating the domain representation to a program $\Pi(\mathcal{D}, \mathcal{H})$ in CR-Prolog, a variant of ASP. Each *answer set* of $\Pi(\mathcal{D}, \mathcal{H})$ represents the beliefs of an agent associated with Π. Planning and diagnostics are reduced to computing answer sets of ASP programs. ASP programs for our domains are in our repository [11]. For the classification task in our domains, relevant literals in the answer set provide the class label and an explanation for this label. The accuracy of the decisions made depends on the accuracy and extent of the knowledge encoded, but encoding comprehensive domain knowledge is difficult. The decision of what (and how much) knowledge to encode is made by the designer.

Decision Tree Classifier: If ASP-based inference cannot assign class labels, the feature vector is mapped to a class label using a decision tree classifier learned from labeled data. Non-leaf nodes of the tree split the feature vector examples based on values of particular features. Each such node is also associated with samples that satisfy the values of the features along the path from the root node, with the leaf nodes representing class labels. We use a standard implementation of a decision tree classifier based on the Gini measure of information gain. Note that this tree's search space is limited since it only considers samples that could not be classified by ASP-based reasoning.

3.3 Answering Explanatory Questions

Existing software, controlled vocabulary, and templates of language models and parts of speech, are used to transcribe questions to text and a relational representation, and to generate answers as text that may be converted to speech.

If ASP-based reasoning is able to classify the image feature vector, it is also used to answer questions about the underlying scene. To provide such answers, we revise the signature and axioms of $\mathcal{D}$, e.g., sorts such as *query_type* and *answer_type*, relations to represent abstract attributes, and axioms to reason with these attributes and construct answers. The answer set(s) of the corresponding program $\Pi(\mathcal{D}, \mathcal{H})$ are computed and parsed to extract relevant literals that form the answer. If the decision tree is used to classify the image feature vector, an LSTM network-based RNN is trained to answer the questions based on the feature vector, class label, and a vector representing the transcribed query. To build the RNN, we start with one hidden layer and add more layers until the accuracy converges. In our domains, the RNN had as many as $26 - 30$ hidden layers. The code used is in our repository [11].

3.4 Learning State Constraints

In many domains, the encoded knowledge is incomplete or changes over time, resulting in incorrect or sub-optimal decisions, e.g., a traffic sign can be misclassified. Our architecture supports incremental learning of domain knowledge, specifically using decision tree induction to learn state constraints. In the context of VQA, we first identify training examples that are not classified or are misclassified based on existing knowledge, and built a decision tree. Next, we identify paths in the tree supported by a sufficient number of examples; these correspond to partial state descriptions and class labels that occur frequently. These paths are used to create candidate constraints. We then generalize the candidate axioms to remove over-specifications, e.g., the first two axioms (below) generalize to the third one:

$$\neg stable(S) \textbf{ if } num\_blocks(S, 3), \ base(S, wide), \ struc\_type(S, lean)$$
$$\neg stable(S) \textbf{ if } num\_blocks(S, 3), \ base(S, narrow), \ struc\_type(S, lean)$$
$$\neg stable(S) \textbf{ if } num\_blocks(S, 3), \ struc\_type(S, lean)$$

The candidate axioms are validated by adding them to the ASP program and testing that they do not violate any of the relevant training examples.

3.5   Planning with Domain Knowledge

We also extend reasoning to planning in the **Robot Assistant (RA)** domain, in which a simulated robot observes the domain, moves to deliver messages to people, and answers explanatory questions. Figure 2(right) shows a simulated scenario. In other work, we have coupled ASP-based reasoning with probabilistic reasoning to account for the uncertainty in sensing and actuation [13]. Here, we temporarily abstract away the probabilistic models of uncertainty, focus on the interplay between reasoning and learning, and evaluate the effect of added noise.

To support planning in the RA domain, we construct a signature Σ with sorts such as *place*, *robot*, and *object*; fluents such as $msg\_status(mid, person, status)$ and $loc(agent, place)$; statics such as $next\_to(place, place)$; and actions that include relations such as $move(robot, place)$ and $deliver(robot, msg\_id, person)$. For ease of explanation, we assume that the locations of people are determined by external sensors, and the locations of objects are statics. Axioms of $\mathcal{D}$ include:

$$move(rob_1, L) \textbf{ causes } loc(rob_1, L)$$
$$loc(P, L) \textbf{ if } work\_place(P, L), \ not\neg loc(P, L)$$
$$\textbf{impossible } move(rob_1, L) \textbf{ if } loc(rob_1, L)$$

to encode causal laws, constraints, and executability conditions. After adding a goal and helper axioms, answer sets of $\Pi(\mathcal{D}, \mathcal{H})$ include a plan of actions, and missing constraints can be learned as described in Sect. 3.4.

4   Experimental Setup and Results

We experimentally evaluated four hypotheses:

- (**H1**) Our architecture outperforms an architecture based on just deep networks for classification and VQA with small training datasets;
- (**H2**) Our architecture provides intuitive answers to explanatory questions;

- (**H3**) Our architecture uses learned constraints to improve the ability to answer questions; and
- (**H4**) Our architecture supports planning and uses learned axioms to improve plan quality.

Hypotheses $H1$, $H2$ and $H3$ are evaluated in the SS and TS domains in the context of VQA; $H4$ is evaluated in the RA domain in the context of planning and VQA. Accuracy was used as the primary performance measure. Accuracy was measured by: (a) comparing the assigned labels with the ground truth labels for classification; and (b) heuristically computing whether the answer mentions all image attributes relevant to the question posed (for VQA); relevance was established by a human expert, one of the authors of this paper. Plan quality was measured as the ability to compute minimal and correct plans that achieves the goal on execution. Two-thirds of the available data is used to train the deep networks and other models, using the remaining data for testing. For each image, we randomly chose from the suitable questions for training and testing, and report the average of multiple such trials. Also, unless stated otherwise, all claims are statistically significant.

Execution Example 1 *[Question Answering, TS domain].* Consider a scenario in the TS Domain with the following exchange for a particular input (test) image.

- Classification question: "what is the sign's message?"
- Architecture's answer: "uneven surfaces ahead".
- When asked to explain the reason for this answer, the architecture identifies the features extracted: (i) triangle-shaped; (ii) main color is white and border color is red; (iii) no background image; (iv) bumpy-road symbol.
- ASP-based inference with domain knowledge and literals of image features is unable to classify the sign.
- Extracted features were processed using the trained decision tree, which only used the sign's colors to assign class label. Colors are normally insufficient for classification, but the decision tree is only trained to classify signs that cannot be classified using existing knowledge.
- The decision tree output, feature vector, and question, were processed by trained RNN to provide the answer.

For other examples such as the image of SS domain in top left of Fig. 2, domain knowledge is sufficient for classification and answering questions.

4.1   Experimental Results: VQA + Learn Axiom

To evaluate $H1$ and $H2$, we ran trials in which we varied the size of the training dataset, and compared the accuracy of our architecture with a baseline CNN-RNN architecture. Due to space constraints, we only summarize VQA accuracy in Fig. 3. We observe that our architecture is better than the baseline architecture based on just deep networks for small training datasets. Classification accuracy (not shown) increases with the size of the training set but VQA accuracy does not because it also depends on the complexity of the questions. The accuracy improvement is more pronounced in the more complex (TS) domain.

Next, we designed an ASP program for the SS domain with eight axioms related to stability, randomly chose four to be removed, and examined the ability to learn these axioms and use them for classification and VQA, with number of labeled training examples ranging from 100 to 2000. Since the TS domain has many more axioms and labeled examples, each experimental trial examines the effect of removing a quarter of the axioms (randomly), with the number of training examples varying from 100 to 4000. Results averaged over 30 such trials are summarized in Fig. 4; the blue ("Original KB") bars represent baseline and the orange ("Learned KB") bars show results with the learned axioms. Our approach incrementally learns previously unknown axioms, and using axioms improves VQA (and classification) accuracy significantly; these results support $H3$.

4.2   Experimental Results: Learn Axiom + Plan

We evaluated the ability to learn axioms and use them for planning in the RA domain. The robot had to use domain knowledge to plan, classify, and answer questions. Results (100 trials) indicate a VQA accuracy of 82% with just 500 labeled images. We first examine an execution trace.

Execution Example 2 *[Question Answering, RA Domain].* The robot has to deliver messages from John to Sally, and return to John to answer questions.

- The robot was initially in John's office. The computed plan had the robot move through the library and the kitchen to Sally's office, deliver the message to Sally, and return to John's office through the same route.
- During plan execution, the robot captures and processes images of the scenes. After returning to John's office, the robot discusses plans, observations, and beliefs with the humans. Some statements in the exchange:
  John's question: "is Sally's location cluttered?"
  Robot's answer: "Yes".
  When asked, robot provides an **explanation** for this decision: "Sally is in her office. Objects observed are Sally's chair, desk, and computer, and a cup, chair, and plate. The room is cluttered because the cup, chair and plate are not usually in that room."

Next, we evaluated the ability to learn and use axioms. In this domain, there is default knowledge about the initial locations of people (i.e., their office) and objects, unless the defaults are negated by other knowledge or observations. Including such knowledge allows the robot to efficiently compute minimal and correct plans, e.g., when trying to deliver messages to a particular person. However, this default knowledge may not be known in advance and may change with

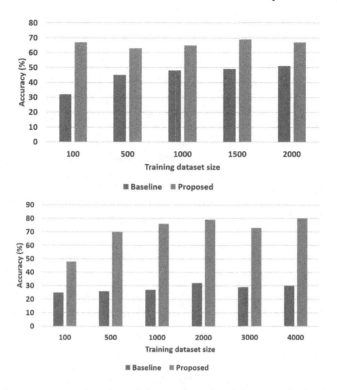

Fig. 3. VQA accuracy as a function of the number of training samples in the SS domain (top) and TS domain (bottom). (Color figure online)

time. In all our trials, our approach was able to accurately and efficiently learn unknown information about such defaults and their exceptions.

Finally, we ran 100 paired trials to explore the impact of learned axioms on planning. In each trial, we randomly chose a particular goal and initial conditions, and measured the ability to computer minimal and correct plans before and after learning previously unknown axioms. The validity of a plan is established by executing it in simulation. Results obtained without the learned axioms were computed as a ratio of the results with the learned axioms. Before axiom learning, the robot often explored an incorrect location (e.g., for a person) based on other considerations (e.g., distance to the room) and ended up having to replan. After learning the axioms, the robot eliminated irrelevant paths in the transition diagram from further consideration; we observe a (statistically) significant improvement in performance. For instance, in the absence of the learned axioms, the robot computes four times as many plans taking more than six times as much time in any given trial (on average) as when the learned axioms were used for reasoning. Even the time taken to compute each plan is significantly higher in the absence of the learned axioms. For a more detailed description of results of additional experiments conducted in simulation and on physical robots, please see [15].

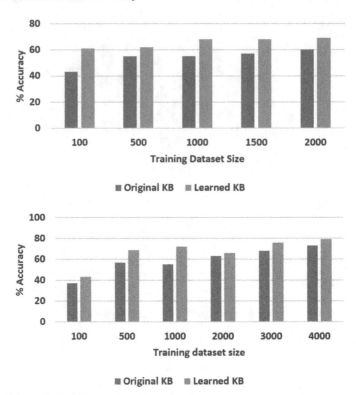

Fig. 4. Comparison of VQA accuracy with and without axiom learning in the SS domain (top) and TS domain (bottom). Reasoning with the learned axioms improves accuracy. (Color figure online)

5 Discussion and Conclusions

For many critical problems in robotics and AI, explainability can help identify errors, design better algorithms, and improve trust in automated reasoning and learning algorithms. In this paper, we considered VQA as a motivating example of such a problem that requires explainability in reasoning and learning. Deep networks represent state of the art for VQA, but they are computationally expensive, require large training datasets, and make it difficult to support explainability. Inspired by research in cognitive systems, our architecture couples representation, reasoning and interactive learning, and exploits the complementary strengths of deep learning, non-monotonic logical reasoning with commonsense knowledge, and decision tree induction. Experimental results on benchmark datasets and simulated images indicate that in comparison with baseline deep networks, our architecture provides: (i) better accuracy, sample efficiency and time complexity on classification problems; (ii) more reliable answers to explanatory questions; and (iii) support for learning unknown state constraints. Future work will further explore the use of reasoning with commonsense knowledge to direct and better understand the operation of deep network architectures, and evaluate our architecture in more complex domains.

References

1. Baral, C., Gelfond, M., Rushton, N.: Probabilistic reasoning with answer sets. Theory Pract. Logic Program. **9**(1), 57–144 (2009)
2. Erdem, E., Gelfond, M., Leone, N.: Applications of answer set programming. AI Mag. **37**(3), 53–68 (2016)
3. Gelfond, M., Kahl, Y.: Knowledge Representation, Reasoning and the Design of Intelligent Agents. Cambridge University Press, Cambridge (2014)
4. Gil, Y.: Learning by experimentation: incremental refinement of incomplete planning domains. In: International Conference on Machine Learning, pp. 87–95 (1994)
5. Goyal, Y., Khot, T., Stay, D.S., Batra, D., Parikh, D.: Making the V in VQA matter: elevating the role of image understanding in visual question answering. In: International Conference on Computer Vision and Pattern Recognition, pp. 6325–6334 (2017)
6. Koh, P.W., Liang, P.: Understanding black-box predictions via influence functions. In: International Conference on Machine Learning (ICML), pp. 1885–1894 (2017)
7. Law, M., Russo, A., Broda, K.: The complexity and generality of learning answer set programs. Artif. Intell. **259**, 110–146 (2018)
8. Li, Q., Fu, J., Yu, D., Mei, T., Luo, J.: Tell-and-answer: towards explainable visual question answering using attributes and captions. Technical report (2018). https://arxiv.org/abs/1801.09041
9. Malinowski, M., Rohrbach, M., Fritz, M.: Ask your neurons: a deep learning approach to visual question answering. Int. J. Comput. Vision **125**, 110–135 (2017). https://doi.org/10.1007/s11263-017-1038-2
10. Riley, H., Sridharan, M.: Non-monotonic logical reasoning and deep learning for explainable visual question answering. In: International Conference on Human-Agent Interaction (2018)
11. Riley, H., Sridharan, M.: Software for paper (2018). https://github.com/hril230/masters_code
12. Selvaraju, R., Cogswell, M., Das, A., Vedantam, R., Parikh, D., Batra, D.: Grad-CAM: visual explanations from deep networks via gradient-based localization. In: International Conference on Computer Vision, pp. 618–626 (2017)
13. Sridharan, M., Gelfond, M., Zhang, S., Wyatt, J.: REBA: a refinement-based architecture for knowledge representation and reasoning in robotics. J. Artif. Intell. Res. **65**, 87–180 (2019)
14. Sridharan, M., Meadows, B.: Knowledge representation and interactive learning of domain knowledge for human-robot collaboration. Adv. Cognit. Syst. **7**, 69–88 (2018)
15. Sridharan, M., Riley, H.: Integrating non-monotonic logical reasoning and inductive learning with deep learning for explainable visual question answering. Front. Robot. AI, Spec. Issue Comb. Symb. Reason. Data-Driven Learn. Decis.-Mak. **6**, 125 (2019)
16. Timofte, R., Mathias, M., Benenson, R., Gool, L.V.: Traffic sign recognition - how far are we from the solution? In: International Joint Conference on Neural Networks (IJCNN), pp. 1–8 (2013)

17. Wagner, M., et al.: Answering visual *what-if* questions: from actions to predicted scene descriptions. In: Leal-Taixé, L., Roth, S. (eds.) ECCV 2018. LNCS, vol. 11129, pp. 521–537. Springer, Cham (2019). https://doi.org/10.1007/978-3-030-11009-3_32

18. Wang, P., Wu, Q., Shen, C., van den Hengel, A., Dick, A.R.: Explicit knowledge-based reasoning for visual question answering. In: International Joint Conference on Artificial Intelligence (2017)

19. Yang, Z., He, X., Gao, J., Deng, L., Smola, A.J.: Stacked attention networks for image question answering. In: IEEE Conference on Computer Vision and Pattern Recognition (CVPR), pp. 21–29 (2016)

Multiagent Task Coordination as Task Allocation Plus Task Responsibility

Vahid Yazdanpanah[1]([⊠]), Mehdi Dastani[2], Shaheen Fatima[3],
Nicholas R. Jennings[4], Devrim M. Yazan[5], and Henk Zijm[5]

[1] University of Southampton, Southampton, UK
V.Yazdanpanah@soton.ac.uk
[2] Utrecht University, Utrecht, The Netherlands
M.M.Dastani@uu.nl
[3] Loughborough University, Loughborough, UK
S.S.Fatima@lboro.ac.uk
[4] Imperial College London, London, UK
N.Jennings@imperial.ac.uk
[5] University of Twente, Enschede, The Netherlands
{D.M.Yazan,W.H.M.Zijm}@utwente.nl

Abstract. In this work, we present a dynamic Task Coordination framework (TasCore) for multiagent systems. Here task coordination refers to a twofold problem where an exogenously imposed state of affairs should be satisfied by a multiagent system. To address this problem the involved agents or agent groups need to be assigned tasks to fulfill (task allocation) and the behavior of these agents needs to be monitored to evaluate whether their tasks are fulfilled so that responsibility for dismissing tasks can be determined (task responsibility). We believe the allocation of tasks should regard both the strategic abilities of agents and their epistemic limitations. To date, however, existing work on the application of logical strategic reasoning for task allocation assumes perfect information for agents (dismissing imperfect information settings) and allocates tasks to individual agents (dismissing task allocation to agent groups). In TasCore, we address this gap by modeling *task allocation* using imperfect information semantics for strategic reasoning and integrate it with a notion of *task responsibility*. We formally verify properties of TasCore: on validity as well as stability of task allocations and fairness as well as non-monotonicity of task responsibilities.

Keywords: Multiagent systems · Task coordination · Responsibility and accountability · Strategic reasoning · Temporal and modal logic

1 Introduction

The focus of this paper is on the *task coordination (TC)* problem in Multiagent Systems (MAS). Given a state of affairs (exogenously imposed to, and to be fulfilled by, a MAS) it is crucial to have a systematic method for *allocating tasks*

© Springer Nature Switzerland AG 2020
N. Bassiliades et al. (Eds.): EUMAS 2020/AT 2020, LNAI 12520, pp. 571–588, 2020.
https://doi.org/10.1007/978-3-030-66412-1_37

to involved agents (prospectively) and *ascribing responsibilities* to agents based on what they were tasked to do and what they actually did (in retrospection). This way, TC consists of two stages: Task Allocation (TA) and Task Responsibility (TR) [36]. Given a collective state of affairs (to be fulfilled by the MAS) TA is concerned with how the state of affairs should be distributed among agent groups in terms of *tasks*. Then TR is about evaluating the behavior of the MAS in fulfilling the tasks and ascribing (a degree of) *responsibility* to agents for dismissing/fulfilling tasks. In other words, following the allocation of a task to an agent or agent group, we see the group as being responsible for fulfilling the allocated task. In a MAS, there might be tasks for which no *single* agent has the required capabilities. Our work allows such tasks to be allocated to capable agent *groups* (instead of dismissing the task).

We believe that ascribing responsibility to agents is justified only if the task allocation process takes into account the *strategic abilities* of the agents and their *epistemic limitations*. In brief, strategic abilities of agents or agent groups determine what they can do in the MAS (e.g., in terms of properties that they can ensure or preclude), while epistemic limitations are about their potential (lack of) knowledge about the MAS. Capturing these two aspects for allocating tasks and ascribing responsibilities in MAS are focal points of this work.

In general, the TC problem relates to studies on Multiagent Organizational (MAO) frameworks, task allocation methods in MAS, and responsibility reasoning concepts in multiagent settings. Reviewing MAO frameworks in [13,21,24,32], their focus is on how the MAO is organized in terms of its organizational structure and high level constructs to enable role/task allocation. They abstract from the exact procedure of task allocation and in some cases assume the availability of agents that are capable of fulfilling any assigned task. In MAO—as a whole or within any of its organizational units—task allocation techniques are often employed as a module to determine who should do what task(s) to ensure the organizational goals (as a collectively defined state of affairs). For instance, given the goal to have a picnic in the countryside for a two-member organization, one agent can be responsible for driving while the other one is responsible for food (i.e., allocating the task to drive to one agent and to prepare the food to the other one). Then some relevant questions are: "which one is able to drive (*strategic* ability)?"; "who knows about potential food allergies (*epistemic* limitations in *imperfect information* settings[1])?"; "who is able to cook/drive at what time, as the journey/picnic evolves (*temporal* dynamics)?". In most real-world environments, the task allocation procedure should capture all three aspects, i.e., addressing strategic, epistemic, and temporal aspects. However, no such method currently exists [3,9,11,16,26,29]. In [16], authors capture *strategic* abilities but

---

[1] By *imperfect information* settings, we refer to the generic class of multiagent settings in which agents do not (necessarily) have perfect information about their environment and all the potential consequences of their actions (also referred to as agents with *epistemic limitations*). In most real-life applications of MAS, agents are epistemically limited. Thus, it is crucial to develop a model that is capable of capturing imperfect information settings.

under a perfect information assumption. The presented approach in [29] relaxes this assumption for *team formation*—as a related problem to TC—but has less temporal expressivity than [16].

Recall that in the picnic example, we said that an agent is *responsible* for food or for driving. That is, when we arrive at the picnic spot with no food, we can justifiably see the agent (to whom we allocated the task of providing food) as being responsible for the (undesirable) outcome. We argue that dealing with autonomous agents, allocating tasks (prospectively) needs to be complemented by a (retrospective) phase of responsibility allocation. In TasCore, the TR component answers this question by ascribing a degree of responsibility to each agent, for an outcome φ. This means seeing an agent as being responsible (for φ) to a degree proportional to its contribution to the occurrence of φ. To model task responsibility, we apply multiagent responsibility reasoning methods [2,35], in particular the notion of *strategic responsibility* [37], for ascription of responsibility in such imperfect information settings.

To overcome these shortcomings, we develop TasCore: a dynamic task coordination method based on formal methods for multiagent strategic reasoning. TasCore is a two-part method: its prospective part is focused on task allocation, while the retrospective part is focused on task responsibility. For task allocation, we allocate a task to an agent or agent group that is capable of handling it. One aspect that we see as being crucial to capture is the fact that the agents' ability is limited to their knowledge about the environment. It is therefore necessary to capture strategic abilities in imperfect information settings and to avoid assuming perfect information for all agents. In imperfect information settings, agent A may be able to guarantee the fulfillment of a task τ today, but not necessarily tomorrow—due to the information and strategies that it possesses today and may miss tomorrow[2]. This is a missing aspect in most task allocation methods for MAS. It also motivates our approach to use the semantic machinery of multiagent logics that are expressive for modeling temporal and strategic properties in imperfect information settings. The retrospective part of TasCore is focused on the history and is about ascribing responsibility to agents—considering what they did and what they had to do. As we allocate tasks by taking into account agents' abilities, the fulfillment of an allocated task is a justified expectation, hence agents that violate this expectation are justifiably responsible for it. Against this background, for the first time, this paper captures strategic abilities *under imperfect information* for task allocation in multiagent settings and applies *responsibility reasoning* for task coordination in organizational settings.

We present a conceptual analysis on the TC problem and recall formal preliminaries in Sect. 2. Then, in Sect. 3, we specify TasCore and its components. In Sects. 4 and 5, we focus on the allocation of tasks and ascription of responsibil-

---

[2] For instance, an agent may be perfectly capable of planning a chain of actions to prepare a meal at home—given all the equipment—but not able to do so if she moves to a picnic camp the day after, e.g., due to inconvenient weather and the lack of equipment.

ities, respectively. We formally verify properties of TasCore: on validity as well as stability of task allocations and fairness as well as non-monotonicity of task responsibilities. Finally, Sect. 6 discusses the relevance and implementability of TasCore and presents the concluding remarks.

2 Conceptual Analysis and Formal Preliminaries

In this section, we present the intuition behind our work, analyze conceptual aspects of TC, and recall key formal notions that form the basis of the TasCore framework.

2.1 Conceptual Analysis

Imagine a family picnic scenario in which parents allocate different picnic-related tasks to their children *Alex*, *Bob*, *Cathy*, and see them responsible for organizing a picnic that satisfies some expectations. They expect the picnic to be organized in a clean picnic spot in the country side and to have home-made food for the day. In this case, having a desirable picnic is a collective state of affairs. Then the first bit of the task coordination problem is to see *"who is able to do what"* in a temporal, strategic, and imperfect information setting. The second bit is about *"seeing who did what"* and ascribing responsibility to agents for the outcome. We deem that the second phase (task responsibility) is justified only if in the first phase (task allocation), the strategic, temporal, and epistemic aspects of the setting are captured. For instance, if we give the task of driving to the spot to Cathy while she has no driving licence, it is not reasonable to blame her for dismissing the allocated task. The analogous case is valid for giving the task of cleaning to Bob, if he cannot distinguish clean from unclean (e.g., due to a visual impairment). We later show how these aspects can be modeled and verified using the semantic machinery of logics for multiagent strategic reasoning. In addition to these aspects, there are a number of high-level principles that are essential to effective task coordination:

Suitability of the collective state of affairs: given the set of agents and their available actions, fulfilling some states of affairs are impossible in principle, regardless of how we allocate tasks among the agents. For instance, in our picnic scenario, a modest picnic is reasonable to expect but seeing the small group organize a festival might not be a *suitable* (collective) state of affairs.

Validity of task allocation: given a *suitable* state of affairs, the process of task allocation ought to be such that all that should be done is allocated, neither more nor less (i.e., if all agents fulfill their tasks, the collective state of affairs will be fulfilled). For instance, if we tell Alex to take care of driving and give the task of cleaning the place to Bob and Cathy, the allocation is not valid as preparing food is dismissed. Basically, we see an allocation of tasks as *valid* if by assuming that all agents fulfill their allocated task, we can see the collective state of affairs will ensure.

Justifiability of task responsibility: task responsibility should be consistent with task allocation. In other words, seeing a group as being responsible is not independent of what tasks they were given in an earlier stage. For instance, if we give the task of preparing food to Alex, then it is not *justifiable* to see Bob responsible for the food quality even if he is able to cook. This shows that verifying task responsibility is not merely based on agents' ability but builds upon the implemented task allocation and the history of realized actions (i.e., the evolution of the multiagent system).

In subsequent sections, we provide a formal account of these principles and then fulfill them using TasCore. To specify the multiagent setting, we use *Concurrent Epistemic Game Structures* (CEGS) [1] as it allows: modeling the behavior of a MAS, specifying strategic abilities of agents, and representing agents' knowledge. Then we focus on task and responsibility allocation in TasCore.

2.2   Concurrent Epistemic Game Structures

To model multiagent systems and analyze their strategic behavior under imperfect information, we use *Concurrent Epistemic Game Structures (CEGS)* [1] as an epistemic extension of Concurrent Game Structures [4]. In addition to being expressive for specifying temporal, strategic, and epistemic aspects of MAS, models that use CEGS can benefit from standard model checking platforms (e.g., ATL-based model-checking tools in [23,25]) to verify properties of the modeled MAS.

Concurrent Epistemic Game Structures: Formally, a *concurrent epistemic game structure* is a tuple $\mathcal{M} = \langle \Sigma, Q, Act, \Pi, \pi, \sim_1, \ldots, \sim_n, d, o \rangle$ where: $\Sigma = \{a_1, \ldots, a_n\}$ is a finite non-empty set of *agents*; Q is a finite non-empty set of *states*; Act is a finite set of atomic *actions*; Π a set of atomic propositions; $\pi : \Pi \mapsto 2^Q$ is a propositional evaluation function; $\sim_a \subseteq Q \times Q$ is an *epistemic indistinguishability relation* for each agent $a \in \Sigma$ (we assume that $\sim_a$ is an equivalence relation, where $q \sim_a q'$ indicates that states q and q' are indistinguishable to a); function $d : \Sigma \times Q \mapsto \mathcal{P}(Act)$ specifies the sets of actions available to agents at each state (we require that the same actions be available to an agent in indistinguishable states, i.e., $d(a, q) = d(a, q')$ whenever $q \sim_a q'$); and o is a deterministic transition function that assigns the outcome state $q' = o(q, \alpha_1, \ldots, \alpha_n)$ to state q and a tuple of actions $\alpha_i \in d(i, q)$ that can be executed by Σ in q.

To enable the specification of a collective state of affairs, we adopt the standard language of LTL (Linear Temporal Logic [30]). Formulas of the language $\mathcal{L}_{LTL}$ are defined by the following syntax, $\varphi, \psi ::= p \mid \neg\varphi \mid \varphi \wedge \psi \mid \bigcirc\varphi \mid \varphi\mathcal{U}\psi \mid \square\varphi$ where $p \in \Pi$ is a proposition, $\neg$ and $\wedge$ are standard logical operators, $\bigcirc\varphi$ means that φ is true in the next state of $\mathcal{M}$, $\psi\mathcal{U}\varphi$ means that ψ has to hold at least until φ becomes true; and $\square\varphi$ means that φ is always true. For convenience, $\diamond\varphi$ is defined as an equivalent to $\neg\square\neg\varphi$ meaning that φ is eventually true. To represent and reason about *strategies* and *outcomes* in agent systems with imperfect information, we make use of the following auxiliary notions. (References to elements of $\mathcal{M}$ are to elements of a CEGS $\mathcal{M}$ modeling a given multiagent system, e.g., we write Q instead of Q in $\mathcal{M}$.)

Successors and Computations: For two states q and q', we say q' is a *successor* of q if there exist actions $\alpha_i \epsilon d(i, q)$ for $i \epsilon \{1, \ldots, n\}$ in q such that $q' = o(q, \alpha_1, \ldots, \alpha_n)$, i.e., agents in Σ can collectively guarantee in q that q' will be the next system state. A *computation* of a CEGS $\mathcal{M}$ is an infinite sequence of states $\lambda = q_0, q_1, \ldots$ such that, for all $k > 0$, we have that q_k is a successor of q_{k-1}. We refer to a computation that starts in q as a q-*computation*. For $k \in \{0, 1, \ldots\}$, we denote the k'th state in λ by $\lambda[k]$, and $\lambda[0, k]$ and $\lambda[k, \infty]$ respectively denote the finite prefix $q_0, \ldots, q_k$ and infinite suffix $q_k, q_{k+1}, \ldots$ of λ. We refer to any two arbitrary states q_k and q_{k+1} as two *consecutive* states in $\lambda[k, \infty]$. Finally, we say a finite sequence of states $q_0, \ldots, q_n$ is a q-*history* if $q_n = q$, $n \geq 1$, and for all $0 \leq k < n$ we have that q_{k+1} is a successor of q_k. We denote a q-history that starts in q_k and has n steps with $\lambda[q_k, n]$. The set of q-histories for all $q \epsilon Q$ is denoted by $\mathcal{H}$.

Strategies and Outcomes: A *memoryless imperfect information strategy*[3] for an agent $a \in \Sigma$ is a function $\zeta_a : Q \mapsto Act$ such that, for all $q \in Q$: (1) $\zeta_a(q) \in d(q, a)$, and (2) $q \sim_a q'$ implies $\zeta_a(q) = \zeta_a(q')$. For a group of agents $\Gamma \subseteq \Sigma$, a *collective strategy* $Z_\Gamma = \{\zeta_a \mid a \epsilon \Gamma\}$ is an indexed set of strategies, one for every $a \epsilon \Gamma$. Then, $out(q, Z_\Gamma)$ is defined as the set of potential q-computations that agents in Γ can enforce by following their corresponding strategies in Z_Γ. We extend the notion to sets of states $\chi \subseteq Q$ in the straightforward way: $out(\chi, Z_\Gamma) = \bigcup_{q' \epsilon \chi} out(q', Z_\Gamma)$.

Uniform Strategies: A uniform strategy is one in which agents select the same actions in all states where they have the same information available to them. In particular, if agent $a \in \Sigma$ is uncertain whether the current state is q or q', then a should select the same action in q and in q'. Formally, a strategy ζ_a for agent $a \in \Sigma$ is called *uniform* if for any pair of states q, q' such that $q \sim_a q'$, $\zeta_a(q) = \zeta_a(q')$. A strategy Z_Γ is uniform if it is uniform for every $a \in \Gamma \subseteq \Sigma$. Realistic modeling of strategic ability under imperfect information requires restricting attention to uniform strategies only.

3   Specification

To specify TasCore, four components are required: a behavior modeling machinery, a collective state of affairs (given to the MAS), the task allocating component, and the task responsibility component.

   Given a CEGS $\mathcal{M} = \langle \Sigma, Q, Act, \Pi, \pi, \sim_1, \ldots, \sim_n, d, o \rangle$ that models the behavior of the multiagent system, a collective state of affairs G_q (given to MAS in state

---

[3] We relax the assumption that agents have a perfect memory. Thus, as a natural choice in imperfect information settings, we focus on memoryless strategies and avoid other forms of strategy that assume the ability of agents to recall the evolution of the MAS, e.g., perfect recall strategies (see [8]). This captures a more generic class of agents as we do not expect them to have the capacity to strategize based on their memory of events.

q) is a set of formulae from $\mathcal{L}_{LTL}$.[4] Then the aim of the task allocation process is to ensure that all $\varphi \in G_q$ hold. Finally, the task responsibility process ascribes a (backward-looking) degree of responsibility to agents given a history $h \in \mathcal{H}$.

In this approach, $\mathcal{M}$ is a standard component (adapted from [1]) for modeling the behavior of a MAS in imperfect information settings. Then G_q specifies the set of properties that are expected to be satisfied by the agents collectively (we call it the collective state of affairs). Then what each subgroup ought to do is determined by *task allocation* and who is responsible to what extent by *task responsibility*. We present the exact specification of both in upcoming sections. This means TasCore is built on a behavior-modeling CEGS, a local state of affairs, and allocates (forward-looking) tasks as well as (backward-looking) responsibilities to agent groups. Note that all the elements of TasCore are defined independently of any desirable properties. So, how an element should be specified such that desirable properties emerge is not intrinsic to the model but will be discussed in the following sections. This is to allow a level of flexibility and to enable capturing context-dependent concerns. TasCore supports task coordination using two forms of prospective and retrospective organizational reasoning. The former is about allocating tasks to agents (Sect. 4) while the latter is about verifying what went wrong/right and who is responsible to what extent (Sect. 5).

4   Allocating Tasks in TasCore

Following the specification of TasCore components, and given a local state of affairs G_q (to be fulfilled collectively by agents in the MAS), *"who should do what, and why?"* is the main question that we aim to answer in this section[5]. We deem that the ascription of tasks to agents or agent groups (with the aim to fulfill a collective state of affairs) should take into account the *temporal, strategic*, and *epistemic* aspects of multiagent systems. Temporality is both about the specification of tasks (e.g., whether some property should be maintained or only

---

[4] One may opt to specify the collective state of affairs simply using propositions from Π. However, this will limit the expressivity. Our LTL formulas enable the specification of temporally-bounded tasks. E.g., simply giving a task to ensure that food is ready may lead to giving the task to someone with a strategy to ensure it in the next week while we aim to have the picnic during the weekend (e.g., this can be achieved by ensuring that food is prepared before the weekend using the *"until"* modality in LTL). Moreover, for task specification, it is necessary to be able to express a dynamic behavioral (semantic) form of task (which is more expressive than a static propositional (syntactic) notion of a task). For instance, one may give (an agent) the task of not only ensuring the tidiness of a place but also to maintain it. Such a notion of task is not about ensuring a state or a set of states (where tidiness holds) but about ensuring a chain/path/computation of states (through which the tidiness is maintained). In general, temporal modalities of LTL enable capturing such temporal subtleties.

[5] *"Who gets what, and why?"* is the focus of the next section (we acknowledge the title of [33]).

achieved once) and also about the state of the environment (e.g., whether a task can be allocated at a current state q_1 (today) or at potential states that follow q_1 (tomorrow)). Then it is reasonable to allocate a task to who—either a single agent or a group of agents—is *capable* of fulfilling it. While some consider this as strategic ability, we emphasize the importance of knowledge in *"being capable of doing something"*. Basically, as highlighted by [1], the strategic ability of an agent group is limited to their knowledge of the system and its dynamics (e.g., in a physical confrontation, even if agent a_i is strong enough to capture an adversary agent a_j, not knowing that a_j is located in front of a_i, avoids it exercising its potential). This is why we focus on *uniform* strategies (see Sect. 2.2).

Prior to allocating tasks and building on the notion of a uniform strategy, we say a local state of affairs G_q is *suitable* for a multiagent system (the *suitability* principle) only if the grand coalition Σ has a uniform strategy in state q to ensure it (note that we are referring to components of a particular CEGS $\mathcal{M}$ that models a given MAS). Then given a suitable G_q, a task allocation is *valid* (the *validity* principle) only if we assume the compliance of agents with allocated tasks entail that G_q.

In the following, we specify the task allocation component of TasCore and show its desirable properties.

Definition 1. *Given a multiagent system $\mathcal{M}$, a local state of affairs $G_q = \varphi_1 \wedge \cdots \wedge \varphi_m$, and the assignment of $\varphi_i (1 \leq i \leq m)$ to agent group $\Gamma_i \subseteq \Sigma$, the assignment set $\{\langle \varphi_1, \Gamma_1 \rangle, \ldots, \langle \varphi_m, \Gamma_m \rangle\}$ is a TasCore task allocation iff (1) Γ_i is a minimal group with a uniform strategy in q to ensure φ_i and (2) for any two intersecting groups Γ_i and $\Gamma_j (1 \leq j \leq m)$, $\Gamma_i \cup \Gamma_j$ is a minimal group with a uniform strategy in q to ensure $\varphi_i \wedge \varphi_j$.*

As discussed earlier, this approach for allocating tasks captures the strategic abilities of agents and their epistemic limitations for allocating tasks. (We highlight that the allocation process is based on perfect information about agents, their abilities, and knowledge. Our reference to imperfect information is to the information that is available to involved agents in the MAS.) The following theorem shows that for a suitable state of affairs, there exists a task allocation that satisfies the two conditions in Definition 1. In q, we modelcheck to find minimal agent groups capable of ensuring propositional components of G_q and generate a task allocation that gives the task of ensuring each component φ_i (the ith components of G_q) to an agent group Γ_i which has a uniform strategy to ensure φ_i. This procedure generates a valid allocation if G_q is a suitable state of affairs.

Theorem 1. *Given a suitable G_q, there exists a valid task allocation in q.*

Proof. We provide a constructive proof by presenting a task allocation procedure based on ATL_{ir} model checking. First, for all $\varphi_i \in G_q = \{\varphi_1 \wedge \cdots \wedge \varphi_m\}$, we use standard ATL_{ir} model checking [23] and apply a minimality-checking loop to generate the set, denoted by Φ_i, of minimal agent groups $\Gamma \subseteq \Sigma$ with the ability to ensure φ_i from q. Given all Φ_i, the set of allocation tuples $\{\langle \varphi_1, \Gamma_1 \rangle, \ldots, \langle \varphi_m, \Gamma_m \rangle\}$ in which the two conditions of Definition 1 are satisfied is non-empty thanks to the suitability of G_q. ∎

Note that we take the collective state of affairs and allocate each component to capable groups—with a uniform strategy to fulfill it. Recalling the notion of uniform strategy (in Sect. 2.1), given that the group has a collective strategy, each agent has an individual strategy that contributes to the fulfillment of the task. This way of allocating tasks to group, leaves it to the group to decide what ultimate individual action (in each state) individuals should take to see to it that the task is fulfilled. This is to see agents in an organizational setting as autonomous entities to whom we do not tell what exact action to take. We see each agent as a group member able to collaborate to execute a strategy, based on a repository of actions, such that the task that is allocated to the group is fulfilled. We later show how we can (retrospectively) ascribe a degree of responsibility to each individual based on what they did (outcome of collective actions) and what they had to do (allocated tasks).[6]

As discussed, the notion of the *collective state of affairs* G_q is a local notion to specify what properties are valuable in an organizational setting. Hence they ought to be satisfied by agents in Σ collectively. G_q says what is expected to be satisfied being in state q assuming that it contains expectations that were given previously and are not yet satisfied but valuable. In other words, agents are not required to keep a repository of tasks. This enables the expression of real-life situations where dynamic task allocation is desirable (i.e., it allows changing the state of affairs as the system evolves, hence gives the ability to give a different task to a group). Our approach to consider a local state of affairs gives a form of deterministic Markov property [27] to task allocation in TasCore. In other words, local suitability can be extended and if satisfied globally (in all states) guarantees the existence of a valid task allocation in all states of MAS.

Proposition 1. *If G_q is suitable for all states $q \in Q$, the procedure presented in (the proof of) Theorem 1 generates a valid task allocation in all states regardless of the evolution of the system, represented by a materialized q-history $h \in \mathcal{H}$.*

Proof. Note that G_q is a local notion (on state q) and that its suitability is independent of any q-history h. Then to prove, we need to show that having a G_q, suitable in all $q \in Q$, there exists a valid task allocation in each q. This is given by Theorem 1. ∎

Under TasCore, agent groups to which we allocate a task may intersect. E.g., if we allocate φ_1 to Γ_1 and φ_2 to Γ_2, agents in $\Gamma_1 \cap \Gamma_2$ ought to take a part in ensuring both φ_1 and φ_2. Then one may ask whether in such cases, agents in the intersection are supposed to choose between two alternatives and only satisfy one task while dismissing the other one. The following proposition shows that

---

[6] One may argue that task allocation is unnecessary as we can simply allocate G_q to Σ. While such a suggestion works under the perfect information assumption, the epistemic limitations of agents means such a simplistic approach will not work under imperfect information. This is because a uniform strategy for Γ to ensure a property is not necessarily uniform for all super-groups $\Gamma' \supset \Gamma$ as knowledge does not necessarily grow monotonically in groups.

using the proposed procedure in Theorem 1, allocated tasks are not mutually exclusive.

Proposition 2. *Given a suitable G_q, there are no two exclusively satisfiable tasks allocated to a group.*

Proof. Follows directly from the second condition (in Definition 1) that any generated allocation—by the procedure presented in Theorem 1—satisfies. Note that the concern is not only about mutual exclusivity in a *logical* sense, but in a *strategic* sense (i.e., that the available strategies for a group to fulfill two properties are coherent). ∎

In organizational settings, agents are assumed to be a part of a collaborative practice, hence ought to fulfill their set of allocated tasks. But a valid question is whether they have any rational reason to avoid fulfilling and deviate from their tasks. In other words, whether an allocation is stable (in game-theoretic terminology). The following theorem shows that a TasCore task allocation is stable as no group has a rational incentive for deviation.

Theorem 2. *Given a suitable collective state of affairs G_q, a TasCore task allocation under the procedure presented in Theorem 1 is stable in the sense that no agent group has a rational incentive to deviate from its allocated task(s).*

Proof. Building on Proposition 2, for any allocated task to a group Γ—under the proposed procedure—any group Γ has a uniform strategy to fulfill the task. Hence, no group in Σ has a rational incentive to deviate from the allocation (i.e., to not fulfill the tasks). Note the assumption that agents are a member of the organization, hence prefer to deliver their tasks if they are able to do so. ∎

Note that we are focused on the availability of a "task-fulfilling" strategy to agent groups—assuming that allocated tasks ought to be fulfilled if such a strategy exists—and abstract from agents' preferences.

Example 1. In our example (see Fig. 1), there are various ways (with different levels of control) which the parents can use to express their expectation. One way would be to have $G_{q_0} = \{\bigcirc f, \bigcirc \bigcirc s, \bigcirc \bigcirc \bigcirc t\}$ which is an explicit form with temporal limitations. Another more-relaxed form is $G_q = \{\bigcirc f, \diamond s, \diamond t\}$. For both forms the first element can be allocated as a task to $\{A, B\}$, the second one to $\{C\}$, and the last one to $\{A, C\}$. Note that for a strategy to be uniform for a group, it should be accessible to them from all the indistinguishable states. In this case: $\{A, B\}$ has a strategy to ensure $\bigcirc f$ from both q_0 and q_1; $\{C\}$ can ensure s either eventually ($\diamond s$) or in the state after the next ($\bigcirc \bigcirc s$); and $\{A, B\}$ can ensure tidiness.

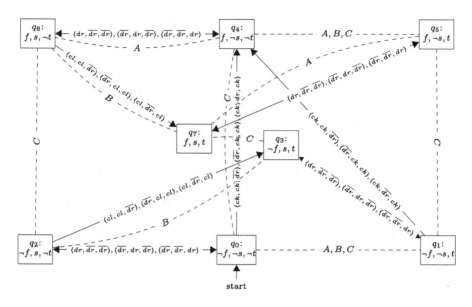

Fig. 1. Set of agents $\Sigma=\{A,B,C\}$ (Alex, Bob, Cathy), set of actions $Act=\{ck,dr,cl,id\}$ (cooking, driving, cleaning, idle, and for any $act \in Act$, $\overline{act}$ denotes any action in $Act \setminus \{act\}$), and set of propositions $\Pi = \{f,s,t\}$ (ready food, being at spot, tidiness). For any unmentioned action profile α and arbitrary $q \in Q$, we have that $o(q,\alpha) = q$ (i.e., we avoided an α self-loop on every node). To model epistemic limitations, we assume that cooking (act ck) is only possible at home while cleaning (act cl) is only possible at the picnic spot. To model epistemic limitations, some states are indistinguishable for some agents represented by dashed lines labeled with the agent(s) who can not distinguish the states that the dashed line connects.

5   Ascribing Responsibility in TasCore

Assuming that the allocation of tasks to agents definitely results in the fulfillment of tasks—and in turn brings about the collective state of affairs—is unreasonable in real-life environments. This is because autonomous agents are not artifacts but entities that may opt to exercise their autonomy and do otherwise. In organizational settings, such undesirable behavior is possible. But in addition—and based on the assumption that agents are a member of the organization, hence expected to deliver their allocated tasks—we can ascribe a degree of responsibility to agents. In particular, to those who contributed to a collective state of affairs being unfulfilled. This form of reasoning is known in the literature on responsibility as *backward-looking responsibility* [31,37]. Basically, the reasoner observes the materialized history of events/actions (that lead to a given outcome situation S) and with the knowledge about agents' available actions, ascribes responsibility to agents who contributed to the occurrence of S or to those who could avoid $\neg S$ but apparently did not exercise their avoidance potential. The former causality-oriented approach is known as *causal responsibility* [12] based on the potential to bring about, while the latter is known as *strategic responsibil-*

ity [37] based on the potential to avoid. One may refer to this backward-looking form of responsibility reasoning as evaluating the blameworthiness if S is known to be a normatively undesirable state of affairs.

In our picnic scenario, imagine that the whole group arrives at the picnic spot with no food (states q_2 or q_3 in Fig. 1). Who is responsible for such an undesirable outcome? Which agent(s) or agent group(s) can be blamed? And to what extent? One can look at the history of events (i.e., who did what at any state in the chain of states that ends in the current state), check the list of allocated tasks in those states, and justifiably blame a group of agents that ought to deliver the task of preparing food. This procedure is in particular a justifiable one in imperfect information settings if the agents' strategic ability and their epistemic limitations were taken into account in the preceding task allocation procedure.

To ascribe responsibility to agents, we adopt the approach described in [37]. The responsibility reasoning notion of [37] is in-line with our approach in TasCore as we both focus on imperfect information settings. Following this, we see a group Γ as being responsible for an outcome φ in state q given a history h if φ holds in q while ensuring $\neg\varphi$ was among the allocated tasks to Γ in a state (other than q) in h. Formally:

Definition 2. *Given a multiagent system $\mathcal{M}$, TasCore task allocation, and the materialized q-history h, an agent group Γ is q-responsible for φ iff (1) φ does not hold in state q and (2) φ is among the allocated tasks to Γ in a state $q' \in h$ for $q \neq q'$.*

In this view, a group that is tasked to ensure φ is responsible for it until φ becomes true. Note that being responsible for φ does not imply any negative connotation here. (That is why we avoid using the negatively-loaded term "*blameworthy*" here.) This is crucial to note because a group might have the plan to bring about φ in a next state or maybe they are assigned a new task in the dynamic setting of TasCore. Moreover, note that a φ being unfulfilled in q directly implies that any state of affairs that contains φ is not satisfied. For instance, in our picnic scenario, having no food in q_2 implies that the collective state of affairs "*well-organized picnic*" $G_{q_0} = \{f, s, t\}$ that was given to the multi-agent system in q_0 is unsatisfied in q_2. This notion of responsibility can be seen as a measure of the collective state of affairs satisfaction in organizational settings. If ensuring G_q is given to a MAS, a state in which no group is responsible for any $\varphi \in G_q$ is a state where G_q is fulfilled completely.

Proposition 3. *Given a suitable state of affairs G_q, the TasCore task allocation, and the materialized history $h = q, \ldots, q'$, we have that G_q is satisfied in q' if no agent group Γ is q'-responsible for any $\varphi \in G_q$.*

Proof. Having no group Γ being q'-responsible for any $\varphi \in G_q$ implies that for all φ, either of the two conditions in Definition 2 does not hold in q'. As TasCore task allocation is applied, the second condition holds for all φ. Thus the first condition does not hold for all φ, i.e., that all the elements of G_q are satisfied in q'.   ∎

Theorem 3. *Given a suitable G_q, there exists a nonempty set of states $S \subseteq Q$ such that for all $q' \in S$, no group Γ is responsible for any arbitrary $\varphi \in G_q$ based on history $q, \dots, q'$.*

Proof. In q, such a set in which $\bigwedge_{\varphi \in G_q} \varphi$ holds is foreseeable as, for ensuring a suitable G_q, a uniform strategy is available to Σ. ∎

As we discussed, responsibility ascription is to agent *groups*. Then a problem that we face in multiagent systems—known as the *responsibility gap* problem—concerns situations where a group of agents is responsible for an outcome but the share of each individual agent is not clear [28]. In principle, the question is about the extent of responsibility of each agent for an unfulfilled task. This is a translation from group responsibility to individual responsibility. We highlighted that as we are dealing with tasks in TasCore, responsibility sharing techniques for MAS (e.g., [12,37]) are not directly applicable. In TasCore, an agent might be in two different groups with different tasks (coalitional dynamics) and moreover, may get involved in different tasks as the system evolves (temporal dynamics). Note that if agent group Γ with n members is found to be responsible for a given φ, sharing the responsibility equally is not a reasonable approach as each individual possesses different levels of knowledge and ability, and hence had different levels of contribution to φ. A standard approach is to consider *fairness* properties[7]:

Theorem 4. *Given a suitable collective state of affairs G_q, TasCore task allocation, and q'–history $h = q, \dots, q'$, the degree of q'-responsibility of agent $a \in \Sigma$ for $\varphi \in G_q$, denoted by $\Re(a, \varphi, h)$, satisfies the fairness properties if $\Re(a, \varphi, h) = \Phi(a, \rho)$ where Φ returns the Shapley value of agents in the cooperative game $\langle\ \rangle \Sigma$, ρ in which $\rho(\Gamma \subseteq \Sigma)$ is equal to 1 if $\Gamma' \subseteq \Gamma$ is q'-responsible for φ based on h and 0 otherwise.*

Proof. The game is such that—using the Shapley value—each agent receives a degree of responsibility with respect to its contribution to responsible groups. ∎

Thanks to the properties of the Shapley value, this degree of responsibility is a fair way for bridging the responsibility gap and distributing the responsibility of each individual in TasCore. As a direct result we have:

Proposition 4. *For a given $\varphi \in G_q$ and history h, we have that $\sum_{a \in \Sigma} \Re(a, \varphi, h) \in \{0, 1\}$.*

Proof. Having h, either q is a state in h or not. If not, then φ is not among the allocated tasks to any agent group in Σ hence the degree of responsibility for all agents $a \in \Sigma$ is zero. The same holds if q is in h and φ holds in the last state of

---

[7] By fairness, we are referring to *Shapley*-based notion of fairness that possesses the properties of symmetry, additivity, efficiency, and dummy player [34].

h. The only case in which some agent groups are responsible for φ based on h is when φ does not hold in the last state of h; and in this case, the summation is equal to one thanks to the efficiency property of the degree.   ∎

Based on this result we have that in organizational settings, for any allocated but unfulfilled task, there exists a responsible group if the task manager follows TasCore. Note that as we are assuming suitability (for the collective state of affairs) and discussing the ascription of responsibility degrees in the context of task coordination, impossibilities for which no group is responsible are avoided automatically. The next property is about the evolution of the notion of task responsibility and the degree of responsibility though a given history.

Proposition 5. *For a given $\varphi \in G_q$ and history h, the notion of responsibility and its degree are non-monotonic through the temporal evolution of h: formally, (1) being q_i–responsible for φ (for a $q_i \in h$) does not imply being q_{i+1}–responsible for φ. Moreover, (2) $\Re(a, \varphi, h'')$ (for $h'' = q, \ldots, q', \ldots, q''$) is not necessarily higher or lower than $\Re(a, \varphi, h')$ (for $h' = q, \ldots, q'$ as a part the materialized history h'').*

Proof. For part (1), we have that φ may hold in one state of the history but not in the next one. In the states where it holds, no group is responsible for it. For (2), we can rely on part (1) but also have that due to dynamism of TasCore, the task to satisfy φ can be given to new groups through h (e.g., to ensure a level of fault-tolerance). Therefore the number of responsible groups is not fixed temporally (through the history h).   ∎

Note that TasCore is neither aware of nor requires agents' preferences as it respects a *separation of concerns* in the process of responsibility ascription (i.e., it is not designed based on the knowledge about agents' internal settings, hence is operational in multiagent organizational settings under imperfect information). Moreover, we assume that being involved in TasCore implies that the agent is expected to dedicate its resources (represented in terms of its available actions in each state) to the organization and is expected to fulfill its allocated tasks.

Example 2. Having the allocation of tasks according to Example 1 and the history q_0, q_2, q_3, the collective state of affairs G_{q_0} is not yet fulfilled. Going back through the steps of history, the task of preparing food was allocated to $\{A, B\}$ and they had a uniform strategy to avoid it remaining unfulfilled. They each have the degree of responsibility of $1/2$ due to their symmetric contribution.[8]

6   Discussion and Concluding Remarks

We discuss the relevance of task coordination under imperfect information, argue the implementability of TasCore by showing steps toward operationalization, and relate our contribution to past work.

---

[8] Note that in general, agents may have various forms of (asymmetric) contribution. Thus, it is not the case that the degree of responsibility of group members is equal in general (see [37]) for a discussion on various responsibility reasoning cases.

Perfect vs. Imperfect Information Settings: Although assuming perfect information is realistic for closed environments (e.g., in production processes or data-base systems), in most real-life applications, an agent's knowledge of the environment, hence of the consequences of its acts, is limited. In our model, we allow the representation of agents with imperfect information and consider uniform collective strategies to capture the epistemic aspect of the notion of strategic ability. This means we can both allocate tasks in imperfect information settings and ascribe responsibility in a justifiable manner. Note that TasCore is also operational in perfect information settings—simply by assuming an empty indistinguishability relation (in CEGS $\mathcal{M}$) for all the agents in Σ. In this way, the presented complexity and experimental results in [16] for the perfect information scenarios can be applied to TasCore if one intends to deploy it in a perfect information task coordination case. In our running example, if agents had perfect information, we could dismiss indistinguishability relations (i.e., by deleting the dashed lines in Fig. 1). Then in the task allocation part of TasCore, agents may have more strategies available to ensure the components of a given state of affairs—as they are not epistemically limited. This in turn affects the responsibility ascription process.

Implementability: As we presented our task coordination concepts and tools using concurrent game structures, then the logical characterization of TasCore is standard. To that end, one can use the epistemic variant of ATL proposed in [22] that adds indistinguishably relations to explicitly specify the epistemic uncertainty of agents. This allows reasoning about the abilities and responsibilities of agent groups under imperfect information. Providing such a logical characterization of our notions also enables the systematic verification of the two parts of TasCore (for task and responsibility allocation). Building on this, one can use standard model-checking tools [25] to implement TasCore as an operational task coordination tool and in turn enable its application in real-life problems (e.g., in the context of business management or collaborative industrial systems).

Given a state of affairs to be ensured by the MAS, TasCore enables tasks to be allocated to agents or agent groups such that their fulfillment leads to the overarching state of affairs being ensured. For task allocation, TasCore is the first model that considers both the epistemic limitations and strategic abilities of agents. Moreover, we allow the allocation of tasks not only to individuals but also to agent groups. We argue that allocation is not enough if we deal with autonomous agents. Thus, following the task allocation, one can use TasCore to ascribe a degree of responsibility to agents with respect to a state of affairs. This work is the first to employ the notion of strategic responsibility for task coordination in MAS.

Our approach to allocate tasks to agents is complementary to *(group) role assignment* in robot systems and open societies [15, 17, 19, 38]. While they generally assume that roles are to be taken by agents, in TasCore we allocate tasks to agents based on their ability to ensure a task and accordingly see them as being responsible for the outcome. In this way TasCore can be used in combination with multiagent organizational frameworks such as *Moise* [21] (more precisely, within each organizational unit and assuming the availability of knowledge about the unit to TasCore).

In relation to the multiagent responsibility and accountability literature [5, 12,35,37], our work applies responsibility reasoning (in specific, the ATL-based notion of strategic responsibility) for task coordination. Based on TasCore's degree of responsibility, one can ascribe blameworthiness and sanctioning penalties to agent groups (e.g., to enforce a given norm in MAS). We also highlight a related but distinguishable approach to this problem that is based on the notion of *causal responsibility* in [2,12,18]. Basically, causal responsibility (as presented in [12]) ascribes a degree of responsibility to agents based on their potential to *provide* a situation while strategic responsibility (as presented in [37]) ascribes responsibility based on their ability to *preclude*. We see these two perspectives as complementarily applicable in different domains.

In TasCore, we dismissed incentivization. We see that an interesting extension is to consider rewarding agents per task fulfillment to provide strategy-proofness. Otherwise, an agent may strategically block its own strategies to avoid the allocation of a task. Rewarding can encourage agents to employ their most *"effective"* strategy, and by effectiveness we are referring to a strategy that enables them to fulfill as many tasks as possible. In principle, rewarding agents following the fulfillment of a task (and sanctioning otherwise) nudges the behavior of economically-motivated and rational agents towards the fulfillment of collective-level organizational goals. To address this, we aim to integrate norm-aware *incentive engineering* techniques [6,7,14] into TasCore and consider *coalition forming* aspects [10,20]. In such a line, the degree of responsibility can be used as a basis to formulate normative notions of blame/praiseworthiness which in turn enables developing sanctioning/rewarding mechanisms. Moreover, in TasCore, we merely focused on physical actions of agents. Thus, another extension is to enrich the repository of actions by adding an explicit representation of communicative actions. Basically, through communicative actions, the agents' epistemic level may change. This extends TasCore and enables us to reason about subcontracting, delegation, commitment-based agreements, and in general scenarios in which agents have *mixed* strategies, consisting of physical and communicative actions.

Acknowledgements. The authors would like to thank the anonymous referees and the conference participants for their valuable comments and suggestions.

References

1. Ågotnes, T., Goranko, V., Jamroga, W., Wooldridge, M.: Knowledge and ability. In: Handbook of Epistemic Logic, pp. 543–589 (2015)
2. Alechina, N., Halpern, J.Y., Logan, B.: Causality, responsibility and blame in team plans. In: AAMAS-2017, pp. 1091–1099 (2017)
3. Alechina, N., van der Hoek, W., Logan, B.: Fair allocation of group tasks according to social norms. In: Bulling, N., van der Torre, L., Villata, S., Jamroga, W., Vasconcelos, W. (eds.) CLIMA 2014. LNCS (LNAI), vol. 8624, pp. 19–34. Springer, Cham (2014). https://doi.org/10.1007/978-3-319-09764-0_2

4. Alur, R., Henzinger, T.A., Kupferman, O.: Alternating-time temporal logic. J. ACM **49**(5), 672–713 (2002)
5. Baldoni, M., Baroglio, C., Micalizio, R.: Accountability, responsibility and robustness in agent organizations. In: Workshop on Responsible AI Agents, pp. 1–8 (2019)
6. Boella, G., Hulstijn, J., Van Der Torre, L.: Virtual organizations as normative multiagent systems. In: HICSS-2005, p. 192c (2005)
7. Boissier, O., Gâteau, B.: Normative multi-agent organizations: modeling, support and control. In: Dagstuhl Seminar Proceedings (2007)
8. Bulling, N., Jamroga, W.: Comparing variants of strategic ability: how uncertainty and memory influence general properties of games. JAAMAS **28**(3), 474–518 (2014). https://doi.org/10.1007/s10458-013-9231-3
9. Campbell, A., Wu, A.S.: Multi-agent role allocation: issues, approaches, and multiple perspectives. JAAMAS **22**(2), 317–355 (2011). https://doi.org/10.1007/s10458-010-9127-4
10. Chalkiadakis, G., Elkind, E., Markakis, E., Polukarov, M., Jennings, N.R.: Cooperative games with overlapping coalitions. J. Artif. Intell. Res. **39**, 179–216 (2010)
11. Chapman, A.C., Micillo, R.A., Kota, R., Jennings, N.R.: Decentralised dynamic task allocation: a practical game theoretic approach. In: AAMAS-2009, pp. 915–922 (2009)
12. Chockler, H., Halpern, J.Y.: Responsibility and blame: a structural-model approach. JAIR **22**, 93–115 (2004)
13. Coutinho, L.R., Sichman, J.S., Boissier, O., et al.: Modeling organization in mas: a comparison of models. In: SEAS-2005, pp. 1–10 (2005)
14. Criado, N., Julián, V., Botti, V., Argente, E.: A norm-based organization management system. In: Padget, J., et al. (eds.) COIN -2009. LNCS (LNAI), vol. 6069, pp. 19–35. Springer, Heidelberg (2010). https://doi.org/10.1007/978-3-642-14962-7_2
15. Dastani, M., Dignum, V., Dignum, F.: Role-assignment in open agent societies. In: AAMAS-2003, pp. 489–496 (2003)
16. Fatima, S.S., Wooldridge, M.: Adaptive task resources allocation in multi-agent systems. In: AGENTS-2001, pp. 537–544 (2001)
17. Frias-Martinez, V., Sklar, E., Parsons, S.: Exploring auction mechanisms for role assignment in teams of autonomous robots. In: Nardi, D., Riedmiller, M., Sammut, C., Santos-Victor, J. (eds.) RoboCup 2004. LNCS (LNAI), vol. 3276, pp. 532–539. Springer, Heidelberg (2005). https://doi.org/10.1007/978-3-540-32256-6_49
18. Friedenberg, M., Halpern, J.Y.: Blameworthiness in multi-agent settings. In: AAAI-2019 (2019)
19. Giordani, S., Lujak, M., Martinelli, F.: A distributed algorithm for the multi-robot task allocation problem. In: García-Pedrajas, N., Herrera, F., Fyfe, C., Benítez, J.M., Ali, M. (eds.) IEA/AIE 2010. LNCS (LNAI), vol. 6096, pp. 721–730. Springer, Heidelberg (2010). https://doi.org/10.1007/978-3-642-13022-9_72
20. Habib, F.R., Polukarov, M., Gerding, E.H.: Optimising social welfare in multi-resource threshold task games. In: An, B., Bazzan, A., Leite, J., Villata, S., van der Torre, L. (eds.) PRIMA 2017. LNCS (LNAI), vol. 10621, pp. 110–126. Springer, Cham (2017). https://doi.org/10.1007/978-3-319-69131-2_7
21. Hannoun, M., Boissier, O., Sichman, J.S., Sayettat, C.: MOISE: an organizational model for multi-agent systems. In: Monard, M.C., Sichman, J.S. (eds.) IBERAMIA/SBIA -2000. LNCS (LNAI), vol. 1952, pp. 156–165. Springer, Heidelberg (2000). https://doi.org/10.1007/3-540-44399-1_17
22. Jamroga, W.: Some remarks on alternating temporal epistemic logic. In: FAMAS-2003, pp. 133–140 (2003)

23. Jamroga, W., Dix, J.: Model checking strategic abilities of agents under incomplete information. In: Coppo, M., Lodi, E., Pinna, G.M. (eds.) ICTCS 2005. LNCS, vol. 3701, pp. 295–308. Springer, Heidelberg (2005). https://doi.org/10.1007/11560586_24

24. Kota, R., Gibbins, N., Jennings, N.R.: Decentralized approaches for self-adaptation in agent organizations. TAAS **7**(1), 1:1–1:28 (2012)

25. Lomuscio, A., Qu, H., Raimondi, F.: MCMAS: a model checker for the verification of multi-agent systems. In: Bouajjani, A., Maler, O. (eds.) CAV 2009. LNCS, vol. 5643, pp. 682–688. Springer, Heidelberg (2009). https://doi.org/10.1007/978-3-642-02658-4_55

26. Macarthur, K.S., Stranders, R., Ramchurn, S., Jennings, N.: A distributed anytime algorithm for dynamic task allocation in multi-agent systems. In: AAAI-2011, pp. 701–706 (2011)

27. Markov, A.A.: The theory of algorithms. Trudy Matematicheskogo Instituta Imeni VA Steklova **42**, 3–375 (1954)

28. Matthias, A.: The responsibility gap: ascribing responsibility for the actions of learning automata. Ethics Inf. Technol. **6**(3), 175–183 (2004). https://doi.org/10.1007/s10676-004-3422-1

29. Nair, R., Tambe, M., Marsella, S.: Team formation for reformation in multiagent domains like robocuprescue. In: Kaminka, G.A., Lima, P.U., Rojas, R. (eds.) RoboCup 2002. LNCS (LNAI), vol. 2752, pp. 150–161. Springer, Heidelberg (2003). https://doi.org/10.1007/978-3-540-45135-8_12

30. Pnueli, A.: The temporal logic of programs. In: SFCS-1977, pp. 46–57 (1977)

31. Van de Poel, I.: The relation between forward-looking and backward-looking responsibility. In: Vincent, N., van de Poel, I., van den Hoven, J. (eds.) Moral responsibility. LOET, vol. 27, pp. 37–52. Springer, Dordrecht (2011). https://doi.org/10.1007/978-94-007-1878-4_3

32. da Rocha Costa, A.C., Dimuro, G.P.: A minimal dynamical mas organization model. In: Handbook of Research on Multi-Agent Systems: Semantics and Dynamics of Organizational Models, pp. 419–445. IGI Global (2009)

33. Roth, A.E.: Who Gets What, and Why: The New Economics of Matchmaking and Market Design. Houghton Mifflin Harcourt, Boston (2015)

34. Shapley, L.S.: A value for n-person games. Contrib. Theory Games **2**(28), 307–317 (1953)

35. Yazdanpanah, V., Dastani, M.: Distant group responsibility in multi-agent systems. In: Baldoni, M., Chopra, A.K., Son, T.C., Hirayama, K., Torroni, P. (eds.) PRIMA 2016. LNCS (LNAI), vol. 9862, pp. 261–278. Springer, Cham (2016). https://doi.org/10.1007/978-3-319-44832-9_16

36. Yazdanpanah, V., Dastani, M., Fatima, S., Jennings, N.R., Yazan, D.M., Zijm, W.H.: Task coordination in multiagent systems. In: AAMAS-20, pp. 2056–2058 (2020)

37. Yazdanpanah, V., Dastani, M., Jamroga, W., Alechina, N., Logan, B.: Strategic responsibility under imperfect information. In: AAMAS-2019, pp. 592–600 (2019)

38. Zhu, H., Zhou, M., Alkins, R.: Group role assignment via a Kuhn-Munkres algorithm-based solution. IEEE Trans. Syst. Man Cybern. Part A: Syst. Hum. **42**(3), 739–750 (2011)

Anytime and Efficient Coalition Formation with Spatial and Temporal Constraints

Luca Capezzuto$^{(\boxtimes)}$ ⓘ, Danesh Tarapore ⓘ, and Sarvapali Ramchurn ⓘ

School of Electronics and Computer Science, University of Southampton,
Southampton, UK
{luca.capezzuto,d.s.tarapore,sdr1}@soton.ac.uk

Abstract. The *Coalition Formation with Spatial and Temporal constraints Problem* (CFSTP) is a multi-agent task scheduling problem where the tasks are spatially distributed, with deadlines and workloads, and the number of agents is typically much smaller than the number of tasks. Thus, the agents have to form coalitions in order to maximise the number of completed tasks. The state-of-the-art CFSTP solver, the *Coalition Formation with Look-Ahead* (CFLA) algorithm, has two main limitations. First, its time complexity is exponential with the number of agents. Second, as we show, its look-ahead technique is not effective in real-world scenarios, such as open multi-agent systems, where new tasks can appear at any time. In this work, we study its design and define an extension, called *Coalition Formation with Improved Look-Ahead* (CFLA2), which achieves better performance. Since we cannot eliminate the limitations of CFLA in CFLA2, we also develop a novel algorithm to solve the CFSTP, the first to be simultaneously anytime, efficient and with convergence guarantee, called *Cluster-based Task Scheduling* (CTS). In tests where the look-ahead technique is highly effective, CTS completes up to 30% (resp. 10%) more tasks than CFLA (resp. CFLA2) while being up to four orders of magnitude faster. Our results affirm CTS as the new state-of-the-art algorithm to solve the CFSTP.

Keywords: Coalition formation · Spatial and temporal constraints · Anytime · Efficient · Convergence guarantee · Disaster response

1 Introduction

Disasters, man-made and natural, can cause severe loss of life, damage to infrastructure and cascading failures in energy systems [1]. In the aftermath of a disaster, first responders have to be deployed to meet the needs of the community. They are responsible for complex tasks such as first aid and infrastructure restoration, which they must perform during periods of high stress and in environments with strict time constraints [4]. During these operations, it is fundamental to act as fast as possible, since any delay can lead to further tragedy and destruction.

© Springer Nature Switzerland AG 2020
N. Bassiliades et al. (Eds.): EUMAS 2020/AT 2020, LNAI 12520, pp. 589–606, 2020.
https://doi.org/10.1007/978-3-030-66412-1_38

We focus on a class of disaster response problems that has been characterised by Ramchurn et al. [23] as *Coalition Formation with Spatial and Temporal constraints Problem* (CFSTP). We use the definitions of *coalition* and *coalition formation* given in [13,23,26]. Hence, a coalition is a flat and task-oriented organisation of agents, short-lived and disbanded when no longer needed, while coalition formation is a consequence of the emergent behaviour of the system [20]. In the CFSTP, the agents (e.g., ambulances or fire brigades) have to decide which tasks they are going to execute (e.g., save victims or extinguish fires). The decision is influenced by how tasks are located in the disaster area, how much time is needed to reach them, how much work they require (e.g., how large a fire is) and their deadlines (e.g., estimated time left before victims perish). Given these conditions, and considering that there could be many more tasks than agents, it is necessary that agents cooperate with each other by forming, disbanding and reforming coalitions over time [26]. Coalitions enable agents to complete tasks more efficiently than working individually. In fact, some tasks may have constraints that could not be satisfied by single agents. For instance, a fire is extinguished faster when multiple fire brigades work on it together, rather than in sequence. Hence, the objective of the CFSTP is to schedule the right coalitions (e.g., the fastest ambulances and fire trucks with the largest water tanks) to the right tasks (e.g., sites with the most victims and the strongest fires) to ensure that as many tasks as possible are completed.

Our interest is in algorithms that are *anytime* (i.e., which can return partial solutions if they are interrupted before completion), have *theoretical properties* and can solve the CFSTP *efficiently* (i.e, approximation algorithms [21]). The reason is that anytime and approximate solutions are fundamental in real-world domains, where it is necessary to have theoretical guarantees, but it may be computationally not feasible or economically undesirable to produce an optimal solution [31]. In particular, as we said above, the faster the disaster response, the lower the losses incurred. We also assume that the agents are situated in an *open* [12] system, that is, at any time agents can join in or leave, and new tasks can appear.

To date, the most effective way of solving the CFSTP is to reduce it to a *Distributed Constraint Optimisation Problem* (DCOP) [9] and solve it with the Max-Sum algorithm [8]. The variants relevant to our scope are *Fast Max-Sum* (FMS) [23] and *Binary Max-Sum* (BinaryMS) [22]. FMS has exponential time, but it can find optimal solutions when the problem is represented by an acyclic factor graph On the other hand, BinaryMS can only find approximate solutions, but it has polynomial time. Nonetheless, since they are both based on binary decision variables, they require a pre-processing phase with exponential time to solve CFSTP instances with n-ary decision variables. Multi-agent approaches that solve problems similar to the CFSTP make use of social insects [7], automated negotiation [10,11,29] and evolutionary computation [30], but without considering the anytime property. In the iTax taxonomy of Korsah et al. [17], the CFSTP is defined as a *Cross-schedule Dependent Single-Task Multi-Robot Time-extended Assignment* (XD [ST-MR-TA]) problem [17].

To date, the approaches proposed to solve XD [ST-MR-TA] problems utilise linear programming [2,15,16], automated negotiation [18] and memetic algorithms [19]. However, either they do not produce anytime solutions [18,19], or do not have theoretical properties [2], or are based on a simpler model [14,16].

Against this background, we focus on the state-of-the-art algorithm to solve the CFSTP, namely, the *Coalition Formation with Look-Ahead* (CFLA) algorithm [24]. Our rationale is that CFLA is anytime and, although its computational time is exponential in the worst case, due to its design [24, Section 6] and to the performance of current computers, a well-engineered implementation can obtain a complete solution to problems with dozens of agents and hundreds of tasks in minutes, when it is not necessary to terminate early. Specifically, this paper advances the state of the art in the following ways.

- We design CFLA2, a novel variant of CFLA that minimises limitations and improves performance.
- Since we cannot eliminate the limitations of CFLA in CFLA2, we propose CTS, the first CFSTP solver to be simultaneously anytime, distributed and with convergence guarantee. CTS asymptotically outperforms both CFLA and CFLA2.

The rest of the paper is organised as follows. In Sect. 2, we give our CFSTP model, while Sect. 3 details CFLA2. Given that CFLA2 keeps the main limitations of CFLA, Sect. 4 presents the CTS algorithm. Section 5 reports an empirical evaluation of CTS in settings where CFLA is very competitive, and Sect. 6 concludes.

2   Problem Formulation

In this section, we present a refined model of the CFSTP [24]. More precisely, we extend the definition of coalition value, define the constraints with fewer and simpler equations, and introduce the concept of solution degree.

2.1   Basic Definitions

Let $V = \{v_1, \ldots, v_m\}$ be a set of m tasks and $A = \{a_1, \ldots, a_n\}$ be a set of n agents. Although not necessary, it is typically assumed that $m \gg n$. Let L_V and L_A be respectively the set of all possible task and agent locations, not necessarily disjoint. Hence, more than one agent or task can be at the same location. Time t is discrete, that is, $t \in \mathbb{N}$, each problem starts at $t = 0$ and agents travel or execute tasks in measurable time units. The time units needed by an agent to travel from one location to another are given by $\rho : A \times (L_A \cup L_V) \times L_V \to \mathbb{N}$. Unlike [24], we put A in the domain of ρ to characterise agents with different speeds. In real-world scenarios, this avoids approximating different speeds to the same one. Task locations do not change over time, while agent locations can. Each task v has a *demand* $D_v = \{w_v, d_v\}$, where $w_v \in \mathbb{R}^+$ is the *workload* of v, or the amount of work required to complete v, and $d_v \in \mathbb{N}$ is the *deadline* of v, or the time until which agents can work on v. Our notion of work will be clear in Sect. 2.3. Hence, workloads can only be positive, and some tasks may have a deadline of zero. In other words, a problem may have tasks that cannot be completed in time, independently of the algorithm chosen to solve it. Tasks can be heterogeneous, in the sense that they may have different demands. We denote the location of agent a at time t by $l_a^t \in L_A \cup L_V$, the times at which a starts and finishes working on task v by $s_a^v \in [0, d_v]$ and $f_a^v \in [s_a^v, d_v]$, respectively, and the *latest deadline* by $d_{max} = \max_{v \in V} d_v$.

2.2   Coalition Allocations

Agents are cooperative [28] and can work together to complete a task. A subset of agents $C \subseteq A$ is called a *coalition*. At time t, the rationale for allocating coalition C to task v is that C completes v in the fewest time units. An *agent allocation* is denoted by $\tau_t^{a \to v}$ and represents the fact that agent a works on task v at time t. The *set of all agent allocations* is denoted by:

$$T = \{\tau_t^{a \to v}\}_{a \in A, v \in V, t \in [0, d_{max}]} \tag{1}$$

and contains all possible agent allocations. A *coalition allocation* is denoted by $\tau_t^{C \to v}$ and represents the fact that coalition C works on task v at time t. Given a set of agent allocations $T' \subseteq T$, and a time $t' \le d_{max}$, the *set of coalition allocations corresponding to T'* over the time period $[0, t']$ is denoted by:

$$\Gamma(T', t') = \{\tau_t^{C \to v} \mid C = \{a \mid \tau_t^{a \to v} \in T'\}, t \le t'\} \tag{2}$$

Furthermore, the *set of all coalition allocations* is denoted by:

$$\Gamma = \Gamma(T, d_{max}) \tag{3}$$

Similar to T, Γ contains all possible coalition allocations. An agent allocation $\tau_t^{a \to v}$ is also denoted as a *singleton coalition allocation* $\tau_t^{\{a\} \to v}$.

2.3   Coalition Values

Each coalition allocation has a *coalition value*, given by the function $u : P(A) \times V \to \mathbb{R}_{\ge 0}$, where $P(A)$ denotes the power set of A and $\mathbb{R}_{\ge 0}$ denotes the set of non-negative real numbers. Unlike [24], we put V in the domain of u to characterise the fact that the same coalition may execute different tasks with different performances. Hence, given a coalition allocation $\tau_t^{C \to v}$, the value $u(C, v)$ expresses the amount of work that coalition C does on task v at each time t. The workload w_v decreases linearly over time, depending only on $u(C, v)$. Coalition values are not necessarily superadditive [25], that is, in general $u(C, v)$ is not required to increase with $|C|$.

2.4   Constraints

There are three constraint types: structural, temporal and spatial. Structural constraints require that each task v can be allocated to only one coalition at a time. This is characterised by the following sets:

$$\forall v \in V, \Gamma_v = \left\{ \Gamma' \subseteq \Gamma : \tau_t^{C_1 \to v}, \tau_t^{C_2 \to v} \in \Gamma' \implies C_1 = C_2 \right\} \qquad (4)$$

With an abuse of notation, we write $\tau_t^{C \to v} \in \Gamma_v$ to indicate that $\tau_t^{C \to v}$ belongs to a not specified set of Γ_v.

Temporal constraints require that each task v can be completed only within its deadline d_v. This is characterised by the function $\Delta : V \times \Gamma \to \{0,1\}$, defined as follows:

$$\Delta(v, \Gamma) = \begin{cases} 1, & \text{if } \exists t \leq d_v : \sum_{t' \leq t,\ \tau_{t'}^{C \to v} \in \Gamma_v} u(C, v) \geq w_v \\ 0, & \text{otherwise} \end{cases} \qquad (5)$$

Equation 5 utilises Γ_v (Eq. 4) to count only well-formed coalition allocations (i.e., that satisfy the structural constraints).

Spatial constraints require that an agent will not start working on a task before reaching it. This is characterised as follows:

$$\forall a \in A, \forall v \in V, \forall t \leq d_v,\ s_a^v \geq t + \rho(a, l_a^t, l_v) \qquad (6)$$

$$\forall a \in A, \forall v_1, v_2 \in V,\ f_a^{v_1} + \rho(a, l_{v_1}, l_{v_2}) \leq s_a^{v_2} \qquad (7)$$

A set of agent allocations $T' \subseteq T$ is called *legal* if it exists a time $t' \leq d_{max}$ such that $\Gamma(T', t')$ satisfies Eq. 5. A set of coalition allocations $\Gamma' \subseteq \Gamma$ that satisfies Eqs. 5, 6 and 7 is called *feasible*. Consequently, at time t, if $\tau_t^{C_1 \to v_1}$ and $\tau_t^{C_2 \to v_2}$ are feasible coalition allocations and $l_{v_1} \neq l_{v_2}$, then $C_1 \cap C_2 = \emptyset$.

2.5   Objective Function

The objective function of the CFSTP is to find a feasible set of coalition allocations that maximises the number of completed tasks:

$$\arg \max_{\Gamma' \subseteq \Gamma} \sum_{v \in V} \Delta(v, \Gamma') \text{ subject to Equations 6 and 7} \qquad (8)$$

To solve Eq. 8, an exhaustive search may require to verify all the possible agent allocations until d_{max}. Consequently, the time complexity of solving the CFSTP is $O(|A| \cdot |V|! \cdot (d_{max})^{|V|})$ [24].

A feasible set of coalition allocations $\Gamma' \subseteq \Gamma$ is called a *solution with degree* k if $\sum_{v \in V} \Delta(v, \Gamma') = k$, with $0 < k \leq |V|$. Moreover, Γ' is called a *partial solution* if $k \leq |V|$ and an *optimal solution*[1] if $k = |V|$. Hence, the argument of the maxima in Eq. 8 is a solution with the highest degree.

Ramchurn et al. [24] proved that the CFSTP is NP-hard [21], and a generalisation of the Team Orienteering Problem [3], which is a generalisation of the Travelling Salesman Problem [27]. As we said in Sect. 1, CFLA is the state-of-the-art CFSTP solver. In the next section, we show how to improve it.

---

[1] Optimal solutions might not exist (Sect. 2.1).

3   Coalition Formation with Improved Look-Ahead

We now present the *Coalition Formation with improved Look-Ahead* (CFLA2), an extension of the CFLA algorithm [24]. More precisely, its look-ahead technique (Sect. 3.4) has two modifications that, as we shall see in Sect. 5, enhance the overall performance.

The concept of CFLA2 is the same as CFLA, but for completeness we briefly report it in Sect. 3.1. After that, we detail the procedures that compose CFLA2, explaining how they differ from the ones of CFLA. Finally, we list the limitations that CFLA2 continues to keep from CFLA, which are the rationale for our new algorithm in Sect. 4.

CFLA and CFLA2 have the same four phases, but [24] describes them in three algorithms. For readability purposes, we describe them in four algorithms.

3.1   The Concept of CFLA2

CFLA2 is a centralised, anytime and greedy algorithm that solves Eq. 8 by maximising the working time of the agents and minimising the time required by coalitions to complete tasks. It is divided into four phases:

1. Defining the legal agent allocations (Sect. 3.2).
2. For each task v, choosing the best coalition C (Sect. 3.3).
3. For each task v, doing a 1-step look-ahead (Sect. 3.4) to define its *degree* δ_v, or the number of tasks that can be completed after the completion of v.
4. At each time $t \in [0, d_{max}]$, allocating a task not yet completed and with the highest degree (Sect. 3.5).

3.2   Phase 1: Defining the Legal Agent Allocations

At time t, Algorithm 1 determines which free agents[2] (A^t_{free}) can reach which uncompleted tasks (V_{unc}) before their deadlines. The resulting set of legal agent allocations is denoted by L_t. This phase is identical in CFLA.

3.3   Phase 2: Selecting the Best Coalition for Each Task

Given a task v and a set of legal agent allocations L_t (computed by Algorithm 1), Algorithm 2 returns the *Earliest-Completion-First* (ECF) coalition C^*_v that can be allocated to v. More precisely, the algorithm minimises both the size of C^*_v and the time at which it completes v. This is achieved by iterating from the smallest to the largest possible coalition size (Line 5) and iterating through all the possible coalitions of each size (Line 6). When the procedure finds a coalition C that can complete v within its deadline d_v (Line 7), then $|C|$ is the minimum size of the coalitions that can complete v. Hence, C^*_v is identified among the coalitions that have size $|C|$ (lines 8–11).

---

[2] That is, agents who neither are travelling to nor working on a task.

Algorithm 1: getLegalAgentAllocations (Phase 1 of CFLA2)

Input: time t
Output: the set of legal agent allocations at time t
1 $L_t \leftarrow \emptyset$
2 **for** $a \in A_{free}^t$ **do** // for each free agent a
3   **for** $v \in V_{unc}$ **do** // for each uncompleted task v
4   **if** $t + \rho(a, l_a^t, l_v) \leq d_v$ **then** // if a can reach v at t within d_v
5              $L_t \leftarrow L_t \cup \{\tau_{t'}^{a \rightarrow v}\}_{t+\rho(a,l_a^t,l_v) \leq t' \leq d_v}$

Algorithm 2: ECF (Phase 2 of CFLA2)

Input: task v, a set of legal agent allocations L_t
Output: ECF coalition C
1 $A_v^t \leftarrow$ define from L_t the agents that can reach v at t within d_v
2 $C_v^* \leftarrow \emptyset$ // the ECF coalition
3 $t_v^* \leftarrow d_v + 1$ // time at which C_v^* completes v
4 $i \leftarrow 1$
5 **while** $i \leq |A_v^t|$ and $C_v^* = \emptyset$ **do**
6   **for** $C \in$ all combinations of i agents in A_v^t **do**
7   **if** $\sum_{\tau_{t'}^{C \rightarrow v} \in \Gamma_v,\ C' \subseteq C,\ t' \in [t, d_v]} u(C, v) \geq w_v$ **then**
8              $t_{minmax} \leftarrow \min_{t_{max}} \left(w_v - \sum_{\tau_{t'}^{C \rightarrow v} \in \Gamma_v,\ C' \subseteq C,\ t' \in [t, t_{max}]} u(C, v) \right)$
9   **if** $t_{minmax} < t_v^*$ **then**
10                 $t_v^* \leftarrow t_{minmax}$
11                 $C_v^* \leftarrow C$
12     $i \leftarrow i + 1$

Unlike the original formulation [24, Algorithm 2], Algorithm 2 clarifies that the minimum coalition size has to be determined by iterating through the subsets of the combinations[3] of A_v^t, which is the set of free agents that at time t can reach v within d_v.

3.4 Phase 3: Defining the Degree of Each Task

Given a task v, Algorithm 3 performs a 1-step look-ahead technique (i.e., a brute force procedure) to define its degree δ_v (Sect. 3.1). At Line 8, with a procedure similar to Line 5 in Algorithm 2, it checks how many tasks can be completed after the completion of v.

Algorithm 3 differs from the original [24, Algorithm 3] in two points. First, it only considers uncompleted tasks that have a deadline greater or equal to d_v (Line 4). This prevents from counting tasks that can be completed before the

---

[3] To date, the most efficient technique to enumerate all such combinations is the Gray binary code [6, Section 7.2.1.1].

Algorithm 3: lookAhead (Phase 3 of CFLA2)

Input: task v, its ECF coalition C_v^*, the set of all agent allocations T
Output: the degree δ_v of task v

1   $\delta_v \leftarrow 0$
2   $f_v \leftarrow$ time at which C_v^* completes v
3   **for** $v_2 \in V_{unc} \setminus \{v\}$ **do**
4   **if** $d_{v_2} \geq d_v$ **then**
5          $A_{free}^{f_v} \leftarrow$ agents that are free at f_v // derived from C_v^* and T
6          $A^{d_{v_2}} \leftarrow$ select from $A_{free}^{f_v}$ the agents that can reach v_2 within d_{v_2}
7          $i \leftarrow 1$
8   **while** $i \leq |A^{d_{v_2}}|$ **do**
9   **for** $C \in$ *all combinations of i agents in $A^{d_{v_2}}$* **do**
                 // if C can complete v_2
10   **if** $\sum_{\tau_t^{C' \rightarrow v} \in \Gamma_v,\ C' \subseteq C,\ t \in [f_v, d_{v_2}]} u(C, v) \geq w_v$ **then**
11                      $\delta_v \leftarrow \delta_v + 1 + (1 - \eta_{v_2})$
12                      $i \leftarrow |A^{d_{v_2}}|$ // break external loop too
13   **break**
14              $i \leftarrow i + 1$

---

completion of v. In fact, as defined in Sect. 3.1, δ_v represents the number of tasks that can be completed only after the completion of v. Second, at Line 11, δ_v is not just incremented by 1, but also by $1 - \eta_{v_2}$, where η_{v_2} is the normalisation of w_{v_2} in the interval $[w_{min}, w_{max}]$, with w_{min} and w_{max} being respectively the minimum and maximum task workloads. Hence, δ_v is also a measure of how much total workload is left after the completion of v. When δ_v is maximised (Line 12 of Algorithm 4), it leads to the remaining tasks with the smallest workloads, thus increasing the probability of completing more.

3.5   Phase 4: Overall Procedure of CFLA2

Algorithm 4 shows the overall procedure. The repeat-until loop is performed until all tasks are completed or the latest deadline is expired (Line 22). At each time t, first the set of legal agent allocations is updated (Line 8), then a task allocation is defined (Lines 9–18). If no other tasks can be allocated, the algorithm stops early (Line 19).

3.6   Analysis and Discussion

Algorithm 1 iterates through all free agents and uncompleted tasks. Assuming that Line 4 requires constant time, the time complexity is $\alpha = O(|A| \cdot |V|)$.

     Algorithm 2 iterates (Line 5) from coalition size 1 to $|A_v^t|$, where A_v^t is the set of agents that can reach task v at time t. This requires $O(|A|)$ time in case

---

Algorithm 4: Overall procedure (Phase 4 of CFLA2)

---
1 $t \leftarrow 0$
2 $T \leftarrow \{\tau_t^{a \rightarrow v}\}_{a \in A,\, v \in V,\, t \in [0,\, d_{max}]}$ // the set of all agent allocations
3 $V_{unc} \leftarrow V$ // uncompleted tasks
4 **repeat**
5       $\delta_{max} \leftarrow 0$ // maximum task degree
6       $v^* \leftarrow$ NIL // next task to allocate
7       $C^* \leftarrow \emptyset$ // coalition to which v^* is allocated
8       $L_t \leftarrow$ getLegalAgentAllocations(t) // Algorithm 1
9   **for** $v \in V_{unc}$ **do**
10          $C_v^* \leftarrow$ ECF(v, L_t) // Algorithm 2
11          $\delta_v \leftarrow$ lookAhead(v, C_v^*, T) // Algorithm 3
12   **if** $\delta_v > \delta_{max}$ **then**
13              $\delta_{max} \leftarrow \delta_v$
14              $C^* \leftarrow C_v^*$
15   **if** $v^* \neq$ NIL *and* $C^* \neq \emptyset$ **then**
16   Allocate C^* to v^*
17          $V_{unc} \leftarrow V_{unc} \setminus \{v^*\}$
18   Reduce T according to new agent locations and availability
19   **if** $A_{free}^t = A$ **then** // all agents are free
20   **break**
21      $t \leftarrow t + 1$
22 **until** $V_{unc} = \emptyset$ *or* $t > d_{max}$

$A_v^t = A$. For each $s \leq |A_v^t|$, all possible coalitions of size s could be examined (Line 6), which requires $O(2^{|A|})$ time. Assuming that Line 8 requires $O(d_{max})$ time, the total time complexity is $\beta = O(|A| \cdot 2^{|A|} \cdot d_{max})$.

Algorithm 3 iterates through all uncompleted tasks, which requires $O(|V|)$ time, while Line 8 is computationally identical to Line 5 in Algorithm 2. Hence, the time complexity is $\gamma = O(|V| \cdot 2^{|A|})$. Since it uses all the previous algorithms, Algorithm 4 has a time complexity of:

$$O\left(d_{max} \cdot (\alpha + |V| \cdot (\beta + \gamma))\right) = O\left((d_{max} \cdot |V|)^2 \cdot 2^{|A|}\right) \tag{9}$$

Therefore, despite having a lower complexity than an optimal CFSTP solver (Sect. 2.5), CFLA2 has a run-time that increases quadratically with the number of tasks and exponentially with the number of agents, which makes it not suitable for systems with limited computational power or real-time applications. Other limitations are as follows.

1. It can allocate at most one task per time unit [24, Section 7]. More formally, at each time unit, the best-case guarantee of CFLA2 is to find a partial solution with degree $k = 1$.
2. In general, greedily allocating a task with the highest degree now does not ensure that uncompleted tasks can all be successfully allocated in future.

This is particularly relevant in an open system, where there is no certainty of having further uncompleted tasks (Sect. 1).

3. The more the tasks can be grouped by degree, the more the look-ahead technique becomes a costly random choice. In other words, at time t, if some tasks $V' \subseteq V$ have all maximum degree, then Algorithm 4 selects v^* randomly from V'. Hence, the larger V' is, the less relevant Algorithm 3 becomes.

4. In Algorithm 4, all tasks have the same weight. That is, tasks with earlier deadlines may not be allocated before tasks with later deadlines. This is independent of the order in which the uncompleted tasks are elaborated (Line 9). In fact, the computation of δ_{max} (Line 12) would not be affected.

To overcome the limitations of CFLA2, in the next section we present CTS, a CFSTP solver that is simultaneously anytime, efficient and with convergence guarantee, both in closed and open systems.

4   Cluster-Based Task Scheduling

The *Cluster-based Task Scheduling* (CTS) is a centralised, anytime and greedy algorithm[4] that operates at the agent level, rather than at the coalition level. It is divided into the following two phases.

1. For each agent a, defining a task v such that v is the closest to a and d_v is minimal.
2. For each task v, defining the coalition of agents to which v has to be allocated.

Algorithm 5 is used in Phase 1, while Algorithm 6 enacts the two phases. We describe them respectively in Sects. 4.1 and 4.2.

4.1   Selecting the Best Task for Each Agent

Given a time t and an agent a, Algorithm 5 returns the uncompleted task v that is allocable, the most urgent and closest to a. By *allocable* we mean that a can reach v before deadline d_v, while *most urgent* means that v has the earliest deadline. The algorithm prioritises unallocated tasks, that is, it first tries to find a task to which no agents are travelling, and on which no agents are working ($v_a^t[0]$). Otherwise, it returns an already allocated but still uncompleted task such that a can reach it and contribute to its completion ($v_a^t[1]$). This ensures that an agent becomes free only when no other tasks are allocable and uncompleted.

Algorithm 5 does not enforce temporal constraints. As we shall see in Sect. 4.2, it is Algorithm 6 that does it, by allocating a task v to a coalition C only when C has the minimum size and can complete v within d_v.

---

[4] Both CFLA2 and CTS are greedy. However, as we show below, only CTS can be proven correct in general settings.

Algorithm 5: getTaskAllocableToAgent (used in Phase 1 of CTS)

Input: time t, agent a

1 $v_a^t \leftarrow (\text{NIL}, \text{NIL})$ // array in which $v_a^t[0]$ (resp. $v_a^t[1]$) is the unallocated (resp. allocated) task allocable to agent a at time t

2 $t_{min} \leftarrow (d_{max} + 1, d_{max} + 1)$ // array in which $t_{min}[0]$ (resp. $t_{min}[1]$) defines the time units required by agent a to reach $v_a^t[0]$ (resp. $v_a^t[1]$)

3 $d_{min} \leftarrow (d_{max} + 1, d_{max} + 1)$ // array in which $d_{min}[0]$ (resp. $d_{min}[1]$) is the deadline of $v_a^t[0]$ (resp. $v_a^t[1]$)

4 **for** $v \in V$ **do** // for each uncompleted task

5      $i \leftarrow 0$ // v is unallocated

6   **if** *other agents are travelling to or working on v* **then**

7          $i \leftarrow 1$ // v is allocated but still uncompleted

8      $t_{arr} \leftarrow t + \rho(a, l_a^t, l_v)$

9   **if** $t_{arr} \leq d_v$ *and* $t_{arr} < t_{min}[i]$ *and* $d_v < d_{min}[i]$ **then**

10          $v_a^t[i] \leftarrow v$

11          $t_{min}[i] \leftarrow t_{arr}$

12          $d_{min}[i] \leftarrow d_v$

13 **if** $v_a^t[0] \neq \text{NIL}$ **then** // prioritise unallocated tasks

14   **return** $v_a^t[0]$

15 **return** $v_a^t[1]$

4.2   Overall Procedure of CTS

The overall procedure is described in Algorithm 6. The repeat-until loop is the same as CFLA2, to preserve the anytime property. Phases 1 and 2 are represented respectively by the loops at Lines 5 and 16.

Phase 1 loops through all agents. Here, an agent a may either be free or reaching a task location. In the first case (Line 6), if an uncompleted task v can be allocated to a (Lines $7-8$), then v is flagged as allocable (Line 9) and a is added to the set of agents A_v^t to which v could be allocated at time t (Line 11). In the second case (Line 12), a is travelling to a task v, hence its location is updated (Line 13) and, if it reached v, it is set to *working on v* (Line 14).

Phase 2 visits each uncompleted task v. If v is allocable (Line 18) then it is allocated to the smallest coalition of agents in A_v^t (defined in Phase 1) that can complete it (Lines $19-32$). In particular, at Lines $24-27$, φ_v is the amount of workload w_v done by all the coalitions formed after the arrival to v of the first $i-1$ agents in Π_v^t (defined at Line 19). After that, if there are agents working on v (Line 33), its workload w_v is decreased accordingly (Line 34). If w_v drops to zero or below, then v is completed (Lines $35-37$). The algorithm stops (Line 39) when all the tasks have been completed, or the latest deadline is expired, or no other tasks are allocable and uncompleted (Sect. 4.1).

Algorithm 6: Overall procedure of CTS (Phases 1 and 2)

Input: tasks V, agents A, task locations L_V, initial agent locations L_A, task
demands $\{D_v\}_{v \in V}$

Output: A set of coalition allocations Γ'

1   $t \leftarrow 0$

2   $\Gamma' \leftarrow \emptyset$ // the partial solution to return

3   $V_{allocable} \leftarrow \emptyset$ // allocable tasks

4   **repeat**

5   **for** $a \in A$ **do** // Phase 1

6   **if** $a \in A^t_{free}$ **then**

7          $v \leftarrow$ getTaskAllocableToAgent(t, a) // Algorithm 5

8   **if** $v \neq$ NIL **then**

9   **if** $v \notin V_{allocable}$ **then**

10             $V_{allocable} \leftarrow V_{allocable} \cup \{v\}$

11          $A^t_v \leftarrow A^t_v \cup \{a\}$

12   **else**

13   Update a's location

14   **if** a reached the task v it was assigned to **then**

15   Set a's status to *working on* v

16   **for** $v \in V$ **do** // Phase 2

17        $C^t_v \leftarrow$ all agents working on v at time t

18   **if** $v \in V_{allocable}$ **then**

19          $\Pi^t_v \leftarrow$ list of all agents in A^t_v sorted by arrival time to v

20          $C^* \leftarrow \emptyset$

21   **for** $i \leftarrow 1$ **to** $|\Pi^t_v|$ **do**

22            $C^* \leftarrow$ first i agents in Π^t_v

23            $\lambda_i \leftarrow$ arrival time to v of the i-th agent in Π^t_v

24   **if** $i + 1 \leq |\Pi^t_v|$ **then**

25             $\lambda_{i+1} \leftarrow$ arrival time to v of the $(i+1)$-th agent in Π^t_v

26   **else**

27             $\lambda_{i+1} \leftarrow d_v$

28            $\varphi_v \leftarrow \varphi_v + (\lambda_i + \lambda_{i+1}) \cdot u(C^* \cup C^t_v, v)$ // w_v done at λ_{i+1}

29   **if** $(d_v - \lambda_i) \cdot u(C^*, v) \geq w_v - \varphi_v$ **then**

30   **break** // C^* is the minimum coalition to complete v

31          $T_v = \bigcup_{a \in C^*} \{\tau^{a \to v}_{\lambda_a}\}$ // λ_a is a's arrival time to v

32          $\Gamma' \leftarrow \Gamma' \cup \Gamma(T_v, t)$ // add $\Gamma(T_v, t)$ (Section 2.2) to Γ'

33          $V_{allocable} \leftarrow V_{allocable} \setminus \{v\}$

34   **if** $C^t_v \neq \emptyset$ **then**

35          $w_v \leftarrow w_v - u(C^t_v, v)$

36   **if** $w_v \leq 0$ **then**

37   Set free all agents in C^t_v

38            $V \leftarrow V \setminus \{v\}$

39      $t \leftarrow t + 1$

40 **until** $V = \emptyset$ or $t > d_{max}$ or all agents are free

---

4.3 Analysis and Discussion

The approach of CTS transforms the CFSTP from a $1 - k$ task allocation to a series of $1 - 1$ task allocations. In other words, instead of allocating each task to a coalition of k agents, we have that coalitions are formed by clustering (i.e., grouping) agents based on the closest and most urgent tasks. This enacts an 'elegibility' criterion: unlike CFLA2, CTS exploits the distances between agents and tasks and the speeds of agents to reduce the time needed to define coalition allocations. Algorithm 5 runs in $\psi = O(|V|)$ time, assuming that the operation at Line 8 has constant time. In Algorithm 6, the time complexity of Phase 1 is $O(|A| \cdot \psi) = O(|A| \cdot |V|)$, while Phase 2 runs in $O(|V| \cdot |A| \log |A|)$ because: in the worst case, $A_v^t = A$ and Line 19 sorts A in $\Omega(|A| \cdot \log |A|)$ time using any comparison sort algorithm [5]; the loop at Line 21 runs in $O(|A|)$ time. Since the repeat-until loop is executed at most d_{max} times, the time complexity of Algorithm 6 is:

$$O\left(d_{max} \cdot |V| \cdot |A| \log |A|\right) \tag{10}$$

If both phases are executed in parallel, the time complexity is reduced to:

$$\Omega\left(d_{max} \cdot (|V| + |A| \log |A|)\right) \tag{11}$$

CTS does not have the limitations of CFLA2 because:

1. It can allocate at least one task per time unit. More formally, at each time unit, if one or more tasks are allocable, CTS guarantees to find a partial solution with degree $1 \leq k \leq |A|$.
2. It runs in polynomial time and does not use a look-ahead technique. Thus, it is efficient and can be used in open systems.

Theorem 1. *CTS is correct.*

Proof. We prove by induction on time t.

At $t = 0$, a task v is selected for each agent a such that v is allocable, the most urgent and closest to a (Sect. 4.1). This implies that the agent allocation $\tau_0^{a \to v}$ is legal (Sect. 2.4). Then, Phase 2 of Algorithm 6 (Sect. 4.2) allocates v to a only if it exists a coalition C such that $|C|$ is minimum, $\tau_0^{C \to v}$ is feasible (Sect. 2.4) and $a \in C$.

At $t > 0$, for each agent a, there are two possible cases: a task v has been allocated to a at time $t' < t$, or a is free (i.e., idle). In the first case, a is either reaching or working on v (Lines $12 - 15$ in Algorithm 6), hence $\tau_t^{a \to v}$ is legal and $\tau_t^{C \to v}$ is feasible, where $a \in C$. In the second case, a is either at its initial location or at the location of a task on which it finished working at time $t' < t$. Thus, as in the base case, if it exists a coalition C and a task v such that $|C|$ is minimum, $\tau_t^{C \to v}$ is feasible and $a \in C$, then v is allocated to a.

As shown in the two previous sections, Algorithm 5 iterates exactly once over a finite set of uncompleted tasks, while the repeat-until loop of Algorithm 6 is executed at most d_{max} times. Hence, Theorem 1 also implies that CTS converges to a partial solution, if it exists.

The counterexample given by Limitation 2 in Sect. 3.6 does not allow to prove the convergence of CFLA and CFLA2 in general settings. Since no current algorithm that solves the CFSTP is simultaneously anytime, efficient and with convergence guarantee (Sect. 1), CTS is the first of its kind.

5   Comparison Tests

We implemented CFLA, CFLA2 and CTS in Java[5], and replicated the experimental setup of [24] because we wanted to evaluate how well CFLA2 and CTS perform in settings where the look-ahead technique is highly effective. For each test configuration, we solved 100 random CFSTP instances and plotted the average and standard deviation of: percentage of completed tasks; agent travel time (Sect. 2.1); *task completion time*, or the time at which a task has no workload left; *problem completion time*, or the time at which no other tasks can be allocated.

5.1   Setup

Let $U(l, u)$ and $U^I(l, u)$ be respectively a uniform real distribution and a uniform integer distribution with lower bound l and upper bond u. Our parameters are defined as follows:

- All agents have the same speed.
- The initial agent locations are randomly chosen on a 50 by 50 grid, where the travel time of agent a between two points is given by the Manhattan distance (i.e., the taxicab metric or ℓ_1 norm) divided by the speed of a.
- Tasks are fixed to 300, while agents range from 2 to 40, in intervals of 2 between 2 and 20 agents, and in intervals of 5 between 20 and 40 agents.
- The coalition values are defined as $u(C, v) = |C| \cdot k$, where $k \sim U(1, 2)$. Hence, coalition values depend only on the number of agents involved, and all tasks have the same difficulty.
- Deadlines $d_v \sim U^I(5, 600)$ and workloads $w_v \sim U^I(10, 50)$.

Unlike [24], we set the number of maximum agents to 40 instead of 20, because it allows in this setup to complete all tasks in some instances. We did not perform a comparison on larger instances due to the run-time of CFLA and CFLA2 (Sect. 3.6). In fact, while CTS takes seconds to solve instances with thousands of agents and tasks, CFLA and CFLA2 take days. Consequently, the purpose of these tests is to highlight the performance of CTS using CFLA and CFLA2 as a baseline. We aim to verify the scalability of CTS in future investigation.

5.2   Results

In terms of completed tasks (Fig. 1a), the best performing algorithm for instances with up to 18 agents is CFLA2, while the best performing algorithm for instances

---

[5] https://gitlab.com/lcpz/cfstp

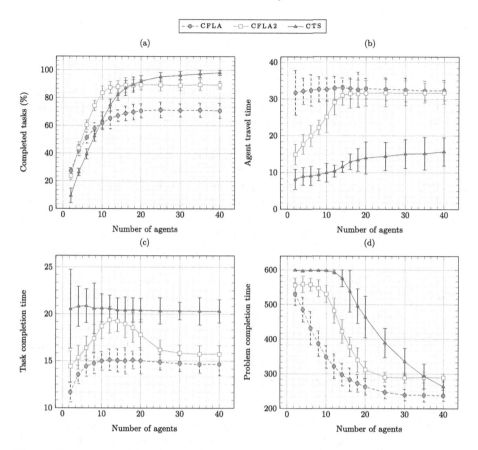

Fig. 1. Comparison of CFLA, CFLA2 and CTS on CFSTP instances with linear coalition values. In each figure, each point is the $avg \pm std/2$, where avg is the average over 100 problems of the value indicated on the Y-axis and std is the standard deviation of avg. The tasks are fixed to 300, while the number of agents is denoted by the X-axis.

with at least 20 agents is CTS. CFLA is outperformed by CFLA2 in all instances except those with 2 agents, and by CTS in instances with at least 10 agents. The reason why the performance of CFLA and CFLA2 does not improve significantly starting from instances with 20 agents is that the more agents (with random initial locations) there are, the more tasks are likely to be grouped by degree[6]. CFLA2 has a trend similar to that of CFLA because it has the same limitations, but it performs better due to its improved look-ahead technique. CTS is not the best in all instances because its average task completion time is the highest (see the discussion on Fig. 1c below). This implies that the fewer the agents, the more tasks may expire before they can be allocated. In our setup, 10 (resp. 20)

---

[6] See Limitation 3 described in Sect. 3.6.

is the number of agents starting from which this behaviour is contained enough to allow CTS to outperform CFLA (resp. CFLA2).

Regarding agent travel times (Fig. 1b), it can be seen that CTS is up to three times more efficient than CFLA and CFLA2. This is due to Algorithm 5, which allocates tasks to agents also based on their proximity. CFLA2 has lower agent travel times than CFLA for the following reason. The degree computation in CFLA2 also considers how much total workload would be left (Sect. 3.4). Higher degrees correspond to lower workloads, and the tasks with lower workloads are completed first. Thus, the tasks are less grouped by degree, and more are likely to be completed. This means that the average distance between task locations in a CFLA2 solution may be lower than that of a CFLA solution. The agent travel times increase with all algorithms. This behaviour is also reported, but not explained, by Ramchurn et al. [24]. To explain it, let us consider a toy problem with one agent a_1 and one task v. If we introduce a new agent a_2 such that $\rho(a_2, l^0_{a_2}, l_v) > \rho(a_1, l^0_{a_1}, l_v)$, then the average travel time increases. In our setup, this happens because the initial agent locations are random.

In general, task completion times (Fig. 1c) decrease because the more agents there are, the faster the tasks are completed. The completion of task v is related to the size of the coalition C to which v is allocated: the highest the completion time, the smallest the size of C, hence the highest the working time of the agents in C. Task completion times are inversely related to agent travel times. Since CTS has the smallest agent travel times and allocates tasks to the smallest coalitions, it consequently has the highest task completion times. Therefore, in CTS, agents work the highest amount of times, and the number of tasks attempted at any one time is the largest.

The problem completion times (Fig. 1d) are in line with the task completion times (Fig. 1c) since the faster the tasks are completed, the less time is needed to solve the problem. The reason why the times of CFLA and CFLA2 do not decrease significantly from 20 agents up is linked to their performance (see the discussion on Fig. 1a above). On the other hand, the fact that the times of CTS decrease more consistently than those of CFLA and CFLA2 indicates that CTS is the most efficient asymptotically. In other words, CTS is likely to solve large problems in fewer time units than CFLA and CFLA2.

In terms of computational times, CTS is significantly faster than CFLA and CFLA2. For example, in instances with 40 agents and 300 tasks, on average[7] CTS is $45106\% \pm [2625, 32019]$ (resp. $27160\% \pm [1615, 20980]$) faster than CFLA (resp. CFLA2). The run-time improvement of CFLA2 is due to Line 4 of Algorithm 3, due to which the look-ahead technique elaborates fewer tasks.

6 Conclusions

In this paper, we proposed two novel algorithms to solve the CFSTP. The first is CFLA2, an improved version of the CFLA, and the second is CTS, which is

---

[7] On a machine with an Intel Core i5-4690 processor (quad-core 3.5 GHz, no Hyper-Threading) and 8 GB DDR3-1600 RAM.

the first to be simultaneously anytime, efficient and with convergence guarantee. CFLA2 can be used in place of CFLA in offline situations or for small problems, while CTS provides a baseline for benchmarks with dynamic and large problems. Because it significantly outperforms CFLA and is more applicable than CFLA2, we can consider CTS to be the new state-of-the-art algorithm to solve the CFSTP.

The limitation of CTS is that it cannot define the quality of its approximation (Sect. 4.3). Moreover, the fact that it maximises the agent working times (Sect. 5) implies that some agents may take longer to complete some tasks and therefore may not work on others. Thus, if an optimal solution exists, in general CTS cannot guarantee to obtain it.

Future work aims at creating a distributed version of CTS, and extending it to give quality guarantees on the solutions found. We also want to test on hard problems generated with the RoboCup rescue simulation, and to define a large-scale CFSTP benchmark from real-world datasets.

Acknowledgments. We thank Mohammad Divband Soorati, Ryan Beal and the anonymous reviewers for their helpful comments and suggestions. This research is sponsored by the AXA Research Fund. Danesh Tarapore acknowledges support from a EPSRC New Investigator Award grant (EP/R030073/1).

References

1. Alexander, E.D.: Principles of Emergency Planning and Management. Oxford University Press, Oxford (2002)
2. Bogner, K., Pferschy, U., Unterberger, R., Zeiner, H.: Optimised scheduling in human-robot collaboration-a use case in the assembly of printed circuit boards. Int. J. Prod. Res. **56**(16), 5522–5540 (2018)
3. Chao, I.M., Golden, B.L., Wasil, E.A.: The team orienteering problem. Eur. J. Oper. Res. **88**(3), 464–474 (1996)
4. Coppola, D.P.: Introduction to International Disaster Management. Elsevier, Amsterdam (2006)
5. Cormen, T.H., Leiserson, C.E., Rivest, R.L., Stein, C.: Introduction to Algorithms, 3rd edn. MIT press, Cambridge (2009)
6. Donald, K.E.: The art of Computer Programming. In: Fascicle 2: Generating All Tuples and Permutations, vol. 4. Pearson Education (2005)
7. Dos Santos, F., Bazzan, A.L.C.: Towards efficient multiagent task allocation in the robocup rescue: a biologically-inspired approach. AAMAS **22**(3), 465–486 (2011). https://doi.org/10.1007/s10458-010-9136-3
8. Farinelli, A., Rogers, A., Petcu, A., Jennings, N.R.: Decentralised coordination of low-power embedded devices using the max-sum algorithm. AAMAS **2**, 639–646 (2008)
9. Fioretto, F., Pontelli, E., Yeoh, W.: Distributed constraint optimization problems and applications: a survey. JAIR **61**, 623–698 (2018)
10. Gallud, X., Selva, D.: Agent-based simulation framework and consensus algorithm for observing systems with adaptive modularity. Syst. Eng. **21**(5), 432–454 (2018)
11. Godoy, J., Gini, M.: Task allocation for spatially and temporally distributed tasks. In: Lee, S., Cho, H., Yoon, K.J., Lee, J. (eds.) ICAS. AISC, vol. 194, pp. 603–612. Springer, Heidelberg (2013). https://doi.org/10.1007/978-3-642-33932-5_56

12. Hewitt, C.: The Challenge of Open Systems, pp. 383–395. Cambridge University Press, Cambridge (1990)
13. Horling, B., Lesser, V.: A survey of multi-organizational paradigms. Knowl. Eng. Rev. **19**(4), 281–316 (2005)
14. Koes, M., Nourbakhsh, I., Sycara, K.: Heterogeneous multirobot coordination with spatial and temporal constraints. In: AAAI, vol. 5, pp. 1292–1297 (2005)
15. Koes, M., Nourbakhsh, I., Sycara, K.: Constraint optimization coordination architecture for search and rescue robotics. In: Proceedings of International Conference on Robotics and Automation, pp. 3977–3982. IEEE (2006)
16. Korsah, G.A.: Exploring Bounded Optimal Coordination for Heterogeneous Teams with Cross-Schedule Dependencies. Ph.D. thesis, Carnegie Mellon University (2011)
17. Korsah, G.A., Stentz, A., Dias, M.B.: A comprehensive taxonomy for multi-robot task allocation. Int. J. Robot. Res. **32**(12), 1495–1512 (2013)
18. Krizmancic, M., Arbanas, B., Petrovic, T., Petric, F., Bogdan, S.: Cooperative aerial-ground multi-robot system for automated construction tasks. IEEE Robot. Autom. Lett. **5**(2), 798–805 (2020)
19. Liu, C., Kroll, A.: Memetic algorithms for optimal task allocation in multi-robot systems for inspection problems with cooperative tasks. Soft Comput. **19**(3), 567–584 (2015). https://doi.org/10.1007/s00500-014-1274-0
20. Mataric, M.J.: Designing emergent behaviors: from local interactions to collective intelligence. In: Proceedings of the Second International Conference on Simulation of Adaptive Behavior, pp. 432–441. MIT Press (1993)
21. Papadimitriou, C.H.: Computational Complexity. Pearson, London (1993)
22. Pujol-Gonzalez, M., Cerquides, J., Farinelli, A., Meseguer, P., Rodriguez-Aguilar, J.A.: Efficient inter-team task allocation in robocup rescue. In: AAMAS, pp. 413–421 (2015)
23. Ramchurn, S.D., Farinelli, A., Macarthur, K.S., Jennings, N.R.: Decentralized coordination in robocup rescue. Comput. J. **53**(9), 1447–1461 (2010)
24. Ramchurn, S.D., Polukarov, M., Farinelli, A., Truong, C., Jennings, N.R.: Coalition formation with spatial and temporal constraints. AAMAS **3**, 1181–1188 (2010)
25. Sandholm, T., Larson, K., Andersson, M., Shehory, O., Tohmé, F.: Coalition structure generation with worst case guarantees. Artifi. Intell. **111**(1–2), 209–238 (1999)
26. Shehory, O., Kraus, S.: Methods for task allocation via agent coalition formation. AI **101**(1–2), 165–200 (1998)
27. Tsiligirides, T.: Heuristic methods applied to orienteering. J. Oper. Res. Soc. **35**(9), 797–809 (1984). https://doi.org/10.1057/jors.1984.162
28. Weiss, G. (ed.): Multiagent Systems, 2nd edn. MIT Press, Cambridge (2013)
29. Ye, D., Zhang, M., Sutanto, D.: Self-adaptation-based dynamic coalition formation in a distributed agent network: a mechanism and a brief survey. IEEE Trans. Parallel Distrib. Syst. **24**(5), 1042–1051 (2013)
30. Zhou, J., Zhao, X., Zhang, X., Zhao, D., Li, H.: Task allocation for multi-agent systems based on distributed many-objective evolutionary algorithm and greedy algorithm. IEEE Access **8**, 19306–19318 (2020)
31. Zilberstein, S.: Using anytime algorithms in intelligent systems. AI Mag. **17**(3), 73 (1996)

Author Index

Printed in the United States
By Bookmasters